SCHOOL BUSINESS ADMINISTRATION

A COMPARATIVE PERSPECTIVE

by

Guilbert C. Hentschke

University of Rochester

with

Frederick L. Dembowski, James H. Faux, Shirley J. Hansen, Ellen Kehoe, Lionel Meno, Michael J. Murphy, Richard P. Vigilante, and John Yagielski

McCutchan Publishing Corporation
2526 Martin Luther King Jr. Way
Berkeley, California 94704

To Peg, Peter, Jen, and Mike . . .
for reasons that should be obvious, but aren't

ISBN 0–8211–0768–2
Library of Congress Catalog Card Number 84–61507

Contents

Preface

School business administration is a very old profession that today is undergoing fundamental changes in conception. It began with formal schooling, when people first felt the need to act collectively to educate their children. Throughout most of our nation's history, schools (coupled later with colleges and universities) were *the* means whereby deliberate, widespread collective efforts were made to pass on to children and young adults the knowledge, skills, and attitudes deemed important in our culture. Despite the idiosyncratic differences of a few institutions during specific periods of history, schools and colleges were considered the only places where formal, organized teaching and learning took place on a large scale. Students who excelled in these organized settings were assumed to be simply better equipped to learn than those who did not.

With the passage of time, especially in recent years, we have come to acknowledge two departures from this stereotype of how and why schooling occurs—one from the perspective of the learner and the other from the perspective of the teacher. First, we are increasingly acknowledging that nonschool settings have a major impact on the learner. Formal efforts to train and educate are greatly aided (or hindered) by a myriad of competing environmental forces from which people today also learn. As we learn more about differences among learners, we have modified, and made more complex, the processes of formal education. The one-room school with one teacher and several dozen children of all ages has been replaced by age- and ability-graded classes and specialized programs for gifted, handicapped, bilingual, unmotivated, vocationally oriented, college-aspiring, even "general" students. Second, rising up beside the traditional institutions of formal schooling are growing numbers of other organizations whose primary missions initially may not have included formal education services, but which have added education to the list of other services they provide. For example, early childhood education programs teach important cognitive and social skills to children long before they enter kindergarten. Post-compulsory schooling takes place in a wide variety of nontraditional school settings—businesses, the military, professional associations, labor organizations, and proprietary schools, to name a few. It has been estimated that expenditures for corporate training alone now equal those for all of the nation's colleges and universities. In sum, educators are acknowledging differences in students, which requires more differentiation in pedagogy; also, the places and contexts of teaching and learning are more varied. The challenges and opportunities for the educator have never been greater.

These relatively recent developments in formal schooling affect today's school business administrators, who are at once educators and managers of the people who provide schooling services. As educators, school business administrators must incorporate into pedagogical processes a flexible, more comprehensive understanding of the learner. With the exponential growth of knowledge to be taught, they must continually modify existing pedagogical processes. As managers of pedagogical processes, school business administrators are found working within any one of an increasing variety of educational organizations over their professional lifetimes. The form of the organization can no longer be usefully "held constant" (for example, public school districts), because schooling is taking place in too many different settings. Greater varieties of schooling services are provided through greater varieties of organizations. This book attempts to be particularly sensitive to this; we seek to address not only business functions but also those dimensions of different organizations that are most likely to affect the way school business administrators manage those functions.

Part 1 and part 6, the conclusion, deal with what we feel is a useful way of examining the many specialized functions of school business administration and of understanding *why* school business administrators perform these functions differently in different organizations. Parts 2 through 5 address the major functional responsibilities of the school administrator—management of finances, human resources, logistics, and information—and explain *how* school business administrators in different organizations perform these functions differently.

Part One: Toward a Comparative Perspective

This part of the book makes explicit those propositions about human behavior that provide our basis for studying the administration of schools as businesses. Each of the three chapters in this part describes propositions and themes that recur throughout the book.

Chapter 1, "Schools as Businesses: Four Perspectives," traces three perspectives through which school business administration has been described and understood. The school business official perspective is drawn largely from practicing school business officials. The schools as business analogue perspective grew mainly out of the scientific management movement as adopted by leading education administrators and professors. The management systems in schools perspective is traceable to more recent thinking about organizations as interacting systems. This text builds on these three perspectives and at the same time focuses on a fourth perspective called property rights. This perspective originated from the work of economists studying organizational behavior, and it not only provides us with a way of describing how school business administration varies across organizations but also helps us to understand why.

Chapter 2, "Schooling as a Three-Sector Industry," is coauthored by Ellen Kehoe of Teachers College, Columbia University. In this chapter we seek to apply some of the more basic concepts of the property rights perspective to the precollegiate schooling industry in the United States. We examine the amount and kinds of such schooling as supplied by each of the three major economic sectors in society, and we show how the systems of rights in each sector influence the production (and, hence, consumption) of schooling. We describe how managers pursue utility through competition both within and among sectors for the rights to use resources.

The first two chapters provide a semantic framework for understanding differences in managerial behavior. Chapter 3, "Planning and Control in Schools," focuses more directly on managerial behavior per se. The distinction is drawn here among strategic planning, managerial control, and operational control. How managers pursue these activities differs depending on the system of rights within which they operate.

Part Two: Fiscal Systems

This part, the longest in the text, consists of six chapters and reflects the primary emphasis of both the book and the profession. Chapter 4, "Variations in the Financial Environment," coauthored by Ellen Kehoe, discusses the major sources and applications of financial resources in the schooling industry. This is followed by a discussion of sector-by-sector differences that occur largely because of differences in the systems of rights among sectors. The appendix to chapter 4 describes the major mechanisms employed to allocate financial resources from state governments to public school districts.

Chapter 5, "Fiscal Strain in Public Schools," is an elaboration of the discussion in chapter 4, with primary attention given to public schools. It is coauthored by John Yagielski, Superintendent of Greece, New York, Central Schools. Whereas school administrators in the two private sectors can avail themselves of a variety of options for improving their financial position and can relatively easily create or dissolve their school organization, public-sector administrators have fewer rights in these areas. The major short-run response to changes in the financial environment of public-sector administrators is on the expenditure side; specifically, they can change capacity and service levels.

Chapter 6, "Variations in Budgeting Processes," views budgeting as the major managerial control activity in any schooling organization. It begins with a portrait of predominant budgeting processes in public schools and explains why budgeting is logically a much less elaborate and formal process in private schools. The last part of the chapter describes two popular departures from predominant practice: program-oriented budgeting and site-oriented budgeting. The rationale and perceived costs and benefits of each of these "reforms" is discussed.

Chapter 7, "Cash Management," is written by Fred Dembowski of the State University of New York at Albany. The chapter describes the major objectives and processes of cash management, includes separate discussions of how efficiency of cash management is measured, and discusses procedures for operational control.

Chapter 8, "Financial Accounting Requirements," describes the foundations of financial control through accounting. Basic accounting concepts are presented along with descriptions of procedures for operating systems of financial reporting and control.

Chapter 9, "Managerial Uses of Accounting Data," builds on the material in the previous chapter but focuses more on managerial decisions that require financial information and on how financial data from the accounting system is converted for use by management.

Part Three: Human Resource Systems

This part is devoted most directly to the analysis of systems of rights of both instructional and noninstructional employees in schools. Both chapters in this part are written by Michael Murphy of the University of Utah. Chapter 10, "Employment Relations and Personnel Management," describes the major issues associated with securing and using the services of individuals who desire to enter into exchange relationships with schools. Topics include staffing, recruiting, evaluating, and compensating personnel. Major differences between the systems of rights in public and private schools are described.

Chapter 11, "Employment Relations and Collective Bargaining," examines the evolution of processes employed by collections of individuals to determine the systems of rights in schooling organizations. Although directed largely at trends in organized labor in the public sector, differences between public and private schools are also pointed out.

Part Four: Logistics Systems

Traditionally, most texts on school business administration devote extensive coverage to the separate "businesses" of schools, such as student transportation, school lunch, insurance, maintenance and operations, facilities planning and management, and purchasing. In this text we attempt to extract the major management decisions associated with most logistics systems and focus attention on the general nature of those decisions rather than on the more obvious, but less important, differences among logistics systems themselves, such as student transportation and school lunch programs.

Chapter 12, "Services Management," describes the differences between school "businesses" that are predominantly services and those that require significant proportions of capital goods. Trends in three major school services—student transportation, school lunches for students, and purchasing—are described to point out differences in sponsorship, regulation, and obligatory provision, and between public and private schools with regards to whether services are rationed by pricing and whether they are cost or profit centers. Following the discussion of this "sampler" of school services, two major classes of service decision problems are described: minimizing the sum of competing costs and increasing net revenues through evaluation of the relationships between price and demand.

Chapter 13, "Capital Goods Management," treats logistics systems that require expenditures and produce benefits over a time period longer than one year. The difference between service management and physical assets management is that decisions about the latter require a consideration of time. Similar to chapter 12, a "sampler" of major assets used in schooling, such as school facilities, buses, and computing equipment, is described. Each of these assets reflects unique trends in its use and in management requirements. Two classes of problems affecting decisions are then described: incorporating the effects of time in decisions about alternative investments in capital goods and incorporating the effects of time into replacement decisions (decisions about points in time). This chapter concludes with a comparison of differences in how public and private schools finance capital goods acquisitions.

Chapter 14, "Energy Management," describes an emerging logistical responsibility of the school business administrator—the planning and controlling of energy use. It is written by Shirley Hansen, an energy consultant in Maryland. Energy management receives separate treatment in this book for several reasons in addition to its relatively recent rise in importance. First, it illustrates classic economic behavior resulting from changes (in this case, increases) in the relative prices of inputs. Second, the field relies heavily on specialized language that has not yet found its way into mainstream usage. Additional coverage is needed to define terms. Third, it provides the single example in this text of the range of activities required of school business administrators as they manage. Administrators not only face the decision problems described in chapters 12 and 13 but also employ numerous planning, managerial control, and operational control activities as they "manage energy." There is little comparison of schools across sectors in this chapter because there is little systematic variance in this field among sectors.

Part Five: Information Systems

Information provides the basis for decisions, and decisions enable school business administrators to pursue utility only to the degree that this information "informs" decisions. This seeming tautology causes the school business administrator to pursue information as a necessary step in utility maximization. Similarly, sponsors require information from school business administrators as they seek to align the administrators' behavior with their own preferences.

Chapter 15, "Managing Information Requirements," written by Richard Vigilante of Teachers College, Columbia University, describes the characteristics of information and computing machinery, which is now the primary means of information storage and retrieval. He describes the activities that school business administrators undertake to create and use information systems.

Chapter 16, "Emerging Technologies in Information Management," written by James Faux, the Assistant Superintendent for Business in the Spencerport, New York, Central Schools, complements the previous chapter. He presumes familiarity with the concepts described in chapter 15, and he describes in detail the information requirements of the "average" public school system and how these are being met through microcomputing machinery coupled with generic, widely available software packages.

Part Six: Conclusion

The concluding chapter, "School Business Administration: Toward Continued Improvement," is coauthored by Lionel Meno, the Superintendent of the Syracuse City Public Schools. We summarize previous chapters by contrasting three prototypical, or "pure form," school administrators, whom we call "Public," "Nonprofit," and "For-Profit." In order not to give the impression that the individual manager is totally constrained by the sector in which he or she works, we examine ways in which managers in each sector strive to acquire the advantages of managers in other sectors. We point out, finally, how the traditional role of school business administrator as fiscal conservator contrasts and conflicts with the newer role of school business administrator as revenue-producing entrepreneur.

The characteristic of schooling organizations that we feel most dramatically differentiates the jobs of various school business administrators is the economic sector in which the school is located. Examining sector differences —public versus private nonprofit versus private for-profit—provides a useful way of contrasting ways in which people interact with each other and how those differences affect the school business administrator's job. We think these differences are more important than even, say, the level of schooling in determining what constitutes successful school business administration. We have deliberately downplayed differences among elementary schools, secondary schools, junior colleges, colleges, universities, and so forth. For convenience we have focused our attention on schooling during the compulsory schooling ages of children.

We hope this volume opens up the specialized field of school business administration to serious questioning about those characteristics of schools that make managing one school fundamentally different from managing another and that make managing some schools similar to managing some nonschool organizations but not others.

I am indebted to the authors and coauthors of sections of this book. They have lent their considerable expertise and helped to reformulate how we educators think about the business of schooling. Collectively they exemplify how productive scholarship can result from collaboration between professors and administrators.

I am particularly indebted to Professor J. William Garett for the many hours we have spent trying to think through the implications of property rights theory for human organizations such as hospitals and schools. I look forward to our continuing collaboration.

My thanks to Kim Sharrar for her thoughtful editorial comments and sensitive insights into the readability of the prose, and to Betty Drysdale for her careful preparation of the manuscript.

Special mention should be given to William Meckling and Michael Jensen for their help in exposing me to the rudiments of property rights theory. Any faults in the applications of those concepts in this book are solely mine.

Guilbert C. Hentschke

PART I

Toward a Comparative Perspective

This book concerns management in educational organizations and seeks to provide the reader with an understanding of what differentiates managers in one educational setting from those in others. The management settings in education include public, private nonprofit, and private for-profit schools; these settings form the empirical basis for comparing differences among managers.

In this part we explain how we can examine these differences through the application of property rights theory. We will note differences in what managers in education can do and cannot do as well as differences in what they are likely to do and are not likely to do; that is, we can examine the different rules that govern managers in different settings as well as the actions, governed of course by both the setting and rules, that managers in different settings take. As we compare different settings and rules, however, we keep in mind that the goal of educational managers in any setting is the same—to provide students with an education.

1

Schools as Businesses: Four Perspectives

•

Overview

Chapter 1 reviews the various perspectives from which the business characteristics of schools have been analyzed. Three of these perspectives have existed for some time: the school business official perspective emphasizes the ethical and technical norms of public school business officials; the schools as business analogue perspective grew out of the scientific management movement of the early twentieth century wherein efficiency in schools was compared to efficiency in manufacturing firms; and the management systems in schools perspective encompasses more contemporary rational management models, including management by objectives, long-range planning, and zero-base budgeting. A fourth perspective, which is emphasized in this book, is the property rights perspective. It departs from the other perspectives by emphasizing the rights and preferences of the individual as well as systems of rights among individuals and how these systems of rights create incentives that cause individuals to behave in predictable ways. The property rights perspective facilitates our comparison of school business administration in the three major economic sectors of our society—public, private nonprofit, and private for-profit.

•••

Introduction

Thinking about the business characteristics of schools usually includes a consideration of three familiar perspectives or themes—the school business official perspective, the schools as business analogue perspective, and the management systems in schools perspective. The way in which we analyze school business administration in this text derives but departs from these perspectives; we call this fourth perspective the property rights perspective, which we describe in detail in this chapter. First, we will compare similarities and differences between the first three perspectives and the fourth.

The School Business Official Perspective

The school business official perspective is largely the creation of leading public school business officials and their professional counterparts in higher education. As part of the gradual process of "professionalizing" school business administration, these individuals distinguished school business administration from general school administration and from general business administration and provided the new field with an identity. They sought to define school *business* (not general) administration as "that phase of school administration having responsibility for the efficient and economic management of the business affairs of the schools" (Linn 1956, p. 21). It included "most of those aspects of school administration *not* directly related to classroom instruction, the training and supervision of teachers, the selection of textbooks, [or] the determination of the subject matter of the curriculum" (Engelhardt and Engelhardt 1927, p. 11, emphasis added).

Through the efforts of these and other national leaders, such as Frederick Hill, areas of noninstructional specialization were identified and crystallized into a separate profession requiring specialized expertise. Specialized tasks most often associated with the school business official's role include budgeting and financial planning, purchasing and supply management, plant planning and construction, personnel management, operation and maintenance of school buildings, student transportation, insurance, food services, accounting, office management, and more recent hybrids of these, such as labor relations and data processing.

The school business official perspective is normative. That is, these skill areas are described in terms of "best practices"; in other words, the perspective defines what the ideal business official ought to do, not what the average business official actually does. Following are examples of these best practices.

1. "The first consideration (in emergency maintenance) should be the safety and health of the building occupants" (Hill 1967, p. 193).

2. "School debt should be incurred only for legal purposes, in strict compliance with prescribed legal procedures and limitations" (ibid., p. 124).
3. "Purchasing's role is coordinated with those of other phases of the school's activities, . . . working closely with other departments toward an optimal educational program" (Candoli 1973, p. 241).
4. "Since education is essentially a human enterprise, major emphasis must be given to the development and administration of sound personnel programs" (Jordan 1969, p. 35).
5. "Skillful planning by school administrators, school lunch directors, and architects is required to serve the maximum number of pupils at minimum costs for suitable plant and equipment" (Linn 1956, p. 468).

Spanning a period of over half a century, at least a dozen major texts have been produced that have served this dual function of defining a field and establishing its ethical, normative basis. Perhaps the most influential and widely read texts were those by Hill (1967), which ran to six printings, and by Hill and Colmey (1964). Even more recently published texts on school business administration reflect the following three distinguishing characteristics of the school business official perspective: (1) despite acknowledgement of the need for "teamwork," school business is a field distinct from general school administration; (2) this separate field is described normatively, that is, in terms of what ought to constitute the best practice in the field as opposed to what actually constitutes current practice; and (3) school business means *public* school business.

The school business official perspective continues to serve two important functions today. First, it provides the major definitions of the technical skills required of school business officials. Second, it formalizes the professional norms for individuals performing business functions in schools, that is, it provides an ideal against which to judge behavior.

On the other hand, it leaves unclear what constitutes average behavior, that is, what most school business administrators actually do rather than what they should do. By shifting the focus from normative (should do) to descriptive (does), we open up for discussion and analysis a wide range of problems in schools, and thus we can begin to work toward solutions. For example, instead of examining the logical division of authority between state and local governments for providing public education, we can ask why some very large public school systems are on the verge of bankruptcy and why others have had to close their doors months before June. Instead of expounding on the importance of local school administrators providing educationally sound facilities, we can seek to understand why some school district officials are responding to enrollment declines by selling their newest buildings. Instead of describing the financial controls designed into the accounting operations of schools, we can seek to understand how a superintendent can be caught misappropriating school equipment only after a jealous neighbor saw the equipment in the superintendent's backyard and blew the whistle on him.

In short, we seek to complement the school business official perspective by looking at what is actually done as much as by examining what ought to be done. This does not imply that by so doing we hope to find that all school officials are spendthrifts, poor planners, or crooks. We argue, however, that to understand school business we have to examine actual behavior, not ideals; even though on the rare occasion we may find some socially undesirable behavior.

The School as Business Analogue Perspective

The mere mention of schools as analogues to business is sufficient to elicit heated discussion from many experienced educators. It is not, however, a recently discovered analogue. The concept of schools as business took form during the first two decades of this century, almost as a by-product of the scientific management movement identified with the work of Frederick W. Taylor (1911). Franklin Bobbitt (1913) of the University of Chicago and Ellwood P. Cubberley (1916) of Stanford were chief among the educators of the times calling for greater efficiency and more scientific management of schools:

> Every manufacturing establishment that turns out a standard product or series of products of any kind maintains a force of efficiency experts to study methods of procedure and to measure and test the output of its works. Such men ultimately bring the manufacturing establishment large returns, by introducing improvements in process and procedure, and in training the workmen to produce a larger and a better output. Our schools are, in a sense, factories in which the raw products (children) are to be shaped and fashioned into products to meet the demands of life. The specifications for manufacturing come from the demands of twentieth-century civilization, and it is the business of the school to build its pupils according to the specifications laid down. This demands good tools, specialized machinery, continuous measurement of production to see if it is according to specifications, the elimination of waste in manufacture, and a large variety in the output. [Cubberley 1916, p. 325]

Some educational administrators today feel schools can be understood by comparing their operation to the idealized operations of commercial and industrial firms. These administrators often resort to comparisons with business to argue for changes in schools. For example, Frank Spaulding, superintendent of the Newton (Massachusetts), Minneapolis, and Cleveland schools and a leading advocate of scientific management, championed the benefits of unit-cost analysis under different conditions as a useful method for reducing costs and improving quality.

> Why is a pupil recitation in English costing 7.2 cents in the vocational school while it costs only 5 cents in the technical school? Is the "vocational" English 44 percent superior to the "technical" English or 44 percent more difficult to secure? Why are we paying 80 percent more in the vocational than in the technical school for the same unit of instruction in mathematics? Why does a pupil recitation in science cost from 55 percent to 67 percent more in the Newton High than in either of the other schools? [Spaulding 1955; also in Callahan 1962, p. 74]

Educators were by no means unanimous in their adoption of this perspective. The most thorough and critical commentary on the adoption by educators of the basic values as well as the techniques of the business-industrial world was provided in the early 1960s in *Education and the Cult of Efficiency* (Callahan 1962). According to Callahan, school administrators adopted the analogue not because of its inherent appeal but because they were vulnerable to pressure from businessmen.

> A "profession" of school administration, vulnerable to the pressures of the community and with no solid tradition behind it to counteract these strong pressures, being criticized for inefficiency at the very time when the community's most influential group, the businessmen, were adopting a new panacea for this very problem, the panacea of scientific management. No wonder that schoolmen sought to emulate the efficiency of business and use whatever methods business had used to attain it; and no wonder that "scientific management" appeared in the forefront of these methods. Its appearance, however, was an unhappy one for our educational system. For instead of approaching the study of administration through the social sciences, school administrators applied the "science" of business-industrial management as they understood it. [P. 245]

For Callahan this "tragedy" was fourfold: ". . . that educational questions were subordinated to business considerations; that administrators were produced who were not, in any true sense, educators; that a scientific label was put on some very unscientific and dubious methods and practices; and that an anti-intellectual climate, already prevalent, was strengthened" (p. 246). Educational decisions made on economic or noneducational grounds included, according to Callahan, eliminating Greek from the curriculum, instituting the "platoon" (schedule) school, and increasing class size and teacher load.

Many experienced educators reject the analogue of schools as business for several of the reasons Callahan discusses: children are not widgets, the education process is too complex to meter and control, and so on. Yet, despite its misapplications and inherent shortcomings, the school as business analogue perspective has had a major impact on our thinking about schools.

The perspective we use to analyze the business characteristics of schools in this text—the property rights perspective—derives from the schools as business analogue perspective, but the differences are quite evident. Today, cost-control measures and reporting requirements of the type bemoaned by

Callahan are actually much more prominent in public education than in today's profit-seeking businesses and industries. If "borrowing" from business was a common practice in previous years, certainly cost containment, efficiency, and control continue to be important concerns of education administrators today. Pressure from businessmen, however, simply does not completely explain all or most of the emphasis over the last several decades on attempts to control costs and increase efficiencies within public schools.

Our second point of departure from the schools as business analogue perspective results from the assumption that all business practices should maximize efficiency. The difference here lies not with the concept of schools as businesses but with the assumptions about businessmen's behavior. As we discuss later, efficiency, or "producing the finest product at the lowest cost" (Callahan 1962, p. 244), is only one of many objectives pursued by both business executives and educational administrators. Efficiency will be encouraged more in some organizations than in others, but comparing all schools to all businesses will not help to differentiate between school organizations very well, nor will it reveal all of the other common goals for which business executives and school administrators strive. There is so much variation among schools and among businesses that comparison of the *groups* masks important similarities between *some* businesses and *some* schools that can be instructive. Public schools, for example, share many operating characteristics with other public organizations, especially those human service organizations that receive relatively large proportions of their income from tax revenues as opposed to client fees. On the other hand, private schools (both proprietary and nonprofit) resemble profit-seeking businesses in many important respects.

The property rights perspective is similar, however, to the schools as business analogue perspective in at least two respects: one regarding the limited usefulness in distinguishing between business and educational functions and the other regarding causes of individual behavior. The presumption in this text is that business functions *cannot* be usefully separated from educational functions in schools. The business of schools is education, and to separate thinking about support functions from the main business of education is impossible. This is not to say that separate departments cannot be set up to perform accounting, custodial, and other functions in schools, that people working in these units do not have unique concerns, or that those functions cannot be separately evaluated. Rather it is an acknowledgment that educational goals and requirements define business goals and requirements, and vice versa, and that these mutually defining relationships differ among different types of schools.

The frequent, I may say the prevalent, effort to distinguish the problems of the school into financial or business on the one hand, and educational on the other, results in two groups of problems barren of significance. Those school boards who insist on reserving to themselves, or committing to a special business manager, supposedly an expert, the business administration of a system of schools, while they impose on a superintendent, presumably an educational expert, the so-called professional administration of that same system of schools, and those superintendents who advocate this plan, or meekly acquiesce in it, give evidence of about as sound and comprehensive a grasp of the real problem of educational administration as the would-be manufacturer of shoes must have of that industry who would put his factory in charge of two independent experts, one of whom knew all about shoes as a finished product and all about the processes of their manufacture but knew little and was expected to know less about costs, while the other knew nothing about shoes but was a past master of business and finance. [Spaulding 1955; also in Callahan 1962, p. 76]

The second major similarity between his text's perspective and that of the schools as business analogue is that both acknowledge the importance of self-interest in motivating behavior. As pointed out by Callahan (1962), school administrators did not adopt business methods *solely* to improve the schools—"the adoption of business procedures [also] strengthened the position of the superintendent." Public school superintendents during the early decades of this century experienced a variety of incentives to adopt "efficiency language" and practices. Spaulding (1955), for example, acknowledged years later that he landed the very high-paying Minneapolis superintendency by cleverly convincing the school board that he was an efficient, businesslike, cost-conscious administrator—which was exactly what they wanted.

One of the central themes of our examination of schools is that educators respond to the incentives, both positive and negative, with which they are faced, and that when two administrators behave apparently differently, it is in large part explained by the different incentives as well as by the different sets of opportunities available to them. Points of comparison in our examination are not between schools and businesses but between the behavior of administrators in one type of school and those in another type. The type of school creates the set of opportunities available to an administrator. Emphasis is placed on what are traditionally thought of as the business functions within schools, and these business functions affect any educator who has responsibility for financial management.

The Management Systems in Schools Perspective

A more contemporary manifestation of the schools as business analogue might be called the management systems in schools perspective. If the schools as business perspective emphasized technical efficiency (perhaps, many critics would say, ineptly applied), management systems corrected this narrowness by encompassing an analysis of the processes and outcomes of schooling as well as an examination of the costs. Management systems go by a variety of more specific proper names familiar to most members of the education profession: management by objectives, cost-benefit analysis, systems analysis, planning-programming-budgeting systems, long-range planning, zero-base budgeting, and others. Many of these management systems originated in other business and government settings. Schools have adopted these systems to varying degrees and with numerous modifications.

This text's perspective also derives from the management systems perspective, but again there are several differences. Although we discuss management systems, the goal in this text is to attempt to understand why certain systems show up in some educational settings and not in others. In other words, we will examine how they are actually used as opposed to how they were designed to be used.

In *The New Cult of Efficiency and Education*, James (1968) captured the flavor of these systems, and from his work we have drawn both an important conclusion and a question. Briefly, our conclusion is that the unifying characteristic of these techniques is that they help educational administrators to think through problems more clearly. But, we must ask, if this is so, is there sufficient evidence that the ability to think clearly and the resulting thoughts have fostered better, or at least different, behavior?

> Much of the usefulness of the [cost-benefit analysis] technique rests in the orderly and disciplined attention given to analyzing the situation surrounding a problem, to finding ways to quantify as many of the relevant variables as possible, to devising simplified models within which the variables can be manipulated, and to changing—as imagination dictates and as capacity for calculation and procurement allows—the materials, personnel, and even purposes to be achieved, in order to arrive at proposals for alternative courses of action and their consequences. [James 1968, p. 35]

This conclusion raises for us the following question: How and why do situations, problems, and courses of action differ among different kinds of schools? Are extensive, systematic planning and analysis the major factors that distinguish schools, or are other factors more significant? Are we hearing variations on a theme or are we hearing different themes? Despite great overall variance in the adoption of management systems, we see broad similarities across schools in similar situations. For example, the problems and courses of action among large-city public schools are remarkably similar, as are the problems and courses of action among selective coeducational private day schools. However, the problems facing administrators in large public schools are quite different from those facing administrators of selective coed boarding schools. Do the seeming advantages of thinking through a problem carefully really result in better, or even different, courses of action? Or rather do the opportunities facing school administrators in their varied settings so shape their behavior that more formal, extensive analysis leads to behavior that differs little from the "seat-of-the-pants" approach taken by others? The presumption in this text is that management systems techniques *can* aid educational administrators as they select among alternative courses of action, but that the range of alternatives is severely constrained within the context of a particular setting. The resulting choices within similar settings have been and can only be marginally different. Since settings make a considerable difference, we would do well to examine how they differ and which differences most influence administrators' behavior.

The Fourth Perspective: Property Rights

All three of the previously described perspectives presume the following objectives: to improve schooling, to explain the organization of schooling, and to help educational administrators manage schools.

How the Property Rights Perspective Differs

Although the property rights perspective shares these same objectives, we suggest three points of departure that should more readily accomplish the objectives. First, adopt a means to describe and explain what actually goes on in schools, not what should go on. A consideration of the desired activities should be complemented by examining predominant practices. Second, the perspective should include a way of explaining behavior in a wide range of school settings, not merely in urban, large, or public schools. If there are important differences between settings, such as between public and private schools, they should be examined, because these differences provide the clues to what is managerially possible in each setting. Three, the perspective should attend to individual—as opposed to organizational—behavior, because managers are individuals and operate as individuals in schools.

The perspective employed throughout this book derives most directly from a branch of study in economics called "property rights." A relatively new school of thought pioneered by Ronald Coase (1960) and others, it incorporates elements of the legal rules on liability into a revised theory of production and exchange. It refers to a system of legal rules, both stated and implied, that includes the legal rights, privileges, and duties of individuals (Pejovich 1979). The property rights approach differs from the standard theory of production and exchange in two respects: motives and costs.

Whereas the standard theory of production and exchange holds that an organization will attempt to maximize revenues over costs, the property rights approach focuses on individual self-interest in the form of utility maximization. Utility differs from profit in that it can be derived from nonpecuniary-related sources, while profit, by definition, cannot. Furthermore, under the standard theory of production the organization is subject to only the costs of production—that is, the purchase of inputs—while transaction costs are nonexistent. The property rights approach assumes the existence of transaction costs, which include costs for exchanging property rights, and that a penalty-reward system occurs within the organization structure that constrains the individual's behavior.

As a result of these modifications to the standard theory of production and exchange, the unit of analysis shifts from the organization to the individual decision makers. The idea of using the concept of property rights to examine organizational behavior is one that is growing among certain economists. We have borrowed from this school of thought because we feel it helps us to better understand school administration. The perspective has grown out of dissatisfaction with both the concepts of "economic man" and the "theory of the firm" arguments about how individuals behave in organizations. This perspective also provides an alternative to the three schools of thought discussed earlier. Among the individuals who have made major contributions to this approach to thinking about organizations are Michael Jensen and William Meckling of the Graduate School of Management at the University of Rochester (see Jensen and Meckling 1976; Meckling 1976). A discussion applying their ideas and those of others to education follows.

Individual Versus Organizational Behavior

Today it is natural to think of organizations as having lives of their own: Chicago public schools close early because of lack of money; St. Anne's School opens a new wing; the Harrell School raises its tuition 12 percent this year. The organization is alive! Upon reflection, however, we realize that it is not the schools but certain groups of people within those organizations who make these and other kinds of decisions. Other groups of individuals within the same schools are not a part of those decisions, and they would not likely make the same decision if they had the right to decide. For example, the school board decides to close schools early for lack of funds against the desires of teachers; a majority of the board of trustees at St. Anne's School opens a new wing against the desires of the faculty and a minority of board members who wish, instead, to improve salaries; the board adopts the headmaster's recommendation to raise tuition at Harrell against the wishes of many parents, some of whom will be forced to withdraw their children from the school.

We can turn up the microscope to even greater levels of magnification and, looking even closer, see that in fact no two individuals have identical interests or opportunities; and even if they were in precisely the same circumstances, they would not behave in precisely the same way. School administrators are not an exception. Although there are a variety of qualities that we could examine, we are concerned here with only two groups of characteristics that set individuals apart from each other: (1) their desires or preferences and (2) their rights or opportunities to make decisions about resources. (In this context, a right and an opportunity are roughly equivalent. Some people have the right to determine how to spend a budget, for example. This implies that they may avail themselves of the spending opportunities associated with budgetary decision rights.) We will look at individual desires, or wants, first.

Individual Desires

Each individual, at any point in time, possesses a unique set of wants or desires. This set is often called a preference function, not only because a person's preferences are a function of a variety of desires but also because the individual's *behavior* is determined by (is a function of) a set of preferences. These desires are often associated with, for example, food, shelter, leisure, education, work, travel, religion, power, love, and self-esteem.

Sets of Desires Are Unique. Although many of us seem to be striving to satisfy similar desires, it is unlikely that any two individuals have identical preference functions, both in terms of the mix of desires and the intensity with which each desire is wanted. An individual's wants are usually unlimited, but few individuals relentlessly pursue a particular desire to the exclusion of others, because each want is subject to "diminishing marginal satisfaction" and desires sometimes conflict. ("Diminishing marginal satisfaction" means that each *additional* unit of consumption of a good or service provides a little less satisfaction than did consumption of the immediately preceding one; for example, the second lobster for dinner is not quite as satisfying as the first.) A specific example will help us to explain these characteristics.

Consider a school district business official who during the coming year wants (among many other desires) to (1) reduce the turnaround time required in the purchasing process; (2) improve reading scores in the school district; and (3) improve his golf score. We can imagine several reasons why the business official has these three desires. He is interested in reducing the turnaround time for purchasing because he gets a lot of complaints from teachers and administrators about the long delays between when something is ordered and when it is received—he wants to avoid complaints. He wishes to improve school attendance because the school district receives revenues from the state based on average daily attendance—he wants greater revenue. He wishes to improve his golf score because golf is one of the few activities in which he is totally responsible for his performance—he derives great personal pleasure from playing golf.

Changing Desires. The importance he attaches to these desires changes over time. If through working with the school principals, his initial efforts to increase attendance from, say, 83 to 89 percent paid off, his desire to improve attendance will diminish—that is, improving attendance will not seem as important as it once was. He would still like to improve attendance, but each additional percentage point will not be quite as important as the previous one; this is an example of diminishing marginal satisfaction.

Conflicting Desires. A school business official's desires sometimes conflict with each other. The time he spends trying to improve attendance and reduce the turnaround time of purchasing is time he cannot spend on the links. Thus, his various desires in a sense compete for his time and other scarce resources. Time acts as a constraint in this case, but it is not the only constraint. For example, there will always be a certain percentage of children who, for various reasons (such as sickness or emergencies), will not show up at school; therefore his desire for a much higher attendance rate will ultimately be restricted by a constraint inherent in that desire—a *physical* constraint. The two kinds of constraints are different. The first limits the availability of resources at hand to satisfy the wants, and the second deals with the limitations inherent in the desire.

How individuals behave is determined in part by their preference function. Therefore, if we want to understand or to influence behavior, it is certainly important that we understand the different sets of preferences of each individual. But how do we go about this? We can ask, but this is not a very good measure for several reasons. The answer is likely to depend on who we are and on the circumstances of our asking. If we were to ask the official about his plans to improve his golf game, his responses might vary depending on whether we were the superintendent of schools, a subordinate, or a golfing partner. His behavior, then, is more revealing than what he says.

Sources of Desires. An individual's unique set of desires may emanate from a variety of causes perhaps best explained by a developmental psychologist. Job-related wants stem only partly from the fact that they represent problems or opportunities; for example, attendance is low, resources are scarce, more kids means more income. They are problems or opportunities only when an individual perceives them as such. Specifically, individuals perceive a problem when they feel that their welfare may be affected or that losses to welfare may be reduced and that the costs incurred from identifying a problem are less than the costs of not identifying a problem. Problems are not constraints; they can be acted on, while constraints cannot. How people acquire their current set of desires is a complex issue. For our purposes, it is sufficient to understand that these desires exist, that they are unlimited, that they are often in conflict, that they change over time, and that they contain both job-related and non-job-related elements.

Individuals' Property Rights

The second characteristic of individuals that affects their behavior is a unique set of "property rights." This term is used here to describe the rights an individual has over a particular set of resources—it is decision-making authority in the broadest sense of the term. Property can include people as well as physical objects such as land, a house, tools, cash. Property rights give the possessor of the property freedom to make decisions as to how to use the property or how its physical attributes will be altered. This could include options to exchange some property rights for others.

Job-Related and Non-Job-Related Rights. The individual has rights over job-related as well as non-job-related resources. The school administrator, for example, has rights regarding how budgets are spent, how subordinates' time is used, and what goods the school purchases.

Consider again our example of the school business official. Certain decision rights accompany his position. He probably has a budget about which he decides on expenditures. He also likely supervises other personnel and makes decisions about how they will spend their time, and he has some discretion over how he will spend some of his own time. Finally, he has a personal claim to a portion of the school district's assets (his salary). These decision rights have value to our business official because they can be used by him to help him satisfy his wants. For example, he may have the right to decide to leave work early on Wednesday afternoon to shoot a round of golf. (We will be saying more about how he uses these rights a little later.) Our business manager exercises non-job-related rights when he decides what personal goods and services to purchase for his family, what civic and social functions to allocate his time and money to, and so forth.

Sources of Rights. How did he acquire these rights? Decision rights are acquired in a variety of ways. First, some *rights accompany a position.* The business manager, for example, has the right to determine how budget appropriations for the school business functions will be spent. He then claims a right to determine the disposition of some district assets. Second, some *rights are inherited.* This manager acquires rights over the use of a set of golf clubs because his father willed the set to him. Third, many *rights are traded.* He exchanges with a country club his rights over $2,000 for the right to purchase playing time on the golf course. Fourth, some *rights are expropriated.* The business manager assumes control of instructional as well as administrative data processing when the district purchases a new computer. He persuaded the school superintendent that dual control over the computer was "dysfunctional."

Shared Rights. In both job and nonjob settings individual rights may be shared with other individuals. Off the job, the business official shares his playing rights on the country club golf course with other individuals who have paid the initiation fee. He shares the rights to rent a campsite in the state park with a much larger set of individuals. He shares the right to smoke his favorite pipe, however, with no one.

On the job, rights run the gamut from being totally shared to being wholly owned. Shared rights implies that others have some say in the manager's decisions. The manager may share, for example, decision rights over the computer with the assistant superintendent for instruction. Sometimes rights are shared because it is not clear who owns the rights: for example, who has the right to decide whether the school district should purchase a new computer for both business and academic computing purposes? Sometimes it is clear who has the right, but other individuals can and do choose to share in the decision. For example, the school board has the right and responsibility for determining the tax rate on real property in order to raise money for the school district. However, the school business official, because of his expert knowledge and command of information, can greatly influence the decision if he chooses to, and he should attempt to if he perceives that it is in his interests to do so.

Delegated Rights. Broadly shared property rights are usually delegated and end up in the control of relatively few individuals. All adults residing in a state share the right to determine how public education will be provided. Rights are delegated from state legislatures to state agencies, to local school boards, down to local school district employees such as our school business administrator. Rights, then, are assigned to individuals who act as agents for larger segments of society.

Changing Rights. To say that rights are assigned to individuals in no way implies an immutable allocation. On the contrary, their distribution is contantly changing. We continually seek to modify the existing system of rights because rights are limited, rights are in conflict with each other, and, most important, rights are the major means by which we satisfy our desires.

Limited Rights. Individual desires and individual rights differ in one crucial respect: desires are not limited, whereas rights are. The school business official has the right to spend his budget appropriation within specific guidelines only. He can not, for example, use $2 million of his $4 million school district budget to buy his own golf course! He can not send out an order to his operations and maintenance staff to get over to his house to repair the leaky roof. He may be able to leave work early once a week to play golf, but if he started leaving early, say, three times a week, then he might find the superintendent and board members, for example, suggesting that (1) he might not have enough work to do or (2) he is damaging the morale of the other administrators who feel compelled to stay until 4:30. These responses might inhibit the business manager from achieving his desires. Alternatively, there may be a school policy that all central office administrative staff work until 4:30 P.M. unless they have a valid reason for leaving early, and the business official may feel duty bound to stay until then even though he could leave if he chose to.

These examples point up limits to the rights we might exercise. There are a number of ways that rights are limited, including, for example, legal prohibitions, social constraints, and one's own sense of right and wrong. The common characteristic of these limits on the individual's exercise of his rights is that the individual perceives that his *set* of desires cannot be obtained if he insists on achieving a particular desire either within or outside of his rights. For example, he may derive pleasure from getting in a golf game by leaving work early, but the pleasure would not be sufficient to compensate for the guilt he would also feel—in this case he is experiencing conflicting desires. The school business administrator wants to play golf, but, in our example, he also wants to be perceived as a hardworking, moral individual. And in this instance the trade-offs between the benefits of leaving work early to play golf and those of staying on the job to work were such that he chose to exercise his right to stay at the office!

Constraints limit our rights, just as they limit our wants. The rights available to us are defined legally and socially, but what usually delimits our rights are both legal and social sanctions. For example, the school business official does not have the right to purchase a good exceeding a certain dollar amount, without seeking competitive bids. In order to expedite the purchasing process for certain items, he may *wish* to bypass this time-consuming requirement. If he bypasses the bid requirement, he knows that there is a chance that the auditors will note his action and report him to the board of education. This sanction may be sufficient to stop the business official from bypassing the bid procedure. On the other hand, the business official may so desire the educational benefits of getting the goods earlier that he is willing to break up the purchase order into small amounts, thereby circumventing the bid process and taking his chances with the auditor. In this later instance the sanctions that constrained the rights of the school business official were insufficient to prevent his exercising the right to bypass bid procedures.

This particular example might be considered an ethical question: Should the business official obey the bidding requirements of the state, or should the business official knowingly bypass these laws in this one instance to ensure that crucial educational materials arrive in time to be incorporated into the educational program? Although this example includes ethical issues, our purpose is to illustrate the limits of individual rights and the sanctions that enforce those limits.

Conflicting Rights. An individual's rights are often in conflict with the rights of other individuals. The school administrator may feel that he has the right to decide to play golf on Saturday morning, but his children may feel that they have the right to use his time to transport them to the zoo. How he decides to use Saturday mornings will depend on which set of behaviors will maximize his preference function (set of desires). For various reasons, he may decide to take the kids to the zoo.

On the job, he may feel that greater efficiency would result from his assuming control of all data-processing functions, but the assistant superintendent of instruction may feel that this would reduce his own rights in managing instructional programs that require data-processing capabilities. Rights can be lost as well as gained! Or, the superintendent may want him to spend more time on buildings and grounds problems that the business manager feels do not warrant added time.

Satisfying Desires Through the Exercise of Property Rights

Up to this point we have tried to treat individual desires and rights as independent, but they are intimately related. We satisfy our wants through making decisions about property—this proposition is central to our analysis, and it helps us to understand why people behave the way they do. We will now discuss the characteristics of individuals as they make property rights decisions.

First, each individual has the capacity to envision and consider alternative ways of employing property rights (Meckling 1976). That is, each individual views his rights as an *opportunity set* to be considered. Individuals are by nature resourceful, creative, and innovative within their opportunity set. The opportunity set can include options that imitate existing ways of doing things—(that is, we can copy others)—as well as options that are created anew. The school business official, for example, may work with the principals to set up a system that rewards students for good attendance. Individuals are creative when they consider alternative ways of gaining new property rights that they want, of keeping from losing their current property rights, or of discarding rights they do not want.

Second, individuals have the *ability to make decisions* about or choose among the alternatives in their opportunity sets. These decisions are made according to what maximizes their preference functions. They are evaluators—the capacity to evaluate options involves knowledge and abilities that may be gained in different ways. Individuals' intuition, the arguments of others, and quantitative analysis might affect the decision alternatives. Decisions, however, are never completely quantitative because only a subset of information about individuals' preference functions is quantified.

Third, individuals seek and use information. Information is an important ingredient in decision making, and one of the options that individuals continually face is whether to postpone a decision in order to gather more information. In both securing and measuring options, individuals can choose to obtain more information than is available at the time the opportunity for the decision is offered (Alchian and Demsetz 1972). Why then do people sometimes make bad decisions? Bad not only as others might see them, but bad as the person making the decisions might see them in retrospect! Often at this point the issues associated with ethics enter into the discussion of decisions, that is, the "right or wrong" of a decision as opposed to the "good or bad" of a decision. Ethics are really "built in" to each of our individual sets of preferences. Albert Schweitzer "preferred" to bring his medical services to people in the jungles of Africa. We can look at his decision and call it highly ethical, even moral, but the fact remains that he was behaving based on *his* preferences. The answer, in a word, is *imperfect* information. As a president of General Motors once said, "There are no bad decisions, just insufficient information." If our school business administrator knew ahead of time that the president of the school board and the superintendent were going to be passing through his office the day he was on the golf course, he may well have postponed his trip to the course. If he knew that it would take a large amount of his resources to reduce the purchasing turnaround time by 10 percent and that this would yield absolutely no decrease in complaints, he might have made different choices. If he and the school board submitted a budget to the voters with a 4 percent increase in taxes and had known in advance that the community would have approved as much as a 10 percent increase, it is possible they would have asked for a larger increase. In each case the business official could have secured more information, probably with added costs, prior to acting. To say that imperfect information is the cause of bad decisions does not imply good decisions result from perfect information. For all practical purposes, decisions are based on incomplete information. We often do not know, even long after a decision was made, whether a decision was the best, or even a good one. Individuals maximize their preferences in creative ways through their exercise of property rights, and the information they choose to use helps them to determine what action to take.

Educational Organizations as Collectives of Individuals

Although the basic building blocks of property rights are individual rights and preferences, we can also examine "organizational behavior." Property rights provides us with a useful, if partial, perspective for analyzing and understanding schools as organizations. In this perspective, organizations are a nexus of contracts with which utility-maximizing individuals exchange rights to resources. One of the ways in which individuals satisfy their desires is by joining—that is, by contracting with—organizations. An organization is a collection of individuals, each of whom perceives that the personal benefits of affiliation with the organization outweigh the costs of disassociation (Arrow 1971). Furthermore, each individual participates simultaneously in a number of organizations. An individual's participation in multiple organizations may directly or indirectly link organizations, a fact that also affects an individual's behavior.

A fundamental purpose of organizations is to allow members to pursue their desires by exchanging property rights. In a sense, then, schools are simply special organizations. Schools may have unique missions, and each school will have a unique set of services and technology. These facts do not suggest, however, that the building blocks of property rights and personal preferences are any less applicable in schools than in other organizations.

The organizations that individuals form in order to pursue their interests are many and varied: factories, banks, clubs, hospitals, schools, churches, libraries, art galleries, retail establishments, fire departments, cocktail parties, demonstrations, meetings, courts, transportation systems, and the like. School organizations may be classified as profit-seeking, nonprofit, and public.

Similarities and Differences Among Organizations

Unique and identifiable characteristics distinguish schools from other organizations. They differ in their clientele and in the services they provide. We certainly can identify the differences between schools and a fire department, a blood bank, a neo-Nazi group, or a nunnery. There are also perceivable differences between organizations having ostensibly the same purpose; for example, no two universities are identical. As we have said, it is easy to think of organizations as entities in their own right—as if they were individuals with their own preference functions, property rights, and personalities. A school or school district has a "personality" only because its members share common characteristics or behave similarly, which reflects the fact that an organization attracts a certain type of individual and offers incentives to its members to behave in ways that help the organization achieve its goals. However, it is each individual in the organizations, not the organizations per se, that has these attributes.

The property rights perspective would be of little use in our study of school business administration if it did not help us to understand how groups of individuals behave as well as how the single individual behaves. Fortunately it is useful in this regard—it helps us to understand (1) how individuals act collectively through a system of contracts, and (2) how that system affects what the organization produces.

Systems of Contracts. Most of us have unique relationships with many other people. If we can think of a relationship with someone else in terms of what each party can expect from the other, a kind of informal "contract," we can view ourselves as working and living within a web of contractual relationships. This web of relationships is complex when we consider our own individual contracts with all the other people we work with. The web can become *very* complex when we attempt to map the contracts of all of those people as well!

Even if we limited our discussion to the most basic contracts in the workplace, we could devote the entire length of this book to a map for one school district. The "system of contracts" is, essentially, a map of the major relationships among people in an organization. "System" here is meant to suggest the interrelatedness of these relationships. "Contracts" implies that the expectations of the relationship are somewhat like the "rights" of individuals as identified in legal contracts. Like legal contracts, contracts here defines rights of individuals, how rights can be exercised, and, as well, what the probable rewards will be for honoring the contract terms and the probable penalties for breaking the contract.

An examination of the systems of contracts of different organizations is useful in comparing the organizations and in providing an understanding of why people appear to behave differently in different organizations. Compare, for example, public school teachers with teachers in an independent school. Generally, public school teachers enjoy the right to their positions through tenure (at least until recently in some districts), are paid on the average 50 percent more in salary than independent school teachers, and teach children with a wide variety of intellectual and motivational levels. Contrast this to independent school teachers who receive less compensation, do not have tenure rights, and who teach students with, on the average, higher levels of aptitude and motivation. Public school teachers do not possess the right to try to increase their following year's salary through "good teaching." Salary increases in the public schools are determined by units of course work taken and years of experience. Private school teachers in many instances can influence their salary because performance is evaluated by their superiors as a basis for a wage increase. These two groups of teachers work within organizations that fundamentally differ in their systems of contracts. As a result, the rewards and penalties of each are as different as their opportunities.

The names we usually use to distinguish among different types of organizations, such as profit-seeking corporations, partnerships, nonprofit entities and government agencies, imply major differences in contract systems and, therefore, differences in the behavior of their members. Two of the most important distinctions deal with how decision rights concerning assets and liabilities and primary sources of revenues differ. Consider the difference between XYZ school district, QED independent school, and ABC secretarial school. Marty Burger, as the sole proprietor of ABC secretarial school, has a right to the profits of ABC when assets exceed liabilities, but she must also cover any deficits. If ABC does well, then Marty does well—Marty's financial future is intimately tied to ABCs financial future. The school derives virtually all of its revenue from student fees.

The owners of QED independent school are not as clearly identified. QED is governed by a board of trustees who serve without pay. To the extent that assets exceed liabilities, the board can increase the school's endowment or in some other way direct the residual money into the school. The welfare of the trustees of the organization is improved because, for example, the education for their children is improved or they achieve enhanced status, but individual board members do not benefit financially. A significant proportion (75 percent) of the revenues of QED are derived from student fees.

XYZ school district is yet a different case. School board members are acting as agents for the state, and the degree to which assets exceed liabilities is not within their control. Yet, when XYZ school district does well, school board members themselves might feel that they are doing well. The source of revenue for XYZ school district is largely derived through tax revenue obtained either directly from local property owners or from the state, and very little revenue is generated through student fees. Some public school board members receive salaries, but most do not.

From these examples, we see that in each instance personal preference functions of educational administrators are tied to the performance of organizations. In some instances the benefits may be largely financial, as in Marty's case. In the case of both ABC secretarial school and QED independent school, individuals can accumulate more assets than liabilities (that is, profit), but they must accomplish this mainly through selling services. They are also able to control the enrollment in their organizations; the XYZ school district, however, must expand and contract its capacity according to demographic changes. XYZ does not have the right to restrict enrollments simply because there is no room for the extra students. These and other differences among ABC, QED, and XYZ are important for us because they represent different opportunity sets for administrators in those schools. These opportunity sets help explain why administrators behave differently in different organizations, and they also provide a way to understand the effects of changes in the systems of rights within these different kinds of organizations.

Systems of rights are interesting theoretical constructs, but they have little meaning to the practicing educational administrator unless they are applied to concrete, specific instances in familiar school settings. It is difficult to talk about rights systems within schools without at the same time describing the production processes that tend to dominate in these organizations.

Production Processes. Because schooling is a service, schools' production processes define the nature of their output. The organization of schools defines how students are educated. Schools are usually organized in age-grouped cohorts, and students move from grade level to grade level and from teacher to teacher as they learn what is required in each level. Intermediate outputs are, for example, fourth graders going on to fifth grade and freshmen becoming sophomores. ("Intermediate output" here means that the fourth-grade teachers educate children to a level sufficient to send them on to the fifth grade next door. They are not part of the final stage in compulsory schooling, like twelfth-grade teachers are.) It does not, of course, reflect the kinds of skills, values, and attitudes that have been taught to students. In another sense, the production process represents a specific example of how rights have been distributed within the organization. A fourth-grade teacher exercises a variety of rights over instruction of pupils in the class, but gives up those rights at the end of the year.

Production processes are also the activities by which physical resources and human skills produce a product or service. These are purposeful, goal-directed activities; they need not be stated, but they should be observable. It is easy to visualize the organization as a collection of physical objects (land, building, equipment, trucks, materials, cash, human bodies). It is less easy to visualize how these are combined with human skills into a production process. Inputs (resources) are transformed by the production process into outputs (products or services). Some services are invisible, such as knowledge (education) or psychological change (counseling, religion).

All organizations have a production technology. The technology may be understood by relatively few people (for example, the technology of nuclear power plants, genetic factories, research hospitals) or by many people (the technology found in, for example, fast food services, motels, grocery stores). Each organization's technology is unique, even for organizations that produce the same kinds of outputs. No two schools or school districts operate in exactly the same way.

An individual is related to the technological process in two ways: (1) as a consumer of raw materials or intermediate products and (2) as a producer of intermediate products or finished goods. In other words, services and goods flow among members of the organization. Since most organizations are divided into suborganizations, each with its own output (product or service), participants are often simultaneously producers and consumers (producing for some members and acquiring from others). Members contract with each other, and members of school organizations are no exception.

Consider, for example, four of the typical suborganizations under the direction of the school business official: accounting, purchasing, transportation, and data processing. The flow of work among these units is multifaceted and high in volume. Individuals in the accounting department record transactions associated with those in the other three units; individuals in purchasing require services from those in the other three units, and data processing provides services for the other three units.

Implications for Managerial Behavior

How does all of the preceding affect the way we look at managerial behavior? Specifically, what are the implications of our assumptions about

(1) individual behavior being determined by rights and preferences and (2) organizations being little more than systems of contracts among individuals? There are at least two implications. First, managers operate in settings most often characterized by conflict. The specialization and division of labor inherent in organizations coupled with the utility-maximizing behavior of individuals makes conflict inevitable. Second, one of the fundamentally important parts of a manager's job is to seek to partition decision rights (alter the system of contracts) in such a way that other people are more likely to behave in ways that maximize his own preferences.

Decision Rights and Preferences in Conflict

The professional norms developed through the school business official perspective emphasize the overall good of the educational organization. This perspective would suggest, for example, that the job-related preferences of the four directors of the suborganizations (accounting, purchasing, transportation, and data processing) discussed before should be consistent with the overall good of the public school district. However, in practice it is rarely clear whose definition of what is good for the district the four directors should, or do, follow. Is it their immediate supervisor's definition (perhaps the chief business official)? The superintendent's? A consensus of the members of the board of education? Of course, there are times when these people all agree on what is the common good, or there are various combinations of groups in agreement.

Presume we could agree that the objectives of the four directors should match, say, the objectives of the superintendent (who, we could argue, is the embodiment of the operational goals of the district). The problem of how to bring this about still remains. The individuals involved do not have identical job-related wants; the opportunities (decision rights) available to each director differ, and each does not have access to the same information with which to make decisions because it is very costly to provide all directors with the same information.

It is certainly *desirable* that all of the employees of an organization march to the same drummer (presuming a "good" drummer). Unfortunately such complete consensus on *all* issues not only never happens in practice, but our "in theory" arguments also force us to conclude that consensus can never be *totally* achieved.

The problem of agreement is more pronounced when we consider horizontal relationships (for example, the director of data processing versus the director of accounting and finance) as opposed to vertical ones (for example, the director of data processing versus the superintendent). The job-related desires of the director of data processing will be more distinct from (and at odds with) the job-related wants of the director of accounting than they will be with those of the superintendent. For example, the director of accounting and finance will be more likely to want—

1. a wide variety of report formats from data processing;
2. an ability to modify automated systems rapidly and at will in response to internally or externally imposed mandates; and
3. numerous error or checking controls built into automated financial systems.

The director of data processing, on the other hand, would prefer to—

1. create fewer, more general report formats;
2. make few changes to systems and only those that are absolutely necessary; and
3. supply simple, easily maintained software (with more responsibility for checking for errors given to accounting).

This is not to say that these two directors will not very often be in agreement and work toward mutual objectives; rather we must recognize the inherent limits of achieving totally cooperative behavior. With an awareness of limits, administrators can create incentive systems and partition decision rights in ways that will encourage subordinates to behave more in accord with behavior that administrators think will help achieve higher goals. Preferences of individuals are sometimes in conflict. As a result, where decision rights are not clearly described and enforced, these rights will also be in conflict. The job of the educational administrator is to partition decision rights in such a way that individuals will find it in their interest to behave in a manner that will also maximize the preferences of the administrator. Getting others to behave the way you want them to is, of course, a fundamental problem facing any manager. The problem is so widespread that property rights economists have a name for it—the "agency problem." This term applies especially to how owners of a business get managers to do what the owners want.

Partitioning Decision Rights Among Individuals

Property rights to the physical objects of production are assigned to the participants in an organization (producers, consumers) through the contract system. In our example, each of four directors is assigned rights with the accompanying system of contracts in each of four production units: accounting, purchasing, transportation, and data processing. Services and some goods are constantly flowing between these and other units as children are being educated. Contractual agreements between these units may call merely for giving up rights on demand (for example, if the purchasing unit buys accounting supplies at the request of the accounting unit) or through some form of exchange (for example, the accounting unit "buying" computer time from the data-processing unit). At the same time, employees are exchanging varying levels of skilled labor for various things, for example, wages, working conditions, promises of future promotions, and ensurance of the right to continue the exchange (tenure). Each of the four directors is maximizing his or her preferences through contracts with the others. Their wants and rights are partly common and partly in conflict.

In pursuit of their preference functions school business administrators partition decision rights among their nominal subordinates and others in the organization and through markets to people in other organizations (Williamson 1975). Examples of how decision rights are partitioned follow:

1. The administrator allocates decision rights over physical resources. For example, the director of transportation grants limited rights to use the bus to the bus driver. They are limited because the bus driver, in our example, is not permited to use the bus for personal use on weekends or after five. Also, the bus driver cannot sell the bus or rent it.
2. The administrator allocates decision rights over money: who spends how much and on what. For example, the superintendent grants limited rights to a sum of money to the principal. Rights in this case are limited in terms of what can be purchased (for example, $X for books and $Y for supplies). Although this type of limited control over money is most common, administrators can grant more extensive decision rights. The principal could be allowed to choose to spend the sum of $X + $Y on any combination of books and supplies. Or, the food service director could be allowed to overexpand on the condition that expenditures over budget must be covered by some fraction of unplanned revenues.
3. The administrator partitions decision rights over job-related behavior. A subordinate may not be allowed to hire more than a specified number of employees, or a subordinate may not be able to pay employees more than a specified wage.

Of the four perspectives on school business administration discussed in this chapter, the property rights perspective predominates in the book. Chapters 2 and 3 use the property rights perspective to compare differences in school business administration in the public, private for-profit, and private nonprofit sectors. Fundamental differences in rights across the three sectors are described in chapter 2, and the implications of these differences for planning and control of schools are discussed in chapter 3.

References

Alchian, Armen, and Demsetz, Harold. "Production, Information Costs, and Economic Organization." *The American Economic Review* 62:5 (December 1972): 772–795.

Arrow, Kenneth J., ed. "Control in Large Organizations." *Essays in the Theory of Risk-Bearing*. Chicago: Markham Publishing Co., 1971.

Bobbitt, Franklin. "The Supervision of City Schools: Some General Principles of Management Applied to the Problems of City-School Systems." *Twelfth Yearbook of the National Society for the Study of Education, Part 1*. Bloomington, Ill.: The National Society for the Study of Education, 1913.

Callahan, Raymond E. *Education and the Cult of Efficiency*. Chicago: University of Chicago Press, 1962.

Candoli, I. Carl, et al. *School Business Administration*. Boston: Allyn & Bacon, 1973.

Coase, R. H. "The Nature of the Firm." *Economica* 4 (1960): 386–405.

Cubberly, Ellwood P. *Public School Administration*. Boston: Houston Mifflin, 1916.

Engelhardt, N. J., and Engelhardt, F. *Public School Business Administration*. New York: Teachers College Press, Columbia University, 1927.

Hill, Frederick W. *School Business Administration*. Minneapolis: T. S. Denison & Co., 1967.

Hill, Frederick W., and Colmey, James W. *School Business Administration*. Minneapolis: T. S. Denison & Co., 1964.

James, H. Thomas. *The New Cult of Efficiency and Education*. Pittsburgh: University of Pittsburgh Press, 1968.

Jensen, Michael C., and Meckling, William H. "Theory of the Firm: Managerial Behavior, Agency Costs, and Ownership Structure." *Journal of Financial Economics* 3: 4 (October 1976): 305–360.

Jordan, K. Forbis. *School Business Administration*. New York: The Ronald Press Co., 1969.

Linn, Henry H. *School Business Administration*. New York: The Ronald Press Co., 1956.

Meckling, William H. "Values and the Choice of the Model of the Individual in the Social Sciences (REMM)." Center for Research in Government Policy and Business, reprint no. C-57. New York: University of Rochester, 1976.

Pejovich, Svetozar. *Fundamentals of Economics: A Property Rights Approach*. Dallas: The Fisher Institute, 1979.

Spaulding, Frank. *School Superintendent in Action in Five Cities*. Ringe, N. H.: R. R. Smith, 1955.

Taylor, Frederick W. *The Principals of Scientific Management*. New York: Norton, 1911.

Williamson, Oliver. *Markets and Hierarchies: Analysis and Antitrust Implications, A Study in the Economics of Internal Organization*. New York: The Free Press, 1975.

2

Schooling as a Three-Sector Industry

with Ellen Kehoe

Overview

Historically, educators have recognized important differences between public and private schools. Unfortunately, descriptions of these differences have too often been couched in value-laden phrases such as "better than" and "worse than," and little thought has been given to the causes of the differences. In recent years, for example, a growing number of critics of public schools not only have been pointing to problems within the public school sector but also have been increasingly supporting private education as a viable alternative. In *Public and Private Schools* James Coleman (Coleman, Hoffer, and Kilgore 1981) concluded that private schools outperformed public schools in the areas of cognitive outcomes and character and personality development and in the provision of safer, more disciplined, and orderly environments. The report has drawn intense criticism from other members of the education community.

Regardless of its merits, this particular study and the heated reaction it has generated suggest that many educators and other citizens hold views about public and private schools that are essentially emotional and are intellectually unexamined. Little serious attention has been given to how "privateness" or "publicness" affects managerial behavior. To say that private schools are better or elitist, or that public schools are for all of our children or are more inefficient, is to fan emotions without increasing understanding of either the potentials or shortcomings of either sector. The policy recommendations that accompany these ad hominem descriptions of schools—"Work harder!", "Develop new policies!", and the like—will probably not have a major effect, because symptoms of problems, and not their causes, are at issue.

We will be comparing management in public and private schools throughout the book, not to make value judgments, but to attempt to identify and understand differences in the behavior of managers in those settings. In our attempt to develop descriptive generalizations about the business of schooling, we emphasize the causes of individual behavior. Individuals pursue preferences, we argue, within a system of rights in organizations called schools. Therefore, we should expect to see the greatest differences in behavior when the systems of rights available to individuals vary in major ways. Naturally, the rights of individuals within a particular schooling organization vary. A principal in a public school district, for example, has a different set of rights from a teacher in that district. (This is discussed at length in chapters 10 and 11.) In this chapter we examine rights more superficially by focusing on the collective rights of individuals in schools, which vary by virtue of the sector in which they work. While we postpone discussing the rights of teachers vis-à-vis principals and others, we are presuming that the systems of rights of teachers, principals, and others vary in major ways from sector to sector and that these differences will be reflected in differences in what the schools in the different sectors "produce," that is, in the education they provide. The overall concerns of this chapter are to examine those major differences in rights across schooling organizations and to describe variations in managerial behavior that seem to be associated with those differences.

●●●

Definition of the Schooling Industry

One of the reasons that differences in rights have only recently been seriously examined is because in the past our attention has been riveted on schools located in only one sector—the public sector. This is reasonable if only because about 90 percent of our nation's children are currently educated in the public sector. So, when people speak of "schools," they usually mean only the public schools, although this definition is by no means inclusive.

A more inclusive definition would include private nonprofit (typically grouped as independent and parochial) schools. Private nonprofit schools provide some services that are roughly equivalent to some of the services provided in some public schools, and they can be considered substitutes for public schools. An even more comprehensive definition would include formal schooling programs that provide education that only partially substitutes for the schooling services of either the public or nonprofit sector. Examples include part-time religious schools for children and youth; educational activities of out-of-school groups such as YMCA and YWCA swim classes, Boys' Clubs, arts and crafts classes, Boy Scout and Girl Scout activities, Future Farmers of America training and vocational agriculture, and summer soccer leagues; part-time specialty schools providing private lessons in both vocational and avocational subjects (for example, piano lessons); proprietary vocational schools providing trade, technical, business, cosmetology, and barbering training; high school education in military and proprietary schools; and instruction by civilian employers that includes both training under apprenticeships by unions and training of employees by employers. In some way or another all these diverse schooling organizations represent partial substitutes for services provided in the public school. Although we shall emphasize public schools, other organizational forms of schooling will be referred to when by so doing we can distinguish among systems of rights and their effect on managerial behavior.

Organization of the Chapter

Although no single taxonomy or categorization scheme will unambiguously distinguish among all schooling organizations according to their systems of rights, one useful means of classification is the sector in which each organization is located. The sector of a school defines in a most elementary manner the rights of the individuals associated with that school. We discuss first the fundamental differences in rights associated with the private for-profit, public, and private nonprofit sectors. Second, we briefly examine how these differences in rights affect the behavior of three groups of individuals—sponsors, operators, and clients—toward each other. We then pose the question: If the organizations in different sectors are partial substitutes for each other, what role do schools in each sector play? If they play different roles, then we should see this reflected in the types and breadth of services rendered and in the technology or ways in which resources are organized to provide services.

Organizational Rights from Sector to Sector

We often link the differences among sectors to the specific organizations with which we are only generally familiar. We know that School No. 3 is public; St. Agnes is private nonprofit; and the Sayward Business School is private for-profit, or "proprietary." However, schools in each sector experience certain "advantages" and are constrained by certain "disadvantages," which are often associated with the rights of managers in those organizations. Five of the most fundamental differences in the rights of schools in these sectors are associated with treatment of an organization's net earnings and equity, access to tax revenues, exclusion from tax costs, access to student markets, and pricing of services.

Equity Treatment

Most schooling organizations have a positive market value, that is, they are worth something. This value is represented not only by the land and buildings but also by the whole operating enterprise, including the value of the "human capital" of those who work there. In other words, a school organization has equity. In the private for-profit sector, individuals (including employees) can own and transfer shares of the organization's equity. Although there are a variety of organizational forms within the private for-profit sector, such as single proprietorships, partnerships, and corporations, all share the characteristic of permitting individuals to share residual cash flows (profits). Individuals can appropriate or distribute to themselves profits and can suffer economic loss during periods of negative cash flow.

Private nonprofit organizations differ from private for-profit organizations in that ownership of the organization cannot be held and traded by individuals. A nonprofit organization is barred from distributing its net earnings, if any, to the individuals who exercise control over it, such as members, officers, directors, or trustees. This does not mean that a nonprofit organization is barred from earning a profit. Many nonprofit organizations, including schools, consistently show an annual cash surplus. It is only the distribution of profits to individuals that is prohibited. Any net earnings must be retained and "devoted in their entirety to financing further production of the services that the organization was formed to provide" (Hansmann 1980, p. 838).

Most nonprofit schools are incorporated, and the constraint on distributing profits is imposed as a condition of the organization's corporate charter. Thus, a nonprofit school is distinguished from a for-profit school primarily by the absence of indicators of ownership that give for-profit owners a simultaneous share in both profits and control.

Public schools, like nonprofit schools, prohibit distribution of equity to individuals. Unlike nonprofit schools, public schools are agencies of state legislative bodies that are legally charged with the responsibility of providing public schooling and have elected to fulfill that charge in large measure by operating schools through local school districts. Net revenues cannot be distributed to individuals, and it is also difficult for surplus revenues to be plowed back into the organization without cost. Most often, any operating surplus in one period is merely used to reduce revenue-generating requirements in the subsequent period.

Claims on Tax Revenues

For-profit educational organizations have no direct or continuing claim on general appropriations from public legislative bodies. However, proprietary schools have on occasion benefited from publicly funded training or education programs, especially those where the aid "follows" the pupil.

Public schools, of course, do have access to tax revenues from local, state, and federal sources. Currently, about 43 percent of the operating revenues of local school districts are raised by taxing real estate property in the district and about 49 percent comes from general revenues of the state in which the district is located. The remainder comes from federal agencies. (The means by which taxes are collected and made available to public school officials is dealt with in chapter 4.)

Although private nonprofit schools do not have the same broad claim on tax revenues, managers of these schools have indirect claims on various categorical sources of public money. Recent amendments to legislation authorizing federal assistance programs in elementary and secondary education require that private school pupils be given an opportunity to participate in programs and services supported by federal grant funds. Generally funds are not given directly to private nonprofit schools (with the exception of school lunch and other food programs for children).

Bearing Tax Costs

Neither public nor private nonprofit schools bear tax costs, although both are being increasingly required to pay "user fees" for municipal services. For-profit educational organizations pay both local real estate taxes and federal and state corporate income taxes. Their corporate income tax liability is mitigated in part by the right of for-profit school managers to depreciate the value of their capital assets.

Access to Markets for Students

School-age children are currently compelled by law to attend either a public or a private nonprofit school. Until recently, for-profit schools have been locked out of the K–12 market (see exhibit 2.1). This may be about to change. Recently, public schools in Illinois and Arizona have been allowed to subcontract with for-profit schools to provide instruction. One of these for-profit providers is Ombudsman in Illinois, a for-profit secondary school that grants high school diplomas. Ombudsman managers are prohibited from contracting directly with students as their nonprofit counterparts can. Rather, they must and do subcontract with public school districts (to educate potential school dropouts).

The student market for public school administrators is usually limited by the boundaries of their school district. Beyond those boundaries they may attract students who are willing to pay a price in the form of tuition. In their pursuit of students, managers in the two private sectors are less constrained by political boundaries than they are by economic boundaries, distances beyond which it is unlikely that sufficient numbers of students will enroll to justify the costs incurred in recruiting and transporting them. Administrators

Exhibit 2.1

Exclusion of For-Profit Organizations from the Schooling Market

	Enrollment (in thousands)			Percentage of Organization by Sector		
	1967	1989	Change from 1967 in percent	For Profit	Non-profit	Public
Category of Student						
Preprimary; ages 3–5	3,868	6,559	170	40.7	45.1	14.2
Kindergarten to Grade 8	49,891	45,393	91	–	12.2	87.8
Grades 9–12	13,649	12,300	90	–	10.4	89.6
Post-Secondary in 2-year Schools	1,792	5,773	322	6.8	15.8	77.5
Post-Secondary in 4-year Schools	5,721	8,766	153	0.8	70.9	28.3

Sources: Adapted from Nancy Dearman and Velena Plisko, *The Condition of Education, 1980 Edition* (Washington, D.C.: National Center for Education Statistics, 1980) pp. 56, 114, and 196; and from Martin Frankel and Debra Gerald, *Projections of Education Statistics to 1988–89* (Washington, D.C.: National Center for Education Statistics, 1980), pp. 25, 26.

in the two private sectors can restrict the entry of children into their organizations and can compel them to leave much more easily than can public school administrators.

Public school administrators have generally been restricted in the age span of the student markets they serve (K–12), although many run auxiliary education programs. Administrators in the two private sectors can provide services to children both younger and older than state-mandated compulsory attendance ages. Although public school administrators are permitted access to markets of students who are over eighteen years of age, their recruiting efforts must be funded through user fees and net revenues (profits); administrators are generally not allowed to use tax revenues for these efforts.

Pricing Services

Public school officials are not permitted to charge students for educational programs that students are required to attend. On the other hand, administrators in the two private sectors are free to set prices and to price discriminate (charge students differing prices for the same service). For-profit schools must usually charge a price that reflects cost. In many private nonprofit schools, the gift and endowment income can partially offset costs, which results in prices somewhat less than cost. Although "free" to the students, the cost of education in public schools is on the average at least as much as that of private schools.

These five differences in managerial rights—rights relating to equity treatment, tax revenues and costs, markets, and pricing of services—are generalizations, and exceptions can be increasingly found in specific instances. Nonetheless, these rights determine the broad parameters within which school administrators seek to pursue their preferences. Other major differences in systems of rights have evolved not through the legal *definition* of sector but through the evolution of systems that tend to be associated with the type of sector. Teacher tenure and uniformity of compensation for teachers based on credit hours of education and years of experience, for example, are rights associated primarily with the public sector, although there is nothing inherent in the "publicness" of these schools that formally stipulates these rights. Differences in rights of school managers in different sectors are reflected in the kinds of roles we expect schools in each sector to play in education and in how managers of schools in the three sectors compete and cooperate with each other.

Competition and Cooperation Among Schools in the Three Sectors

So far we have examined basic differences in rights available to managers in each of the three sectors, and our arguments have focused more on differences that might apply to any industry than those that apply specifically to schools. Although schooling is by no means a unique industry, it embodies characteristics that, when coupled with the differences in rights, help to delimit the roles of each sector in providing education services.

Production of Private Versus Public Goods

The arguments in this section are based on somewhat hypothetical presumptions about the degree to which schooling is perceived as a "private" versus a "public" good. The meanings of these two terms in this context need to be clarified. If the benefits of schooling accrue largely to the individual client, such as through more earnings over a lifetime, schooling would be viewed as a private good. If, on the other hand, the major benefits of sending that individual to school accrued largely to society, for example, by producing a more productive citizen, then we would describe schooling as primarily a public good (referred to also as having high positive externalities).

Naturally, this distinction about who benefits from the first dozen or so years of an individual's education is for analytical purposes only. It is, in reality, very difficult to separate individual from social benefits. The prevailing arguments about this tend to attribute to society the benefits of earlier years of schooling, which coincidentally include both more basic and less vocationally oriented instruction. The benefits from later years of schooling—which are more recent and thus temporally proximate to an individual's work as well as more vocational in content—are presumed to accrue largely to the individual.

This theory can help explain how schools in each of the three sectors respond to the purposes of the schooling industry, because the assumptions we as society make about the externalities of schooling guide us as we continually revise the rules under which educational administrators must operate in each sector. If we happened to feel that, for example, only the individual, and not society, benefits from schooling, then there would be little reason for the public sector to involve itself in schooling.

The Role of the Private For-Profit Sector in Schooling

Private for-profit school managers, like other school administrators, enter the profession to pursue a variety of preferences, including educating young people and receiving a paycheck of satisfactory size. However, they enter the for-profit sector of schooling because of the additional benefits of possible ownership and claims on profits. Like other businesspersons, for-profit school managers would in general offer only schooling services that had a potential for profit. Likewise, consumers would purchase only those schooling services that both benefited them personally and were cost-effective. They would not be interested in buying schooling that mainly benefited society at large, even if a well-educated citizenry were considered desirable. In addition, the price to the buyer of schooling services in this sector would need to be sufficient to cover all the costs of the inputs, or factors of production.

The net impact of all of these forces is that, left to their own devices, managers in the for-profit sector would not offer sufficient schooling services and therefore children would not learn enough for these schools to be *socially* optimal. Because education has so many positive externalities, the argument goes, individuals left to their own devices would not choose to "consume" sufficient schooling services to benefit society—"Not only am I worse off without schooling, but *you* are also worse off if I don't have schooling." Although this kind of thinking is termed "private (for-profit) market failure," it is not meant to imply a "fault" of the sector. Rather it suggests that if the full costs of the schooling service were reflected in the price consumers had to pay for schooling, they would buy much less than society wants them to consume. As a result, the private for-profit sector, *by itself*, would fail to produce as much schooling as society feels children should have.

The Role of the Government in Providing Education

In theory, the government steps in to ensure provision of that quantity of schooling that is not being provided by the private for-profit sector. The rationale of government provision of education evolves from the propositions that: (1) education is a collective good in that the benefits from consumption of it accrue to society in general as well as to the individual consumer; and (2) given this, if education were provided solely by the private sector, society would be worse off because individuals would consume only those amounts of education that were best for them and not the additional amounts that would lead to benefits to society.

"Private market failure" has been used to justify government provision of certain services "consumed" by society, including schooling, certain health services, and civil and national defense services. Government provision of education (largely through ownership but also by purchasing or by contracting outside services) is financed through tax systems that do not permit all consumers to equate the taxes they pay for education (and for other government services) with the incremental benefit of education (or such other government services) to them. This is true because client preferences vary. Consequently, the political process of raising money through taxes and providing public schooling leaves significant numbers of voters dissatisfied with the education supplied by government *and* with taxation levels.

This situation is not due to bad management in specific school districts nor to inadequate schooling, but it is an inevitable outcome of the general political process, which by definition leaves some sponsors overtaxed and some clients underserved. In the jargon of public finance:

> Whatever cost-distribution rule taxpayers expect to be used, few persons expect a rule that (even roughly) equates tax liability with the value of benefits from a marginal unit of the good. This is especially true for the host of governmentally provided goods for which there are no user charges (for example, schools). [Weisbrod 1977]

Because of this fact, the level of education produced by the government is likely to leave some clients of schooling dissatisfied with public schools. Among the dissatisfied will be those who are receiving and paying for more education than they desire and those who are dissatisfied because they are receiving too little and would prefer more even if it meant more taxes. The inevitable difficulty in satisfying demands for services provided by government is termed "public market failure." Again, "failure" here implies not fault but the inherent limitations of the sector.

The proportions of each group as well as the intensities of each individual's dissatisfaction will vary from school district to school district. The greater the homogeneity within the school district is (in terms of income, wealth, religion, ethnic background, education level, and other factors that influence the demand for education), the smaller the expected variation in individual demands is, and the dissatisfaction with the politically determined level and quality of public schools will be less.

Because the political process leaves segments of the community dissatisfied with schooling provided by government, several adjustments can occur. Individuals might migrate to other school districts or, in large school districts, to other parts of the city. They might also choose to receive schooling from private nonprofit or "voluntary" organizations. None of the alternatives are cost-free or straightforward. Migration, for example, involves substantial moving costs and exchanging entire sets of services provided by the local governments (such as libraries, roads, fire and police protection, trash collection as well as schooling). Private alternatives require fees that under the current system of rights cannot be recouped by withdrawing from the "free" public schools. (This need not imply a purely one-way sequential process. Individuals frequently elect to transfer from private to public schools. This occurs when the perceived quality and quantity differences are diminished while the cost differential remains the same or when private school tuition is raised to a level clients can no longer afford.)

The Role of the Private Nonprofit ("Voluntary") Sector in Providing Education

The private nonprofit sector fills a void left by the other two sectors. Many individuals are either over- or undersatisfied by government-run schools, and society as a whole underinvests in the collective-good components of education provided by the profit-seeking sector of the schooling industry. Weisbrod (1977) argues that nonprofit or "voluntary" schools arise as "extra-governmental providers of collective-consumption" schooling. These schools supplement whatever level of schooling is provided by government (including the possibility of none) and provide alternatives to the profit-seeking sector of education, which produces schooling largely as a private good. In other words, the nonprofit sector provides largely the same kinds of education as the public-sector schools, yet provides it to undersatisfied consumers. It becomes, in effect, the "second best" solution for consumers of schooling. It is because this sector provides schooling that is largely a collective good that tax subsidies are granted to nonprofit schools.

Flow of Clients Across Sectors

Although we described these three sectors sequentially, they are best seen as forces always seeking equilibrium. If any argument must be marshaled for sequential development of the sectors in schooling, Weisbrod argues that the nonprofit organizations preceded governmental schools historically. This is currently the case with prekindergarten educational programs. The critical point here, and one of the reasons for including this discussion in the text, is that the rules that govern which sector provides what kinds of schooling to which students are always changing.

> The varying roles of government over time ... are not a consequence of ... (externally) determined "attitudes" toward government; rather ... such attitudes are themselves ... determined by changes in incomes, in other demand variables, and in the state of technology and factor prices. [P. 64]

A variety of evolving forces affect the demand for schooling within and across the three sectors. At any point in time, changes in these forces may have the effect of "favoring" schools in one sector over schools in the other two sectors. The strategic position of educational administrators in a particular school is affected by the sector of the school. The ability of administrators to understand and read these forces will, regardless of the sector, enhance their ability to pursue their preferences.

Consumers of schooling services ("clients") find choices within and across sectors. Each schooling option is unique, embodying differences in cost, in the mix of services, and in the degree to which externalities are private or public. Weisbrod's principal hypothesis about sector-based differences in production seems at first glance to apply to schooling:

> In such industries in which government is providing essentially a *private* good, the undersatisfied demand will be manifest principally in the private for-profit sector, and the voluntary [private, nonprofit] sector will be comparatively small. Similarly, if the government services are substantially collective, then implementation will tend to be in the voluntary sector, with the private for-profit sector component being relatively small. [Ibid., p. 69]

Early childhood education is currently one of the few rapidly growing segments of schooling. Early growth in the private nonprofit sector has been complemented by subsequent growth in the for-profit sector, which suggests that there are both high collective and high private benefits to early childhood education. The emergence of firms such as Ombudsman suggests also that the for-profit sector may have an increased role in the future in serving K–12 clients. However, recently a number of school districts and states have provided funds to increase the number of early childhood programs available in the public-school sector, creating additional competition and greater choice for consumers of early childhood education.

Each sector responds to demands for schooling in unique ways because managers in each sector have unique sets of rights that influence how they behave. As various forces—economic, social, political—evolve, managers in different sectors will face new threats and opportunities, which will determine both the size of the schooling industry and the share of schooling services provided by each sector.

Factors Affecting the Size and Shares of the Schooling Sectors

Unambiguous figures on the size of the schooling industry by sector are not readily available. We estimate that approximately 46.9 million students were enrolled in public schools and about 5.1 million were enrolled in private elementary and secondary schools in fall 1979. During the 1978–79 school year, public schools received over $88 billion in revenues.

Demographic Factors

Enrollment trends suggest that the size of the schooling industry as a whole will increase between 1985 and 2000. Due to the impact of a "baby boomette," the school-age population is expected to increase by over 18 percent by 2000. However, enrollments in New England and the mid-Atlantic states are expected to continue to decline, or at best to remain stable (Sherman 1982). Concurrently, the proportion of adults over age sixty-five is expected to increase as is the proportion of adults over the age of twenty-five. This means that the education sector is less likely to command as high a proportion of tax dollars as it had in the past because other public services such as health, recreation, and care for the aged are likely to receive a greater share of public resources in the future.

Philip Piele, who has conducted extensive research regarding voter behavior and support for public schools, has recently analyzed demographic trends in order to predict future changes in financial support for public schools. He noted a number of factors that are likely to contribute to diminished levels of public financial support for public education. First, the proportion of voters with children in public schools, whom previous research has shown to be "more likely to vote in favor of school tax and bond referenda than those without children or with children in private schools" (1981, p. 5), will be lower in the eighties than in the previous two decades. Second, more recent studies indicate that parents of public school children may no longer be such relatively strong supporters of public education (Hall and Piele 1976; Rubinfeld 1979). This change in sentiment was also apparent in a recent Gallup poll that showed little difference between parents of public school students and those of private school students in their willingness to support a voucher plan that could include private as well as public schools (Gallup 1981).

However, Piele also points out that not all demographic changes over the past decade contribute to decreased voter support for the financing of public schools. There now exists a higher proportion of minority public school parents than in previous decades. Analyses of voting records or predominantly minority and nonminority precincts indicate that minorities are more likely to vote in favor of school referenda (Piele and Hall 1973). Given increasing voter turnout among blacks and Hispanics in recent years, this influence may help to slow otherwise decreasing public support for public schools.

The hypothesis that voters will be less concerned with support for education and more concerned with financing other public services seems to be supported by research on nonschool referenda. Piele writes that "whereas public support for school referenda declined recently, support for certain other public services apparently held firm—perhaps even increased" (1981, p. 8). On another level, a similar type of phenomenon seems to have had an impact regarding state and federal support for public schools. Public schools now face strong competition for scarce dollars from manpower-training institutions and day-care centers. The impact of these and other potential competitors for public resources may not be fully realized by the public school system until the late 1980s.

Revised Access to Tax Revenues

A variety of political factors now on the horizon have the potential to greatly alter the present relative sizes of the three sectors of schooling. Voucher plans and tuition tax credit plans, proposed at the state and federal levels, could effect a shift of enrollments and funds from public schools to private schools.

Voucher Plans

A voucher plan would allow parents to send their child to a school of their choice using a voucher equal to, for example, the average per pupil expenditure for the districts in the state, depending on the scope of the plan following that child to the pacticular school. The plan might be smaller in scope and provide a smaller dollar amount, or it might be larger. School managers, therefore, would have an incentive to offer educational programs that will attract students. Voucher plans, however, can be developed with a variety of different contingencies, and not all plans proposed in the past included private schools as an option. Therefore a voucher plan per se may or may not have an impact on the relative sizes of the public and private school sectors.

Controversy has surrounded voucher proposals that would allow parents to choose from both public and private schools. R. Freeman Butts argues that "a full-scale voucher scheme will promote *private* purposes rather than *public* purposes" (1979, p. 7). In addition, his hypothesis—that greater choice among both private and public schools may result in a larger degree of racial and social class segregation and lack of a common educational background for students—can also be applied to a situation where choice is limited to the public arena. Coons (1979), a proponent of vouchers, has argued that voucher plans that include private as well as public schools would be more equalitarian than present school-financing systems, which effectively eliminate private schools as a choice for low-income parents.

Tuition Tax Credit Plans

Tuition tax credits, which would result in lower taxes for those paying private school tuitions, have also been a current source of heated debate. The tuition tax credit controversy spans a wide range of issues including:

1. Should a tuition tax credit be given?
2. If so, how much?
3. Would a tuition tax credit plan be constitutional?
4. Would a tuition tax credit plan that in effect provides public subsidies to private schools increase government regulation of those schools?
5. Who would benefit from tuition tax credit plans?
6. Would a tuition tax credit plan result in a major shift of students from public to private schools?

A basic argument in support of tuition tax credits is that parents of children attending private schools pay twice for schooling: in private tuition and in local and state taxes to support public schooling. Therefore, proponents of a federal plan for tuition tax credits make the case that parents of private school students should be given, in effect, a "rebate" in the form of lower federal income taxes to compensate for this double payment.

Opponents of tuition tax credits argue that such a plan may cause a substantial shift of students from public to private schools, which would threaten the existence of the public school system. Albert Shanker (1982), president of the American Federation of Teachers, has opposed tuition tax credit plans on the grounds that public schools could then become a "dumping ground" for students whose parents still could not afford private school tuitions or who may have been rejected by the private schools due to discipline problems, learning handicaps, and the like.

Other Shifts in Subsidies

As Encarnation (1982) notes, public support for private schools is not a new concept. In fact, private schools may currently receive up to a fourth of their total costs in direct and indirect public subsidies. Under indirect funding he includes property tax exemptions for nonprofit schools and the tax deductions donors receive for charitable contributions to private schools. Encarnation also describes two types of public financial aid to private schools in the form of "direct budgetary expenditures for specific categories of assistance" as follows:

> Most is distributed by state and local agencies as "in kind" services, defined as the extension of existing publicly funded and publicly administered programs to include certain students attending nonpublic schools, though no direct transfer of public funds actually occurs. The "in kind" services include the extension of student transportation, textbook loan, dual enrollment, and other "child benefit" programs. Over thirty-three states each offer up to seven child benefit programs that account for over two-thirds of all programmatic expenditures from state, federal, and local sources.
>
> The remainder of government programmatic expenditures reimburse selected nonpublic school personnel for services rendered to students with special educational needs. These include, for example, the provision of services to nonpublic school students enrolled in special education or compensatory education (Title I) programs. [1982, p. 1.]

Due to the level of public subsidies for private schools already in existence today, the appropriate question is not whether to have public funding for private schools; rather the question is how much public funding private schools should receive and in what forms. Although much of the debate on public aid to private schools has focused on the potential impact on public schools of public aid to private schools, this funding will also affect private schools because, as in the past, increased levels of government regulation accompany increased levels of government financing.

Elasticity of Demand

It is difficult to estimate the degree of change in enrollments from the public to private sector that might result from a voucher or tuition tax credit plan or other shift in rights. Albert Shanker (1982) has suggested that a small fluctuation in attendance rates (upward for private schools, downward for public schools in one year) may result in a chain of similar movements in subsequent years, resulting in "skimming-off" the students from the higher socioeconomic status families into private schools. Gemello and Osman (1982), who have attempted to measure how changes in income might affect private school attendance, estimate that shifts to private schools due to tuition tax credits will be relatively minor:

> Public policies to increase family income through tax credits or educational vouchers would increase nonpublic school attendance rates by about two-thirds of a percent for every one percent increase in family income. For example, in a community with an average family income of $13,000 and where 10 percent of the children attend nonpublic schools, an increase in income of 10 percent (to $14,300) would lead to a nonpublic school attendance rate of approximately 10.67 percent. [P. 3]

While such research helps to enlighten us as to the possible ramifications of changing the present methods of financing education to include plans such as vouchers and tuition tax credits, future predictions based on present data will not likely be wholly accurate. The Gemello and Osman results, for example, may not be equally applicable to both tuition tax credits and voucher plans, insofar as income-related benefits derived from vouchers must be spent on education whereas a tuition tax credit plan acts to change the price of private education. The point to consider here, rather, is that political influences, including voucher and tuition tax credit plans, have the potential to shape the future size of the three elementary and secondary education sectors.

Macro-economic Factors

Economic factors also have the potential to influence not only the relative sizes of these three sectors but also the size of the schooling industry as a whole. The condition of the United States economy may affect the size of the schooling industry (measured in terms of dollars), by the way it affects individuals' willingness to allocate resources to education. In times when incomes are increasing relative to inflation, citizens are generally willing to spend more money to improve the quality of educational services. However, in times of recession the opposite trend is likely to prevail. The economic outlook may also affect the size of enrollments as sixteen-year-olds decide whether to quit school and work full time in a relatively unskilled job or to continue their education to receive a high school diploma. Economic trends that differentially affect fluctuations in income among various economic groups are likely to have an impact on the relative size of the public, private nonprofit, and private for-profit sectors of the schooling industry (Bendick 1977).

Technological Factors

Recent technological advances in the computer and telecommunications industries are likely to have a major influence on the relative sizes of the three sectors of elementary and secondary education, though the type of influence is very difficult to predict at this time. One might expect that with the growth of the home computer industry more parents may choose to educate their children primarily at home, perhaps sending them for private schooling in specific course areas. Such a scenario would likely entail growth first in the private for-profit and private nonprofit sectors. While this has not yet happened to any noticeable degree, private nonprofit schools have been hiring private for-profit computer software companies to come into the schools to teach computer literacy courses to elementary and secondary students. If the number of students who stay home to learn by using the microcomputer increases tremendously, one might argue that public schools are all the more important to complement the private benefits derived from computer-assisted instruction and to provide a common background to students to help make them informed citizens.

These technological, economic, political, and demographic trends that shape the nature of the schooling industry have been mentioned to underscore the point that such forces are continually influencing education. We do not mean to imply that any one of these trends will have a permanent impact on the sizes of the three sectors of schooling, but rather we want to suggest how these trends might influence or direct schooling during the remainder of the century.

Differences in the Behavior of Managers

The "appropriate" role of each of the three sectors in schooling is relevant to us only to the degree that it affects managerial behavior. To see if the hypothetical incentives operate, we need to examine the relationship between behavior and incentives. Stated simply: if these incentives operate, we should see them reflected in comparisons between sectors of the types of services offered by schools, the breadth of service mix offered by schools, and the technologies employed by schools in providing services.

Service Differentiation

If our theories are true, private for-profit school managers will specialize in individual-consumption goods to a greater degree than will public school managers and to a lesser degree than will private nonprofit school managers. In his examination of secondary data, Bendick (1977) found that student enrollments in advanced or specialized courses in nine fields of study (as a proportion of the total enrollment in each field) were highest in profit-seeking schools, with the other two sectors alternating between second and third place.

Service specialization in for-profit schools is not restricted to academic, college-preparatory curricula; these schools also offer more advanced and specialized courses in business education, home economics, and vocational arts than do schools in the other two sectors. This same type of service differentiation seems to hold for noncollegiate post-secondary schools as well. Schools that provide education with relatively higher individual-consumption value (relatively fewer positive externalities) such as business office, cosmetology/barber, flight, and trade schools are also those offered principally through for-profit schools. Alternatively, schools that provide education services with higher positive externalities, such as *basic* vocational/technical, hospital, and allied health, are public and nonpublic organizations (see exhibit 2.2).

Service Mix

The range of educational services offered within the average public school is broader than the range of educational services offered in the average

Exhibit 2.2

Sector Differentiation in Noncollegiate Post-Secondary Schools

Type of School	Public	Private	
		Distribution (by percentage)	
		Proprietary	Nonprofit
Vocational/technical	62.1	1.3	2.6
Technical institute	0.9	1.4	1.0
Business/office	0.5	20.7	4.4
Cosmetology/barber	0.0	37.2	0.1
Flight	0.6	18.1	0.4
Trade	1.7	10.6	8.6
Arts/design	0	3.9	2.6
Hospital	18.1	.3	75.3
Allied health	14.0	3.4	4.6
Other	2.1	3.2	0.5
Total	100.0	100.0	100.0

Note: Percentages may not total 100 because of rounding.

Source: Evelyn Kay, *Enrollments and Programs in Noncollegiate Post-Secondary Schools, 1978* (Washington, D. C.: National Center for Education Statistics, 1979), p. A-1.

private school (either profit or nonprofit). Private school managers pursue narrower missions, and, in fact, public school missions are usually so broad that parts of their service mix resemble services offered by a wide range of private schools: college preparatory, business, vocational, athletic, and the like.

Although the service mix in a public school is much broader than the service mix in a private school is, the private *sector* as a whole is not more narrowly focused. Rather, while the private schools have narrower missions, the breadth of services available in the private sector is no less than that which is available in the public sector. In fact, some schooling services are available only in the private sector, for example, religious instruction.

The actual mix of services and the proportion of resources devoted to each service defines the mission of the school. Regardless of what we say we do, our mission is defined by what we actually do. Religious instruction is part of the service mix of some schools, but not of others. Similarly, vocationally oriented courses are offered in some schools but not in others.

The mere presence or absence of a service does not, however, adequately describe the level of service. Two schools may provide college counseling services for high school juniors and seniors, but one school might have a full-time counselor for every two hundred students while the other might have a part-time counselor for all of its five hundred students. (The two schools employ a different "technology" for college counseling.) Although both schools provide the service, it is a more important part of the service mix in the first school.

Course Offerings

The range of course offerings in private schools differs from that found in public schools. There are, in addition, major differences within each sector. For example, when Coleman and his colleagues compared service mixes of public and private schools, they found several major differences between "high-performance" public and private schools on the one hand and other public, Catholic, and other private schools on the other. Nearly all students in high-performance public and private schools have access to a calculus course as compared with 63 percent in other public schools, 71 percent in Catholic schools, and 61 percent in other private schools (1981, p. 78).

Both public and private high-performance schools have more extensive language offerings than the other public, Catholic, and other private schools. In language offerings, Catholic schools rank first, ahead of both the public and other private schools. More than three-quarters of the Catholic schools offer third-year French and even more offer third-year Spanish. Less than half of the public schools and less than a quarter of the other private schools offer these courses.

Finally, public schools offer significantly more technical, vocational, and practical courses than private nonprofit schools offer. In the public sector, about 66 percent of the students have access to an auto mechanics course, 94 percent to a wood or machine shop course, and 96 percent to a home economics course. The lowest accessibility to technical or vocational courses is found among Catholic schools in the nonprofit sector, where wood and machine shop or auto mechanics courses are each available to only about 10 percent of the students (ibid., p. 84).

Actual Programs of Study

Access to courses does not necessarily imply that students take those courses. Indeed, the service mixes of schools may be more accurately described in terms of courses the average student takes than in terms of courses offered. In general, however, similar patterns prevail. Students in Catholic schools and other private schools take more semesters of academic course work than do students in public high schools (ibid., 104); "academic" here is defined as mathematics, English, science, history, and foreign languages. Students in public high schools take more business, trade, technical, and other vocational courses than do students in private nonprofit schools.

These differences would be reduced if we controlled for students' higher education plans.

Extracurricular Services

Extracurricular activities constitute another set of services that schools incorporate into their service mix. Specific activities at the high school levels include athletics, cheerleading, debate, drama, chorus, band, subject matter clubs, hobby clubs, honorary society, school newspapers, and student government. The major differences in participation across schools appear between public schools and Catholic schools on the one hand and other private (especially high-performance private) schools on the other. Among the latter group, the number of activities undertaken by students appears to grow over time, with seniors participating considerably more than sophomores. In the former group, levels of participation are in general slightly lower at the sophomore level, and growth does not occur.

Coleman and his colleagues suggest that these differences may be attributable to differences in technology:

> One might conjecture that extracurricular activities are organized differently in the Catholic and public schools than in the other private schools. In particular, there are two approaches a school may take to the organization of extracurricular activities. One is a selective orientation, which recruits younger students into, say, less selective choruses, with subsequent narrowing down for the more selective choruses, or into junior varsity athletics with only the best going on to the varsity. Another approach, the intramural orientation, holds to the philosophy that everyone ought to try everything. This latter approach may be seen in elite English schools that aspire to develop a "well-rounded" individual.
>
> If the public and Catholic schools have the selective orientation to extracurricular activities, and the other private schools more often have the intramural orientation, this would explain the participation decline from sophomore to senior in public and Catholic schools and the growth (or at least the absence of decline) in the other private schools. [P. 114]

Technology

The technology of schooling employed by managers differs across sectors. Because data on for-profit schools are so scarce, most comparisons are between public and private nonprofit schools.

Staffing Ratios

One measure of technology—staffing ratios—reveals major differences between these sectors as well as within the nonprofit sector. Catholic and public high schools have a student to professional staff ratio of sixteen to one and fifteen to one respectively, whereas other private nonprofit schools have,

Exhibit 2.3
Staffing Ratios for Public and Private Schools in Spring 1980
(X number of students per staff type*)

Staff	Major Sectors: Public	Major Sectors: Catholic	Major Sectors: Other Private	High-Performance Schools: Public	High-Performance Schools: Private
Total number of schools	16,051	1,572	3,123	12	11
Mean enrollment	757	546	153	1,386	310
General professional staff:					
Overall ratio	15	16	8	15	7
A. Teachers	16	18	7	18	8
B. Assistant principals, Deans	503	410	120	433	163
C. Counselors	323	235	55	284	182
D. Librarians and Media specialists	597	340	212	696	163
E. Remedial specialists	504	891	382	563	0
F. Psychologists	2,025	4,579	1,177	2,064	1,033
Other staff:					
A. Teacher aides	349	2,549	124	380	1,033
B. Volunteers	839	385	101	312	344
C. Security guards	1,824	17,055	780	1,868	1,395

$$\text{*Ratio} = \frac{\text{weighted enrollment}}{\text{weighted number of full-time-equivalent staff}}$$

Source: James Coleman et al., *Public and Private Schools*. ED 197 503 (Chicago: National Opinion Research Center, 1981), p. 40.

on the average, six students for each full-time professional staff person (ibid., p. 85). Nearly all of this difference is attributable to the student to teacher ratio (line two of exhibit 2.3). Catholic schools have the highest student to teacher ratio (eighteen to one), followed closely by public schools, while the other private schools have less than half as many students per teacher.

Instructional Support

Differences in technology also exist in areas of instructional support. There are significantly fewer students per remedial specialist and teacher aid in other private schools. High-performance private schools provide the greatest number of librarians and media specialists. The number of students to counselors is quite low in the other private schools (55 to 1 as compared with 323 to 1 in the public schools and 235 to 1 in Catholic schools).

The ratio of security guards to schools is approximately 1 for every 2.4

public schools, 1 for every 31 Catholic schools, and 1 for every 5 other private schools. Volunteers (relative to student enrollment) provide the least service to public schools, where there is on the average 1 full-time volunteer for every 841 students. At the other extreme, other private schools have the greatest intensity of volunteer service—about 1 full-time for every 100 students (ibid., p. 88).

The available data on the technology employed in for-profit schools is mixed, and it is not clear whether the technology is more or less expensive than that employed in the other two sectors. Bendick (1977) found that profit-seeking schools offer "significantly more inputs to schooling than do either government or nonprofit schools (for example, class size, credentials of teachers, availability of books and equipment, teachers' salaries, and expenditures per pupil)". A large part of these differences is probably attributable to the fact that differences in services were not controlled for.

The data from Ombudsman suggest the opposite, that is, for comparable service, for-profit schools are likely to assemble a less-expensive technology (which may, incidentally, be more capital intensive). The fact that they can educate a student for less than what it costs a public school district can be traced to three major factors, one of which is less-expensive technology. Closely related, the wages paid to teachers are on the average less, and services not directly related to education (such as compliance with state reporting requirements) are not provided for as readily as in the public sector.

Up to this point we have focused our attention on one "variable" of school managers—the sector in which they work. We have seen that some individuals obtain certain rights by virtue of the legal definition of the organization in which they work, and that schooling behavior (measured by service mix and the like) also varies by sector. The rights of individuals (managers and others) *within* each sector differ as well. The preferences and incentives of these individuals also vary. We now turn our attention to the three broad categories of people who are associated with schools in each sector: sponsors, operators, and clients.

Sponsors, Operators, and Clients in the Three Sectors

Rights associated with the type of sector affect the incentives and rights of individuals in the schooling organization. We cannot discuss the particular rights of each individual in the organization, but we can make some generalizations about three groups of people: sponsors, operators, and clients. (There are many subgroups within each group, of course, which we will examine more in subsequent chapters.) As these labels suggest, sponsors provide some of the resources necessary to finance the organization, and they determine the organization's mission; operators rent their services to the organization to carry out its mission; and clients are those individuals who receive the services of the organization, for which they may or may not pay.

Sponsors

For-Profit Schools

The sponsors of for-profit schools own those schools. They may be sole proprietors, partners, or stockholders. They enter into contractual agreements with operators whereby they exchange their time and money for claims on future net earnings. Because of their personal investment, they have incentives to monitor the behavior of the operators to ensure that operators carry out the owners' mission.

In many cases sponsors may also assume operator roles and operators may acquire equity in the organization. In these cases the "agency problem" (the need for sponsors to monitor operators) is lessened. To the extent that operator compensation is linked to overall organizational profitability, sponsors and operators will share similar preferences and the agency problem is less than it otherwise would be.

Nonprofit Schools

Sponsors of nonprofit schools, usually called a board of trustees, do not have equity claims on the school. They provide time and money resources to their school and shape its mission. Even without equity shares, these sponsors have incentives to monitor the behavior of operators in order to maximize the present value of future revenue—for example, most of them have children attending the school, they may be alumni of the school, or they may have a business relationship with the school.

In private nonprofit schools, sponsor and client roles sometimes overlap, which implies that the incentives of sponsors overlap with those of clients. Although the financial incentives of sponsorship are absent in this sector, they are replaced with incentives of clients for receiving good services and with a means of satisfying general philanthropic preferences.

Public Schools

Sponsorship of public schools is more complex. In some fundamental sense, the public sponsors public schools. Because of the inherently unworkable nature of this sponsorship, government officials act as agents for the public, carrying out on behalf of the people the roles of financial supporter and mission director. Sponsors come from all three levels of government—local, state, and federal—and thus their sponsor role often overlaps with their operator role. In the public sector, managers often find themselves acting as operators for higher-level sponsors and as sponsors for operators below them. Their behavior is controlled from above and they seek to control those below.

School board members in public schools function in all three roles. In their roles as "community representatives" they exhibit preferences characteristic either of clients who use school services or of local sponsors who pay, in part, for school services. As legal extensions of state government, they act as operators under state sponsorship, and the majority of their rights are those typically assigned to operators.

Operators

Operators are created and sustained in large part by their sponsors. Operators are responsible for producing educational services and for doing so within the system of rights assigned to them by sponsors. Operators "rent" their educational expertise to sponsors in return for monetary and nonmonetary compensation. The value of operators to sponsors and to clients is their professional skills, sometimes called their human capital. Like all other individuals, operators pursue their preferences within a system of rights.

For-Profit Schools

Private for-profit operators either rent their expertise to sponsors or, if they are also sponsors, exchange their expertise for claims on future earnings of the school. As they pursue their preferences, they have incentives to maximize long-run profit. This does not mean that they have incentives to offer "cheap" or "shoddy" educational services. Rather it means that operators and sponsors in the private for-profit sector are not usually willing to invest resources into schooling services for which there is not some reasonable financial return in the near future.

Nonprofit Schools

Operators in private nonprofit schools are limited to renting their expertise to sponsors and cannot exercise equity options. To the exent that the school's revenue for renting operator services comes from client fees, operators will face the same incentives as their counterparts in for-profit schools. In nonprofit schools there is little overlap between operator roles on one hand and either sponsorship or client roles on the other.

Public Schools

Operators in the public sector are also limited to renting their expertise to sponsors. However, unlike their counterparts in the other two sectors, client and sponsor roles are more clearly separated. Although operators in the public sector are subject to the control of sponsors, they are not coincidentally and automatically as subject to control by clients. Control by clients represents a built-in or self-monitoring control device in the private sectors. Because clients exert less control in the public sector, sponsors must exert control over operators by other means such as extensive and specific rules of operation and by the use of monitoring mechanisms.

Clients

"Client" is a label we have given to individuals who are the most direct recipients of schooling services. Clients include children as well as the parents or guardians of school-age children because decisions about where and what schooling a child receives are heavily influenced by these adults. To a much lesser degree, adults who partake in the ancillary "continuing education" programs of schools are also clients.

Like all other people, clients vary in terms of preferences and information and, as a result, do not behave uniformly. Most clients receive some schooling (perhaps because the legal penalties for not receiving an education are perceived by some individuals to be not worth the benefits of quitting). However, because they vary in fundamental ways, clients of education do not constitute a single market.

Characteristics of clients that most likely influence the quantity and kind of education they consume include family income, religious background, physical or mental condition, race and cultural background, parents' education, and number of children in the family unit. These and other client characteristics combine to account for schooling preferences, and research on how schooling preferences are traded off against all other preferences when choosing schools is, at best, incomplete. Despite the complexity of causes of client preferences, those preferences, which might include the decision to attend the most convenient school, affect their choice of schooling.

Some of the relationships between an individual's characteristics and choice of school are obvious. The family income of clients in private nonprofit schools, for example, is somewhat higher than that of clients in the public sector (the median family income of private school students is $23,200 compared to a family income of $18,700 for students in the public sector [Coleman et al. 1981, p. 53]). That some families with relatively more income are, in general, inclined to spend more than they have to in order to purchase preferred education services is not surprising.

Similarly, geographic proximity to the school, all else being equal, appears to heighten a school's attractiveness. More black clients live in areas surrounding Catholic schools (13.2 percent) than in areas surrounding other private schools (11.0) percent, and thus this fact may partially account for the greater number of blacks in Catholic schools (5.6 percent compared to 3.0 percent in other private schools) (ibid., p. 35).

Because the characteristics of clients that affect their schooling preferences come in sets, it is difficult if not impossible to isolate a single characteristic, such as income level, place of residence, or race, and then suggest causal relationships. Clients have sets of personal characteristics that empirically suggest certain schooling characteristics they would prefer. Preferences, too, are difficult to pinpoint in reality. The client may desire a school with low cost, proximity to home, safety, a particular philosophical orientation, and the "appropriate" amount of classroom discipline. Client choice entails evaluation of alternatives, both public and private, each of which contains a unique mix of these and other elements.

Multiple Roles for the Educational Manager

Managers are generally thought of as operators (no slight intended). They possess more formal training in education, usually rent their services and take their direction from sponsors, and provide direct services to clients. While not all operators are managers, all managers are at least operators. Sometimes they also assume roles as sponsors. When they create missions and contract with other operators for educational services to be provided to clients, managers assume the responsibilities of a sponsor, including the monitoring of operators. For example, the public school managers that contract with Ombudsman in Illinois to teach potential dropouts are acting as sponsors.

Repartitioning Rights Among Sponsors, Operators, and Clients

The division of schooling into three sectors and three major roles could suggest a certain orderly view of managing schools. After all, certain rights are associated with each sector and certain preferences are associated with each role. It would seem reasonable to create a neat three-by-three matrix whereby sponsors, operators, and clients participate in producing and consuming schooling in each sector. To be sure, we have alluded to a number of generalizations that would fit our grid, including:

1. Public-sector sponsors have more formal controls over public school operators than is the case in the other two sectors.
2. Private school operators offer more limited service mixes to clients per school than do public school operators.

While these and other generalizations may be descriptively accurate, it would be misleading to conclude that managers simply "manage" within a set of rights. An important and complicating part of a manager's job is making decisions on when to play within the existing systems of rights, when to attempt to change the systems of rights in his or her favor, and when to impose negative externalities on others. Consider recent cases involving the provision of free schooling to alien children in Texas and the provision of state aid to public schools in Pennsylvania.

Attempts to Shift Costs and Obligations

In the first example, managers of public schools in Texas were alarmed at the flow of illegal alien children into the public schools, which caused increases in costs without commensurate increases in operating revenues. State legislators enacted a state law that gave local school district managers the right to charge tuition to illegal alien children or to bar them from school altogether. This law was enacted "to ease the financial burdens caused by the federal government's inability or unwillingness to stem a flood of illegal immigrants from Mexico" (*New York Times* 12/2/81, p. A28). The districts receive no state money to cover the cost of educating children they choose to admit. Civil rights groups and clients challenged the law, and it was found unconstitutional by the courts (see *Doe v. Plyler*).

In the second example, the governor of Pennsylvania, recently faced with an election year, a 4.9 percent increase in state tax revenue, and an 8 percent rate of inflation, pledged that he would not increase state tax rates. During the fiscal year, he held the line on personal income, on corporate and sales taxes, and did not measurably increase state aid to schools. As a consequence, 87 percent of the state's five hundred and one school districts had to raise their property taxes. Local education managers and union leaders publicly protested the low levels of state aid.

These current events are repeated in one form or another every day across the county at all levels of government and in all sectors. Managers pursue their preferences by seeking to ameliorate the impact of external forces on them. This means attempting to shift negative externalities to others either through existing rights or by changing systems of rights. The processes of attempting to avoid negative externalities imposed by others or to capture positive externalities are called planning and control, the subject of the next chapter.

References

Bendick, Marc Jr. "Education as a Three-Sector Industry." In *The Voluntary Nonprofit Sector*, edited by Burton A. Weisbrod. Lexington, Mass.: D. C. Heath & Co., 1977.

Butts, R. Freeman. "Educational Vouchers: The Private Pursuit of the Public Purse." *Phi Delta Kappan*, January 1979, pp. 7–9.

Coleman, James; Hoffer, Thomas; and Kilgore, Sally. *Public and Private Schools*. Chicago: National Opinion Research Center, 1981. ED 197 503.

Coons, John E. "Of Family Choice and 'Public' Education." *Phi Delta Kappan*, January 1979, pp. 10–13.

Encarnation, Dennis J. "Public Support, Public Regulation: The Dilemma for Nonpublic Schools." *Policy Perspectives*, Winter 1982, p. 2. Stanford, Calif.: Institute for Research on Educational Finance and Governance.

Gallup, George H. "Taking Education's Pulse: The 13th Annual Gallup Poll of the Public's Attitude Toward Public Schools." *Principal*, September 1981, pp. 21–36.

Gemello, John, and Osman, Jack W. "Factors Influencing Choice: Estimating the Enrollment Shift." *Policy Perspectives*, Winter 1982. Stanford, Calif.: Institute for Research on Educational Research and Governance.

Hall, John S., and Piele, Philip K. "Selected Determinants of Precinct Voting Decision in School Budget Elections." *Western Political Quarterly* 29 (1976): 440–456.

Hansmann, Henry B. "The Role of Nonprofit Enterprise." *The Yale Law Journal* 89: 5 (April 1980): 835–900.

James, Thomas, and Levin, Henry M., eds. *Public Dollars for Private Schools: The Case of Tuition Tax Credits*. Philadelphia: Temple University Press, 1983.

Piele, Philip K. "Public Support for Public Schools: The Past, the Future, and the Federal Role." Paper prepared for the School Finance Project, U.S. Department of Education, July 31, 1981. Contract No. NIE-P-81-0131.

Piele, Philip K., and Hall, John S. *Budgets, Bonds, and Ballots: Voting Behavior in Financial Referanda*. Lexington, Mass.: D. C. Heath & Co., 1973.

Rubinfeld, R. B. "Voting in a Local School Election: A Micro-Analysis." *The Review of Economics and Statistics* 59 (1979): 30–42.

Shanker, Albert. "The Risk Is Too Great." *Policy Notes* 3:1 (1982). Stanford, Calif.: Institute for Research on Educational Research and Governance.

Sherman, Joel D. *Prospects for Financing Elementary/Secondary Education in the States: Congressionally Mandated Study of School Finance*. Final Report, Vol. 1. Report to Congress from the Secretary of Education, December 1982.

Weisbrod, Burton. *The Voluntary Nonprofit Sector*. Lexington, Mass.: D. C. Heath & Co., 1977.

Supplementary Reading

Abramowitz, Susan. "Private High Schools: A Descriptive Profile and Comparison with Public High Schools." Paper presented at the Annual Meeting of the American Educational Research Association, San Francisco, 1979. EA 172 358.

Abramowitz, Susan, and Stackhouse, E. Ann. *The Private High School Today*. Washington, D.C.: National Institute of Education, 1980. ED 202 125.

Sullivan, Daniel. "Comparing Public and Nonpublic Schools: The Difficulty of Measuring Efficiency." *Policy Perspectives*, Winter 1982. Stanford, Calif.: Institute for Research on Educational Finance and Governance.

Sullivan, Daniel J. *Public Aid to Nonpublic Schools*. Lexington, Mass.: D. C. Heath & Co., 1974.

3

Planning and Control in Schools

•

Overview

Chapter 3 builds on the discussion in the previous chapter of schooling as a three-sector industry, and focuses on how the emphasis on the formal processes of planning and control vary from sector to sector. On a most general level, school business administrators plan and control; they determine what they want to do and how to do it, and then they attempt to ensure that what they wanted to do is in fact done. Planning and controlling are "umbrella" concepts; each encompasses many more specialized activities. The most general and fundamental planning and controlling concepts are described in this chapter. Although planning and control concepts apply to management of all organizations, we see that they take on a somewhat different meaning and refer to slightly different behavior from sector to sector in education.

• • •

Introduction

In the first two chapters we have discussed the systems of rights of school business managers. Rights, we have argued, define the broad parameters within which educational managers work and live. In this chapter we turn our attention to more specific constraints on managers' rights and to what managers do—that is, how they maximize their utility—within these constraints.

There are numerous ways of looking at behavior, and each taxonomy of management behavior emphasizes only part of the school business administrator as manager. Some emphasize functional responsibilities such as purchasing and preparing the school budget; others emphasize observable behaviors such as attending meetings and talking on the phone. Still others focus attention on the "formal" versus the "informal" aspects of the job such as attending board meetings versus hanging around the water cooler to pick up the latest gossip. We will use a three-part classification to categorize planning and control activities not because it captures all of what administrators do but because it helps to describe differences between school business administration across the three sectors.

As they pursue preferences, educational managers spend some of their time determining the goals or purposes of the schooling organization, deciding which activities the organization should undertake to more efficiently and effectively achieve the goals; and making sure that the desired activities are carried out as intended. Robert Anthony (1965) has distinguished and named these functions:

1. *Strategic planning* is the process of deciding on objectives, on the resources used to attain these objectives, and on the policies that are to govern the acquisition, use, and disposition of these resources. . . .
2. *Management control* is the process by which managers assure that resources are obtained and used effectively and efficiently in the accomplishment of the organization's objectives. . . .
3. *Operational control* is the process of assuring that specific tasks are carried out effectively and efficiently. [Pp. 24, 27, 69]

Implicit in these distinctions among processes are two assumptions: (1) that strategic planning constrains management control because the objectives are already established, and (2) that management control constrains operational control because activities or tasks have already been determined. Although planning appears to be eminently more important than the other two functions because it deals with the big issues (such as reassessing the educational organization's goals, considering major environmental threats to and opportunities of the educational organization, and determining the broad strategies the educational organization will follow), it is not—each of the three functions is equally important.

Planning is of little use unless it is linked to managerial control and operational control. Subsequent to the planning stage, goals and objectives are given, and the focus of the educational administrator's effort is on determining the most effective and efficient means for accomplishing those objectives. These means are usually called programs or projects or decision packages. They are the organized activities that the educational organization engages in.

Operational control is a natural extension of managerial control. Both the objectives and the means or activities to achieve the objectives are given, and the focus of the educational administrator's efforts is to assure that the specific tasks are carried out effectively and efficiently. The utility and importance of planning, then, are determined in part by the degree to which plans are applicable to programs and programs are carried out as intended. This is why most of the work in educational planning deals with both planning and management systems. There is rarely a useful description of a school planning process that has not evaluated procedures for managerial and operational control as well.

These three processes are very broad and overlap one another. Often a particular activity, such as closing a school building, entails elements of all three processes, and where one process begins and another leaves off is not always clear. Implicit in the three-part classification is the primacy of planning over managerial control and the primacy of managerial control over operational control. In other words, administrators decide what to do before deciding how best to do it and decide how best to do it before making sure it is done that way. Moreover, each function is associated with activities in which the business official is either the project leader or is in some other way a major actor. These activities are usually called long-range planning (strategic planning), budgeting (managerial control), and administrative systems' management (operational control).

Which of these activities, however, is the school business manager usually involved in? The answer will likely vary with the individual, regardless of the sector. Budgeting is probably more important for most managers because it is done annually, provides the major method for reviewing strategic plans and controlling activities, and, in effect, partitions managers' rights to resources. Although budgeting processes are examined separately in chapter 6, they should be seen within the context of this chapter as a major means by which management controls schooling organizations.

Strategic planning and operational control are considered together in this chapter for two reasons. First, an individual manager both plans and controls within the same system of rights. For example, if a manager can terminate an employee only at great financial cost to the organization and emotional cost (disutility) to herself, this will influence both the plans she makes and the mechanisms she uses to control operations. Second, plans made in a particular setting must ultimately be linked to control devices, which ensure that the plans are carried out. When they are apparent, we identify relationships between planning and control processes, especially when they seem to vary between sectors.

The sector in which a manager works influences planning and control decisions if only because the sector determines the set of regulations under which the manager must operate. These differences are outlined in the next section of this chapter. The incentives for planning are discussed next, followed by a description of the major activities of planning and then a discussion of operational control.

Planning and Control in a Regulated Environment

Government regulation is old news. Attempts by higher levels of American government to influence the behavior of lower levels, whether through sanction or inducement—the working definition of regulation in education—form an indispensable part of a federalist system of government. [Kirp 1982, p. 1]

The school business administrator views state and federal government both as a revenue source and as a constraining force, a regulator. In other words, some state and federal government officials are school sponsors. The controls imposed by officials in higher levels of government on school organizations are not unlike controls imposed by central office administrators on building-level educational administrators. (The latter controls, however, represent constraints on much simpler systems of rights than in even the biggest public school systems.) Both state and federal regulation and central office regulation represent behavior of educational managers to increase the likelihood that their preferences are carried out. Educational administrators, regardless of location, will institute controls when they act as sponsors and perceive that operators do not share their preferences.

Early federal funding and regulation of programs in public schools were characterized by relatively few controls, because the sponsors (especially government officials) perceived that operators (local superintendents) shared roughly similar preferences. As state and federal preferences became dissimilar from local preferences, additional controls were implemented. Consider, for example, vocational education. The Smith-Hughes Act of 1917 required that if a student was taught one class by a teacher paid from federal vocational funds, that student had to spend 50 percent of his or her course time in shopwork, 25 percent in closely related subjects, and 25 percent in academics. As Charles Benson points out:

Given the unity of the vocational educational leadership . . . there was no special concern about monitoring vocational education programs for compliance with Congressional intent. There existed general agreement on goals and there were no insurmountable difficulties in achieving the desired results, so that the activity was virtually self-monitoring. [1982, p. 4]

From 1963 nearly up to the present, the federal role in vocational education grew and controls were increased, including using the system of vocational education to provide training specifically for disadvantaged persons;

requiring each state to spend at least 25 percent on training for people who had completed or left high school, on construction of area vocational school facilities, or on both; requiring set-asides to train youth in economically depressed communities; dispersing funds only to local agencies that proved to be economically efficient; creating state advisory councils charged with evaluating programs and preparing long-range and annual program plans; appropriating money for bilingual vocational education and other special-interest programs; emphasizing sex equity; and establishing a national vocational education data system (ibid., p. 5). What also changed during this period, as Benson points out, was the growing sense in Congress that educators at the local level were not able or willing to enforce these new regulations. The net result over the last several decades has been an increase in the rights of Congress to control vocational education at the expense of the rights of local educators.

The cause of these shifts in rights is the increasing incongruence between the preferences of state and federal sponsors of education and those of local educational managers. Efforts by local educational managers to repeal control imposed from higher government stem from an absence of shared goals. Proponents of wholesale deregulation of schools are more critical of the goals of federal intervention than they are of the means.

Where the preferences and incentives of the sponsor and the operator are congruent, the sponsor can rely on the operator's self-monitoring as a control device. The sponsor does not need to set up elaborate mechanisms to monitor the operator's behavior because the operator can be counted on to do the "right thing." On the other hand, when the operator does not share the preferences and incentives of the sponsor, self-monitoring will not work.

The same issue arises between superiors and subordinates in an organization. The superior is able to rely on the subordinates' self-monitoring as the superior's control device to the extent that the subordinate shares *all* of the superior's preferences and incentives. Because this rarely occurs, superiors install control devices over subordinates, and sponsors install control devices over operators. Centralization (within an organization) and regulation (within an industry) are responses to the same perceived need to control.

When developing plans and controlling their implementation, educational managers work within a system of rights, which, although they may evolve over time, are fixed in the short run. We have outlined the most basic rights available to managers in the previous chapter; those rights are associated with the legal status of the organization within which managers work, whether schooling or some other activity is the organization's primary mission. We now consider those rights available to managers that more directly affect the ways they plan and control.

State Regulation of Schooling

Unlike the federal government, state governments possess the right and obligation to provide schooling. They largely discharge this responsibility through publicly operated school districts. Within this public structure, state-level educational managers possess a broad set of rights that act to constrain the planning and control activities of local officials.

In most states, state regulations govern virtually every major function of schooling, including instruction, transportation, services to the handicapped, facilities, personnel, finance, and physical education. Regulations are for the most part designed to control the behavior of public school educators. State-level education officials control much of the technology of public schooling by prescribing the system of rights within school districts. They determine to a large extent what services the district shall offer, the pool of individuals eligible to provide those services, the manner in which services are provided, the amounts of the resources that are spent on these services (within certain parameters), and the rights of employees and students who engage in providing and receiving the service. (Labor contracts, which are described in chapters 10 and 11, are the other major device for defining systems of rights.)

State regulations affecting management of public schools could (and do) fill volumes of books and are too numerous and variable across states to describe here. Along with federal regulations, they define many of the systems of rights within which the school district manager acts. (School-board policies are "residual" in that they define local-level rights within the constraints imposed by state and federal governments.) An administrator whose preferences differ from those imposed by regulations must determine whether to comply with regulations and, if so, to what degree. Sometimes the perceived disadvantages of compliance with a specific regulation are less than those associated with noncompliance. As the number and kind of regulations grow, the district-level manager may find that it is not even possible to totally comply with all regulations and has no choice but to determine how to minimize the disadvantages resulting from various forms of noncompliance.

To increase the probability that school district managers will "play within the rules," state and federal government officials and legislators devise various mechanisms for increasing the disutility of noncompliance (the proverbial stick) or increasing the utility of compliance (the proverbial carrot). Perhaps the most pervasive control mechanism used by state and federal educational managers to promote compliance with mandates is the combination of reporting requirements and external auditing. We turn now to the status and nature of reporting requirements in public schools. (Audit concepts—another form of control—are discussed separately in chapter 8 because of their detailed financial focus.)

Reporting as a Means of Control

One of the most pervasive control mechanisms is that of collecting information about the behavior of managers to be controlled. Information can describe managers' behavior with regard to inputs, processes, and outputs of schooling. School administrators, like most other managers, are both collectors and providers of data. They would prefer to have access to more (meaning "better" or, perhaps, "different") data than they have, and they would prefer to report less data to others than they currently have to. Because useful data (information) provide the basis for decisions and because there is almost always some information managers wish they had when forced to make a decision, managers pursue information.

Managers would rather not have to supply data to others for several reasons. The reports managers prepare are often helpful to others, but not to the managers. More important, reporting processes require managers' scarce time and other resources.

School business administrators find themselves in an unusually onerous position of being the major providers of data that outside interests use for monitoring the organization. Costs to the agency are incurred in three ways: (1) the direct costs of monitoring incurred by the monitoring agency, (2) the (usually indirect) costs incurred by the school district in complying with reporting requirements, and (3) the costs incurred by both organizations for missed opportunities, that is, the activities not undertaken because scarce resources were expended on monitoring and reporting. Costs of missed opportunities are, by definition, difficult to assess because they are hypothetical. There is also little comprehensive documentation on the costs of monitoring and the costs of compliance, but the anecdotal evidence that does exist suggests that none of the costs is trivial.

The reporting required of school districts by their state education agencies is usually at least as comprehensive as the state's regulation of schools. As indicated by the lists of some of the major federal reports required of school districts in California (exhibit 3.1), there are few school district services of which some aspect need not be reported. As part of her study of a 30,000-pupil school district in California, Mary Bankston (1982) found that district administrators were required to prepare 153 reports for federal and state departments of education during the fiscal year 1979–80 (not including many short forms prepared due to special circumstances or on an "as-required" basis). Most of the reports were lengthy; some were longer than fifty pages.

> Some [reports] also possessed several long components. For instance, "School Level Plans," identified as one report, was actually a conglomerate of plans for each school

Exhibit 3.1

Required Reports California School Districts to U.S. Department of Education

July 1980 – December 1980

Title

Development of Competency Measures for Vocational Skill Areas (OE-755)
Districtwide Advisory Committee Final Report
Application for Federal Assistance: Career Education Incentive Act (OE-692)
Application for Migrant Education Program: ESEA, Title I (OE-362)
Financial Status and Performance Report for Migrant Education Program ESEA, Title I
Nationwide Study of the Distribution, Utilization, and Impact of Research and Development Products in Vocational Education
Needs Assessment Survey for Handicapped Populations in Vocational Education
Teachers' Language Skills Survey, 1980–81
Indian Student Enrollment Certification: LEA (OE-506)
Quarterly Program Progress Report: EEOP (OE-361)
Right to Read Financial Status and Performance Report (OE-361)
ESEA, Title VII Basic Program Profile (OE-770)
Evaluation of the Classroom Instruction Component of ESEA, Title VII Bilingual Education Program
Program Administrative Review System for Handicapped Programs (OE-9066)
Evaluation of School Health Education Programs
Handicapped Children Receiving Special Education and Related Services (OE-9058)
EEOP Instructions for Financial Status Report and Performance Report (OE-116-2-1)
Financial Status and Performance Report: Part B of Education for All Handicapped Children Act (OE-9039)
A National Evaluation of School Nutrition Program
  Survey of Food Program Administrators
  Survey of Students
  Household Survey of Parents
  Longitudinal Survey of Students (FNS-1106)
Survey of Private Elementary and Secondary Schools
Career Information Systems in Secondary Schools: A Comparative Assessment of Alternative Types
Financial Status and Performance Report for Adult Basic Education Programs for Indo-Chinese Refugees (OE-571-1)
Management Evaluation Review for Quality Adult Education Programs (OE-750-1 through 5)

Source: Mary Bankston, "Organizational Reporting in a School District: State and Federal Programs" (Stanford, Calif.: Institute for Research on Educational Finance and Governance).

participating in a state-sponsored School Improvement Programs. Each of those separate plans was approximately fifty pages long. [P. 1]

Each report prepared by the district was routinely passed through the school district's business division for both fiscal and programmatic review.

Although precise measures of the cost of compliance are difficult to derive, Bankston developed several proxy measures. Of the fifty-three central office administrators in the school district, seventeen were retained specifically for and were funded by categorical programs. Report writing for state and federal agencies in the district was spread throughout the district in twenty different departments: ". . . this task [report writing] appeared to be the primary activity of many departments" (p. 1).

Not surprisingly, public school districts will allocate proportionately more staff to the task of report preparation to comply with the mandates of state and federal sponsors. The findings of Scott and Meyer (1985) are instructive here. They found that:

> Districts receiving more types of federal and state funds had larger numbers of administrators after taking into account the effects of site. . . . Shifting to the school level, . . . schools participating in more public programs had larger numbers of administrators.

The relationship between financial sponsorship and reporting requirements is not uniform. School districts are required to report data to agencies that may provide no money to the district (agencies at the federal level include the Department of Education's Office of Civil Rights, the Veteran's Administration, the Census Bureau, the Equal Employment Opportunity Commission, the Bureau of Labor Statistics, and the Federal Energy Commission). These data are then used for (among other things) monitoring compliance with regulations.

Managerial Incentives and Behavior

Managers seek to gather more data and to report less. That is, managers seek to be free of regulation (someone else's control devices) and at the same time to exert additional control over their environment; both activities have the effect of increasing managers' rights. Increased rights provide managers with greater opportunities to pursue their preferences. Efforts to curtail data reporting rarely change the incentives to gather more data, whether the administrator is a school business official, the manager of a firm, or a Washington bureaucrat. (Pressure to curtail reporting requirements comes from two interrelated sources: operators who have to prepare the reports and policy analysts who feel that the "gains" from reporting are more than offset by the costs.) It is not surprising that there has been little progress in curtailing efforts to gather data through required reports, even if the order comes from the President of the United States. In 1976 President Ford ordered departments to cut the number of reporting forms that they made organizations fill out by 10 percent. This was achieved within a year, but during the same time the reporting burden measured by the man-hours needed to complete the forms had increased. The Office of Management and Budget had stipulated that an agency could add a reporting form only if it withdrew another, but many agencies apparently replaced the short form with a longer, more detailed one.

The reporting requirements of public school managers are much more onerous than those of private school managers, because the systems of rights of public school managers are much more constrained by regulation than those of their counterparts in private schools. This fact does not suggest that the job of either public or private school managers is "harder" or "easier." The jobs are, however, different. Extensive external regulations certainly limit the choices and behavior of public school officials. They reduce the probability that any particular public school will fail in any spectacular way (such as going out of business), but they also reduce the likelihood that the same public school district will achieve remarkable success (such as a radical turnaround within two years).

Private school managers have a wide range of decisions they can (and must) make, and consequently they have a better chance of doing very well or very poorly as individual organizations. They exercise greater control over staffing, mission, and technology. In addition, they have to make decisions about pricing, marketing, and the division of current revenues between current expenses and future expenses. The distinction between "fewer decisions, less room to maneuver" versus "more decisions, more room to maneuver" implies differences in incentives and behavior between public and private school managers that are almost counterintuitive. Because public school managers are, relatively speaking, hemmed in on all sides by regulations, contracts, and externally determined funding mechanisms, they are largely occupied with trying to develop feasible "solutions" within seemingly (and sometimes actually) mutually exclusive constraints. The strategic posture of these individuals requires ingenuity and a wide information base, not because they have to make basic decisions about mission, service mix, clientele, organizational structure, and so on, but because they *cannot* make these decisions. The challenge is to succeed in a situation where laws, contracts, and regulations eliminate many of the possible moves in the game of management.

Private school managers are also constrained by rules, but they are different rules emanating from a different source—the marketplace. Their challenge is to succeed by determining service mix, marketing strategy, pricing policies, mission, and target clientele. Their rules are derived within a more classical economic setting and deal with, for example, relationships between changes in price and changes in demand, between current and future preferences of clients and current service mix, and between investments for the future and current expenditures.

Managers in both public and private schools have incentives to plan, but because they face somewhat different systems of rights, both the purposes of planning and the processes employed will differ in emphasis across sectors, as will the purposes and processes of control. We consider planning first.

Planning

Managers use planning to guide the educational organization as it responds to environmental influences. To say that the current fiscal, demographic, and regulatory factors affecting schools are complex and interrelated is, of course, an understatement. We have only briefly touched on the regulatory factors, yet even a thorough understanding of both these and the other factors would not automatically suggest solutions or responses that are appropriate for all educational institutions. In this section we want to examine the ways in which managers organize to respond to these and other environmental conditions. In other words, we want to examine how school managers plan.

There are almost as many different definitions of planning as there are planners. Handler defines planning as "a series of related steps organized around and moving towards an accomplishment of an objective." To Gulich, planning is "working out, in broad outlines, the things that need to be done and the methods for doing them to accomplish the purpose set for the enterprise." The American Association of School Administrators sees planning as "an attempt to control the future in the direction of the desired goals through decisions made on the basis of careful estimates of the probable consequences of possible courses of action." Joseph Hannon, past Superintendent of Schools in Chicago, calls planning "a means of steering our school system in a focused, rather than a scattered, direction."

It is certainly difficult not to argue that under any of these definitions planning certainly sounds "good." As Stephen Robbins (1980) has indicated, recommending that administrators engage in formal planning is akin to the story about a little old lady, who upon hearing of the death of David Ben Gurion, the Israeli statesman, suggested that he be given some chicken soup. A friend said, "The man is dead! What good will chicken soup do?" To which the little old lady replied, "It couldn't hurt!" A similar reply is usually given in regards to the benefits of formal planning: It certainly couldn't hurt. And yet, of course, we must ask the question, To what degree does it help, and are the benefits worth the costs incurred?

As we progress through this section we first want to acquaint ourselves with what is typically thought of as the major purposes and processes of planning in educational organizations, and then we will evaluate those elements of planning that appear to have most utility for educational organizations.

Purposes of Planning

Planning is an attempt to be aware of those systems of rights affecting the school and to anticipate changes in rights and the impact of alternative decisions on the school. Forecasting, by the way, is part of planning because forecasting is the process of determining trends, which is useful in planning. Both external and internal trends are evaluated as the manager seeks to anticipate the major threats as well as the major opportunities that might face the organization. Threats are those external or internal factors that may greatly reduce the ability of the school to achieve its goals. Opportunities, on the other hand, are those factors that, if capitalized on, may enable the school to achieve its goals to a much greater degree.

The list of major threats and opportunities facing a school will vary from school to school and change over time. They often grow out of changes in client demographics, finance, and external regulations. Sometimes it is not always clear whether (or the degree to which) a trend represents a threat or an opportunity. Enrollment decline, for example, may represent a series of threats to program enrichment and staff quality as well as a series of opportunities for closing obsolete facilities and containing total expenditures.

As managers evaluate threats and opportunities, they simultaneously consider actions that will avert or capitalize on the threats. As they do this, they engage in planning on two fronts: the public and the private.

Planning to Provide Public Direction

The purpose of planning is to determine a direction; the purpose of a public plan and resulting document is to provide a directional guide for future decisions as well as to communicate that direction. As one state education department official colloquially put it:

> The superintendent, like the minister, needs a bible to give him guidance and direction. Some superintendents have a bible. It may be the board policy handbook; or it may become, if it is not already, the board-teacher negotiated agreement. It should be neither of these. It should be the District Long-Range Development Plan.

Over the last decade an increasing fraction of public school districts have developed or revised public documents called long-range plans. Usually these plans for public school districts contain most of the following:

1. Mission statements, goals, objectives, and other indicia of what the authors agree are the desired outcomes or behaviors of the school

2. Plans for instructional program development, staff development, support services development, and capital facilities improvement
3. Trend data including projections of key variables such as enrollments, assessed valuation, tax rates, expenditures, and revenues

Publicly circulated plans for private schools differ from those developed in public schools primarily in that there would be different variables in trend data projections. For example, assessed valuation and tax rate information would not be found, but estimates of tuition changes, lengths of waiting lists, and ratios of inquiries to applications would be included.

Consideration of categories one and two in the previous list is desired before number three, trend data, is assembled. In order for expenditure and revenue forecasts to be created, assumptions must be made about changes in enrollment, staffing, salaries, state aid, local tax base, price levels, service mix, and so on. (These specific topics are discussed in more detail in other chapters. Our goal here is simply to describe how they fit into planning.)

When the purpose of planning is to provide public direction, the content of plans tends to be comprehensive in the treatment of programs that will help the organization and to avoid topics that could threaten the organization. Mission statements will attempt to encompass all or most of what the school managers desire to undertake. All expenditures and revenues are projected. In addition, every effort will be made to mask the "losers," that is, those who are likely to be hurt from the plan. The overwhelming emphasis will be on "winners." The content of the plan will reflect its purpose, which is to align preferences of all who read it and to broaden the base of support for the school.

Planning for Private Direction

While a public long-range plan may be a necessary bible for the school administrator, it is by no means sufficient. The contents of publicly circulated long-range plans do not contain all, or even the most important, plans of the school administrator. There are certain elements of plans and planning that managers pursue privately because to "go public" would jeopardize the plan. For example, the manager may determine that, over the next three years, every three secretaries should be replaced by two secretaries, a clerk, and a word processor; or perhaps the manager will determine that school X should be closed. All of the information this manager has at hand suggests that these actions should be taken, but if the manager broadcasts those strategies in a public plan, forces opposed to the plan (such as secretaries and the School "X" PTA in these cases) would immediately coalesce and attempt to sabotage the plan before it even got off the ground. Or, consider the issue of intersector competition. Because of declining enrollments, the public school manager may determine that an extensive campaign should be conducted to convince parents of children enrolled in private schools that they should reconsider public school magnet programs. Again, to publicize this plan could well stir up more negative reaction initially than it would generate positive action.

Staff development plans represent perhaps the most fundamental case for having a private plan as a complement to a public plan. Administrators usually wish to develop and ultimately promote only a subset of employees whom they supervise. Plans identifying specific manpower needs, including plans for "grooming" some employees and not others, are among the most potent in the sense that they will have a major impact on the future success of the school. However, in most instances these plans should not find their way into a public document.

Throughout these examples of private plans the identities of people who stand to lose and those who stand to gain are relatively clear. In terms of managers' preferences, the "net" gain should always be positive. To publicize these plans would be to undermine the very purpose of other publicly presented plans, that is, to generate goal consensus and align preferences. Private plans, if known, would divide the work force, but they still need to be made. Unless managers have attempted to evaluate the impact of the plans on other peoples' preferences, they will not be in a very good position to carry out either their public or private plans. Just because certain issues best remain unpublicized is no reason not to develop plans for those issues. Indeed, a private promotion, demotion, or reassignment plan is just as valuable as a public, comprehensive plan for the school.

In many respects the private plan is like the public one: they both result in written documents, assumptions are enumerated, threats and opportunities are evaluated, and courses of action are considered. Unlike the comprehensive public plan, however, the private plan has a selective focus, and the threat of the plan to individuals is explicitly considered. While the net financial impact is less explicitly stated in a private plan, the political impact is more carefully considered.

Developing a formal, public long-range plan for their schools can help managers to (1) learn a good deal quickly about a new job; (2) influence employee behavior; and (3) increase client support. Formal long-range planning is not, however, always perceived as being worth the costs incurred. Just over a decade ago about half of the school business officials in one state perceived that long-range planning was important for their school districts, but only about 5 percent actually undertook formal public planning processes. Formal long-range planning is usually undertaken for one or more of the reasons cited above or is limited to revenue and expenditure analyses. Increasingly public school district managers are preparing formal plans because state legislatures are requiring that it be done (which makes long-range planning more of a reporting requirement than a plan). In most instances where long-range plans have been prepared, managers presume that by involving community and labor representatives in the decision problems facing the school, these groups will gain an appreciation for management's problematic trade-offs and will be more supportive of the necessary but sometimes no-win choices that management must make.

Processes of Planning

Planning processes usually consist of several interrelated activities: (1) establishing goals for the future; (2) collecting information about the environment, including external events and trends as well as internal strengths and weaknesses; (3) devising several paths toward meeting goals; (4) selecting the best paths to follow; and (5) evaluating movement to attain the specified goals. All three of Anthony's (1965) managerial behaviorals are included: planning (1, 2, 3), management control (4), and operational control (5).

Review Goals

Where planning is done, members of the board of education and the superintendent (or in the case of private schools, boards of trustees and headmaster) review and in most cases reaffirm the overall goals of the school system with minor modifications. These goals are usually statements of long-range purposes, which provide continuity and definition for the organization. They do not specify a period of time in which to achieve the goals, nor do they employ quantitative measures. In some instances, school districts have adopted comprehensive goal statements, that is, statements that are collectively designed to deal with all operations of the school system. One large school system, for example, has eleven major goal statements that deal with student achievement, pupil services, community relations, human relations, the learning environment, equality of opportunity, personnel, management, finance, relationships with government, and conservation. Within each of these broad areas, of course, there is a wide variety of more detailed goal statements, such as the following:

1. Implement a proficiency test to ensure minimum student achievement on graduation
2. Reduce the high school dropout rate
3. Expand educational options for out-of-school youth
4. Strengthen the interaction between local schools and parents
5. Provide trained crisis-intervention teams
6. Ensure that tenure policies provide for realistic procedures for terminating employees who are rendering unsatisfactory services
7. Develop recommendations for maximum utilization of space

8. Maintain an effective relationship with the state board of education
9. Fuse concepts of conservation into the curriculum

At this level of generality, goals function in a manner not unlike an organization's statement of its mission. That is, they describe in very general terms their intended business. For that school district, goals were designed to provide the broadest, most public outlines for the direction of the organization. Other districts will achieve this function by developing statements of their missions. Consider the following statement from a large suburban school district:

Education is a human project performed by humans for other humans. As such, it requires not merely the imparting of knowledge from one brain to another, but also the attitude of caring. An education based on the sharing of knowledge and the caring for individuals, whether they are very young or very old, is essential for the human relationship.

The rapid changes in our society establish our belief that a program for all individuals should be devised and implemented which is designed to provide life-long education and to convey the importance of, and the need to develop, each individual to his or her maximum as a human being. This should include developing healthy attitudes, self-reliance, self-discipline, respect for one's self and others.

Opportunities should be made available to all individuals in the district which will enable them to develop and pursue a personal educational plan, including learning about the world in which they live, its people, its social, physical, and biological environment—both past and present; it should include study of the arts and literature—both historically and creatively, and the manner in which human interaction takes place.

Ideally, the educational process should begin at the earliest moment of awareness, and continue through life, utilizing all available human and physical resources, and should offer maximum flexibility for entry and re-entry into the world of work and the world of education.

Broad statements of purpose as the one above seldom change dramatically in educational organizations. In most cases their missions are established for them by state charter or state legislation. However, these most broad statements of purpose are reviewed from time to time to incorporate relatively recent developments (for example, energy conservation) and to ensure that the language is contemporary.

Assess the Environment

The second major step in most planning processes involves collecting information about the environment that affects the schools. The term *environment* defines those forces that affect the performance and development of the school system. It includes an assessment of external conditions, especially political, social, economic, technological, and, of course, demographic. These external factors may affect the entire district or some specific aspect of the district. For example, federal and state legislation on special education is likely to be felt throughout the district, whereas the construction of a housing development within one attendance area may have a more localized impact.

Information is also collected regarding the internal environment. Typically it deals with issues of manpower, revenues, expenses, and capital. It includes such items as the number and background of employees, the condition of physical plants, curriculum requirements, and contractual obligations. Both the strengths and weaknesses of the internal environment should be considered. *Strengths* in this context means those positive aspects of the organization that can serve as the foundation for further development. *Weaknesses*, on the other hand, are problems that are not being corrected in an efficient manner and can be compensated for, corrected, or eliminated. For example, strengths of the faculty of a particular district could include a large number of employees who are bilingual, who have an excellent attendance record, and who have consistently volunteered for extracurricular activities. Weaknesses of the same group might include the fact that certification locks many of the teachers into areas of reduced demand and inhibits their ability to move into higher-demand areas.

Develop Strategies

Once goals and objectives have been established and the environmental data have been collected, several approaches, called strategies, toward accomplishing the goals are developed. These are courses of action involving people, time, money, and other resources. In many respects strategies force educational administrators to define their organizations' purposes much more than the process of goal-setting does. Strategy formation involves broad commitments of resources in certain directions and withholding of those resources in others. (Private plans can come into play here.) The Chicago Board of Education's decision to combat racial isolation and inadequate learning conditions through an intricate, comprehensive program of voluntary enrollment measures (called the "Access to Excellence" program) was a strategic decision in broad terms. It committed resources toward the development and marketing of new, innovative instructional programs and away from "standard" programs currently used in the schools. This particular example highlights several important characteristics of strategic decisions. First, these decisions are inevitably the response to major threats and opportunities facing the organization. The threat of federally mandated "forced busing" was assured unless the district could show "all deliberate speed" in its desegregation efforts. On the other hand, strictly mandatory busing measures would speed the flight out of the school district of white and middle-class student populations, who were gradually declining as a proportion of the total school population. To achieve desegregation, white students needed to be attracted back into the schools, not driven out. Segments of the white and black communities were adamant in their opposition to busing, but for different reasons. The development of a program offering voluntary enrollment in attractive programs was the district's response.

Second, strategies capitalize on the strengths and minimize the weaknesses of the organization. In the case of Chicago, the "best and the brightest" among the faculty were recruited to start up new language, technical, scientific, and performing arts programs. They were located in school facilities with excess space. The extensive school transportation systems were used to transport children to sites out of their attendance areas. As much as possible, per-pupil costs for these programs were kept at or below the average for the district.

Third, some people will undoubtedly be helped, but others will be hurt. Virtually no decision today can be made that does not affect *someone* negatively, even though many others are helped. In Chicago, brighter students and those with more concerned parents were enrolling in the programs. They perceived a greater opportunity to excel than existed in their current schools. So far, so good. However, the parents of students in the schools that were losing students, along with many members of the faculty and administration of those schools, objected strongly to the "creaming" of their schools, that is, the deliberate efforts to pull the best students out of their classrooms. They argued that it inevitably lowered the quality of education in these schools. As is the case with most strategies, some groups of individuals were helped at the expense of others. The "task" is to estimate beforehand who will be negatively affected by strategies and then to determine whether the strategy is still preferable to the current course of action.

Fourth, strategies both commit and withhold resources. In Chicago, incremental amounts of resources were committed toward the development and marketing of new, innovative programs and away from current programs in the schools.

Strategies like the one just discussed identify ways for the organization to match its capabilities with potential opportunities, avoiding as much of the negative impact of threats as possible. Strategies can deal with a wide range of issues. Most often they involve one or more of the following: the kinds of programs and courses to be offered, methods of internal organization and operation, identification of changes in various clientele (characteristics of students to be served), and financial issues such as cost reduction or revenue-producing methods.

Strategies also vary with different stages in the "life cycle" of the organization, that is, within the context of growth, stability, retrenchment, or some combination. Many organizations, especially school districts, are facing what could be termed *retrenchment*. A retrenchment strategy would include plans for reducing the scope of current operations or scaling down objectives.

Key ingredients of such strategies would include plans for school closings, reductions in force, consolidation of positions, and elimination of instructional programs.

Although retrenchment strategies could characterize the strategies of some school districts, they are by no means universal. In fact, most districts pursue what is more accurately termed a combination of retrenchment, stability, and growth. School districts are expanding programs in early childhood development, adult education, and education of the handicapped. In many instances, entirely new populations are being served. These changes are occurring within the context of declines in the numbers of "traditional" students.

Link to Management and Control

Following the planning activities (goal analysis, environmental analysis, and broad strategy formation), activities of managerial control (developing action plans, budgeting) and operational control (including various evaluation activities) are built into the planning process so that the "loop is closed." In other words, goals influence activities; activities are monitored; and, to close the loop, the information gained from monitoring activities influences goals.

Planning processes are attempts to direct the diverse energies of a wide variety of employees who work in a variety of different offices, departments, and schools. Planning is not a natural occurrence in an organization and usually requires a relatively high degree of formal action (even informal arm-twisting), including recruiting nonemployee volunteers, developing calendars of activities with deadlines, filling out forms, attending in-service training, and formal allocation of responsibility for managing the planning process to some individual.

In many respects the formal planning processes in educational organizations are like those in most other programs: they are in a perpetual state of evolution. They undergo evaluation and some modification annually. Administrators who have attempted to implement long-range or comprehensive planning have had as much difficulty reconciling the wide variety of existing but fragmented planning activities as they have had in implementing new ones. Often the problems of design and implementation become ones of reconciling many existing planning activities more than installing new ones.

Evaluating the Costs and Benefits of Planning in Schools

As we discussed earlier, planning processes sound so "rational." To question their utility and efficacy is to cause at a minimum raised eyebrows, if not scorn. The evidence supporting the usefulness of planning, however, is indeed mixed. Although many administrators and academics support the assumption that formal planning improves organizational performance, at least one study questions this simple, generalized relationship. Fulmer and Rue (1974) found that in durable goods industries the planners outperformed the nonplanners; however, the reverse was true in service industries (such as schools). They concluded that "such variables as timing, and the immeasurable quality of 'overall managerial competence' have a more direct relationship on a firm's performance/success than the formality of [its] long-range planning activity" (p. 7). Although the study was restricted to business firms, and measures of performance were defined in financial terms, it does suggest to us that perhaps we should be examining the "overall managerial competence" of the administrators in an educational organization, as distinct from the formal mechanism of putting together a planning process. Just because a school district or private school assembles a mission statement, goals, objectives, action plans, lists of strengths and weaknesses, and so on, does not mean that it is assured of reasonable performance, or even of improving on current performance. On the other hand, it is entirely possible that educational organizations with a relatively high proportion of "competent" administrators are likely to have instituted a successful long-range planning process.

The School Business Administrator: A Passive Facilitator Versus an Active Participant

During the planning process, a wide variety of individuals and individual preferences are channeled in order to focus the energies and ambitions of these individuals toward organizationally appropriate ends. The participants in the planning process include various constituencies within the organization and frequently external constituencies as well. These diverse participants, then, express their conflicting preferences, and through bargaining they enter into what might be termed an "agreement" on the general purposes and priorities of the organization. It is easy for us at times to deride the very general goal statements and the lack of specificity of missions, such as described earlier. They have no specific time line for completion, and no criteria against which to measure performance. However, the purpose of these nebulous statements is to achieve a consensus among diverse groups of individuals. Such a consensus would not be possible if the goals were highly specific and their relative importance had to be determined. As Cyert and March (1959) point out, behind agreement on rather vague objectives is considerable disagreement and uncertainty about subgoals. This explains why it often appears that various parts of an organization are pursuing different and partially inconsistent goals.

More than a few school business officials have commented that they feel their appropriate role in planning and budgeting is to be responsible for the process, that is, to ensure that a thorough planning process is in operation and that plans and budgets are developed as a result. This is an entirely appropriate public position. In fact, however, the business official, by virtue of being one of the top administrators in the educational organization, is bound to have a major influence on the goals and objectives selected for the schools. In the vast majority of organizations, the decision-making coalition is predominately made up of top administrators. According to James B. Thompson (1967), "organizational goals are established by individuals—but interdependent individuals who collectively have sufficient control of organizational resources to commit them in certain directions and to withhold them from others" (p. 120).

Although it may be politically convenient to talk about the business official's role as financial analyst and facilitator of the planning process, it would be inaccurate to indicate that the business official does not nor should not have a major influence in the plans that a school or school district undertakes. Many of the more "technical" domains of education are under the direction of the school business official. On complex matters involving, for example, transportation, insurance, data processing, and purchasing, the manager's opinions can greatly influence the decisions of the school board. The business administrator usually must play at least two often-conflicting roles in goal setting and strategy formation. As chief spokesperson and individual responsible for business functions, the business official lobbies for goals and general strategies that will ensure that he can accomplish his responsibilities in a manner consistent with his personal preferences. However, as part of the team of top administrators, the business official is compelled to consider district-wide goals and strategies, some of which may even be detrimental to the "subgoals" of the school business office.

It is good theory to suggest that the business official consider what is good for the district as a whole. In practice this is not always the case, and probably should not be. To paraphrase William Hall (1977), it is nearly certain that all educational administrators involved in the planning process will disagree as to what the objectives of the schools should be. Conflict between district-level goals, building goals, and departmental goals are legend, as are conflicts between individual goals and the goals shared by the coalition of individuals within the school district. Thus, it is not surprising that individuals and groups of individuals bias their analyses in favor of those alternatives that are in their self-interest.

The goals of the educational organization evolve through coalition and negotiation. The resulting objectives represent the views of senior administrators and the school board, but they rarely perfectly match the goals of any one administrator. The objectives that are finally arrived at tend to be vague due to compromise and the desire of participants to avoid subordinating their personal interests to those of the departments that they represent. This vagueness gives the appearance of agreement on overall objectives, but it can create operating problems when any of the administrators attempt to develop subgoals for their divisions and departments (Robbins 1980, p. 144).

While many of the activities of planning apply to almost all organizations, the purposes of planning in education differ at least in degree, if not in kind, among the sectors of schooling. Most public education organizations do not plan for the purpose of improving profitability or share of the market as do private schools. The concept of measuring the percentage of return on the capital invested or measuring performance in terms of the relative market share is simply not applicable for the most part to public elementary and secondary educational organizations. Often private profit-seeking, and to some extent nonprofit, organizations plan with the purpose of improving productivity. This is defined as an organization's ability to transfer inputs into outputs at a lower cost. Often this result is turned around in the public sector, and lower costs for services are sometimes viewed correctly as reduced service. Consequently, public entities more often pursue *service-enhancing* plans, not plans to increase productivity.

On the assumption that, with or without the assistance of long-range plans, the goals of the school have been established, we would logically progress to issues of managerial control, such as budgeting. Because budgeting is covered in chapter 6, we will assume for the moment that the most appropriate ways of achieving those goals have also been decided on. Our interest at this point is merely to make sure that those activities are carried out as intended.

Controlling

The word *control* conjures up a variety of images, many of them negative. Within the context of school business management, however, control is neutral; control consists of the forces that guide the educational organization through a predetermined set of objectives by means of predetermined policies and decisions. The key word here is *predetermined.* Not only have the goals of the organization already been determined, but the specific activities or means for carrying out those goals have already been decided. When we speak of control, then, we are speaking of a process of ensuring that specific tasks are carried out effectively and efficiently.

When educational administrators control, they monitor the activities of other administrators (and they themselves are monitored by other administrators) to determine whether individual units in the organization are obtaining and utilizing their resources effectively and efficiently so as to accomplish the organization's objectives. Where this is not being achieved, the administrators implement corrective action (Robbins 1980, p. 376). The control process is made up of three separate and distinct steps: measuring actual performance, comparing actual performance with a standard to determine if there is any difference, and correcting any significant deviations through remedial action.

Described this way the controlling process sounds deceptively simple. However, it is rarely entirely clear what ought to be measured, against what standard these measurements ought to be compared, how deviations should be corrected, or even when the costs of control are worth it. In order to get a feel for these issues related to control, we present the following five cases and then analyze them to determine where there is a need for controls, where controls exist and seem to be working, and where controls exist and seem not to be working.

Case 1. In one medium-sized urban public school district a routine physical audit of school food service turned up the fact that hourly food service workers uniformly received significant amounts of overtime during the first week in December, which showed up in paychecks just before Christmas vacation. Although overtime work is not uncommon in the school system, the fact that it was so widespread at one particular point in time every year raised questions. Further investigation revealed that school food service supervisors were using their authority to allocate overtime as a means for distributing unauthorized Christmas "presents" in the form of bonuses prior to Christmas each year. Once this was discovered, the director of food services was notified and immediately put a stop to the practice.

Case 2. Telephone calls from taxpayers in a small school district to the assistant district attorney in the area led to the following events: (1) a man was arrested for petty larceny, accused of charging the school district for three hours of work at the time he was wallpapering his brother's kitchen; (2) more than $3,700 worth of school district equipment (drills, sander, chemical sprayer, two-hundred pound landscaping rake, and the like) was returned from the homes of individuals to the school district; and (3) one of the district administrators pleaded guilty to falsification of business records and faced a maximum of one year in the county jail.

Case 3. "As many as 28,000 high school students who have not been immunized against five childhood diseases will be barred from classes this morning, the Board of Education announced yesterday. . . . Notices have been sent home, students have been informed over loudspeakers, principals have made announcements in several different languages, a school official said. The Board of Education receives state funds based on daily attendance figures and therefore the exclusion of uninoculated students could result in a financial loss for the city. At the current rate—$4.40 a day for each student—the uninoculated students could cost the city $26,000 a day" (*New York Times*, October 3, 1980, p. 81).

Case 4. "The (urban) school system, beleagured by administrative, budgetary and labor disputes, may face punitive action by the (state) Board of Education if those conflicts are not resolved. The State Board had 'reached a peak of frustration' at a meeting the night before and was reviewing ways of withholding state and federal money that accounts for more than half the (school) system's expenditures. State Board officials said they might seek legislative approval of a commission to oversee the school system if it did not 'put its house in order.' They plan to meet within two weeks to determine their course of action" (*New York Times*, Friday, October 31, 1980, p. A15).

Case 5. "The financial crisis in the (Midwest City) Public Schools in 1979–80 was inevitable. . . . In 1973 . . . school officials began dipping into the savings accounts by using restricted funds (set aside to make bond and note payments) to meet operating expenses. For the school district the end came in November of '79 when Moody's slashed its credit rating, eliminating its access to the financial markets. . . . Among the measures recommended by the State Board of Education to the General Assembly Investigating Committee in 1980 was the requirement that school districts evaluate regularly and periodically change their audit firms, that is, every five to seven years" ("Chicago Financial Crisis Why it Happened," *School Business Affairs*, February 1981, pp. 20–21).

These cases highlight in different ways many of the features of control systems in schools. Control processes often deal with financial matters; financial controls act to protect against loss resulting from errors or irregularities in processing transactions and in handling the related assets. (The term *errors* refers to unintentional mistakes, while the word *irregularities* refers to intentional distortions of records or financial statements.)

In some instances the absence of controls is apparent (cases 1 and 2). The Christmas presents in the urban school system were found accidentally, and the improprieties in the small district were uncovered by perhaps envious neighbors. In case 3 it appears that controls were not only implemented but were also working. These controls ensured that schoolchildren indeed got immunized. In the final two cases it appears that the controls in place somehow were not adequately functioning. The state boards of education have legal authority over their state's school districts, but in case 4 the state seemed unable to exercise its authority. Similarly, in Midwest City independent financial audits designed to determine the financial health of school districts were not sufficient to predict or control the financial crisis that erupted.

We will return to the three questions asked at the beginning of the chapter. For purposes of control, what is to be measured? Against what will these measures be compared? How will corrections be implemented? Measurement is perhaps the most fundamental of the three ingredients of control. Measurement can take place in a variety of ways, including personal observation, statistical reports, oral reports, and written reports. The measures themselves do not imply controlling actions. Rather, measurements provide facts and information that form a basis for making judgments. The act of measuring is the act of generating facts. As one high-level official once said, "There are no hard decisions, just insufficient facts. When you have the facts, the decision comes easy." In many of the strictly financial areas, the process of technical or operational control is conceptually relatively straightforward (though still difficult to implement), primarily because there is little disagreement about the appropriate link between measurement, comparison, and control.

Purposes of Control

Previous uses of the term *control* in management have likened managerial control to simple electromechanical servo-mechanisms. Since these control systems are designed to maintain a level of performance (for example, temperature) between predetermined limits, it was assumed that "preventiveness is the essential attribute of a control system. . . . The existence of a control system is justified by its ability to enforce its norms. Precision in the determination of norms is of elementary importance in industrial control" (McKenna 1955, p. 180). While applicable to management generally, this description becomes clearer when it is linked to the variety of ways in which controls are typically used in educational organizations.

Controls are used *to standardize performance* in order to increase efficiency and to lower costs. Examples include inspections, written procedures, and work schedules. With the custodial work schedule in exhibit 3.2, the supervisor of operations and maintenance is attempting to ensure that the performance of each custodian who cleans school classrooms and laboratories is uniform. (It is *not* evident from that exhibit whether the schedule is enforced, how it is enforced, or whether it has resulted in greater efficiency and lower costs.)

Controls are also used *to safeguard the assets* of the school organization from theft, wastage, or misuse. These controls are designed to protect both liquid assets such as cash and less liquid assets such as microcomputers. In controlling rights to liquid assets, managers often rely on division of responsibilities (and rights), such as the separation of operational, treasury or custodial, and accounting activities. Within these control devices are systems of authorization and recordkeeping. (The general mechanics of financial control processes are discussed later in this chapter.) Nonliquid physical assets are controlled largely through inventory recording and monitoring systems.

Exhibit 3.2
Standardizing Performance Through Uniform Work Schedules Daily Custodial Schedule

School ....
Employee ....
Hours Worked ....

Assignment for Day Custodian

Morning	*Types of Duties*
7:30- 8:30	Assignments related to the opening of school.
8:30- 9:30	Sweep entrances, police grounds, preventive maintenance.
9:30-12:00	Assignments related to corridor, restroom, grounds areas.
Afternoon	
12:00-12:30	Lunch.
12:30- 1:30	Assignments related to cafeteria, corridors, special rooms, and restrooms.
1:30- 2:15	Cafeteria cleaning.
2:15- 4:00	Assignments related to classroom cleaning or care of grounds.

Assignment for Evening Custodian

Evening	
3:30- 6:30	Assignments related to daily cleaning (sweep classroom, etc.) or care of grounds.
6:30- 7:00	Supper.
7:00-12:00	Assignments related to daily (sweep classrooms, etc.) and periodic cleaning (scrubbing, waxing, etc.). Providing building service for evening activities.

Source: Frederick Hill and James Colmey, *School Business Administration* (Minneapolis: Dennison & Co, 1964), p. 180.

Controls are used *to standardize services* in order to meet program requirements and specifications. Curricular guides, individual educational plans, and lesson plans are examples of these controlling devices. Controls are also designed to set limits within which delegated authority can be exercised without the approval of higher-level management. Board policy manuals and policy and procedure directives often contain examples of this type of control.

Controls are used *to measure and increase the job performance* of individuals. Examples include evaluation of teaching, internal audits, reports of counseling loads, number of accounting transactions posted in a period, and number of calls for repairs responded to in a period. These controls are sometimes used in conjuction with controls designed to motivate individuals. "Motivational" controls consist of positive reinforcers such as promotions, bonuses, awards, and merit-based compensation.

Controls come in many forms and are applied in a variety of ways. All share two common characteristics: the range of desired or preferred activities has been determined a priori, and the methods of control are designed to ensure that these activities are carried out. Again, the second characteristic is the purpose of controls, but the actual impact of controls is another matter entirely.

As with any other manager, the school business official has incentives to use all of the controls discussed up to the point at which the advantages that result from their use are less than the effort it takes to implement controls. School business administrators have particular incentives to emphasize controls, such as safeguarding of assets and ensuring the productivity of noncertificated school personnel, that are best suited to their specific systems of rights.

Controlling Personnel Behavior

Even within these specific areas of responsibility, there is seldom a simple relationship between behaviors that the manager seeks to control and the most appropriate controlling devices. For example, managers generally wish to reduce or eliminate certain behavior of personnel, yet it is not always clear what controlling devices are most applicable. Consider the more blatant forms of misconduct by employees, which could include fighting; disorderly conduct; verbal abuse or intimidation of others; insubordination; damage or spoilage of property, equipment, or material (either willfully or through negligence); sleeping on the job; attempting to commit immoral acts on the premises; failing to report the correct amount of time worked; use of telephones for other than school business; being drunk on the job; failing to use protective equipment or devices where required; leaving the job during working hours without permission; excessive tardiness or absenteeism; exceeding specified rest periods; and on and on.

Although there would be general agreement that these behaviors are not preferred, there would not necessarily be agreement among managers about the best way of controlling either the frequency or the severity of their occurrence. Should these behaviors be penalized? If so, then how severely? Should persons who do not exhibit undesirable behavior be rewarded? What kinds of resources should be allocated to monitoring the organization for these occurrences?

All of the control devices could be brought to bear, in one way or another, to control these types of personal misconduct. (Many school districts attempt to combat these problems through employee handbooks describing a series of "shalts" and "shalt nots" and through personnel evaluation mechanisms. (Control devices built into personnel policies are described in chapter 10.)

Controlling for Intended Use of Liquid Assets

Financial control is one of the major responsibilities of school business officials, although that responsibility is shared with other members of the business office, the superintendent, and the board. In pursuing their preferences to ensure that liquid assets are used as intended, business administrators, perhaps more than other school managers, build control measures into the information systems of the organization as well as into the systems of rights of those over whom they have authority. What are referred to as accounting, personnel, payroll, and other "systems" are largely controlling devices to improve the likelihood that intended activities take place—especially that money is spent and received as intended.

Processes of Control: Financial Control Methods for Payroll and Personnel

Because major rights and responsibilities of the business official are associated with the financial management of the school, the most important controlling devices for the official will be those with the most direct implications for the intended use of money. The subject we want to deal with here, and to some extent in the next section, is how controls are implemented to ensure that money is used as intended. The process of controlling can best be described by examining a specific example. Perhaps the most important activities in a school that require financial control are those associated with payroll and personnel. Payroll expenditures for most schooling organizations account for about 70 percent of their total expenditures. The required activities of establishing, maintaining, and carrying out contractual relationships of the work force require that financial control be permanently part of personnel practices. Control devices are usually found in at least five payroll and personnel areas: (1) creating positions, (2) hiring and staffing employees, (3) recording employee attendance and calculating pay, (4) distributing payroll costs to appropriate accounts, and (5) creating miscellaneous personnel reports that have implications for the intended use of financial resources. The purpose of looking at a "typical" or "hypothetical" payroll and personnel system here is to point out how controls are (or could be) used. Controlling mechanisms that have been incorporated in the payroll and personnel system are denoted by "*".

Defining Personnel Positions

Schools, like most other organizations, are continually modifying personnel positions and dropping positions as regulations change, as new programs are established, as existing programs are merged or otherwise modified, and as missions shift. In many respects the right to define a position can directly affect the right to use financial resources. The process of controlling personnel positions begins when a school manager initiates a request to open, change, or close a position. At the point when a change in position is requested, its projected cost is calculated and funding availability is determined. If funds are not available, the request to open the position is rejected*. If funding exists, top-level instructional managers are given a week to deny the request on other than financial grounds*. If no action is taken within the one-week limit, the position will be automatically approved for staffing*.

Hiring and Staffing Employees

The staffing process links people to positions. Managers responsible for filling positions are provided lists of vacancies that they are authorized to fill*. Once they make a final staffing decision, the projected cost of salary and fringe benefits allocated for the position is recomputed*. Budgetary adjustments are made based on the person's actual payroll data as opposed to the averages used when the position was opened.

Recording Employee Attendance and Calculating Pay

In order for the employee to be paid, attendance must be reported for the position into which the employee is staffed*. The process begins when employees sign in on a daily basis at the school or office where they are working*. One week prior to the end of the pay period, all timekeepers prepare attendance reports based on the sign-in sheets. Because most school payroll systems are now automated, computer programs are used at this point to cross-check relationships between positions, employees, and work locations to identify any unusual attendance conditions*, which are then printed out for the manager to evaluate. Once evaluated, the attendance data are entered into the system for payment calculation. Most schools require a variety of payment calculation routines and deduction procedures. Any retroactive pay adjustments that may be required are also processed at this point.

Distributing Payroll Costs

Personnel expenditures are accumulated and reported according to organizational unit, educational program, special project, and type of expenditure. It may also be desirable for the system to enable many people to report to a single position. (This is most commonly used in implementing special short-term programs where many teachers are teaching in the same educational program funded out of a single source. Also, substitutes can report their time from each of the locations where they are working. The system consolidates all substitute attendance data and uses them to distribute substitute charges for appropriate locations and programs.)

The concept of control of personnel expenditures is not limited to making sure that people are paid exactly what they are due. Higher-level controls are usually required as well. For example, in the event that a position has been opened but not filled, the system of control would have procedures for reprojecting the costs of the position and releasing those funds that are not used*. These released funds would then be recorded in a special account to be reallocated by some manager to a portion of the organization where personnel expenditures may be running higher than originally anticipated.

In addition, the system of control would also incorporate processes for automatically encumbering additional funds when changes have occurred that were not recognized at the time the position was opened and staffed. For example, an additional encumbrance would take place in the event of a general increase in pay rates for all employees or when there is a change in one or more of the organization's benefit programs*. Without this ongoing reprojection and encumbrance capability, top-level managers would not become aware of a possible deficit-spending situation until it was too late to take appropriate corrective action.

Generating Personnel Reports

Financial control, as we can see, extends far beyond controlling dollars directly. A variety of personnel control and reporting devices are required that are not directly linked to dollars but are no less important. Reports could be generated that indicate when an automatic transfer of funds had been made in order to open a position, or that indicate names of employees who either are on probation and must have examinations for their positions within the next month or have a recent history of unusual absences.

In this brief description of a payroll system, we see examples of control measures, tempered by a few measures that attempt to expedite processes and keep controls from completely constraining management's work. Implicit in this process is the fact that different managers have different rights and different incentives in the payroll and personnel area. Some managers have rights to open positions, others to staff positions, others to pay personnel, and still others to monitor problems or exceptions to intent. A wide variety of types of controls can be applied to this and the many other processes under the jurisdiction of the business administrator. The questions of which controls to apply to which processes and at what point the costs of controls (direct and opportunity) outweigh the benefits require ongoing management attention. A central part of the job of school business managers is seeking answers to these questions.

Linking Control of Payroll and Personnel to Control of Other Financial Systems

The payroll and personnel system is linked to a variety of other financial and nonfinancial reporting and control systems. Without those other systems it would indeed be difficult to exert more than marginal control over payroll and personnel. Stated another way, the ability of the educational manager to control payroll and personnel is only as good as his or her ability to control all major systems that are linked to payroll and personnel, such as program cost control, government-funded claims, and, of course, the general accounting system.

Program Cost Control

Payroll and personnel control is affected by program costs. Much of managerial control involves allocating resources on the basis of the program. In order to be able to control programs, it is necessary to monitor both the financial and nonfinancial aspects of most day-to-day activities, including opening, changing, or closing positions; staffing employees; authorizing and issuing purchase orders and contracts; paying vendors; and preparing status and exception reports for all levels of management and operating personnel. The managerial reports generated by this control system are designed to provide administrators with the budgetary and financial information they need to manage their units. ("Unit" is the level at which budgetary control is exercised, and it is the basic foundation for managerial reporting.)

On a regular basis (usually every month), a program-budget status report is distributed to each administrator, which shows the cumulative effect of business decisions in the results of operations for the previous month and the fiscal year to date, in comparison to current and original appropriations. A transaction report would accompany the status report and show the financial details of each event that affected the unit's appropriation during the month. For each budget line, these reports would show the amount of funds set aside and committed for planned spending requests, but that have not been approved by higher levels of management. Also displayed are the amounts that have been encumbered or expended once the available balance for each budget line would be listed.

Budgetary controls are also imposed over revenues. Since a shortage of revenues can have the same effect on fund balances as excessive spending does, this approach makes it possible to assign organizational responsibility for revenues of a categorical nature, including such items as reimbursable program claims, nonresident tuition, and building rentals.

Middle and upper levels of administration receive summary and exception reports that permit them to monitor decisions at the unit level. Each manager above the unit level receives reports showing the overall fiscal planning and control status of each person reporting to him. Other key reports are provided to highlight specific areas where management attention may be required.

Government-Funded Claim System

The cost of service of many personnel in schools can be recaptured through reimbursement from third parties. State and federal mandates require services, partially reimburse the cost of service, and, hence, require extensive reporting. Consequently, particular attention is paid (particularly in public schools) to the process of claiming revenues from higher levels of government. Reimbursement is not necessarily based on the number of students enrolled in the program or on any particular formula. Sometimes programs are strictly reimbursable on a dollar-reimbursed-for-a-dollar-spent basis. For every such program adopted by a school system, a claim must be prepared and financial data for that claim must be maintained. In order to protect its cash position, a school board must also closely monitor the reimbursement for each claim submitted. The programs funded by the state and federal governments have to meet and are measured against special qualifications set by the sponsoring or funding organizations. Consequently, the measuring and reporting process must be prompt, accurate, and auditable. Within this system, a master list is maintained showing all reimbursable projects for which a claim is required. This list contains information on the nature of the program, the date the claims are due, and the funding agency. It is the primary control for ensuring that claims are filed promptly, and that the board does not lose funds by allowing a claim to exceed its expiration date. On a regular basis (approximately each month), a claim exception would be prepared showing significant claim preparation or collection problems. It contains a description of the project, the date the claim is due, the amount of the original claim, the number of days it is late, and the total dollars still outstanding.

One of the more difficult aspects of the claiming process is ensuring that the claim includes all funds, supplies, and equipment. School districts employ accrual accounting techniques to ensure that reimbursable funds are identified at the time a purchase order is issued rather than when the final invoice is paid. This ensures that each fiscal year's reimbursable costs are recorded in the proper year and are not disallowed by virtue of having been claimed in the wrong fiscal period.

General Accounting System

The payroll and personnel system is further controlled through the general accounting system. This system anchors all other systems, including payroll and personnel, in place. Each of the other financial systems must balance to the amounts maintained by the general accounting system. These intersystem balancing requirements are an integral part of the operation of each system. The final proof of the integrity of this balancing process is assured at the conclusion of each month when the general accounting system closes out the financial operations for that month. The accounting system maintains control ledgers for each of the funds used by the school system. The number of funds can vary from half a dozen in a small school district to nearly a hundred in very large school systems. The two primary operating reports produced by the general accounting system are the results of operations and the balance sheet (discussed in detail in chapter 8). The system also produces a trial balance, which contains a more detailed identification of the items summarized on the first two reports. At the end of the month all three of these reports are produced for every fund.

There are several features of the general accounting system that enable school districts to control their operation. Cash flow is monitored as it is received, and various subsidiary ledgers are kept that provide supporting detail for the general ledger (cash management is the subject of chapter 7). Examples of such ledgers include the claims-receivable ledger for reimbursable projects; taxes-receivable ledger for control and analysis of local property tax collections; interfund-receivable ledger for use in setting up temporary advances to another fund; bid-deposit ledger to facilitate control over good faith deposits made by vendors seeking to do business with the board; unclaimed warrants-payable ledgers to facilitate control over payroll and vendor warrants; and suspended-transactions ledgers that maintain a detailed record of all transactions with errors that must be corrected before further processing in the general accounting system. All of the control mechanisms described above are described in their *ideal form.* Many control systems in the "real world" operate far less perfectly than these.

Conclusion

In one respect planning and control are simply a multiperson extention of individual purposeful behavior: considering preferences, evaluating options, exercising rights, and maximizing utility. The word "simply" is, however, very misleading, because business administrators are not acting only for themselves; they are also attempting to cause many people to act as a single entity. Both planning and control are unifying endeavors. As they initiate long-range planning processes and implement control mechanisms, school business administrators are acting as the agents of sponsors as well as individuals who are seeking to maximize their utility.

The rules of the game under which they play will vary from sector to sector, and they may behave differently as a result. However, regardless of sector location, they try to respond to the preferences of sponsors because to some degree their utility is usually directly correlated with their sponsor's preferences.

References

Anthony, Robert N. *Planning and Control Systems: A Framework for Analysis.* Boston: Graduate School of Business Administration, Harvard University, 1965.

Bankston, Mary. "Organizational Reporting in a School District: State and Federal Programs." Stanford, Calif.: Institute for Research on Educational Finance and Governance, 1982.

Benson, Charles. "Changing Goals Spawn New Rules." *IFG Policy Notes* 3: 4 (Fall 1982): 4–5.

Cyert, Richard M., and March, James G. "A Behavioral Theory of Organizational Objectives." In *Modern Organizational Theory*, edited by Mason Haire. New York: John Wiley & Sons, 1959.

Fulmer, Robert M., and Rue, Leslie W. "The Practice and Profitability of Long-Range Planning." *Managerial Planning*, May–June 1974.

Hall, William K. "The Impact of Managerial Behavior on Planning Effectiveness." *Managerial Planning*, September–October 1977.

Kirp, David. "Controls and Consequences: Balancing Regulation and Education." *IFG Policy Notes* 3: 4 (Fall 1982): 1–2.

McKenna, J. V. "The Basic Theory of Managerial Control." *Mechanical Engineering* 77: 8 (August 1955): 180ff.

Robbins, Stephen P. *The Administrative Process*, 2d ed. Englewood Cliffs, N.J.: Prentice-Hall, Inc., 1980.

Scott, Richard, and Meyer, John W. *Environmental Linkages and Organizational Complexity: Public and Private Schools.* Stanford, Calif.: Institute for Research on Educational Finance and Governance, July 1984. Report no. 84 A16.

Thompson, James B. *Organizations in Action.* New York: McGraw-Hill, 1967.

Supplementary Reading

Berkeley, William D; Foster, Jerry; and Zajchowski, Richard A. *Long-Range Planning for Independent Schools.* Boston: National Association of Independent Schools, 1979.

Colley, John L., Jr.; Landel, Robert D.; and Fair, Robert R. *Operations Planning and Control.* Oakland, Calif.: Holden Day, 1978.

Commissioner's Advisory Committee for School Business Administration. "Financial Planning as a Component of School District Long-Range Planning." Albany, N. Y.: State Education Department, 1975.

Hussey, D. E. *Corporate Planning*: Theory and Practice. Oxford, Eng.: Pergamon Press, 1976.

Jerome, William T. *Executive Control—The Capitalist*, pp. 31–34. New York, John Wiley & Sons, 1961.

"The Planning and Control Concept." *The Controller*, September 1954.

Weinwurn, Ernest H., and Weinwurn, George F. *Long-Term Profit Planning.* New York: American Management Association, 1971.

PART II

Fiscal Systems

The system that best defines the business characteristics of schools and distinguishes among schools is that of finance. Financial systems describe how school managers acquire, spend, keep track of, and invest money. These are the subjects of chapters 4 through 9.

4

Variations in the Financial Environment

with Ellen Kehoe

•

Overview

School business administrators facilitate and monitor how funds flow into and out from their schools. Differences in systems of rights among schools are reflected in differences among the sources and applications of funds and in the manner in which "operators" (school business administrators) secure revenue from "sponsors" (such as the federal government). The inflow of funds to and within the public sector is more complex if only because the mechanisms for distributing these funds vary significantly among federal, state, and local governments. Although inflow of funds from individual sponsors (those who pay tuition and donors) to private schools is conceptually straightforward, private-sector managers face additional decisions regarding future income generation through creating or adding to endowments. (They have to decide how much income in the current year should *not* be spent and, instead, be invested to produce income in future years.) Sources of revenue influence where administrators devote their attention. For example, the large city school district that gets the bulk of its operating budget from city government will have its school business administrator working very closely with the mayor's office. The private school that receives major gifts through bequest will have its headmaster spending a lot of time with rich, old alumni. Appendix 4.1 discusses in detail the variations in mechanisms for allocating financial aid from state governments to public school districts.

• • •

Introduction

School business administrators work in a largely financial environment. Although school programs, staff morale, and the like are part of school business managers' jobs and may even determine their success or failure, the activities that occupy most of their time are financial. Differences in the financial environment distinguish the opportunities available to educational administrators across schools, and, hence, influence their behavior. These differences are more a matter of degree, but the relative emphases vary so greatly that the differences become ones of kind.

The term *financial environment* suggests a selective and abstracted view of the real world, a view that consists largely of revenues and expenditures; of efforts to increase revenues and to channel expenditures in such a way that preferred (rather than required) goods and services are purchased. This view includes planning and control activities that directly affect the financial health of the school. Exhibit 4.1 portrays a highly abstracted view of the school business administrator's financial environment by depicting the major sources of revenue and the major items for which expenditures are made. (Not all inflows and outflows, however, are portrayed.) The importance of each flow varies greatly from school to school. Public-sector school managers derive the bulk of revenues from local (1), state (2), and federal (3) governments (in decreasing amount of revenue), whereas private school managers derive the bulk of their revenues from tuition and fees (4), donations (5), and, for many schools, endowment income (6) (also in decreasing amount of revenue). Amounts of revenues from the different sources are listed in exhibit 4.2. Most managers derive revenues from borrowing (7) and from short-term investments of idle cash (8) (discussed in chapter 7). Major items of expenditure for most schools are salaries and wages (9) (discussed in chapter 6), purchases of goods (10), and debt service (11).

The flow of school funds is unextricably linked with the general economy, and sponsor support is determined by many factors, only a few of which the school manager can control. Nonetheless, one of the principal concerns of the business administrator is monitoring the financial implications of managerial behavior and, where feasible, attempting to modify sponsor behavior so that it favors the operators' preferences.

This chapter examines the major elements of the schools' financial environments and describes briefly how they vary over time and across sectors. The general theoretical framework of the financial relationship between sponsors and operators is discussed first, followed by a more detailed analysis of the four major sources of revenue: the three levels of government and individuals.

Exhibit 4.1
Simplified Flow of Funds in Schools

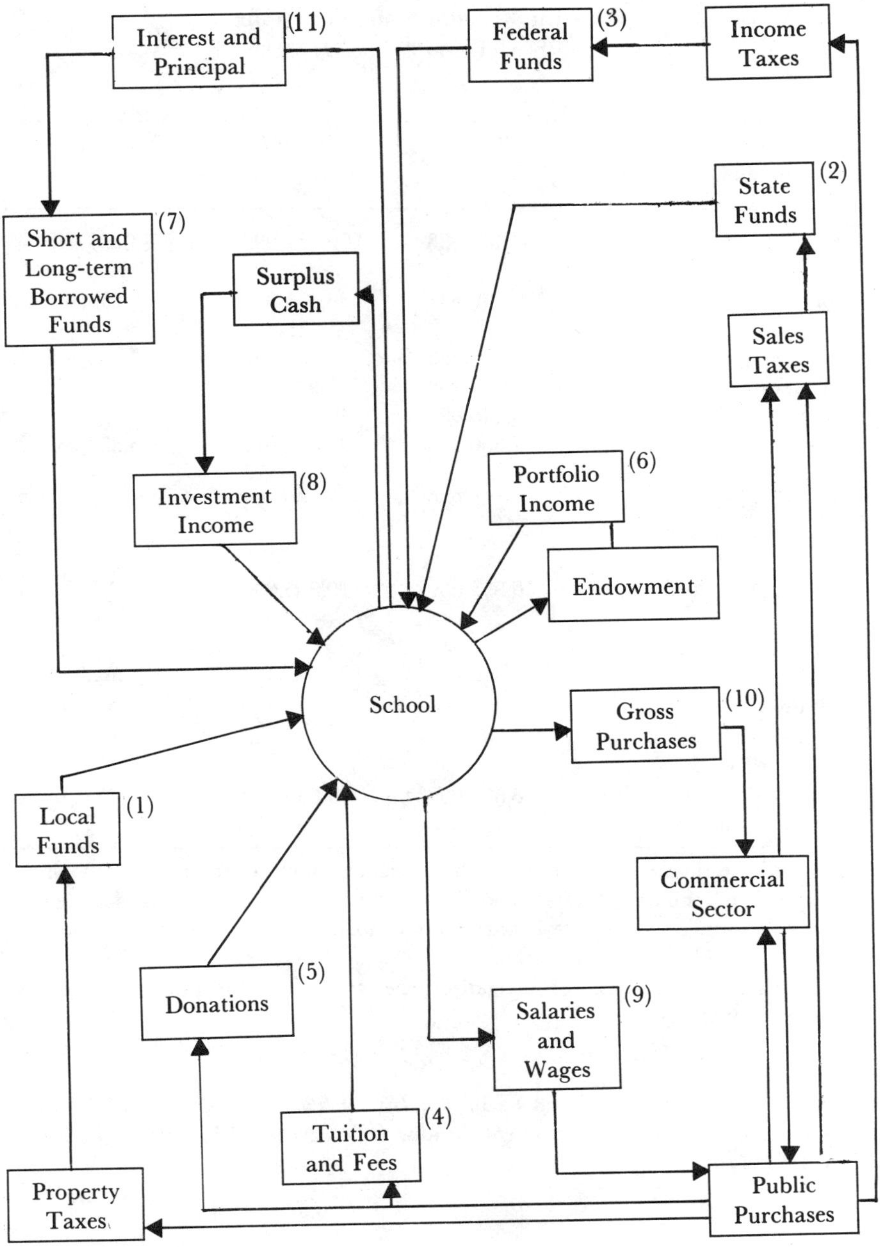

Exhibit 4.2

Receipts of Elementary/Secondary Educational Institutions,* by Control of Institutions and Source of Funds

(School Year 1978–79)

Control of Institution and Source of Funds	Total	Revenue (in thousands)	Nonrevenue
Total	$103,145,483	$99,311,997	$3,833,486
Publicly controlled	92,290,483	88,456,997	3,833,486
Government	92,090,483	88,256,997	3,833,486
Federal	8,994,493	8,994,493	—
State	40,245,891	40,245,891	—
Local	42,850,099	39,016,613	3,833,486
Student fees	—	—	—
Private gifts and grants	200,000	200,000	—
All other sources			
Privately controlled	10,855,000**	10,855,000**	***
Government	—	—	—
Federal	—	—	—
State	—	—	—
Local	—	—	—
Student fees			
Private gifts and grants	10,855,000**	10,855,000**	***
All other sources			

*Includes estimated income for "other" schools, such as residential schools for exceptional children, federal schools for Indians, and federal schools on federal installations. Subcollegiate departments of institutions of higher education are included under higher education.

**Estimated on the basis of expenditure per teacher in the public elementary/secondary schools.

***Included in revenue.

Source: Nancy Dearman and Valena Plisko, *The Condition of Education, 1981 Edition* (Washington, D.C.: U.S. Government Printing Office, National Institute of Education, 1981).

Financial Relations Between Operators and Sponsors

Operator behavior vis à vis that of sponsors varies with the sponsor. The most pronounced differences are between government sponsors on the one hand and individual sponsors on the other, and accordingly these differences reflect differences between public and private schools.

Relations Between Public Schools and Sponsors

To paraphrase Niskanen (1973) in his analysis of bureaus, school districts offer a promised set of activities and expected outputs of these activities in exchange for a budget. Exchanges between a public school district and its sponsors and a private school and its sponsors differ because a public school district offers a *total* output in exchange for a *budget*, whereas a private school offers *units* of output at a *price*.

Federal, state, and local governments' demands for public schooling relate to those of their constituents through the political process (elections, political decision making), but their demands will not necessarily be identical to those of their constituents. The demands of the populus for schooling are never directly revealed to administrators of the school district. That is, people do not generally decide what will be offered in schools by choosing among alternatives within a school district. Rather, through budget votes, elections, and lobbying, they attempt to influence the decisions of public school administrators. School district administrators, on the other hand, may appeal to the constituents of its sponsoring (governmental) organizations in an attempt to increase the sponsors' demand for the district's educational services; but the preferences of the individual constituents are not important to the school district; rather the school district is concerned with their influence on the preferences (and behavior) of its sponsor (Niskanen 1973, p. 15). School district sponsors, that is, the various levels of government, are essentially "passive." They know the budget they are prepared to grant for a given quantity of services, but they do not have either the incentive or the opportunity to obtain information on the minimum budget necessary to obtain those services. Consider, for example, state legislators, who provide revenues not only for public schools but also for a wide variety of other public goods and services ranging from highways to welfare, from water projects to jails. They simply cannot become expert enough in schooling to identify the minimum that each district "needs" for its schools. Even if they could, their opinions would carry no more weight than those (higher estimates) from district administrators.

Characteristic behavior of administators in public school districts and state and federal education agencies is to maximize budgets subject to constraints imposed by the sponsors. Public school administrators, like the rest of us, seek to maximize personal utility, but why does this necessarily imply budget maximization in their particular case? Niskanen advances two arguments to support this notion: rationality and survival. Among the several variables that may enter the school administrators' preference function are salary, perquisites of the office, public reputation, power, schooling outcomes, patronage, ease of making changes, and ease of managing the school district or agency. All except the last two are a positive function of the total budget of the school district or education agency, that is, the bigger the budget, the bigger the salary, perks, and so forth. (The last two are more a function of *increases* in the budget.) This does not imply that the school administrators' interests are other than "professional." Again to paraphrase Niskanen, most school administrators, by either predisposition or training, undoubtedly try to serve their perception of "the public interest." School administrators, however, are neither omniscient nor sovereign. They can not acquire all the information on individual preferences and production opportunities that would be necessary to divine "the public interest," and they do have the authority to order an action that is contrary to either the personal interests or the different perceptions of "the public interest" by other bureaucrats or higher level education officials" (ibid., p. 23). Rationally, bureaucrats pursue their preferences via larger and larger budgets.

The survival argument also suggests why public school administrators seek to maximize budgets. Two groups of people significantly influence school administrators' tenure in office: the employees of the school district and the sponsors (local taxpayers and state and federal legislatures). To varying degrees, individuals employed by the education agency desire budget maximization for reasons similar to school administrators, and they also can influence school administrators to seek increased budgets. As Niskanen points out, for all public bureaus, employees "can be co-operative, responsive, and efficient. Or, they can deny information to the [school administrator], undermine his directives, and embarrass him before the [public]. Their behavior depends on their perceived rewards of employment in the [school district]" (ibid., p. 24). The administrator who seeks operating efficiencies without budget increases will have difficulty "buying the cooperation" of employees.

Sponsors (local taxpayers and state and federal education officials and legislators) also have an interest in (public) school district budget maximization, although their reasons are less obvious. Parents' interests in increased spending are a major force for increased budgets, although parents of school-age children constitute a declining proportion of taxpayers in many school districts. (Individuals who want to combat budget-maximizing behavior, such as taxpayer groups, are defeating school budgets in increasing numbers. These efforts, however, do not appear to have measurably slowed the rise of public schooling costs nor halted the steady decline in student-teacher staffing ratios.) Local, state, and federal legislators fully expect local, state, and federal school administrators to aggressively propose additional funding based on increased needs and new activities. State and federal legislatures often lack the time, the information, and the staff necessary to formulate new programs; they depend on local, state, and federal education officials to propose them. "At every stage in a multistage review process, the review officers are dependent on the bureaucrat to make a forceful case for his proposed budget, in part to determine whether a previous review had made too large a reduction" (ibid., p. 25).

For some school administrators in school districts, budget maximization may not be consistent with the maximization of personal utility. Nonmaximizing behavior is likely to be for the short run only, and is more appropriately understood as a response to a tightening constraint on the budget that limits funds. (They would spend more if taxing and spending constraints were relaxed.) The constraint that ultimately limits the fiscal size of school districts and other public education agencies is that, on the average, public administrators must supply that output expected by the sponsor on its approval of the budget. By extension, a school district that consistently promises more than it can deliver, or at a cost that is greater than the minimum cost required as perceived by the sponsor, will be penalized because future promises will not be taken seriously and therefore they will receive lower budgets (ibid., p. 26).

Relations Between Private Schools and Sponsors

In contrast to public schools, which derive a large proportion of their revenues from taxing authorities, profit-seeking and private nonprofit schools derive substantial proportions of their revenue from student fees and gifts. Just like the public school administrator, the private school administrator seeks to maximize personal utility. However, because of the differing set of rights systems in private schools, the focus is not on budget size, but on the net present value of future flows of funds. (Decisions are made to invest as well as to spend so as to increase net revenues over the long run.) The private school administrator's behavior is similarly motivated by rationality and survival criteria. The sponsors of private schools include fee-paying students as well as donors of money, goods, and services.

Decisions by private school administrators will not necessarily be consistent with budget maximization. Net present value is enhanced by internal operating efficiencies (cost control) in at least three major ways. First, direct savings through effecting internal efficiencies will enhance the value (equity) of the school. Savings can be added to endowment. Second, private school administrators are motivated to create the *impression* of fiscal integrity and internal operating efficiency in order to attract donor support. Third, they are motivated to minimize unit costs for a given quality level in order to be able to price the educational services of their schools competitively. The behavior of administrators in profit-seeking and private nonprofit schools is similar. Although the administrators in private nonprofit schools are less able than their for-profit counterparts to appropriate excess revenues that result from efficiency to themselves, their personal utility is directly tied to the net present value of future flows of funds within their term of tenure. The scope of these differences between the three sectors is now discussed.

Flow of Funds from Government Sponsors to Public Schools

The flow of funds greatly influences the behavior of educational administrators, because strategic opportunities are shaped by current and potential sponsors. In the public sector, intergovernmental aid to schools has declined proportionately over the last decade as competing demands for education-related services have grown. Public schools find themselves having to compete for scarce public dollars with other government-sponsored education-related programs. The structure of public funding for schools, coupled with proportionate reductions in funding and increased budget maximizing behavior by school administrators, suggests that their strategic options at present are largely efficiency oriented. That is, budget-limiting constraints imposed by sponsors are increasing.

Federal Government Sponsorship

Federal aid to local and state governments has increased in recent decades; it rose by a factor of eight between 1964 and 1980 from $10 billion to $80 billion. Between 1946 and 1978 the percentage of the gross national product represented by this aid rose from about .5 percent to about 3.5 percent. The percentage of state and federal funds made up of federal revenues rose from about 10 percent to over 25 percent between 1950 and 1980.

Over the last two decades the federal government has also provided increasing support for education in the areas of employment, training, and social services when measured not only in actual amounts but also as a proportion of total federal aid to state and local governments. The specific federal legislation that resulted in this increased role included GI Bills, the National Defense Education Act, the Manpower Development and Training Act, the Economic Opportunity Act, the Elementary and Secondary Education Act, and the Education of All Handicapped Children Act (P.L. 94–142). Despite these increases, the proportion of federal aid to state and local governments for programs in public schools has, following a nearly two-fold increase, declined over the last decade from 9.9 percent to 5.6 percent (see exhibit 4.3).

State and Local Government Sponsorship

Following a similar "inverted bowl" pattern, state and local governments increased spending for education from 36 percent to about 40 percent of their expenditures during the 1960s, and decreased this proportion during the 1970s and early 1980s (see exhibit 4.4). As the proportion of the school-age population declines, so will public support for expenditures in this area. The overall demographic shifts in society are reflected in the decrease in the federal funds given to state and local government as well as in the proportionate diminution of state and local governmental support for public schools.

At the same time that the share of publicly collected dollars earmarked for schooling has declined, the relative share of public education revenues has also shifted among the three levels of government. Over the last several decades the federal share has approximately doubled to about 10 percent. The state share has steadily increased to the point where, in 1978–79, revenues for public elementary secondary schools from state sources slightly exceeded revenues from local sources and has been gradually increasing since then (see exhibit 4.5).

The mechanisms for raising government revenues are similar at each of the three levels of government only in that money is always raised through taxation. The mechanisms for raising tax revenues for education and for distributing it to education organizations vary in major ways across levels of government.

Revenues from the Federal Government

The content of the federal legislation discussed previously and other federal legislative initiatives changes continually as the preferences of federal sponsors change. The planning and control problems of federal sponsors are not unlike those faced by any sponsor: to create systems of rights that will maximize the preferences of sponsors as state and local operators receive and spend the money. When creating mechanisms for providing noncompetitive revenue, federal sponsors have relied on variants of three funding mechanisms: categorical grants, block grants, and revenue sharing.

Categorical Grants

About three-quarters of the federal transfers of funds to state and local governments are through categorical grants. A categorical grant has the following characteristics: (1) its purpose is to meet the very specific program objectives of federal sponsors; (2) it is usually accompanied by extensive

Exhibit 4.3
Federal Education-Related Aid to State and Local Governments: 1970–1984

	Aid (in millions) 1970	1975	1980	1984 (est.)
Elementary and secondary education	$1,470	$ 2,276	$ 3,536	3,961*
School assistance in federally affected areas	622	577	622	613
Occupational, vocational, adult education	285	653	854	771
Library resources	105	210	261	88
Work incentives	81	304	383	259
Human development	390	803	1,548	1,751
Comprehensive manpower assistance	421	2,504	6,191	2,818
Employment and training assistance	—	319	1,796	—
Social services–block grants to states	574	2,047	2,763	2,772
Other	2,442	2,440	3,908	4,371
Total Education, Employment, Training, and Social Services	6,390	12,133	21,862	17,404
Percentage of Total Federal Aid to State and Local Groups	23.9%	24.4%	27.4%	
Federal Aid to State-Local Governments	26.6%	24.3%	23.9%	17.7%
Percentage of Total Federal Aid for Categories 1–3	9.9%	7.0%	5.5%	5.4%

*Total of aid programs for compensatory education for the disadvantaged, special programs and populations, and bilingual education.

Source: U.S. Department of Commerce; *Statistical Abstracts of the United States 1985* (Washington, D.C.: U.S. Government Printing Office, 1984), p. 267.

monitoring and control devices to help ensure that the preferences of federal sponsors override those of state and local managers; (3) it is used when federal sponsors seek to establish and support innovative or controversial programs that will likely represent a shift in services and service mix at the local level; and (4) operators have relatively little discretion over how the funds are to be raised. Title I of the Elementary and Secondary Education

Exhibit 4.4

State and Local Governments—General Revenues and Education–Related Expenditures: 1970–1982

	1970	1975	1980	1982
General Revenue (billions)	$135.4	$237.7	$386.1	$441.9
Percentage from:				
Federal government	16.7	20.6	21.7	19.1
All taxes	66.4	62.0	58.4	58.4
Property	26.0	22.6	17.9	18.0
Sales and gross receipts	23.2	21.8	20.9	20.5
Individual income	8.3	9.4	11.3	11.1
Other	8.9	8.2	8.3	8.8
Charges and miscellaneous	16.9	17.4	19.8	22.6
General expenditures (billions)	$133.5	$232.2	$355.5	$409.0
Percentage to education	40.1	38.2	36.3	35.7

Source: U.S. Department of Commerce, *Statistical Abstracts of the United States 1985* (Washington, D.C.: U.S. Government Printing Office, 1984), pp. 293 and 270.

Act and P.L. 94–142 are two of the well-known examples of the use of categorical grants.

The principal advantage of categorical grants to operators is that such grants enable them to undertake costly, controversial programs with the federal government taking the financial and political risks.

Block Grants

Federal sponsors use block grants when supporting established national programs. In these cases they feel that national preferences will be pursued, but they seek to share decision rights over use of funds with state and local operators. Block grants result from a bundling of specific programs into one "block" for purposes of funding. Block grants require less monitoring and control by federal sponsors than do categorical aid grants, and state and local operators assume more of a sponsor role as they, in turn, allocate block grants to other operators under their sponsorship. One recent example of block grants to education is "Chapter Two," a federal aid program to school districts where numerous categorical grant monies (with extensive reporting requirements) were put into one simple-to-administer block grant.

Federal sponsors also use block grant mechanisms as a means of reducing the financial level of financial sponsorship to schooling. By shifting aid from categorical to block mechanisms, federal sponsors grant more decision rights to state and local operators and provide operators with increased flexibility

Exhibit 4.5

Revenue Receipts of Public Elementary and Secondary Schools from Federal, State, and Local Sources

(1959–60 compared to 1978–79 and 1980–81)

	1959–60	1978–79	1980–81[2]
Total ($000)	$14,747	$87,994	$105,905
Federal Share (%)	4.4	9.8	9.3
State Share (%)	39.1	45.6	47.4
Local Share (%)[1]	56.5	44.6	43.3

In 1978–79, for the first time, revenues for public elementary and secondary schools from state sources exceeded revenues from local sources.

[1]Includes revenues receipts from local and intermediate sources, gifts, and tuitions and fees from patrons.

[2]Preliminary data source: Nancy Dearman and Valena Plisko, eds., *The Condition of Education, 1982* (Washington, D.C.: National Center for Education Statistics, 1982), p. 56, and W. Vance Grant and Thomas D. Synder, eds., *Digest of Educational Statistics 1983–84* (Washington, D.C.: National Center for Education Statistics, 1984), p. 77.

and efficiency in pursuing their own preferences as well as in carrying out the preferences of federal sponsors. Yet if local operators receive less federal revenue in the process of gaining more decision rights, they may not perceive that they have gained in the trade. Although they may have more opportunity to maximize their preferences, federal sponsors have provided fewer total resources.

Revenue Sharing

The revenue-sharing mechanism is merely a transfer of money from federal to state and local governments accompanied by a transfer of all of the rights over that money. Federal sponsors use this mechanism when they feel their preferences and those of state and local operators are aligned and when fiscal (as opposed to programmatic) concerns are paramount. Monitoring and control are transferred to lower levels of government. Of the three forms of federal grants to schools, this is the least common.

Revenues from State Governments

Although local, state, and federal levels all contribute to the operation of public schools, the financial environment at the state level is most critical. States provide nearly half of the revenues to operate public school districts, and for a variety of reasons their contribution has, on the average, been increasing.

Capacity and Effort of State Sponsors

The amounts of revenues flowing to public school districts is in large part a combination of the fiscal capacity of the state and locality to raise money and of the effort they exert in raising this money. *Capacity* in this sense is a measure of the ability of state and local governments to obtain revenues through taxes. *Fiscal effort* is the extent to which governments actually use their capacity to tax.

Capacity is a theoretical construct difficult to measure in the real world of schooling, and each operational definition has its own bias. Per-capita personal income and tax revenues collected per capita are poor measures of inherent or potential resources. Residential personal income, for example, fails to reflect closely the revenue potential of such taxable wealth as the oil and mineral deposits in Alaska, Louisiana, West Virginia, Texas, New Mexico, and Wyoming; the disproportionately large amount of farm land in agricultural states such as South Dakota, Montana, and Iowa; and the expanded hotel and amusement business in Nevada and Florida. Tax revenues collected are also a poor measure of actual or potential resources because they reflect fiscal effort as well as capacity. Thus a basically poor state such as Maine, by levying heavy taxes, appears relatively well off, but economically it is not. On the other hand, because some truly rich states such as Nevada, Wyoming, and Texas levy low taxes, they appear less wealthy than they actually are.

School District Capacity and Effort. School districts are situated within state and local taxing jurisdictions that vary greatly in terms of both effort and capacity. Although much of the study of school finance has focused on interdistrict variations within states (as we shall do later in this chapter), it is important first to understand that the relative fiscal capacity and effort of the state goes a long way in defining the strategic financial options of school districts in that state. The fact that sponsors of public schools in Alaska spend over $4,500 per student per year whereas public school sponsors in Arkansas spend less than $1,500 per student per year suggests large variations in the combined impact of public-sector *capacity* and *effort* to purchase schooling.

State-level capacity and effort are inextricably linked in complex ways to local capacity and effort. There is a common demand throughout the United States for localized public services. Public schools in a sense "compete" with police protection, roads, water and sewer systems, and other services recognized as major responsibilities of government. Although these needs are common, there is no uniform provision of such services by local governments. There are and will continue to be relatively "rich" communities readily able to raise public revenues because of local economic strength, and impoverished communities with little capacity for fund raising will lack comparable services.

Trends in Fiscal Capacity and Effort. The most recent study of relative tax wealth among the fifty states shows strong but declining variances on measures of both fiscal capacity and effort (Halstead 1978). In this study, tax capacity is defined as the amount of revenue a state and its local governments could raise (relative to other state and local governments) if all fifty state and local systems applied identical tax rates (national averages) to their respective tax bases. Tax effort is defined as the extent to which a given state makes use of its fiscal or taxable capacity.

State and local tax collections in fiscal 1975 totalled $141.5 billion, or $664 for every American. By far, the largest source of state and local government tax revenues (over two-thirds) is derived from property taxes. Combined with general sales (21 percent), these two funding sources provide nearly six of every ten tax dollars. Individual income and selective sales taxes each provide about 15 percent, with corporate income taxes and license taxes providing between 4 and 5 percent (Halstead 1978, p. 11). The trend over the last fifteen years has been toward increasing dependency on general sales and individual income taxes and decreasing dependency on selective sales and property taxes (see exhibit 4.6).

Within this overall pattern, Halstead found major differences between states. The extreme values in relative tax capacity range from $970 per capita (51 percent above the national average) in Nevada to $448 per capita (30 percent below the national average) in Mississippi. This means that Mississippi has only 46 percent of the inherent tax wealth of Nevada. Stated differently, Nevada has $2.16 in potential taxes for every $1.00 in Mississippi. When the five highest ranking and the five lowest ranking states are disregarded, the range between states is much smaller—$1.4 to $1.

Five states with high per-capita tax capacity—Alaska ($143) Delaware ($122), District of Columbia ($120), Illinois ($114), and Nevada ($151)—exhibit similar revenue-producing potentials. All have a large volume of retail trade and services per capita as a base for general sales taxes, relatively high personal income subject to taxation, large corporate tax bases (except the District of Columbia and Nevada), high residential property values per capita (except Alaska), and high corporate property values (except Nevada). The five states with the lowest tax capacity—Alabama ($78), Arkansas ($78), Maine ($74), Mississippi ($70), and South Carolina ($77)—have less than average potential in all of the major tax areas, that is, retail trade and services, individual income, corporate income, and property (except farm real estate in Arkansas and Mississippi).

"*Fiscal Blood Pressure.*" For public school administrators that must seek to raise revenues through budget referenda, the interaction of capacity and effort (especially the local sponsors' perception of it), is a strategic variable. Residents are more likely to feel that tax burdens are heavier when taxes are high and rising than when they remain relatively constant or at a fixed percentage of income. Analysts sought a measure not unlike Halstead's, and came up with the concept of "fiscal blood pressure" to explain this public perception. A state's fiscal blood pressure is measured as the ratio of current tax effort to recent relative changes in effort—two numbers similar to the blood pressure readings for humans. States with currently high and rising effort include New York, Massachussetts, California, Maine, and Rhode Island. States with currently low and falling effort include Texas, Oklahoma, Wyoming, Alabama, and West Virginia. All other factors being equal, public school administrators in the former group of states will devote more attention to revenue-raising behavior.

This will be particularly true where locally derived revenues constitute a relatively large proportion of total public school revenues. This varies greatly among the states, from over 86 percent in New Hampshire and over 76 percent in Nebraska down to under 19 percent in Alaska and New Mexico and 0 percent in Hawaii.

Within this broader framework of state and local governmental finance, public school districts face the tasks of raising revenues locally and exerting as much influence as possible to increase state (and, to a lesser degree, federal) revenues. Generally, however, administrators from individual districts cannot exert influence over the manner in which general operating aid is allocated to them, although many of the constituents from larger districts in a state will be encouraged to lobby directly with sponsors in the state's capital.

State-level Revenue Allocation Mechanisms. State aid to individual public school districts is determined through the political mechanism of a state aid formula. The formula defines relationships between local capacity, effort, and demographic variables. An individual district receives revenues based on its unique set of capacity, effort, and demographic values. The formula is derived and modified through political negotiation among state legislators. The normative principles guiding the allocations are equal treatment of equals (that is, students of equal ability and need should receive equivalent educational services), efficiency of operation, and freedom for individual district decision making (Garms, Guthrie, and Pierce 1978). The major means by which these principles are made operational in formulas are discussed in the appendix.

Sponsor Preferences and Operator Behavior

The actual preferences of sponsors are reflected in the mechanisms they employ to transfer money among the levels of government. Some mechanisms place high emphasis on reducing interdistrict expenditure inequities.

Exhibit 4.6

Trends in Tax Revenues by Source

Type of Tax	Amount (millions)	Percentage Distribution		
	1975	1975	1967	1960
All Taxes	$136,830	100.0	100.0	100.0
A. Sales and gross receipts taxes	48,463	35.4	34.4	33.5
1. General sales or gross receipts taxes	29,101	21.3	16.5	14.2
2. Selective sales and gross receipts taxes	19,363	14.1	17.9	19.3
a. Motor fuels	8,324	6.1	8.0	8.3
b. Alcoholic beverages	2,059	1.5	2.5	2.9
c. Corporations in general	3,395	2.5	2.8	2.7
d. Insurance	1,751	1.3	–	1.5
e. Public utilities	3,059	2.2	1.7	1.8
f. Pari-mutuels	676	0.5	–	–
g. Amusements	99	0.1	0.8	0.2

B. Licenses	5,720		4.2		5.4		6.3	
1. Motor vehicles		3,951		2.9		5.4		6.3
2. Motor vehicle operators		284		0.2				
3. Corporations in general		1,042		0.8		–		–
4. Alcoholic beverages		147		0.1		–		–
5. Hunting and fishing licenses		296		0.2		–		–
C. Individual income taxes	21,451		15.7		9.5		6.7	
D. Corporation net income taxes	6,642		4.9		5.6		4.4	
E. Property taxes	51,496		37.6		40.4		43.6	
1. Residential property (nonfarm)		23,938 est.		17.5		20.1		–
2. Commercial and industrial		19,785 est.		14.4		16.2		–
3. Farm real estate		2,855		2.1		3.3		–
4. Public utilities		4,817 est.		3.6		–		–
F. Death and gift taxes	1,418		1.0		1.3		1.3	
G. Severance taxes	1,741		1.3		0.9		–	
					2.5 (other)		4.2 (other)	

Others seek to induce local operators to generate additional local revenues for schooling. Still other mechanisms provide incentives for local sponsors to reduce the share of local revenues for schooling (as through property tax relief).

Most state aid formulas are complex combinations of the pure types discussed above. Even in a jumbled form, aid formulas set up incentives that influence operator behavior. This is particularly true where sponsors perceive that their preferences are not aligned with those of operators. Categorical aid mechanisms of the federal and state level are designed to override the preferences of lower-level operators, but in so doing may set up operator incentives that are costly to sponsors.

One of the more recent examples of this phenomenon can be seen as state education managers create mechanisms to enforce state-level versions of the Education for All Handicapped Children Act. Formulas for special education funding differ only in degree from most mechanisms for intergovernmental transfer of funds. Funds are transferred according to formulas tied to resources used for special education services, number and classification of children served, and the costs of the program. Usually one of the factors serves as the basis for the special education funding formula, while the other two factors are used to regulate the amounts and uses of the funds generated under the formula (Hartman 1980, p. 139).

Hartman describes the kinds of clashes between sponsor preferences and operator incentives in special education with regard to both classification of students with handicapping conditions and their placement:

> A potential for abuse exists—overclassification—in which excessive numbers of students are classified (by operators) as handicapped in order to increase the special education funding allotment. . . . There will be a tendency (on the part of operators) to place children in those programs in which the funding amounts are greatest relative to program costs and to minimize those placements in which the reverse is true. [Ibid., pp. 140 and 141]

The issue here can be viewed from two perspectives: (1) operators will pursue their own preferences and not those of sponsors when it is in their interest to do so, and (2) operators are responsive to the incentives created by sponsors. Both are true to a degree and, thus, the "goal" of the sponsors is to create incentives for operators that cause operators to do what sponsors want. The "goal" for operators is to behave within the incentives set up by sponsors in such a way that their own preferences are maximized.

The activities of operators vis à vis state (and federal) sponsors are those of lobbying, persuasion, and negotiation over allocation rules. Operators join together in these activities when they can; at times they also may abandon persuasion and adopt litigation as a tactic. Regardless of the tactics employed, operators seek to modify the system of rights over public resources in ways that enhance their own opportunities.

Revenues from Local Government

Relationships between public-sector sponsors and operators at the local level are developed through voting mechanisms, as opposed to lobbying for formula revisions. (There are notable exceptions to this general rule. For example, fiscally dependent school systems, which rely on appropriations from their city government, lobby city governments for more funds. They constitute about 5 percent of all school districts and serve about 15 percent of all public school children.)

Operators must present voters with requests for income. The specific request may be for passage of a bond (usually to finance capital improvements) or for an increased level of tax levy or school budget (usually to finance current operations).

The number of voters required to pass a bond issue is often more than a simple majority, in part because a "yes" vote commits operators of the school district to long-term debt. For the same reasons, most states limit the bonding capacity of public school administrators to a percentage (usually 5 to 10 percent) of the assessed valuation of real property in that district. (Garms, Guthrie, and Pierce 1978, p. 374). The immediate goal of the bond election is to seek approval to sell bonds. The bids from bond purchasers resulting in the lowest net interest rate to the district are accepted. (A more complete discussion of the bond process is presented in chapter 7).

Budget and levy elections are similar to each other in the sense that the relationship between the outcome of the election and the revenue to the district is more direct. Both processes are built on the equation: revenues equal tax rate times assessed valuation, although the budget vote focuses attention on the revenues while the levy focuses attention on the tax rate.

The difficulty in generalizing on this subject stems from the major variations in local voting mechanisms from state to state (as with state aid formulas). The most definitive description of voting on local school finances is the 1974 publication by Hamilton and Cohen. Although specific changes in mechanisms have taken place since then, the diversity of approaches presented there is still generally accurate:

> Bond elections occur in all states except Alabama, Hawaii, and Indiana; however, some school systems are exempt from (bond) referenda in fourteen states. . . . Tax levy elections occur in . . . twenty-seven states, including the five states with school budget elections, which are functional equivalents of levy elections. . . . Historical circumstances largely explain the distinct pattern in the geographic distribution of levy referenda. New England has few independent school districts and no tax levy elections; school budgets and taxes have always been voted at town or school

> meetings or by city councils and town boards. New York and New Jersey have school districts, but the school meeting tradition has been retained by annual budget elections in the districts outside large cities. West of the Appalachians, whether or not a state has fiscal referenda depends on whether an antiproperty tax movement ever developed sufficient strength to write tax rate limits into the state constitution on statutes. [Ibid., p. 3]

This brief summary, although generally accurate, masks many variations in both the voting mechanisms and the financial and demographic environment in which they are employed.

Variations in Voting Mechanisms

The specific set of rights of operators shapes their ability to extract revenue from owners (real estate owners) of "assessed valuation" (the appraised value of real estate, which is used as the basis for levying property taxes). Three of the most fundamental rights are discussed here: revenue limits imposed by state governments; the level of revenue within which the school district must operate should the election fail (called the reversion level); and the right to call for repeat elections.

Revenue Limitations. Some states have attempted to control the revenue-seeking behavior of public school administrators by placing restrictions on the property tax levy or revenue yield per pupil; the maximum (and minimum) level of property tax rate; and per-pupil operating expenditures or growth in those expenditures. Some form of legislation limiting revenue acquisition has been considered or adopted by a majority of state governments. These measures may constrain local operators seeking more local revenues, which is, of course, the preference of taxpayer groups who helped put revenue-limitating measures into place. These measures have not, however, been effective in reducing differences in expenditures between rich and poor districts. Clients select residential location in part because of the level of public schooling offered. Successful attempts to reduce that level of schooling through revenue-limiting legislation have had the effect of reducing the value of that school district in the eyes of voters who favor more than the median level of schooling.

Reversion Levels. In the general case of local elections, the school board proposes a budget or tax levy that requires approval by a majority of voters. If the proposal fails, the level of expenditure, that is the revenues available to schools, is a legislatively or constitutionally-specified *reversion level.* (Rosenthal 1980, p. 8). The reversion level can take one of a variety of forms: last year's tax rate (Arkansas), last year's budget plus a certain percent (Colorado), a specific millage rate (Idaho), or simply a sufficiently small budget to require that schools be closed early (for example, Ohio, Oregon, Illinois, Connecticut, and Virginia)(ibid., p. 5).

The level of the reversion affects the tactics of the local administrators when they seek revenues. The reversion level reflects in the eyes of the voter the consequence of a "no" vote outcome. As Rosenthal points out, the lower the reversion level, the greater the consequences of a no vote. The operator, argues Rosenthal, "is able to threaten the electorate with the reversion. . .", and as a general rule, the ability of the operator to acquire local tax revenues increases as the level of the reversion decreases (ibid., p. 7).

Repeat Elections. The right of the operators to resubmit their proposal to the electorate affects their ability to raise local revenue. In most states, operators are entitled to more than one attempt to pass a proposal. The right to repeat elections gives operators an advantage over local sponsors, because operators can never be worse off than they would be if only one election were permitted, and they can always choose to hold but one election. *Resubmitted* budgets tend to be reduced versions of original budgets, although frequently the same budget level is proposed a second and a third time (ibid., p. 13).

Other variations in voting mechanisms contribute to the ease (or difficulty) with which the public school operator can raise local revenues. For example, the outcomes of some positive votes can remain unchanged until a subsequent election, while others have a fixed duration after which they must be voted on again. The requirements for revoting also vary in some states that limit the items of expenditure at the reversion level.

Managerial Behavior

Public administrators as budget maximizers behave in ways that will yield positive votes in local school elections. Evidence has been accumulating for many years on the strategies and tactics employed by public school administrators to pass elections. Two intimately related focuses are the characteristics of sponsor-clients (these are individuals whom the schools serve and who also can allocate revenue to schools through voting) and the election strategies of operators.

Characteristics of Sponsor-Clients. The need to understand the characteristics of the sponsor-clients that correlate with their voting behavior is purely a pragmatic one: it provides the basis for planning campaigns to achieve a majority of "yes" votes. Sponsor-clients, like all other individuals, will go to the polls to vote when the anticipated benefits to them of voting exceed the costs. The benefits are associated with the voter's preferences for a particular outcome coupled with some feel for the impact of his or her single vote on the outcome. The costs are associated primarily with the value of voter's time—

time to register, time to seek out information, time to deliberate, and time to mark the ballot (Hatley and Ritter 1981, p. 5). Using this rationale, parents would be interested in increased school spending while property owners would be interested in decreased spending. This paradigm of voter behavior is too simplistic, however, to be of use to the school administrator when seeking revenues through ballot initiatives.

More helpful are the specific attitudinal and background characteristics that have been found to be associated with voting behavior, such as having voted in the past (habit); interest in the community; high income and education; middle-age; married; white-collar employment; strong partisan preference; high sense of citizen duty; and high interest in the campaign. Hatley and Ritter helped to synthesize the wide variety of findings in pursuit of characteristics of people who both voted and voted positively on school referenda. Within five categories of characteristics they found attributes of individuals that were common both to voters and to "yes" voters.

> Common to both criterion variables of active voter participation and supportive patterns in the voting booth are having children at home and enrolled in the public schools, having a history of relatively low geographic mobility, and having middle to upper economic status. [Ibid., p. 28]

Unique to the "yes" voters are variables associated with political party affiliation and orientation, education attainment, home ownership, trusted sources of information about the public schools, and markedly positive attitudes about the efficiency and effectiveness of the public schools. These data are presented in exhibit 4.7.

Not voting or voting against referenda are not always simply the "flip side" of a "yes" vote. Factors that have been found to be associated with negative voting include specific school policies, personalities of school officials, tax resistance, the presence of unresolved controversies in an election, and a sense that schools have few needs.

Implications for Election Strategies. Although local conditions may well negate any generalizations about the implications of the foregoing description of voter characteristics in a particular instance, several generalizations seem warranted. First, continual communication with the community through formal means is better than that limited to the few months before an election. Second, needs as well as accomplishments of the district should be kept in the public eye. Third, budget formats should be intelligible to the average voter. Fourth, representative voters should be encouraged to participate "meaningfully" in budget deliberations. Fifth, the first announcement of a campaign should be the most carefully planned and widely publicized. (Some studies suggest that most voters make up their minds the first time they hear of the proposal.)

Perhaps the most important generalization is that the campaign should be directed toward those who already support the budget, not toward those who are opposed to it: ". . . it's more productive and easier to find ten 'yes' votes than to turn one 'no' voter around" (Jones 1977, p. 7). This strategy suggests that emphasis be placed more on improvements in service levels and program quality than on tax rates and expenditure levels.

Flow of Funds from Individual Sponsors to Private Schools

In most cases, private schools derive a large proportion of their operating revenue from the tuition, fees, and gifts from individuals. Before discussing the implications of this for managerial behavior, we should underscore that "large proportion" does not mean "all." Most private schools receive some form of public aid, even those that are religiously affiliated. In fact, all but three states (Georgia, Florida, and Oklahoma) provide some type of aid to church-related schools. Some states, for example, give or lend instructional materials to church-affiliated schools. Other services include providing building loans for construction or maintenance of school facilities; subsidies for testing and recordkeeping; and school transportation for students both to and from school and for some field trips. Federal aid to private schools includes money for special education and food. Nonetheless, the proportion of private school revenues from these sources is generally small. (Among the exceptions, which we will discuss separately, is Ombudsman, which is a private, for-profit school that markets to school districts and, as a result, receives mostly public revenues.) Tuition revenues per child per year range from nothing for students on complete scholarships to over $7,000 at several boarding schools. About a fifth of the students attending private schools pay under $200 in tuition and fees, and about the same proportion pay over $1,000. Much of the variance in tuition payments is attributable to variances in family income levels of students served, religious affiliation of schools, and level of schooling provided (see exhibit 4.8).

Even with broad categories of private schools (including religiously affiliated and nonreligiously affiliated), there exist major differences in the education services offered, markets served, and tuition charged. Consider, for example, the schools affiliated with the National Association of Independent Schools (NAIS). This association of about 880 schools serving approximately 370,000 students consists of various combinations of day and boarding schools, single-sex and coed schools, and elementary, secondary, and K–12 schools. It is difficult to generalize about revenue patterns among this group of schools, not to mention among all private schools. However, by examining two types of these schools, we can see not only how they differ, but how private school administrators, as a group, do in fact behave differently from their counterparts in the public sector in acquiring funds. Comparing, for

Exhibit 4.7

Construct Dimension Profiles of Those Who Tend to Vote and Who Tend to Vote "Yes" in School Financial Referenda

The Active Voter	The "Yes" Voter
The Personal Dimension	
Have children residing at home and enrolled in the public schools.	Have children residing at home and enrolled in the public schools.
The Sociological Dimension	
Are less mobile than their counterparts, having lived in the district and at their current addresses for extended periods of time.	Are less mobile than their counterparts, having lived in the district and at their current addresses for extended periods of time.
	Are registered Democrats or Independents and describe themselves as "liberals" or "moderates."
The Economic Dimension	
Are in an income class that is above the average for the community.	Are in an income class that is the average for the community; have a high level of education, including some college; and work in professional, clerical, or homemaker roles.
	Are renters or homeowners who have not yet retired their mortagages.
The Informational Dimension	
Have an extensive and comprehensive knowledge base about the public schools, or at least they believe this to be the case.	Regardless of the extent of the knowledge base, desire still more information about the schools, and look to school sources for this information rather than to the mass media.
The Attitudinal Dimension	
Participate in the financial referenda somewhat independent of their attitudes about the conditions, operations, and effectiveness and efficiency of the schools.	Have highly positive attitudes regarding the public schools' teaching staff, administration, program efficiency and effectiveness, and overall operations and conditions.

Sources: Richard Hatley and James R. Ritter, "Prediction of Voting Behavior in Local School District Financial Referenda" (Paper presented at the Annual Meeting of the American Educational Research Association, Los Angeles, Calif., April 13–17, 1981), p. 30. Reprinted by permission.

example, coed elementary-secondary day schools with coed boarding schools (exhibit 4.9), we see that day schools rely more on tuition and fees, income from auxiliary services, and affiliated enterprises (such as tennis and swim clubs) for revenue than the boarding schools do. Boarding schools rely slightly less on tuition and fees and more on endowment, gift income, and net summer school income.

The figures illustrate major differences in the opportunity sets between public and private school administrators with regard to raising revenues. Whereas public school administrators are heavily engaged in raising revenue from governmental sponsors, private school administrators are more engaged in raising revenues through gifts, grants, and enterprises as well as through recruiting and pricing services.

Part of the behavior of private school managers includes allocating resources (money, employees' time, and so forth) that are devoted to fund raising, recruitment, and the like. For example, private schools, according to a NAIS survey concerning the schools' receipt of annual gifts, expended a little over 24 percent of the revenues from annual gifts on costs directly associated with annual gifts. Fund raising includes both securing annual giving and campaigns to raise money for capital improvements. Over half of the out-of-pocket costs for fund raising for these schools went to salaries; other expenditures were for items that include travel, printing, supplies, postage, and fund-raising counsel.

Flow of Funds from Donors to Endowments and Foundations

An endowment is money that has been set aside and invested, and schools consider income from the investment as revenue. The degree to which the principal can be spent varies. *True endowment* refers to funds whose principal must remain invested and whose income is available for the support of the institution. *Term endowment* funds are like endowment funds, but all or part of the principal may be expended after a stated period of time or on the occurrence of a certain event. In a *quasi-endowment* fund, the principal may legally be spent at the discretion of the governing board (Herzlinger and Taylor 1979, p. 2).

Creating and Increasing Endowments

Managers of private nonprofit schools often both create and seek to increase endowments to their schools. Increased endowments are a hedge against future uncertainties for both operators and sponsors and create the image of quality and stability in the eyes of clients. Public school managers are largely prohibited by law from creating endowments, although they are permitted to set aside sums of money from their operating funds in anticipation of future, usually capital, expenditures. There are no incentives for

Exhibit 4.8
Annual Tuition and Fees
(October 1979)

	Percentage Distribution of Tuition and Fees				
	Under $ 200	$200 to $ 499	$500 to $ 999	$1000 and over	Not reported
Total	19.8%	21.0%	27.1%	20.4%	11.8%
By income:					
$10,000 to $25,000	23.1	26.7	27.8	5.5	16.5
$25,000 and over	17.2	17.9	25.2	32.6	7.2
By religious affliation:					
Affiliated	22.8	24.2	29.0	14.0	10.1
Unaffiliated	3.8	4.3	20.9	62.2	8.9
By grade level:					
Elementary	26.2	26.8	21.7	13.4	11.8
Secondary	1.6	4.2	42.6	40.0	11.6

Exhibit 4.9
Income per Student for Sample of Private Schools
(1979–80)

Source of Income	Coed Elementary and Secondary Schools		Coed Boarding Schools	
	$	%	$	%
Tuition and fees	2,472	78.0	5,717	66.7
Auxiliary service	217	6.8	430	5.0
Endowment	108	3.4	1,131	13.2
Gifts	218	6.9	665	7.8
Public aid	11	0.3	33	0.4
Net summer school	29	0.9	236	2.7
Other affiliated enterprises	10	0.3	0	0
Other	101	3.2	358	4.2
Total income	3,166	100.0	8,570	100.0

Source: National Association of Independent Schools, *NAIS Statistics, Spring 1981* (Boston: NAIS, 1981), p. 15.

for-profit managers to create endowments because no one would be likely to donate money to an organization whose stated purpose is to make money for sponsors.

Any school manager, regardless of sector, can create or receive money from a foundation. A foundation is a legal mechanism for the contribution of private wealth to public purposes. Under this broad definition there are five classes of foundations—general purpose, special purpose, company sponsored, community, and family. Foundations were frequently established by the founder's donation of a large block of stock from a portfolio. In some cases, the desire of the donor to avoid capital gains and estate taxation without losing effective control was as much a motivating factor to establish a foundation as the pursuit of philanthropic activities.

In most private nonprofit schools, endowments provide a small proportion of revenues. In all three sectors, foundations provide an even smaller and much more sporadic source of revenue for schools. Their importance is not adequately measured by the current dollar volume of revenue income. For the nonprofit manager, however, endowment income can mean the difference between being price competitive and investing in new programs or not: these funds provide a margin of freedom to the manager that would not otherwise exist. Likewise, a foundation grant that gives the manager leverage to pursue an otherwise neglected interest can have great utility.

Currently public school managers are actively considering creation of foundations to tap donor markets and to bring resources to public schools from this typically nonpublic revenue source. There are actually a variety of mechanisms that can be used to accomplish this purpose. One is to create a separate organization that can accept donations and spend money on programs closely associated with the public schools. (These are usually private nonprofit charitable organizations created to comply with section 501.C.3 of the tax code. The corporate income of these organizations is not taxed.) Another is to establish a fund within a community foundation. A third way is to create a department within the public school system that would act as a foundation. (Public schools can accept gifts, and donors can retain a tax-deductible status for the gift.)

Portfolio Spending Policy

The perceived costs and benefits of using these three mechanisms or any other alternative will vary from setting to setting. On the premise, however, that school managers find themselves in a setting where they have (or can acquire) rights over invested resources from either endowment or foundation mechanisms, they face trade-offs on the issue of present versus future spending. What managers spend from an endowment today cannot be invested, earn interest and dividends, and be spent in the future. The issue is made complex by a variety of factors, including the level of uncertainty regarding the amount of future returns on investment of the portfolio; future nonportfolio income from tuition payments, annual gifts, and so on; and the school's future expenses (see Meckling and Jensen 1970.)

On initial consideration, it may seem intuitively obvious that the logical spending policy should be to spend interest earned, that is, to treat any endowment strictly as a true endowment. However, there are a number of arguments against such a policy (which was in fact used by many managers of endowed education institutions as recently as the 1960s). The most fundamental problem associated with this policy is that it forces simultaneous specification of both the investment and the expenditure policy. By specifying that income from endowments will be tied precisely to earnings, portfolio managers are constrained to invest in low-risk securities, such as bonds, that generate relatively large, predictable cash flows from dividends and interest. The school manager can pursue this strategy, but at the cost of foregoing the possibility of even larger capital gains. If he invests in high-risk securities, he will earn smaller cash flows, but may find the market value of his portfolio growing significantly. Thus, a school that follows a relatively aggressive investment policy could find its overall rate of return, including capital gains, higher than it would have been, but it will also find its dividend and interest income less than it could have been. A manager who restricts spending to interest and dividends (and not to capital gains) on high-risk investments will end up spending less currently than with a low-risk portfolio. Most school managers who work with endowment funds have adopted various rules for spending that incorporate capital gains in the concept of yield (called *total yield*) and that act to dampen the effects of market fluctuations.

The five guidelines set down by Meckling and Jensen for forming rules on spending in higher education apply equally to elementary and secondary schools with endowments: (1) Rules on expenditure decisions should provide a stable, gradually growing level of expenditures from the portfolio. A rule that results in major fluctuations in operating revenue available to finance budgets would make planning and budgeting difficult. (2) It should make it possible to separate investment decisions from expenditure decisions. The portfolio manager should be free to maximize the yield of the portfolio (including capital gains) at appropriate levels of risk without having to produce a specified cash flow each year. (3) A rule should improve the likelihood that the school could continue the existing level of education in the future. It should take into account inflationary trends and thereby endeavor to ensure the ability to carry on existing programs. (4) It should have the characteristic that increases in the market value of the portfolio will result in increases in expenditures from portfolio yields. (5) It should be simple.

Most school managers and sponsors have developed policies on spending that specify a fixed percentage (for example, 7 percent) of the total value of the portfolio will be spent as measured by a moving average of some number (for example, 4) from *previous* years. In other words, the moving average is the average annual yield of the endowment. For example, if the endowment earned annually over the last four years 4 percent, 8 percent, 10 percent, and 6 percent, this year's draw *from* endowment would be 7 percent (4 + 8 + 10 + 6 ÷ 4 years). Such a policy creates stability for the budget planner, provides freedom to the portfolio manager, and assures a continuation of growth. Like any other policy, it requires periodic evaluation.

Raising Donor Dollars

Campaigns for donor dollars for annual giving or capital campaigns involve formal strategies and tactics, including designation of a committee to plan a sequence of activities; recruitment of volunteers to carry out activities; development of the data base of target populations; printing and mailing literature; following up with phone calls; and reporting results. Money-raising campaigns in private schools are comparable to local budget elections in public schools only in the sense that to succeed, both require marketing skills and extensive coordination of many related activities.

Revenue-Generating Behavior and "Responsiveness"

Both public and private educational administrators maximize personal utility by behaving in ways that generate revenue. For the public school administrator this means maximizing budgets, and for the private school administrator this means maximizing the present value of future flows of revenues. Public school administrators mobilize constituencies to put pressure on sponsors for more resources, whereas private school administrators develop and retain markets of individuals who purchase private education services and who contribute resources to the school. Significant proportions of resources in both public and private schools are devoted, either directly or indirectly, to revenue generation.

The private school administrator is likely to appear to be much more sensitive to personal needs, because individuals represent specific unit contributions of money (or purchases of services) to the school. Public school administrators are less likely to behave in ways that appear responsive for several reasons. First, the diversity of constituents is usually much greater, and hence it is inherently more difficult to satisfy any single person. Second, the monetary consequences of not responding individually to constituent concerns are not nearly as severe because of the quasi-monopoly position of public schools and because the revenue lost from the departure of one single student is proportionately quite a bit less than is the case in private schools.

Public school administrators are not less "humane," or "sensitive," than their colleagues in the private sector are. Rather, the personal benefits (rewards) that accrue to public school administrators for responding to individual client concerns are somewhat less.

Conclusion

Revenue sources as much as any other single descriptor differentiate the role, and hence behavior, of school business administrators across the three sectors. In all cases the school administrator is *marketing* sponsors, but the manner in which this is done varies across different sources of revenue (and, consequently, across sectors). The private for-profit school administrator focuses heavily on revenue from direct sales and those factors that influence direct sales, for example, campaigns, endorsements, and word-of-mouth comments of students to potential clients. He may as well pursue government training subsidies and also seek loan programs for his students. The subsidies are often per-capita payments to the school and show up as a direct revenue item, whereas the loan program may simply show up as tuition revenue.

The private nonprofit school administration seeks, in addition to direct sales, donor dollars. Both of these revenue sources require convincing the individual to exchange money for something that the individual values personally. (Individuals are also encouraged to donate time and material goods that can be converted into revenues, as is the case with "next-to-new" sales.)

The public school administrator may pursue "yes" votes in local elections or appropriations from city government, but his or her overall orientation is to secure a large lump of money from sponsors, many of whom do not use the service. Marketing sponsors in the public sector creates incentives for the school administrator to convey three messages at the same time: one, money is being spent wisely; but, two, not appropriating sufficient quantities of money can do harm to necessary programs in the schools; and, three, there are educational problems facing the schools that require remediation. Private school sponsors, on the other hand, tend to focus on the strengths of their schools. Even when pursuing donors, the private nonprofit administrator has to blend the messages of institutional "need" with those of institutional strength and quality.

Appendix 4.1: Allocating State Financial Aid to Public Schools

Although the financing of elementary-secondary public education is both complex and constantly changing, a simplified model is presented in exhibit 4.10 to provide a basis for introducing state aid allocation formulas. As exhibit 8.9 shows (see page 271), school districts receive revenue from a wide variety of sources. However, local taxes and state assistance are by far the largest sources of revenue. The local dollar contribution to education is raised by taxing property at a specified rate, and state contributions to local school districts are often a function of the local contribution. The allocation formulas discussed here represent several of the major methods of determining the state contribution that have evolved over the last three-quarters of a century. Simplified versions of the formulas are given for purposes of comparison.

The Flat-Grant Approach

In its most basic form, the flat-grant form of state assistance amounts to a fixed sum of money:

$$\text{school district revenue} = \text{local contribution} + \text{state contribution as a fixed amount of money per unit.}$$

The state pays a fixed amount to the district based on some unit of measure (for example, average daily attendance of pupils or number of teachers employed). The unit of measure used is important in determining the impact of the flat-grant formula (such as a flat grant based on average daily attendance versus a flat grant based on number of teachers employed). The differences are shown in exhibits 4.11 and 4.12. In exhibit 4.11 the distribution has been uniformly shifted upward. That is, in terms of dollar amounts the difference between the richest and poorest districts is the same (although the percentage difference has been reduced). This is because the average daily attendance in a district is not a function of either local wealth or local effort.

In exhibit 4.12 the distribution has been shifted in favor of the wealthier districts. In terms of dollar amounts, the difference between the richest and poorest districts has increased. This is because the number of teachers (the unit of payment of the flat grant) that a district purchases is clearly a function of the financial ability of the district. As a consequence, the rich get richer when the state agrees, in effect, to pay part of the cost of a service. A description of how this works follows.

The flat grant was developed around the turn of the century by Ellwood P. Cubberley (1906). One of the main objectives of Cubberley's plan was to expand educational offerings in communities. He was anxious for secondary school instruction to become more widespread, and he also sought the institution of kindergartens, manual and physical training classes, evening schools, special classes, and vocational schools. He believed that the efforts of

Exhibit 4.10

Financing Elementary-Secondary Public Education

		Local contribution				State contribution
Revenues for the operation of local school districts	=	Local tax rate (local effort)	×	Assessed valuation of local real property (local wealth)	+	Assistance from state

Exhibit 4.11

State Aid Distribution from a Flat-Grant Formula Based on Average Daily Attendance

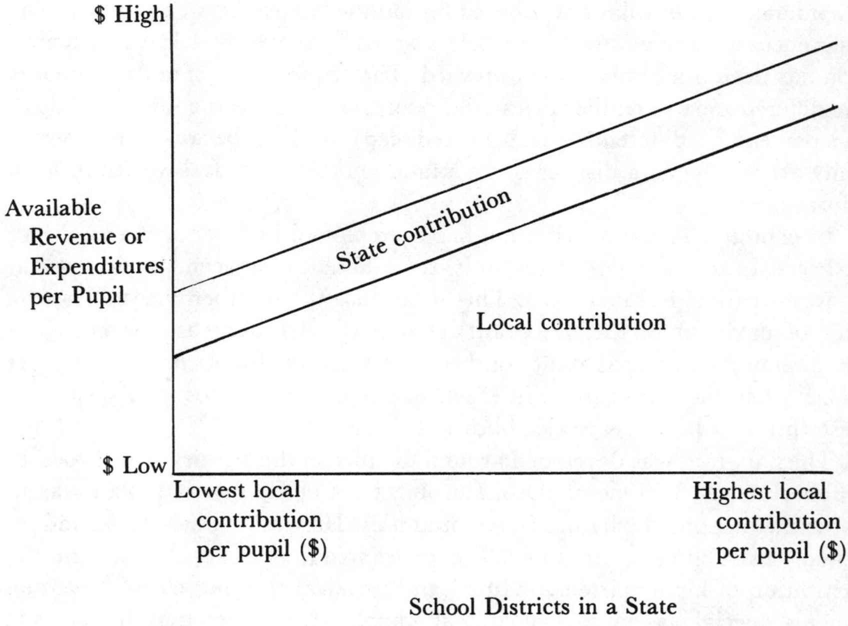

Exhibit 4.12

State Aid Distribution from a Flat-Grant Formula Based on Teacher Revenue Units

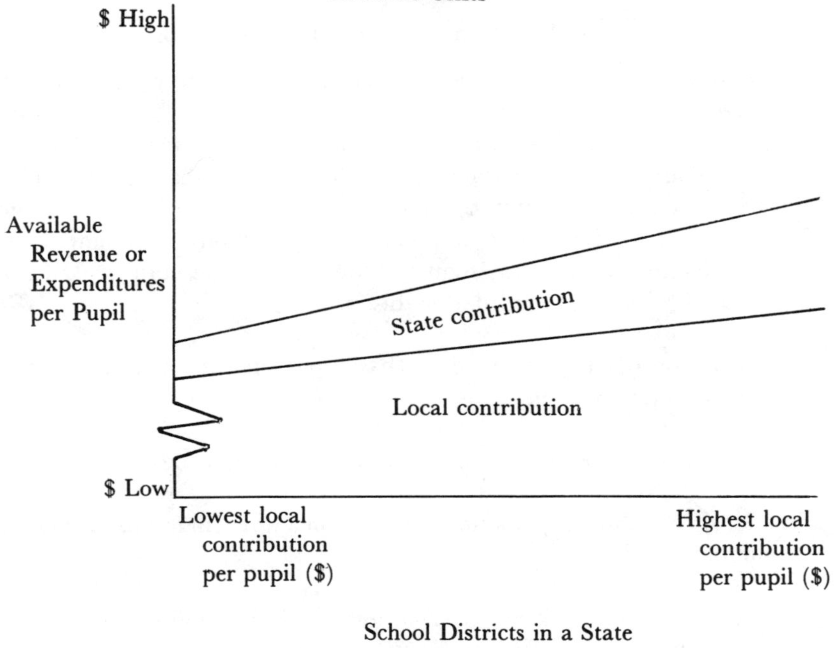

school districts to expand their offerings should be rewarded on a "teacher-employed" basis. That is, for every teacher employed by a district, the state paid a portion of that teacher's cost, and there was no limitation on the use of teachers. Thus, districts could hire new teachers and have the costs shared by the state. Such a financial incentive usually stimulates local expenditures. It is also important to note that allocating flat grants on the basis of teacher, rather than pupil, units benefited rural districts, which had higher teacher-to-student ratios, for reasons beyond district control. However, in Cubberley's program the stimulation of expenditures in any district is limited by the wealth of that district. (For an extended discussion of the effects of the flat-grant and other formulas, see Benson 1968, pp. 154–90.)

Another of Cubberley's objectives was to promote local property tax relief. However, in the early twentieth century the property tax was the major source of state, as well as local, revenue; and the property tax is regressive, that is, it has a disproportionately heavy impact on the poor (because the poor spend a high proportion of their income on housing). Thus, poorer districts had already paid a disproportionate share of state revenue, and Cubberley's state aid program did not promote local tax relief. Today, however, when many states rely on nonproperty taxes, a flat grant promotes some local tax relief.

The Foundation Program Approach

The foundation program is a mechanism designed to guarantee a minimum fixed amount of revenue per student in a school district. It is determined in three steps. First, a minimum (or foundation) level of revenue per pupil necessary for an "adequate" educational program is determined by the state. Second, a local district, by taxing itself at a specified level, determines if its local contribution is more or less than this foundation amount. Third, if the local contribution is less than the foundation, the state makes up the difference. The general formula for this is:

If the local contribution per student (based on a uniform tax rate) is greater than the foundation, then

local revenue per student = local contribution per student.

If the local contribution per student (based on a uniform tax rate) is less than the foundation, then

local revenue per student = local contribution per student + (foundation minus the local contribution per student).

The impact of this formula is shown in exhibit 4.13. The level of the foundation is very important in determining the degree to which the program succeeds in equalizing per-pupil revenues among school districts. The foundation is determined by picking a *key district*, one whose local contribution at the fixed tax rate equals the amount of the foundation. If the key district is the richest district in the state, revenues are equalized throughout the state, as shown in exhibit 4.14. If the key district is a district of average expenditure, as shown in exhibit 4.13, then per-pupil revenues are equalized only up to the point of the foundation. In choosing a key district, state legislators attempt to negotiate a compromise between those who wish to choose a wealthy district in order to equalize for wealth differences and others who wish to choose a less-wealthy district in order to limit the state's financial commitment to education.

Since in practice the level of the foundation is invariably below the real cost of schooling, the district must raise additional funds to cover the costs not provided by the foundation funds. Because of the varying degrees of district, wealth, poor communities must exert a proportionately greater tax

Exhibit 4.13

State Aid Distribution from a Foundation Plan (key district is district with average local contribution)

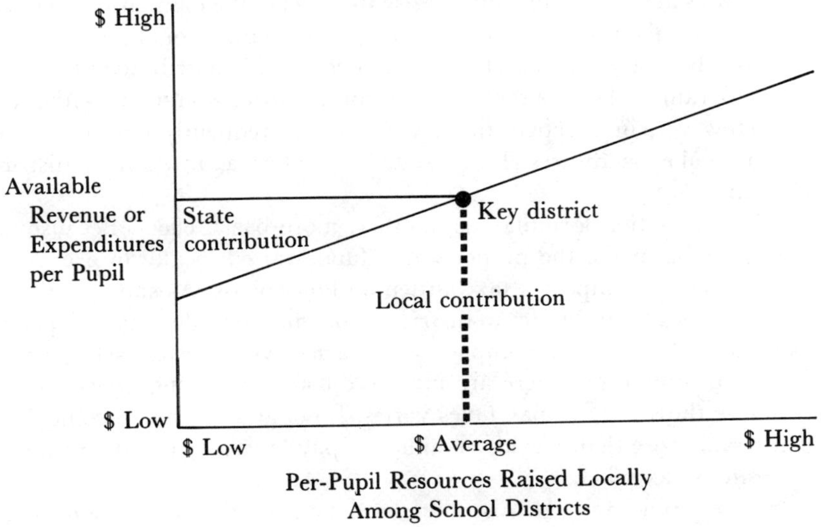

Exhibit 4.14

State Aid Distribution from a Foundation Plan (key district is district with highest local contribution)

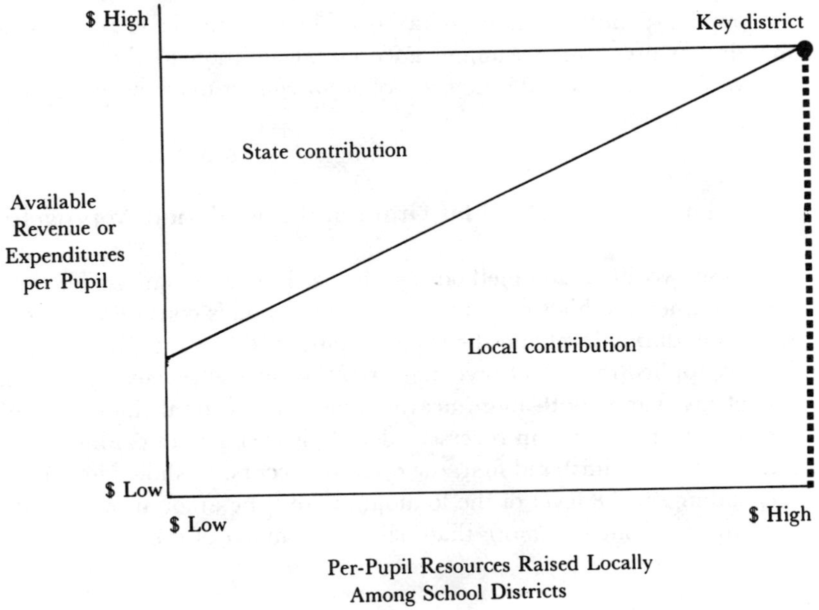

effort than rich communities in order to obtain the same amount of local funds. In inflationary periods, poor districts are further disadvantaged. State legislatures are often reluctant to raise the level of the foundation, permitting inflation to take away the buying power of the educational dollar.

It has been argued that all communities should contribute to the foundation program at the rate that the wealthiest district would pay without state aid. However, in practice, the key district is frequently one with average educational expenditures. This results in a higher tax rate among districts in the state.

The foundation formula has another, more basic, effect. Because of the regressive nature of the property tax, funds raised locally in excess of the foundation level impose a tax burden on households. As stated earlier, this impact varies from district to district, depending on differences in per-pupil assessed valuation. The impact also varies within each school district. Within communities, there are income differences among households, and therefore the ability to pay taxes varies. Low- and average-income families will strain more than wealthy families to pay taxes. Again, the result is the opposite of tax relief.

Strayer and Haig (1923), the developers of the foundation program approach, believed that incentive payments were inconsistent with the equalization objective. Therefore, the foundation program does not provide for the stimulation of local expenditures. The initiative for expanding educational offerings resides with the state. If the state decides a new offering is necessary, funds will be included in the foundation program. If a local district wants to initiate a new offering of its own, or in other ways increase per-pupil expenditure, it must tax itself beyond the level required for the foundation program (assuming an optimal addition to the set tax rate is allowable). Therefore, districts are often unwilling to experiment with innovative programs.

The Combination Flat Grant and Foundation Approach

These two allocation methods can be used in combination. The impact of the combined methods depends on which formula is considered first (for the same foundation level and the same amount of flat grant). If the foundation level is applied to district revenues first, the general revenue pattern among school districts is both more nearly equal and, in total, higher than if the formulas were applied in reverse order. This is shown in exhibit 4.15. If the flat grant is administered first, the opposite occurs, as shown in exhibit 4.16. Depending on the level of the foundation and the amount of the flat grant, the impact of one can more than offset the impact of the other.

Exhibit 4.15

State Aid Distribution from Administering a Foundation Plan (key = average district) Followed by a Flat Grant

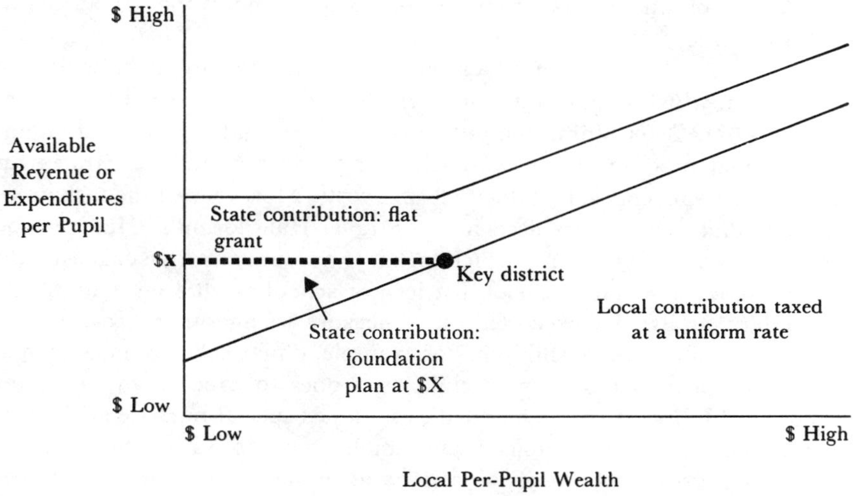

Exhibit 4.16

State Aid Distribution from Administering a Flat Grant Followed by a Foundation Plan (key = average district)

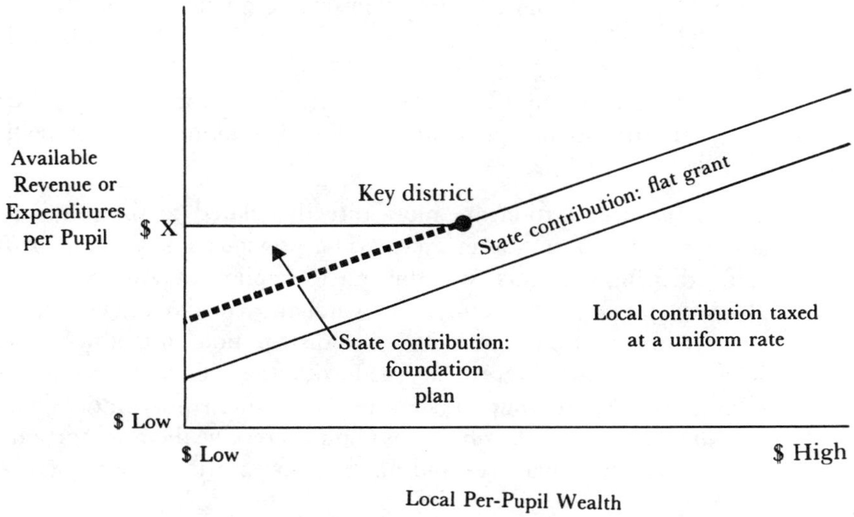

The Weighted-Pupil Measures Approach

The formulas discussed so far are calculated on the basis of equality of revenue among students. The concept discussed here deals with providing for groups of students (such as the physically handicapped) who require extra revenue.

Paul Mort (1960) advanced a number of refinements to the basic Strayer-Haig plan, which might be termed *weighted-pupil measures* (see Benson 1968, pp. 157–67). Determining the unit cost (cost per student) of the minimum educational program caused problems for Cubberley and for Strayer and Haig. Different schools had different unit costs. Mort refined the task unit of average daily attendance used in the Strayer-Haig formula. He developed the weighted-pupil measure, which took into account any unusual costs (that is, transportation, small school districts, or schools with a large number of secondary pupils). The weighted-pupil measure assumes that it costs more to educate certain types of children. For example, it may cost 1.3 times as much to educate a secondary school child as it does to educate an elementary school child, because of such added expenses as special-purpose facilities for vocational and science subjects and smaller class sizes in these subjects. There is a great amount of variation among states regarding the relative weights assigned students of differing grade levels. Some states provide more aid (that is, higher weightings) to secondary students (including Nebraska, North Dakota, and Illinois), while others provide more aid to elementary school students (Florida and North Carolina), presumably because of the importance placed on the value of early childhood education. Still other states (South Carolina and Tennessee) provide more aid for both early elementary school students and high school students than they do for those in the middle grades. (For more information on the finance plans of specific states, see "School Finance at a Glance: 1983–84" from the Education Commission of the States.)

When the weighted-pupil measures for its finance formula were first adopted, Utah educational policymakers found a number of compelling advantages:

1. The costs of education are more directly related to the number of students than to any other factor. The previous system used in the state (distribution units) was difficult to implement, since it was not always related to the number of students. It is relatively easy to convert weighted-pupil measures into distribution units if necessary.
2. Recent court cases were concerned with the inequality of cost per pupil. The weighted-pupil system tends to build equity into a finance formula, because all classifications of pupils receive their proportionate share of revenue increases and all share proportionately if there are revenue decreases.

3. This approach reduces the number of categorical grants required in the financing of educational programs.
4. A number of other states were moving in this direction, because it usually results in a formula that is relatively easy to understand and apply.

In Utah, weighted-pupil measures are incorporated in a foundation plan. Mort's influence is clearly present in the Utah finance plan: he established the *largest* wealthy district as the key district on which the foundation program is based. This alteration eliminated the small, idiosyncratic district that was extremely wealthy. Such unusual districts necessitated large amounts of state aid to support the foundation programs, assuming the richest district was chosen as the key district. Mort also adjusted the rate of local contribution downward so that almost all districts received some state aid, making the plan more politically feasible.

By refining the task unit, Mort more accurately depicted the costs of educating a pupil. A higher degree of equalization is attained by this refinement, because the more accurate the description of the costs, the more appropriate the tax rate that produces the revenue.

Mort also provided local tax leeway, which resulted in some stimulation of local expenditure. Larger amounts of state aid may serve to increase local expenditure, because localities do not entirely reduce spending as the state contribution increases.

In summary, Mort's refinements of the Strayer-Haig plan further the equalization objective by more accurately describing the costs of educating a pupil. They also promise a degree of local tax relief but do not offset the overall tax burden of the Strayer-Haig plan when the key district is not the largest and wealthiest district. And they provide for the stimulation of local expenditures for education.

The Percentage-Equalizing Approach

The percentage-equalizing grant is a device by which the state government shares in supplying funds to meet a locally determined volume of school expenditure. It is like a matching grant except that this term often is interpreted to mean dollar-for-dollar matching; under the percentage-equalizing grant, the state's share varies from one district to the next, being small in rich districts and large in poor districts.

In theory, the percentage-equalizing grant promises to attain equalization, local tax relief, and the stimulation of local expenditures. Equalization of tax burden is accomplished because all districts taxing themselves at a certain rate receive the same amount of state financial support (assuming the key district is the wealthiest district in the state). Each district determines its tax rate, and for each rate levied the state supplies a specific amount of aid, determined by the following formula:

$$Ai = (1 - C \cdot Yi \div Y)\ Ei,$$

where Ai is the state grant to district i, C is a constant representing the local share for the key district and normally having a value of between 0 and 1, $1 - C$ is the percentage of the cost of local education services that the state is willing to pay, Yi is the assessed valuation per pupil in district i, and Y is the assessed valuation per pupil of the key district. Y is often calculated as the state average,

$$\frac{\Sigma Yi}{n}, \quad i = 1, n.$$

Ei is the school expenditure in district i.

Assume that a state is willing to pay 60 percent of the cost of local educational services ($1 - C = .60$), that the key district is defined as the average per-pupil assessed valuation in the state ($50,000), and that the expected per-pupil revenue level is $3,000. The percentage of state aid to a poor district with $25,000 in per-pupil wealth is calculated as follows:

$$1 - .40 \times \frac{25{,}000}{50{,}000} =$$
$$1 - .40 \times .50 =$$
$$1 - .20 =$$
$$.80 \text{ or } 80 \text{ per cent}$$

This means that the state's share is 80 percent of $3,000, or $2,400. Therefore, the local share for this relatively poor district is 20 percent, or $600. The local share for this district with an average per-pupil assessed valuation of $25,000 (half the state average) can be raised with uniform local tax rate of .024 (in other words, $2.40 in property taxes per $100 of assessed valuation, or $24 per $1,000). One can see that $25,000 (assessed valuation per pupil) multiplied by .024 will raise the local share of $600 per pupil.

Consider a relatively rich district ($112,500 in per-pupil wealth) under comparable circumstances. The state share in that district's budget is determined as follows:

$$1 - .40 \times \frac{112{,}500}{50{,}000} =$$
$$1 - .40 \times 2.25 =$$
$$1 - .90 =$$
$$.10 \text{ or } 10\ \%$$

The state's share is 10 percent of $3,000, or $300, while the local share for this relatively wealth district is 90 percent of 3,000, or $2,700. The local share for this wealthy district can be raised with the same .024 tax rate used for the relatively poor district. Again when one multiplies the assessed valuation per pupil ($112,500) by the tax rate (.024), it will equal the respective district's local share ($2,700).

Thus, a poor district, in levying a certain tax rate, receives the same amount of total funds as the key district would if it taxed itself at the same rate. Local tax relief is attained, for the level of expenditure in a district is directly related to the effort a community wishes to exert rather than to its tax base. In addition, a community can decide to increase its educational expenditure without undue economic hardship.

Where the percentage-equalizing grant has actually been implemented, however, the results leave much to be desired. First, the key district is the district with an average level of educational expenditure in the state. Thus, equalization of the tax burden cannot occur unless the rich districts pay into a state fund in order to adjust their wealth downward. No state using the percentage-equalizing grant has used this approach to equalization. Thus, every district taxing at a certain rate will receive in local and/or state funds only the amount of funds the key district can raise at the same rate. When more funds are needed, which is usually the case, districts richer than the key district can raise more revenue at a lower tax rate than poor districts can. Generally then, the percentage-equalization approach has much the same effect as the foundation approach: when the key district is the average district, revenues are equalized only up to that point.

Another factor inhibiting total equalization is the provision in many percentage-equalizing plans (such as in Rhode Island) for a minimum-aid ratio for every district in the state. Thus, both rich and poor districts are guaranteed state aid. This obviously benefits rich districts, since poor districts receive support under the equalizing program anyway.

Because the key district represents the average level of expenditure—rich districts do not pay to the state excess funds—and a ceiling is usually imposed on state aid, equal expenditures among districts are assured only to the point where the costs of education are equalized by the formula. Expenditures beyond this point must be raised by the local property tax, and the advantages of rich districts in obtaining funds are obvious when it is known, for example, that in New York State in 1984–85 (which has a percentage-equalizing formula) most districts expended more funds per student than the maximum level at which the state would provide reimbursement.

The Power-Equalizing Approach

In recent years several alternative school finance plans have been developed that could serve as guides for a new system for financing public education. One such plan is district *power equalizing* (Coons, Clune, and

Sugarman 1970). In the power-equalizing plan, instead of the educational offering being a function of effort alone, the legislature specifies a given revenue yield for a certain tax a district chooses to impose on itself. That is, whatever the amount of local collection, the district is permitted to spend per pupil only that amount fixed by statute for the tax rate locally chosen. The formula describing this plan amounts to a schedule of operating revenues guaranteed for different tax rates. For example,

if a district taxes itself at:	it is guaranteed (based on local and state revenues):
less than 5 mills	no aid
between 5 and 14 mills	$1,500 plus $100 for each mill over 5
between 15 and 25 mills	$2,500 plus $50 for each mill over 15

Power equalizing promotes interdistrict equalization of tax burdens because each effort produces a specific amount of revenue for education. Power equalizing also promotes the stimulation of local expenditures because a community does not suffer economic hardship if it wants to increase its support of education. The effect of power equalizing on tax relief depends on the source of state revenue. If the state relies on the property tax, poor households bear a heavier burden than wealthy households because of the regressivity of the property tax.

A number of state legislatures have found the power-equalizing approach appealing in recent years, for several reasons. In addition to offering potential for great equalization of revenue, it does not place a rigid constraint on local effort, as do plans with uniform tax rates. Further, while not forcing districts to spend at a particular level, it can encourage them to do so. The sample formula presented above, for example, encourages all districts to spend at the level of $2,500 per pupil (by taxing themselves at 15 mills). For every mill added to the tax rate below 15 the district receives an extra $100 per pupil. But for every mill added to the tax rate above 15 the district receives only an extra $50 per pupil.

The Philosophical Bases of State Aid Formulas

The philosophical bases of state assistance can be obscured by the objectives, mechanisms, and impact of the different approaches. Implicit in each of the finance plans is a set of objectives. In most plans the main objective is to reduce financial inequalities in per-pupil operating expenditures within school districts. In addition, the plans of Cubberley and Mort include the objective of promoting the expansion of educational offerings. A third objective implicit in several plans is local tax relief. It is apparent that some of these objectives can conflict with each other.

Clear-cut distinctions among the methodologies can best be expressed in terms of mechanisms. Certain plans provide for supplementation of local resources after the district taxes itself at a maximum level. In other plans, the dispensation of aid is tied to the kinds of expenditures incurred (such as number of teachers hired) or students served ("weighting" various classifications of pupils).

The impact of each of the formulas varies greatly in terms of the stated objectives. Failure to completely accomplish objectives usually can be traced to the particular administration of the formula rather than the formula's abstract design. For example, the concept of leveling up to the key district could, in theory, accomplish the objective of equalizing expenditures. Making the key district an average district instead of the wealthiest district, however, precludes this.

There is an assumption that underlies the formulas discussed above: the benefits of public education do not accrue only to the individual who is educated. All the formulas imply that some of the benefits of education accrue to society. These social benefits may be described in terms of a more productive labor market, a citizenry more active in governmental affairs and less prone to criminal acts, and so on. It is because of the perceived benefits to society that the state assumes some of the responsibility for funding education. The argument is that if the individual were solely responsible for purchasing his own education, without any state assistance, he would consume only enough to benefit himself, given the resources at his disposal. The state must subsidize education, thereby making it possible for the individual to receive enough to benefit society.

Acknowledging that society benefits in some ways by an individual's education, there are, nevertheless, different conceptions of the role of the state in contributing to public education. One is that the state is responsible for providing a minimum amount of education (defined in terms of course offerings, expenditure levels, or some other measure). That minimum amount is required of all students. Above that minimum amount, localities may purchase whatever additional educational resources they want. (Elements of this idea are found in the flat grant and the foundation plan approaches.)

Alternatively, the state may feel that a large proportion of the benefits of education accrue to society. Therefore, from the state's perspective education is very important, and all individuals should have equal access to all levels of education. This idea implies that the state is fully for funding school operations rather than for developing funding plans that permit variations in revenue among localities.

Finally, the state may feel that the social benefits of education are large but that local control is also important. The state's position in this conflict is to guarantee each locality that taxes itself at a particular rate the same amount of revenue for education (the power-equalizing and percentage-equalizing approaches).

References

Benson, Charles S. *The Economics of Public Education.* Boston: Houghton Mifflin, 1968.

Coons, John; Clune, William; and Sugarman, Stephen. *Private Wealth and Public Education.* Cambridge, Mass.: Harvard University Press, 1970.

Cubberley, Ellwood P. *School Funds and Their Apportionment.* New York: Teachers College, Columbia University, 1906.

Garms, Walter I.; Guthrie, James W.; and Pierce, Lawrence C. *School Finance.* Englewood Cliffs, N.J.: Prentice-Hall, 1978.

Halstead, D. Kent. *Tax Wealth in Fifty States.* Washington, D.C.: National Institute of Education, 1978.

Hamilton, Howard D., and Cohen, Sylan H. *Policy Making by Plebiscite: School Referenda.* Lexington, Mass.: D.C. Heath & Co., 1974.

Hartman, William T. "Policy Effects of Special Education Funding Formulas." *Journal of Education Finance* 6 (Fall 1980): 135–159.

Hatley, Richard, and Ritter, James R. "Prediction of Voting Behavior in Local School District Financial Referenda." Paper presented at the Annual Meeting of the American Educational Research Association, Los Angeles, California, April 13–17, 1981. ED 203 509.

Herzlinger, Regina, and Taylor, Tabb. "Note on Endowment Management." Mimeographed. Cambridge, Mass.: Division of Research, Graduate School of Business Administration, Harvard University, HBS #79–36, 1979.

Jones, J. William. *Budget/Finance Campaigns: You Can't Afford to Lose.* Arlington, Va.: National School Public Relations Association, 1977. ED 140 428.

McGuire, Kent, and Dougherty, Van, "School Finance at a Glance: 1983–84". Denver: Education Commission of the States, 1984.

Meckling, William H., and Jensen, Michael C. "University Endowments and Spending Policies." Mimeographed. New York: University of Rochester, 1970.

Mort, Paul R.; Reusser, Walter C.; and Polley, John W. *Public School Finance.* 3rd ed. New York: McGraw-Hill, 1960.

Niskanen, William A. *Bureaucracy: Servant or Master?* London: The Institute of Economic Affairs, 1973.

Rosenthal, Howard. "Institutional Structure of School Finance Elections." Washington, D.C.: National Institute of Education, 1980. ED 203 477.

Strayer, George, and Haig, Robert. *Financing of Education in the State of New York.* New York: MacMillan, 1923.

Sugarman, Stephen D. "The Current System of Financing Public Education in California." In *Equality of Educational Opportunities*, edited by Guilbert C. Hentschke, pp. 17–45. Denver: Department of Education, 1972.

Talbot, Walter. "Utah's School Finance Program." In *Financing Educational Opportunity*, edited by Guilbert C. Hentschke, pp. 57–82. Denver: Department of Education, 1973.

Supplementary Reading

Barkin, E., and Hettich, W. "The Elementary and Secondary Education Act: A Distributional Analysis." ERIC, no. ED022244, 1969.

Harris, Marshall A. "Description and Analysis of the Process and Methodology of a School Finance Study in Florida." ERIC, no. ED084698, 1974.

Keyserling, Leon H. "Achieving Nationwide Educational Excellence. A Ten Year Plan to Save the Schools." ERIC, no. ED033879, 1970.

Lee, Robert D., Jr., and Johnson, Ronald W. *Public Budgeting Systems.* Baltimore: University Park Press, 1973.

5

Fiscal Strain in Public Schools

with John Yagielski

•

Overview

This chapter is an extension of the discussions in chapters 2, 3, and 4 but focuses solely on public schools. In chapter 2 we described the budget-maximizing incentives of public school officials. In chapter 3 we described the extensive regulatory environment that constrains public school managers as they seek to plan and control their organizations. And in chapter 4 we observed how public school managers pursue revenue largely by promising a set of activities and outcomes in return for a budget allocation. In this chapter we examine the combined implications of these discussions when public school administrators operate in districts experiencing fiscal strain.

We open the chapter with a definition and discussion of fiscal strain, emphasizing, as we have in earlier chapters, how behavior results from the interaction of preference functions and rights, represented in this instance by budgetary constraints. We then discuss the three major causes of fiscal strain: enrollment decline, price increases, and imposed changes in the mix of resources. (A fourth cause of fiscal strain, reductions in the budget, decreases the level of discretionary income available to the public school administrator. This has the same effect as the three factors we focus on, and it rarely occurs in practice.)

In appendix 5.1 we portray how the process of adjusting to fiscal strain affects curricular offerings in the public high school and how these school offerings are modified through school closings. In each section of this chapter we see the public school administrator as a budget maximizer who over the years faces fiscal strain: the administrator must make decisions, the results of which are less preferable to those of the previous period.

• • •

Definition of Fiscal Strain

Few issues have captured the attention of educators more than those regarding retrenchment in public school districts. Educators have been forced to deal with the statistics of projecting school enrollments, the economics of declining enrollments, facility closings, staff reductions, and the use of surplus space (see Stefonek 1979). Efforts to gain greater understanding of retrenchment have proceeded along many lines, covering such diverse topics as the study of school district policymaking (Nolte 1976), the analysis of enrollment changes on operating costs (Hentschke 1977), changes in service levels, the impact of inflation, reductions in course offerings, school closing, administrator behavior, and teacher mobility (see Zerchykov, Heleen, and Weaver 1982; Zerchykov and Weaver 1983). Despite the apparent variety of subject matter, two phenomena are implicit in each study: (1) conditions over which district decision makers have no direct control change in such a way as to reduce the decision makers' discretion; and (2) the "decision alternatives" (choices available to district decision makers) that remain are, as a group, less preferable than those that were available in the recent past. District decision makers are forced to choose among progressively less preferable alternatives. We will use these two phenomena as a basis for our definition of fiscal strain.

The mechanism that enforces these choices is the balancing equation of revenues and expenditures, that is, the budget. It is not that districts are legally prohibited from engaging in once-legal activities; rather, districts are financially prohibited from engaging in once-affordable activities. This can happen in one or more of three major ways: (1) changes in the volume of students, (2) changes in the prices of goods and services, often called *inputs* or *resources*, and (3) changes in the manner in which inputs are combined for service. To understand why this is so, we need to understand how public school administrators act as consumers of education inputs, that is, how their behavior results from the interaction between preference functions and budget constraints.

School Boards and Superintendents—Decision Makers With Preferences

The school board and superintendent make the major decisions that affect how resources are allocated in a school district. These decisions are varied and include how much revenue to secure through tax levies, how large a budget should be, what clauses to approve in a contract, whether to keep a school open, and what purchases to authorize. Before arriving at a decision, these district-level decision makers consider a range of alternatives during their deliberations. They hold hearings, receive and give tentative opinions, analyze data, and ultimately take votes. They face fiscal strain when all the alternatives they currently face are, as a group, less preferable than the alternatives they faced in the immediate past. Consider the hypothetical example of the school board that had to approve a district budget that was identical in *all* respects to the previous year's budget with one exception—fuel oil had doubled in price. In this case we know that this year's set of choices is less preferable than last year's set of choices, because our hypothetical school board would avoid paying more for fuel if it could.

The preferences of these decision makers play a major role in defining and explaining fiscal strain. School boards and superintendents do not consider alternatives without at the same time evaluating their own preferences. In fact, most of the testimony and acrimony surrounding budget proposals, school-closing proposals, and contract proposals reflect the facts that individuals have preferences and that those preferences vary from individual to individual.

When district decision makers vote on budgets, school closings, and the like, they are expressing preferences. In particular, they are buying preferred goods and services, assembling them in preferred combinations, and using them to provide schooling in their district. Although not purchased simultaneously, the goods and services purchased by these decision makers are the most preferred, *given what they perceive are the available options*. In the purchasing process they "buy" teachers at a specified level of compensation, put them into classes of specified sizes and compositions, hire administrators for a specified number of school buildings, approve a specified array of courses, and so on. In all instances school boards and superintendents choose among alternative purchases. Decision makers choose because they have to. The mechanism that forces these choices is the balancing equation of revenues and expenditures, that is, the amount of money that can be used to purchase these inputs is limited by the amount of revenues.

In most instances the district decision maker would obtain as many inputs as possible (to a point), but is prohibited by a budget constraint. The budget constraint determines the level at which the decision maker can consume goods and services for schooling, but it does not determine the specific mix of goods and services. For a given budget constraint, district decision makers decide on the combination of schooling inputs that maximizes their collective preferences. They do this by evaluating their choices and purchasing the set of inputs that gives them the greatest overall satisfaction (or which most reduces dissatisfaction) *and* is equal to but not greater than their budget constraint.

School Boards and Superintendents Behave Like Consumers

District decision makers behave like "household decision makers," or consumers, who think about whether to buy a new car, pay off old bills, insulate the house, go on a vacation, add to savings, take in a boarder, and so on. The alternatives considered at any one time are usually not comprehensive, nor are they of equal financial magnitude or consequence, and the relative importance or utility of each alternative to the individual is often difficult for him or her to articulate. Nevertheless, decisions do get made somehow, and the preferences of the decision maker determine what decisions are made.

Viewing the educational decision maker as a consumer of schooling inputs implies several characteristics of decision making in school districts. First, because their desires are, for all practical purposes, unlimited and because consumption is constrained by budgets, the preferences of the decision makers are revealed by their behavior. Rather than having to ask them what they prefer, we can observe their consumer behavior. In particular we can see what they are "willing" to give up in order to gain additional units of the preferred input. The arguments put forth for closing a school building, for example, are often portrayed in terms of this "opportunity cost," for example, the instructional programs that would have to be eliminated in order to pay for keeping the school open.

Second, like other consumers, educational decision makers have what economists call "diminishing marginal utility," which simply means that the satisfaction (utility) that results from purchasing one unit of a good or service is greater than the satisfaction resulting from purchasing the second (marginal) unit of that good or service. For decision makers this means that the more they consume of one input, all other things being equal, the less they value an additional increment of that input. For example, getting one set of new band uniforms for $\$X$ will give the decision maker a certain amount of satisfaction. Getting two new sets of band uniforms (one for home games and one for away games) at $\$2X$ will not give the district-level decision maker twice the satisfaction.

Third, the consumer analogy suggests a general cause and description of fiscal strain in school districts. Budgets always constrain, that is, no amount of money is enough, but the negative effects are greater under some circumstances than others. A budget constraint that permits increasing levels of consumption is preferred to one in which the level of consumption is merely maintained; and, one in which the current level of consumption is maintained is preferable to one that forces a reduced level of consumption. *Fiscal strain in school districts occurs when district-level decision makers are forced to purchase sets of schooling inputs in the near future that are less preferred than the current set of inputs.*

Causes of Fiscal Strain

At first glance it may appear that there are many different causes of fiscal strain in school districts, if only because district decision makers face a large number of choices. As we have defined it, however, fiscal strain can emanate from one or more of only four general causes: changes in enrollment levels; changes in the prices of schooling inputs; changes in the way in which inputs are combined for schooling (changes in the set of inputs); and changes in the budget constraint.

Fiscal Strain Through Enrollment Decline

Consider first the widely documented relationships between enrollment decline and fiscal strain. Four major effects of enrollment declines cause fiscal strain: increasing fixed costs per pupil, declining staff-to-pupil ratios, average salary bracket increase, and district per-pupil wealth bracket increase. Each focuses on a different manifestation of the fact that, in the short run, enrollment changes "drive" both expenditures and revenues in school districts. The first three drive up costs facing the district, while the last one acts to drive down state revenues. In order to provide a common basis for discussion, a brief explanation of each cause follows.

As enrollments decline, the fixed costs per pupil increase, everything else being equal. Many costs of schooling are not totally variable. When a district's enrollment changes from four hundred to three hundred, each of the remaining students "carries" a little more of, for example, the superintendent's salary, because that fixed cost is distributed among fewer students. Fixed costs per pupil, and hence total costs per pupil, go up when enrollments decline. Though widely acknowledged, few studies have attempted to derive fixed-variable cost ratios for individual districts. The declining staff-to-pupil ratio effect is similar to the fixed-variable one. For example, if a district with four hundred pupils and one teacher for each of twelve grades loses one student in each grade (for a total enrollment of 388 students), it cannot very well let a teacher go without combining grades in a classroom. The net effect is a reduction in teacher-to-pupil ratios from 1:33.3 to 1:32.3.

As seniority rules force younger, less expensive, teachers out of schools (or at least reduce their rate of entry), the average age and expense of staff increase disproportionately. This results in a higher average teacher salary, which is determined by the salary schedule.

At the same time the first three factors are at work driving up costs, the fourth factor (district wealth bracket creep) is driving down revenue. School districts across the United States receive about one-half of their operating revenues from state and federal governments. This aid is awarded largely on the basis of the number of children per district (counted either as enrolled in school or as attending). Consequently, with fewer pupils the district receives less total financial assistance. In some instances this aid is further reduced because the district appears to be wealthier and hence deserving of less state financial aid. Districts with low amounts of property wealth per pupil usually receive more aid than districts of the same size with greater property wealth per pupil because state governments attempt to equalize revenues available to "rich" and "poor" districts. Because most enrollment-based aid formulas are based on average rather than on marginal (additional) cost concepts, districts that lose enrollment must retrench, despite the fact that retrenchment is not intended by state-level decision makers when they reduce state aid to the districts.

These familiar occurrences bring about fiscal strain in two ways. First, because of the decrease in state revenues resulting from the loss of enrollments, the budget is reduced (or not increased as much as it would otherwise be with no enrollment loss). Because of the reduced budget, district decision makers are forced to consume inputs at a lower level. Second, they must also acquire a less-preferred set of inputs because many of the inputs are consolidated, that is, they cannot be sold or acquired in part. Although buildings, computers, and central office staff are obvious examples of consolidated inputs, it is even difficult to reduce some teaching staff in proportion to enrollment reductions. The net result is that district decision makers have to settle for a less-preferred set of inputs. They are consuming at a lower level and are forced to overconsume inputs that cannot be divided.

Fiscal Strain Through Price Increases

Increases in prices cause fiscal strain because, without a corresponding increase in the budget, district decision makers are forced to consume lower quantities of inputs. Although all prices are rising (including budget amounts), some prices are rising faster than other prices or budget levels are. The most striking examples in school districts include fuel and health insurance costs and teachers' salaries. (Teachers' salaries are included here because of the compound effect of wage settlements and an aging work force.) Fiscal strain is caused through price increases in two ways. First, attempts are made to reduce consumption of those inputs whose prices have risen most dramatically. (The utility to the decision maker of consuming those inputs is intimately associated with their opportunity costs, that is, their value compared with that of the other inputs that could not be purchased). Second, not all of the reduction falls on the disproportionately high-priced inputs, and consumption of other inputs is also reduced. Declining marginal utility works in reverse here: the utility of the last unit of an input foregone or sold off is less than the utility attached to those not yet foregone or sold off. It hurts more to forego each additional increment of an input. Cutting back energy consumption by 10 percent is easier the first time than is the second cutback of 10 percent. As a result, consumption of other inputs will be reduced often before an input already reduced is reduced again.

Fiscal Strain Through Changes in the Mix of Inputs of Resources

If changes in the input mix are forced legislatively by other than local decision makers without a corresponding increase in the budget, district decision makers are (in this case by definition) forced to shift to a less-preferred set of inputs. Examples include passage of P.L. 94–142, which mandates the mix of resources to be used in instructing children with learning difficulties. Various statutes and court decisions influence districts in this way; that is, they cause the district to shift, from acquiring preferred to less-preferred mixes of inputs, which includes inputs related not only to instructional programs but also to personnel practices, student rights, building requirements, and support services.

Fiscal Strain Through Reductions in the Budget

Various causes can force a reduction in the budget *independent* of the three causes discussed above. The two most obvious are an absolute reduction in the amount of state aid granted per pupil and an absolute reduction in the amount of local property tax revenue. The impact of these reductions on the budget will be reflected in decreased expenditures, which is the focus of this chapter. Hence, the impact of the first three factors is our major concern.

The three causes of fiscal strain emanate from different sources and are reflected differently as they affect the decision-making behavior of district administrators (summarized in exhibit 5.1). They do, however, have the same type of impact on school district decision makers: in each case decision makers are forced to purchase less-preferred sets of inputs; in other words, much of what administrators do is to make trade-offs among things (inputs) they desire (preferences). They try to make those trade-offs that they think are "best."

How Causes of Fiscal Strain Interact

It is common in many school districts for educational administrators to understand and to communicate the impact of demographic changes on the operation of their school districts. Yet, in reality, demographic changes are not the only (and perhaps not even the major) factors affecting operating costs. Other important factors include changes in negotiated labor settlements, inflation, fluctuating amounts of state level and other aid, local tax rates, and "resource mixes" reflected in class size, building use, and the like.

Exhibit 5.1
Fiscal Strain Resulting in Consuming Less-Preferred Sets of Inputs

How Caused	How Reflected
1. Enrollment declines	a. — Budget constraint reduced b. — Disproportionately greater reductions in variable costs c. — Disproportionately fewer reductions in fixed costs
2. Price increases	a. — Reduced quantity of inputs purchased, especially of more costly inputs
3. Legislation external to district	a. — Forced changed in input mix

These too are fluid factors that must be considered simultaneously when estimating the district's fiscal future, in particular as reflected in local tax rates. All of these factors are "blended" in a very specific way here, and that special blending models the general ways these factors interrelate.

The model is presented like a recipe. It has a list of basic "ingredients" (data) followed by a set of "cooking instructions" (data relationships). The ingredients, or data, include: (1) cost-to-volume relationships for major items of expenditures, (2) estimates of change in enrollment over the next several years, (3) estimates of changes in the costs of groups of items due to inflation or contractual agreements, (4) estimates of changes in nonlocal revenues, and (5) estimates of changes in assessed valuation of local property. The "cooking" of these five ingredients requires six basic operations:

Step 1. Determine short-run, fixed, and variable cost elements. The expenses of operating any enterprise may be divided into two groups: (1) those that do not vary within a relevant range of changes in activity (fixed costs), and (2) those that vary in direct proportion to the volume of operations. Together these costs describe how total costs vary with changes in volume (see exhibit 5.2). If average unit costs (in our case, per-pupil costs) are considered rather than total costs, the situation is reversed: the fixed costs are variable when expressed as unit or average costs (exhibit 5.3); this is so because a portion of total costs will rise as enrollment declines.

Costs are not inherently fixed or variable. They acquire these characteristics as a result of managerial decisions. Consequently, any discussion of the

Exhibit 5.2

Short-Run Total Cost Variation with Respect to a Relevant Range of Volume

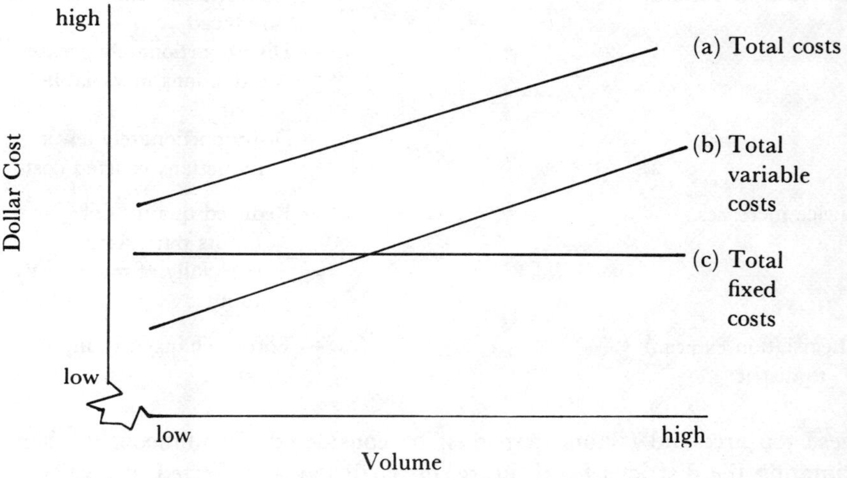

Exhibit 5.3

Short-Run Average Unit Costs Variation with Respect to a Relevant Range of Volume

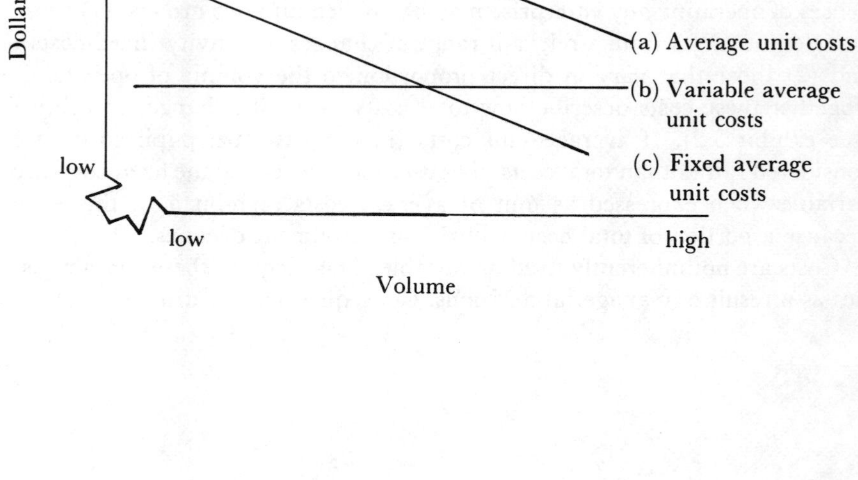

short-run costs of a school district must incorporate a rather definitive statement of which costs management considers fixed, and which it considers variable.

Some fixed costs may be relatively "pure" in that they will continue regardless of current management policy or level of enrollment (for example, capital financing costs, certain insurance expenses, and executive salary expenses). Other fixed costs may be determined by management policy or union contract (for example, supervisory salary expenses, building management expenses, and certain utility costs). These costs are fixed in the sense that, based on present managerial policy as expressed in the current budget, these costs will not change with limited variations in the volume of operations.

Variable costs may include such items as direct labor and certain supplies. These costs will vary as some function of increasing and decreasing enrollments. However, this will occur only when district decision makers establish and enforce procedures that will appropriately affect the size of the labor force in relation to the size of student enrollment.

The concept of fixed versus variable cost elements, then, is based as much on managerial policy as it is on accountants' inferences. The first step to take in estimating the impact of enrollment decline on costs is to determine how certain costs vary with volume (ingredient one in the model). An example of how costs can be classified and tied to volume is shown in exhibit 5.4.

In this particular district, costs were aggregated into eleven "classifications," two of which were considered "pure" and fixed. The other nine varied with different ranges of enrollment. The rates of changes in these cost classifications are used to construct the short-run *total* cost relationships of the district (portrayed in exhibit 5.5). Exhibit 5.6 portrays the short-run *unit* cost relationships facing the district over a relevant range of enrollment.

Step 2. Construct the short-run cost relationships that will face the district over the next several years. In step 1 the purpose was to develop a general relationship between costs and uniform changes in volume. In order to get a "pure" picture of this relationship, arbitrary but uniform changes in enrollments were used (+1 percent, +2 percent, and so on). For the same reason, it was assumed that the current mix of students remained constant.

Step 2 involves substituting estimates of changes in enrollment actually facing the district over the next three years (ingredient two in the model). An example of this is shown in exhibit 5.7. In that example, overall enrollment in the district declines from the previous year at rates of about 5 percent, 2.4 percent, and 1.4 percent respectively. The declines in total costs facing the district over this same period are about 0.2 percent, 1.1 percent, and 0.9 percent respectively in terms of the current year's dollars.

However, per-pupil costs occurring in this same period are expected to increase by 3.8 percent, 1.3 percent, and 0.5 percent, again holding every-

Exhibit 5.4

Calculation of Basic Ratio Formula Based on 1976–77 Cost Structure ($ in thousands)

Cost Determinants	Other Costs ($)	Salaries ($)	Total ($)	Students per Buildings	Teachers	Basic Ratio Formula
Elementary—Ratio 1/27	347	1,238	5,585	6,391	238	$23.5/27 students
—Building Staff	1,955	573	2,528	13		$194.5/building
Jr. High—Ratio 1/19	2,068	570	2,638	2,085	113	$23.2/19 students
—Building Staff	412	129	541	3		$182.2/building
Sr. High—Ratio 1/19	4,117	1,296	5,413	4,286	227	$23.8/19 students
—Building Staff	1,022	437	1,459	3		$486.4/building
Guidance—Ratio 1/350	431	128	559	6,371	18	$31.1/350 students
Transportation	521	691	1,212	13,213		$9.2/100 students
Facilities	1,371	1,635	3,006	20		$150.3/facility
Educational Operations	1,208	884	2,092			Fixed
District Operations	1,018	3,678	4,696			Fixed
Operating Cost	18,468	11,261	29,729			
Nonoperating Costs	166	1,219	1,385			
Total Budget	18,634	12,480	31,114			
	(60%)	(40%)				

Exhibit 5.5

Short-Run Total Cost Relationships Facing the District

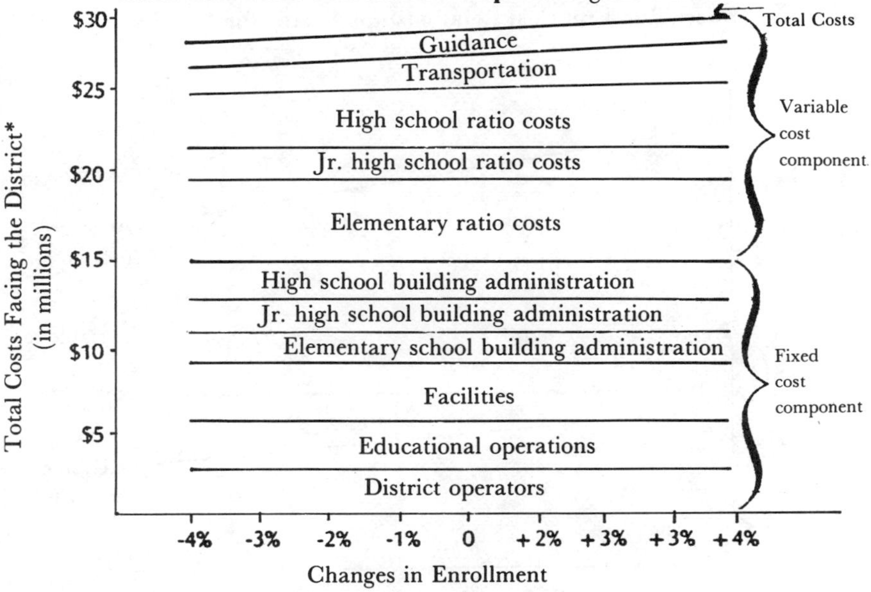

*All costs are stacked on top of one another; total costs are read as the top variable cost line.

thing else constant. While this estimate is by itself important, it does not convey the reality of the problem: other important factors will also be changing at the same time. These factors and the effects of inflation need to be included in the estimates.

Step 3. Incorporate estimates of change in expenditures due to inflation and contractual settlements. Constant dollar estimates must be adjusted to reflect the impact of inflation in order to be relevant for district decision makers. However, the cost classifications most appropriate for fixed-variable analysis may not be as appropriate for estimating inflation effects. Their criteria for grouping are different. Costs should be accumulated on the basis of similarity of estimated effects. Hence, grouping costs into labor versus nonlabor categories, as in this example, may be more useful when estimating inflation effects.

It would be possible to determine the impact of new wage settlements using a single estimate. The same could be done to estimate the effect of inflation on nonlabor costs. (Some administrators may be more comfortable with this approach.)

Often, administrators wish to incorporate a range of possible estimates into a single "expected" value. For example, labor settlements could result in

Exhibit 5.6

Short-Run Unit Cost Relationships Facing the District

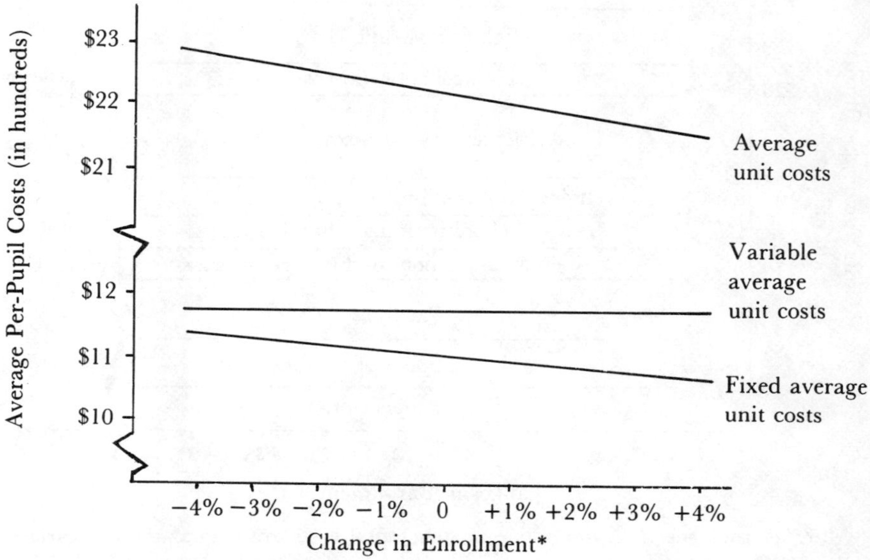

*Assumes uniform mix of grade levels.

a 4 percent increase in the average salary of personnel (an optimistic estimate). On the other hand, a more expensive contract might result in an annual 10 percent salary increase. It is possible to incorporate these and other possible outcomes into a single expected value by specifying the probability of occurrence of each possible outcome. (The probabilities of occurrence should add up to 1.00, which means that all possible outcomes have been considered.)

Examples of three separate estimates of increase in labor and nonlabor costs are illustrated in exhibit 5.8. Labor costs are estimated to increase between 4 percent and 10 percent; each has a 20 percent chance of occurring. (The likely increase in labor cost is 7 percent, with a 60 percent chance of occurring.) Nonlabor costs are estimated to increase 10 percent, 8 percent, and 6 percent. These increases have the probabilities of occurrence of 20 percent, 60 percent, and 20 percent respectively. (These estimated increases and probabilities of occurrence compose variable 3.)

The actual process of projecting expenditures involves two parts. First, adjust labor and nonlabor costs to reflect changes in enrollment. (These are represented in exhibit 5.8 as reductions in total cost in the column labeled "less reduction per ratio formula.") Second, that reduced amount is then

Exhibit 5.7
Unit Costs Facing the District Over the Next Three Years (current dollars)

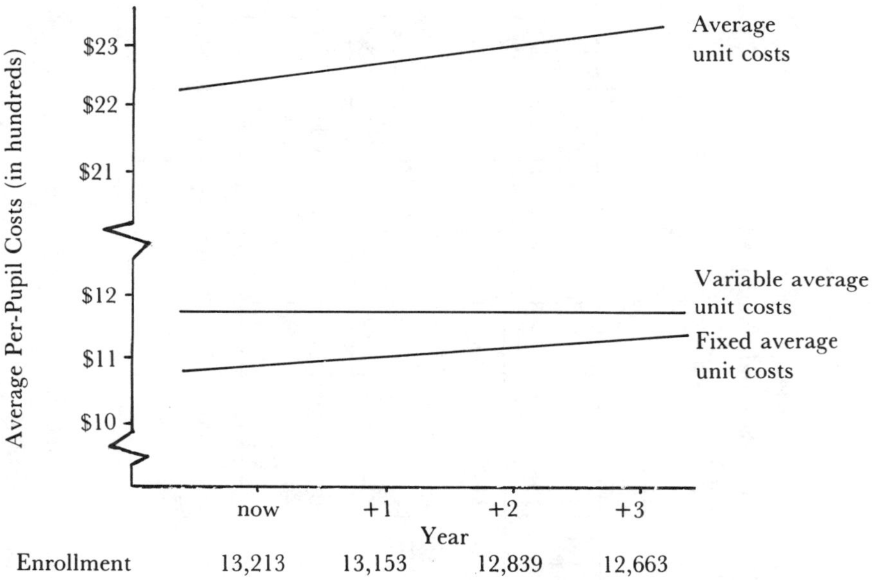

adjusted back up to reflect the effects of inflation and contracts. The resulting projected expenditures, or expected values, are simply the estimated changes weighted by the probabilities of occurrence.

The process is then repeated for the second and third planning years. Notice that between planning years, the reductions subtracted from each possible occurrence are placed in the corresponding box for the following year. For example, between planning year 1 and planning year 2, $204,000 is subtracted from the "pessimistic planning year 1 salaries" figure of $20,430,000, and the remaining $20,226,000 is placed in the "pessimistic planning year 2 salaries" box.

Step 4. Estimate the impact of changes in nonproperty tax revenue (exhibit 5.9). Using much the same general approach described in step 3, estimates of revenue from nonproperty tax sources can be made (variable 4 in the model). In this particular example all changes in state aid estimates are negative or zero. Other revenues are expected to change between minus 5 percent and plus 2 percent over the next three years. (The "fund balance" figure represents carryover money from the previous year, which would be used to offset taxes.)

Exhibit 5.8

Estimated Changes in Expenditures for Labor and Nonlabor Inputs
(in thousands)

	Current	Year +1					Year +2					Year +3				
	Base	Less reduction per ratio formula	Pessimistic	Most likely	Optimistic	Expected value	Less reduction per ratio formula	Pessimistic	Most likely	Optimistic	Expected value	Less reduction per ratio formula	Pessimistic	Most likely	Optimistic	Expected value
Assigned probability			0.2	0.6	0.2			0.2	0.6	0.2			0.2	0.6	0.2	
Salaries																
Base	$18,630	−$96	$18,534	$18,534	$18,534		−$204	$20,226	$19,666	$19,106		$166	$22,084	$20,874	$18,940	
Estimated change			+ 10%	+ 4%	+ 7%			+ 10%	+ 7%	+ 4%			+ 10%	+ 7%	+ 4%	
Total projected			20,430	19,310	19,870	$19,870		22,250	21,040	19,870	$21,050		24,290	22,340	19,700	$22,200
Other Costs																
Base	$12,480	−$64	$12,416	$12,416	$12,416		−$136	$13,484	$13,234	$12,984		−$111	$14,729	$14,175	$13,649	
Estimated change			+ 10%	+ 6%	+ 8%			+ 10%	+ 8%	+ 6%			+ 10%	+ 8%	+ 6%	
Total projected			13,620			$13,370		14,830	14,290	13,760	$14,290		16,200	15,320	14,470	$15,320
Projected																
Expenditures	$31,110		$34,050	$33,240	$32,480	$33,240		$37,080	$35,330	$33,630	$35,340		$40,490	$37,660	$34,170	$37,520
Change from prior year			+ 9%	+ 7%	+ 4%	+ 7%		+ 9%	+ 6%	+ 4%	+ 6%		+ 9%	+ 7%	+ 2%	+ 6%

Exhibit 5.9
Estimated Changes in Revenue and Required Tax Levy
(in thousands)

	Current	Year +1				Year +2				Year +3			
	Base	Pessimistic	Most likely	Optimistic	Expected value	Pessimistic	Most likely	Optimistic	Expected value	Pessimistic	Most likely	Optimistic	Expected value
Assigned Probability		0.2	0.6	0.2		0.2	0.6	0.2		0.2	0.6	0.2	
State Aid													
Estimated change	$11,600	−17%	−10%	−5%		−5%	0%	0%		−5%	0%	0%	
Total projected		$9,630	$10,440	$11,020	$10,390	$9,150	$10,440	$11,020	$10,300	$7,699	$10,440	$11,020	$10,300
Other Revenue													
Estimated change	$2,200	−5%	0%	−2%		−5%	0%	2%		−5%	0%	+2%	
Total projected		$2,090	$2,200	$2,240	$2,180	$2,000	$2,200	$2,280	$2,170	$1,900	$2,200	$2,320	$2,160
Fund Balance	$1,500	$690	$690	$690	$690	–	–	–	–	–	–	–	–
Req. Tax Levy	$16,500	$21,640	$19,910	$18,480	$19,980	$25,930	$22,690	$20,330	$22,870	$28,789	$25,020	$20,830	$25,060
Change from prior year		+31%	+21%	+12%	+21%	+20%	+14%	+10%	+14%	+15%	+10%	+2%	+10%
Total Revenue	$31,800	$34,050	$33,240	$32,430	$33,240	$37,080	$35,330	$33,630	$35,340	$40,490	$37,660	$34,170	$37,520
Assessed Valuation													
Estimated change	$180,000	+ 2%	+ 3%	+ 4%		+ 2%	+ 3%	+ 4%		+ 2%	+ 3%	+ 4%	
Total projected		$183,600	$185,400	$187,200	$185,400	$187,300	$19,100	$194,690	$191,000	$191,000	$196,730	$202,500	$196,730
Tax/$ Valuation	$491.67	$117.86	$107.39	$98.72	$107.77	$138.44	$104.42	$119.74	$119.74	$156.49	$127.18	$102.86	$127.38
Change from prior year		+29%	+17%	+8%	+18%	+17%	+11%	+6%	+11%	+13%	+7%	−2%	+6%

Step 5. Estimate necessary changes in property tax revenues and rates. At this stage of the process we want to be able to see what the net effect of all the previous changes is likely to be on the tax levy. (We are viewing the local property tax as the revenue source that "fills in" the gap between planned expenditures and other sources of revenue.) The tax levy is calculated by subtracting the estimates of state aid and other revenue from projected expenditures. Total revenue equals total expenditures. In this example, the tax levy must yield at least 21 percent more revenue in the next year despite a nearly 1 percent decline in enrollment(!).

Some of this increase will be offset by increases in assessed valuation. Estimated changes in assessed valuation are calculated by incorporating the three values into one expected value (variable 5 in the model). Having incorporated these estimates into the model, we can now proceed to estimate the required changes in the local property tax rate. As shown in exhibit 5.9, the tax rate would have to be increased by 18 percent, 11 percent, and 6 percent respectively over the next three years, if all of our assumed changes come true.

Step 6. Adjust as necessary. If the combined impact of enrollment changes and the other factors on local tax rates is acceptable, and if no changes in variable cost ratios is desired, the analysis is complete. If this is not so, the model is put to work to determine the appropriate adjustments necessary to bring tax rates into an acceptable range. This was the case with the school district in our example.

Expenditures can be reduced by reducing the amounts of fixed costs or by reducing the variable cost ratio. Strategies for reducing costs are not discussed here. This involves concerted effort at the negotiations table, in the board room, and among district personnel. However, cost reduction alternatives can be incorporated into the model, and their effect can be assessed.

The district in our example has used the model to evaluate a wide range of cost-reduction alternatives. The impact of one cost-reduction alternative on per-pupil costs is portrayed in exhibit 5.10. The alternative involves increasing instructional ratios by one each and increasing the counseling ratio by fifty. Although the direction of unit costs after adjustment continues to rise as enrollment falls, the overall level of cost has been greatly reduced. These new ratios are fed back into the projected expenditure and revenue calculations shown in exhibits 5.8 and 5.9.

Under the existing ratios, we subtracted $96,000 in expenditures for personnel due to enrollment decline between the current year and planning year 1 (see exhibit 5.8). Under the new ratios of cost reduction, $674,000 would be subtracted instead. Hence, in planning year 1 the base salary figure would be $17,956,000 rather than $18,534,000. That change would work its way down through the projected expenditure calculations and would end up reducing the percentage change in local tax expenditure calculations, which

Exhibit 5.10
Unit Costs with Existing (—) and Adjusted (---) Inputs
(1976–77 dollars)

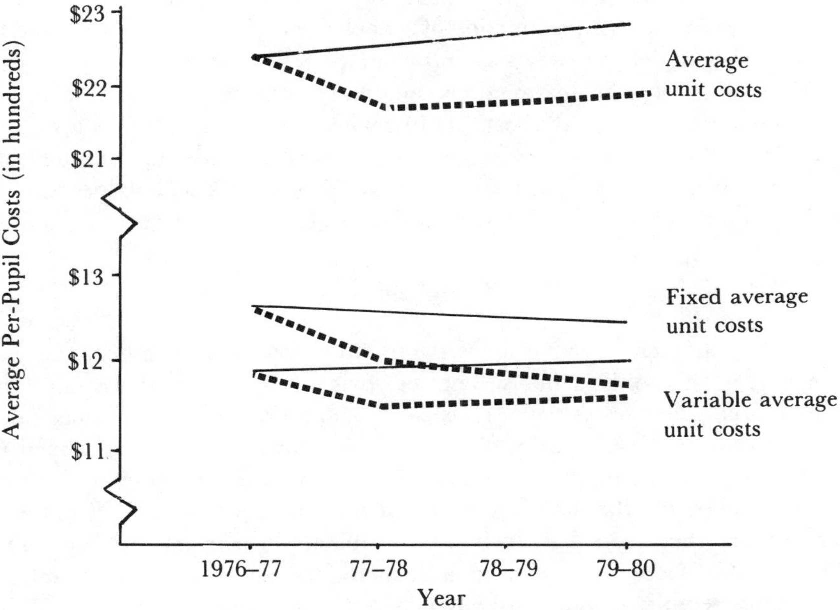

in turn would reduce the percentage change in local tax effort. Other cost-reduction alternatives would be worked through the model in the same way.

Note

The models discussed at the end of this chapter and in the appendix suggest some ways that major trade-offs are made by school district decision makers. A few caveats should be added here about them. First, models do not always completely translate from one setting to another because each of us has a slightly different sense of "reality," including what the most important pieces of that reality are. It is not only possible but probable that modifications in these (or any other) models would be required for them to be useful in a given school district.

Second, these models are designed to portray major trade-offs for the decision makers in an "objective" and "rational," even "logical," format. This is *not* to suggest that models are neutral. On the contrary, the models you choose and the variables you select and include in the models both define the problem at hand and capture the solution choices. The model in the appendix, for example, is formulated to make people aware of some of the trade-offs of keeping all high schools in the district open. It is more likely to be used by individuals who are more concerned with curricular erosion than with neighborhood schools, although both concepts are implicit in the model. (Someone with the opposite set of preferences would be more inclined to develop models that attempt to portray, say, student and parent disaffection with a school as a positive function of school size and distance from home to the school.) Models are weapons in debate as well as tools for inquiry.

Third, models indicate directions but do not build roads. This is merely a way of pointing out that the costs of *carrying out* alternative decisions are often overlooked in models, including the ones discussed in this chapter. To portray how much of the curriculum we save by closing a school does not tell us how much trouble it will cost us to implement such a decision.

Conclusion

In this chapter we have focused our attention entirely on managerial behavior in the public schools. The set of rights in that sector is such that demographic changes *determine* physical capacities of districts to house (and thus serve) various quantities of students. As enrollments have declined in many school districts, administrators have had to make trade-offs among preferred activities that have resulted in shrinking district capacity (just as in other times they have had to increase capacity as enrollments increase). Their major focus of attention is reducing capacity, not, for example, increasing recruiting and marketing in order to maintain capacity. That strategy is much more in the domain of school administrators in the private sectors.

Appendix 5.1: Curricular Implications of Fiscal Strain*

One of the major "hidden" effects of retrenchment is on the curriculum itself, especially at the high school level. Beneath the general problematic decisions associated with changing tax rates, staffing ratios, and so on are those associated with adapting these changes into the curricular offerings in the schools. Unfortunately, the impact of decline on the curriculum is sometimes not clearly understood or simply not presented because it is not strictly a financial issue. In fact, however, the breadth and depth of curricular offerings are greatly affected by changes in a *school's enrollment* and hence by decisions on how school programs will be housed (see Dembowski and

---

*I wish to acknowledge here my indebtedness to the staff of the Sequoia Union High School District (Redwood City, California) for access to their records from which this appendix was developed.

Gay 1980). Consider, for example, the reductions in curriculum over the last several years in the five high schools of one California school district that was losing enrollments (exhibit 5.11). It is hard to argue in these instances that the quality of the curriculum has been maintained over the last several years.

The purpose of the model presented here is to formulate relationships between decisions about curricular offerings and school closings at the high school level. We are more concerned here with the *long-run* effects on curriculum of the closing of schools (or of leaving them open) than with the effects on the costs of administering or maintaining buildings.

Specifically, we seek to provide initial answers to the following questions. First, what will be the likely effect on your high school curriculum of keeping all high schools open and revising your curriculum as necessary? Second, what will be the likely effect on your high school curriculum of closing one or more high schools? Although easy to ask, both questions require answers to prior questions, most of which are associated with assumptions about probable changes in curriculum. Curricular offerings in high schools are constantly evolving due to a variety of forces including attempts to improve or upgrade the curriculum, availability of staff, and student demand. This is not a treatise on curriculum development; rather it is merely a statement that one of the "givens" in this model is some determination about current course offerings regarding their future utility and feasibility and whether they can be reasonably modified. The major ingredients in this model include both current curricular offerings and proposed changes, enrollment changes, staffing ratios, and numbers and capacities of buildings.

Step 1. Determine the changes possible in the high school curriculum that would reduce staff requirements yet provide a minimum course framework for an average high school in your district. One of the political liabilities associated with working on school-based problems and models is the readiness of all of us to begin early to make comparisons about the characteristics of specific schools in a district. For example, School A may have a more academically oriented student body, program, and physical plant than School B. The leadership of School B, however, may be better than School A's. Although such comparisons must inevitably be made, every effort should be made to suppress comparative specifics at this stage, because the goal at this point is to evaluate and redesign the general high school curriculum.

The process of redesigning a high school curriculum is both difficult to undertake and to describe precisely. The general guidelines for those undertaking the redesign include: (1) comply with any major assumptions such as board policies; (2) costs should be no more than the present arrangement; (3) maintain, preserve, and possibly strengthen the program of instruction. Easy to say, but hard to do. In the following example, the district developed a hypothetical "average high school" whose program of instruction they redesigned. The school district has five regular high schools with an average

Exhibit 5.11

Courses Dropped in Five High Schools over the Last Seven Years

School A	*School B*	*School C*	*School D*	*School E*
Art Studio I, II	Animal Science	Crafts I	Fundamental Economics	Ethics and Logic
Consumer Economics	Floriculture	Fashion Merchandising	Drafting	A capella Choir
Retail Merchandising	Ornamental Horticulture	Ethics and Logic	East Asian Affairs	F.E.A.S.T.
Speech I	Speech I, II	Beginning Band	Business Law	Consumer Economics
Contemporary Writing	Intro. to Data Processing	Electronic Music	Business English	Fine Art
Textile Arts	Italian I-V	History of Films	Textile Arts	Figure Drawing
World Literature	Anthropology	Ilios	Retail Merchandising	Marketing
Child Development	History and Art	Reading-Typing	TV Production	Office Practice
Wood I, II	Choral I	Textile Arts	Child Development	Food, Facts, and You
Orchestra	Humanities in Three Cities	Harmony	AV Techniques	Life Styles
Solo Voice	Law Enforcement	Jewelry	Sculpture	Italian II
Choral I, II Advanced	Harmony	Fundamentals of Economics	Music Drama Workshop	French V
Harmony	Commercial Art I, II	Office Practice	Consumer Protection	Textile Arts
Medical Careers	Sculpture	Art*/Art Studio*/Photography*	Stage Band	AP Math
A.P. Biology	Art Studio	All Drafting Courses Combined	Orchestra	Art*/Commercial Art*/Lettering*/Painting*
Anthropology	Retail Merchandising	Shorthand I, II*	Harmony	Accounting I, II*
Black Studies	Foods II	Accounting I, II*	German III, IV	Shorthand I, II*
California Experience	Contemporary Writing	Drama II, III, IV*	Sociology	All Levels of Woods into One Course*
Ecology	Textile Arts	German III, IV*	Social Psychology	AP Biology**
Fine Arts	Boating Operations	French III, IV, V*	Japanese	Shorthand**
Office Practice	Drafting IV	Orchestra/Jazz Ensemble*	Crafts	
English S.O.L.	Home Mechanics	Yearbook I, II*	Sheet Metal	
Journalism	Motorcycle Operations I, II		Readings in the Content Area	
Latin			General Art	
Metals I, II				

Jazz Band I
Crafts
SAT Prep/English III
Foods I*
Creative Arts*/Guitar*
Yearbook**
Spanish Spanish IV/V**

Dance Production
Employment Readiness
Modern Media I, II
Orchestra
Guitar
Music-Drama Workshop
Piano I, II
Survival Skills/Living Skills
A capella
TV Production I, II
Stage Band
Fundamentals of Economics
Latin I, II, III
Business English
Mini-Science
Super Market*/Consumer Economics*
Journalism I, II, III, IV*
Journalism**
French III, IV, V**
German I, II**

Clothing I-V*
Wood II/Advanced Wood*
Metal II/Advanced Metal*
Italian I**

F.E.A.S.T.
Ceramics I, II*
All Machine Shop Courses*
Some ESL Classes**

*Combined with other courses
**May be dropped or combined next year

current enrollment of 1,750 students each. The average student took 5.6 classes (not including such nonclassroom assignments as student clerk, attendance assistant, and the like). The average class size was 28.6 excluding special education and other classes supported by project funds or special staff allotments. In this average high school the total number of class sections was 344 (1,750 ÷ 28.5 × 5.6).

Twelve general alternatives were developed and evaluated by the curriculum task force in this district. The alternatives and their evaluation are presented in exhibit 5.12. In the process of their deliberations, the curriculum task force started with the current program in their composite high school, and proceeded to "slim it down." There is no formula for achieving this; many trade-offs must be made. Exhibit 5.13 portrays a "straw vote" of the committee in the example district when it was nearly done with its work. At that point they had reduced their alternatives to consolidating courses, staggering courses, having teachers travel to different schools, and keeping the current courses in the basic curriculum.

Exhibit 5.12

Evaluating Alternatives to Current Curricular Organization

Alternatives to Current Curriculum Organization

If small-sized schools are considered to be desirable and worthy of preservation, then means must be found to present the optimum instructional program in a more economical way. The suggestions listed for alternative consideration comply with a few key priority assumptions. The alternatives suggested must not cost more than the present arrangement, could actually produce income, or could save money. The alternatives suggested maintain, preserve, and possibly strengthen the program of instruction.

1. Consolidate choral and instrumental classes and offer them at one or two locations only.
2. Increase lecture-type classes double- or three-fold and schedule them for large-area facilities (music or multi-use rooms).
3. Assign certain teachers to travel to more than one school so that specialized subject matter (e.g., advanced foreign language) could be offered.
4. Designate certain schools as specialized learning centers where only pertinent electives are offered (High School of Math/Science).
5. Combine adult education and high school student programs into the same classes.
6. Convert to community center schools where recreation department and social service rental income augments budgets. Lease unused classrooms to compatible community and private agencies.
7. Schedule significant numbers of elective offerings at community colleges.

8. Use Independent Study as an alternative to scheduled electives. These "courses-by-arrangement" could allow for higher student/teacher ratios.
9. Stagger school schedules and provide transportation so that electives could be consolidated at a few schools.
10. Convert elective offerings to a semester schedule so that more elective variety and less student time commitment are possible.
11. Reduce scope of electives to a few offerings to maintain cost-effective class sizes.
12. Deliberately consolidate electives so that several related subjects and levels are offered simultaneously in one classroom.

Advantages and Disadvantages of Alternative Suggestions

While some of the proposed alternatives may extend the life of some elective areas, only speculation is possible on the success of some approaches and the ramifications for the teacher workload of others.

Will students and parents in sufficient numbers accept the concept of a district orchestra, drama, or industrial arts program in lieu of their traditional school orchestra, drama, or industrial arts program? If not, offering these programs at one site, as opposed to five, could accelerate the demise of the program rather than prolong its life. Transportation problems and a lack of identity with the district program could discourage enrollment in a consolidated program. A survey that questions the receptiveness of parents and students to this proposal should be undertaken before courses are consolidated at one school.

Certain schools could be designated as specialised learning centers where only certain electives such as math-science are offered. Offering a narrow range of electives to a student body would ensure that classes in the specific areas could be kept filled. Students would be deprived, however, of the variety of courses that a true comprehensive high school offers.

Combining adult education with high school programs probably would boost the enrollment in electives. Some disagreement exists as to the desirability of combining adults with minors in the same classroom.

Leasing unused classrooms to compatible community and private agencies has met with mixed success in a nearby elementary district. While that district has avoided closing schools despite declining enrollment, it faces a financial crisis this spring because budgeted rental income may not materialize as a result of zoning and other legal difficulties.

Redesigning suitable courses to learning package or individual student contract formats could allow some courses in danger of being eliminated to survive. There would be some initial expense in developing the materials for such programs. The numbers in such programs would have to be kept at a manageable level if students were to receive adequate assistance and supervision.

One strategy curriculum planners use to preserve courses with declining numbers is to combine compatible courses in one room. Thus, French 2, 3, and 4 or Jewelry and Ceramics are taught simultaneously in one classroom. This increases the number of preparations for the teacher, however, and can decrease effective teaching.

Very few courses can be offered successfully in alternate years because continuity is often necessary to ensure the continuation of a program. Some courses require skills obtained from a more basic course, while other continue to attract numbers of students because of positive word-of-mouth. Removing the course from the curriculum for a year could seriously reduce student interest in the program. Some college requirements, however, might be staggered successfully.

Assigning teachers to two schools also has been proposed as a method of saving curriculum. Traveling teachers sometimes have difficulty maintaining continuity when moving from one campus to another. Under current contract provisions, classes are arranged so that teachers who travel do so on a preparation period, and those teachers are excused from supervising extracurricular activities at either school. This latter compensation rarely replaces the preparation time lost on a daily basis. Removing teachers from the extracurricular pool of teachers at a school places the increased burden of supervision on the steadily declining population of remaining teachers. While the enrollment of a school may decline, the demand for supervision of cocurricular activities may not necessarily experience a corresponding decline. This places an increased burden on the staff at a time when they find their number of course preparations increasing. Also, as a result of enrollment decline and the resulting reduction of course offerings, many teachers will be assigned to teach courses out of their area of expertise. Time-consuming, costly retraining may be necessary. These pressures could result in increased absenteeism stemming from anxiety and stress-induced illness.

Step 2. Project the number of class sections by departments for the composite high school. District enrollment projections are used here to derive the projected enrollments for the composite high school in the district over the next decade. In making the projections, a number of assumptions were made. First, projections in each academic department would drop in the same proportion during each projected three-year period as did the total enrollment. Second, the "minimum course framework" was to be offered, and courses listed that are not part of the minimum are shown below the dotted lines in exhibit 5.14. Third, as enrollments decline, students will increasingly have to settle for second choices in order to take a full schedule of classes. Courses will be offered during fewer and fewer periods and will be closed more rapidly and frequently due to maximum enrollment having been reached. Four, value judgments were made and noted that resulted in nonlinear, mechanistic projections. Sections were added, for example, to reduce scheduling problems such as academic singletons, to provide a richer variety of elective options, and to maintain some advanced academic or specialized sections. Five, where it becomes apparent that in order to staff the projected program in the composite high school, teachers would have to be "bought" over ratio to maintain the program in a particular year, the need is recorded in the plan.

The curricular projections of the composite high school for planning years three, six, and nine are presented in exhibit 5.15. These data are summarized by department in exhibit 5.16, including the number of sections over ratio that must be staffed. In the composite high school, the total number of sections would drop from 344 to 213 over the next decade. If no over-ratio teachers were permitted in the plan, the number of sections would drop to 196.

Step 3. Portray the trade-offs in the curriculum of closing one or more high schools. In general terms this can be done by contrasting the effects on average school enrollments of closing one or more schools. This is portrayed in Exhibit 5.17. In this example, the district would have to close one of its five high schools in the second planning year and another in the eighth planning year simply to maintain its current level of curricular offerings. Alternatively it could keep its five schools open and operate its "minimum acceptable" curriculum.

Earlier, in exhibit 5.11, we saw the effects of enrollment declines on the curriculum in five high schools. In the previous four years the average enrollments of these schools declined from 2,129 to 1,749, or a little less than 400 students per school. In about four years those schools are projected to lose a little over another 400 students per school—if all schools stay open. In the same set of five high schools we have portrayed the reductions required in the curriculum for keeping each school open over the next decade. The question, "Is it worth it?," is answered on an individual basis by comparing the "slimmed down" curriculum of the composite school with the current program in the five schools today. The reduction in offerings over the next decade will be at least as severe as those portrayed in exhibit 5.16.

Although space does not permit elaboration here, two other sets of data could also be used at this point to portray the curriculum trade-offs of school closings. The first deals with faculty "quality," by which we attempt to describe both the degree of "fit" between teacher and teaching assignment as well as working conditions conducive to "good" teaching. Under assumptions about the composite school when keeping all five schools open, closing one, and closing two, the following data could be developed, although with some difficulty: (1) number of sections taught by faculty not initially trained in that subject, (2) number of different subjects taught by each teacher, and (3) the number of sections in which combined subjects are taught.

The second set of data would attempt to measure student access to the curricular program. Elements would include the number of students who had all first choices in their program as well as the percentage of the average student's program that is not his or her first choice. All of these data take on meaning only when portrayed as trends (past compared to present, present compared to future).

Exhibit 5.13

"Straw Vote" of the Committee on Curriculum Reorganization

	Consolidation	Staggering Courses	Traveling Teachers	Maintain at Home School as Basic	Comments and Questions
Art					
Ceramics Jewelry Freehand Drawing Adv. Art Courses	Students not likely to travel to a school for Art only		Possible, but there are problems with prep. time & lab cleanup	Preferred if possible	Might be better to consolidate to a basic program at a home school
Business					
Accounting Business Law Business Math Shorthand Typing I Typing II/Word Proc. BEST Personal Typing					Certain basic Business courses desirable at each school—i.e. Typing I&II, BEST, perhaps others
English					
English I, II, III, IV English Skills English Lab English AS Program			Not feasible for basic curriculum		Basic to curriculum Should not be cut.

Drama		Elective areas need creative attention to save them.
Journalism		
Yearbook		
Reading		
Home Economics		
Child Development		
Clothing 1, 2, 3		
Foods		
Fashion		
Merchandising		
On Your Own		
Industrial Arts		
Auto		
Electronics		
Drafting 1, 2, 3		Drafting needed for engineering prerequisite at college
Metals 1, 2, 3		
Woods 1, 2, 3		
BIA – M & W		
Language	Not viable for language	Adv. classes at community college? Traveling courses
French I, II		
Advanced Fr. III-V		
Spanish I, II		
Spanish III, IV, V		
German I, II		
Advanced German III-V		
Latin I, II, III, IV		

Exhibit 5.13, continued

	Consolidation	Staggering Courses	Travelling Teachers	Maintain at Home School as Basic	Comments and Questions
Music					
Advanced Band		Not viable for			Orchestra may
Orchestra		music			best be handled
Stage Band					by referral to
Choral					Peninsula Youth
Band I, II					Symphony or
					other groups
Math					
Basic Math					
Pre Algebra					
Algebra I					
Geometry					
Algebra II					
Advanced Math					
AP Math					Canada Course
Computer Problems					
Physical Education					
Fresh		Not feasible for			May eliminate PE
Soph/Jr/Sr		PE			requirement for

Age Exempt	12 and possibly 11.
PE Modified	
PE Sub	Could reduce to intramurals
PE Sports	
Science	
Adv. General Sci. *	*Could consolidate the lower-level sciences into a single course
Life Science *	
Earth Science *	
Physical Science *	
Biology	Maintain as quality a program as possible
Human Biology	
Chemistry	
Physics	
AP Biology	
Social Studies	
World Studies I-III	
US History	
Government	
Psychology	Could open to juniors to increase population
Economics	
IR	
Anthropology	
Safety Ed.	May be out of our hands if state legislature withdraws funds
Work Experience	
Educationally Handicapped	

Exhibit 5.14

Minimum Curriculum of Prototypical High School

Art Department
- General Art
- Two Dimensional, Beg. & Adv.
  - (Fr. Hnd. Dr., Cartooning, Fine Art, Photog., etc.)
- Three Dimensional, Beg. & Adv.
  - (Ceram., Jewel., Crafts, etc.)

English Department
- English 1, 2, 3
  - (Rem., Reg., AS)
- English 4
  - (Rem., Reg. and AP)
- Reading
- Drama, Beg. & Adv.
- Yearbook
- Journalism, Beg. & Adv.
- Speech, Beg. & Adv.

Math Department
- Basic Math (Math Lab)
- General Math (Pre-Alg.)
- Algebra .5, 1.0, 1
- Geometry
- Algebra II
- Advanced Math

- AP Math *
- Computer Prob. *
- Calculus *
- Consumer Math *

Business Educ. Department
- Typing, Beg. & Adv.
- Shorthand, Beg. & Adv.
- Accounting, Beg. & Adv.
- Off. Prac./Best
- Wk. Exper.

- Business Law *
- Business Math *
- Reading/Typing *
- Typing/Rec. Keeping *
- Personal Typing *
- Bus. Leadership *
- Consumer Econ. *
- Business Eng. *

Foreign Language Department
- French (I, II, and III)
- German (I, II, and III)
- Spanish (I, II, and III)

- French (IV and V) *
- German (IV and V) *
- Spanish (IV and V) *
- Italian *
- Latin *
- Japanese *

Science Department
- Gen. Science
- Biology
- Chemistry
- Physics

- Human Biol. *
- Adv. Biol. *
- Environ. Physics *
- Adv. Gen. Sci. *

Consumer Home Econ. Dept.
- Clothing, Beg. & Adv.
- Foods, Beg. & Adv.
- Survival/Living Skills (inc. Ch. Dev./Parenting)

Fashion Merchand.*
Interior Design*
On Your Own*
Textile Arts*
Feast*

Industrial Arts Department
- Basic Ind. Arts
- Drafting, Beg. & Adv.
- Metal, Beg. & Adv.
- Wood, Beg. & Adv.

Auto*
Plastics*
Tech. Illus.*
Machine Shop*
Intro. Electronics*

Social Studies Department
- World Studies 1, 2, 3
- U.S. History
- Gov't.
- Electives

Driver Safety Education

*Beyond minimum, but desirable

Exhibit 5.15
Projection Table

	Number of Class Sections Projected by Departments			
	(1,750)	(1,390)	(1,225)	(1,000)
	(average enrollment in each high school)			
	now	year +3	year +6	year +9
Art Department				
General Art	0	0	0	0
Two Dimensional, Beg. & Adv. (Fr. Hnd. Dr., Cartooning, Fine Art, Photog., etc.)	8	6	6	5
Three Dimensional, Beg. & Adv. (Ceram., Jewel., Crafts, etc.)	6	5	4	3
	14	11	10	8
Business Educ. Department				
Typing, Beg. & Adv.	9	8	7	6
Shorthand, Beg. & Adv.	1	1?	1*(0)	1*(0)
Accounting, Beg. & Adv.	3	2	1	1
Off. Prac./Best	5	3	3	3
Wk. Exper.	5	5*(4)	5*(4)	5*(3)
Business Law, Business Math, Reading/Typing, Typing/Rec. Keeping, Personal Typing, Bus. Leadership, Consumer Econ., Business Eng.	3	3	3	2
	26	22	20	18

*? To maintain the minimum offering in Shorthand and accommodate anticipated enrollment in Work Experience, 0.2 of a teacher over ratio must be "bought" in 1982–83, 0.4 in 1985–86, and 0.6 in 1988–89.

	now	year +3	year +6	year +9
Consumer Home Econ. Dept.				
Clothing, Beg. & Adv.	3	2	2	2
Foods, Beg. & Adv.	5	4	4	3
Survival/Living Skills (inc. Ch. Dev./Parenting)	1	1?	1*(0)	1*(0)

Exhibit 5.15, continued

	Number of Class Sections Projected by Departments			
	(1,750)	(1,390)	(1,225)	(1,000)
	(average enrollment in each high school)			
	now	year +3	year +6	year +9
Fashion Merchand. / Interior Design / On Your Own / Textile Arts / Feast	3	3	2	2
	12	10	9	8

*? To maintain the minimum offering of Survival/Living Skills, 0.2 of a teacher over ratio would have to be "bought" in 1985–86 and 1988–89; that 0.2 may also have to be bought in 1982–83.

	now	year +3	year +6	year +9
*English Department**				
English 1, 2, 3 (Rem., Reg., AS)	50	41	36	28
English 4** (Rem., Reg., and AP)	4	6	6	5
Reading	12	10	8	7
Drama, Beg. & Adv.	3	2	1	1***(0)
Yearbook	1	1***(0)	1***(0)	1***(0)
Journalism, Beg. & Adv.	1	1***(0)	1***(0)	1***(0)
Speech, Beg. & Adv.	1	1***(0)	1***(0)	1***(0)
	72	62	54	44

* No attempt has been made in English or any other department to isolate bilingual classes; they are accounted for in the total counts.

** As shown, English 4 represents a series of courses at the fourth-year, not necessarily English 4 as traditionally thought of. Although enrollment decreases, fourth-year English sections begin to increase in 82–83 due to the fourth-year University of California requirement and recycling necessary because of failures in competencies (course minimum objectives tests).

*** To maintain the minimum offerings of Yearbook, Journalism, and Speech, 0.6 teacher over ratio would have to be "bought" in 1982–83, 0.6 teacher over in 1985–86, and 0.8 teacher in 1988–89.

Exhibit 5.15, continued

	Number of Class Sections Projected by Departments			
	(1,750)	(1,390)	(1,225)	(1,000)
	(average enrollment in each high school)			
	now	year +3	year +6	year +9
Foreign Language Department				
French (I, II, III)	6	5	4	4
German (I, II, III)	3	2	2	2*(1)
Spanish (I, II, III)	13	10	9	9
French (IV and V), German (IV and V), Spanish (IV and V), Italian, Latin, Japanese	2	2	2	2*(0)
	24	19	17	17

* One section, or 0.2 of a teacher over ratio, must be "bought" in German in 1988–89 to provide 1 section of German 1 and 1 section of German II–III. To maintain advanced language offerings in two languages, 0.4 of a teacher over ratio must be "bought" in 1988–89.

	now	year +3	year +6	year +9
Industrial Arts Department				
Basic Ind. Arts	3	2	2	2
Drafting, Beg. & Adv.	3	2	2	1
Metal, Beg. & Adv.	2	2	2	1
Wood, Beg. & Adv.	2	2	1	1
Auto, Plastics, Tech. Illus., Machine Shop, Intro. Electronics	1	1	1	1
	11	9	8	6

* This portion of the list does not include fifteen courses located at one or more schools.

	now	year +3	year +6	year +9
Math Department				
Basic Math (Math Lab)	6	5	5	4
General Math (Pre-Alg.)	7	6	5	4
Algebra .5, 1.0, 1	15	12	10	9
Geometry	8	6	6	5
Algebra II	5	4	4	3
Advanced Math	3	2	2	2*(1)

Exhibit 5.15, continued

	Number of Class Sections Projected by Departments			
	(1,750)	(1,390)	(1,225)	(1,000)
	(average enrollment in each high school)			
	now	year +3	year +6	year +9
AP Math Computer Prob. Calculus Consumer Math	2	2	2*(1)	2*(0)
	46	37	34	29

* To maintain advanced and specialized math sections, 0.2 of a teacher over ratio must be "bought" in 1985–86 and 0.6 in 1988–89.

Music Department	now	year +3	year +6	year +9
Choral, Beg & Adv.	2	2*(1)	2	2*(1)
Instrum. Group, Beg. & Adv.	2	2	2*(1)	2*(1)
Instrum. Individ., Beg. & Adv.	1	1	1	1
	5	5	5	5

* To maintain a viable minimum music offering, 0.2 teacher over ratio must be "bought" in 1982–83, 1985–86, and 0.4 over in 1988–89.

P.E. Department	now	year +3	year +6	year +9
P.E. 9th, 10th, 11th	38	30	27	23
P.E. 12th	9	3*	3*	2*
	47	33	30	25

* These section numbers are calculated at one-third of the seniors continuing optional P.E. in 1982–83 and one-half in 1985–86 and 1988–89.

*Science Department**	now	year +3	year +6	year +9
Gen. Science	9	8	8	7
Biology	9	7	6	5
Chemistry	4	3	3	2
Physics	3	2	2	2**(1)
Human Biol. Adv. Biol. Environ. Physics Adv. Gen. Sci.	3	2	1	1
	28	22	20	17

* This list does not include five district classes in Science.

** Physics was maintained at one section higher than ratio for scheduling; 0.4 teacher over ratio would be needed, therefore, in 1988–89.

Exhibit 5.15, continued

	Number of Class Sections Projected by Departments			
	(1,750)	(1,390)	(1,225)	(1,000)
	(average enrollment in each high school)			
	now	year +3	year +6	year +9
Social Studies Department				
World Studies 1, 2, 3	27	22	19	17
U.S. History	14	11	10	9
Gov't	6	5	4	3
Electives	4	3	3	2
	51	41	36	31
Driver/Safety Education	8	7	6	5

Exhibit 5.16
Summary Table

Number of Class Sections Projected

	Number of Class Sections*			
	(1,750) Now	(1,390) Year +3	(1,225) Year +6	(1,000) Year +9
Art	14	11	10	8
Business Education	26	22	20	18
Consumer Hmk.	12	10	9	8
English	72	62	54	44
Foreign Language	24	19	17	17
Industrial Arts	11	9	8	6
Math	46	37	34	29
Music	5	5	5	5
Physical Educ.	47	33	30	25
Driver/Safety Educ.	8	7	6	5
Science	28	22	20	17
Social Studies	51	41	36	31
Total No. of Sections	344	278	249	213

Exhibit 5.16, continued

Estimates of the Number of Sections Required Based on Projected Enrollments

	Now	Year +3	Year +6	Year +9
Projected Enrollments	1,750	1,390	1,225	1,000
Total Class Enrollments, Based on 5.6 Classes/Student	9,800	7,784	6,860	5,600
No. of Class Sections Needed, Based on 28.5 Students per Class	344	273	241	196
No. of Additional Class Sections Needed for the Proposed School	0	+5	+8	+17

*These sections do not include EH, EMR, SED, or District Commute Classes

Exhibit 5.17

Average Size of High Schools in the District Projected Through Year +9 and Compared with School Plant Capacity

			Five Schools		Four Schools	Three Schools
Year	Total Enrollment	Total Capacity	Average Capacity	Average Enrollment	Average Enrollment	Average Enrollment
–4	10,646	11,937	2,387	2,129		
–3	10,337	NA	NA	2,087		
–2	9,810	NA	NA	1,962		
–1	9,418	9,748	1,950	1,884		
now	8,743	9,156	1,831	1,749		
+1	8,148	8,476	1,695	1,630		
+2	7,588	8,191	1,638	1,518	1,897	2,529
+3	6,960	8,191	1,638	1,392	1,740	2,320
+4	6,511	8,191	1,638	1,302	1,628	2,170
+5	6,263	8,191	1,638	1,253	1,566	2,088
+6	5,962	8,191	1,638	1,192	1,491	1,987
+7	5,539	8,191	1,638	1,108	1,385	1,846
+8	5,141	8,191	1,638	1,028	1,285	1,714
+9	4,815	8,191	1,638	963	1,204	1,605

Note: All enrollments and capacity figures exclude students in the self-contained special education classes.

References

Dembowski, Frederick, and Gay, Geneva. "Instructional Effects of Declining Enrollments." *Educational Leadership*, November 1980, pp. 173–175.

Hentschke, Guilbert C. "Assessing the Impact of Enrollment Decline on Operating Costs." *Educational Economics*, May–June 1977, pp. 10–15.

Nolte, M. C. "How to Tell Which Teachers to Keep and Which to Lay Off." *American School Board Journal*, June 1976, pp. 28–30.

Stefonek, Thomas. "Cutback Management in Public Organizations." *Information Series*, 7:3. Madison: Wisconsin State Department of Public Instruction, Division of Management and Planning Services, 1979. ED 192 441.

Zerchykov, Ross; Heleen, Owen; and Weaver, W. Timothy. *A Review of the Literature and an Annotated Bibliography on Managing Decline in School Systems*. Boston: Institute for Responsive Education, March 1982.

Zerchykov, Ross, and Weaver, W. Timothy. *Managing Decline in School Systems*. Boston: Institute for Responsive Education, 1983.

Supplementary Reading

Bernhardt, V. B. *Projecting Student Enrollments: A Basic Step in Comprehensive School District Planning for Declining Enrollment*. Eugene,: Oregon State Division of Research, Development, and Evaluation, 1980. ED 187 020.

ERIC. *The Best of ERIC — School-Based Management*, No. 53. Eugene, Ore.: Educational Resources Information Center, 1980.

Gideonse, Henrick. "School Site Budgeting: Abstracting the Literature." A Project for the Education Panel of the Cincinnatus Association, February 1981.

Hentschke, Guilbert C., and Yagielski, John. "School District Fiscal Strain: Implications for State and Federal Financial Assistance." *Journal of Education Finance* 8 (Summer 1982): 52–72.

Hentschke, Guilbert C., and Yagielski, John. "School District Fiscal Strain: Past and Future." *Educational Horizons* 6:1 (Fall 1982): 12–17.

6

Variations in Budgeting Processes

•

Overview

Budgeting describes the ways school administrators determine how best to use money to accomplish predetermined goals. Many budgeting processes, such as fundamental estimating activities associated with budgeting, are common to schools regardless of the sector. The formality of budgeting processes increases as the size of the organization increases. Differences do, however, exist that can be attributed in part to the sector. For example, budgeting processes are much more of an issue in public schools than in private schools, partly because the political competition for scarce discretionary dollars is dominant in that sector. The major criticisms of and subsequent reforms in school budgeting treat *public* schools. Major reforms have attempted (1) to link expenditures with goals and with schooling services or programs, (2) to create explicit expenditure alternatives, and (3) to push more decision rights down to the building level. Reform efforts in public school budgeting are designed largely to attract sponsor support, and they reflect the incentives of public school business administrators to provide extensive detail to justify and explain to sponsors the manner in which revenues will be spent.

• • •

Introduction

Budgeting is a special case of management control, which was discussed at the beginning of chapter 3. There, management control was described as

---

Pages 193 to 197 are reprinted, by permission, from *Journal of Education Finance*, Vol. 4 (Fall 1978), pp. 235–245 "the process by which managers assure that resources are obtained and used effectively and efficiently in the accomplishment of the organization's objectives" (Anthony 1965, p. 27). Anthony used the term *management control* to describe managers' determination of *activities* that most nearly will permit management to achieve its *objectives*. Budgeting is the most important example of management control processes, because it is *the* major means by which strategic planning processes (deciding objectives) are linked to operational control processes (assuring that desired activities are carried out).

Superficially, budgeting is similar across many different school organizations: given some assumptions about objectives (utility), managers set about to determine the activities that maximize utility subject to a budget. (As we discussed in chapter 4, public-sector managers maximize utility by trying to maximize budgets, while private-sector managers maximize utility by trying to maximize the present value of future flows of net revenues. In both cases they have to put into their budget those activities that maximize their utilities.) The budget limits what can be expended in a year, and this is usually determined by estimating the amount of revenue available for school operation during that year. Most managers are concerned primarily with the expenditure side of budgeting, because their utility is maximized by purchasing inputs (services or goods) for schooling. The term *budgeting* refers largely to determining expenditures, and that is the emphasis in this chapter. The document resulting from the budgeting process, the budget, is often the most comprehensive description of what the school organization, be it a public or private school, intends to do. The rhetoric of intent is affirmed or contradicted by the actual budgets. Because of this, the budget is of fundamental interest to sponsors and clients of both public and private schools. It also provides the blueprint for the behavior of school operators.

Despite these basic similarities, there are notable differences in budgeting practices among schools. Budgeting in public schools, for example, differs from budgeting in private schools in part because of the major differences in size between the average public school district and the average private school. Larger public school organizations require more formal procedures because more people are involved and (as we shall discuss near the end of the chapter) because public sponsors *by virtue of the system of rights in public organizations* require more documentation. In this chapter we will focus the bulk of our attention on budgeting trends in the public schools before comparing them with private schools.

This chapter is organized into four parts. In the first part we summarize the basic budgeting practices found in most schools and describe why these, by themselves, are usually inadequate for most school managers. In the second and third parts we describe two extensions of the basic budgeting practices that are fundamentally competing—programmatic budgeting and site budgeting. The fourth part is an analysis of the first three parts and is intended to show how variations in budgeting processes and even budget outcomes are largely a function of the distribution of decision rights among managers in different school settings.

Basic Budgeting Practices

The major steps in school district budgeting represent a series of estimates of revenues and approval of proposed expenditures. In preparing next year's revenue budget, public school district budget makers count the anticipated aid from the federal and state governments, arrange the district's expenditures to give the appearance of fulfilling all matching requirements, and add in miscellaneous revenue. In determining expenditures, they look at the enrollment projections for the district and personnel salary adjustments that have been mandated or negotiated, make an allowance for the impact of inflation on the cost of materials, supplies, and maintenance; and account for bond amortizations and interests. The typical gap between revenues and expenditures can be closed in one of two ways: class size can be increased, thereby reducing the requirements for instructional staff, or property taxes can be increased (Burkhead 1976, pp. 23–24).

These general steps have been disaggregated in the PERT (Program Evaluation Review Technique) chart in exhibits 6.1 and 6.2. In that more detailed map of school district budgeting, a variety of district employees interact to revise programs, prepare expense requests for all manner of items and personnel, conduct negotiations, present preliminary budget estimates and hold budget hearings, and conduct the vote on the budget. The resulting document is a list of objects of expenditure accompanied by dollar amounts that portray last year's expenditures and next year's requested budget.

Allocation Rules

The preceding "web" of activities, though factually representative, gives the erroneous impression that school district administrators wade through an almost infinite number of possible expenditure alternatives in order to develop a budget. Although there are in theory an extremely large number of choices, school administrators, like other managers, employ mechanisms that greatly reduce the number of choices required while attempting not to rule out choices that may be much better than current practice. To simplify the decision process associated with budget building, most school district administrators have developed line-item allocation formulas. The formulas or rules are designed to provide answers to the following kind of problem: with X many (or much) of Item A, plan on requiring Y many (or much) of item B.

A different formula is used for each of the major budgetary items found in

Exhibit 6.1
Activities in the Budgeting Process

Activity	Who Performs	Start-Finish (PERT Events)
Evaluate last year's program	Superintendent	1–3
Conduct (update) district census	Administrative assistant	1–2
Review debt-service schedule	School business official Bank official	1–4
Conduct individual school plant surveys	Principals	1–5
Revise education and recreation programs	Principals, coordinators, directors	3–6
Estimate anticipated state and federal revenue	School business official	2–7
Estimate anticipated local nontax revenue	Cafeteria manager, principals, directors of special areas	2–8
Estimate total revenue and expense for budget period	School business official	8–9
Revise education and recreation programs	Assistant superintendent of instruction	6–9
Determine educational objectives and policy	Superintendent and school board	9–10
Prepare estimates of school board and central administration expense requests for supplies, equipment, and personnel	District clerk	10–13
Distribute budget preparation information	School business official	9–11
Revise school board and central administration expense requests	Assistant superintendent and business official	13–22
Revise school board and central administration expense requests	Superintendent	22–62
Review school board and central administration expense requests	Citizens' advisory committee	62–23
Tentatively approve board of education and central administration expense requests	School board	23–24

Exhibit 6.1, continued

Activity	Who Performs	Start-Finish (PERT Events)
Prepare building-level administration and instruction expense requests for supplies, equipment, and capital improvements	Principals, coordinators, directors	10–14
Prepare building-level conference expense requests	Coordinators	10–15
Prepare building-level personnel expense requests for both classified and certificated personnel	District-level administrators, principals, coordinators, directors	10–16
Revise building-level certificated personnel requests	Assistant superintendent of instruction	16–25
Revise building-level budget requests for certificated personnel, supplies, and equipment	Assistant superintendent of instruction and school business official	25–27
Revise building-level classified personnel requests	School business official	16–27
Revise instruction expense requests for regular and special schools and community services	School business official	27–30
Prepare building-level expense requests for supplies, equipment, and maintenance	Principals	11–17
Prepare building-level expense requests for supplies, equipment, and maintenance	Administrative assistant for buildings and grounds	17–26
Revise building-level expense requests for plant personnel	Administrative assistant for buildings and grounds	26–27
Prepare estimates for fuel, utilities, contracted services, and miscellaneous plant expenses	Administrative assistant for buildings and grounds	26–29
Revise plant operation and maintenance expense requests	School business official	29–31

Exhibit 6.1, continued

Activity	Who Performs	Start-Finish (PERT Events)
Revise plant operation and maintenance expense requests	Superintendent	31–32
Revise instruction expense requests for regular and special schools and community services	Superintendent	30–33
Revise instruction expense requests for regular and special schools and community services	School board	33–42
Revise plant operation and maintenance expense requests	School board	32–43
Prepare and exchange professional staff/school board negotiation proposals	Instruction staff and school board	42–44
Conduct professional staff/school board negotiations	Instruction staff and school board	44–46
Review instruction expense requests for regular and special schools and community services	Citizens' budget advisory committee	42–46
Tentatively approve instruction expense requests for regular and special schools and community services	School board	46–49
Adjust central administration personnel salary expense requests	School business official	46–24
Develop and exchange secretarial staff/school board negotiation proposals	Secretarial personnel and school board	42–45
Conduct secretarial staff/school board negotiations	Secretarial personnel and school board	45–46
Develop and exchange custodial staff/school board negotiation proposals	Custodial personnel and school board	43–47
Conduct custodial staff/school board negotiations	Custodial personnel and school board	47–48

Exhibit 6.1, continued

Activity	Who Performs	Start-Finish (PERT Events)
Review plant expense operation and maintenance requests	Citizens' budget advisory committee	43–48
Tentatively approve plant operation and maintenance expense requests	School board	48–49
Prepare regular transportation expense requests	Public and parochial principals and directors of special areas	11–18
Prepare special transportation expense requests	District clerk, principals	11–19
Revise transportation expense requests	School business official	19–34
Prepare expense requests for oil, gas, insurance, and maintenance of vehicles	School business official	34–35
Revise all transportation expense requests	Superintendent	35–36
Revise all transportation expense requests	School board	36–50
Review transportation expense requests	Citizens' budget advisory committee	50–51
Tentatively approve transportation expense requests	School board	51–52
Prepare expense requests for cafeteria personnel, supplies, and equipment	Cafeteria manager	11–20
Revise expense requests for cafeteria personnel, supplies, and equipment	School business official	20–37
Revise expense requests for cafeteria personnel, supplies, and equipment	Superintendent	37–38
Revise expense requests for cafeteria personnel, supplies, and equipment	School board	38–40
Prepare and exchange cafeteria staff/school board negotiation proposals	Cafeteria staff and school board	40–28
Conduct cafeteria staff/school board negotiations	Cafeteria staff and school board	28–63

Exhibit 6.1, continued

Activity	Who Performs	Start-Finish (PERT Events)
Prepare capital improvement expense requests	Administrative assistant for buildings and grounds	5–12
Revise capital improvement expense requests	School business official	12–21
Revise capital improvement expense requests	Superintendent	21–39
Revise capital improvement expense requests	School board	39–40
Review capital improvement and cafeteria expense requests	Citizens' budget advisory committee	40–41
Tentatively approve interfund transfer expense requests	School board	54–49
Calculate retirement, social security, health insurance, and other undistributed expense requests	School business official	49–52
Revise debt service expense requests	School business official	52–53
Approve financing plan for approved tentative budget	School board	53–54
Approve budget for presentation to public	School board	54–55
Publish required legal notices	District clerk	54–56
Develop plans for registration and voting on school budget	School board	55–57
Print detailed tentative budget	Administrative assistant	57–59
Distribute detailed tentative budget to public	Administrative assistant	59–58
Present completed tentative budget to public	Citizens' budget advisory committee and school board	55–58
Conduct public hearing on budget	School board, superintendent, school business official	58–56
Hold annual meeting on budget	Superintendent	56–60
Conduct vote on school budget	District clerk	60–61

Source: Guilbert C. Hentschke and John Shaughnessy, "The Budgeting Process," *Research Bulletin* 13: 3 (April 1973): 1, 3–13, and 14:1 (November 1973): 1, 4–15. Reprinted by permission.

Exhibit 6.2

PERT Chart–District Budgeting Process (with time estimates)

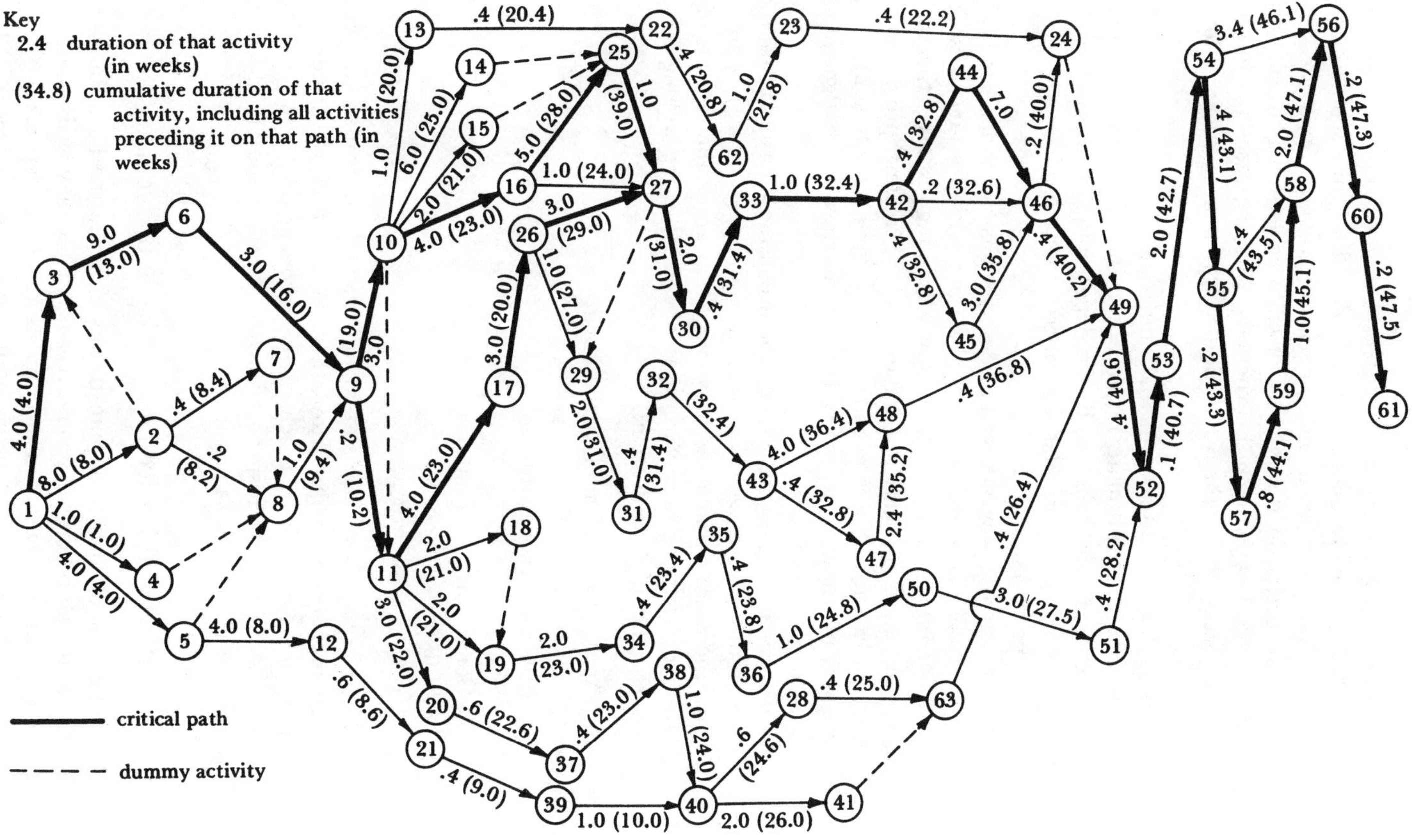

a school building. Examples of the items and allocation formulas are listed in exhibit 6.3. Each formula refers to a major "line" in a school budget. Some items are allocated on a one-per-school basis (for example, librarians). Others are based on the number of children enrolled in each school (for example, other expenses of instruction). In some cases the formula is not apparent because only the results of the formula are indicated (for example, custodians).

Although the building principals and staff of each of the schools in this district may have ultimate responsibility for program development, the central office is clearly responsible for determining the mix of resource inputs in the schools. If the formulas are adhered to, each school will have its share of each type of resource.

If instructional programs can be described as components in budget lines, then a school plans and operates programs within a given distribution of such components. A chief argument for allocating resources this way is equal treatment; another is ease of administration. Personnel projections are more easily made; there is less negotiation in staffing schools; and at the school level, less planning is necessary because much of the budget request each year is predetermined.

The primary arguments against the use of these formulas are the reverse of the arguments for them. Equal treatment, for example, is a double-edged sword; there are possible circumstances that argue the benefits of unequal treatment. Consider how variations of the following among schools in a district would affect education:

1. Age and condition of the building
2. Building utilization rates
3. Student turnover rate
4. School location
5. Community expectations
6. Staff performance
7. Instructional program

There are many variables that could make the operating circumstances of a particular school unique. How, then, can the need to consider the unique requirements of individual schools be reconciled with the equally worthy goals of avoiding favoritism in resource allocation and of reducing administrative work as much as possible?

Perceived Inadequacies of Basic Budgeting Practices

Many school district administrators enhance the basic budget practice outlined in exhibit 6.1 for several reasons. They may wish to use the budget to market the revenue request to sponsors (local taxpayers). Or, they may wish to use the budget document to communicate "desired" behavior to school employees. Finally, they may simply want to broaden participation in the budgeting process in the belief that by so doing a better budget will emerge. The basic budget document, by itself, often is neither sufficient to convince sponsors of the cost-worthiness of proposed schooling activities nor to provide direction to district employees. In other words, formula allocations do not ensure maximization of utility.

Consequently, the basic budgeting process and the resulting document suffer from a variety of shortcomings. First, there is no formal relationship between strategic planning and management control; that is, there is no relationship between organizational objectives and expenditures. Second, alternative means of accomplishing objectives are neither formally developed nor considered. Rather, the major mode of planning is to carry on with current operations. Third, the orientation of the basic budget is, by definition, short-term because it requires consideration of only the coming year (see Hartley 1968, p. 83).

In attempts to increase the utility of the budget to the school manager, a variety of budget "reforms" have been proposed (and implemented to varying degrees). In schools these reforms center around two seemingly contradictory themes: one emphasizes the primacy of *programs* (services) offered in the schools; the other emphasizes the primacy of the groups of clients (children) and operators (teachers and building administrators). This dichotomy is the education version of the ubiquitous function versus product debate in other organizations: whether managers responsible for functions should form the organizational budget hierarchy or whether managers responsible for products should. In schools, functions take the form of "programs" (for example, reading, mathematics, advanced placement science, third-grade English, second-year Spanish, and so on. "Products," on the other hand, refer to the organizational units (school sites) through which students receive educational services (for example, Franklin High School, School No. 3, Wilson Magnet School, Monroe School for the Performing Arts). Often the program–site categories are blended (for example, Franklin High English), but one pattern of budget organization usually predominates, and that determines, for example, whether subject matter supervisors or school principals have the final say over what is taught and how in the schools. The inherent interdependency of both sets of managers implies that the issue is never solved in a totally satisfactory manner. The rationale and processes of budgeting reforms in each area are the subject of the next two sections.

Program-Oriented Budgeting

Determining budgets through evaluation of program needs evolved primarily during the 1960s and 1970s. The conceptual base in education (as well as in other public agencies) for this approach was provided by planning,

Exhibit 6.3

Line Allocation Formulas for Selected School Accounts

Account Code	Account Description	Formula
210	Instructional salaries	
211	Principals' salaries	One principal and three vice-principals in each school, except as designated in article VI, section 11-C, page 62, of the Board Policy Manual.
212	Supervisors' salaries	One curriculum assistant for two periods each day in school. District personnel as determined by Board of Trustees.
213	Teachers' salaries	
213.1	Regular certificated staff	A ratio of one certificated staff member for every 22 students except as follows: School A, 21.5; School B, 19.5. The following assignments are exempt from the above ratio and are in addition to basic staff allowance: special education, driver training, curriculum assistant, and teachers given out-of-class assignments by the superintendent of schools. Students enrolled in classes exempt from ratio formula should be deducted from total enrollment figures. Nonteaching activities are deducted from above figure and budgeted under 214.
214	Other certificated salaries of instruction	
214.1	Librarians' salaries	A certificated librarian for each school on basis of actual placement on salary schedule.
214.2	Counselors' salaries	One hour of counseling time for every 75 students. Total counseling salaries are part of basic ratio in 213.1.

220	Classified salaries of instruction	
221	Regular clerical salaries	The following are maximum allowances: Five secretaries and clerks (including mimeo clerk) are allowed as basic staff for each school up to 1,000 enrollment. One of above clerks to be assigned as school treasurer. Add one-fifth time of clerical person for each 100 students in excess of 1,000. Library staff is assigned on basis of formula allowing for two classified persons for each school as basic staff and one-fifth time of clerical person for each additional 200 students in excess of 1,000 up to total enrollment of 2,000. Maximum clerical staff for school of 1,000 is 9. Maximum clerical staff for school of 2,000 is 13.
222	Student clerical salaries	Maximum allowance for student clerks for all services should not exceed 80 cents for each student enrolled. Maximum allowance for school of 2,000 enrollment is $1,600.
230	Textbooks	Maximum allowance of $4.00 per student plus $250.00 for book replacement, plus $6.50 per unit of growth over previous year for new schools that have not previously reached capacity. This allowance may be adjusted by borrowing from or adding to the 240 account. The combined total for the two accounts should not exceed the combined allowance for each account.
290	Other expenses of instruction	Total maximum allowance for each school based on the following allowance for each student enrolled: School A, $22.50; School B, $22.50; School C, $22.50; School D, $22.50; School E, $25.50; School F, $28.50; plus additional allowance of $5.00 per unit of growth over

Exhibit 6.3, continued

Account Code	Account Description	Formula
		previous year in new schools that have not previously reached capacity. Include in the above allowances for attendance office. Additional allowance for conventions as established by administrative policy, article VI, section 1-D. Allow $300 additional for EMR classes and allow for blind students on basis of previous experience.
400	Health service	
410	Certificated salaries of health personnel	A full-time nurse in each school.
490	Other expense of health service	Allow 15 cents per unit of enrollment.
600	Operation of school plant	
610-620	Classified salaries of operation	Two gardeners assigned to each school.
	Gardening salaries	District staff to consist of a gardener, foreman, three equipment operators, a gardener leadman, and five gardeners, for a total of ten.
730	Replacement of equipment	Not to exceed five percent of total assessed value of school equipment as reflected on inventory of previous fiscal year. Limitations are placed on school total and not on departmental figures. If total inventory values are not available, limitation of $4.00 per unit of enrollment. Individual items to be listed.
791	Repairs of buildings	Based on survey of needs as shown on work requests but limited to a total cost of $15.00 per unit of enrollment.
793	Repair of equipment	Based on survey of actual need as reflected on work request and experience of previous years but not to exceed a total cost of $3.50 per unit of enrollment.

Exhibit 6.4
Major Tasks of ZBB and PPBS

Zero-Base Budgeting	Planning, Programming, Budgeting System
1. Formulate decision packages	1. Develop goal-objective hierarchy
a. Purpose of activity	2. Develop programmatic classifications
b. Consequences of not performing	3. Sort organization's activities into programs
c. Measures of performance	4. Analyze alternative programs through cost-benefit analysis
d. Alternative courses of action	
e. Cost and benefits	5. Develop multiyear program and financial plans
2. Rank decision packages	

programming, and budgeting systems (PPBS). During those years, much was learned about the utility of PPBS for public school administrators. More recently interest has increased in so-called "alternative" budget reforms, most notably zero-base budgeting (ZBB). The evolution in interest first in PPBS then from PPBS to ZBB reflects management's pursuit of utility through changes in budgeting processes.

Differences Between ZBB and PPBS

Perhaps the most fundamental and important difference between the two systems is in the degree of behavioral orientation; ZBB is much more behaviorally oriented than is PPBS, and PPBS is more theoretically or conceptually oriented. An analogy may help here. Consider two books of matches with "safety first" printed on one and "close cover before striking" printed on the other. The phrases are related to each other, but one describes the underlying concepts without describing the appropriate behavior; the other is a statement of the appropriate behavior with only an implicit inference to the underlying concept. PPBS represents the "safety first" approach to budgeting; ZBB represents the "close cover before striking" approach. This difference will become more apparent by examining the specific tasks in each system. ZBB can be described in terms of two major tasks and PPBS in terms of five major tasks. The tasks of both systems are outlined in exhibit 6.4

ZBB Described

The first task in ZBB is to formulate a decision package. A decision package "identifies a discrete activity, function, or operation in a definitive manner for management evaluation and comparison with other activities"

(Phyrr 1973, p. 6). The definition of a decision package includes: (1) stating the purpose of the activity, (2) drawing out the consequences of not performing it, (3) listing measures of performance, (4) specifying alternative courses of action, and (5) delineating costs and benefits.

These packages are created at the lowest level of management or administration for each current and proposed function. The line manager describes in behavioral terms in each decision package both the program operations needed to carry out the function and the goals that performing the function achieves. The manager initially develops a base-case (for example, "business as usual") decision package and then considers two types of alternative decisions: (1) different ways of performing the function and (2) different levels of effort of performing the function. The complete decision package then consists of a "business as usual" proposal plus alternatives that may consist of different ways of performing the function or different levels of effort. These levels of effort may include those that are "preferred," "current," "reduced," "minimum," and so on.

The second task in the zero-base budgeting process entails ranking the decision packages in order of decreasing benefit or importance (Blodgett 1973, p. 15). The ranking process is repeated at each hierarchical level of management up through the organization as decision packages are aggregated and scrutinized. The initial ranking occurs at the level at which the packages are developed. Each line manager evaluates and ranks the importance of his own activities. The manager at the next higher level reviews these rankings and uses them as guides to produce a single, consolidated ranking for all the packages presented to him from managers below him.

Packages may be, for example, elementary English, student transportation, high school mathematics, and, for purposes of comparison, they may be numbered: 1,2,3, . . . *n*. The level of service (level of effort) for each package may be represented as follows:

P (preferred level of service) is higher than current cost
C (current level of service) is the current cost
R (reduced level of service) is less than current cost
M (minimum level of service) is the minimum cost

Each package, therefore, has four price tags (P,C,R, and M). Managers then determine the desired level of each package (P,C,R, or M) and then also rank the packages from most desired to least desired. For example, for packages 17, 18, 19, 20, and 21, a manager may determine that these packages, from most desired (or necessary) to least, should be 20, 17, 21, 19, and 18 (all are desired but some are desired relatively more). Remember, each package has a price tag. Once the decision packages have been ranked (with desired levels of effort), available revenues are examined. For example, a manager finds that there are X dollars available to spend. He then asks how many decision packages he can fund with those revenues. Say he has fifty packages and X dollars to spend, but he can fund only the forty most desired packages (each at the preferred level of effort or service). He must then start analyzing alternatives and making trade-offs. For example, if he wants to fund packages 41 to 45, he will have to reduce levels of effort (and hence spending) among the first forty packages. To do that, he may decide to reduce the levels of effort to "current levels" in five packages, to "reduced levels" in three others, and to "minimum" in one. These savings might then be enough to fund packages 41 to 45, which did not make the first cut. In doing so, the manager is saying that including packages 41 to 45 was worth more to him than operating nine of the first forty packages at preferred levels.

Various heuristics are recommended to implement the ranking process. The volume of packages should be kept small enough by limiting the number of packages ranked at any level. Managerial attention should be focused on the packages about which serious questions remain as opposed to all packages. A decision package that is ranked below expected revenue levels can be included only by giving the package a higher priority (thus eliminating another package) or by reducing the levels of effort of higher-priority packages (thus freeing up money that could be allocated to the low-priority package). There is a variety of differences between ZBB and PPBS, not the least of which are the places of origin (industry and state government versus federal government). The major differences between ZBB and PPBS, however, lie in the treatment within each system of three central elements: goals and objectives, programmatic structure, and analysis of alternatives.

Goals and Objectives

PPBS is a "top-down" process designed by top management. Goals and objectives are developed: (1) before designing programs, (2) in a hierarchical manner, and (3) not necessarily in clear or singular relation to the existing organizational structure.

The ZBB process, by contrast, is a "bottom-up" system. Line managers develop the objectives and goals when describing courses of action in their decision packages. Goals and objectives are expressed in terms of activities, actually or potentially performed, and are not organized in an *a priori* hierarchical fashion. Goals do not cut across the existing organizational structure. The hierarchy of goals emerges out of operational experiences. The description of the purpose of each activity, division, agency, program, or profit center identifies how it relates to the organization as a whole. Ideally, each decision package states the relation of the purpose of the activity to the overall purpose of the total organization, identifying either the goals and objectives of the activity, the problem the activity is attempting to solve, or the service the activity is attempting to provide (Phyrr 1973, p. 70). Top management neither develops nor imposes goal–objective structures for the line units in the organization. The function served by goal–objective statements in ZBB is generally to inform top management how a given line activity empirically relates to other line activities and to the organization as a whole (p.71). In ZBB, since goals of the organization develop from the line units up to top administration, the goal hierarchy is literally constrained by the operating structure of the organization. In PPBS the goal hierarchy is constrained only by the intelligence and creativity of the top managers.

Programmatic Structure

The organizing concept in both systems is a programmatic structure. A program structure is a grouping of activities that is oriented toward a strategic objective. However, the criteria for its development in ZBB and PPBS differ. In PPBS the total program structure stands in a direct one-to-one relation to the goal-objective hierarchy. Another characteristic of programmatic classification under a PPBS system is its hierarchical nature. This is a direct logical result of specifying that programs will follow from the goal–objective hierarchy. As Steiss pointed out, "the design of a program structure can be viewed as a *hierarchical* ordering problem" (1972, p. 161, emphasis added). The program structure, therefore, constitutes low-level entities that, when aggregated, constitute middle-level entities that in turn, when aggregated, constitute higher-level entities (ibid., pp. 102–121; Hartley 1968, p. 156).

Keeping the possible disjunction between goal hierarchy and organization hierarchy in mind, the resulting program structure may only incidentally resemble current operating relationships in the educational organization. However, many educational organizations that have attempted to implement PPBS have built program structures around existing organizational structures such as grade level or subject matter-curricular combinations. Program structures based on such foundations represent the *status quo*. They can be used "mindlessly" without a careful analysis of the needs and problems of the individual students of the school district (Curtis 1971, p. 204). "Although it will be difficult to abandon traditional thinking, creative planners may find it desirable to dismiss the departmental concept. *Inasmuch as a program will cut across departmental lines*, the notion of departmentalization may inhibit systems (or programmatic) thinking" (Hartley 1968, p. 165, emphasis added). In PPBS "programmatic thinking" is held as a desirable objective in and of itself.

The "cross organizational" and hierarchical features of program categorization that are present in PPBS systems are not present in the decision package categorization of ZBB. The criterion for developing decision packages in ZBB, stated simply, is that they "must be meaningful for both those preparing the packages and those reviewing and evaluating them" (Phyrr 1973, p. 45). "Meaningful" criteria are pragmatic, not directly related to goals, and include, for example, size of the organization, its range of activities, and the availability of accounting and workload data (Blodgett 1973, p. 15). These relatively loose criteria leave open the particular subjects about which decision packages are organized (such as programs, people, or service provided). However, in order to meet the criterion of "meaningfulness," it is necessary that existing organizational structure and areas of responsibility be considered. The basic premise in operation here is that the expertise at the level of performance of an activity must be formally included in the process of budgeting for that activity. While a decision package may contribute to some larger goal of the organization, no attempt is made formally to aggregate packages in terms of overall organizational purposes.

Analysis of Alternatives

Analysis of alternatives is a formal part of both budgeting systems, but the two systems differ in the manner by which they assess alternatives. Each system's logical structure for analyzing alternatives is internally consistent (that is, the methods of analyzing alternatives follow logically from other characteristics of the system). In a PPBS, alternative programs are analyzed by cost-benefit, cost-utility (Steiss 1972, p. 165), or resource-effectiveness criteria (Carpenter and Haggart 1969, p. 3). The production relationship between inputs and outputs of the program must be understood. Alternatives are considered that differ only in terms of costs or benefits. Potential alternatives will vary either system cost or its effectiveness, but not both.

> Cost-benefit analysis . . . is useful in comparing alternatives when either the *cost* (budget level) or the *effectiveness* (achievement) is held constant . . . . To do this meaningfully, specify the level of effectiveness and then examine the *cost* of alternative means to achieve that effectiveness. Conversely, you can fix a single *budget level* and examine the levels of effectiveness that can be achieved through different alternatives because of these problems in comparing programs. The best way to use cost-effectiveness analysis is to construct *equal-cost alternatives*, that is, to adjust the dimensions of each program (such as the number of students enrolled) so that each program will incur approximately the same total cost over some appropriate period of time. In this way the educational planners will be freed from having to consider . . . [differences in magnitude among programs] . . . when choosing among alternatives and can concentrate on the more difficult aspects of effectiveness, the phasing of dollar requirements, and the requirements for scarce resources. [Carpenter and Haggart 1969, pp. 6, 10 emphasis added]

The consideration of effectiveness within PPBS requires that programs be described in terms of (among other things) the output measures that are achieved through the program, which in education implies largely learning outcomes (that is, changes in pupil behavior) or degree production. The conceptual and technical difficulties of estimating production functions are seen as being outweighed by the benefits that accrue from cost-benefit analysis. A basic assumption in cost-benefit analysis is that methods for measuring outcomes are available. In many academic areas there are tests of student achievement that may be used with some confidence. But if program goals included such objectives as changes in a child's conception of his own self-worth or improvements in the child's relationships with his peers, it may be more difficult to obtain or devise instruments that are valid and reliable. Sometimes very expensive techniques such as individual observation by trained psychologists must be used. Output levels (that is, any end products) are stressed, but service levels (that is, production processes) are used when necessary. As an example, for a decision package in tenth-grade science, a preferred level might be four sections with sixteen students and with lab twice a week. A minimum level might be three sections with twenty-two students each and with lab only once a week. In PPBS, emphasis is placed on the determination of production relationships, which are used as a basis for evaluating programmatic alternatives. A *single* statement of costs and benefits should be made for each program. Furthermore, each should be stated from the perspective of the entire organization (as distinct from the perspective of a division or department).

Program alternatives are incidental results of cost-effectiveness analysis but are not intended as formally stated end products of PPBS. The generation of new and sometimes better alternatives is often an important by-product of the analytical part of the program budgeting process.

The internal logic of program analysis in PPBS follows from the existence of a hierarchy of goals and objectives as well as from a hierarchy of programs that parallels those goals and objectives. Given the parallel, it is possible to evaluate a program in terms of an overall welfare function.

Alternatives that are generated and evaluated in ZBB also follow a logical procedure that leads to internal consistency. As mentioned earlier, alternatives to each decision package are prepared simultaneously along with the "base case." The alternatives included different ways of performing the same function (only the preferred alternative is presented in detail) and different levels of effort of performing the function. Alternative levels of effort are described in terms of information required for management to evaluate the decision package and compare it with other packages. This information includes statements of purpose, consequences of not performing the activity, meaningful measures of performance, and costs. At this stage of preparation, information about the "production relationship" implicit in the activity is presented by line managers. As a decision package is scrutinized at different stages up through the hierarchy, it is compared with successively additional packages. Consequently, *different* amounts of overall organizational utility are ascribed to those productive relationships.

Cost-benefit analysis is accomplished in radically different ways within each budgeting system. Alternative programs in PPBS are evaluated against all other programs by means of a cost-utility relationship. For example, the cost of the alternative is calculated as an incremental cost to the cost of all other district programs (Carpenter and Haggart 1969, p. 1). In ZBB, the cost-utility of a decision package is not expected to be viewed uniformly by all managers. The line managers who develop decision packages (it is argued) are best equipped, because of their detailed knowledge of their particular functions, to identify and evaluate the cost-benefits of levels of efforts. It should be the responsibility of these managers to advise higher management of these relationships. It then becomes higher management's responsibility to avaluate the relative importance of functions and the different levels of effort within each function (Phyrr 1973, pp. 7–8).

Formal analysis of alternative levels of effort for a given activity is the basic activity of zero-base budgeting, and not budgeting from zero each year. In PPBS, cost-benefits of whole programs constitute the basis for analysis. In ZBB, analysis is directed much more toward incremental changes.

Implementation Problems with Programmatic Budgeting

ZBB and PPBS have similar basic characteristics, each of which differs operationally, which causes us to ask whether the similarities between the two systems imply similar implementation problems or whether the differences between the two systems imply differing probabilities of successful implementation. This is not an easy question, in part because there is no consensus about the degree to which programmatic budgeting systems have been successfully implemented in education or elsewhere.

Proponents of PPBS cite widespread adoption of PPBS: "approximately 20,000 school districts in this country, as well as the state education budgets (sic), are rapidly turning to program budgeting" (Novick 1973, p.v). Opponents state that adoption cannot be equated with successful implementation and, further, that "PPBS has failed everywhere and at all times. Nowhere has PPBS (1) been established and (2) influenced governmental decisions (3) according to its own principles" (Wildavsky 1975, p. 363). Proponents counter this argument by stating that PPBS has not really been tried; if it would be, it would succeed. Opponents of PPBS reply by stating that the requisite conditions for "really trying" simply cannot be made to exist: the faults of PPBS are:

> not merely those of program implementation but also of policy design . . . [I]ts defects are defects of principle, not of execution. PPBS does not work because it cannot work. Failure is built into its very nature because it demands abilities to perform cognitive operations which are beyond present human (or machine) capacities." [Wildavsky 1975, p. 364]

The jury is similarly "out" on ZBB.

The purpose here is not to attempt to reconcile the two different orientations to programmatic budgeting, but rather to summarize the major criticisms of programmatic budgeting in order to understand why it has not been widely adopted.

Many separate problems have been identified in an attempt to explain why PPBS implementation efforts have not been totally successful. These problems are of two general yet distinct types: these can be termed problems of environment and problems of conception. Problems of environment refer to those problems that can be traced to the conditions within which PPBS implementations have been attempted. These problems carry with them the unstated assumption that the problems of PPBS are the result of factors external to PPBS. Problems of conception, on the other hand, represent a more serious indictment in that they are seen as problems inherent in the design and structure of PPBS.

Problems of Environment

A variety of distinct environmental problems have been identified, some more substantive than others. One of the most often cited environmental problems is lack of executive leadership. When top management fails to support PPBS implementation efforts, the chances for its successful implementation are greatly reduced. This factor has been cited in regards to implementation efforts at the federal level (Botner 1970, p. 426), at state and local levels (Mushkin 1969, p. 178), and in school districts in particular (van Geel 1973, p. 4; Fogel 1979, p. 74). While this is an important observation, it begs the question of why top management might not be supportive. Major innovations in organizations require top management support to succeed, but the lack of top management support is essentially a diagnosis of a symptom rather than of a cause.

This problem is actually an important special case of the second problem: some PPBS implementation efforts have lacked support *anywhere* in the school district. The reasons often attributed to lack of support are fear of loss of power, lethargy, fear of the unknown, and other, essentially individualistic, personality-based reasons. In one study of PPBS implementation in several school districts, "PPBES faced resistance within the central office insofar as one part of the central office, the existing business office, saw PPBES as taking power away from them and giving it to another division which had the computer expertise necessary to make PPBES work. . . . PPBES was resisted by teachers, for they saw the move to PPBES as part of a long-term effort of the board to make teachers accountable for student performance. . . . Principals . . . resisted PPBES because they saw no benefit coming to them from the system, but they did foresee themselves saddled with extra paperwork" (van Geel 1973, p. 4). Other, more organization-focused, motives have also been used to explain resistance by staff, perhaps the most compelling of which is *experience*. School district staff are, typically, already familiar with the strengths and weaknesses of existing programs. This familiarity is based on years of experience with the programs. As Wildavsky (1975) has pointed out, the most dramatic changes introduced in the Pentagon, where PPBS got a major start, had to do with questions of avoiding or limiting nuclear war, in which no one had a claim to experience and in which the basic purpose of analysis was "to make certain that we do not have to learn from experience" (p. 193). Such has not been the case with subsequent implementation efforts in school districts. Experienced personnel know something about the consequences of what gets proposed. They have tried or at least already considered a variety of alternatives and can point to a variety of reasons why each one will not work.

Lack of staff support in school districts has also been attributed to rather high-handed introductions of the concept by management. Staff were not involved in setting up the system, and no attempt was made to show how PPBS could improve the teaching-learning process. For this reason, teachers opposed it (Hartley 1968, p. 9). Further, PPBS could well have been introduced not only poorly, but prematurely: "PPBS is a good idea whose time has not quite come." It was introduced government-wide, the argument goes, before the requisite concepts, organizational capability, political conditions, informational resources, and analytical techniques were adequately developed (Schick 1969, p. 150). Time is required not only for adapting organizations to PPBS, but for adapting the economic and planning concepts inherent in PPBS to the realities of different organizations (Mushkin 1969, p. 169). The implication of this environmental problem is that there will be a continual upgrading in the sophistication of systems budgeting. Early implementation efforts outside of the Department of Defense, including those in school districts, were undertaken without the benefit of adequately trained analytical staffs capable of conducting the necessary cost-benefit studies and special analyses and of developing long-term program and financial plans (Fogel 1979, p. 75). Relatedly, early implementation efforts were characterized by undue emphasis on technique coupled with excessive documentation (Schick 1969, p. 149; Botner 1970, p. 426). The net result has been "reams of unsupported, irrelevant justification and description" (Botner 1970, p. 428). Implementation strategies suitable for other innovations were simply not well suited for implementation of PPBS. For example, standard procedures for installing a new computer call for a period of transition when the new and old systems operate in parallel. This did not work well for PPBS. In fact, one of the chief reasons attributed to the demise of PPBS at the federal level was the fact that PPBS was introduced as a system running parallel to the existing budgeting and decision-making system (ibid., p. 425). The implication is that PPBS did not replace so much as add on to current practices and, hence, was not *really* given a chance to operate on its own. If the old system continued to exist, budget decisions would continue to be made under it.

Yet centralized implementation of PPBS throughout governmental agencies has failed for reasons more complex than those related to how the old system is disposed of. In tracing the "rise and fall" of the efforts of the state of California to implement PPBS in school districts, Kirst (1975) identifies a number of factors subverting implementation. Generally, during early pilot phases of implementation, technical issues were broadened to include issues of basic values, such as what the goals of education should be and who should set them. These issues mobilized opposition forces from numerous corners. This more than any single factor caused the rapid demise of legislative support.

The failure of PPBS has even been linked to the change between the 1960s and the 1970s from "growth" to "no growth." Demographic and economic conditions have forced many governmental agencies into a retrenchment mentality. This changing climate has reduced the probability of successfully implementing PPBS. PPBS is more easily implemented in a time of rising levels of appropriations. If change means that things must be taken away from people, resistance may be expected (Wildavsky 1975, p. 193). This phenomenon has affected all governmental units to a degree, but it has had a particular impact on municipalities. The structural and fiscal idiosyncracies of different governmental bodies explain, in part, why implementation efforts below the federal level have met with limited success. Because they differ from the federal government in legislative power and revenue-generating ability, local governmental units, including school districts, are simply ill-fitted for PPBS, at least as currently conceived (Mushkin 1969, p. 169). Because balanced budgets for cities are required and revenues are inelastic, there exists an almost control orientation, with less strategic room to maneuver than within the federal government, and generally little scope for decision making. Budgeting becomes a form of revenue behavior; income determines outputs (Wildavsky 1975, pp. 10–11). Revenue-oriented budgeting at the local level of government has been documented for school districts (Gerwin 1969) as well as cities (Crecine 1969). Its cause is largely structural, that is, expenditures can be precisely determined only after revenues from different sources have been determined.

Local governmental units are closer to the pluralistic pressures that are generated in a political system and, at the same time, must reconcile their aims with those of other local and higher-level bodies that act through the local government (Mushkin 1969, p. 169). The complexity resulting from conflicting expectations of sponsors at the local level is *greater* than at the federal level, and, hence, PPBS is all the more difficult to implement locally.

Problems of Conception

These environmental problems, while severely affecting the likelihood of successful implementation of PPBS, are seen as essentially extrinsic to PPBS.

They are distinct from a second set of problems that are seen as stemming directly from PPBS. In these instances, unsuccessful implementation of PPBS is attributable to flaws inherent in PPBS, not in the environment surrounding implementation efforts. At least three different but interrelated types of inherent problems have been identified. They are conceptual, structural, and economic.

Optimal allocation policy by means of cost-benefit analysis, it is argued, cannot be accomplished without specifying, unambiguously, an acceptable social welfare function that would allow administrators to make comparisons between widely diverse programs (Capron 1969, p. 157; Wildavsky 1975, pp. 92, 104). If the principal budgeting task is to resolve conflict over goals (as opposed to the more technical one of selecting the best means or programs within largely agreed-on ends), it is simply not useful to prescribe that the goals of the organization should be decided on as one step in budgeting. Even if goals could be agreed on, very few alternatives can be considered in any real decision-making situation. This is intellectually impossible given the limits of our knowledge, intellectual capacity, and time.

One structural problem relates to the impossibility of aligning program definitions with a goal hierarchy. Most school district activities are oriented toward more than one end. For example, a reading program may contribute to the role of general education, comprehension of the English language, drop-out prevention, and vocational education. This problem applies equally to the work of other governmental agencies, and it is intimately related to the overall conceptual problem mentioned above. Even one of the structural "strengths" of PPBS—formally linking planning and budgeting—has recently been viewed as both a weakness and a reason for nonadoption (Simmons and Barkdull 1967). Linking the strategic-planning function to the budgeting function places an unwarranted emphasis on the financial aspects of new ideas, directions, and programs. This is reminiscent of arguments made by Anthony (1965) distinguishing strategic-planning and managerial control functions.

The third type of problem inherent in PPBS really stems from positive theory in economics, which can be termed the economics of information in school systems. Stated simply, any benefits that might be gained by educational administrators through the formal methods of PPBS are perceived to be more than offset by the added costs associated with the undertaking. Advocates of PPBS have been accused of defining a rational executive as one who applies cost-effectiveness techniques to all important programs with the exception of PPBS programs. The opportunity cost of additional analysis is seen as being particularly high in local governments (Gross 1969, p. 128). Yet supporters of PPBS in education have relied on the "spare-no-cost" argument when advocating implementation of PPBS (Weiss, 1973 pp. 24–25). The economic argument is particularly intriguing, because it implies that given the circumstances surrounding administration of public schools, the current amount of managerial effort devoted to analytical and budgeting tasks is "rational." Economists advocating adoption of PPBS for school districts must at the same time seek to explain why it has *not* been adopted to date.

The Future of Programmatic Budgeting in Education

The factors hindering the successful adoption of PPBS in school districts are manifest and pervasive. It often appears that only a few factors are needed in combination in a particular instance to sufficiently subvert successful implementation. There is some reason to suspect that many of these factors would also hinder attempts to implement zero-base budgeting. For example, its implementation could well be perceived as threatening or as an unhelpful burden. Or, insufficient attention may be devoted to preparing the district for ZBB, including attention to reorganization and staff training. Mandated implementation of ZBB could succumb to most of the problems that befell PPBS. Assumptions that the economy is not growing, and the structural perversities of municipal governments, will not likely change the revenue orientation of school officials.

Despite the persistence of these factors, there is reason to suspect that the rate of successful voluntary adoption of ZBB by school districts will be greater than the rate of adoption of PPBS was. There are at least three reasons. First, the problems perceived as inherent in PPBS are largely missing in ZBB—ZBB does not require an agreed-on goal hierarchy. Decision-package objectives are weighed and rationalized during the budgeting process, not beforehand. Strategic planning, greatly de-emphasized in ZBB, is seen as a more selective, less periodic process involving a much smaller portion of the total organization.

Second, ZBB appears to "fit" current school district budgeting behavior more closely. ZBB uses the current organizational structure and the experience of existing staff to a greater degree. More emphasis is placed on intuitively estimated (as opposed to quantitatively derived) production relationships. Bargaining about both means and ends is incorporated into the budgeting process. Perhaps most significant, the process of ZBB is compatible with revenue-oriented behavior. It is better suited to describing (to city council, voters, the state) what incremental changes in services can be expected with changes in expenditures. ZBB is a concrete manifestation of the "consumer orientation" of district administrators described in the previous chapter.

Third, several reports of successful budget reform in school districts (Alioto and Jungherr 1969; Robinson, Yagielski, and Brueningsen 1976) cite improved ability to communicate these relationships between expenditures and services to an expenditure-conscious, hostile community as the major reason for undertaking ZBB and the major benefit of the budget reform. It is because of (not despite) the no-growth mentality that school districts will be resorting more to budget reform efforts in general (and ZBB in particular). The ability to secure funds for education is more difficult now than a decade ago. It is in this context that the rational district administrator will evaluate the benefits of budget reform as outweighing the costs.

These positive forces should also be viewed in context. ZBB will likely be implemented in some school districts across the United States. Following the initial fanfare, however, the rate of successful implementation will be slow to moderate. Even though the "pure form" of either PPBS or ZBB has not gained widespread use, the analysis and reporting of past and budgeted expenditures on a programmatic basis seems to be common among most public school districts.

Site-Oriented Budgeting

School site budgeting emerged at about the same time as programmatic budgeting. It was designed to address many of the same deficiencies in basic budgeting practices, but with greater emphasis on differences among sets of clients (schools) than among instructional services (programs). The arguments for school site budgeting rest on a set of assumptions about the primacy of managerial decision rights at the school building level as opposed to the district level, a philosophy sometimes referred to as school site management (see Garms, Guthrie, and Pierce 1978, p. 278).

School Site Management

> The essence of school site management is a shift of decision-making responsibility from the school district to the individual school. Under current state laws, school districts are legally responsible for providing educational services. They are empowered to raise money and are the recipients of state school support funds. School site management would not remove the district's responsibility for providing educational services or its power to raise money or receive state school support funds. In order to provide families greater control over school affairs, however, important aspects of educational decision making would be delegated to the schools. [ibid., pp. 278–279]

In addition to reallocating decision rights from the district to the school level, decision rights at the school level would be shared between employed school personnel and parent advisory councils (ibid., pp. 279–280). Such councils would "select and advise school principals, approve school site budgets, and participate in negotiations with teachers on the details of the school's educational program" (ibid.)

Under the design of school site management, the principal would be subject to two bodies, the central administration and the parent advisory body. He or she "would be accountable . . . to the school district for operating the school within state and district regulations, and to the parent advisory body for tailoring the school's program to the council's policies." However, the principal would "have discretion over three important areas of school management: personnel, budget, and curriculum" (ibid., p. 281).

School Site Budgeting

This rather dramatic reallocation of decision rights provides the backdrop for budgeting processes known as school site budgeting. As with program-oriented budgeting reforms, school site budgeting is a general concept that embodies a variety of specific manifestations. Some definitions are all-encompassing, as "[s]chool site budgeting may be said to be present when discretion to allocate funds across a variety of budget categories according to priorities established at the local level in fact exists" (Gideonse et al. 1981, p. 2). If a principal, for example, can decide to spend fifty dollars of the equipment allocation for staff development, school site budgeting is argued to exist. Other definitions are more constraining, requiring discretion among the all-important personnel categories: "[a] total operating budget for the district would be established, then funds would be allocated to each school in *unrestricted*, lump sums" (Garms, Guthrie, and Pierce 1978, p. 282, emphasis added).

Allocation Rules in School Site Budgeting

The methods employed for determining the allocation to a school would not vary greatly from the formula-based allocations already in place. The difference in school site budgeting comes in deciding how to spend the lump sum allocation at the building level. A variety of mechanisms are proposed for deciding how to allocate resources within the school, including the creation of extensive information systems describing "work flows" in schools and annual school-based performance reports. These mechanisms and others would be used to assist the school building-level staff in determining the proportion of the appropriated sum that is to be spent for each line item in the budget.

The following example may clarify how this approach works. For the sake of brevity, the example is limited to personnel allocation to high schools in a district.

All personnel allocations to the high schools in XYZ School District are made in units, a unit being equivalent to the average annual salary of a high school teacher. A single allotment of units provides for all personnel services—instructional and support—for each school.

The formula for the distribution of units in specific high schools is in four parts: support services; basic instruction and supervision; additional support services for pupils reading at least two years below grade level; and a discrete allotment for optional programs and special needs.

1. *Support services.* A constant twenty units is allocated to each school for minimum services common to all schools regardless of size. This is to provide the basic organizational structure, such as a principal and a minimum number of supportive positions. In addition, each school will be allocated eight units per one thousand pupils for registers in excess of one thousand, with a maximum of thirty-five units. This provides additional support services for larger high schools. From this formula, School A is allocated forty-four units. (See sample computation in exhibit 6.5.)

Exhibit 6.5

Computing Personnel Units for Support Services

Two schools of 2,000 and 4,000 pupils respectively would receive 20 units each, plus 8 for the 2,000-pupil school and 24 for the 4,000-pupil school.

School of 2,000 pupils: $\frac{8\ (2{,}000 - 1{,}000)}{1{,}000} = 8$ units additional

Total: $8 + 20 = 28$ units for support services

School of 4,000 pupils: $\frac{8\ (4{,}000 - 1{,}000)}{1{,}000} = 24$ units additional

Total: $24 + 20 = 44$ units for support services

2. *Basic instruction and supervision.* The formula to calculate the number of units for this area is:

$$\frac{1.05 \times \text{weighted estimated register} \times \text{weighted daily pupil load}}{\text{average class size} \times \text{number of academic or basic instruction periods per day.}}$$

Based on experience in the district, a constant of 1.05 is written into the formulas to provide for relief periods for the assistant principals in charge of supervision. The weighted estimated register is the total number of pupils estimated to be in the school, some of whom have been given special weightings because of their characteristics. In one example there are only two types of students: regular students, whose weight is 1.0, and students reading more than zero but less than two years below grade level, whose weight is 1.07. Of the three thousand pupils who will be at the high school next year one thousand will be reading at least two years below grade level.

The weighted daily pupil load is the principal's estimate of the daily average number of periods per pupil required for next year's programming.

The subjects are weighted for varying contractual class size maximums:

Academic	1.00
Physical education and music	0.68
Industrial arts and home economics	1.32

See exhibit 6.6 for computation of the weighted pupil daily load, and exhibit 6.7 for computation of units for basic instruction and supervision.

Exhibit 6.6

Calculating Weighted Pupil Daily Load

Subject	Factor	Proportion of daily Load	Weighted Number
Academic	1.00	4	4.00
Physical education and music	0.68	1	0.68
Industrial arts and home economics	1.32	1	1.32
Weighted daily load		6	6.10

Exhibit 6.7

Computation of Units for Basic Instruction and Supervision

Given:

School register: 3,000 pupils (2,000 regular + 1,000 with between 0 and 2 years of reading retardation)

Average daily pupil load: 6 periods (1 physical education or music, plus 1 industrial arts or home economics, plus 4 academic subjects)

Weighted register: $2{,}000 + (1{,}000 \times 1.07) = 3{,}070$

Computation:

$$\text{Units} = \frac{\text{relief factor} \times \text{weighted register} \times \text{weighted daily pupil load}}{\text{average class size} \times \text{number of academic or basic instruction periods per day}}$$

$$= \frac{1.05 \times 3070 \times 6.00}{32 \times 4}$$

$$= 151.1 \text{ or } 151$$

3. *Additional support services for pupils reading at least two years below grade level.* This part of the formula is based on perceived needs for services such as

guidance and remedial reading. For every one hundred severely retarded readers in the school, an additional 1.64 are allocated. For example, two hundred severely retarded readers would qualify a school for an additional 3.28 or, rounded off, 3 units.

4. *Discrete allotment for optional programs and special needs.* This part of the formula is initiated at the request of the school and the discretion of the superintendent. A certain amount of the total allotment of units (say, 3 percent) is set into this category for distribution to specific schools on an application basis.

The number of units available to School A would be determined by totaling the units to which it is entitled under each of the four formulas above. In the example we have been using, assume the school qualified for no units under the fourth formula; it would be credited with 44 + 151 + 3 = 198 personnel units.

Once building administrators know the number of personnel units that are allocated to them, they can plan, cooperatively or otherwise, the staffing patterns best suited to the individual needs of their schools. This model allows the principal broad discretion.

A sampling of titles and conversion factors of people who might be employed in a large high school is shown in exhibit 6.8. If School A was allocated 198 personnel units, for example, the program would be staffed with a number of different job types, the total "value" of which would be 198 units.

Exhibit 6.8

School Personnel Conversion Factors
(Weighted Unit Value of Sample Titles)

Sample Titles	Weighted Unit Value
Pedagogic titles	
Principal	2.1
Assistant principal	1.4
Guidance counselor	1.1
Teacher (basic unit)	1.0
Laboratory specialist	0.8
School secretary	0.7
Sub. school secretary interns	0.4
Industrial arts technician	0.5
Administrative titles	
Account clerk	0.4
Accountant	0.7
Accountant (assistant)	0.6

Exhibit 6.8, continued

Sample Titles	Weighted Unit Value
Accountant (senior)	0.8
Administrative assistant	0.8
Assistant stockman	0.4
Budget examiner	1.0
Business officer	0.9
Clerk	0.4
District business officer (fiscal and accounting)	1.0
Machinist helper	0.8
Nurse's aide	0.5
Senior audio-visual technician	0.7
Senior human resources specialist	0.8
Senior intergroup relations officer	0.7
Special officer	0.6
Stockman	0.6
Paraprofessional hourly employees	
Educational assistant	0.2
Family assistant	0.2
Family worker	0.2
Health service aide	0.2
Junior neighborhood worker	0.4
School aide	0.2
School neighborhood worker	0.3
Senior school neighborhood worker	0.7
Teacher aide	0.2
Per-session personnel	
Major nonathletic extracurricular (per 2-hour session)	.0015
School secretary (per day)	
Summer service	.003
Peak load	.003

Although subject to constraints of unions and the "politics of planning," principals and faculty have greater staffing flexibility under site budgeting than when each personnel type is allocated individually to schools. This leads to a final observation on the use of formulas and negotiation in budgeting: although formulas are developed primarily for ease of administration, the presence of complex allocation formulas is not necessarily synonymous with centralized planning and decision making.

Comparing Budgeting in Public and Private Schools

Virtually all of the preceding discussion on budgeting refers to *public* schools. Additional ways to improve public school budgeting have continued to emerge over the previous several years and will likely continue to be proposed (see, for example, Brackett, Chambers, and Parrish 1983). It is unlikely that fundamental budgeting processes will be radically altered or that resources will be allocated much differently than they have been in the past. Regardless of the particular organizing theme, public school budgets will likely continue to be heavily documented, program oriented, highly participative processes, designed to secure sufficient consensus to convince sponsors to provide tax revenues.

One of the reasons that normative theories of public school budgeting are not widely accepted is that budget reformers make faulty assumptions about the preferences of public school administrators and the importance of existing systems of decision rights. Budget reformers presume that public school administrators greatly desire more information in order to make better budget allocation decisions. In fact, they feel that there is little discretion available in the budget process, and their preference is to pass a budget, not to make better budget decisions. Without changes in decision rights, it is probably naive to suspect that changes in budgeting processes *per se* will lead to significantly improved decisions.

Budgets in private nonprofit schools are much less detailed, often only a page in length (see exhibit 6.9). They are usually created by a subcommittee of the board of trustees in partnership with the business administrator, and they are passed at one of the monthly board meetings. Budgets in private for-profit schools are even less public, constituting in themselves short-run plans designed by and for managers. In both types of private schools the two major budget decisions are usually rates of increase in tuition on the revenue side and faculty salaries on the expenditure side.

Conclusion

Whereas public schools are extensively preoccupied with budgeting processes, budgeting procedures are much less formal in nonpublic schools. Variations in the complexity of budget documents parallel variations in the complexity of budget processes. Public school budgets are more complex than private processes are. Public school budgets are more complex than private school budgets are by a factor of about twenty, even after adjusting for differences in budget size. These differences are representative of differences in the systems rights in schools across sectors.

Public school district administrators derive the bulk of their revenues from sponsors who have very little first-hand knowledge of the school district's

Exhibit 6.9

Example of Private School Budget 1983–1984

(Reported as of September)

	Budget 82–83	Actual 82–83	Budget 83–84	Projected 83–84
Income				
1 enrollment (equiv.)	445	442	415	433
2 gross tuition	1,908	1,842	1,883	1,983
3 endowment	32	32	33	37
4 state aid	17	19	19	19
5 tennis and swim	113	99	93	93
6 athletic store	6	5	6	5
7 day camp	25	41	41	45
8 summer school	10	9	9	10
9 driver education	27	25	26	24
10 music school	14	10	10	10
11 rental of facilities	7	11	7	7
12 interest earned	61	77	58	75
13 miscellaneous	4	4	2	4
14 total before gifts	2,224	2,174	2,187	2,312
15 annual sale	90	86	90	86
16 annual giving	130	123	140	140
17 special gifts	0	0	0	0
18 arts grants	5	33	5	5
19 total income	2,449	2,416	2,422	2,543
Expense				
1 equiv. full-time faculty	53.8	53.8	50.8	50
2 aver. full-faculty salary	16	16	17	18
3 scholarships	220	220	220	225
faculty remissions	33	36	44	50
4 faculty salaries	941	882	914	911
5 staff salaries	321	323	340	342
6 benefits	188	185	207	200
7 educational supplies	100	93	100	100
8 food service	60	62	65	65
9 buildings and grounds	195	188	230	214
10 administrative	114	90	102	102
11 financial	28	29	26	26
12 capital/depreciation	60	58	40	130
13 mortgage principal	30	30	32	32
14 community programs	154	183	143	140
15 search/relocation	5	1	0	0
16 total expense	2,449	2,380	2,463	2,537

Exhibit 6.9, continued

	Budget 82–83	Actual 82–83	Budget 83–84	Projected 83–84
total income before giving	2,224	2,174	2,187	2,312
total expense	2,449	2,380	2,463	2,537
deficit before giving	(225)	(206)	(276)	(225)
gifts	225	242	235	231
net surplus (deficit)	-0-	36	(41)	6

overall operation. This is certainly true of sponsors at the state and federal levels of government, and is increasingly true of the local level. The budget process (and document) in the public sector has to carry a relatively large share of the information to sponsors that justifies school expenditures. The process is designed to convince local sponsors that a scientific, rational analysis of school spending plans has taken place. Much of the budget document format is mandated by state sponsors and, coupled with financial accounting controls, helps to assure those sponsors that public school officials spend state money in desired ways.

Budgeting does not carry the same burden in the private sectors. Sponsors, being largely clients, are informed about school performance and "quality" in ways other than through the budget. Decisions to support or not to support the school are based on a wide variety of personal experience and perceived school reputation. For a for-profit school this may include a reputation for speedy job placement and the existence of modern-looking facilities. For a nonprofit school this may include a reputation for high proportions of college placement and a warm, friendly atmosphere when the school is visited.

All this is not to say that school budgeting in the private sectors is any less thoroughly deliberated. Rather, private school managers can (must) rely on many indicators of performance other than budgets to secure resources from sponsors.

References

Alioto, R. F., and Jungherr, J. A. "Using PPBS to Overcome Taxpayers' Resistance." *Phi Delta Kappan*, November 1969, pp. 138–141.

Anthony, Robert N. *Planning and Control Systems: A Framework for Analysis*. Boston:

Graduate School of Business Administration, Harvard University, 1965.

Blodgett, Terrell. "Steps to Success with Zero-Base Budgeting Systems." *Management Controls* 24: 6 (1973): 15.

Botner, S. "Four Years of PPBS: An Appraisal." *Public Administration Review* 30 (July/August 1970): 423–431.

Brackett, John; Chambers, Jay; and Parrish, Thomas. "The Legacy of Rational Budgeting Models in Education and a Proposal for the Future." Stanford, Calif.: Institute for Research on Educational Finance and Governance, August 1983.

Burkhead, Jesse. "The State of the Economy: Resources and Costs for Educational Services." Paper delivered at the Conference on the Changing Politics of Education: Prospects for the 1970s. University of Virginia, November 23–24, 1976.

Capron, William M. "PPBS and State Budgeting." *Public Administration Review*, March/April 1969, pp. 155–167.

Carpenter, M. B., and Haggart, S. A. *Cost-Effectiveness for Educational Planning*. Santa Monica, Calif.: Rand Corporation, 1969. P–4327.

Crecine, John P. *Governmental Problem-Solving: A Computer Simulation of Municipal Budgeting*. Chicago: Rand McNally Co., 1969.

Curtis, William H. *Educational Resources Management System*. Chicago: Research Corporation of the Association of School Business Officials, 1971.

Fogel, Richard. "Conditions for the Use of PPB." *Journal of Research and Development in Education* 3 (Summer 1979): 72–79.

Garms, Walter I.; Guthrie, James W.; and Pierce, Lawrence C. *School Finance, The Economics and Politics of Public Education*. Englewood Cliffs, N.J.: Prentice-Hall, 1978.

Gerwin, Donald. *Budgeting Public Funds: The Decision Process in an Urban School District*. Madison: University of Wisconsin Press, 1969.

Gideonse, Henrick, et al. "School Site Budgeting: Abstracting the Literature." A Project for the Education Panel of the Cincinnatus Association, February 1981.

Gross, Bertram M. "The New Systems Budgeting." *Public Administration Review*, March/April 1969, pp. 113–137.

Hartley, Harry. *Educational Planning—Programming—Budgeting: A Systems Approach*. Englewood Cliffs, N.J.: Prentice-Hall, 1968.

Kirst, Michael W. "The Rise and Fall of PPBS in California." *Phi Delta Kappan* 56: 8 (April 1975): 535–538.

Lee, Robert C., and Johnson, Ronald W. *Public Budgeting Systems*. Baltimore: University Park Press, 1973.

Mushkin, Selma J. "PPBS in Cities." *Public Administration Review*, March/April 1969, pp. 167–178.

Novick, David, ed. *Current Practice in Program Budgeting (PPBS), Analysis and Case Studies Covering Government and Business*. New York: Crane, Russak, 1973.

Phyrr, Peter A. *Zero-Base Budgeting*. New York: John Wiley and Sons, 1973.

Robinson, David; Yagielski, John; and Brueningsen, Arthur. "Using Zero-Base Budgeting in Effecting Cost Reductions." *Educational Economics* 1: 4 (September 1976): 14–18.

Schick, Allen. "Systems Politics and Systems Budgeting." *Public Administration Review* (March/April 1969): 137–151.

Simmons, William, and Barkdull, Charles W. "Why Is Response to PPBS Mostly

Bad? An Answer or Two." *School Business Affairs* 42: 11 (November 1967): 280–282.

Steiss, Alan W. *Public Budgeting and Management.* Lexington, Mass.: D. C. Heath and Co., 1972.

van Geel, Tyll. "PPBES and District Resource Allocation." *Administrator's Notebook* 22: 1 (1973).

Weiss, Edmond H. "PPBS in Education." *Journal of General Education* 25 (April 1973): 17–27.

Wildavsky, Aaron. *Budgeting, A Comparative Theory of Budgetary Processes.* Boston: Little, Brown and Co., 1975.

Supplementary Reading

Cheek, Logan M. *ZBB Comes of Age.* New York: Amacon (Division of American Management Association, 1977.

ERIC. *The Best of ERIC—School-Based Management*, No. 53. Educational Resources Information Center, 1980.

Hentschke, Guilbert C. "Evaluating Zero-Base Budgeting in the Light of Earlier Budget Reforms." *Journal of Education Finance* 4 (Fall 1978): 234–247.

Hentschke, Guilbert C. *Management Operations in Education.* Berkeley: McCutchan Publishing, 1975.

Lawrence, Pierce. "Decentralization and Educational Reform in Florida." Educational Resources Information Clearinghouse (ERIC), 1978. ED 153 368.

Schick, Allen. "The Road to PPBS: the Stages of Budget Reform." *Public Administration Review* 26: 4 (1966): 243–258.

Schick, Allen. "The Road From ZBB." *Public Administration Review* 38: 2 (1978): 177–180.

7

Cash Management

by Frederick L. Dembowski

•

Overview

The feature that distinguishes cash management from general financial management is timing. Funds flow into schools in varying amounts at different points in time, and they flow out in a pattern usually quite unlike that of the inflow pattern. The result of different inflows and outflows of cash is the creation of unique sets of problems and opportunities. The problem of being temporarily short of needed cash is often solved through short-term borrowing. The opportunity created by temporarily possessing excess amounts of cash takes the form of short-term investments that yield additional revenues. This chapter describes the major activities associated with cash management, highlighting the differences between public and private schools where they exist.

•••

Introduction

Approximately $1.5 billion is earned annually by public school districts nationwide through cash management. Another half billion dollars is earned by private schools.[1] With these large amounts of revenue at stake, it is no wonder that cash management has become recognized as an increasingly important function in school business operations. The purpose of this chapter is to discuss the major aspects of a cash management program and to demonstrate how an effective cash management system may be established or improved in public school districts and private schools.

Cash management represents an important component of financial management in an educational organization. It is the process of managing the monies of a school in order to ensure maximum cash availability and maximum yield on investments of idle cash. It is concerned with what happens between the time cash is received as revenue and when it is expended. More specifically, cash management is concerned with the conversion of accounts receivable to cash receipts and of accounts payable to cash disbursements, the rate at which cash disbursements clear the bank, and what is done with cash in the meantime.

The goals of cash management may be subdivided into financial and nonfinancial goals. The primary financial goals of cash management are as follows:

1. *Availability*—to maximize cash available to meet daily needs and to increase the cash available for investment
2. *Yield*—to earn the maximum return on cash invested

These goals conflict with each other to the extent that cash invested is not available to meet current obligations. Since bills must be paid, the yield goal is necessarily secondary. However, the timing of cash inflows and outflows may be manipulated to affect yield favorably.

The nonfinancial goals include building the trust and goodwill of the taxpaying community or tuition-paying parents, promoting favorable business relations with vendors and banks, and ensuring the orderly conduct of the financial aspects of the district's operations.

A cash management program encompasses seven interrelated elements designed to attain the two cash management goals of availability and yield. The impact of these elements on each other and on the cash management goals is shown in exhibit 7.1.[2] Each of these components is discussed in the following sections.

---

1. Based on estimates derived from Frankel and Gerald (1980, p. 113).
2. Exhibit 7.1 and a portion of the text on pages 215–217 were adapted from Patitucci and Lichtenstein (1977).

Exhibit 7.1

The Elements and Goals of a Cash Management Program

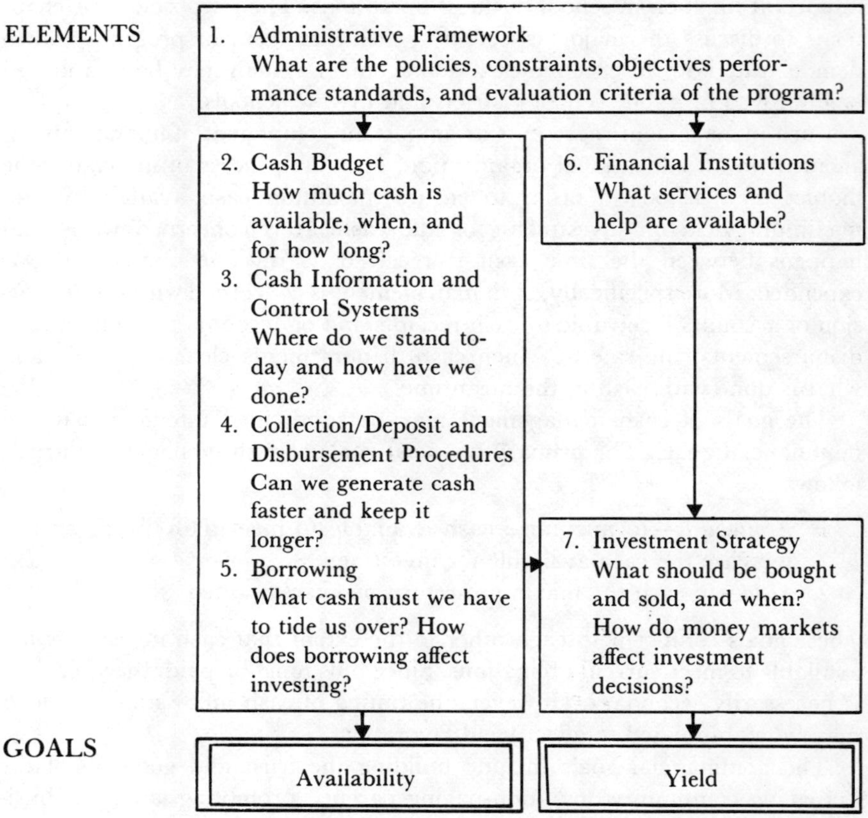

Source: Adapted from F. M. Patitucci and M. H. Lichtenstein, "Improving Cash Management in Local Government: A Comprehensive Approach" (Municipal Finance Officers Association 1977).

The Administrative Framework of Cash Management

The administrative framework describes the policy, legal, and procedural requirements for carrying out an effective cash management program on a day-to-day basis. In order to contribute to the achievement of cash management goals, the business administrator must have the following:

1. A set of federal, state, and local laws that affect the operation of a cash management program

2. A written district policy approved by the board governing the conduct of the cash management program (see appendix 7.1 for a sample board policy)
3. A cash investment "pool" consisting of the cash balances of different funds
4. An ongoing evaluation process that reviews progress periodically throughout the fiscal year and provides appropriate historical performance data

Every state has a number of restrictions on the cash management activities of educational organizations, particularly on local school districts. These state laws generally restrict cash management in three areas. First, they stipulate the dates and procedures to be followed in collecting taxes and fees. For example, they may specify the dates that property taxes may be collected and the procedures to be followed for delinquent taxes. Second, they restrict the kinds of securities and obligations a school district may use. Finally, many states limit the types of financial institutions with which local districts may do business. For example, some states prohibit the use of mutual savings banks and out-of-state banks. These statutory restrictions vary from state to state.

The school business administrator should help establish a written statement that defines the organization's policies on cash management. A typical policy adopted by the board of education might cover the following items:

1. The delegation of authority for the cash management activities to one district official
2. A listing of the types of investments in which the district may invest
3. The criteria for selecting a depository bank
4. The specification of the frequency and types of financial reports that must be submitted to the board
5. Local district limitations on cash management

In writing a policy, the specification of policies, constraints, and limits is necessary, but the specification of procedures should be avoided and left to administrative personnel. A sample board policy is given in appendix 7.1.

The pooling of cash resources consists of consolidating the cash accounts of separate funds into one or a few bank accounts for investment purposes. There are many advantages to pooling: it permits larger investments, it tends to smooth out fluctuations in the cash flow, it simplifies the investment process, and it reduces paperwork. Under a typical pooling process, accounting records are kept for the pooled account but they also attribute cash and investments to each fund. Interest earnings are apportioned accordingly.

The evaluation of cash management performance completes the administrative cycle. It tells interested parties how successful the program has been and establishes a basis for developing objectives for cash management programs in future years.

The rate of return on investments of cash varies greatly. Various studies indicate that the average rate of return is somewhere between 0.1 percent and 0.5 percent of total expenditures, with individual educational organizations earning between nothing and nearly 4 percent of total expenditures. (McCanless 1952; Carr 1971; Rothrock 1972; and Welliver 1974). The rate-of-return measure reported in these studies is calculated by dividing the net interest earnings by the total expenditure of the school district. The total expenditure figure should include all of the school district's expenses. If the school district borrowed money during the fiscal year, the interest paid on the note should be included in the total expenditure, but the principal used to pay off the note should not be included. In determining the net interest earning of the school district, any interest paid out on borrowed money should be subtracted from the total interest earnings on investments.

Measuring the Efficiency of the Cash Management Program

Apparently some cash management programs are yielding proportionately more revenue than others. How can the school business administrator determine whether his cash management program could yield more revenue? One approach would be to compare actual performance to a standard of perfect performance. The optimally efficient cash management program would maintain a zero balance in the cash accounts, placing all cash into interest-bearing investments. The optimal amount of interest earnings could be obtained through the use of mathematical programming techniques.[3] Interest earnings from the previously determined optimal investments plus interest earnings from the savings account (assuming a zero cash balance in the checking account at all times) would yield a benchmark of the highest possible interest earnings available to that educational organization. The actual interest earned could be divided by the optimal amount of interest, which yields a percentage that reflects the efficiency of the program. The more efficient the program, the closer the percentage is to 100 percent. In other words, the efficiency rating is calculated by:

$$E = \frac{I_a + S_a}{I_o + S_o}$$

where:

E = the efficiency of the financial management operation of the district expressed as a percentage

3. See the linear programming problem in the appendix to this chapter.

I_a = the actual interest earnings from investments
S_a = the actual interest earnings from the savings account
I_o = the optimal interest earnings from investments
S_o = the optimal interest earnings from the savings account.

Through the use of the efficiency rating, the cash manager can judge performance over time, which is improved by keeping the balances of the cash accounts to a minimum while optimizing investments. For example, suppose a business manager earned \$300,000 in interest from investments and \$65,000 in interest from the savings account during the previous year. Through a review of the year's cash flow, he determined (either variably or through a mathematical programming technique) that the potential interest earning from investments was \$350,000 and if all remaining cash were placed in a savings account, he would have earned an additional \$75,000 in interest. The calculation for the efficiency rating would be:

$$E = \frac{I_a + S_a}{I_o + S_o} = \frac{\$300{,}000 + \$65{,}000}{\$350{,}000 + \$75{,}000} = \frac{\$365{,}000}{\$425{,}000} = .857$$

Thus, the cash management program was 85.7 percent efficient. The rating should be interpreted with caution because there are a number of factors that will hold the rating down—factors that do not necessarily indicate that the cash management program is inefficient. For example, most cash managers in educational organizations do not invest the "float" in their cash accounts. Second, they are often required to maintain large cash balances in compliance with the minimum balance requirements of the depository bank. Finally, the cost of additional analysis (especially by manual methods) may be greater than the possible additional yields.

Efficiency, as determined here, is but one of numerous ways to monitor and evaluate the cash management program.[4] Each has strengths and weaknesses. The ratio of investment earnings to total expenditures, mentioned earlier, is a case in point. It is easy to understand and calculate, and it is especially useful for interdistrict or interschool comparisons. It is not, however, a good measure of one program's performance over time because interest *rates* vary from year to year.

Cash Budgeting

Cash budgeting involves the estimation of receipts and disbursements in order to determine cash requirements and possible cash surpluses and to develop a cash management strategy. Cash budgeting seeks answers to the following questions: When are cash receipts expected? How long will cash be

4. For a complete discussion of this topic, see Dembowski (1980, pp. 51–67)

Exhibit 7.2

The Cash-Flow Pattern of the Sample District
(in thousands of dollars)

Period	1	2	3	4	5	6	7
Month	Jan. 1	Feb. 1	Mar. 1	Apr. 1	May 1	June 1	July 1
Inflow	400	250	400	150	100	50	50
Outflow	200	200	200	200	200	400	100
Netflow	+200	+50	+200	−50	−100	−350	−50

Period	8	9	10	11	12	13
Month	Aug. 1	Sept. 1	Oct. 1	Nov. 1	Dec. 1	Dec. 31
Inflow	50	150	400	400	50	0
Outflow	100	200	200	200	300	0
Netflow	−50	−50	+200	+200	−250	0

Note: All revenues are received by the district on the first day of the month.
— All expenditures occur on the first day of the month.
— The beginning cash balance of the district on the first day of the year is $50,000.

available? Is borrowing required? Are there opportunities for investment? If so, when?

Cash budgeting is different from revenue and expenditure budgeting in that it is concerned with the timing of the receipts and disbursements as well as with their amounts. Revenue and expenditure budgeting is concerned with budgeting commitments and obligations, and it usually precedes cash budgeting. Furthermore, while the revenue and expenditure budgeting process culminates in a budget document, cash budgeting is a continual process with periodic updates.

An important tool in cash budgeting is the cash-flow schedule. A cash-flow schedule may be as simple as a table that lists the total expected receipts, disbursements, and net balance by month (exhibit 7.2), or it may be as detailed as a listing of major receipts and disbursements by fund and source on a weekly or even daily basis (exhibit 7.3). In constructing a cash-flow schedule, two parameters must be determined. First, a time horizon must be selected; the school business administrator usually develops an annual cash-flow schedule for the fiscal year. This annual schedule will indicate periods of major borrowing and investment requirements. Once an annual schedule has been developed, cash-flow schedules for smaller time horizons (that is, biannually, monthly, weekly, and so on) may be devel-

Exhibit 7.3
Cash-Flow Chart
(for the period July 1 to October 1)

Date	Explanation	Estimated Expenditures	Estimated Revenues	Running Balance
July 1	Openish cash balance (not fund balance)	$	$	$ 247,000
14	Payroll	37,000		210,000
28	Payroll	40,000		170,000
31	Bills	30,000		140,000
Aug. 1	Debt, principal and interest	63,000		77,000
11	Payroll	37,000		40,000
15	Bills	40,000		0
25	Tax anticipation note (TAN)		400,000	400,000
25	Payroll	40,000		360,000
31	Bills	50,000		310,000
Sept. 1	Debt, principal, and interest	63,000		247,000
1	Payroll	200,000		47,000
10	Bills	40,000		7,000
15	State aid		350,000	357,000
15	Payroll	200,000		157,000
20	Bills	60,000		97,000
29	Property taxes		1,400,000	1,497,000
29	Pay TAN	400,000		1,097,000

oped. In general, the smaller the time horizon, the more time consuming and costly the cash-budgeting process becomes. Thus, the school business administrator must weigh the additional costs of more detailed cash budgeting against the anticipated benefits of increased earnings.

The second parameter essential to cash budgeting is the selection of the level of specification involved in the cash-flow schedule. The cash manager must decide on a level of aggregation in specifying receipts and disbursements and the time interval for reporting. For example, exhibit 7.2 represents a cash-flow schedule in which the cash manager has made three decisions. First, it is an annual cash-flow chart representing a fiscal year. Second, total receipts and disbursements are reported, as there is no disaggregation of the data. Finally, the receipts and disbursements are reported in monthly intervals. In contrast, exhibit 7.3 is a three-month cash-flow chart with receipts and disbursements disaggregated into major categories reported on the day of anticipated receipt and disbursement. This more detailed cash-flow schedule will enable the cash manager to make a more precise estimate of cash needs for the school district.

In order to develop a cash-flow schedule, the timing and amounts of the cash receipts and disbursements of the district must be anticipated. Historical cash-flow information is helpful for this purpose, for example, the previous years' cash accounts. (Records of the dates and amounts of major receipts and disbursements should be kept as a memorandum account.) Public school districts receive most of their revenues through property taxes and state aid payments. Both of these payments accrue to the school district in large lump sums periodically throughout the fiscal year. The property taxes, which often account for between 40 percent and 60 percent of the total district revenues, are usually received by the school district once or twice a year. Thus, these annual or semi-annual payments are quite large.

State aid payments are usually the second largest source of school district revenue. The timing and amounts of state aid payments vary from state to state. Together, the property tax receipts and state aid payments constitute the majority of school district receipts, typically accounting for between 80 percent and 90 percent of the total revenue of the district. Since school business officials know with a high degree of certainty both the timing and amounts of these funds, they are able to plan accordingly for the receipt of the funds.

Private schools business officials, who rely heavily on tuition receipts from individual families, face a different pattern of revenue receipt. Because they face a much larger number of accounts receivable and because many families pay in installments, the revenue receipt pattern is more even. However, greater provision must also be made for uncollectable accounts.

Expenditure patterns of public and private schools are more similar to each other than are revenue patterns. In both instances expenditures are composed primarily of salary and fringe benefit expenses. The typical educational organization allots approximately 80 percent of the expenditures for these purposes. Once the number of employees is determined and the salaries are negotiated, the flow of most expenditures may be anticipated fairly accurately. During the school year, the expenditure pattern for personnel is relatively stable. Other major expenses, such as debt service payments and utility bills, may also be anticipated through a review of previous years' expenditure patterns. This review would show, for example, that June was a high-expenditure month because social security and other tax payments were made to the federal government.

A graphic portrayal of the data in exhibit 7.2 is presented in exhibit 7.4. October and January revenues are large because of property tax receipts,

Exhibit 7.4
A Cash Budget and Cash-Flow Pattern

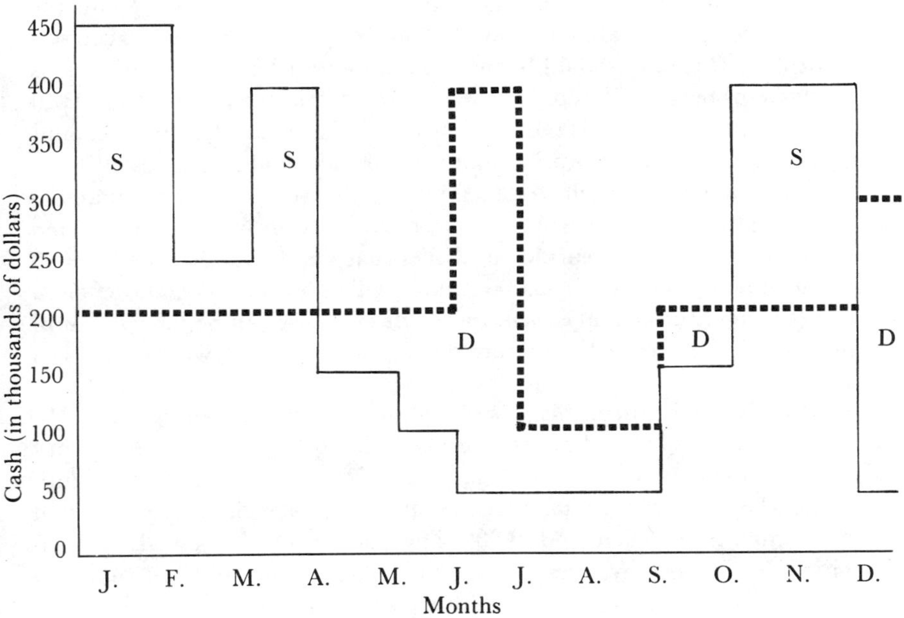

S—indicates a cash surplus
D—indicates a cash deficit

---------- expenditures
__________ revenues

and November and March revenues are large because of state aid payments. Expenditures for most months are stable at $200,000 per month, with a high amount in June and low amounts for the summer months. Because of the differences in the timing of revenues and expenditures, the school business administrator faces periods of surplus cash, denoted by *S* (January through March in exhibit 7.4). From April through October, however, the school has more expenditures than revenues. These periods of cash deficit are denoted by *D*.

The primary task of the school business administrator is to determine what borrowing and investing decisions should be made. If investments are to be made, three questions have to be answered: When should investments be made? What amounts should be invested? For how much time should the cash be invested? If it is necessary for the school district to borrow money until its revenues arrive, the same three questions about timing, amount, and maturity need to be answered.

This financial planning task is usually approached in the following manner. The net cash flow is determined by subtracting the monthly expenditures from revenues. A positive net flow indicates a cash surplus, and, accordingly, a negative flow indicates a deficit. Exhibit 7.1 presents the monthly cash flows in tabular form. The month of January has a $200,000 cash surplus. This cash should be invested in interest-bearing assets such as a certificate of deposit or repurchase agreement. Since the month of April shows a cash deficit of $50,000, a short-term investment of $50,000 should be made from January to April. Another $100,000 could be invested from January to May to cover the $100,000 deficit in May, and the remaining $50,000 from the January surplus should be invested until June, in addition to investing the $250,000 surplus from February and March. The $50,000 beginning balance plus the $300,000 surplus will cover the $350,000 deficit in June. When revenues equal expenditures, this process can be followed until all surplus cash is invested to mature during the months in which there is a cash deficit.

As you may have noted, this process will work until the month of July. In July the school business administrator needs $50,000 to meet expenses, but all available revenue has been used. This deficit situation continues until October, when the property tax revenues arrive. By that time the school will have accumulated a deficit of $150,000. The district must borrow $150,000 in anticipation of future revenues. In October sufficient revenues will arrive to allow for both the repayment of the anticipation note and the investment of an additional $50,000. Thus, the investment process starts again. The actual process of making investments and selecting the appropriate security will be discussed in a later section.

Cash Information and Control

Information required to control the cash management process includes data on the cash balances in the various depository accounts and on anticipated current expenditures and revenues. The cash information system includes three kinds of records: (1) that which records actual financial events as they occur, that is, a record of investments made; (2) that which assists in making investment decisions, that is, the current cash balance by account; and (3) that which permanently accounts for cash by fund.

The cash information system consists of accounting processes that routinely record and process data for six interrelated purposes. A cash accounting system keeps track of daily receipts and disbursements, provides cash balances by fund and account, and provides daily average-cost balances. A cash budget reporting system provides a budgeted-compared-to-actual report of receipts and disbursements. This system provides information to update the cash-flow schedule and to evaluate the cash manager's forecasting abilities.

An investment status and earnings system is useful in providing a summary performance record of cash management activities. Three key sets of information on investment transactions that should be recorded are the purchase (date, amount, rate, and so on), the sale (date, amount), and receipt of interest. An extension of this system, the earned interest apportionment system, is sometimes needed. It is used when the interest or posted funds need to be redistributed to the appropriate funds or accounts.

A reconciliation system provides the data to undertake a monthly reconciliation between the balance in the district accounting records and the actual cash balances in the bank accounts and other liquid assets. The reconciliation usually follows this basic format: ending cash balance equals cash in treasury plus investment principal plus cash in banks minus outstanding checks and deposits not recorded.

Finally, a performance reporting system provides the information required to assess how well the district cash management system is attaining the four objectives of availability, yield, dollars earned, and efficiency. Performance reporting is particularly useful when estimating future interest during the budgeting process.

A well-administered cash information and control system also has less formal processes. The informal processes consist of close working relationships between the school business administrator and administrators in the various (cash receiving and spending) departments of the school. They can provide the school business administrator with information on anticipated cash flows that the formal system may not furnish. The school business administrator will also attempt to keep abreast of potential changes in the earnings of various investment instruments.

Collection and Disbursement Procedures

Cash collection, deposit, and disbursement procedures are possibly the most important factors in determining the maximum availability of funds and whether funds will meet cash needs or there will be surplus funds to invest. The development of procedures to immediately deposit dollars in the school accounts and to keep those dollars there as long as possible can mean a significant increase in the investment dollars earned. To ensure that these processes will contribute to the achievement of the school business administrator's cash management goals, a school should have—

1. revenue collection policies and procedures for each major source of revenue;

2. special deposit procedures to handle major revenue-processing problems, such as tax collections;
3. established deposit procedures for each type of revenue and collection location; and
4. disbursement policies and procedures for each category of expenditure and vendor.

Collection procedures can be accelerated in the public sector if the school business administrator develops procedures designed to encourage the speedy payment of property taxes. Some suggested procedures are as follows:

1. Increase the frequency of property tax collections. This will allow the receipt of cash to align more closely with expected disbursements, and it will smooth out the cyclical cash flow, thereby permitting larger and longer investments.
2. Raise the penalties for delinquent payments. This will discourage the practice of deferring payment and holding money for more personally productive reasons.
3. Offer discounts to encourage prepayments. This is especially advantageous to the district if the discounts did not cost more than the expected earnings on the cash made available by the prepayments.
4. Provide preaddressed and prepaid postage on the return envelopes to encourage rapid payment.

The public school districts could accelerate receipt of many other types of taxes by working closely with administrators at those federal, state, or local government agencies responsible for distributing the funds. For example, lobbying with other school districts at the state level might be effective in producing earlier collection of state aid monies. Also, the required forms and claims should be submitted complete and in a timely manner so that revenues are not delayed on technicalities.

School business administrators in the private sector can create similar incentives to speed tuition payments:

1. Add interest charges to parents electing to pay tuition on the installment basis. This, in effect, is a discount for paying the full amount early.
2. Add penalties for late payments.
3. After an appropriate waiting period, personally contact the parent to ascertain why payment has not been received.
4. Develop and carry out policies on actions to be taken for nonpayment of tuition. (Some private schools actually "carry" a delinquent account for several years, allowing the student to stay in school.)

Deposit procedures affect the rate at which money already on its way to the school gets deposited into a bank account. Sometimes it makes sense to intervene to shorten the deposit time. School districts in the far western portion of New York State, for example, send a courier to the state capital (two hundred miles away) to collect the state aid checks for the districts instead of having them mailed. While this may sound trivial, it is clearly worth the effort. It would probably take three days by mail for the district to receive a $2 million state aid check. If the district picks up the check, drives it back on the same day, and deposits it into a savings account, the district could earn $822.00 in interest, minus the cost of the driver and trip!

There are a number of special arrangements that can be made to speed up deposits. Some banks will accept direct deposits of property tax payments mailed in by taxpayers in envelopes addressed to a lock-box. With a lock-box arrangement, cash is immediately deposited into the school's accounts. This removes a step in the deposit process, and consequently payments become immediately available for use or investment upon receipt. Wire transfers of cash may be used to eliminate delays caused by mailing if the funds are received in a location other than the school. Depositing funds in branch offices of the main bank will also speed up the collection and deposit process.

School business administrators may also use a number of methods to disburse cash in a manner favorable to the school's cash management program. From the cash management standpoint, disbursements should be timed so that they remove cash from the district accounts at the last possible moment. However, bills should be paid in a timely fashion. Unhappy vendors may raise prices or perform poorly, and administrators may spend an excessive amount of time responding to complaints. One approach to disbursement is to schedule two payrolls and two vendor payment days per month. Over time, this practice will result in a routine of scheduled disbursements that are tailor-made for cash management procedures. An accounts payable system that allows the payables to "age" before payment can improve disbursement control. As invoices are received, they should be briefly analyzed and a payment date affixed. They can then be paid on the later date instead of immediately. Some factors that affect the payment date decision are discounts available, the history of a particular vendor requiring immediate payment, and the method of payment, that is, payment by mail or direct delivery. The trade-offs for discounts should be examined. For example, a discount of 1 percent for repayment in ten days, as opposed to no discount when the full bill is due in thirty days, is equivalent to an interest rate of 18 per cent per year.

Warrants can be used to improve cash availability in certain instances. A warrant is a promise to pay a sum of money at some future date upon which the warrant is presented to the issuer (the school) by the vendor. Under a warrant system, funds need not be available until the date on which the warrant is presented back to the issuer for payment. One disadvantage of this method is that banks usually charge higher handling charges for warrants than for checks. Vendor relations is also an important consideration in changing disbursement procedures. Frequent communication and a history of cordial relationships with vendors can carry a school district over a rough financial period. For example, instead of borrowing cash for a very short period of anticipated deficit, a school district might delay payments to vendors in order to cover the deficit.

A final important issue regarding disbursements is the direct deposit of payrolls. Direct payroll deposit promotes favorable employee-district relations because employees can more easily gain access to their money. Banks like direct payroll deposit because it brings them new customers and increases their cash balances. However, direct payroll deposit is unfavorable to the school district from a cash management standpoint because it significantly speeds up the flow of cash from the district accounts, thus shortening the time available to the district for investing that cash.

Borrowing

There are times when the school business administrator may require cash in excess of anticipated revenues. At such times, the district may borrow cash through a variety of means. There are two classes of borrowing: long term and short term. Long-term borrowing provides the district with a large sum of money, which is usually expended for a particular purpose. Short-term borrowing allows the district to meet current obligations for a period prior to the receipt of anticipated cash. Both types of borrowing are integral components of cash management.

Long-Term Borrowing

Long-term borrowing allows a school to finance a capital improvement project by making payments over a long period of time. The ability of public school districts to engage in long-term borrowing is regulated by statutory law that stipulates the conditions under which a district may engage in long-term borrowing. These regulations cover four areas: (1) debt limits on borrowing; (2) time periods allowable before maturity; (3) bond payment timing and limitations; and (4) legal steps for issuance of bonds.

Many states have legal debt limits that must be recognized. Such limits are usually tied to the assessed valuation of the school district. For example, a school district may have a 10 percent debt limit. If the school district has a total full valuation of $100 million and an outstanding bonded debt of $4 million, the school district is eligible to incur an additional $6 million of bonded indebtedness.

If a school district has not exceeded its debt limit, it must then decide what the total bond requirement is and over what period of time the obligations will mature. The principal of the bond is determined by the anticipated cost of the capital improvement project. The life of the bond is typically the period of probable usefulness of the capital investment, which usually ranges from three to fifty years. Once the period of probable usefulness has been determined, the maturities of the bonds are established. Long-term bonds usually have serial maturities in annual installments, with the first installment occurring between eighteen months and three years from the date of the bond and the last maturity occurring no later than the expiration of the period of probable usefulness. While the amounts of the annual bond payments may be unequal, there are usually state regulations that limit the payment differences. One example is the "50 percent rule," which stipulates that no installment of a bond issue may be more than 50 percent in excess of the smallest previous installment. (Commissioner's Advisory Committee for School Business Administration 1976, p. 3) Thus, if the first installment of a bond was $20,000, no later issue may exceed $30,000. This rule prevents the ballooning of bond issue installments during the last maturities; in this case the amount of the earlier maturities are kept to a bare minimum as a matter of political expediency—the elected officials supporting the bonds would benefit politically by providing improvements at low initial costs, and the burden of higher subsequent payments would fall on those people elected in perhaps fifty years. A nonschool example of this is the seventy-year paving bonds in New York, most of which were paid in the sixty-ninth year. By that time, the people who built the streets and those who were elected for paving the city had long since departed, along with, in some cases at least, the roads themselves. Incidentally, the 50 percent rule usually does not work in reverse. A $500,000 installment can be paid the first year, and a payment of $1,000 in the following year may be made if desired.

Because the amounts of money involved in bond issues are usually quite large, most state laws mandate a number of procedural steps designed to ensure protection of the local taxpayers. These steps include:

1. Public advertisement of the capital project and financial requirements
2. Voter authorization
3. State approval of the plans and specifications for the capital improvement projects
4. Procedural steps for the sale of the bonds
5. Reinvestment of the bond proceeds

Many states require that bond issues be subject to public referenda.

The uncertainty of raising revenues by means of fiscal referenda, be it for a bond, tax levy, or budget approval, is evident in daily newspaper headlines—repeated defeats of school budgets and bond proposals; tax levies are defeated four, five, and six times—and numerous other school district fiscal crises. While the fiscal crises of school districts make good copy for newspapers, the results of many public referenda are positive. In thirty-two states, voter approval is required before any general obligation bonds can be issued for public school purposes (Hamilton and Cohen 1978). In fifteen states, voter approval is required in most, but not all, districts. Only three states (Alabama, Hawaii, and Indiana) do not require voter approval for school bond issues. In fiscal year 1976, 770 school bond elections were held nationwide proposing school bond issues that totaled $2.1 billion. In those elections, 391 bond issues totaling $970 million were approved. However, the 50.8 percent voter approval rate was markedly lower than the approval rate during the 1940s and 1950s, which was a period when school proposals rarely lost.

There is a wide variety of laws governing voter approval of bond issues in the various states. Besides voter approval, the state government must approve the project. The plans and specifications of the capital improvement project are evaluated to assure compliance with state building and safety codes.

Once voter and state approval has been obtained, there are a number of procedural steps to be followed in the legal sale of the obligation. Typically, the debt statement must be filed with the state government, and the nature of sale of the bonds must be posted and advertised. The sale of the obligation usually follows a bidding procedure in which bids are opened publicly and awarded to the lowest responsible bidder.

The cash management process begins with the receipt of the proceeds of the obligation. Since these proceeds are rarely expended immediately, they should be invested. Provisions for investing these funds should be made well in advance of their receipt so that not a day on interest is lost. (Ten percent annual interest per day of $1 million comes to $274!)

Where cash from bond issues for capital projects makes up a large percentage of the cash balances, the public school district should treat the bond proceeds separately for cash-budgeting purposes. Ideally, the maturities should match with the cash requirements for the project, but this seldom occurs. Thus, the cash manager should monitor these funds closely to ensure the maximum yield while meeting the project's cash requirements. Often, each project has a separate account to prevent pooling with other district monies.

Private school business administrators face fewer requirements and different constraints when entering long-term capital markets. Endowed institutions can borrow from endowment funds for capital projects. Many private schools at one time or another finance major capital improvement projects through capital fund drives. Finally, they seek loans from banks for capital improvements much the same way a private individual secures a home-improvement loan. Although legal requirements are fewer, the private school business administrator can borrow only those amounts that bankers are willing to lend or which donors are willing to concede is an "appropriate" use of endowment funds. In general, the private school business official must convince the sources of capital that investment in a project will yield greater long-term benefits to the school than no investment.

Short-Term Borrowing

The purpose of short-term borrowing is to provide sufficient cash to meet current obligations during the interim between when cash is needed and enough revenue is received. Again, the restrictions placed on (and opportunities available to) public school business administrators differ from those facing the private school business administrator. The private school business administrator establishes a line of credit at a bank against which short-term loans can be made. The public school business official has as many as five types of notes available:

1. Revenue anticipation notes—used for general-purpose expenditures in anticipation of collected revenues other than property taxes
2. Tax anticipation notes—used for general-purpose expenditures in anticipation of taxes or assessments levied or to be levied
3. Budget notes—used to provide revenues during the fiscal year for any unforseeable public emergency and are usually paid off with taxes collected in the succeeding year
4. Capital notes—used to finance all or part of the cost of any object or purpose for which serial or sinking-fund bonds may be issued
5. Bond anticipation notes—which may be issued whenever bonds have been authorized, the proceeds of which may be used only for the same object or purpose as the bond

Short-term (and long-term) borrowing by public officials is subject to federal arbitrage regulations. Generally the interest rates obtainable on investment instruments are higher than the rate at which districts borrow, although there have been periods when this is reversed. The point spread between the borrowing rate and the investing rate offers public school districts the opportunity to "make money" by borrowing and then investing a portion of the proceeds. This process is commonly referred to as *arbitrage.*

The following is an example of arbitrage. A school district develops a cash-flow schedule and determines that it will experience an anticipated cash deficit of $100,000 over the summer months. The school district is able to borrow through their local bank at 5 percent annual interest. The current interest rate for certain investment instruments is 15 percent annually. The district then decides to borrow $500,000 for a full year; it uses $100,000 to cover the deficit in the first two months of the year and invests the remaining $400,000 until the end of the fiscal year. Sufficient revenues arrive in September, but instead of paying off the note, the district invests the remaining $100,000 of the note until the end of the fiscal year. Through this process, the district earns $72,500 in interest revenue and pays $25,000 in interest on the note, which yields a net interest earning of $47,500. Arbitrage has been discouraged by the Internal Revenue Service. Why? The school district administrators gain because it affords them the opportunity to earn interest revenues for their district. Local property-tax payers gain because the added interest income offsets taxes. Bankers favor the process for three reasons: (1) the interest paid on the school district's investment is deductible as a cost of doing business; (2) the interest earned on the note borrowed by the school district is tax exempt, yielding a much higher yield to the bank than the 5 percent rate; and (3) the note may be used by the bank as collateral for all investment instruments.

The only "loser" in this process is the federal government, which collects fewer tax revenues due to the tax exemptions and deductions of the banks. Because of IRS admonishments and court opinions, most states have statutory provisions limiting the arbitrage opportunities.

Private school business officials are not affected by arbitrage regulations because they do not have access to money at below market rates such as their public counterparts do.

Financial Institutions

Educational organizations vary in the fervor with which they pursue assistance from financial institutions. In one state, 60 percent of its public school districts made use of only one bank, and 54 percent of the districts did not use savings accounts.[5] The majority of schools do not choose banking services by competitive bid. Many educational organizations are being assessed an annual fee for banking services and are required to maintain a minimum or minimum-average cash balance in their depository account to compensate the bank for its services. This is not to imply that banks are doing schools a favor by providing financial services.

On the contrary, schools have been among commercial banks' favorite customers. There are a number of reasons for this. Often, an officer of the local bank is a school board member and, less frequently, local superintendents are on the board of trustees of the bank. Handling the funds of the local school district has some public relations value to the bank, for as a manager of a commercial bank stated, "When other depositors know that the school district maintains all of its accounts in the bank, they feel that the bank must be very 'safe' because school districts are very careful with their money." School district accounts are likely to be among the largest accounts that the bank handles. In addition to the volume of funds that flows through the

---

5. For an extended discussion of this topic, see Demboski (1981).

bank, school districts typically maintain large cash balances in their checking accounts. For these reasons, banks have traditionally sought out the business of schools, particularly public school districts.

Different banks use different methods of determining the profitability of the accounts they service. The following example illustrates how a depository bank might conduct an analysis of a school district. XYZ School District used one bank for its checking and savings accounts and also invested money in certificates of deposit through the bank. The school district made all payments to vendors by check. The bank incurred expenses in servicing these checking accounts; these expenses were primarily labor costs for performing various tasks required to service the accounts, such as check reconciliation, accepting deposits, and check clearing. Banks are usually recompensed for these expenses by requiring that a minimum or minimum average cash balance be maintained in the checking account or by charging the school district an annual fee.

In determining how much of a fee to charge or at what level to set the compensating balance requirement, a bank performs a "profitability analysis" of the checking account, which includes determining the expenses of servicing the school district accounts over a period of time. For the XYZ School District, the total expenses for a five-month period were:

Number of checks:	17,646 @ \$.10 each	\$1,764.60
Number of deposits	6,094 @ \$.05 each	304.70
Fixed monthly charge:		
(1 account × 5 months × \$2.00 per account per month)		10.00
Stop-payment requests	11 @ \$4.00 each	44.00
Master Charge sales	208 @ \$.95 each	197.00
Check reconciliation fees:		
\$.01 for first 1,000 per month (3 months only)		30.00
\$.015 per check per month		219.69
Total Expenses		\$2,569.99

Once a bank estimates these charges or expenses of servicing the school district accounts, it then determines whether there is a net profitability for the bank by calculating the earnings allowance of the account. The earnings allowance of the account accrues to the bank because the money sitting in the checking account may be partially invested by the bank in interest-earning assets. The earnings allowance is determined as follows. First, the bank records showed that for the five-month period in question, the gross average daily balance for the checking account was \$359,200. In order to meet governmental liquidity requirements, the bank stated that only 75 percent of this cash balance was available for investment purposes. Thus, the bank could invest \$269,400 of the \$359,200. The bank then stated that it could earn only 2.4 percent annual interest on this money by investing it. Thus, for the five-month period, the bank determined that it could earn \$269,400 × 5/12 × 0.024 or \$2,694 in interest on the school district checking account. The net profitability of the checking account is equal to the earnings allowance credit minus the account expenses, that is, \$2,694 minus \$2,570 equals \$124.00. Thus, the bank would be making a profit of \$124 for the five-month period, or \$297.60 annually. In addition, the bank is charging the XYZ School District \$870 annually as a fee for banking services, which results in a net profit to the bank of \$1,168 annually after expenses. By calculating the bank's net profit from providing service to the district, the business administrator was able to shop for less-expensive service at other banks or negotiate a lower annual fee.

Options in School Banking Relations

The school district could do a number of things to ensure cordial, professional working relationships with financial institutions. First, when selecting a bank, the school business administrator can solicit bids for banking services. Another alternative would be to discuss the account profitability requirements with a number of banks before making a selection. The desire for cordial relations should not inhibit the business administrator from reducing the size of the average daily balance in the checking account to a minimum. Some business administrators feel constrained by the compensating balance requirement set by the bank, and leave more than this amount of cash in the checking account. If the business manager can invest the idle cash in the checking account efficiently, he should negotiate an annual fee and a much lower average daily cash balance requirement with the depository bank.

In the previous example (taken from an actual situation), the bank stated that it could earn only a 2.4 percent annual interest rate on investments. The business administrator could invest funds at rates higher than these. The lowest rate available to school districts is that of U.S. treasury bills currently at about 7 percent per annum. Daily savings accounts rates are usually 5 percent, with certificates of deposit yielding a higher rate. Since the checking account will usually have some money in it because of "float," the estimated average daily balance could be calculated with the assumption that all money was invested, leaving only the "float" in the account. The amount of a "float" is typically between \$50,000 and \$100,000. The district can have the bank use this amount as the compensating balance requirement and pay the bank an annual fee that equals the difference between its earnings allowance on the cash balance and the expenses of servicing the account. By using this method, the school district could invest the rest of the cash in interest-bearing assets. If the XYZ School District had used this technique, it could have earned 5 percent annually on a savings account of approximately

$250,000, which would come to $12,500 minus the cost of the time it took the school business administrator to execute the plan.

The Use of Available Banking Services

To increase the productivity of the school organization's resources, the school business administrator can make use of additional banking services. Most banks offer telephone transfers of cash between checking and savings accounts. The business administrator can call the bank daily to determine the checking account balance and decide whether to transfer money from the savings account to the checking account or vice versa. By evaluating the checking balance, the amounts of outstanding checks, and the cash needs of the school, the business administrator could then maintain only the amount of cash in the checking account that is required to meet immediate expenses. The surplus could be invested in interest-bearing assets. The administrator would routinely deposit daily receipts in the savings account and not in the checking account. All large deposits, such as state aid checks or property tax payments, should at least be deposited in the savings account but preferably be put in higher yield assets. The daily interest earning on $1 million in a 5.25 percent savings account is $144.00. Why leave this cash in the checking account overnight before deciding what to do with it when it could be earning additional interest?

Another service offered by banks that school administrators can use to manage cash flow is the commercial line of credit. In some states, public schools are prohibited from using this method of financing, but private schools are not. If it is not prohibited, public school districts should consider its use. Lines of credit offer an overdraft protection that replaces the need to leave excessively large cash balances in the checking accounts as a margin of safety. This margin of safety is likely costing the school much more per year in lost interest than it saves by not paying interest on overdrafts.

Through the use of a line of credit, the bank lends the school district cash to cover any overdrafts. The loan is made at a specified rate of interest, payable when the overdraft is covered. Because the bank would be loaning money to a tax-exempt institution, the rate of interest is likely to be low. Since many long-term investments such as certificates of deposit or repurchase agreements have relatively higher interest yields, any cash left in the checking account as protection against overdrafts should be invested in 180- or 360-day Certificates of Deposit that earn substantial interest revenues. By monitoring checking balances daily and using telephone transfers of cash as outlined above, the chance of overdraft would be minimized. Any overdrafts that might occur could be paid from interest earnings of the investments made from cash previously left in the checking account for overdraft protection.

Another argument for borrowing through the use of lines of credit is to eliminate the necessity for "cashing in" invested assets before they mature. Suppose a school has a bill due, but has no cash to pay for the bill. (All its cash is invested in interest-bearing assets.) The school business administrator could redeem an interest-bearing asset to pay the bill. In so doing, however, the school would pay an interest penalty for redeeming the asset before it matures. Another option for the school business administrator would be to borrow the necessary cash through the line of credit. Using this option would allow the district to keep its interest-earning asset invested until it matures.

As schools become more restricted financially, there will likely be a tendency to place more of the school's excess cash in interest-bearing assets. This will reduce the average daily cash balances in the depository accounts. Banks will soon note this reduction in their earnings ability, and they probably will perform an account profitability analysis similar to the one previously described. Based on this analysis, a new cash balance level or annual fee will be set by the bank. The school business administrator of the local school district should be aware of what is happening and take an active role in the process. Thus, in the future, school-banking relationships will play an increasingly important role in the financial picture of schools.

Investment Strategy

An investment strategy should govern the actions that are taken in the day-to-day cash management program of the school. The strategy emphasizes the cash management goal of yield and takes the other goal—availability—as a given. The three major factors affecting the investment strategy are available cash, money market conditions, and mix of securities.

1. How much money is available to invest—the cash budget combined with information on current investments determines the forecast of the amount of cash available for investment.
2. Money market conditions—an analysis of the historical and present money market conditions helps forecast the expected increase or decrease in the yield rates of various types of securities.
3. Mix of securities—the cash control and reporting systems should provide information about the current mix of investments (what investments have been made for what periods of time) representing the investment portfolio at the beginning of the period covered by the strategy.

One investment strategy was implied in the cash-budgeting section above. In that discussion, the cash flow of a sample school (see exhibit 7.1) was determined, and investments were selected based on a prediction of cash availability and need in later periods. This strategy is the most basic procedure for investing, and it represents a reasonable "first approximation." However, because of the differences in the terms and yields of investment instruments, there is no guarantee that this basic strategy could not be markedly improved on.

For example, suppose the financial planners were concerned with the period from January to June only, which would eliminate the necessity of including borrowing in its determinations. During this six-month period, there are a number of opportunities to invest surplus cash. The important question for the financial planners to answer is: What investments should be made in order to maximize interest earnings while making sure that all bills get paid? This is a classic constrained optimization question. Strategies that produce greater yields but require more complex mathematics are discussed in appendix 7.1.

As with borrowing, the investment of idle cash is regulated by statutory law to a much greater extent in public schools than in private schools. The public school business official acts within the constraints of all the laws and legal opinions that regulate the investing process. Only within the scope of what is legally permitted do the other considerations of risk, liquidity, and yield apply.

The risk of financial loss should temper all school investments, but in the public sector many of the more speculative investments are prohibited. To reduce the risk of default or loss, many states require 100 percent collateral on all investments in the form of United States treasury securities or other obligations backed by the "full faith and credit" of the United States government.

Once the legality and risk of an investment are determined, the school business administrator next considers liquidity and yield. Liquidity is the ability to quickly convert a security to cash without the loss of principal or accrued interest. The school business administrator should include some highly liquid (usually lower yield) securities in the portfolio to be assured that all bills will be paid on time in case of an unanticipated cash deficit. The yield of the investment varies with the type of security used. Competitive yields for comparable investments may indicate the different rates available. Comparable certificates of deposit (CDs), for example, may be purchased at three different yield rates from three different banks. There are a number of factors that affect the yield of an investment. Generally, the yield is higher when the time to maturity is longer, risk is greater, liquidity is less, denominations are larger, and interest is taxable.

The yield of each security is calculated by a specific method. The interest earned is calculated on either a 360- or a 365-day basis, which causes slight differences in actual interest earnings between two instruments with the same maturity schedule. Instruments available to public school business officials are usually limited to certificates of deposit, treasury bills, repurchase agreements, savings accounts, and federal agency securities. Private school business administrators are not limited to a specific list of instruments, but in practice they usually rely on these instruments as well as on money market funds. A brief discussion of each of these instruments follows.

Certificates of Deposit (Time Deposits)

The maturities on these certificates can range from fourteen days to one year or longer. The rates are regulated by the Federal Reserve System and, at times, rate ceilings are imposed. These certificates can be either negotiable or nonnegotiable. Most districts buy nonnegotiable certificates and pick a maturity date that coincides with the time when they need the money. However, certificates can also be negotiable and may be sold if the money is needed sooner. The rates paid by the bank are subject, of course, to current money market conditions. The certificates are also a safe investment because the bank is required to pledge treasury securities against the deposit. In actuality a district enjoys the same protection as if the money were invested in treasury securities.

Treasury Bills

Treasury bills are probably the safest form of investment for a school district. They are very flexible instruments that can be purchased to mature practically any week of the year. They are also very marketable since they are obligations of the United States.

However, it is not practical to invest small sums of money in these securities because surcharge or odd-lot fees are imposed on purchases of less than $100,000. For bills that are held a short period of time, these extra fees can eat quite heavily into the interest that would otherwise be earned on the investment.

Repurchase Agreements

Another form of investment, which is relatively new, is called a "repurchase agreement." It is an investment vehicle presently used by only a few local municipalities and school districts. Basically, in this form of investment the bank sells government or agency bonds, which it holds, and agrees to buy those same bonds back on a specified day. The district will be paid interest at a stated rate over the entire period of the contract. Since this transaction involves the purchase and resale of a United States government security, the district has the same safety as if it purchased the security outright or deposited the funds in a certificate with the bank. The rates on these agreements are tied to the short-term money market. Generally, the rate of interest fluctuates with the federal funds rate.

The advantages of repurchase agreements are that they are simple to handle, they are safe, and they can be used for periods as short as one day. All it takes is a phone call to a bank. Securities do not change hands; rather they are set aside in a segregated trust account. The district does not receive physical delivery, but it does receive advices of the purchase, sale, and interest paid.

Savings Accounts

Depending on the interest rates available on the aforementioned investment vehicles, you might find it advantageous to place the surplus funds in a savings account in a commercial bank.

Prior to investing school funds in a savings account, you should consider the advantages and limitations of all of the investment options available to you and then pick the one that best suits your district's cash-flow needs and produces the best interest income.

Federal Agency Securities

These securities vary greatly depending on the issuing agency. Although they are not technically legal obligations of the United States government, they do not present a significant credit risk because the government closely supervises the issuing agencies. Maturities range from several months to several years. One key advantage of securities for smaller school districts is the lower minimum-denomination requirements. The secondary markets are active, and the liquidity is excellent. The principal federal agency securities are as follows:

1. Banks for Cooperatives Debentures (Coops)
2. Federal Home Loan Bank Discount Notes (FHLB)
3. Federal Intermediate Credit Bank Debentures (FICB)
4. Federal Loan Bank Notes
5. Federal National Mortgage Association (FNMA)
6. FNMA Discount Notes

The different securities purchased from different kinds of institutions require different procedures for purchasing and selling the security. Some control questions the business administrator typically wants answered concerning each transaction include:

1. Have the terms, principal, and discount and accrued interest amounts been confirmed and recorded?
2. Is the description of the security in question clear?
3. Has the method by which funds are to be delivered been specified?
4. Has the location where the security will be held for safekeeping been specified?

5. Has the place where settlement will take place been specified?
6. What bank accounts will be credited or debited as a result of the transaction?

Answering these questions will help ensure the accurate completion of a transaction without excessive administrative complications and without the risk of failure to complete the transaction.

Summary

The purpose of this chapter was to provide an overview of the terminology and processes of a school district cash management program. While the scope of cash management can become complex, even the smallest school district could benefit from designing and implementing a cash management program. By taking deliberate actions to increase cash availability and investment yield, the school business administrator can reduce the costs (of borrowing) and increase the revenues (from investing) for his or her school.

Appendix 7.1: Mathematical Models for Cash Management

Linear programming is a mathematical technique used primarily to solve constrained optimization problems. Constrained optimization problems are concerned with the attainment of specified objectives given certain limitations. Smythe and Johnson (1966, p. 187) list the following steps in formulating a linear-programming model:

1. Recognition of the problem
2. Formulation of the mathematical model
   a. identification of the decision variables
   b. choice of a measure of effectiveness
   c. symbolic representation of the objective function
   d. identification of constraints
   e. algebraic representation of constraints
3. Estimation of the parameters of the model

These steps can be followed to formulate and solve investment and borrowing problems. Only the investment applications are discussed here. (A linear program that covers both borrowing and investment is somewhat more complex. See, for example, Dembowski and Schwarz 1980, pp. 147–153.)

Using only the first six-month period of the XYZ School District's cash flow pattern (exhibit 7.1), we see that there are opportunities for investment of surplus funds. The school business administrator's task is to determine when to make investments, how much cash to invest, and when the investments should mature. For simplicity of notation, we call January "month 1," February "month 2," and so on, with June being "month 6." Any investments that can be made will be denoted as "NP_{tk}," which stands for "notes purchased in month *t* that will mature in *k* months from the time of purchase." Thus, the notation NP_{15} would represent an investment note purchased in the first month that will mature at the beginning of the sixth month.

In the planning period in question, there are fifteen possible investments: NP_{11} to NP_{15}, NP_{21} to NP_{24}, NP_{31} to NP_{33}, NP_{41}, NP_{42}, and NP_{51}. Which of these investments should be made, and in what amounts? If all investments earned the same annual rate of interest, neither the timing nor the amounts of the investments would make a difference to the investment analysis. The total interest earning would be the same regardless of the investment made. However, there is often a term structure to interest rates, that is, the longer the duration of the investment, the higher the annual rate of interest the financial market will offer.

A call to the local bank will obtain the current term structure of interest rates. In our example, an investment of one to two months' duration will earn 7 percent annually, or 0.07/12 = 0.0058 monthly interest. An investment of three to four months' duration will earn 9 percent annually, or 0.09/12 = 0.0075 monthly, and an investment of five to six months' duration will earn 11 percent annually, or 0.11/12 = 0.0092 monthly.

Using this term structure, NP_{11} would earn 0.0058 NP_{11} interest (1 month × 0.0058/month). NP_{15} would earn 0.046 NP_{15} interest (5 months × .0092/month). Thus, if NP_{15} equals \$250,000 invested in period 1 and maturing at the beginning of period 6, it would earn (5 × 0.0092 × 250,000) = \$11,500 interest. Likewise, if NP_{32} was \$150,000, it would earn (2 × .0058 × \$150,000) = \$1,740 interest.

Given the existence of the term structure of interest rates, there is usually only one set of investments that will maximize the total interest earning possible for the school district. It is quite difficult to determine the optimal set of investments by trying out different combinations of investments. This is where linear programming can be useful. So far we have accomplished step one, recognition of the problem—that is, realizing that there is an optimal solution that cannot be determined by manual methods!

To accomplish the second step, formulation of the mathematical model, we need to identify the decision variables. This requires developing a system of notation to represent the variables used in this problem. NP_{tk} has been established as a notation for the investment possibilities. Likewise, ID_{tk} will be used to represent the interest due on investment NP_{tk}. Thus, the interest due on investment NP_{24} is denoted as ID_{24}. The monthly revenue inflows will be denoted as I_t. So, using the information from exhibit 7.2, the revenue that arrives in period 4 = I_4 = \$150,000. The monthly expenditure that flows out of the school district is denoted as O_t. The monthly expenditure in period 6 = O_6 = \$400,000. The last necessary notation represents the cash balance at the end of the period. The cash balance will be represented by C_t. Because there is a beginning cash balance at the start of period one, this will be denoted as C_o. Thus, the cash balance left at the end of the second period is C_2. In summary, the variables used in the linear program are as follows:

NP_{tk}— investment noted purchased in month t maturing in k months
ID_{tk} — the interest due on investment NP_{tk}
I_t — the inflow of revenue in month t
O_t — the outflow of expenditure in month t
C_t — the cash balance left at the end of month t

The next step in the formulation of the linear-programming problem is the selection of a measure of effectiveness. Since the objective is to maximize total interest earnings, the measure of effectiveness is dollars. Given the measure of effectiveness, the objective function is to maximize the dollars earned in interest on investment. Since there are fifteen possible investments, there are fifteen possible interest earnings. If Z represents the total interest earnings, then the objective function is stated mathematically as:

$$\text{Maximize } Z = \Sigma ID_{tk}$$

or

$$Z = ID_{11} + ID_{12} + ID_{13} + ID_{14} + ID_{15} + ID_{21} + ID_{22} + ID_{23} + ID_{24} + ID_{31} + ID_{32} + ID_{33} + ID_{41} + ID_{42} + ID_{51}$$

With the objective function stated, the next steps are to identify and mathematically state the constraints. For this simplified problem, there is only one constraint: the cash balance constraint. At the beginning of this section it was noted that the purpose of the linear program was to maximize interest earnings while making sure that all bills are paid. For each period (t), the following sequence of events takes place: the inflow of revenue, I_t, is added to the cash balance remaining from the previous period, C_{t-1}. Investments from previous periods may mature, so the principal, NP_{tk}, plus interest due, ID_{tk}, is added to the available cash. Bills are paid, so the monthly expenditure, O_t, is deducted from the available cash. If there is surplus cash, investments that will mature in future periods will be made, so these sums are subtracted from available cash. After all these transactions are finished, there may be a cash balance remaining. This sequence of transactions is represented mathematically as:

$$C_{t-1} = I_t + \sum_{t=1}^{t-1} (NP_{tk} + ID_{tk}) - \sum_{t=k}^{t+k} NP_{tk} - O_t - C_t = 0.$$

This constraint would be required for each period. For this example, this constraint is represented as a series of six equations, one for each of the periods. Exhibit 7.5 lists this set of constraints for the sample school district. To complete the linear program formulation, the term structure of interest

Exhibit 7.5
The Formulation of a Linear-Programming Model For School District Financial Management

The objective function:

$$\text{Maximize } Z = ID_{11} + ID_{12} + ID_{13} + ID_{14} + ID_{15} + ID_{21} + ID_{22} + ID_{23} + ID_{24} + ID_{31} + ID_{32} + ID_{33} + ID_{41} + ID_{42} + ID_{51}$$

Subject to:

The "cash balance" constraints for each period:

$$C_0 + I_1 - 0_1 - C_1 - NP_{11} - NP_{12} - NP_{13} - NP_{14} - NP_{15} = 0$$
$$C_1 + I_2 - 0_2 - C_2 - NP_{21} - NP_{22} - NP_{23} - NP_{24} + NP_{11} + ID_{11} = 0$$
$$C_2 + I_3 - 0_3 - C_3 - NP_{31} - NP_{32} - NP_{33} + NP_{12} + ID_{12} + NP_{21} + ID_{21} = 0$$
$$C_3 + I_4 - 0_4 - C_4 - NP_{41} - NP_{42} + NP_{13} + ID_{13} + NP_{22} + ID_{22} + NP_{31} + ID_{31} = 0$$
$$C_4 + I_5 - 0_5 - C_5 - NP_{51} + NP_{14} + ID_{14} + NP_{23} + ID_{23} + NP_{32} + ID_{32} + NP_{41} + ID_{41} = 0$$
$$C_5 + I_6 - 0_6 - C_6 + NP_{15} + ID_{15} + NP_{24} + ID_{24} + NP_{33} + ID_{33} + NP_{42} + ID_{42} + NP_{51} + ID_{51} = 0$$

The term structure of the interest rates on investment constraints:

$$ID_{11} - .0058NP_{11} = 0$$
$$ID_{12} - .0116NP_{12} = 0$$
$$ID_{13} - .0225NP_{13} = 0$$
$$ID_{14} - .03NP_{14} = 0$$
$$ID_{15} - .046NP_{15} = 0$$
$$ID_{21} - .0058NP_{21} = 0$$
$$ID_{22} - .0116NP_{22} = 0$$
$$ID_{23} - .0225NP_{23} = 0$$
$$ID_{24} - .03NP_{24} = 0$$
$$ID_{31} - .0058NP_{31} = 0$$
$$ID_{32} - .0116NP_{32} = 0$$
$$ID_{33} - .0225NP_{33} = 0$$
$$ID_{41} - .0058NP_{41} = 0$$
$$ID_{42} - .0116NP_{42} = 0$$
$$ID_{51} - .0058NP_{51} = 0$$

The values of the monthly inflows, outflows, and the beginning cash balance (see exhibit 7.1):

$C_0 = 50{,}000$	$0_1 = 200{,}000$
$I_1 = 400{,}000$	$0_2 = 200{,}000$
$I_2 = 250{,}000$	$0_3 = 200{,}000$
$I_3 = 400{,}000$	$0_4 = 200{,}000$
$I_4 = 150{,}000$	$0_5 = 200{,}000$
$I_5 = 100{,}000$	$0_6 = 400{,}000$
$I_6 = 50{,}000$	

rates and the initial inflow, outflow, and beginning balance data must be given. Recall that investments of one to two months' duration would earn 7 percent annual interest or 0.0058 monthly; an investment of three to four months' duration, 9 percent annually or 0.0075 monthly; and an investment of five to six months' duration, 11 percent annually or 0.0092 monthly. Thus,

$ID_{14} = (.0075) \times (4) \times (NP_{14}) = .03\ NP_{14}$. Setting the equation to zero yields $ID_{tk} - yk(NP_{tk}) = 0$, where y is the monthly interest rate. Exhibit 7.5 lists the fifteen interest rate formulations for the sample problem. The initial values of the inflows and outflows of each period are also given in exhibit 7.5, as is the beginning cash balance. This completes the formulation of the linear-programming example.

The solution of the linear-programming formulation can be accomplished through the use of any linear-programming computer program generally available on all computers. For the solution of the example problem, a regular linear-programming computer program based on the simplex technique, the most common of several standard linear-programming methods, was used. The objective function and constraints as listed in exhibit 7.5 were used with the following results.

The optimal solution for the example would be to make the following investments with the resultant interest earned.

$$
\begin{aligned}
NP_{15} &= \$250{,}000 & \text{with } ID_{15} &= \$11{,}500.00\\
NP_{23} &= \$\ 50{,}000 & \text{with } ID_{23} &= \$\ 1{,}125.00\\
NP_{31} &= \$\ 98{,}024 & \text{with } ID_{31} &= \$\ \ 568.54\\
NP_{33} &= \$101{,}975 & \text{with } ID_{33} &= \$\ 2{,}294.45\\
NP_{41} &= \$\ 48{,}593 & \text{with } ID_{41} &= \$\ \ 281.84
\end{aligned}
$$

Thus, the total interest earned equals $15,769.83. Based on the beginning cash balance, the monthly inflows and outflows, and the term structure of interest rates faced by the sample school district, the five investments listed above would yield the greatest amount of interest earnings possible while making sure sufficient cash is available to meet current expenditures.

References

Carr, M. I. "An Analysis of the Distribution of Intergovernment Transfers of Monies and of the Investment of Idle Monies in the Public Schools of Kentucky." Ph.D. dissertation, Indiana University, 1971.

Commissioner's Advisory Committee for School Business Administration. "The Borrowing and Investing of Funds." *The Investment of School Funds*. Albany: The State University of New York, 1976.

Dembowski, F. L. "Alternative Methods in the Evaluation of School District Cash Management Programs." *Journal of Educational Finance* 6 (Summer 1980): 51–67.

Dembowski, F. L., ed. *A Handbook of School Banking Relations*. Albany: The New York State Association of School Business Officials, 1981.

Dembowski, F. L., and Schwarz, L. "An Integer Programming Approach to School District Financial Management." *Socio-Economic Planning Sciences* 14 (Winter 1980): 147–153.

Frankel, Martin M., and Gerald, Debra E. "Projections of Education Statistics to 1988–89." Washington, D.C.: National Center for Education Statistics, 1980.

Hamilton, H. D., and Cohen, S. H. *Policy Making by Plebiscite: School Referenda.* Lexington, Mass.: Lexington Books, 1978.

McCanless, C. A., "The Investment of Idle School Funds." Proceedings of the Association of School Business Officials of the U.S. and Canada." Kalamazoo, Michigan, 1952.

Patitucci, F. M., and Lichtenstein, M. H. "Improving Cash Management in Local Government: A Comprehensive Approach." Municipal Finance Officers Association, 1977.

Rothrock, P. D. "Results of a National Survey on Handling School Funds." Report of the West Virginia Association of School Business Officials Legislative Committee, August 1972. Mimeographed.

Smythe, W. R., and Johnson, L. A. *Introduction to Linear Programming: With Applications.* Englewood Cliffs, N.J.: Prentice-Hall, Inc., 1966.

Welliver, W. A. "An Analysis of the Investment and Related Financial Management Practices of Pennsylvania School Districts." Ph.D. dissertation, Temple University, 1974.

8

Financial Accounting Requirements

•

Overview

Up to this point we have assumed the existence of an organizational "black box" into and out from which flows money. In this chapter we look inside the box. Financial accounting is a discipline with its own terminology, rules, goals, and procedures. As in other chapters in this volume, the emphasis here is on financial accountring in *public* schools because of the complexity of accounting in that sector. Although the concepts of financial accounting apply in all educational organizations, public-sector regulations and incentives as well as the larger size of public school districts foster relatively detailed accounting systems.

• • •

Accounting is concerned with providing financial information about the status and progress of an organization. All segments of economic society have financial obligations to fulfill deriving from legal obligations and requirements placed on them by their sponsors. Accounting is the means of measuring and reporting these obligations. It is analytical in the sense that it takes a great mass of data and, through classification and summarization, reduces that mass of data to a relatively small number of highly significant

---

Special thanks to Clayton W. Harrell, Xerox Corporation, for his helpful comments on this chapter.

and interrelated items, which, if properly presented, tell much about that organization. In order for these analytical classifications to be meaningful to educational managers, the concepts underlying accounting must be understood.

To some people, accounting seems to be primarily procedural in nature, emphasizing recordkeeping and preparation of financial statements rather than conceptually based analysis. This appearance is deceiving—recording of financial transactions is actually preceded by an analysis of those transactions. From the development of a chart of accounts to preparation of financial statements (both discussed in this chapter), accounting is concerned primarily with analyzing the nature and effect of the transactions involved. Therefore, the recognition and development of the conceptual foundation of accounting is presented first in this chapter, followed by a section discussing basic accounting operations. The emphasis will be on public schools because their reporting requirements are most complex. Differences from public-sector practice are pointed out if significant differences exist.

Basic Accounting Concepts

Accounting concepts may be defined as those basic ideas that permit the identification and classification of phenomena or other ideas. As Mautz (1970, p. 20) states, "We must have a concept of an asset to separate assets from those items which are not assets. In turn, we must have a concept of current assets in order to separate current assets from noncurrent assets."

To be complete, a concept must state all that the given classification includes and all that it excludes, which is no small task. For example, one may start with a simple definition of an *asset* as "anything of value owned"—a satisfactory concept for simple situations. Yet there are numerous business situations in which, for example, certain types of leases grant the lessee rights to use property that, for some purposes, give him the equivalent of ownership. The rudimentary concept of an asset is thus accordingly modified to include such lease arrangements. Other arrangements will suggest other modifications of the basic concept until the once simple concept becomes quite complex.

Because so many of the concepts with which accounting deals are both abstract and potentially very complex, they are not easily stated in any complete sense. "We find it necessary to use broad, general terms to describe most concepts and rarely meet the requirements of a complete statement" (Mautz 1970, p. 20). Nonetheless, concisely stated concepts, even if incomplete, do aid in conveying fundamental understanding. It is in this sense that the following accounting concepts are presented and discussed.

Six major accounting concepts, when taken together, provide the foundation on which fiscal systems in educational organizations operate. In order to understand these six concepts, some major subsidiary concepts (appended in parentheses) must also be understood:

1. Financial condition (asset, liability, fund balance)
2. Results of operations (revenue, expense, matching)
3. Enterprise (corporate entity, consolidated financial statements)
4. Continuity
5. Present fairly (generally accepted accounting principles, consistency, materiality, full disclosure)
6. Audit (standards, opinions)

Financial Condition

As used by accountants, the term *financial condition* refers to the impression or conclusion one might draw from a balanced array of a company's assets and the claims against those assets. Although typically applied to profit-directed business enterprises, the concept is also applicable to both public and private educational institutions.

Assets and the claims against those assets are described in a semi-standardized fashion. Without an understanding of the classification and measurement conventions applied in developing the descriptions, one could easily come to erroneous conclusions about their significance. Thus, in order to properly explain financial condition, it is necessary to explain *assets, liabilities*, and *fund balance*.

Asset

An asset may be defined as anything of use to future operations of the enterprise, where the enterprise is seen to benefit from such use (Mautz 1970, p. 5). Assets may be monetary or nonmonetary, tangible or intangible, owned or not owned. As long as they can make a contribution to future operations of the organization, and the organization has the right to use them without expending additional cost in excess of the anticipated amount of that contribution, they constitute assets and are so treated in accounting.

One useful distinction among types of assets is that of current versus noncurrent assets. For accounting purposes, the term *current assets* is used to designate "cash and other assets or resources commonly identified as those which are reasonably expected to be realized in cash or sold or consumed during the normal operating cycle [typically a fiscal year] of the business" (A.I.C.P.A. 1965, p. 38). Assets not meeting the terms of this definition are typically reported under a variety of headings (for example, general fixed assets). Current assets are set off from noncurrent assets because of their importance in the organization's current position. *Current position* refers to the organization's ability to meet its impending financial obligations in the ordinary course of business with the assets at hand. Current assets typically include cash; bank deposits that are readily available; marketable securities about to be converted within an operating cycle; inventories; and any prepaid expense that, had it not been prepaid, would have been a drain on other resources within the next operating cycle.

Assets are generally measured by their *transaction price*—that is, the price of an "arm's-length" exchange transaction between independent parties in which the organization is one of the parties. ("Arm's length" implies that the transaction was a simple exchange of goods or services for money.) This value may be reduced proportionately for observed or estimated consumption of its use value. If no stated price exists (as, for example, with donated goods), a price is inferred from surrounding circumstances. For instance, if foodstuffs are donated to a private nonprofit or public school, a reasonable estimate of their worth may be what they would have cost in the marketplace.

There are, however, significant exceptions to this general rule for measuring assets. If the anticipated recovery from use or sale of an asset falls below the transaction price, accountants generally "write down" the carrying value of the asset to the anticipated recovery amount (that is, record the lesser amount). However, they seldom do the opposite—accountants are much less inclined to "write up" an asset to a higher anticipated recovery value. This practice is an example of the doctrine of *conversatism*, which holds that, given a situation in which exact measurement is not possible, accountants should err on the side of understatement of assets and overstatement of expenses, rather than vice versa. This doctrine is being increasingly challenged as continuing inflation (it is argued) makes transaction price data obsolete over short periods of time. An exception to the practice of listing only the purchase price of an asset on the "books" concerns fixed assets that have a life that is either known or established by good accounting practice. In the case of a fixed asset, it is normal for a depreciation schedule to be established to reduce the carrying costs of the asset. Additionally, assets with a known market value, such as stocks and bonds, can be reevaluated at any time depending on the business cycle of the enterprise. In most private for-profit schools (and a few private nonprofit schools), it is common practice to record the acquisition of assets, and then to depreciate them according to a schedule or to write the assets off as an expense in the current year. For-profit schools record assets carefully for several reasons; for example, to take advantage of government programs such as investment tax credits whereby they can benefit by paying lower taxes as a direct result of the purchase of the fixed asset. Also, depreciation is a tax-reducing expense that the public and private nonprofit schools are not concerned with. Because assets are typically not listed or valued on the books of a public school, the cost of performing its services to the public is understated.

Liability

The claims against the assets of an organization are typically classified under two headings: *liabilities* and *shareholders' equity*. Because of the nonprofit orientation and external funding arrangements of most educational institutions, the concept of fund balance effectively replaces that of shareholders' equity.

Liabilities are claims against an organization payable in cash, in other assets, or in service on a fixed or determined future date (Mautz 1970, p. 8). Like assets, liabilities are generally classified as current or noncurrent. *Current liabilities* are those that will be paid from among the assets listed as current assets. Thus, a direct relationship exists between current liabilities and current assets (generally expressing the current position of the organization). *Noncurrent liabilities* in educational organizations would include such things as bonds for school construction or purchases of sites and large equipment.

Fund Balance

The concept of shareholders' equity is interpreted in a variety of ways, one of which is the arithmetic difference between the total of an organization's assets and the total of its liabilities. (Except in failing companies, this difference is positive.) Relying on this interpretation, then, equity is a balancing figure. In order to reinforce this interpretation of equity, public educational institutions more often use the term *fund balance*, which is the balance of a specified group of accounts. (Funds are discussed in more detail later in this chapter.) It represents the excess of assets of a fund over its liabilities. The three concepts of assets, liabilities, and fund balance are related as follows:

$$\text{assets} = \text{liabilities} + \text{fund balance}$$

Results of Operations

In a profit-making organization, *results of operations* is a general term for the presentation of those accounting data that together indicate how well the organization has succeeded in fulfilling its profit-seeking purpose during a given period of time. The presentation attempts to show what the enterprise has accomplished and what costs have been expended in the process. The term takes on a slightly different meaning in a not-for-profit context: the concept of profit is replaced by the concept of *patterns of benefits* that result from the expenditure of revenues.

Revenue

In profit-seeking businesses, *revenue* is generally defined as the monetary measure of the product or service transferred to customers during the period at the price paid or promised by those customers (Mautz 1970, p. 10). (It can also be derived by disposing of assets other than products or services.) Thus revenue generally represents the accomplishment of business. In nonprofit organizations, such as some educational organizations, the term is more usefully defined as "additions to assets which do not increase any liability, do not represent the recovery of an expenditure, and do not represent the cancellation of certain liabilities without a corresponding increase in other liabilities or a decrease in assets" (Roberts and Lichtenberger 1973, p. 138). Stated more simply, revenues are increases in assets and decreases in liabilities that increase the amount of the fund balance. Examples of revenue received by school districts include state aid, federal aid, and receipts from taxes and tuition.

Expense

This is another term whose use differs according to context. In profit-seeking organizations, *expenses* is used to describe the efforts made by a company to obtain revenues. In this sense, expenses tend to fall into three groups: (1) the cost of goods or services sold to produce the revenues; (2) the costs of selling and administration; and (3) other costs of doing business that do not necessarily have any direct relationship to specific revenues. In most educational institutions, especially public schools and colleges, expenses are viewed as decreases in assets or increases in liabilities that decrease the amount of the fund balance. Because educational spending is goal directed, it is perhaps more useful to define expenses as charges incurred that are presumed to help achieve organizational objectives during the fiscal year.

Results of operations is related to financial condition in the following way:

$$\text{current assets} = \text{current liabilities} + \text{fund balance} + \text{revenues} - \text{expenses}$$

Changes in one category affect other categories; for example, increases in revenue will bring about increases in assets. (For an extended discussion of this, see Adams 1967, pp. 22–24.)

Matching

The term *matching* is used to describe the appropriate association of related revenues and expenses. Accounting presentations strive to associate data on an interpretive basis; that is, those items that are related to one another are presented together and those that are not are separated. This concept leads to the establishment of separate funds in educational organizations, especially in public schools.

A *fund* is an independent accounting entity (like a separate business) with its own assets, liabilities, and fund balances. Fund accounting is the procedure by which economic resources and obligations are segregated into separate account groupings according to the function or purpose the resources serve. Funds constitute a control device that sponsors usually elect to impose on public school districts to help ensure that their legal, financial restrictions designate the funds and their associated accounting activity as separate bookkeeping entities (like a separate business) with its own assets, liabilities, and fund balances.

Private nonprofit schools generally operate a fund accounting system similar in nature to the public schools for similar sponsor-imposed (or legal) reasons. The fund structure of these schools reflects the unique characteristics of the sponsor and include, for example, funds to manage endowments, restricted gifts, or monies set aside to make loans to students, faculty, and staff. Funds acquired by the schools carry obligations to distribute either a fixed income (annuity) or a variable income (life income) to the donor or other designated individuals during their lifetime.

Although fund accounting is common mainly within the public sector, certain governmental agencies and private sponsors who grant funds for retraining to private organizations, either for-profit or not-for-profit, have created situations that come close to fund separation processes found in the public sector. Also, in most large private educational organizations of either type the concept of profit centers has caused fundlike accounting practices to become more common. Again, at the will of the sponsors, and if the private organizations wish to capture the benefits of grants for special purposes, fund separation is required.

Funds used to separate monies designated for private for-profit schools are usually established to record expenditures for, and depreciation of, capital goods for tax purposes, which is a function unique to the private for-profit sector. Financial trade-offs by private for-profit organizations to calculate whether to expense (usually by leasing) a capital investment or to purchase the asset depend heavily on the investment tax credit and potential tax savings that can be gained by the organization. That is unless there are other reasons for leasing, such as product obsolescence. The expensing of assets for tax purposes is a unique situation found only within this sector. (Although private nonprofit and public organizations make these same buy-versus-lease decisions, it is usually done to balance potential investment interest and probable profits against lease costs of the assets.)

This is not to say that nonprofit and public organizations are free from tax laws. Even though they are exempt from federal taxes, nonprofit organizations are required to file annual information returns with the IRS. The IRS assumes allocation of costs into fundlike categories. Additionally, nonprofit organizations may be liable for taxes on funds coming from unrelated businesses, another reason for segregation of costs and incomes. Typically, educational institutions operate from three to ten separate funds, depending on specific needs. In school districts, for example, ordinary operations are financed through the *general fund*. Recorded here are taxes collected, state and federal aid, tuition, payment of teachers' salaries, costs of classroom supplies, utility costs, and so on.

In addition to the general fund, school districts operate *special funds* for a variety of purposes. Two of the most common special funds are the capital project fund (used to account for all resources and for acquisition of capital facilities, including real property) and the school food service fund (used to record financial transactions related to food service operations). The most useful descriptions of special funds identify the function of the fund. *Revolving funds*, for example, describe those special funds that maintain an approximately steady level (of cash, receivables, inventory, or other assets) by restoring the amounts expended from the fund with earnings from operations or with transfers from other funds. *Sinking funds* are for setting aside money for a special use in the future (beyond the current year). Private nonprofit educational organizations often have occasion to set up special *endowment funds*, where income from the principal may be expended although the principal itself may not.

Cash Versus Accrual Accounting

Many nonprofit organizations use the cash basis of accounting because of its simplicity. Cash basis accounting is a system in which transactions of cost and revenue are recorded when they are actually received or paid. This differs from the accrual basis of accounting, which respects the element of time and its affects on the transactions. The recognition of when the organization owes but does not pay a creditor; or the period (in time) when a customer owes (but not necessarily pays) the serving organization is a more accurate way of depicting the element of time in the accounting system. Most private for-profit and large nonprofit organizations use the accrual basis of accounting because of its accuracy.

Some public and private nonprofit schools use a combination of both the cash and the accrual accounting methods or one of several other alternatives, such as fiscal period-end accruals. This system requires transactions to be recorded as cash throughout the period (because it is easier), and at the end of the accounting period, a set of entries are put into the accounting system to establish the accruals. If the organization uses the straight cash basis, a bias is depicted in the books because monies actually earned during a period, for instance, may or may not be shown as earnings depending on when the cash was actually received. Better financial controls can be instituted with the accrual basis than with the cash basis of accounting. For this reason, most for-profit organizations use the accrual method.

Enterprise

Transactions are usually at least two-party propositions, but the accountant is interested in only one side of the transaction. That is, he is always concerned with a specific organization, largely ignoring the effects of the transaction on the other party or parties. It will be helpful to describe precisely what that "specific organization" is.

Corporate Entity

Accounting concerns itself with the transactions of a *corporate entity*. What conditions must exist in an organization for it to be considered a corporate entity and, thus, for accounting to take place? The only requirements for the application of accounting are that a unit be identifiable and that it enter into transactions. Thus, a corporate entity may be defined as a legally constituted organization or some part of it.

Consolidated Financial Statements

Even though separate accounting units may be usefully established within an educational organization, *consolidated financial statements* are also required of these organizations. Generally if a single economic entity includes more than one legal corporate entity, the financial statements of the legal entities must be consolidated into one set of statements to represent the total economic entity. While derived for use primarily in private for-profit enterprises, consolidation of financial statements also applies to the educational organizations with discrete legal subunits.

Continuity

The concept of *continuity* applies to an assumption about the future of an organization: that the organization will continue in its present form, and with its present purpose, far enough into the future so that its assets will be used for the purpose for which they were acquired and the obligations against them will be paid in due course (Mautz 1970, p. 13). If this assumption could not be held in regard to an organization, it would be necessary to treat the organization as if it were about to go out of business (*liquidate*). To do so would fundamentally alter the valuation of assets, the treatment of liabilities, and the preparation of financial statements in general.

Present Fairly

Present fairly is a term used by auditors to suggest that the financial statements examined are presented in a manner that is fair or just. In a broader context it represents a concept of "proper" or "appropriate" representation of financial information and includes a cluster of more specific concepts: *generally accepted accounting principles*, *consistency*, *materiality*, and *full disclosure*.

Generally Accepted Accounting Principles

This term describes those practices and procedures that have been found over time to be most useful. Although they do not necessarily constitute the preferred treatment in every case, in combination they generally do present an agreed-on method for arriving at a picture of the status and progress of an organization.

Consistency

One of the primary purposes of accounting is to present reports on a comparable basis. By themselves, individual accounting figures are seldom informative; coupled with other figures (for example, reports for the same organization for prior years), they become much more useful. If comparisons are to be made, however, it is imperative that reports be prepared in a consistent way over time and across units of the organization. Thus great reliance is placed on consistency as a requirement for good accounting data.

Materiality

It is not required that all transactions, however minor, be handled on a consistent basis; only transactions of material significance require such attention. A material transaction (or event or item) is one the knowledge of which might influence the judgment of an informed reader of the financial statements (Mautz 1970, p. 14). This definition, however logical, has been difficult to put into operation usefully. The materiality of a transaction was more of an issue prior to the advent of the computer. Now with the speed and ease with which a computer handles routine tasks, this factor has become less significant.

Full Disclosure

This means that the presented information includes everything that an informed reader should know to come to appropriate conclusions, nothing of substance having been concealed or omitted. Full disclosure does not necessarily mean that an overwhelming amount of detail need be included in financial statements; rather, that taken as a whole, the financial statements of an organization represent a satisfactory *overall* impression of its current position.

Audit

A major factor in establishing and maintaining confidence in the financial reporting of organizations is the customary *audit*—an annual examination and report by independent certified public accountants (often required by law). The financial information of the organization is examined by an auditor, who applies previously determined *standards* and, on the basis of what is found, renders an *opinion*.

Standards

Auditing standards cover general conditions of the auditing process as well as the result of auditing (that is, the quality of the auditor's report). Standards applied to the auditing process relate to the competence and independence of the auditor and to the rigor and adequacy of the formal audit.

The standards applied to the result of auditing bear separate mention. The generally accepted standards of audit reporting adopted by the American Institute of Certified Public Accountants are:

1. The report shall state whether the financial statements are presented in accordance with generally accepted principles of accounting.
2. The report shall state whether such principles have been consistently observed in the current period in relation to the preceding period.
3. Informative disclosures in the financial statements are to be regarded as reasonably adequate unless otherwise stated in the report.
4. The report shall contain either an expression of opinion regarding the financial statements taken as a whole or an assertion to the effect that an opinion cannot be expressed. When an overall opinion cannot be expressed the reasons should be stated.

One of the most common means for presenting the results of auditing is the short-form report used in conjunction with basic financial statements. The usual short-form report consists of a representation as to the work performed, expressed in an opening paragraph, and a representation as to the independent auditor's conclusions, usually in a closing or "opinion" paragraph. An example of what this report might look like for a public school system is presented in exhibit 8.1.

Opinions

The auditor's opinion is central to the auditing concept. In writing an opinion, the auditor is describing the nature of his examination of the organization and, equally important, the degree of responsibility he is taking for what he says about the organization. An unqualified opinion from an auditor represents in essence a certification of the appropriateness of the financial records of an organization. The short-form report in exhibit 8.1 is an illustration of an unqualified opinion. Qualified opinions arise from conditions that represent departures from the statements in the short form. For example, the auditor's scope of examination may be limited; the financial statements may not present fairly the financial position of the organization; accounting principles may not be consistently applied; unusual uncertainties may exist concerning future developments affecting the organization, and so on.

Exhibit 8.1

Prototypical Short-Form Report to a School District Board of Education

Members of the Board:

We have examined the balance sheets as of June 30, 19 ____, the related statements of revenue and expenditures, the statements of fund balance, and statements of changes in financial position for each fund and group of accounts used in financial administration of the ________________ School System for the year then ended. Our examination was made in accordance with generally accepted auditing standards, and accordingly, included such tests of the accounting records and such other auditing procedures as we considered necessary in the circumstances.

In our opinion, the aforementioned financial statements present fairly the financial position of the ________________ School System at June, 19 ____, and the results of its operation and the changes in its financial position for the year then ended, in conformity with generally accepted accounting principles applied on a basis consistent with that of the preceding year.

Very truly yours,
/signature/

Source: Sam B. Tidwell, *Financial and Management Accounting for Elementary and Secondary School Systems* (Chicago: Research Corporation of the Association of School Business Officials, 1974), p. 424. Reprinted by permission.

While the concept of audit applies largely to an *independent* examination of an organization's financial data, it has more recently been expanded to include *internal auditing* and *governmental auditing* as well. As the term implies, internal auditing is conducted by personnel within an organization; the chief purpose is to test and improve financial operations. Governmental auditing deals with those funds supplied to organizations by various government agencies, typically state or federal. The primary objective of an audit by a governmental agency is to determine whether legal provisions prescribed by that agency are being adhered to. By definition, then, this type of audit is more limited in scope.

Structure of the Accounting Operation

Any activity that changes the financial condition of the educational organization is referred to as a *transaction.* Such activities include buying supplies, paying teachers, receiving tuition, and selling bonds. Transactions are analyzed, recorded, and reported through the use of accounts. Accounts are, to a large degree, the building blocks of financial reports. There are two major classes of accounts: *proprietary accounts* (accounts for assets, liabilities, and fund balances) and *budgetary accounts* (accounts reflecting budgetary operations).

The term *single account* describes a record of "similar" financial transactions. In order to be able to increase the degree of similarity among transactions (and thus be more precise in recording transactions), it is necessary to describe each account in finer detail. This in turn requires the generation of more accounts. For example, one asset account may be labeled *cash,* which might be defined strictly as currency, checks, postal and express money orders, bankers' drafts on hand or on deposit with an official or agent designated as custodian of cash, and bank deposits. Although this is a rather precise description, an educational organization may wish to create an even more specific one—for example, by making a distinction between *petty cash* and *cash.* Petty cash could be defined as a sum of money set aside for the purpose of paying small obligations for which the issuance of a formal voucher and check would be too expensive and time-consuming. It is evident from the definitions that petty cash is a form of cash. However, if the distinction between the two is deemed worthwhile, a separate account for petty cash would be created and the definition of the cash account would include a statement to the effect that "all cash except petty cash is in this account."

Each account is in the form of a *T.* The left side of the *T* is called the debit side, and the right side of the *T* is called the credit side.

debit side	credit side

Actually, account forms vary among organizations according to the complexity of the accounting system and the medium for record-keeping being used (for example, manual versus computer). All accounts, however, record the date of a transaction and give a brief description of it as well as stating the amount of money debited or credited (see exhibit 8.2).

Transactions are usually first recorded in a journal and then "posted" to separate accounts. In order to record a transaction in the journal, however, it

Exhibit 8.2

Prototypical Account

ACCOUNT TITLE IN FULL PAGE

DEBIT SIDE					CREDIT SIDE				
DATE		EXPLANATION	P.R.	AMOUNT	DATE		EXPLANATION	P.R.	AMOUNT
YEAR MONTH	DAY				YEAR MONTH	DAY			

is necessary to analyze the transaction and determine the accounts that will be affected by it. In order to understand how transactions get recorded in accounts, it will be helpful to take another look at an equation discussed previously.

assets = liabilities + fund balance + revenues − expenditures.

Assume for purposes of discussion that a single account is associated with each of the terms in this equation. (In an actual operating system each term would have many accounts associated with it.) The *T* accounts associated with each term would look like exhibit 8.3. A transaction is analyzed in order to determine which of the accounts are affected and whether an account is increased or decreased as a result of that transaction. Notice in the accounts in exhibit 8.3 that increases are not uniformly associated with credits. The particular conventions outlined above can be briefly summarized as follows:

1. To increase asset or expenditure accounts, debit
2. To decrease asset or expenditure accounts, credit
3. To increase liability, fund balance, or revenue accounts, credit
4. To decrease liability, fund balance, or revenue accounts, debit

Exhibit 8.3
Basic Structure of Accounting Operations

assets		=	liabilities		+	fund balance		+	revenues		−	expenditures	
debit	credit		debit	credit		debit	credit		debit	credit		debit	credit
I	D		D	I		D	I		D	I		I	D

I = increased
D = decreased

These conventions are not founded on any theoretical basis. Rather they have been established with a very pragmatic purpose in mind: to create a situation in which (1) each transaction has at least one debit and at least one credit and (2) the total debits equal the total credits. These two facts act as built-in validity checks in the accounting system.

Perhaps the best way to understand the process of recording transactions in accounts is to look at a few examples. Nine transactions are presented in exhibit 8.4; note that in each transaction the validity check rules have not been violated. In each case at least one debit and one credit has been affected, and the debits equal the credits.

Another very important, although less apparent, validity check in this system is that for each transaction the net change in assets equals the sum of the net changes in liabilities, fund balance, revenues, and expenditures. These validity checks, taken together, are not foolproof—for example, they would not flag an increase in the fund balance that should be posted as an increase in liabilities—but they do act efficiently to check many of the possible errors that can arise during the recording process.

Exhibit 8.4
Recording Transactions in Accounts

1. Assume that the assets of the New Hope School System's general fund, at the beginning of a year, are: cash in bank, $1,000; taxes receivable, $6,000; and temporary investments, $3,000. Assets total $10,000, and are shown on the debit side of the account. As these assets exist at the beginning of the period, no revenues are realized nor do liabilities exist. Therefore, fund equity exists in the amount of $10,000. These account balances at the beginning of the accounting period would be shown in the accounts as follows:

Assets		= Liabilities		+ Fund Equity		+ Revenues		− Expenditures	
Increase	Decrease	Decrease	Increase	Decrease	Increase	Decrease	Increase	Increase	Decrease
Debit	Credit	Debit	Credit	Debit	Credit	Debit	Credit	Debit	Credit
$10,000					$10,000				

The debits of $10,000 equal the credits of $10,000 and the assets equal the liabilities plus fund equity.

2. Assume that taxes are assessed and levied in the amount of $30,000. This transaction increases assets by $30,000 and, at the same time, increases revenues by the same amount. Both transactions would appear as follows:

	Assets		= Liabilities		+ Fund Equity		+ Revenues		− Expenditures	
	Increase	Decrease	Decrease	Increase	Decrease	Increase	Decrease	Increase	Increase	Decrease
	Debit	Credit	Debit	Credit	Debit	Credit	Debit	Credit	Debit	Credit
(1)	$10,000					$10,000				
(2)	30,000							$30,000		
	$40,000					$10,000		$30,000		

Exhibit 8.4, continued

Transaction (2) has equal debits and credits. By combining both transactions, debits of $40,000 equal credits of $10,000 plus $30,000. The equation, assets equal liabilities plus fund equity, plus revenues, minus expenditures, has been maintained.

3. Assume that the school system borrows $5,000 from the bank. When the cash is received, assets will be increased by $5,000 and will be recorded by debiting assets. At the same time an obligation is created by the debt owed to the bank. The obligation is recorded by a credit to the liability account. The transaction appears as follows:

	Assets		=	Liabilities		+	Fund Equity		+	Revenues		–	Expenditures	
	Increase	Decrease		Decrease	Increase		Decrease	Increase		Decrease	Increase		Increase	Decrease
	Debit	Credit		Debit	Credit		Debit	Credit		Debit	Credit		Debit	Credit
(3)	$5,000				$5,000									

4. Assume that salaries are paid in the amount of $5,000. When cash is disbursed, assets are reduced and the reduction in assets is shown by a credit to the assets. Expenditures are increased by the same amount and are shown by a debit to expenditures. This transaction appears as follows:

	Assets		=	Liabilities		+	Fund Equity		+	Revenues		–	Expenditures	
	Increase	Decrease		Decrease	Increase		Decrease	Increase		Decrease	Increase		Increase	Decrease
	Debit	Credit		Debit	Credit		Debit	Credit		Debit	Credit		Debit	Credit
(4)		$5,000											$5,000	

5. Assume that $8,000 is collected from the taxes assessed and levied in transaction (2). This is an illustration of a transaction in which a reduction in one asset results in the increase of another. Therefore, to record the transaction, assets are debited for $8,000—the amount of the cash received—and assets are credited for the same amount, which represents the reduction in the asset, taxes receivable. The transaction appears as follows:

	Assets		=	Liabilities		+	Fund Equity		+	Revenues		−	Expenditures	
	Increase	Decrease		Decrease	Increase		Decrease	Increase		Decrease	Increase		Increase	Decrease
	Debit	Credit		Debit	Credit		Debit	Credit		Debit	Credit		Debit	Credit
(5)	$8,000	$8,000												

6. Assume that the school system pays $4,000 to apply on the loan from the bank. The cash payment reduces assets and is recorded by crediting the assets account. The liability to the bank is reduced and a debit in the liabilities account records the reduction of $4,000. The transaction appears as follows:

	Assets		=	Liabilities		+	Fund Equity		+	Revenues		−	Expenditures	
	Increase	Decrease		Decrease	Increase		Decrease	Increase		Decrease	Increase		Increase	Decrease
	Debit	Credit		Debit	Credit		Debit	Credit		Debit	Credit		Debit	Credit
(6)		$4,000		$4,000										

7. Assume that the school system lends $2,000 to the library fund. An investment creates a new asset, shown by a debit, and payment of cash reduces the asset, cash, and is shown by a credit to the asset account. The transaction appears as follows:

	Assets		=	Liabilities		+	Fund Equity		+	Revenues		−	Expenditures	
	Increase	Decrease		Decrease	Increase		Decrease	Increase		Decrease	Increase		Increase	Decrease
	Debit	Credit		Debit	Credit		Debit	Credit		Debit	Credit		Debit	Credit
(7)	$2,000	$2,000												

8. Assume that the school system collects $6,500—representing $6,000 from taxes receivable assessed and levied in transaction (2) and $500 from interest and penalties. The asset, cash, is increased by a debit of $6,500. At the same time the asset, taxes receivable, is reduced by a credit of $6,000. In this transaction, $500 represents a source of revenue from interest and penalties. This revenue is recorded by a credit to the revenue account and the transaction appears as follows:

Exhibit 8.4, continued

	Assets		= Liabilities		+ Fund Equity		+ Revenues		− Expenditures	
	Increase	Decrease	Decrease	Increase	Decrease	Increase	Decrease	Increase	Increase	Decrease
	Debit	Credit	Debit	Credit	Debit	Credit	Debit	Credit	Debit	Credit
(8)	$6,500	$6,000						$500		

9. Assume that the school system pays salaries in the amount of $5,000. This is a repetition of transaction (4) and would be analyzed and recorded in the same way.

The following chart will show the combined effect of the preceding transactions on the accounts.

	Assets		= Liabilities		+ Fund Equity		+ Revenues		− Expenditures	
	Increase	Decrease	Decrease	Increase	Decrease	Increase	Decrease	Increase	Increase	Decrease
	Debit	Credit	Debit	Credit	Debit	Credit	Debit	Credit	Debit	Credit
(1)	$10,000					10,000				
(2)	30,000							30,000		
(3)	5,000			5,000						
(4)		5,000							5,000	
(5)	8,000	8,000								
(6)		4,000	4,000							
(7)	2,000	2,000								
(8)	6,500	6,000						500		
(9)		5,000							5,000	
	61,500	30,000	4,000	5,000		10,000		30,500	10,000	

Source: Sam B. Tidwell, *Financial and Management Accounting for Elementary and Secondary School Systems* (Chicago: Research Corporation of the Association of School Business Officials, 1974), pp. 37–38. Reprinted by permission.

Exhibit 8.5

Trial Balance of Transactions Described in Exhibit 8.4
(gross figures)

Transaction	Debits	Credits
Assets	$61,500	$30,000
Liabilities	4,000	5,000
Fund equity		10,000
Revenues		30,500
Expenditures	10,000	
Total	$75,500	$75,500

Exhibit 8.6

Trial Balance of Transactions Described in Exhibit 8.4
(net figures)

Transaction	Debits	Credits
Assets	$31,500	
Liabilities		1,000
Fund equity		10,000
Revenues		30,500
Expenditures	10,000	
Total	$41,500	$41,500

These validity checks are applied to groups of transactions as well as to single transactions. The process of doing this is called *taking a trial balance*, and it entails summing and comparing the amounts of the transactions in each of the accounts. For example, the transactions described in exhibit 8.4 have been summed at the bottom of exhibit 8.4 and are presented separately in exhibit 8.5. Notice in exhibit 8.5 that, for the sum of all nine transactions, debits equal credits and assets equal liabilities plus fund balance, plus revenues, minus expenditures. These relationships are more apparent in exhibit 8.6. where only the net differences in each account are reported.

As stated earlier, accounts are created to make distinctions between various transactions: similar transactions are clustered and separated from dissimilar transactions. The number of single accounts is proportional to the need for distinction among the various kinds of assets, liabilities, and so on, in an organization. The need for creating these distinctions may stem from data requirements for improved decision making, from externally imposed

Exhibit 8.7

Plausible Distinctions Among Assets

Balance Sheet Accounts	Funds and Groups of Accounts								
	General fund	Special revenue fund	Debt service fund	Capital projects fund	Food service fund	Pupil activity fund	Trust and agency funds	General fixed assets	General long-term debt
Current assets									
Cash	X	X	X	X	X	X	X		
Petty cash	X				X	X			
Cash change funds					X	X			
Cash with fiscal agent			X						
Taxes receivable	X	X	X	X			X		
Estimated uncollectible taxes (credit)	X	X	X	X			X		
Tax liens receivable	X	X	X	X			X		
Estimated uncollectible tax liens (credit)	X	X	X	X			X		
Accounts receivable	X	X		X	X	X			
Bond proceeds receivable				X					
Loans receivable	X						X		
Due from ______ fund	X	X	X	X	X	X	X		
Due from ______ government	X	X	X	X	X	X	X		
Advance to ______ fund	X								
Taxes levied for other governmental units							X		
Interest receivable on investments	X	X	X	X	X	X	X		
Accrued interest on investments purchased	X	X	X	X	X	X	X		
Inventory	X			X	X	X			

Inventory of stores for resale					X	X			
Investments	X	X	X	X	X	X	X		
Unamortized premiums on investments			X	X					
Unamortized discounts on investments (credit)			X	X	X		X		
Deposits	X			X	X	X			
Prepaid expenses	X	X			X	X			
Unamortized discounts on bonds sold			X						
General fixed assets									
Land								X	
Buildings								X	
Improvement other than buildings								X	
Equipment								X	
Construction work in progress								X	
Budgeting accounts and other debits									
Estimated revenues	X	X	X	X					
Revenues (credit)	X	X	X	X					
Bonds authorized—unissued				X					
Amount available in debt service funds									X
Amount to be provided for payment of bonds									X

Source: Adapted from Charles T. Roberts and Allan R. Lichtenberger, *Financial Accounting: Classifications and Standard Terminology for Local and State School Systems* (Washington, D.C.: U.S. Government Printing Office, 1973, OE 73-11800), pp. 5–6.

reporting demands, or from other sources. Plausible distinctions among assets and within different funds are displayed in exhibit 8.7; plausible distinctions among liabilities and fund balances are shown in exhibit 8.8; and plausible distinctions among types of revenue appear in exhibit 8.9.

Plausible distinctions among expenditures are conceptually more complex than those relating to assets, liabilities, and sources of revenue. There are several reasons for this. First, expenditure information is more directly linked to an educational organization's activities and operations than are the other three. Organizational objectives are realized through expenditure. Because of this, classification schemes of one dimension are often inadequate. For example, classification of expenditures on the basis of the objects purchased, while totally inclusive, is not useful by itself in determining the costs of the different departments in a university.

A second complicating factor is that educational organizations are often subject to a variety of external mandates and restrictions from governmental bodies. Often such restrictions are monitored in large part by examining how an educational organization spends its money.

A single expenditure, then, may be classified along a number of different dimensions. One of these dimensions, which has already been mentioned, is fund. Another is object of expenditure. A third dimension is function. Function is a broad and somewhat eclectic classification scheme based on the different activities (or functions) for which expenditures are incurred. *Operational unit* or *site* is a useful expenditure dimension; it serves the purpose of distinguishing expenditures among physical locations. *Program* often refers to a classification scheme based on distinctions among subject matter, levels of instruction, or groups of students served. Additional dimensions may be added because of needs generated by internal decision making or external reporting. Eleven different dimensions for elementary-secondary schools are presented in exhibit 8.10 along with examples of general distinctions among expenditures within each dimension.

Accounts are used to record and show the assets, liabilities, reserves, fund balances, revenues, and expenditures of an organization. Accounts created for these purposes are referred to as *proprietary accounts*. Accounts are also used for budget planning and control: these are called *budgetary accounts* and are used to record and report the implementation of an adopted budget.

When an educational organization adopts a budget, it is committing itself to a rather detailed spending plan based on estimates of revenue from a variety of sources. Various amounts of money are appropriated for specified purposes; that is, specified sums are authorized to be used within a specified time frame (for example, fiscal year). There are two general types of budgetary accounts: those dealing with estimated revenues and those dealing with appropriations.

Exhibit 8.11 illustrates in a highly simplified manner how budget amounts

Exhibit 8.8

Plausible Distinctions Among Liabilities, Reserves, and Fund Balances

	Funds and Groups of Accounts								
Balance Sheet Accounts	General fund	Special revenue fund	Debt service fund	Capital projects fund	Food service fund	Pupil activity fund	Trust and agency funds	General fixed assets	General long-term debt
Current liabilities									
Vouchers payable	X	X	X	X	X	X	X		
Accounts payable	X	X		X	X	X			
Judgments payable	X	X	X	X	X	X			
Contracts payable	X	X		X	X	X			
Construction contracts payable				X					
Construction contracts payable—retained percentage				X					
Due to ______ fund	X	X	X	X	X	X	X		
Due to ______ government	X	X	X	X	X	X	X		
Advance from ______ fund	X	X	X	X	X	X	X		
Matured bonds payable			X						
Matured interest payable			X						
Payroll deductions and withholdings	X	X		X	X	X	X		
Accrued expenses	X	X			X	X			
Deposits payable	X	X		X	X	X	X		
Due to fiscal agent			X						
Unamortized premiums on bonds sold			X						

Exhibit 8.8, continued

Balance Sheet Accounts	Funds and Groups of Accounts								
	General fund	Special revenue fund	Debt service fund	Capital projects fund	Food service fund	Pupil activity fund	Trust and agency funds	General fixed assets	General long-term debt
Revenues collected in advance	X	X	X	X					
Taxes collected in advance	X						X		
Long-term liabilities									
Bonds payable									X
Budgeting accounts and other credits									
Appropriations	X	X	X	X	X	X			
Expenditures (debit)	X	X	X	X	X	X			
Encumbrances (debit)	X	X		X	X	X			
Reserves and fund balance									
Reserve for encumbrances	X	X		X	X	X			
Reserve for inventory	X								
Reserve for ______ (special purposes)	X	X	X	X	X	X	X		
Fund balance	X	X	X	X	X	X	X		
Investment in general fixed assets								X	

Source: Adapted from Charles T. Roberts and Allan R. Lichtenberger, *Financial Accounting: Classifications and Standard Terminology for Local and State School Systems* (Washington, D.C.: U.S. Government Printing Office, 1973, OE 73-11800), pp. 6–7.

Exhibit 8.9

Plausible Distinctions Among Types of Revenue

Revenue from Local Sources
- Taxes
  - Ad valorem taxes levied by LEA
  - Ad valorem taxes levied by another governmental unit
  - Sales and use taxes
  - Income taxes
  - Other taxes
  - Penalties and interest on taxes

Revenue from Local Governmental Units Other than LEAs
- Tuition
  - Regular day school tuition
    - Tuition from pupils or parents
    - Tuition from other LEAs within the state
    - Tuition from other LEAs outside the state
  - Adult/continuing education tuition
    - Tuition from pupils or parents
    - Tuition from other LEAs within the state
    - Tuition from other LEAs outside the state
  - Summer school tuition
    - Tuition from pupils or parents
    - Tuition from other LEAs within the state
    - Tuition from other LEAs outside the state
- Transportation fees
  - Regular day school transportation fees
    - Transportation fees from pupils or parents
    - Transportation fees from other LEAs within the state
    - Transportation fees from other LEAs outside the state
  - Summer school transportation fees
    - Transportation fees from pupils or parents
    - Transportation fees from other LEAs within the state
    - Transportation fees from other LEAs outside the state
- Earnings on investments
  - Interest on investments
  - Dividends on investments
  - Gain or loss on sale of investments
- Food services
  - Sales to pupils
  - Sales to adults
- Pupil activities
  - Admissions
  - Bookstore sales
  - Pupil organization membership
  - Other pupil activity income

continued on page 272

Exhibit 8.9, continued

Other Revenue from Local Sources
- Rentals
- Contributions and donations from private sources
- *Sale and loss of fixed assets
  - Sale of fixed assets
  - Compensation for loss of fixed assets
- Services provided other LEAs
  - LEAs within the state
  - LEAs outside the state
  - *Refund of prior year's expenditures
  - *Transfer from other funds
  - *Sales of bonds
  - Premium on bonds sold
  - Miscellaneous

Revenue from Intermediate Sources
- Grants-in-aid
  - Unrestricted grants-in-aid
  - Restricted grants-in-aid
- Revenue in lieu of taxes
- Revenue for/on behalf of the LEA

Revenue from State Sources
- Grants-in-aid
  - Unrestricted grants-in-aid
  - Restricted grants-in-aid
- Revenue in lieu of taxes
- Revenue for/on behalf of the LEA

Revenue from Federal Sources
- Grants-in-aid
  - Unrestricted grants-in-aid received directly from federal government
  - Unrestricted grants-in-aid received from federal government through the state
  - Restricted grants-in-aid received directly from federal government
  - Restricted grants-in-aid received from federal government through the state
- Revenue in lieu of taxes
- Revenue for/on behalf of the LEA

---

*Revenues with an asterisk are not revenues to a LEA (Local Education Agency).

Source: Charles T. Roberts and Allan R. Lichtenberger, *Financial Accounting: Classifications and Standard Terminology for Local and State School Systems* (Washington, D.C.: U.S. Government Printing Office, 1973, OE 73-11800), pp. 13–15.

Exhibit 8.10

Plausible Dimensions of Expenditure Accounts in Elementary-Secondary Educational Organizations

Fund	Object	Function	Operational unit	Program	Source of funds	Fiscal Year
1 General fund	1 Salaries	1000 Instruction	001 Friedley Elementary	Broad-based goals and subject matter and type of pupils combined with level of instruction or age of learner	1 Local	0 1969–1970
2 Special revenue	2 Employee benefits	1100 Regular programs	501 McLune Middle		2 Intermediate	1 1970–1971
3 Debt service	3 Purchased services	1200 Special	701 Jones High		3 State	2 1971–1972
4 Capital project	4 Supplies and materials	1300 Adult/continuing education	751 Chismore Vocational		4 Federal	3 1972–1973
5 Food service	5 Capital outlay	2000 Support services	781 Curtis Junior College			4 1973–1974
6 Pupil activity	6 Other objectives	2100 Pupil support	901 Central administration			5 1974–1975
7 Trust and agen.	7 Transfers	2200 Staff support	911 Main warehouse			
8 Fixed assets		2300 General administrative support	921 Main bus garage			
9 Long-term debt		2400 School administrative support	990 ——			
		2500 Business support				
		2600 Central support				
		3000 Community services				
		4000 Nonprogrammed charges				
		5000 Debt services				

Exhibit 8.10, continued

Instruction Organization	Assignment	Term	Special Cost Center
1 Elementary school	1 Official/administrative	1 Fall—day	01 Girls' basketball
2 Middle/junior high	2 Professional-educational	2 Fall—evening	02 Drug abuse
3 High school	3 Professional-other	3 Winter—day	03 Special project
4 Adult/continuing education school	4 Technical	4 Winter—evening	99 Other special project
5 Junior college	5 Office/clerical	5 Spring—day	
9 Other school	6 Crafts and trades	6 Spring—evening	
	7 Operative	7 Summer—day	
	8 Laborer	8 Summer—evening	
	9 Service work		

Source: Charles T. Roberts and Allan R. Lichtenberger, *Financial Accounting: Classifications and Standard Terminology for Local and State School Systems* (Washington, D.C.: U.S. Government Printing Office, 1973, OE 73-11800), pp. 63–64.

Exhibit 8.11

Sample Budgeted Revenues and Appropriations in the General Fund

Estimated Revenues from:		
Taxes	$30,000	
Tuition	5,000	
Rentals	5,000	
Total estimated revenues		$40,000
Appropriations:		
Salaries	$28,000	
Supplies	8,000	
Capital outlay	2,000	
Total appropriations		$38,000

Source: Adapted from Sam B. Tidwell, *Financial and Management Accounting for Elementary and Secondary School Systems* (Chicago: Research Corporation of the Association of School Business Officials, 1974), pp. 130–31.

and conditions are recorded in budgetary accounts. Exhibit 8.12 illustrates general journal entries that record the budget in the budgetary accounts.

If conditions under which estimates were made actually develop as anticipated the budgetary accounts will remain unchanged until the end of the accounting period. If changes do occur, however, revisions must be made in the budget and recorded in the budgetary accounts. The following four conditions could develop, any one of which would require adjustments in the budget and budgetary accounts:

1. Estimated revenues are recorded for which no provision exists, such as an unrestricted grant-in-aid from the state.
2. Estimated revenues, as recorded, are found to be in excess of all possible sources of revenue, such as from a tax levy.
3. Appropriations, as recorded, do not provide for an unexpected expenditure (for example, destruction caused by a flood), and additional expenditures would be necessary to replace the asset destroyed.
4. Appropriations, as recorded, are found to be in excess of required expenditures.

In each type of circumstance, budgetary accounts would be adjusted through entries that would have the effect of increasing or decreasing the fund equity in the account.

A system of encumbrances is used to avoid the possibility of overexpenditure of an appropriation. *Encumbrances* have been defined as "obligations or commitments in the form of purchase orders, contracts, salary commitments, and so on, which are chargeable to an appropriation and for which a part of the appropriation is reserved prior to the actual expenditure

Exhibit 8.12

Sample Account Titles for Budgeted Revenues and Expenditures

Revenue Accounts in the General Fund		
Estimated revenue from taxes	$30,000	
Estimated revenue from tuition	5,000	
Estimated revenue from rentals	5,000	
Expenditure Accounts		
Appropriation for salaries		28,000
Appropriation for supplies		8,000
Appropriation for capital outlay		2,000

Source: Adapted from Sam B. Tidwell, *Financial and Management Accounting for Elementary and Secondary School Systems* (Chicago: Research Corporation of the Association of School Business Officials, 1974), p. 130.

of funds for that purpose" (Tidwell 1974, p. 137). Encumbrances are used to "earmark" some portion of the unexpected amount of appropriation.

Taken together, accounting concepts and operations such as those described in this chapter provide a means for ordering financial data. Financial data, systematically derived and organized, can be highly useful in managing educational organizations. It is to those managerial uses of financial data that we turn in the following chapter.

Conclusion

Methods for treating, recording, and presenting financial information on schools are quite similar across the three sectors. Differences among the three sectors, as discussed, include treatment of assets, fund accounting, and accrual versus cash accounting. In practice these and other differences are more differences in degree than differences in kind.

References

Adams, Bert K. *Principles of Public School Accounting*. Washington, D.C.: U.S. Government Printing Office, 1967. OE 22025.

American Institute of Certified Public Accountants. "Inventory of Generally Accepted Accounting Principles for Business Enterprises." *Accounting Research Study No. 7*. New York: The Institute, 1965.

Mautz, R. K. "Basic Concepts of Accounting." In *Handbook of Modern Accounting*, edited by Sidney Davidson, chap. 1. New York: McGraw-Hill, 1970.

Roberts, Charles T., and Lichtenberger, Allan R. *Financial Accounting: Classifications and Standard Terminology for Local and State School Systems.* Washington, D.C.: U.S. Government Printing Office, 1973. OE 73-11800.

Tidwell, Sam B. *Financial and Management Accounting for Elementary and Secondary School Systems.* Chicago: Research Corporation of the Association of School Business Officials, 1974.

Supplementary Reading

Gross, Malvern J., and Martin, D. Edward. "Cost Accounting in Nonprofit Organizations." In *Handbook of Modern Accounting,* edited by Sidney Davidson and Roman L. Weid. New York: McGraw-Hill Book Co., 1978, pp. 25 to 29.

Hay, M., and Mikesell, R. *Governmental Accounting.* 5th ed. Homewood, Ill.: Richard D. Irwin, 1974.

National Association of Independent Schools. *Accounting for Independent Schools.* Boston, Mass.: National Association of Independent Schools, 1977.

Palen, Jennie, M., ed. *Encyclopedia of Auditing Techniques.* Englewood Cliffs, N.J.: Prentice-Hall, 1974. Provides in its early chapters a nontechnical description of financial practices in general, and auditing practices in particular. See especially William S. Woodman's "Audit of a School District" (pp. 1257–1286), which describes in a nontechnical manner the specific activities required of independent auditors engaged in the audit of a typical school district; and D. W. Edens's "Auditing of a University" (pp. 1466–1508), a nontechnical treatment of the required activities of auditing a university, which provides a rather comprehensive overview of the diverse financial dealings required of most universities.

Reason, Paul L., and White, Alpheus L. *Financial Accounting for Local and State School Systems: Standard Receipt and Expenditure Accounts.* Washington, D.C.: U.S. Government Printing Office, 1957. While updated by the Adams and Roberts references, this nevertheless provides a useful overview of school district accounting practices that is not at odds with many existing district accounting operations.

Samuelson, Everett V., and Tankard, George G., Jr. *Financial Accounting for School Activities,* Washington, D.C.: U.S. Government Printing Office, 1962. A guide for the financial accounting of money received by individual schools for school activities, including student clubs, student publications, the sale of merchandise through a school store, rental of textbooks, and so on.

9

Managerial Uses of Accounting Data

•

Overview

Through the procedures of accounting (see chapter 8) financial data are generated to serve a variety of purposes, such as facilitating planning and control decisions and responding to external reporting requirements. The balance sheet and the statement of revenues and expenditures, by themselves, are ways of reporting data that serve both of these purposes. In order to develop cost analyses (including examples discussed in chapters 5, 12, and 13), several general distinctions among types of costs must be made, such as between variable and fixed costs, between direct and indirect costs, and between total and unit costs. Public-sector school business administrators use these tools extensively in claiming third-party payments or reimbursements. Private school managers use these tools more to evaluate the profitability of new and existing programs.

• • •

The description in chapter 8 of the fundamental concepts of accounting systems has paved the way for a discussion of their application of managerial decision making in education. The accounting system is the major quantitative information system in almost every organization. In educa-

---

Special thanks to Clayton W. Harell, Xerox Corporation, for his helpful comments on this chapter.

Exhibit 9.1

Overlap of Accounting Specialties and Organizational Uses of Accounting

	Managerial	Financial
Internal reporting: routine	XX	X
Internal reporting: nonroutine	XX	XX
External reporting	X	XX

XX = heaviest emphasis

tional organizations, as in others, it should provide information for three broad purposes:

1. Internal reporting to managers, for use in planning and controlling routine operations
2. Internal reporting to managers, for use in making nonroutine decisions and in formulating major plans and policies
3. External reporting to outside parties (analogous to stockholders in for-profit concerns), such as government and granting agencies (Horngren 1972, p. 4).

In its attempt to provide information for these and other purposes, the accounting profession has developed specializations, the two most comprehensive of which are *financial accounting* and *managerial accounting*. Financial accounting has been characterized as "the branch of accounting that focuses on the general-purpose reports of financial position and results of operations known as financial statements" (A.I.C.P.A. 1970, p. 6). Financial accounting is the process that culminates in the preparation of financial reports *relative to the enterprise as a whole for use by parties both internal and external to the enterprise*. In contrast, managerial accounting pertains most directly to the accumulation and communication of information *relative to subsystems of the entity for use by internal parties* (American Accounting Association 1971, p. 9).

As implied, the distinctions in the field of accounting overlap to some degree with the organizational purposes of accounting. This overlap is illustrated in exhibit 9.1. It can also be said that financial accounting concerns itself more with "how to do" accounting, while managerial accounting concerns itself more with "how to use" accounting in management. However, even this distinction is not entirely accurate, because there are things that managers *do* that can be properly termed managerial accounting.

While these accounting-related classification schemes are by no means mutually exclusive, they do provide a way for introducing the contents of this chapter and distinguishing this from the previous chapter. In the previous chapter, emphasis was placed more on financial accounting and on how it is done. In this chapter the emphasis is more on managerial accounting and how to use accounting-related information. The first section describes the degree to which accounting in public educational organizations differs in emphasis from accounting in private educational organizations. Despite these differences, a far greater number of accounting concerns are common across organizations. Three of these are discussed in this chapter: (1) internal control, (2) routine decision making, and (3) nonroutine decision making.

Managerial Accounting: Public Versus Private Schools

The accounting emphasis in public educational organizations has been on internal control and external reporting and less on internal planning. There are several reasons for this. The financial activities of public educational organizations—including accounting, reporting, and auditing—are governed by statutes to a much greater extent than those of private educational organizations. Compliance with statutory requirements is mandatory, even though they may, and frequently do, conflict with good accounting practices (Woodman 1974, p. 1258). Second, control of expenditures is considered of paramount importance, especially in those instances where public tax dollars are being spent. Ironically, however, internal control in public educational organizations is often less effective than in for-profit schools because of the academic orientation of administrative personnel, overlapping statutory provisions, and different incentives for control.

Some of the differing emphases in accounting in educational organizations and other businesses can be traced to the relative complexity of each. Educational organizations generally engage in quite diversified activities, including large-scale sports programs; operations of transportation facilities, cafeterias, and bookstores; rental of facilities; and significant construction programs. Clientele and programs are diverse; for example, the basic instructional activities may involve day as well as night students and part-time as well as full-time students.

Although more complex and subject to greater external control than for-profit schools, public educational organizations attach relatively less importance to balance sheets and accounting for fixed assets (Woodman 1974, p. 1259). Balance sheets are less significant because the credit of the public educational organization is defined by its legal position (including, in the case of school districts, its taxing power) rather than by its recorded net worth. Assets are seldom pledged to secure debt, but the pledge of future revenues is common practice. (As a consequence, the statement of revenues and expenditures is of relatively more interest to public educational managers than is the statement of assets and liabilities.)

Since accounting for fixed assets is less important in public educational organizations, it is quite common to find no formal accounting records of property accounts, whereas this is standard procedure in for-profit organizations. Motivation for keeping property accounts in educational organizations stems largely from insurance and external reporting requirements as opposed to taxation requirements (except with respect to those educational organizations devoted primarily to the production of income).

Despite these differences in emphasis, the managerial purposes for which accounting systems are used in educational organizations are much the same as in other organizations. These purposes involve the concepts of (1) internal control, (2) routine management decision making (both within the organization and by external sponsoring and regulatory agencies), and (3) nonroutine decision making.

Internal Control

Internal control is defined by the American Institute of Certified Public Accountants as "the plan of organization and all of the coordinate methods and measures adopted within a business to safeguard its assets, check the accuracy and reliability of its accounting data, promote operational efficiency, and encourage adherence to prescribed managerial policies" (Committee on Auditing Procedure 1963, p. 27). It is the financial part of "operational control," discussed in chapter 3 and elsewhere in this book.

Accounting is an essential instrument for maintaining and enhancing internal control. Internal control is a management function, not an accounting function. However, a number of management principles will help to bring about accounting control and thereby minimize errors, fraud, and waste. *Minimize* is a more appropriate term here than *eliminate* because, as Horngren (1972, p. 668) says, "no framework for internal control is perfect in the sense that it can prevent some shrewd individual from 'beating the system' either by outright embezzlement or by producing inaccurate records."

A checklist for a good internal control system might include the eleven items below (drawn from Horngren 1972, pp. 668–670, and Vatter 1950, chap. 11):

1. Reliable personnel. The accounting system, no matter how elaborate, is only as good as the individuals who operate it. This means that individuals should be given duties and responsibilities commensurate with their abilities, experience, interests, and reliability.
2. Separation of powers. Recordkeeping and the physical control of

assets should not be in the hands of one person. For example, the bookkeeper should not handle cash, and the cashier should not have access to ledger accounts. This removes the temptation for a single person to alter the ledger accounts to hide the theft of cash.

3. Supervision. The typical pyramid organization chart illustrates a common mode of supervision: everyone has a boss who oversees and appraises performance.
4. Responsibility. It is important to track actions as far down in the organization as is feasible, so that results may be related to particular individuals. This might mean, for example, having building-level personnel sign for supplies received from a central warehouse, having workmen sign time cards, and so on.
5. Routine and automatic checks. Establishing routine and automatic procedures for checking on operations is especially important in activities such as order taking, order filling, and disbursements. For example, no check should be written without an accompanying (signed) disbursement voucher that indicates who authorized the check. Forms should be designed so that the absence or incorrectness of key information is automatically uncovered and corrected on the spot. For example, the absence of a head custodian's signature prevents payments of overtime pay to custodians.
6. Document control. This term refers to measures that ensure immediate, complete, and tamper-proof recording of transactions, especially those involving cash. This is encouraged, for example, by having all source documents prenumbered and accounted for.
7. Bonding, vacations, and rotation of duties. Key people who are subject to excessive temptation because of access to money should be bonded. Temptation is reduced when these people have understudies and are forced to take vacations. Improved control is also established by rotating clerks (for example, those handling receivables and payables).
8. Independent checks. These include and extend beyond practices normally undertaken by independent auditors. Such practices should be undertaken by people who do not ordinarily have contact with the operation under review and would include reconciling bank statements with book balances and the physical counting of inventory.
9. Physical safeguards. This would cover all measures taken to physically protect cash, inventories, and records. Locks, safes, and watchmen fall into this category.
10. Cost feasibility. The complexity and costs of an internal control system have to be compared to the expected benefits. Unfortunately, "more" does not always mean "better." While difficult to quantify, these trade-offs must nonetheless be considered.

11. Computer security. To this list of traditional internal controls, one should be added for computer security. Schweitzer (1983, p. 22) suggests that three levels of security for information access should be installed: physical security, which allows access to only those who have a need to enter computer rooms or terminal areas; logical security, including user-changeable passwords and other identification and authentication coding; and procedural security that is intended to oversee who is using the system and what data is being accessed. Although competition is not the driving force in the public sector as it is in the private sectors, misuse of and damage to computer equipment and data can cause considerable expense to the organization if not protected in a cost-effective manner.

Routine Decision Making

The word *routine* as used here does not imply mundaneness or triviality. Rather, routine finance-related decisions are those whose *form* is consistent over time. Many of the recurring, or routine, questions asked of the accounting system are answered via standard, basically unchanging, financial statements. There are at least four such general financial statements that together yield much information about the financial health of an educational organization. These financial statements provide the necessary information in a way that greatly condenses and organizes the mass of detail inherent in an accounting system.

The financial statements discussed here are: (1) the combined balance sheets, (2) the combined statement of revenues and expenditures, (3) the statement of changes in fund balances, and (4) the statement of changes in the overall financial position over time. The examples cited are drawn from elementary-secondary public education (Roberts and Lichtenberger 1973, pp. 167–174).

Combined Balance Sheet

The combined balance sheet summarizes the assets, liabilities, and equity amounts for the entire educational organization. These figures are reported on a fund-by-fund basis and are usually backed up by more detailed statements of each fund. Exhibit 9.2 shows the general form of a combined balance sheet for a school district.

It is possible to garner a wide range of information about the financial state of the organization from its combined balance sheet. In order to highlight different aspects of the combined balance sheet, school districts have started reporting various indices made up from the data. These include indebtedness indices (for example, matured bonds and interest payable

Combined Balance Sheet for All Funds

Funds (End of Year)

Balance Sheet Accounts	Total	General fund	Special revenue fund	Debt service fund	Capital projects fund	Food service fund	Pupil activity fund	Trust and agency funds	General fixed assets	Long-term debt
Assets and resources										
Cash	$ 335,500	$ 40,000	$ 25,000	$ 23,900	$ 235,600	$ 2,200	$ 800	$ 8,000		
Accounts receivable (net)	18,000	15,000	3,000							
Loans receivable (net)	30,000							30,000		
Notes receivable (net)	20,000			10,000				10,000		
Interest receivable on notes	3,200			2,400				800		
Taxes receivable, current (net)	140,000	80,000	30,000	30,000						
Interest receivable on taxes, current	1,400	800	300	300						
Taxes receivable, delinquent (net)	8,400	7,000	400	1,000						
Interest receivable on taxes, delinquent	1,800	1,400	100	300						
Due from other units of government	632,300	60,000	20,000	7,900	454,400	30,000	20,000	40,000		
Inventories	17,700	1,300	6,400			7,000	3,000			
Investments (including premiums and discounts)	1,940,000			1,860,000				80,000		
Bonds authorized and unissued	310,000				310,000					
Amount available and to provide for retirement of bonds and interest	2,400,000									$2,400,000
Land	90,000		8,000				2,000		$ 80,000	
Buildings	3,553,000		100,000			15,000			3,438,000	
Improvements other than buildings	98,000		15,000			1,000			82,000	

Machinery and equipment	1,630,000		20,000			140,000	70,000		1,400,000	
Total assets and resources	$11,229,300	$205,500	$228,200	$1,935,800	$1,000,000	$195,200	$95,800	$168,800	$5,000,000	$2,400,000
Liabilities										
Vouchers payable	$ 80,200	$ 30,000	$ 200		$ 2,000	$ 20,000	$10,000	$ 18,000		
Matured bonds and interest payable	137,200	87,200		$ 50,000						
Contracts payable	370,000	75,000	22,000		273,000					
Due to other units of government	35,100	5,300	16,000		5,000	8,000		800		
Interest payable in future years	800,000									$ 800,000
Bonds payable	1,600,000									1,600,000
Total liabilities	$ 3,022,500	$197,500	$ 38,200	$ 50,000	$ 280,000	$ 28,000	$10,000	$ 18,800		$2,400,000
Appropriations, reserves, and fund equities										
Appropriations	$ 300,000				$ 300,000					
Reserve for encumbrances	421,000	$ 6,000	$ 15,000		400,000					
Investment in general fixed assets	5,000,000								$5,000,000	
Principal or capital	360,000					$160,000	$50,000	$150,000		
Fund equity	2,125,800	2,000	175,000	1,885,800	20,000	7,200	35,800			
Total appropriations, reserves, and fund equities	$ 8,206,800	$ 8,000	$190,000	$1,885,800	$ 720,000	$167,200	$85,800	$150,000	$5,000,000	
Total liabilities, appropriations, reserves, and fund equities	$11,229,300	$205,500	$228,200	$1,935,800	$1,000,000	$195,200	$95,800	$168,800	$5,000,000	$2,400,000

Source: Charles T. Roberts and Allan R. Lichtenberger, *Financial Accounting: Classifications and Standard Terminology for Local and State School Systems* (Washington, D.C.: U.S. Government Printing Office, 1973, OE 73-11800), pp. 168–169.

Exhibit 9.3

Combined Statement of Revenues and Expenditures

Funds (End of Year)

Revenue and Expenditure Accounts	Total	General fund	Special revenue fund	Debt service fund	Capital projects fund	Food service fund	Pupil activity fund	Trust and agency funds
Revenues								
Taxations and appropriations	$2,561,000	$1,521,000		$140,000			$100,000	$800,000
Tuition from patrons	10,000	10,000						
Transportation fees from patrons	14,000	14,000						
Revenue from other units of government	50,000							50,000
Earnings on investments	68,000	20,000		14,000	$ 24,000	$ 1,000		9,000
Revenue from food sales	246,000					246,000		
Revenue from pupil activities	314,000						314,000	
Revenue from other local sources	2,735,000	1,000,000	$ 175,000	60,000	1,400,000			100,000
Revenue from intermediate sources	143,280	43,280		100,000				
Revenue from state sources	2,480,000	1,380,000	1,100,000					
Revenue from federal sources	975,000	100,000	715,000			160,000		
Total revenues	$9,596,280	$4,088,280	$1,990,000	$314,000	$1,424,000	$407,000	$414,000	$959,000

Expenditures								
Elementary programs	$1,890,000	$1,240,000	$ 197,000			$138,000	$ 15,000	$300,000
Middle/junior high programs	1,740,000	1,070,000	188,000			110,000	97,000	275,000
High school programs	2,018,000	827,000	546,000			105,000	300,000	240,000
Special education programs	785,000	175,000	587,500			5,000	500	17,000
Adult/continuing education program	285,000	115,000	158,500			500		11,000
Administration	122,000	107,000						15,000
Facilities acquisition and construction	1,520,000			$280,000	$1,240,000			
Transportation	245,000	15,000	230,000					
Community services	178,000	175,000	3,000					
Nonprogram charges	214,000	214,000						
Total expenditures	$8,997,000	$3,938,000	$1,910,000	$280,000	$1,240,000	$358,500	$412,500	$858,000

Source: Charles T. Roberts and Allan R. Lichtenberger, *Financial Accounting: Classifications and Standard Terminology for Local and State School Systems* (Washington, D.C.: U.S. Government Printing Office, 1973, OE 73-11800), p. 170.

divided by total liabilities) and liquidity indices (for example, cash divided by total assets and resources).

The balance sheet serves two main purposes: (1) to show the organization's liquidity and (2) to show fund or stockholders' equity, depending upon whether the entity is a for-profit, nonprofit, or public enterprise. Private for-profit schools seldom show the results of their divisions or privately held organizations the way public educational entities are required (by fund) to do. But private schools may show more detail in their identification of assets and liabilities, especially if tax implications, such as reserves and depreciation, can be drawn from the data.

Combined Statement of Revenues and Expenditures

This form yields a different but equally useful type of general information: it summarizes the major sources of revenue to the district (by fund) as well as the amounts spent in the major expenditure categories. This summary is often backed up by more detailed revenue-expenditure statements for each fund. Exhibit 9.3 is an example of a combined revenue and expenditure statement. In a sense, this statement reflects the "activity" of each fund during the period. During the year past, the debt service fund, for example, received $300,000 from taxations and appropriations and from other local and intermediate sources. The district earned $14,000 in interest on this money and spent $280,000 of the money on facilities.

Here, too, various indices can be helpful in gaining a more comprehensive picture of the financial condition of the organization—such as indices of the investment activity of the district (for example, earnings on investments divided by total revenues).

In for-profit schools, this report is often referred to as the profit and loss statement, operating statement, or just the income statement. Its purpose is to show the results from operations for the period. If it is a profit-making concern, profit is the measure of success. If the purpose of the organization is not to have a profit, but to show relative equality between income and expenses, as in a private, nonprofit school, the facts will speak for themselves. On the other hand, if the purpose of an educational entity is not to make a profit, the measure of success will be hidden from the reader; consequently, other means must be developed to show success over and above the balances depicted on the statement of revenues and expenses.

Naturally, if there are large differences between revenues and expenses for public and private nonprofit schools, in either direction, explanations for the "loss" or "profit" must be made. Whereas in the private for-profit sector, profits and losses are themselves a central measure for the success of the organization; losses are the death blow if sustained for any period of time.

Changes in Fund Balances

Closely related to the combined statement of revenues and expenditures is the statement of changes in fund balances. Generally, this statement shows for each fund the net differences between revenues and expenditures, both at the beginning and at the end of the period; it reflects the degree of change in revenue-expenditure differences by fund in comparison with the previous year. In the example in exhibit 9.4 all funds (except the general fund) show an increase in net revenue over the previous year.

Changes in Financial Position

This statement describes in summary fashion (for all funds combined) the resources provided the district and to what they were applied. Resources are provided from revenues for each fund; from reduction in assets during the year; from increase of liabilities, appropriations, and reserves during the year; from collection of revenues from the prior year; and from expenditures being refunded. These funds are applied to the operations of the district via funds to increase assets during the year, decrease liabilities during the year, collect expenses for the prior year, and refund excess revenue collected in the prior year.

An example of this statement appears in exhibit 9.5. The statement of changes in financial position is prepared using combined balance sheets at the beginning and end of the period (for example, fiscal year) and the combined statement of revenues and expenditures. (Comparative balance sheets from which exhibit 9.5 was prepared are presented in exhibit 9.6.)

The financial statements described here provide a broad basis from which much of the financial condition of the organization can be inferred. While possibly indicating over time a wide variety of desirable and undesirable conditions in an organization, the financial statements rarely change in format and, as intended, are addressed to the recurring (routine) decisions facing management in educational organizations. They are also used by sponsoring and regulatory agencies as they formulate policy affecting the educational organizations.

Nonroutine Decision Making

Generally, financial information that management knows will be routinely and frequently required should probably be generated through the transactions (accounting) system described previously or through a system that operates directly off it. However, many decisions faced by educational managers differ in form over time. But it would be prohibitively expensive—if not virtually impossible—to design an accounting information sys-

Exhibit 9.4

Changes in Fund Balances for All Funds

(end of year)

Funds

Balances	Total	General fund	Special revenue fund	Debt service fund	Capital projects fund	Food service fund	Pupil activity fund	Trust and agency funds
Beginning of year	$453,250	$ 300,000	$28,000	$ 5,000	$ 45,000	$ 1,100	$ (850)	$ 75,000
End of year	599,280	150,280	80,000	34,000	184,000	48,500	1,500	101,000
Change	$146,030	$(149,720)	$52,000	$29,000	$139,000	$47,400	$2,350	$ 26,000

Source: Charles T. Roberts and Allan R. Lichtenberger, *Financial Accounting: Classifications and Standard Terminology for Local and State School Systems* (Washington, D.C.: U.S. Government Printing Office, 1973, OE 73-11800), p. 171.

tem comprehensive enough to be adequate for all possible future financial information needs.

As a result, the financial information required as input for nonroutine decisions cannot be provided directly by the accounting system. Accounting systems, for example, do not automatically report the cost of expanding an instructional program to serve 50 percent more pupils. In order to generate the information required for this type of decision, and many like it, the educational manager must be able to estimate costs (as well as income). To do this with any degree of validity requires an understanding of cost relationships in the organization.

The manager can use *cost analysis* to arrive at and to implement decisions made in the light of organizational objectives. Consequently, the structure and logic of cost analysis have a major impact on the decisions reached and on the ability of the organization to achieve its goals. It is therefore imperative that top management understand some of the more fundamental classifications of costs and how they are incurred. Among many types of costs that could be discussed, four of the most fundamental are discussed here. They are (1) variable versus fixed costs, (2) direct versus indirect costs, (3) total versus unit costs, and (4) transfer pricing.

Variable Versus Fixed Costs

A total cost may be either *variable* or *fixed* depending on whether or not it changes in relation to fluctuations in the activity of the program or quantity of the cost object under analysis. Many types of activity can be defined in this way: for example, man-hours worked, miles driven, students enrolled, gallons consumed, payroll checks processed. If a total cost changes in proportion to changes in activity, it is variable; if a total cost remains unchanged for a given period despite wide fluctuations in activity, it is fixed. A fixed cost is fixed only in relationship to a given period of time and a given, though wide, range of activity, called the *relevant range* (Horngren 1972, p. 24). For example, a school district may find that, over a 10 percent variation in enrollment, the variable costs include only teachers' salaries and instructional supplies. No additional administrative staff or facilities may be required; these may be considered fixed in this relevant range. Over a wider relevant range, however, these costs would vary. A significant increase in students would require additional facilities and support staff, whereas with a significant drop in existing levels in enrollment, schools may be closed. This is portrayed conceptually in exhibit 9.7. The likelihood of activities being outside the relevant range is usually slight, so the $500,000 in figure 9.7 becomes the fixed-cost level. The three-level refinement shown in this figure is not usually required because the chances are very remote that total enrollment will change more than 10 percent over the year (see exhibit 9.8).

Educational managers find this concept useful for a number of reasons.

Exhibit 9.5

Changes in Financial Position for All Funds

(end of year)

Resources Provided from:			Resources Allocated to:		
Revenue for year			Operations		
General fund	$4,088,280		General fund	$3,938,000	
Special revenue fund	1,990,000		Special revenue fund	1,910,000	
Debt service fund	314,000		Debt service fund	280,000	
Capital projects fund	1,424,000		Capital projects fund	1,240,000	
Food service fund	407,000		Food services fund	358,500	
Pupil activity fund	414,000		Pupil activity fund	412,500	
Trust and agency funds	959,000	$ 9,596,280	Trust and agency funds	858,000	$ 8,997,000
Reducing assets during year			Increase assets during year		
Accounts receivable	$ 12,000		Cash	$ 266,800	
Notes receivable	20,000		Loans receivable (net)	20,000	
Taxes receivable, current (net)	10,000		Interest receivable on notes	1,000	
Interest receivable on taxes, delinquent	100		Taxes receivable, delinquent (net)	600	
Investments	60,000		Due from other units of government	532,300	
Amount available and to be provided			Inventories	3,700	
for retention of bonds and interest	200,000	$ 302,100	Bonds authorized and unissued	310,000	$ 1,134,400

Increasing liabilities, appropriations, and reserves during the year			Decreasing liabilities during year		
Vouchers payable	$ 70,000		Contracts payable	$ 333,000	
Matured bonds and interest payable	137,200		Bonds payable	652,000	$ 985,000
Due to other units of government	25,100		Corrections of prior year		
Interest payable in future years	500,000		Interest expense	$ 2,200	
Appropriations	300,000		Contracts payable	73,080	
Reserves for encumberances	401,000	$ 1,433,300	Due to other units of government	92,000	$ 167,280
Corrections of prior year			Revenue rebates from prior year		
Taxes receivable, delinquent	$ 39,000		Revenue from taxes	$ 79,000	
Interest receivable on taxes, delinquent	87,000		Revenue from state sources	87,000	
Inventories	15,000	$ 141,000	Revenue from federal sources	89,000	$ 255,000
			Total resources applied		$11,538,680
Expenditures refunded from prior year					
Elementary programs	$ 10,000				
Middle/junior high programs	39,000				
Community services	17,000	$ 66,000			
Total resources provided		$11,538,680			

Source: Charles T. Roberts and Allan R. Lichtenberger, *Financial Accounting: Classifications and Standard Terminology for Local and State School Systems* (Washington, D.C.: U.S. Government Printing Office, 1973, OE 73-11800), pp. 172–173.

Exhibit 9.6

Comparative Combined Balance Sheets

Balance Sheet Accounts	Beginning of Year	End of Year	Net Changes: Debits	Net Changes: Credits
Assets and resources				
Cash	$ 68,700	$ 335,500	$ 266,800	
Accounts receivable (net)	30,000	18,000		$ 12,000
Loans receivable (net)	10,000	30,000	20,000	
Notes receivable	40,000	20,000		20,000
Interest receivable on notes	2,200	3,200	1,000	
Taxes receivable, current (net)	250,000	140,000		110,000
Interest receivable on taxes, delinquent	1,400	1,400		
Taxes receivable, delinquent (net)	7,800	8,400	600	
Interest receivable on taxes	1,900	1,800		100
Due from other units of government	100,000	632,300	532,300	
Inventories	14,000	17,700	3,700	
Investments (including premiums and discounts)	2,000,000	1,940,000		60,000
Bonds authorized and unissued		310,000	310,000	
Amount available and to be provided for retirement of bonds and interest	2,500,000	2,400,000		100,000
Land	87,000	90,000	3,000	

Buildings	3,250,000	3,553,000	303,000	
Improvements other than buildings	95,000	98,000	3,000	
Machinery and equipment	1,800,000	1,630,000		170,000
Total assets and resources	$10,258,000	$11,229,300		
Liabilities, reserves, and fund equity				
Vouchers payable	$ 10,200	$ 80,200		70,000
Matured bonds and interest payable		137,200		137,200
Contracts payable	703,000	370,000	333,000	
Due to other units of government	10,000	35,100		25,100
Interest payable in future years	300,000	800,000		500,000
Bonds payable	2,252,000	1,600,000	652,000	
Appropriations		300,000		300,000
Reserve for encumbrances	20,000	421,000		401,000
Investments in general fixed assets	4,861,000	5,000,000		139,000
Principal on capital	250,000	360,000		110,000
Fund equity	1,851,800	2,125,800		274,000
Total liabilities, reserves, fund equity, debits, and credits	$10,258,000	$11,229,300	$2,428,400	$2,428,400

Source: Charles T. Roberts and Allan R. Lichtenberger, *Financial Accounting: Classifications and Standard Terminology for Local and State School Systems* (Washington, D.C.: U.S. Government Printing Office, 1973, OE 73-11800), p. 174.

Exhibit 9.7
Total Annual Fixed Costs—Conceptual Analysis

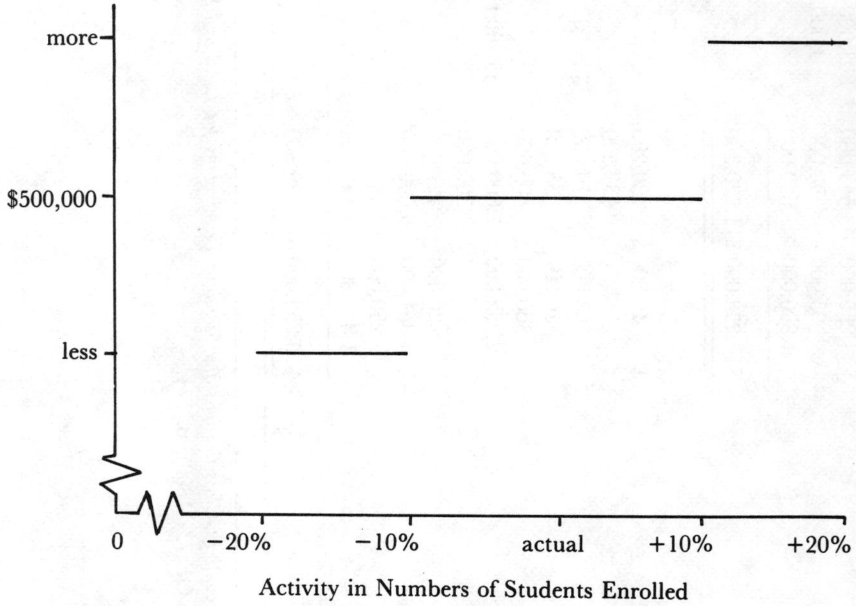

Exhibit 9.8
Total Annual Fixed Costs as Plotted in Practice

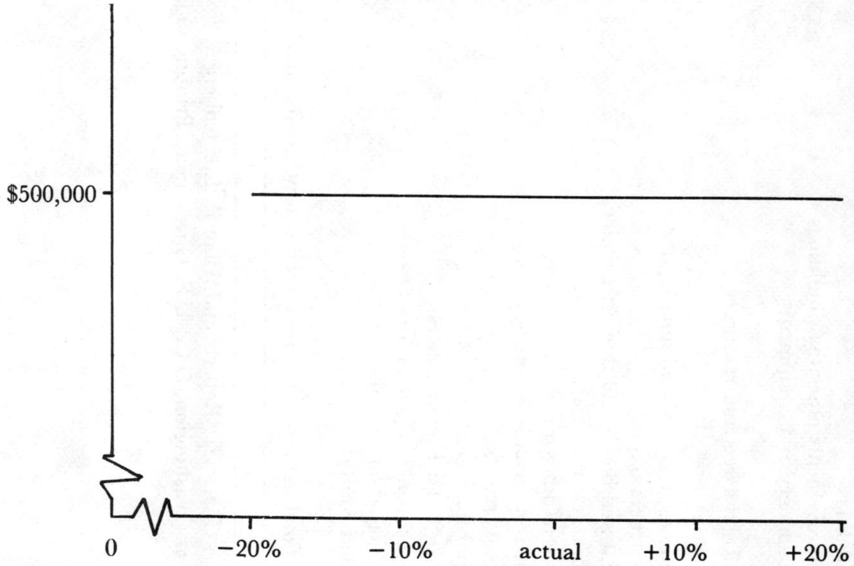

Most importantly it provides them with knowledge of their organization's cost behavior patterns (*cost functions*), which they can use to predict the impact of their decisions on costs and to formulate means for controlling cost incurrence.

Some costs are difficult to categorize as either strictly variable or strictly fixed. In fact, few costs are clearly one or the other. How a cost is identified depends largely on the activity base that is chosen. Central administration of a university, for example, may view telephones as a variable cost if the activity base is the number of professors on the faculty. However, such costs are fixed for an academic department that does not change in size and that uses as an activity base the number of calls made.

Direct Versus Indirect Costs

Closely related to the concepts of fixed and variable costs are the concepts of *direct* and *indirect costs*. None of these terms has a useful meaning apart from its relation to a particular object of costing. The distinction between direct and indirect costs is made on the basis of *traceability*. *Direct* refers to the obvious (traceable) relationship of a cost incurred with respect to an object of costing, whereas an indirect cost does not have this obvious relationship with an object of costing. For example, the salary of a mathematics curriculum coordinator who works at a school district central office would be a direct charge to the mathematics program of a school district. There is an obvious relationship between the math coordinator and the mathematics program he coordinates. However, his salary would be an indirect charge to the various mathematics programs in each of the schools in the district. In order to allocate his salary among the various schools in the district, it will be necessary to determine some intervening allocation mechanism, such as the number of mathematics teachers in each of the schools. The allocation of a portion of the mathematics coordinator's salary to the math program at school A would be determined as follows:

$$\text{Mathematics coordinator's salary} \times \frac{\text{number of mathematics teachers in School A}}{\text{number of mathematics teachers in the district}}$$

= that portion of the mathematics coordinator's salary allocated to the mathematics program in school A.

In program costing, the distinction between direct and indirect costs is determined by the procedures used for the allocation. For direct cost:

1. There is almost always some sort of observable physical identification with the cost object that can be explicitly measured in terms of the quantity of the input used. (In the case of the mathematics curriculum

coordinator, he has actually been defined as part of the mathematics programs in the district.)

2. There is no intervening basis for allocation.

For an indirect cost there would be an intervening basis for allocation. For example, the salary of the mathematics curriculum coordinator would be an indirect charge to the mathematics programs at each of the school sites, and such a cost would be determined on an allocation basis such as that described above.

The issue of determining direct and indirect costs is particularly crucial in educational organizations where external agencies often sponsor specific segments of the organization's operations (such as transportation and food service operations in elementary-secondary education and a wide variety of research and training programs in colleges and universities). In higher education the concern with increased indirect costs and the resulting growth in overhead rates is frequently expressed by sponsors but is shared by both higher education administrators and principal investigators. The impact of these costs on limited institutional funds and the resulting reduction in sponsors' funds available for direct costs are recognized by the college and university community as factors in the overall financial difficulty that has faced higher education since the late 1960s (National Association of College and University Business Officers 1974, p. 2).

In an effort to clarify indirect costing procedures used by the federal government in dealing with institutions of higher education, the American Council on Education summarized both the tentative nature of cost accounting as well as the impact of cost determination on organizational income (Commission on Federal Relations 1969, p. 2).

> Depending upon how an institution organizes the management of its research, some costs may be considered either direct or indirect, *but not both.* These differences in organization for the management of research are the major reason for differing indirect cost rates among institutions, but such differences do not affect total costs. If indirect costs go up, direct costs come down correspondingly; total costs remain unchanged. But the amount of total costs recovered by the institution may be affected by a change in the mixture of indirect and direct cost elements.

Total Versus Unit Costs

Total cost is a necessary but not sufficient piece of cost information for management decision making, especially in education. *Unit cost* information supplements total cost information and aids in selection and pricing decisions. For example, a particular reading program in a school district may cost $80,000 and serve eight hundred pupils. While it has a higher total cost than an alternative that costs $60,000 and serves four hundred pupils, its unit (in this case, per-pupil) cost is less; therefore, if the programs are equally effective, the $80,000 alternative would be preferable. Similar examples in educational organizations might deal with those operations where student choice is a big factor (for example, food service operations, elective programs). Alternative food service options, for example, will attract different numbers of pupils and reflect different unit costs. The volume of demand for a particular food service option (the denominator of our unit cost figure) may, in turn, be particularly sensitive to price. Consequently, in certain circumstances unit costs are important in pricing as well as in program selection decisions.

Transfer Pricing

Goods and services are often exchanged between various departments and divisions of a company or an educational institution. In elementary-secondary education, for example, the maintenance department provides services to school buildings, the data processing department provides services to the accounting department, and so on. These services are supplied at some cost. But the question immediately arises, at what price should these transfers of services and goods be valued?

Ideally, *transfer prices* should guide each manager to choose inputs and outputs in coordination with other subunits so as to maximize the effectiveness of the organization as a whole.

Maximum effectiveness in this context is defined as the best conceivable decision, given top-management objectives. There are at least three criteria that should be considered simultaneously when establishing transfer prices: goal congruence, performance evaluation, and autonomy (Horngren 1972, pp. 714–750). In other words, the aim is to design a transfer-pricing scheme that will point subunit managers (for example, principals, department chairmen) toward top-management goals *and* provide incentive to reach these goals. While no simple pricing mechanism exists for achieving this, there is a general rule that may be applied in a particular situation: the transfer price should be (1) the incremental cost incurred in the transfer plus (2) the opportunity costs for the organization as a whole. *Incremental cost* refers to the cash costs that are directly associated with the production and transfer of the goods or services. (Of course, these cash costs do not necessarily have to be made at a particular instant, but the action of the production and transfer will result sooner or later in some cost.) *Opportunity costs* are defined here as the maximum contribution to organizational goals foregone by the organization as a whole if the goods are transferred internally. The distinction between outlay and opportunity costs is made here because the accounting records ordinarily record the outlay costs of the best of the rejected alternatives (Horngren 1972, p. 734).

One of the more widely used bases for setting transfer prices is *actual cost.* This means that sending units charge the full cost of their services to the receiving units in the organization. If this is done, the performance of the receiving units would bear the accumulated efficiencies or inefficiencies of other divisions not subject to their control. Transfer prices that ensure recovery of actual costs often fail to provide an incentive on the part of the sending unit to control their own costs. In higher education this issue bears most directly on the transfer prices affixed to various computing services. Computer rates vary significantly among universities, reflecting, at least in part, different attempts to encourage computer usage while controlling costs.

Viewed structurally, transfer pricing represents an attempt on the part of management to find some intermediate point between total centralization and total decentralization that will maximize the organization's objectives. Total centralization implies that purchasing functions take place at the top of an organization. Total decentralization in this context implies that units within an organization act as if they were independent of one another. Carried to the extreme, this would mean that each unit could act in its own self-interest, which could be dysfunctional to the organization as a whole. Transfer prices may be viewed as constraints on decentralization because they are designed to link subunits in an organization.

Management's ability to provide and interpret valid cost information for nonroutine decisions depends in large part on its ability (1) to assess costs that are valid and (2) to set prices and resulting levels of service in the subunits of the organization that best reflect the overall goals of that organization.

Conclusion

The fundamental principles and report formats that guide financial management practice in schools are generally similar across the three sectors. However, the principles are applied with different degrees of emphasis across the three sectors. Public school administrators are less concerned with balance sheets and accounting for fixed assets than are their counterparts in the private sectors. All administrators conduct analyses for what we have called nonroutine decision making. In the private sectors cost analysis is used to decide when to start and stop programs, to decide on prices to charge for programs, and to determine future, but indirectly related, expenditures (as for marketing campaigns). In the public schools similar cost analyses are used less for decisions then for claiming third-party payments.

References

American Accounting Association. *Report of the Committee on Courses in Financial Accounting*. Evanston, Ill.: The Association, 1971.

American Institute of Certified Public Accountants. "Basic Concepts and Accounting Principles Underlying Financial Statements of Business Enterprises." *Statement of the Accounting Principles Board No. 4.* New York: A.I.C.P.A., 1970.

Commission on Federal Relations. *Direct and Indirect Costs of Research at Colleges and Universities*. Washington, D.C.: American Council on Education, 1969.

Committee on Auditing Procedure. *Auditing Standards and Procedures*. New York: American Institute of Certified Public Accountants, 1963.

Horngren, Charles T. *Cost Accounting: A Managerial Emphasis*. Englewood Cliffs, N.J.: Prentice-Hall, 1972.

National Association of College and University Business Officers. "Indirect Costs: A Problem in Communication." *Studies in Management* 4: 1 (1974): 1–4.

Roberts, Charles T., and Lichtenberger, Allan R. *Financial Accounting: Classifications and Standard Terminology for Local and State School Systems*. Washington, D.C.: U.S. Government Printing Office, 1973. OE 73-11800.

Vatter, William J. *Managerial Accounting*. Englewood Cliffs, N.J.: Prentice-Hall, 1950

Woodman, William S. "Audit of a School District." *In Encyclopedia of Auditing Techniques*, edited by Jennie M. Palen, pp. 157–1286. Englewood Cliffs, N.J.: Prentice-Hall, 1974.

Supplementary Reading

American Council on Education. *College and University Business Administration*. Washington, D.C.: The Council, 1968. See especially pp. 141–274. Treats financial reports and routine financial decisions commonly found in institutions of higher learning.

Anthony, Robert N. *Planning and Control Systems: A Framework for Analysis*. Boston: Harvard Business School, 1965. A classic text describing the scope of management activities in organizations and distinguishing between strategic planning and operational control. Although written with the private, for-profit sector in mind, it is also relevant to educational organizations.

Anthony, Robert N., and Herzlinger, Regina E. *Management Control in Nonprofit Organizations*. Homewood, Ill.: Richard D. Irwin, Inc., 1975.

Dearden, John. "Interdivisional Pricing." *Harvard Business Review* 38:1 (1960): 117–125. Treats the fundamental issues involved in deciding upon, determining, and evaluating transfer pricing policies in organizations.

Hass, Jerome E. "Transfer Pricing in a Decentralized Firm." *Management Science: Application* 14:6 (1968): B-310–B-317. Presents a technical model for ascertaining optimum pricing decisions.

Hungate, Thad L. *Finance in Educational Management of Colleges and Universities*. New York: Teachers College, Columbia University, 1954. While somewhat dated in a few technical details, this book describes the policy role of financial managers in higher education organizations as well as providing insight into a variety of technical tasks.

Taylor, Philip J., and Thompson, Granville K. *Financial Management of Higher Education*. New York: Coopers and Lybrand, Certified Public Accountants, 1973. One of the most sophisticated yet readable volumes on the subject, it goes beyond descriptions of current practice in higher education financial management to assess weaknesses and trends in the field.

PART III

Human Resource Systems

The implications of property rights theory for understanding human behavior in school organizations are perhaps most explicit when we examine human resource systems in schools. Schooling is labor intensive, and the relationships among individuals in the school labor force define to a great extent formal schooling in our society. Systems of rights in schools affect how individuals are compensated, what claims an individual has to positions and benefits, and even how an individual can pursue justice for perceived violations of his or her rights (through grievance procedures). Chapter 10 examines the predominant patterns whereby systems of rights are determined. Chapter 11 examines the major systems of rights in schools, especially in public schools.

10

Employment Relations and Collective Bargaining

by Michael J. Murphy

Schools are labor-intensive enterprises. Most of the work in schools is done by people—teachers, administrators, secretaries, bus drivers, custodians, and others; comparatively few machines are used in the operation of schools. Wages and benefits amount to as much as 85 percent of a school's operating budget. The work of people—employees—necessarily receives great scrutiny in an analysis of a school's efficiency and productivity.

In this chapter we focus on some ways managers can think about employment relations in schools. Specifically addressed are ways that employment contracts develop from the exchanges of property rights between managers and employees. We also consider how rules that govern behavior in the school workplace are formulated and how these rules affect employment contracts. Because many work rules are now generated through collective bargaining, a significant portion of the chapter is given to the discussion of the structure and process of collective bargaining in school settings.

Property Rights and Employment Contracts

All persons who work in school organizations have control over certain resources and actions. Most individuals control the allocation of their time and effort: their labor. Some have control of fiscal resources, and others can control the deployment of material. Individuals can often exchange resources or the right to control resources and actions for other rights. For instance, an individual may decide to "exchange" a portion of his or her time or energy for a money wage. A manager may see fit to exchange money to gain control of sufficient labor to fulfill the mission of the organization. When a personnel manager hires a fourth-grade teacher, his or her right to control $14,000 is exchanged for limited rights to control that teacher's labor. Thus, hiring transactions represent an exchange of property rights. When individuals agree to an exchange of property rights that includes a labor transaction, they enter into an employment contract. This contract is a basic instrument of personnel relations.

In its simplest form, an employment contract is an agreement between a worker and a manager wherein the worker agrees to give up control of his labor for a fixed period and in return the manager transfers to the worker control over a certain amount of money—a wage. In this contract the worker also agrees to give up the right to do certain things. For instance, a bus driver gives up the right to stay in bed on cold mornings. A teacher gives up the right to become a policeman or a nurse or a truck driver for the contractual period. The manager, on the other hand, agrees to set aside money for the agreed wage and not use it to purchase a new Xerox machine.

Even though the parties may desire to make certain exchanges of property rights, rights transactions as employment contracts may be prohibited by a wide variety of social and legal restrictions. Managers and workers usually cannot exchange labor for any wage price; rather they are bound by an established or the going wage rate. A school manager probably cannot agree to pay a classroom teacher only $900 for a contract year even though a teacher can be found who will work for that rate. Because of collective agreements and governmental minimum-wage policies, unemployed teachers or other potential employees usually cannot bid for jobs by setting lower and more attractive wage prices for themselves. Employment contract terms are restricted in other ways. For example, a school manager may not hire ten-year-old children for grounds maintenance work because of child labor laws; state driving and licensing laws prevent the manager from hiring fifteen-year-old children to drive school buses; teacher certification regulations rule out hiring high school dropouts as mathematics teachers.

Constraints on employment contracts may come from a variety of sources including state and federal governments. For example, states require certification of teachers and administrators and in some cases require them to periodically take additional college courses to maintain certification.

The individuals who will be parties to the contracts may also act to restrict employment-contract terms through collective bargaining. A school district and teachers' unions may agree that teachers have the right to remain in a given school assignment if they so choose. As a consequence, a school manager does not have the right to transfer teachers without their consent.

A school or school district may stipulate conditions in policies adopted by its board of trustees. For example, board regulation may give secretaries the right to a one-hour uninterrupted lunch period and two, twenty-minute breaks during the day.

The definition and transaction of property rights are complicated by other factors. Rights are often unclear or disputed. Conflicts or disagreements over rights may result from ambiguity in the contract. A personnel officer may think that an employee has agreed to labor conditions that the employee is actually not prepared to accept. A manager may believe, for instance, that he is acquiring the rights to an employee's labor between the hours of 8:00 A.M. and 4:00 P.M. The employee, on the other hand, may believe that he is giving up control of his labor only between the hours of 8:00 A.M. and 12:00 P.M. and between 1:00 P.M. and 4:00 P.M. and that from 12:00 P.M. to 1:00 P.M. he maintains the rights to his own time and energy. Principals may insist that the employment contract obligates teachers to attend PTA meetings held at night. On the other hand, teachers may hold that they are obligated to the school and are under the direction of the principal only until 4:30 P.M.

Disputes over rights in the employment contract may also stem from confusion over how rights are conferred. Individuals in organizations acquire rights as a result of their position in the organization, by law or by governmental action, by delegation, or because of their expertise or professional standing. Conflicts can occur when an organization bestows a positional right on one of its officers while employees believe that their own profession bestows on themselves the same right. Among school personnel this confusion is often noted in the area of instructional or curriculum decisions. School principals may believe that they have the right to determine how reading will be taught in their building; or the superintendent and the board of education may conclude that they have the right to determine educational methods that will be employed in the school district. Yet teachers may contend that decisions about educational actions are decision rights belonging to them by virtue of their professional training. The director of buildings and grounds may order members of the maintenance crew to install a piece of playground equipment in a certain way. But the maintenance crew may refuse to do so, claiming that it would be improper and unsafe to place the equipment in that fashion. The maintenance men are implicitly claiming that by virtue of their knowledge they have the right to determine how a particular piece of equipment will be installed.

Sorting out the property rights in employment contracts is complicated and time consuming. For school systems to function smoothly, the rights of administrators, teachers, bus drivers, groundkeepers, maintenance persons, nurses, cafeteria workers, and others must be defined or definable. Employment contracts must be clarified and disputes over rights must be resolved.

The parties to the employment contract devote considerable effort to clarifying property rights, specifying terms for subsequent property right exchanges, and acquiring rights they prefer. Trustees in both public and private schools adopt detailed personnel policies to distribute rights among employees. In general, school managers spend considerable time partitioning rights among employees and seeking to acquire or defend rights they themselves prefer. In recent years collective bargaining has become a major mechanism by which employees seek rights they prefer.

Because ownership or control of rights is a fundamental yet complex issue in employment contracts, a number of agencies are involved in trying to specify those rights. Equal-employment opportunity commissions rule on individuals' property rights to jobs. The Occupational Health and Safety Administration interprets individuals' rights to protection from job hazards. Courts hear cases involving conflicts over rights in order to make certain decisions or take certain actions, such as whether a district may terminate a teacher for employing unconventional teaching methods or violating dress and grooming regulations. Arbitrators interpret contracts and partition rights that stem from the contracts.

Job Rights and Employment Relations

Labor has long been treated as the "property" of workers in industrial societies. Early in this century John R. Commons (1957) noted that the only property workingmen had left was their labor. Property exchanges are often contractually bound, that is, parties to the exchange specify and agree on the terms of the exchange in advance. In employment relationships, even where no formal or written contract exists, courts and arbitrators will recognize an implied contract in the acts of employing and accepting employment. Within the constraints of law and ethics (which may be many), individuals are free to enter into contracts for work as they see fit. No individual teacher, for instance, is compelled to accept work in a particular school district nor is a school district compelled to hire any given teacher.

Workers may acquire more from the employment contract than an opportunity to ply their trade and receive compensation for their labor. They can acquire rights to the job itself, and the literature on labor economics describes and discusses jobs as "property rights" that can be acquired by workers (see Gomberg 1965). As workers acquire property rights to a job, it becomes more difficult for the employer to deprive them of that job property either by unilaterally terminating the employment contract or by modifying the job by technological innovation. These issues have been central to the disputes between longshoremen and shipping companies over automation of containerized cargo and shiploading, between railway workers and railroad companies over the need for firemen in diesel locomotives, and between airline pilots and airlines over the third pilot in the cockpit. In all cases, workers have pressed the property claim to their jobs and have attempted to deny their employer the right to take their properties.

In education, the issue of a job as property presents itself in two ways. One is the current concern with job security. Teachers' unions are pressing for clauses and other contract restrictions that would prevent school districts from eliminating teaching jobs. In New York and other places, the teachers' unions have been active in the area of controlling paraprofessionals and teachers' aides so that some of the teaching job is not taken away from teachers.

Another way teachers have secured their jobs is through tenure or continuing-employment status, which is a legal recognition of teachers' property rights to their jobs. Except in cases of fiscal or program cutbacks, school managers may not deprive tenured teachers of their jobs without due process, which requires procedural fairness and substantive rationality. The employer must show cause for termination, and provisions must be made for holding a hearing on the charges. The hearings are analogous to the condemnation hearings that are required to deprive individuals of their real property when it is necessary to confiscate that property for public purposes.[1] The insistence on due process (that is, the methods that schools must use to protect rights before terminating employees) derives from acceptance of a teacher's property right to his or her job. Many school managers, however, think these protections are a serious constraint on their rights as managers to terminate problem employees.

Although the concept of property rights in a job is widely acknowledged, employment in itself does not establish a property right. The United States Supreme Court has held that for an employee to have a property interest in a job, and hence a due-process claim, there must exist a reasonable expectation of continued employment or a "legitimate claim of entitlement." This claim may arise from "statute, regulation, civil service rules, tenure systems, common law contracts, collective agreements or even obligations implied under state law" (Player 1981, p. 55). Even though private-sector employees, including those in private schools, may be entitled to a property interest in a job, constitutional guarantee of due process applies only to governmental actions that infringe on property interests. Job rights and due-process entitlements in private-sector employment stem primarily from collective agreements. Without an agreement or clause in the employment contract establishing job property rights, private-sector employers are generally not required to provide due-process procedures. Though some private schools have explicit or implicit tenure systems because of policy or agreement, many do not. Thus it may be easier for private school managers to terminate employees than it is for their public school counterparts.

---

1. The United States Constitution guarantees that no person may be deprived of life, liberty, or property without due process of law (Fourteenth Amendment). It has been held that teachers may have certain property or liberty interests in their jobs. See McCarthy and Cambron (1981, pp. 107–144).

Employment Relations System

An employment relations system is the subsystem of a school organization that determines how employer and employee will behave within the context of the work setting. It formalizes and directs employment contracts and defines rights and duties of the employing school system and of its managers, teachers, and other employees. The system specifies terms for compensation, hours of work, the nature of job tenure, the seniority system, and a whole host of other items that govern employment contracts and rights transactions in the employment relationship.

The mechanism used to define property rights between managers and employees and the terms of their exchange is a body of rules and regulations developed by the employment relations system. These rules are both substantive and procedural; that is, they specify what can or must be done as well as who may take certain actions relative to the creation of rules.

Dunlop has said "an industrial relation system at any one time in its development is regarded as comprised of certain actors, certain contexts, an ideology which binds the industrial relations system together, and a body of rules created to govern the actors at the work place and work community" (1958, p. 7).[2] The industrial relations system as envisioned by Dunlop contains three primary sets of actors: (1) a hierarchy of managers, that is, the board of education (or trustees acting in their administrative capacities), administrators, supervisors, and employment relations specialists; (2) a hierarchy of workers, that is, employees and their associations; and (3) specialized agencies concerned with employment relations, that is, employment relations boards, the national labor relations board, and other groups with an interest in the employment relations system.

These actors interact in a context with three principal components of the industrial relations system. One is the technological characteristics of the workplace and work community. Another is the marketplace or budgetary characteristics, and the third is the nature of power distribution in the larger community, which may be concerned in some way with the workplace.

The outcome of the industrial relations system is the *web of rules*. The industrial relations system is bound together by a set of beliefs or ideologies that helps to define roles and defines, as Dunlop says, "the ideas which each actor holds toward the place and function of the others in the system (1958, p. 7). The employment relations system is depicted in graphic form in exhibit 10.1. The outer ring represents the three contextual and the ideological forces that influence both the way actors behave in the system and many of the

---

2. The terms *industrial relations systems* and *employment relations systems* are used interchangeably in this chapter.

Exhibit 10.1
Employment Relations System

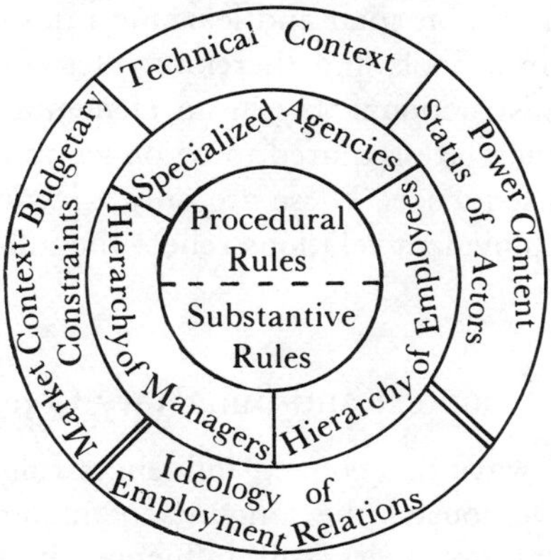

rules of the system. In the middle ring are the three sets of primary actors: managers, workers, and specialized agencies. The inner core consists of the "web of rules" that result from the forces and actions of the system.

Context of Employment Relations in Schools

Technical Context

The technical context of schooling influences rules and categories of rules. For instance, the way work is done in schools influences rules governing supervision of teachers and appraisal of their performance. Teachers usually do their work in isolated, walled-off locations we call classrooms, and many of these classrooms are in operation simultaneously. It is very difficult, therefore, for supervisors or administrators to observe the work as it takes place. Performance appraisals are usually based on indirect evidence of performance or on very limited observations of performance. Typically there are rules governing the collection and use of these data.

The way educational operations are organized has helped to formulate rules about the size of the work group. For instance, it is generally held that any given teacher can work successfully with a limited number of students at a given time (although classroom size may vary from place to place and is also influenced by budgetary constraints). If that number is thirty, then the size of the primary work group is fixed and we have a class-size rule. The number of pupils enrolled in a school determines the number of primary workgroups and therefore the number of teaching jobs.

The fact that the content of jobs in education requires considerable professional input also has a substantial influence on the kinds of rules in schools and colleges. Educators are highly trained and act according to professional tenets. These people require the right to determine appropriate instructional strategies and to make many other work decisions. Technical assumptions about attention span and learning rates of students determine the daily schedules in schools and therefore rules concerning the hours of work. Usually, the instructional day in an elementary school is about six hours long, and teachers are required to be on campus for six and a half to seven hours as a consequence. These are only a few examples of the many ways the rules of employment relations reflect the influence of the technical context.

Market Context and Budgetary Constraints

There are several ways this context influences rules and the behavior of actors in schools. Obviously, the amounts of money made available by legislatures and local taxpayers will influence, in conjunction with the technical considerations, rules for staff hiring, size of the work force, and employee compensation.

The client-demand system and the nature of the marketplace in which the school operates will determine some of the rules as well. Public school systems operate as a governmental monopoly and provide services to school-age children living within the systems' attendance areas free of direct charge. School attendance is mandatory throughout the United States, and if parents opt to have their children attend public schools (as opposed to private schools), they generally cannot choose the particular school. Public schools, therefore, are insulated to some degree from the client-demand market, and the structure of rules reflects this insulation. Elected boards of education are created to oversee schools and are given certain rule-making powers. Teachers are not allowed to bargain collectively with their employer in some states, are prohibited from striking in response to a collective bargaining impasse in most states, and frequently have rights to political action restricted.

Because its monies are appropriated from the public purse, taxpayers and their elected representatives may be able to directly influence the way funds are expended. For instance, if citizens are not satisfied that educational service is essential or efficiently provided, they may reject school budgets and requests for tax overrides and construction bonds. Citizens may also elect board members or governors who will allocate resources according to the preferences of the majority of citizens.

Rules governing the timing of the revision of rules are also influenced by the market context as well as by the technical context of education. Contracts for teachers are usually for an academic year. Negotiations usually take place in the spring and, if necessary, throughout the summer, with the intention of an agreement taking effect in the fall. When teachers are unable to reach an agreement with the employing school district over the terms and conditions of employment, a strike usually takes place in the fall, which is a time that affects the community as it anticipates returning its children to school.

Labor markets also have an influence on the various work rules. Wages are influenced by regional wage rates as well as by the supply of teachers and other employees.

Power Context and Status of the Actors

Two dimensions of this context should be noted, for they have significant influence on the web of rules. First, through its political and administrative structure, society gives certain responsibilities to certain officers. School boards in public school systems are created by legislatures to oversee education in a given region. These boards are usually made up of elected officials, are charged with certain rights and responsibilities, and are given status as an actor in the employment relations system by the larger political arenas. On the other hand, trustees of private schools are chartered under provisions governing incorporation and are imbued with rights and responsibilities under acts regulating business practice.

The type of school provides a status for the school in the legal sense. For instance, in the area of employment relations, private schools, whether they be preschools, elementary and secondary schools, or colleges, are subject to most federal employment regulations. Private colleges and private schools are subject to federal minimum-wage laws, federal health and safety regulations, and, perhaps most importantly, collective bargaining laws and regulations as set forth in the National Labor Relations Act and by the National Labor Relations Board. Though private schools may be subject to state education regulations, they are usually more constrained by federal and state rules governing commerce. Public schools, on the other hand, are not subject to the laws governing commerce and most other federal regulations concerning employment relations.

Ideology

Industrial relations systems exist because both managers and workers lack sufficient property rights to be able to satisfy their needs; one group must exchange some of their rights with those of the other group. Managers cannot accomplish the work of the organization without labor transactions with workers. Workers in an industrial society cannot maintain an existence without a wage, and at the very minimum the two groups must maintain a relationship wherein the manager who has access to money gives that money as a wage to workers who, in exchange, supply their labor. In the school setting, administrators generally do not teach students; they rely on teachers for this function. Hence, administrators have to be able to attract teachers in sufficient numbers and of sufficient quality to meet the instructional needs of the school. Administrators must be willing to pay a wage to guarantee this supply; that is, they must set forth or agree to sufficiently attractive compensation rules in order to accomplish the required labor transactions. These needs bind the system and actors together.

When we think of voluntary exchanges of property rights, we usually think of equivalent or symmetrical exhanges; labor for wage is such an exchange. The terms of the exchange are negotiated between the parties so that the exchange makes sense to both parties; that is, it satisfies their needs and is fair to both parties.

Economic Exchange

There are two kinds of exchanges that individuals can enter into. The first of these is an "economic" exchange that requires reciprocal terms that are specified and agreed to in advance.[3] An economic exchange is a marketplace exchange in which the parties agree to its rules in advance of the exchange. This results in a contract between the parties, which when executed brings about the exchange and leaves the parties with no particular obligation to one another after the exchange is completed. Examples of such an exchange are housing or automobile purchases. The buyer and seller agree to the terms of the purchase in advance, and, after money and property are exchanged, the parties usually do not deal with one another further.[4] Labor exchanges also generally follow this pattern. A teacher sells his or her skills and labor to a school district for a specified period of time for a special wage. Each party understands what it is agreeing to do before the exchange takes place, and at the end of the contract period neither has any continuing obligation to the other unless tenure rights are involved.

Social Exchanges

A second kind of exchange is frequently observed in social systems, however. This might be called a social exchange, where the exchange is temporarily asymmetrical and the precise terms of the exchange are unknown to the parties. This is the kind of exchange that occurs when one party does the other a favor, and although the party does not know when and how the favor will be returned, the party nonetheless is aware that at some point in the future the favor will be returned. In a social exchange one of the parties gives up a property right and expects that the other party will yield some property rights at some future time when needed or appropriate.

---

3. For a thorough discussion of types of exchange and their impact on work relations, see Fox (1974, esp. chap. 2).
4. This simple example of an economic exchange ignores problems introduced by the trust needs if repeat exchanges are anticipated.

Trust and Exchange

It has been noted that rules governing property exchange, work conduct, and trust are related. When managers and workers lack trust in one another, they tend to resort to economic-type exchanges because one party does not expect the other to reciprocate fairly if the exchange is temporarily asymmetrical. In labor transactions there is a tendency under these circumstances to develop increasingly explicit rules to govern the exchange, which specify in advance exactly how the labor will be delivered and under what circumstances. Managers are required to be explicit not only about wages but also about conditions of employment. This yields a labor agreement that specifies in detail the terms of the labor transaction and attempts to cover all contingencies.

There are dangers to relying on specified, symmetrical, or economic exchanges in the workplace. The extensive rules themselves may communicate distrust or concern for lack of common preferences between managers and employees. Parties respond to this lack of trust by requiring greater and greater elaboration of the terms of the exchange, which makes the agreement cumbersome and the exchange less flexible. It is simply difficult to anticipate in advance all the contingencies of an exchange.

Enforcement of Rules as Property to Exchange

The enforcement of rules themselves can be part of the exchange process. School managers may treat the application of rules as an item of exchange. Building principals have frequently suspended rules to allow teachers some personal or professional privilege without specifying an explicit trade-off. For instance, in cases where rules on absences require teachers to take the day off if they must be away from school for any period of time for personal business or illness, a principal might allow teachers to leave their post for an hour or two and arrange a coverage for that period of time instead of making the teachers take off an entire day. This rule bending or being a "good guy" is really an example of a social exchange wherein the principal does a favor for a teacher in the hope that the favor is returned in the future. This may be the expectation of loyalty or support at a future time.[5]

Legitimacy of Conflict

In the ideological context of the employment relationship, there are also views about the legitimate goals of the parties to the exchange and to the communality and hierarchy of preferences. Can employees have different

---

5. In her research on collective bargaining impacts at the school level, Johnson (1981) has observed that building administrators shaped the meaning of the contract to fit circumstances as they saw them.

goal sets from managers? Must preferences of managers be given priority? Do managers have the right to consider their preferences more important? Two ideologies can be identified: the unitary and the pluralist. The two reflect from different outlooks the legitimacy of organization goals and the needs of actors. Fox has said in regard to the unitary view that "the organizational logic of the enterprise is seen as pointing toward the unified authority of loyalty structure, with managerial prerogative being legitimated by all members of the organization. This accords with the emphasis that is placed on serving the common objectives and the common values which unite and bind together all participants" (see Fox 1975, p. 302). The unitary view holds that both school management and teachers share common goals, but only management has the right to develop work rules to accomplish those goals. Deviations from a consensus on rules and rule making are viewed as disloyalty and are considered destructive to the functioning of the school system. The unitary view prevailed in education at least until the 1960s and is still the dominant view of many school administrators.

The pluralist view not only recognizes goal divergence as a distinct possibility but allows that it may be positive to aggressively pursue divergent preferences. Labor unions not only are tolerated in the pluralist ideology but are considered valuable advocates of employees. Management should be forced to develop its position under strong pressure from labor organizations representing the views of the employees. Under the pluralist perspective, administration is seen as a much more political or consensus-building process. Furthermore, the pluralist view supports collective bargaining. In education there has been a shift in the last twenty years toward acceptance of the pluralistic view.

Actors

The actors in the school employment relations systems are members of three distinct groups: managers, employees, and specialized government agencies. Managers in the school employment relations systems include those individuals with the rights to make employment rules or who have supervisory responsibilities. Superintendents and assistant superintendents are part of the managerial set of actors because they have both supervisory responsibilities for employees and the right to help create and to enforce rules. School principals would be part of the managerial set of actors because they have supervisory responsibilities for teachers, custodians, and others. However, they have a much more limited role in the rule-making function. Headmasters in private schools often have both chief executive and direct supervisory responsibilities.

As employment relations systems develop and the body of rules that governs the system becomes more complex, a group of individuals charged with the responsibility for managing the body of rules develops. In larger school systems there are personnel and employment relations specialists who negotiate contracts, codify rules, handle grievances, and the like. The personnel and employment specialists are important actors in the employment relations system.

The employee actors in the school employment relations system are the teachers, custodians, bus drivers, secretaries, and all other nonmanagerial employees, their organizations, and the organizations' spokespersons. The employee organizations may be unions, associations, or local informal bodies that from time to time reflect the needs and interests of their constituents.

Numerous specialized government agencies are concerned with employment relations in education. Employment relations boards have been created in many states to oversee and regulate collective bargaining. State departments of education have a variety of rule-making functions including certification and employment regulations as well as certain responsibilities for instructional systems.

In addition to these primary actors, there are hosts of other organizations that generate regulations that become part of the larger set of rules in the employment relations system. Equal opportunity commissions influence recruitment and employment and promotions. The social security administration and state retirement boards regulate retirement systems, which consequently affects compensation packages and structures. State fire marshals create regulations about the number of individuals who may occupy a given space, and this may affect class size. The Federal Mediation and Conciliation Service and the American Arbitration Association may be involved by statutory requirement or by agreement of the parties in the resolution of impasses that occur during the negotiation of contracts.

The cast of special agency actors involved in the employment relations process varies considerably between public or private school systems. In public school systems, federal agency actors are more limited primarily because of Constitutional interpretations regarding powers reserved to states.

Private schools, however, are treated as private businesses with regard to employment relations provisions, and as a consequence, they are subject to the regulations of a host of federal agencies. The National Labor Relations Board (NLRB) has responsibility for defining bargaining units, certifying elections, and ruling on issues of bargaining behavior. The Occupational Health and Safety Agency (OHSA) has issued a substantial number of rules and regulations governing health and safety in the work environment. The Employee Retirement Insurance Security Act (ERISA) established a mechanism for insuring private-sector employee pension plans and has imposed a number of regulations on private schools.

Rules

Function of Rules

Rules are the outcome of the employment relations systems and result from the forces of the various contexts and the behavior of the actors. The term "web of rules" has been used to suggest the importance and pervasiveness of the large body of employment rules in most organizations. These rules are central to the function of schools for a number of reasons. They define parameters of property rights exchanges between managers and nonmanagerial employees. Compensation rules define the wages and benefits that will be paid to a given teacher who accepts employment. Civil rights and antidiscrimination rules regulate hiring and firing transactions and affect wage structures.

Rules direct the work behavior of employees. Labor agreements specify hours of work, certification and licensing rules set training and skills required, and health and safety rules determine the work environment.

Rules signal minimum expectations for employees' performance (see Anderson 1966). For instance, a rule requiring teachers to be at school fifteen minutes before classes begin and to remain on campus thirty minutes after instruction ceases sets the minimum workday.

Rules define managerial rights or options. Transfer and assignment rules may limit management's right to deploy the work force. Affirmative action rules and certification rules limit hiring options.

And rules are instrumental in creating a system of justice in the workplace (see Selznick 1969). They provide employees with security and predictability, and rules can provide a mechanism for holding management accountable for their actions.[6]

Types of Rules

Rules can be of two types: procedural and substantive. Procedural rules in the employment relations systems are rules about rules and rule making; they define the way employees and employers and special agencies interact to create and interpret rules. For instance, the state legislature may enact a collective bargaining law for public-sector employees. Such a law may create an employment relations board that in turn produces regulations specifying when employers must bargain with unions (duty to bargain) and the items

---

6. Most writers tend to focus on the managerial use of rules as mechanisms to control and regulate employee behavior, and they completely overlook the fact that employees aggressively push for rule adoption as a way of regulating managerial behavior. Grievance uses these rules as the basis for determining the legitimacy of managerial action.

that may be bargained for (scope of bargaining). These rules determine how managers and workers will interact in the formation of additional rules that govern employment relations and hence the exchange of property rights.

Substantive rules are the rules about how work should be done and rules that specify property exchange rates. Compensation rules are examples of these types of rules. They specify what the wage rate will be for each unit of labor and the conditions under which the wage rate will be varied. Rules governing sick leaves and class size are also examples of substantive rules.

Collective Bargaining

In many public school districts a large share of rules that govern work relationships are developed through collective bargaining, which is a bilateral process of making rules in which representative worker and management actors negotiate certain future conditions of employment. The particular conditions of employment negotiated are governed by the procedural rules set in the web of rules of the employment relations system that cover negotiations. These negotiation rules come from state and federal agencies who set forth rules concerning union recognition, duty to bargain, scope of bargaining, and impasse handling. They also include negotiation rules created by the parties through previous agreement or custom and practice.

In the employment relations system, collective bargaining represents only one source of rule making, although it is clearly becoming a more important source of rules governing the workplace as many rules are now bilaterally determined.[7] For many years employees of school systems have been regularly involved in the development of the rules that govern the workplace. For example, it is apparent from a review of the history of educational governance and decision making that rules governing compensation for teachers have always been in effect. In the early days of education in the United States, rules were largely determined by individual negotiations between itinerant teachers and school committees. As school districts grew larger and more complex, rules became more formalized and salary schedules were adopted. School committees and administrators were responsible for enactment of these rules. Later, compensation rules were adopted in school systems by the governing boards of education after considerable consultation with representatives of teachers; this was a widespread practice in the 1940s and 1950s. In the 1960s and 1970s compensation rules began to be made through collective bargaining.[8]

---

7. For documentation of the expansion of contract provisions, see McDonnell and Pascal (1979).
8. For a discussion of the development of collective bargaining and why teachers shifted their preference to collective bargaining, see Cresswell and Murphy (1980, esp. chap. 3).

The development of work rules and of the ideological sets that characterize the principal actors can be followed in the phases through which collective bargaining in American public education passes (see Mitchell et al. 1981). The first phase is to "meet and confer." In this stage, school managers and teachers' union representatives meet and discuss issues of mutual concern, but the school board retains unilateral power for making employment rules. The dominant ideology during this stage is that teachers and managers share common goals, and that through joint discussion, differences can be resolved and the general good of the school educational system is served; in a word, this phase reflects the unitary ideology.

In the 1960s the unitary ideologies on which the employment relations systems in education were based began to deteriorate in some districts. The idea of a common profession in which all professionals shared equally eroded, and managers became suspicious of teachers and teachers grew suspicious of managers. That period was marked by great labor-management unrest and a broad series of strikes, often related to recognition issues. Boards of education insisted they maintain the final authority to make important policy decisions governing the workplace. Teachers, convinced that conflicts with managers over some basic issues were unavoidable, appealed to the pluralist ideology and the tradition of industrial democracy, and stressed the legitimate right of employees to participate formally in the determination of rules and regulations that govern their work life.

The second phase of employment relations is called bargaining in good faith. This phase begins as pluralist views are accepted and some rules are determined through collective bargaining. Compensation rules are usually among the first to be determined bilaterally .

Early in this phase, school managers attempt to keep negotiated agreements as brief as possible. By so doing they preserve the old policy formation arrangement wherein the web of rules governing employment relations is determined mostly by the board of education and school managers. During this second phase, bargaining is characterized by teachers' unions proposing contract items and by management representatives reacting to those proposals and often denying their negotiability.

In the late 1970s managers in some districts took a more active role in bargaining. In this third phase, management proposes changes in the contract that reflect a growing toughness and effort to use the negotiation process to establish or acquire preferred rights. Some school managers, board members, and many members of the public believe that teachers and other school employees have gained an "undue" influence in the rule-making arena and that the balance of power has to be evened out. This belief has led to aggressive attacks by management representatives on various laws and rules protecting teachers and to the promotion of evaluation schemes and termination policies aimed at "weeding out the dead wood."

Available research suggests a developmental hierarchy of rule determination. The first level would be unilateral determination by management, followed by employee input through consultation. The third level would be acceptance of collective bargaining for limited rule making, and the fourth is the consideration of a large array of regulations and their negotiation by the employer and employees.[9]

Extent of Bargaining Activity

There are presently about 16,000 operating public school districts in the United States. Probably about 70 to 75 percent engage in collective bargaining.[10] A survey of a stratified sample of school districts in the United States in 1976 revealed that about 85 percent engaged in some form of collective interaction with teachers' organizations over salary and conditions of employment. These forms of collective interaction ranged from consultation to informal negotiations that produced mutually acceptable policies or policy recommendations to contract negotiations (called bilateral negotiations) that were expressly intended to produce a formal agreement. Seventy-six percent of those districts involved in collective interaction engaged in formal contract negotiations (Cresswell and Murphy 1980, chap. 2). This means that over 10,000 school districts in the United States engaged in formal contract negotiations in 1976. There is no reason to believe that fewer school districts currently participate in formal negotiations. Collective bargaining in public education has clearly become the dominant mode of interaction between teachers and school board representatives in public schools, and it has become a very significant force in the determination of the rules governing the workplace.

Teachers and, to a lesser degree, other employees in educational organizations are highly organized into unions (the term union is used in the generic sense to cover not only those organizations that formally designate themselves as unions but also associations of employees that attempt to influence wages, benefits, and conditions of employment). Research indicates that in the mid-1970s the percentage of teachers belonging to teachers' unions increased to about 93 percent of the teaching work force (see exhibit 10.2). In comparison to the general levels of union organization in the

---

9. Slichter, Healy, and Livernash (1960), in their now classic research on private-sector unions, have identified stages that roughly approximate stages identified by Mitchell et al. (1981).
10. For data on collective bargaining activity in the mid-1970s, see Cresswell and Murphy (1980, chap. 2). Most reliable published data come from this period and no good current data on collective bargaining activity are available.

Exhibit 10.2

Teacher Organization Membership as a Percentage of a Nonsupervisory Instructional Work Force

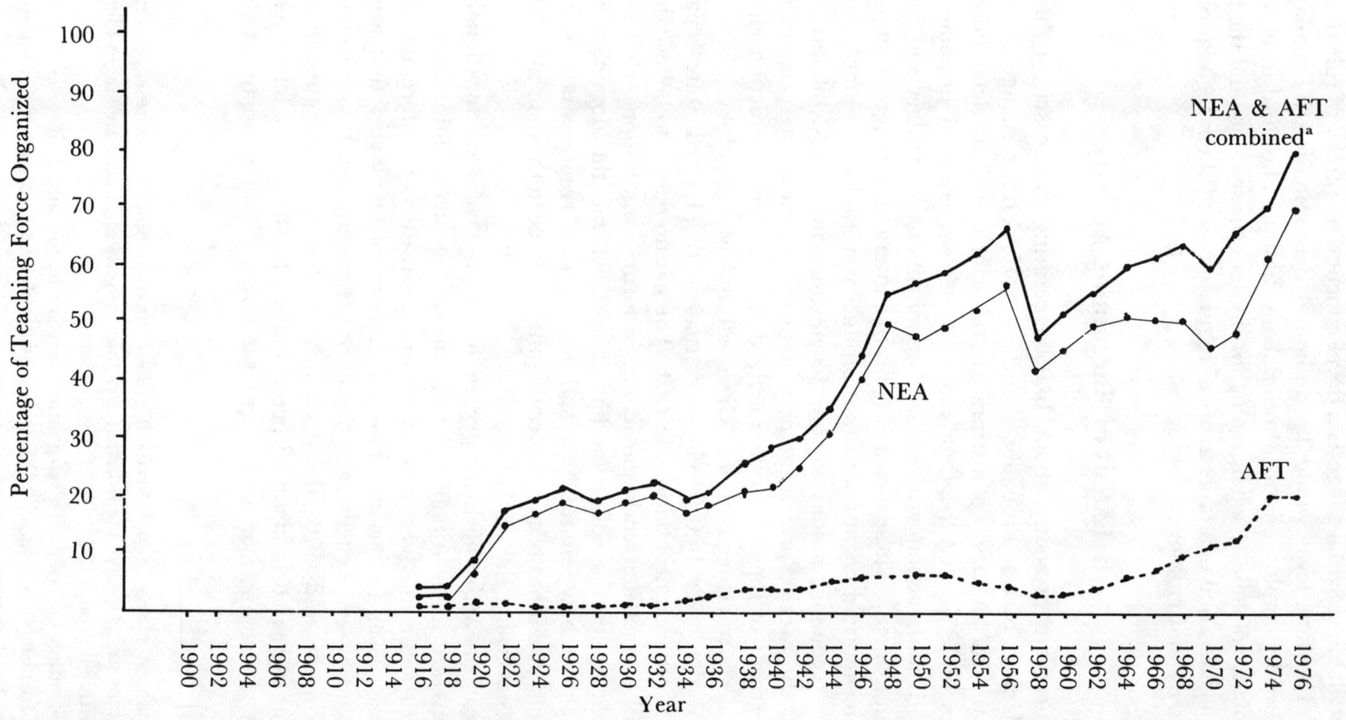

[a]Corrected for joint membership in 1974 and 1976

private sector and in most other areas of government employment, this figure suggests that public school teachers in the United States are one of the most completely organized groups of employees in the nation. No other union, with the possible exception of the fire fighters, approaches the density of membership represented in teachers' unions.[11] Extent of organization and density of membership contribute to pressure for collective bargaining. The widespread collective bargaining in public education can be attributed in part to this pattern of union membership.

As might be expected, collective bargaining activity is in some ways a function of school and district size. Virtually all large public school systems engage in collective bargaining with their teachers, and the very small districts make up the majority of nonnegotiating districts. It is likely that over 80 percent of the teachers working in public school systems in the United States are covered by collective bargaining agreements (Cresswell and Murphy 1980, chap.2).

The process of collective bargaining carries with it substantial costs in time and money both to school districts and to teachers' unions. In 1976 it was estimated that the cost of collective bargaining (that is, the value of the time spent by district employees and district administrators in negotiating and administering the contract plus the costs of employing outside consultants and negotiators and buying information and services from bargaining services) cost the average school district in the United States about fourteen dollars per pupil.[12] This figure did not include the costs of pursuing dispute resolution (that is, the fees paid to mediators, fact finders, and arbitrators), nor did it include the cost to teachers' unions of preparing and pursuing their bargaining agenda and representing their members in hearings. If all of these costs are totaled, it is clear that in 1976 the cost of conducting collective bargaining in school districts would certainly have exceeded twenty dollars per pupil.[13] Adjusting for inflation, costs of collective bargaining probably now range from thirty to thirty-five dollars per pupil.

Process of Collective Bargaining

The social process of bargaining is at once common and complex. It is a central feature in most political systems and in most free-market economic transactions. It is the primary means of making decisions where no universal fair or correct decision exists, where an individual or group of individuals

---

11. For a good comparison of the density of union organization, see Clegg (1976, p. 12).
12. Estimates of process costs of negotiation were derived from a survey of collective bargaining activity reported in Cresswell and Murphy (1980, chap. 2).
13. Kerchner (1979) has estimated process costs of bargaining in California and has arrived at very similar figures.

does not possess sufficient power to make unilateral decisions, and where substantive criteria for establishing price do not exist. The process of negotiation is not limited to institutions or large collective bodies. Families negotiate vacation plans, allocation of family resources, and the like. In most societies where commercial retailing is less developed, nearly all market transactions occur through a process of negotiation.

There are four distinct bargaining processes in employment relations systems (Walton and McKersie 1965). They are as follows:

1. *Distributive bargaining*. This is the bargaining process most generally associated with collective bargaining. It is the process by which fixed or zero-sum resources are distributed. If one party gains more control or rights to more of the resource, the other party loses the same amount. In this type of bargaining, interests are presumed opposite, that is, each party seeks to maximize its rights to the resource.
2. *Integrative Bargaining*. This is problem-solving behavior that occurs within the context of bargaining. It occurs when non-zero-sum items are at stake, and parties try to find solutions that increase benefits to both.
3. *Attitudinal Structuring*. The attitude of negotiators toward each other can be significant in bargaining outcomes. In this bargaining process, negotiators act to influence the way they are perceived by their counterpart party. Perceived states such as trustworthiness, friendliness, cooperativeness, and legitimacy are the focus of attitudinal structuring.
4. *Intraorganizational Bargaining*. Negotiators and bargaining teams represent sides; they speak for constituents who will gain or lose property rights through rules developed from bargaining. Negotiators are accountable to these constituents, but constituents must have realistic expectations and behave in ways that maximize negotiators' bargaining power. The negotiation of expectations, resolve (that is, firmness of stand), and threat strategies between negotiators and constituents is intraorganizational bargaining.

Collective bargaining is composed of a complex set of transactions involving power, information, and skill by which employers and employees reach agreement on terms for future interactions in the workplace. To clarify, the process can be simplified into a series of decisions. The flow chart in exhibit 10.3 presents the bargaining process as a series of related actions and decisions that are repeated to reflect the dynamics of bargaining.

Reason to Bargain (Start of Process)

Of course, a prerequisite to collective bargaining is a reason for the parties to bargain. Fundamental to collective bargaining is the fact that the school

Exhibit 10.3
Flow Chart of the Bargaining Process

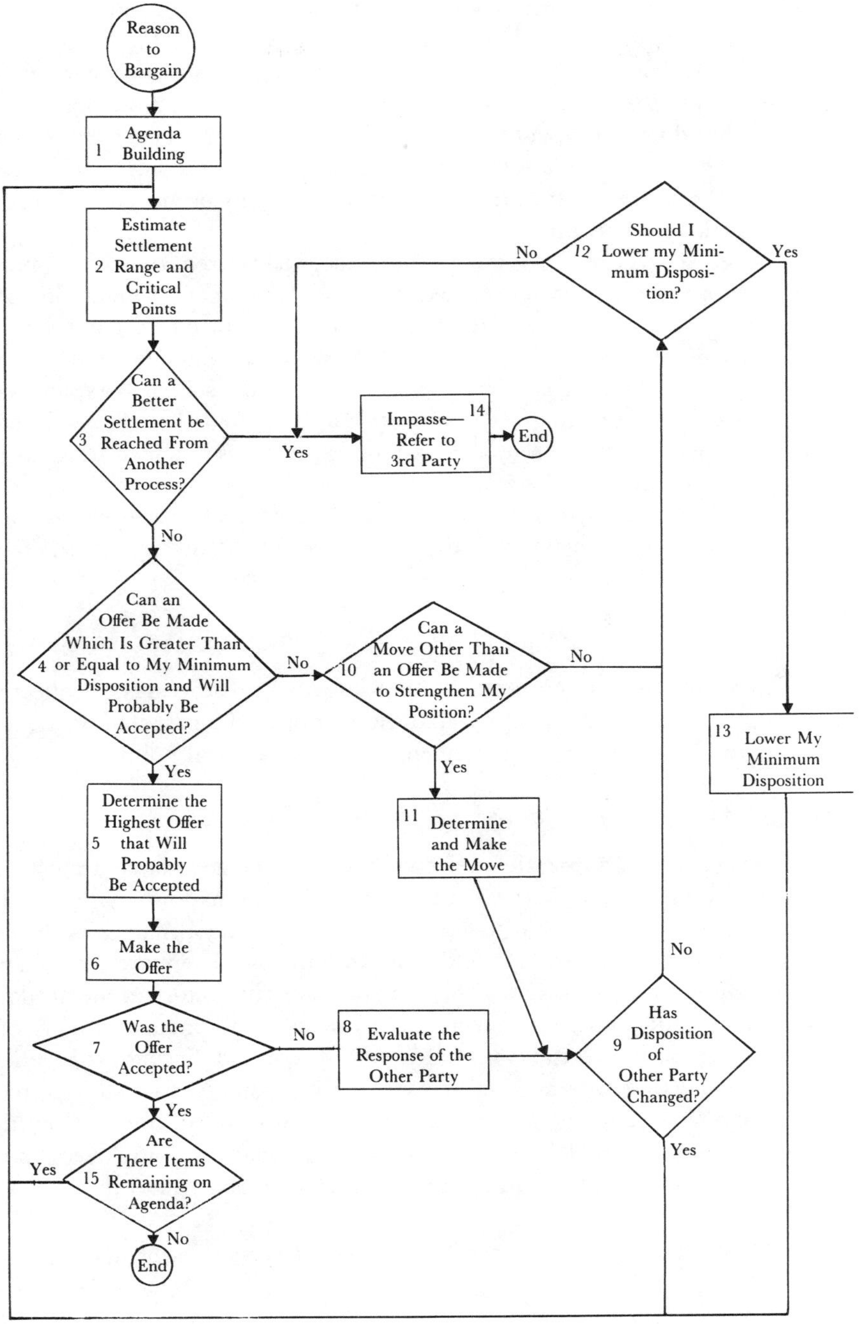

and its employees are voluntarily engaged in a continuing, interdependent employment relationship. Employees depend on the school as a source of employment and, therefore, wages. The school, on the other hand, depends on its employees to perform the basic work activities essential to the district's mission. Furthermore, the employees' organization is a dependent organization—it relies on the school for its members. The union derives its membership dues and operating revenues from the wages of the employees. Usually officers of the union are employees of the school district, and sometimes they are on leave from regular assignments or are given released time to perform their union duties.[14]

In order to carry out its mission, the school district requires the cooperation of its employees. It is in the interest of school managers to maintain good working relations with the employees. Disruptions in educational service caused by employees unhappy with the bargaining behavior of their employer may have serious political consequences for the school. Taxpayers or tuition payers may be angered and they may withhold their financial and political support from the school. Common expressions of anger are refusing to approve the budget in states where the voters must in fact approve an annual budget of the school system, or voting down tax levies or bonds. As a result of employment relations disruptions, superintendents and board members may lose their jobs.

Preparation for Bargaining

Some of the most important but often overlooked processes of collective bargaining are those relating to preparation for bargaining, including agenda building and estimating the settlement range and critical points.

Activity 1: Agenda Building

In collective bargaining the majority of items to be negotiated are usually set forth by the union. There are two primary reasons for this. First, the bargaining relationship is initiated by the union. School managers do not seek a bargaining relationship nor do they initiate one. There are other forms of interaction, such as consultation, that are quite satisfactory to the needs of management, and most managers would prefer not to engage in a serious bilateral negotiating relationship unless one is required. Second, it is generally presumed that rule making not specifically assigned to collective bargaining by legal mandate, agreement, or tradition is a right retained by the board of education and its management. Nonmanagerial employees must succeed in placing an item on the table and negotiating it into the contract

---

14. For a good discussion of the dependency of unions on employing organizations see Tannenbaum (1965).

for it to be a managerial constraint. Naturally managers generally work to avoid constraints that they feel do not serve their interests.

Management teams may also develop a list of proposed items to be negotiated. The development of this list should not be a random process—it should be the result of careful analyses of the bargaining process and general work rules and transactions. Supervisors and middle managers are a good source of information about problem areas in the work relationship and may help develop items. Records of problems with the collective bargaining agreement and its administration provide data on items and clauses that are ambiguous or troublesome in their application. Grievance records are another good source of information about problem items. Unclear contract clauses will often result in grievances. It is the responsibility of the management team to propose a bargaining agenda that will improve interaction between employer and employee and will benefit the work practice and the workplace.

In most bargaining relationships the parties will agree that all items to be negotiated must be submitted at an initial meeting of the two sides. This allows both sides to analyze the items being set forth and permits the bargaining process to go forward smoothly without the possibility of disruption should either side introduce new items as the bargaining unfolds.

Once all items are "on the table," each item must be classified as mandatory, permissive, or illegal.[15] Mandatory items are those that employers must negotiate as specified by law or rulings of the labor relations board. Illegal (or prohibited) items may not be included in a collective agreement and hence not negotiated. All remaining items are permissive. Permissive items may be negotiated if both parties agree to include them in the bargaining agenda. Given the wide variation in states' legislation, interpretations of courts, and public employee relations boards (PERBs) in various states, no general guidelines can be offered here. Bargainers must be familiar with their own state's legislation and public employee relations board's rulings regarding what items are negotiable. Public employee relations boards provide summaries of rulings and guidelines, and they often have telephone consultation or referral. State school board associations and administrator organizations also provide information about classifying the negotiability of items. The National Association of Independent Schools can be of help to private school managers.

The management team must decide which of those items that are permissive to include in the negotiation. There is a strong tendency on the part of many management teams to exclude as many items as possible from the negotiation, because they feel that this best preserves the authority of

---

15. For a discussion of classes of bargaining items and scope of bargaining, see Cresswell and Murphy (1980, pp. 166–173).

management. Although it is often said the best contract is a short contract, there may be reason to question the wisdom of this statement. To refuse to negotiate all permissive items set forth by the teachers' organization or other employee groups will be taken as a denial of the bargaining process itself and certainly will engender bad feelings toward the employer. Rather each item should be analyzed to determine whether its inclusion in the bargaining agenda may result in an agreement that will strengthen the operation of the school district. Many times change can be instituted through the collective bargaining process with the agreement of the employees that could not be successfully brought about by the unilateral action of management. If an item is in the contract, the employees have explicitly agreed to it and are obligated to honor it.

Activity 2: Estimate of Settlement Range and Critical Points

Initial estimates made during the preparation phase include establishing priorities, estimating resistance points, determining initial offers, and estimating the bargaining ranges. Though all of the estimates will be reviewed and perhaps revised as bargaining progresses, care in developing initial estimates and positions will often prevent costly mistakes later. Thorough preparation helps negotiators maintain a focus on goals and helps them guard against being distracted by the emotion of the moment.

Establishing Priorities. Once the agenda for bargaining is established, the next step in the preparation process is setting the priorities of the items to be bargained. This is important homework. It requires examining each of the items that will be negotiated, estimating its possible settlement values, and analyzing the position of the district and the union. It is important that this preparation be done before the bargaining session for two reasons: (1) it will provide essential guidance for bargaining activities to come, for example, future offers and concessions, and (2) it is easier to analyze each item carefully and dispassionately before bargaining begins.

Some items on the bargaining agenda are more important than others. These items will be conceded or traded off more reluctantly than other items with lower priority. Usually certain items in a bargaining session are very important to the parties, and the success of the bargaining session will be largely determined by whether or not the parties have accomplished their goals on these high-priority items. Items may be included in the agenda that the parties have little hope of attaining or really care little about; these are included in the agenda for tactical reasons only. Negotiators will agree to drop these items in return for concession on another, more important item. These low-priority items are usually called "throw-away" items.

Estimating Resistance Points. The value or point beyond which a negotiator will not or cannot accept a settlement is called a resistance point. A lesser settlement would be unacceptable perhaps because it would be too expensive or perhaps because it would cause excessive erosion of managerial authority. For whatever reason, it is the point at which a negotiator will stop conceding and accept the consequences of not concluding an agreement. It is critical that each bargaining team know its limits on each item before negotiations begin.

People buying houses or making major purchases are often advised to set an upper price limit and break off the negotiations if the item cannot be purchased at that price, that is, they should walk away from the deal. The same advice applies to negotiating wages and other items. It is essential for negotiators to establish the point at which they will walk away from the negotiations or "take a strike." Otherwise concessions may drift into ranges that will later be regretted.

The resistance point must be carefully estimated. It is not the point at which you want a settlement nor is it necessarily the point at which you expect the settlement to occur; rather it is the extreme point beyond which you feel you absolutely cannot go.

Establishment of the resistance point requires good knowledge of the resource limits and estimates of the real impacts of the items. For financial items it is important to be able to estimate the monetary consequences of various possible settlement points.

Resistance points for various items may be interdependent and may change in the light of new information or adjustment of other items. For instance, demands for salary increases and district-paid life insurance might both be on the bargaining agenda, and both items require expenditure of the same revenue. It might be possible to pay higher life insurance premiums if the wage settlement is lower. By the same token, it might be possible to offer a higher wage settlement if the life insurance item is withdrawn.

With the advent of small computers, many negotiators and members of their support team have found it appropriate to prepare computer programs to analyze the costs of possible wage settlements and other compensation items. The complexity of the wage schedule in education requires repetitious calculations to estimate the total amount of money that possible wage settlements would cost. Because the wage schedule in education is a matrix, with wage values within the matrix often indexed to the base salary and individual wages computed on the basis of allowed experience and training, it is possible to use the matrix-handling facilities of computers to quickly analyze almost any possible wage settlement. Such a computer package is a worthwhile investment for a school district involved in negotiating with teachers. (See chapter 16 for a discussion of specific computer applications.)

Initial Offer. The decision about the initial offer is something of a balancing act. There are those who advocate beginning negotiations with a relatively extreme offer; in other words, with an offer that is a long way from the expected settlement. The logic is that the extreme allows considerable room for concession. If concessions are matched, those starting with an extreme offer are likely to get a more favorable settlement. Research would seem to support this notion.[16] Yet an extreme initial offer can have undesirable effects on intraorganizational and attitudinal structuring. It can lead constituents to expect unrealistically low or high settlements. An extreme offer can offend the other party and suggest to them that you do not seriously intend to bargain.

Bargaining Range. The bargaining range is generally defined as the range in which settlement is possible. To some, this represents the overlap of the two resistance points. (Obviously if parties sense no overlap in the resistance points, no settlement is possible and both will break off the negotiations before reaching a point that is acceptable to the other party). Others prefer to define the settlement range as the range that represents estimates of where the settlement will probably occur. In any case, it is important at the outset to make some initial estimates of this range because serious bargaining takes place when the negotiations are within that range.[17]

Reed C. Richardson has observed that most bargaining failures are failures of preparation. In response to this problem he has developed a system for bargaining preparation that has been found helpful over the years. The method incorporates the establishment of priorities for each of the items. Instead of establishing and estimating or setting resistance points, however, Richardson advocates the establishment of a range of possible acceptable settlements. He calls the three points on the range pessimistic, realistic, and optimistic. The process developed by Richardson is helpful for two reasons: (1) it forces negotiators to concentrate on the development of a range in which they expect to be working in the final analysis, and (2) because these points have been specified in advance, at the conclusion of bargaining it is easy for the negotiators to go back and evaluate their bargaining in terms of the degree to which they achieved the objectives they had set and the accuracy with which they had been able to estimate the outcomes. A sample preparation worksheet is shown in exhibit 10.4

It is important to be able to estimate the likely outcomes of bargaining

---

16. The mathematician John Nash (1950) has shown that bargainers tend to resolve differences by splitting the difference. Other things being equal, a higher initial offer by one party will yield a higher (that is, more favorable) settlement.

17. For additional discussion of the bargaining range, see Cresswell and Murphy (1980, pp. 248–261).

Exhibit 10.4

Bargaining Preparation Worksheet

COLLECTIVE BARGAINING BY OBJECTIVES

(A GUIDE FOR DATA PREPARATION, STRATEGY, AND EVALUATION OF BARGAINING RESULTS)

BARGAINING* ITEMS	PRIORITIES**	RANGE OF BARGAINING OBJECTIVES			INITIAL*** BARGAINING POSITION	EVALUATION RESULTS		
		PESSIMISTIC	REALISTIC	OPTIMISTIC		P	R	O

* Classify Items in Two Groups: Financial and Nonfinancial.

** Relative Priority of Each Bargaining Item to All Bargaining Items.

*** Actual Visible Position Taken at Opening of Negotiation (Union Initial Proposal or Company Response or Counteroffer)

Source: Reed C. Richardson, *Collective Bargaining by Objectives: A Positive Approach* (Englewood Cliffs, N.J.: Prentice-Hall, Inc., 1977), p. 107.

also because the strategy for bargaining in part depends on what the negotiators believe the ultimate outcomes will be. If the bargaining range is extremely narrow or if the estimated settlement is very close to the resistance point, experienced bargainers know bargaining on that item will be tough. Bargainers may need to make larger concessions on other low-priority items or be willing to be satisfied with the attainment of fewer bargaining goals.

Estimating Opponents' Critical Points. It should be obvious by now that negotiators must not only set priorities and develop initial parameters for their own side but they must also make estimates of the parameters being established by their opponents in order to function within the bargaining context. These estimates are changed constantly on the basis of new information gained during the bargaining process. The estimates of opponents' priorities and parameters need not be mere guesses, for there is usually much available information that would allow sharp negotiators to estimate their opponents' parameters. Union negotiators, for example, can generally estimate fairly closely the revenue picture for a school district. From that amount they can calculate what settlements are likely in wages and benefits. In states where a large portion of the revenue for local school districts comes from the state, percentage changes in state appropriation will often determine or predict quite closely percentage changes in wage rates. District negotiators can examine wage settlements in adjacent or comparative districts, and cost of living changes also provide estimates of what union negotiators are likely to be expecting. If the cost of living change in the previous year was high, union negotiators are going to seek higher increases in wage rates. Likewise, if the cost of living change was low, union negotiators will probably settle for a lower rate of increase. Throughout the bargaining process these estimates will change according to information collected and reactions to and estimates of the concession rate.

Activities 3–13: Bargaining Behavior and Decisions

The reality of bargaining is that it is a continual dyad. In this relationship between the two parties, a series of offers and counteroffers are made until an agreement is reached or the parties see that no settlement is possible and agree to terminate their bargaining relationship. Because bargaining processes normally require multiple sessions (that is, they are iterative), strategic decisions are made throughout the bargaining process by the parties. These decisions are strongly influenced by the behavior of their opponents.

As bargaining unfolds, negotiators evaluate two factors constantly: strategic opportunities and concession rates. In general it is assumed that bargainers are "utility maximizers"; they seek to achieve terms they most prefer from any bargaining relationship. It is also assumed, particularly under conditions of distributive bargaining, that opponent bargainers are unable to simultaneously maximize their utilities. Each party is a "flexible constraint" on the other, and it is generally impossible for both sides to completely achieve their bargaining objectives. In order to achieve a settlement, a series of concessions or a reduction in demands must be made over the course of the bargaining.

Negotiators are sensitive to the strategic consequences of their behavior, and they know that certain actions may speed a settlement or improve the chances of their obtaining a favorable settlement. For example, if a negotiator can irrevocably commit to some action—that is, convincingly threaten some undesired act—he or she may gain a bargaining advantage.[18]

Cost of Agreeing and Disagreeing. Many theoretical explanations focus on calculations made by bargainers during the negotiations. In general these concern the degree to which offers currently "on the table" are satisfactory and the likelihood that offers made by the opponent will become more satisfactory or can be influenced to become more satisfactory.

This analysis frequently revolves around the cost of agreeing and the cost of disagreeing with a particular offer.[19] For example, if management has put forth an offer of a 6 percent increase in new monies available for wages for the coming year and the union has demanded an increase of 8 percent, each side must examine their opponent's proposal to see what costs would be associated with accepting the proposal or rejecting it. If the union has an 8 percent demand on the table, management must examine it to see whether it would be less costly to accept it or to reject it. An obvious cost of accepting the proposal would be the settlement cost of the 8 percent wage rate, that is, the money required to fund the wage bill under that settlement. Other less direct costs of agreeing to the union proposal would be consequences for other wage settlements with other groups of employees in the school system, the impact of that settlement on other wage negotiations in other school systems, and the possible adverse reaction of taxpayers and citizens. On the other side, the cost of disagreeing with the union's proposal may be the possibility of a strike, of losing good teachers, and of becoming unable to recruit effectively in the labor market. If the management team concurs that the costs of agreeing are higher than the costs of disagreeing with the proposal are, they will not accept the proposal at that point in bargaining time.

The union analysis is focused on management's offer of a 6 percent increase. Union bargainers will undertake a similar type of analysis to determine whether they should accept that 6 percent wage offer or hold out

---

18. The classic essay on the use of commitment in bargaining is Schelling (1956).
19. For a discussion of power and the cost of agreeing–cost of disagreeing formulation, see Cresswell and Murphy (1980, pp. 245–247, 348–350).

for the possibility of a settlement closer to their own request for 8 percent. Potential costs to the union of agreeing to a proposal of 6 percent might be the dissatisfaction and defection of members, that the settlement could be voted down by the membership, or that the union itself could be decertified in an election. The costs of disagreeing with the proposal might be having to carry out a costly strike, or after subsequent prolonged negotiation, not being able to raise the management's offer and thus being viewed as ineffective.

Cost calculations are complex. Union and management bargainers are faced with balancing a tremendous number of forces and interests in any given solution or settlement offer that is proposed. Further complicating the analysis is that the precise outcomes cannot be fully anticipated. One of the potential costs of management disagreeing with a union proposal is the possibility of a strike. This requires a certain amount of risk analysis, for it is never certain that the union will carry out a strike threat. Even if the union calls a strike, it may be unsuccessful.

Older theories of bargaining generally assumed that both management and labor bargainers have complete knowledge of both their own preferences and the preferences of their opponents.[20] We know from experience that this is an unrealistic condition; it is obviously in the interest of both parties to exaggerate or understate their preferences in certain instances. For example, in wage negotiations it is to management's advantage to convince the unions that they are absolutely unwilling and unable to exceed a low figure. Because bargainers' decisions are based in part on their expectations of the degree to which opponents will concede and what the settlement will be, each side has a vested interest in distorting parameters in an attempt to affect the responses or concessions of their opponent. Thus, assume that a management team is actually willing to agree to an 8 percent wage increase but has determined prior to the onset of bargaining that there is a good chance it can achieve a settlement of less than 8 percent by convincing the union that it will be unwilling to settle above 6 or 7 percent. Management's bargaining behavior, then, will be such that it transmits signals to convince the union it is willing only to settle for a smaller wage increase when it will actually agree to a larger one if necessary. The deliberate communication of false information about one's position is a tactic used to try to gain bargaining advantage.

Learning and Concession Rates. Several theorists have examined the degree to which bargaining behavior is affected by the signals sent by the opponents. John Cross (1969) has used the concept of "learning" in his analysis of bargaining behavior and has suggested that parties develop expectations of their opponents' concession rates and adjust their own concession rates

---

20. Both Zeuthen (1930) and Hicks (1963) stress information in their models, for example.

accordingly, so that the opponents usually meet at the expected settlement point. These expectations are modified during the course of the bargaining depending on whether the opponent concedes at the expected rate or at a more rapid or a slower rate. Three characteristics of the parties determine or affect concession rate: attitude towards risk, rate of time preference, and learning coefficients. Rate of time preference refers to the degree to which bargainers prefer a payoff today or a payoff at some future time. The preference for immediate settlement would occur, for instance, in the case of a school district that was seeking a favorable vote from the taxpayers on a bond to finance a capital expenditure. The district would not want to have a messy negotiation under way or the possibility of a teachers' strike during the time that they were campaigning for successful passage of the bonds. As a consequence, they would lower or compromise a demand in order to arrive at a settlement more rapidly.

Learning in the bargaining dyad occurs as the parties make judgments about the expectations of their opponents as indicated by their concession behavior and other behavior toward each other (the attitudinal structuring of Walton and McKersie). If, for example, an opponent concedes at a slower rate than was expected, the expected concession rate is revised downward. If the opponent concedes more rapidly than expected, the expected concession rate is adjusted upward. If both parties concede at a slower rate than expected, both parties might be expected to increase their rate of concession in order to achieve a settlement. If one party (management, for example) concedes more rapidly than expected, however, the other party (the teachers' union) will tend to reevaluate its own position and might be expected to renege on its concession offers. However, since revoking an offer is considered an unfair labor practice, the union might instead be expected to cease concession and stand on its current demand or offer. Their standing pat would affect management's assessment of the union's expected concession rate (that is, they would revise their expectation downward and, according to Cross's theory, management would concede even faster in order to reach a settlement). Thus, in this case, one team (management) would do all the conceding, which would suggest that initial rapid conceding may be a bargaining mistake.

The bargaining process can be compared to a video game in which you try to hit a target with a guided missile. There are two important constraints:

1. The guidance mechanism allows you to remain only level (not concede) or descend (concede). You cannot pull up or stop.
2. The target is invisible and its location can only be estimated from the trajectory of another missile (that is, the opponent's concessions).

In bargaining, falling short of the target (optimal settlement) is unacceptable because it results in no settlement and perhaps a strike; overshooting the target is also unacceptable because it represents a suboptimal (that is, too costly) settlement for you. Since your knowledge about your optimal settlement comes in part from your opponent's concession behavior (that is, his concession trajectory indicates his belief about his "best" or optimal settlement, which could be "higher"—for example, closer—or "lower"—for example, farther—than you thought).

The process is complex because each party is tracking the other's "concession missile" and adjusting their own concession path to reach what appears to be the best possible settlement (which is estimated by but unknown to either party).

Impasse and Impasse Resolution

When parties with opposite interests seek agreement through the negotiation process, it is inevitable that at times they will be unable to come to a satisfactory settlement. The lack of resolution may stem from a number of problems that can occur during bargaining. One party might have problems with the "learning" process, and parties can misperceive their opponent's positions or develop unrealistic concession rates, leading to insufficient concessions. Impasse can occur when one party becomes emotional during the bargaining process and feels that it "has something to prove." Impasse can occur when bargainers are unable to convince their constituents of the reality of the situation and those constituents insist on unachievable terms.[21] Impasse can also occur in the bargaining dyad for strategic reasons. In some cases the union might periodically create an impasse situation just to maintain bargaining credibility so that their threats will be taken seriously in future bargaining situations. Impasses can occur because the parties improperly calculate or give credit to the costs of agreeing or disagreeing. It may be that they believe their opponent will not carry out a threat and call a bluff (see Cresswell and Murphy 1980, chap. 9). And even when negotiators reach an agreement, there is no guarantee that the agreement will be endorsed or accepted by their constituents. In the United States, for example, somewhere between 9 and 12 percent of all recommended settlements are rejected by union members in ratification votes (Davey 1982, p. 127).

The Strike. One outcome of a bargaining impasse is a job action. The extreme case is the strike or withdrawal of services by union members or a corresponding lockout by management.

The purpose of the strike is to increase the cost of disagreement. In the private sector its purpose is to impose economic losses on the employer such that it is in the employer's interest to reach an accord with the union rather than sustain the loss of revenue and potential loss of market that will occur in

21. For a good discussion of these problems, see Davey (1982, pp. 312–329).

a competitive arena when the company is not producing goods and services. The strike idles capital equipment and, after inventories are depleted, creates a situation where the employer is unable to meet fixed costs because income from sales and service has been cut off.

A strike not only imposes costs on an employer but also imposes costs on employees. In most circumstances the cost of a strike to employees is in lost earnings, though the economic impacts of the strike on employees may be modified by strike funds and other union benefits.[22]

The ways public schools are financed and are required to operate minimize the direct economic costs of a strike to employer and employee alike. In most states, monies come to public schools as tax revenues or state government appropriations. Property taxes are collected annually and distributed to schools in annual, semiannual, or quarterly installments. Tax collections and distributions are not in any way dependent on the operating calendar of the school but instead depend on the established property tax rate and on the value of property that can be taxed. In the case of state appropriations, many states appropriate money to school districts on the basis of enrollment; thus, the district will receive a set amount of money for the education of each student enrolled in the school district whether or not the school is open or the student is in attendance. As a consequence of funding arrangements, school districts may continue to receive income during the time teachers or other workers are on strike even if the strike has forced closure of the school.

Most states require that school be in operation for a minimum number of days, usually from 180 to 185. School calendars are usually established such that the school year consists of close to the minimum number of days. If employees of a school system strike and schools are closed, it is likely, then, that the school district will have to make up days lost to reach the minimum number of required days. Thus, even though school may close for two or three weeks in the fall due to a strike, the teachers will end up teaching the same number of days and, in most cases, will suffer no real loss of income. Under these circumstances, the economic cost of strikes is low and there is no particular economic incentive for either party to resolve their differences.

The situation is different in private schools because they collect tuitions directly from patrons. In the event the school is closed, two things may happen: (1) the patrons will not pay for a service they did not receive, and (2) they may choose to purchase their education service from another supplier. Parents in a private school that is struck may choose to enroll their children

---

22. Teachers' unions do not usually maintain a strike fund to offset wage losses during a strike. The practice of making up teaching days lost during strikes means that, although teachers may not receive wages during strikes, they will ultimately realize full wage payments.

in public school or in another private school. Thus, a strike in a private school can have significant economic consequences.

The absence of an economic incentive to settle a strike in the public sector does not mean that strikes are totally unimportant or ineffective, however. Strikes by public school employees that cause the system to cease functioning impose costs on patrons and taxpayers, and they modify the political climate in which the school system operates. Schools perform important custodial functions, and when a public school system is struck, most students in the area are deprived of the custodial care that the school has provided. With over 50 percent of married women now in the work force, many families depend on the school to provide child care for a portion of the day. When the school is struck and closed, these families must make alternative child-care arrangements. This added child care must be paid for, and the economic burden shifts directly to the family. The costs and inconveniences of school strikes to parents put a great deal of political pressure on school boards to resolve labor impasses and get the schools open again.

Political pressure is also generated by parents who are concerned that their children will lose out on educational benefits as the result of the schools being closed. For example, if the schools are closed for an extended time in the fall, members of the senior class in high school may find themselves at a disadvantage in collegiate examinations and placements. Problems resulting from child-care costs and loss of educational benefits apply to private school strike closures as well.

Strikes and Public Policy. In most states strikes by public school employees are prohibited, although in some states strikes are allowed under certain limited conditions. There are several arguments set forth to justify strike prohibitions in public employment. First, it is pointed out that many government services are instrumental to public health, safety, and welfare. Interruptions to such vital services cannot be tolerated.

Second, it is argued that most public services are monopoly services; that is, no other service providers are available. In the event of service interruption, no satisfactory alternative source is generally available. The monopoly condition also means that no economic market exists to restrain prices and wages.

Third, some people contend that public employees' organizations operate in the governmental sector as any other interest group does. This enables them to interrupt vital services by striking, which inappropriately increases their political power. (See Wellington and Winter (1969) for a discussion of these perspectives.) The argument is that by means of the strike (and subsequent shifting of costs to the public) teachers can gain greater political power. School boards and managers will be reluctant (or unable) to oppose unions and their demands. In a sense, Wellington and Winter argue that public-sector unions can gain their objectives by holding the public hostage.

Private schools fall under the jurisdiction of the federal government, not the state government. Strike activities therefore are regulated by provisions of the National Labor Relations Act and other federal statutes governing employment relations. Private school employees may strike under these provisions, and they are in a much stronger position than are public school employees to bring their employer back to the table by the use of the strike mechanism.

Strike Activity in the United States. Over the last twenty years the number of strikes by public school teachers has grown and now appears to be stabilizing at around two hundred per year. Though strike activity among private school teachers is generally assumed to be lower, good figures are not available.

Impasse Resolution Alternatives

Because strikes by public employees, including teachers and other employees of boards of education, are banned in almost every state, there has been considerable attention given to alternative ways to resolve impasses. Most states that regulate collective bargaining for public employees have established various third-party mechanisms for resolving impasses. The three main third-party resolution procedures are mediation, fact finding, and arbitration.

Mediation. Mediation is a process during which a neutral third party attempts to help a union and management resolve their differences. (See Cresswell and Murphy 1980, pp. 365–366, for a more thorough discussion.) Mediators have no powers to force a settlement or even to recommend or specify terms for settlement. Mediators characteristically work to discover the reasons for the impasse, try to identify common goals, and help the parties work toward those common goals. Mediators may also help parties identify new solutions or settlement options.

Fact Finding. Many states provide for fact finding if mediation is unsuccessful or does not lead to a resolution of the contract impasse. (See Cresswell and Murphy 1980, pp. 366–367, for a more thorough discussion.) Fact finding may be done by an individual third party or by a fact-finding board. The function of a fact finder or fact-finding board is to establish the facts of the case and make those facts public. The intended effect of fact finding is that the report by a neutral party of the facts in the case will mobilize political actions that will force the opposing parties to accept a rational solution. The literature on public-sector bargaining is very ambivalent on the utility of fact finding.

Arbitration. If meditation is unsuccessful and the parties remain at impasse, some states provide for interest arbitration. (See Cresswell and Murphy 1980, pp. 367–375, for a more thorough discussion.) Some schools have contract provisions that require arbitration in the event that contract negotiations break down. In arbitration, an arbitrator or a panel of arbitrators hears the unresolved contract matters and orders a solution on arbitrator-specified terms. In a sense, an arbitrator is a judge who hears a case to determine the merits of the relative positions and then issues an award or ruling that determines how the parties will resolve their conflict. Thus, the arbitrator establishes the terms of the labor agreement when parties have been unable to achieve an agreement on their own.

There is considerable controversy about the use of arbitration in settling the future terms disputes. Some argue that it detracts from the authority of school boards and puts final decisions in the hands of someone not accountable to the public. There is considerable merit in this argument because arbitrators are not elected officials nor are they directly responsible to elected officials for their actions. Thus, an arbitrator might specify terms that would be totally unacceptable to the governing body of a school district and destructive per se to the school district.

A further problem with arbitration is that if parties expect that they will end up in impasse, they will make less serious efforts to settle their disputes and will instead concentrate on achieving the best possible position for entering arbitration. The record of arbitration suggests that, other things being equal, arbitrators will tend to split the difference. Thus, it is in the interest of the parties to be far apart rather than close together on terms of an agreement when they go to an arbitration hearing.

Although several proposals have been put forth to modify some of the problems inherent in arbitration, they have not been totally successful. In some states arbitration is "advisory" in some circumstances. This means that arbitrators are called in to hear the case and they then issue a report specifying terms for the settlement, but the parties are free to accept or reject those terms, that is, they are not bound by the award of the arbitrator. In this instance, the arbitrator's award has only a political impact and will add to the cost of agreeing and disagreeing in much the same way that other tactics and strategies do. If the arbitrator issues an award that is acceptable to the school board management team but is rejected by the teachers' union, there will be increased pressure on the teachers to accept those terms. If the terms are acceptable to the teachers, then there will be pressure on the board to accept those terms.

Arbitrators by and large do not like advisory arbitration and many professional arbitrators will not serve on advisory arbitrations. They believe that in most cases it is not effective in resolving disputes but simply prolongs the bargaining process. It undercuts the adjudicative nature of arbitration.

Another proposal for solving some of the defects of arbitration has been the so-called "last-best offer" proposal, which requires that arbitrators select for their award the final position of one of the parties. Presumably this causes the parties to enter the negotiations more seriously and with the thought of coming to the arbitration hearing not as far apart as possible but in a position of presenting an offer that is likely to gain the support of the arbitrator because it is the fairest and best offer (see Wheeler 1977).

Summary

Managers and employees each control certain property rights, and because the property rights each controls are initially insufficient to satisfy their needs, exchanges of property rights must occur. The employment relations system is that part of a school or school system that regulates and directs exchanges of property rights between managers and other school employees.

The employment relations system consists of contextual influences, actors, an ideology, and a set of rules. There are three contexts: technical, market or budgetary, and power. These three contexts constrain the behavior of the three sets of actors: managers and their representatives, employees and their representatives, and specialized agencies. An ideology determines how actors view the system and behave toward other actors. The outcome of the employment relations system is a body or "web" of rules that govern work relationships in schools.

Teachers' unions have been instrumental in forcing much determination of employment rules into the bilateral decision arena we call collective bargaining, and by all indications collective bargaining is becoming an increasingly important vehicle for rule making. Bargaining is a complex, dynamic process through which parties (or actors) try to establish rules that allow them to maximize their preferences. In cases where simultaneous maximization cannot take place (that is, in cases of conflict), actors use various strategic behaviors to try to accomplish their preferred ends. Successful bargaining—that is, achievement of rule objectives and maintenance of the employment relationship—requires considerable skill. Bargainers must be able to accurately estimate critical bargaining parameters (for example, resistance points and concession rates) and costs of agreeing and disagreeing with various offers and counteroffers. A major contributor to bargaining success is careful preparation before negotiations begin.

References

Anderson, James G. "Bureaucratic Rules: Bearers of Organizational Authority." *Educational Administration Quarterly* 2:1 (Winter 1966): 7–34.

Clegg, Hugh. *Trade Unionism under College Bargaining*. London: Basil Blackwell, 1976.

Commons, John R. *Legal Foundations of Capitalism*. Madison: University of Wisconsin Press, 1957.

Cresswell, Anthony M., and Murphy, Michael J. *Teachers, Unions, and Collective Bargaining in Public Education*. Berkeley: McCutchan Publishing, 1980.

Cross, John G. *The Economics of Bargaining*. New York: Basic Books, 1969.

Davey, Harold W. *Contemporary College Bargaining*. 4th ed. Englewood Cliffs, N.J.: Prentice-Hall, 1982.

Dunlop, John T. *Industrial Relations Systems*. New York: McGraw-Hill, 1958.

Fox, Alan. "Industrial Relations: A Social Critique of Pluralist Ideology." In *Industrial Relations and the Wider Society: Aspects of Interaction*, edited by Brian Barrett, Ed Rhodes, and John Beishon, pp. 302–324. London: Collier MacMillan, 1975.

Gomberg, William. "The Work Rule Problem and Property Rights in the Job." In *Labor: Readings on Major Issues*, edited by Richard A. Lester. New York: Random House, 1965.

Hicks, J. R. *The Theory of Wages*. 2d ed. New York: St. Martin's Press, 1963.

Johnson, Susan Moore. "Collective Bargaining at the School Site: A Varied Picture." Paper presented at the Conference on Creating Conditions for Effective Teaching, July 17 and 18, 1981, at the University of Oregon.

Kerchner, Charles T. "The Process Costs of Collective Bargaining in California." *Journal of Collective Negotiations in the Public Sector* 8:1 (1979): 39–51.

McCarthy, Martha M., and Cambron, Nelda H. *Public School Law: Teachers' and Students' Rights*. Boston: Allyn and Bacon, 1981.

McDonnell, Lorraine, and Pascal, Anthony. *Organized Teachers in American Schools*. Santa Monica, Calif.: Rand Corporation, 1979.

Mitchell, Douglas E., et al. "The Impact of Collective Bargaining on School Management and Policy." *American Journal of Education* (February 1981).

Nash, John F. "The Bargaining Problem." *Econometrica* 18 (1950): 155–162.

Player, Mack A. *Federal Law of Employment Discrimination in a Nutshell*. 2d ed. St. Paul, Minn.: West Publishing Co., 1981.

Schelling, Thomas C. "An Essay on Bargaining." *American Economic Review* (June 1956): 281–306.

Selznick, Philip. *Law, Society and Industrial Justice*. New York: Russell Sage Foundation, 1969.

Slichter, Summer H.; Healy, James J.; and Livernash, E. Robert. *The Impact of Collective Bargaining on Management*. Washington, D.C.: The Brookings Institution, 1960.

Tannenbaum, Arnold S. "Unions." In *Handbook of Organizations*, edited by James March. Chicago: Rand McNally Co., 1965.

Walton, Richard E., and McKersie, Robert B. *A Behavioral Theory of Labor Negotiations*. New York: McGraw-Hill, 1965.

Wellington, Harry H., and Winter, Ralph K., Jr. "The Limits of Collective Bargaining in Public Employment." *The Yale Law Journal* 78: 7 (June 1969): 1107–11027.

Wheeler, Hoyt N. "Closed-offer: Alternative to Final-offer Selection." *Industrial Relations* 16: 3 (October 1977): 298–305.

Zeuthen, F. *Problems of Monopoly and Economic Warfare*. London: Routledge & Kegan Paul, Ltd., 1930.

11

Personnel Policies and Practices

by Michael J. Murphy

•

Overview

Management of human resources (personnel) is grounded in legal contracts that are voluntarily agreed on by the parties involved. These agreements affect present and future human resource requirements, the kind and amount of recruiting required to fill vacancies, and the criteria used to select employees. Contracts further define how the individual will be evaluated and the relationship (if any) between performance, evaluation, and compensation. When an individual perceives that his or her contractual rights have been violated, several courses of action are open. The process of recourse itself—the grievance procedure—is often a job right guaranteed by the contract.

• • •

Introduction

In the United States, public and private elementary and secondary schools employ about three million persons in instructional capacities. There are perhaps another half million administrators and professional support personnel and a million classified personnel. Thus, the total work force in schools is close to four and a half million people doing different specialized jobs (National Center for Education Statistics 1982, p. 46). The success of the enterprise depends on these people understanding their jobs and doing them well, provided, of course, that rights in the organization have been partitioned and incentives established so that the preferences of top managers and sponsors are achieved when each person does his or her job well.

In any given school year the turnover for most professional positions will be perhaps 10 to 20 percent. Turnover is generally assumed to be somewhat higher for classified personnel. In any year there may be between 300,000 and 800,000 job vacancies to be filled in public and private education. If collegiate job figures are added, it is conceivable that schools in the United States could be recruiting, selecting, and placing as many as one million people yearly. The business of deciding what kinds of jobs there will be, the organizing of recruiting and selecting personnel, the assessing of personnel effectiveness, and the developing of compensation plans are all the business of personnel management.

Personnel management is a set of functions designed to influence the performance of employees in a given job environment. The purpose of these functions is to secure the most capable work force possible for a given school unit and to sustain and improve the capacity of that work force once it is employed.

This is a difficult mission. Personnel managers must operate within a host of technological, legal, labor market, and fiscal constraints. For example, there is a growing shortage of teachers trained in science and mathematics (see Guthrie and Zusman 1982). Public and private schools are competing for mathematics and science talent not only among themselves but with industry, which has increasing technical demands and needs for those with mathematical and scientific training. In this competition for talent, public school personnel managers are constrained by state certification requirements for teachers and single-salary schedules that do not allow for the realities of the labor market. Private school managers, while generally immune from certification restrictions, may not have the financial means to make wage offers attractive to mathematics and science graduates.

Even though a personnel manager is successful in recruiting and hiring able staff, the school may encounter problems in retaining them. This presents additional challenges to the personnel manager. For example, recent studies indicate that attrition of public school teachers is highest among the most able teachers and lowest among the least able teachers (see Schlecty and Vance 1981). This research suggests that over time schools retain less able teachers and lose the services of more able teachers, ending up with the least able of those hired.

In many parts of the country there has been a steady decline in school enrollments. Personnel managers, particularly in large public school systems, have had to design staff-reduction approaches under great union pressure to acknowledge service (seniority) before ability. In other regions, particularly the South and West, some schools have experienced very rapid enrollment growth, and personnel managers have barely been able to recruit sufficient staff to cover classroom needs. In some cases they have taken "any warm body with minimum qualifications" to meet current needs.

In addition to changes in school populations, there have been shifts in the demographics of teacher supply. Beside the already noted shortages in mathematics and science, the general supply of teachers is down substantially. Recent surveys indicate the number of graduates from teacher training programs is down by 40 percent nationally.[1] This means that personnel managers have a much smaller pool from which to recruit candidates and must work harder to ensure an adequate supply of qualified applicants.

This chapter focuses on the work of the personnel manager in schools. It begins with a discussion of the rules within which personnel managers must act. Sources of rules that affect personnel management are reviewed, distinctions between public (or governmental) law and private (or organizational) law are drawn, and the importance of private law is discussed. The chapter then focuses on seven functions of personnel management: human resource planning, recruiting, selecting, evaluating, administering compensation, and administering contracts.

School Organizations and the Rule of Law

The process for rule making and the nature of the body of rules that govern workplaces and work communities is described in the preceding chapter, "Employment Relations and Collective Bargaining." This body of rules (or laws) performs an important function in school organizations. It helps change an organization from one dominated by individuals to a system of government where a rule of law predominates. A rule of law has three distinguishing characteristics: (1) all individuals, including officials, are subject to the rules; (2) the potential for arbitrariness is greatly reduced; and (3) a system of secondary rules—that is, "rules of authoritative determination"—is introduced (Selznick 1969, p. 5).

---

1. In 1973, 194,210 bachelor degrees were awarded in education. In 1980 the number had fallen to 118,102 (National Center for Education Statistics 1982, p. 96). Some of the reduction in teacher supply can probably be explained by career choices made by students anticipating a bleak job market for teachers due to declining enrollments (that is, little demand). However, in Utah, a state with enrollment growth and strong teacher demand, the number of teachers certified by the State Office of Education in 1983 was down 35 percent from 1974 certifications (figures supplied by Utah State Office of Education).

Students of complex organizations have argued that there is an evolutionary trend toward the introduction of legal systems into organizations. In his book *Law, Society, and Industrial Justice*, Selznick argues that organizations have a strong internal urge to develop a legal system or a rule of private law, a system in which all officials, including top management, accept a framework of established rule. In this sense, bureaucratic organization is a constitutional form (Selznick 1969, p. 82).

Personnel policies are an integral part of bureaucratization. Not only does the bureaucratic structure of organizations lead to the development of law but it also promotes the development of formal personnel operations, such as the personnel department and personnel managers. Private law must not only consist of rules that all members of the organization including the officialdom subscribe to, but it must also contain principles and mechanisms for criticism as well as specialized mechanisms for enforcement. To operate under a system or rule of law, the organization's management must do more than create a personnel policy or regulation. There must be mechanisms for testing the legitimacy of that law, which means that the regulation must relate logically to the accomplishment of the organization's accepted goals, must be considered nonarbitrary, and must not violate the rights of the organization's members.

In the United States most legal reasoning regarding organizations is rooted in the notion of voluntarism and primacy of contract (compare Selznick 1969, pp. 144–145). Individuals are free to associate with or to disassociate themselves from organizations and are able to specify the terms of their property exchanges in the form of contracts. The state's role entails enforcing the right of contract, preventing the entry into illegal contract, and enforcing contractual agreements.

In the previous chapter we talked about employment agreements and employment contracts. An employment agreement is an agreement negotiated between a union and an employing organization that specifies the parameters of employment contracts; for example, it indicates the hours that an employee can agree to work and the salary the organization can agree to pay for that work. The employment contract itself is a matter between the individual and the employing organization and must be within the bounds of the collective bargaining agreement as well as other parameters laid down by public policy in statutory law and decisions of the court. Matters in private law agreements represent not only contracts but also systems of constitutional governance (Selzick 1969, pp. 137–154). The process of collective bargaining discussed in the previous chapter serves to redress the power imbalance between employer and employee and allows the principle of voluntarism to work more effectively. Most students of employment relations note that voluntarism is a difficult principle in practice because, although employers are free to dismiss employees within reasonable bounds and employees are free to disassociate themselves from their employment—that is, to quit provided reasonable notice is given—the fact is that most employees cannot freely disassociate themselves from their employer due to the scarcity of other employment opportunities and the need to earn a wage. Collective bargaining enhances the collective power of employees to negotiate equitable employment contracts. It also reinforces the practice of private constitutional government by requiring that changes in the rules or laws that govern the relationship must be discussed with those whom they affect.

Employment Relations Law

Since the 1930s government has been more actively involved in the welfare rights of employees. Often, these federal interventions came about through more general concern for welfare. Social security, for example, arose out of the concern that citizens be able to provide for their needs after retirement. Most job discrimination laws and their interpretation are rooted in civil-rights legislation or in interpretation of basic constitutional rights.

The federal government has endorsed industrial governments or private systems of government based on rules of law by creating legislation such as the National Labor Relations Act. Collective bargaining legislation and judicial interpretation of collective bargaining have greatly restricted the power of managers in both private and public enterprise to act unilaterally on so-called mandatory bargaining items (see Halpenny 1980). Thus the impact of collective bargaining legislation has been to reduce the potential for arbitrary decisions by management and to enhance the potential for industrial democracy or government by consent in organizations.

Public Law and Private Law

Exhibit 11.1 depicts the relationship between public and private employment law as it regulates the workplace. Private law, of course, is bound and governed by public law, which results from the government's or the state's obligations to protect the civil and welfare rights of employees by regulating events in the workplace and to promote public policy by encouraging equitable private government. These rules are interpreted and enforced by special agencies. The National Labor Relations Board applies the National Labor Relations Act; the Occupational Safety and Health Administration oversees the Occupational Safety and Health Act; and the Equal Employment Opportunities Commission administers the civil rights job discrimination law. There is a set of counterpart regulations in private employment law. Both private and public employment law require a mechanism for the interpretation and enforcement (that is, for adjudication and rule clarification) of its system of law. In the area of public employment law, the courts

Exhibit 11.1

Work Place Regulation

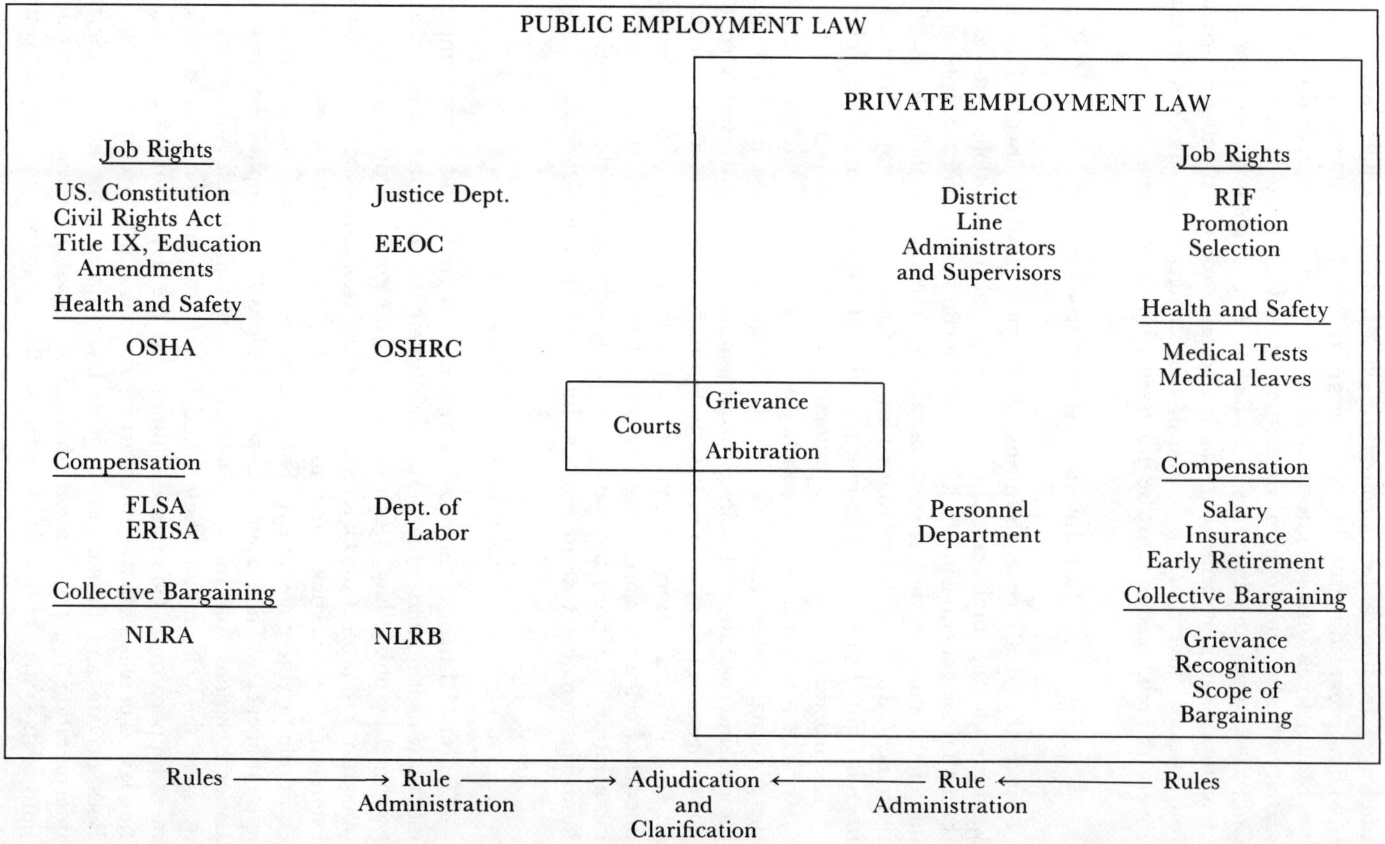

provide these services. Arbitration systems provide these services in the area of private employment law.

Functions of Personnel Management

School organizations and employment relations systems have specialized systems for the administration of personnel rules and policies. This special area is called pesonnel management.

Personnel functions and personnel managers are part of the general management system in schools. As such they subscribe to the general goals of management, which are to preserve the school organization and to help the school to do its job. These are matters of organizational performance; personnel managers enhance organizational performance by influencing personnel effectiveness. Personnel efforts in schools focus on six personnel functions: human resource planning, recruiting, selecting, evaluating, administering compensation, and administering contracts (grievance handling). Each of these will be discussed separately in this chapter.

Miner and Miner observe that personnel functions in organizations can be thought of as a system of inputs, input-output mediators, and outputs that operate within certain environmental constraints (1973, esp. chap. 3). Inputs are functions that identify and enlist personnel (in other words, recruiting and selecting). Mediator functions or activities are classified by their relationship to organizational maintenance or productivity and whether they improve, sustain, or control personnel. Personnel evaluation represents the system output function. This model integrates the main elements of personnel management and provides a useful framework for organizing thinking.

It is also often conceptually useful to consider personnel functions as a more or less natural flow. Human resource planning precedes and sets the parameters for recruitment and selection activities. Recruitment and selection activities result in new personnel who need training, compensation, placement, and evaluation. (Harris et al. 1979, esp. chap. 4).

Human Resource Planning

Human resource planning is the process used to forecast the human resource needs of schools and to develop personnel strategies for attaining the goals of the organization. Because schools are labor-intensive organizations, the accomplishment of the schools' mission requires the schools to employ the necessary quantity and quality of personnel. Increases or decreases in school enrollment may dictate adjustments in teaching staff. The smooth accomplishment of these adjustments with a minimum impact on individuals and program continuity requires that districts anticipate changes in enrollment several years in advance. Adjustments in programs, instructional approaches, ways of managing and delivering food service, instructional media, or transportation may call for changes in the functions and the abilities of personnel. Since time is required for any change, human resource planning activities are designed to provide timely information for making adjustments. Since events that affect personnel are inevitable, personnel managers must project what impact these events will have on personnel in future years.

There are three principal manpower-planning activities in school districts: interpreting the personnel implications of a school's goals and plans, forecasting human resource needs, and developing strategies for satisfying human resource needs.

Interpreting Personnel Implications of Organizational Goals and Plans

Human resource planning is a process of comparing the organization's present human resource position with its desired human resource position. To define the desired human resource position, personnel managers must take into consideration what the school or school system seeks to accomplish, what its student population is currently and what it will be in the foreseeable future, and what kind of educational program the school wishes to operate.[2] Planning must also consider the availability of funds, the political climate, and other things that normally determine what activities occur in the school.

Suppose, for instance, school administrators decided to institute a differentiated staffing model. Human resource planners must estimate the number and qualifications of staff needed and the degree to which present staff are capable of accommodating to the differentiated staffing model. They must also anticipate training needs of current employees that might result from the program revision.

Forecasting Human Resource Needs

In forecasting human resource needs, planners estimate the number of employees that will be required to operate the program or unit effectively. This is known as the demand for labor. Second, they estimate the number and qualifications of employees that will be available to the organization from all sources—this is the supply of labor. In forecasting the demand for labor, personnel managers typically seek to identify things that affect the need for employees. For example, manufacturing firms look at estimates of product sales; governmental agencies might look at population projections.

---

2. A useful, in-depth discussion of considerations in human resources planning can be found in Castetter (1981, chaps. 4 and 5).

Items on which labor demand can be indexed are often referred to as "leading indicators." In schools the leading indicator most frequently used is enrollment, and most staff demand is indexed to pupil enrollment by the personnel staffing policy. The number of fourth-grade teachers required is a function of the number of students enrolled in the school's fourth-grade and the district's policy on class size. The number of high school counselors required is a function of the number of high school students and the caseload assigned to a given counselor. The number of elementary principals required will be determined by the enrollments in elementary schools and policy on the enrollment size of elementary schools.

Estimates of manpower demand require not only that personnel managers establish staffing policy ratios between the leading indicators and personnel but also that they be able to estimate attrition and intrasystem mobility. In school systems, promotions and other job changes will take place. For instance, if the superintendent retires, he or she might be replaced by an assistant superintendent. This creates an assistant superintendent vacancy. That vacancy might be filled by a secondary school principal. The new vacancy at the secondary school might be filled by an assistant principal, and the vacant assistant principal position might be filled by a high school mathematics teacher who has just finished administrative training at the local university. Manpower planners refer to this system of internal promotion as a vacancy chain, and the length of the vacancy chain influences hiring needs. Although there were five vacancies created in the previous example, only one new person needs to be hired—a new high school mathematics teacher to replace the teacher who became the assistant principal.

Using enrollment projection data, staffing ratio plans, and staff-mobility data, a model to project staff needs (demand) for a given position can be constructed. A standard equation frequently used is:

$$V_i = (E_i/SR_i) - (S_{i-1}\ T)$$

where

V_i = Number of position vacancies expected to occur in the ith year.
E_i = Enrollment on which position is indexed for the ith year
SR_i = Position staffing ratio for the ith year
S_{i-1} = Number of staff members in the position in year previous to ith year $(i-1)$
T = Transition coefficient expressed as the percentage of those expected to remain in position.

The demand for new personnel is the residual demand after internal staff mobility or vacancy chain movement is discounted. It may be calculated:

$$NH_i = V_i PNH_i$$

where

NH_i = Demand expressed as new hires required for position in *i*th year
V_i = Estimated position vacancies in *i*th year.
PNH_i = Percentage of vacancies that will not be filled by internal promotions and job mobility; the vacancy chain discount coefficient for the *i*th year.

Shown in exhibit 11.2 are ten-year demand projections for three positions in Utah's public schools. These projections were produced by a computer model using the previous formulas. Enrollment forecasts were made using methods to project cohort sizes. Staffing (pupil-to-position) ratios reflect expected increases in class and building sizes of about 1 percent per year, and turnover and new hire coefficients reflect the five-year hiring experience for the positions.

Estimates of labor supply require an analysis of two dimensions: the internal supply of labor and the external supply of labor. Estimates of the internal supply of labor require personnel managers to give attention to such things as retirement, transfer, voluntary and involuntary departures, and other events that may cause manpower to stay with or leave the organization. It is almost inevitable that a certain number of teachers will not return. Although most schools and school districts require that teachers notify the district of their intentions for the following year in the spring, the amount of time available to recruit replacements is short. Personnel managers must, therefore, be able to estimate internal supply factors in order to schedule recruiting efforts, which include many activities that must be arranged long before teachers give final notice.

The supply of labor available to any given school or school system for any position depends on a number of factors. Exhibit 11.3 gives a model of the external supply of labor for management positions. The external supply of labor depends on conditions in the labor market, including how many people choose to make themselves available for positions, the net gain (or loss) from those leaving and those entering the region, and the competitive position of the organization.

A number of factors affect the external supply of teachers. For instance, the number of college students in teacher preparation programs is declining nationally and the supply of new teachers has declined accordingly. This decline is probably a labor-market correction from recent supply surpluses as well as a decrease in the attractiveness of teaching salaries compared to the salaries of other occupations.

The external supply of available labor may vary from school to school as well, and it reflects the competitive position of the school. In general, beginning teachers prefer schools that pay well and are located in suburban environments. Reputations of school districts, pay scales, and other factors will affect whether or not teachers will apply for jobs in those districts.

Developing Strategies for Satisfying Human Resource Needs

Once the personnel manager has identified the position requirements of the school and has developed a comparison of labor supply and demand, he or she develops plans to ensure that the district has the necessary quantity and quality of human resources required to accomplish its mission. Programs can be developed that target recruiting efforts to locations and specialized labor markets. Training programs can be developed to upgrade skills of existing employees to make them capable of performing new jobs that are expected to become available within the organization. These strategies are taken up in detail in subsequent sections of this chapter.

Recruiting

Recruitment activities within school districts have three purposes: first, to ensure an adequate supply of applicants with desired qualities for anticipated vacancies; second, to promote fairness of opportunity for applicants; and third, to promote appropriate staff diversity and balance by creating a large, diverse pool of candidates. The quality of a school system's personnel will be determined, in part, by the effectiveness of its recruiting efforts. At some point, all members of staff were recruited from an external labor pool. The assistant superintendent may not have been recruited as an assistant superintendent but may have been recruited as a junior high school English teacher. Despite the internal movements of staff, all personnel ultimately came from the external labor pool; therefore, the ability of personnel managers to recruit talented people is vital.

The recruitment process must be cost-effective. Some use the term "yield ratio" to rate the effectiveness of recruiting efforts (see Heneman et al. 1980, pp. 212–213). This is simply a ratio of the amount of energy that is expended on behalf of recruiting compared to the number of technically qualified applicants the efforts produce. Naturally, recruiters recruit in labor markets that will give the highest yield ratio. There is little point in recruiting on a distant college campus where graduates have a history of remaining in the locality. Recruiters often develop informal lists of locations that have high yield ratios.

The concept of yield ratios is also useful in estimating the amount of recruiting that is likely to be necessary for a given type of candidate. In general, recruiting efforts are influenced by the type of personnel that are being recruited. Organizations tend to seek managerial and professional

Exhibit 11.2

State of Utah

Staffing Projections 1981–1990

	Year	Estimated Enrollment	Pupil/ Position Ratio	Estimated Number of Positions	Pct. Staying From Year Previous	Estimated Number of Vacancies	Pct. Vacancies Requiring New Hires	New Hires for Position
Elem. Teacher	80–81	198,148	29	6,895				
	81–82	209,873	29	7,237	0.860	1,307	1.000	1,307
	82–83	221,867	29	7,651	0.860	1,427	1.000	1,427
	83–84	233,683	30	7,789	0.860	1,209	1.000	1,209
	84–85	248,442	30	8,281	0.860	1,582	1.000	1,582
	85–86	262,135	31	8,456	0.860	1,334	1.000	1,334
	86–87	276,463	31	8,918	0.860	1,646	1.000	1,646
	87–88	290,907	32	9,091	0.860	1,422	1.000	1,422
	88–89	303,830	32	9,495	0.860	1,677	1.000	1,677
	89–90	315,914	32	9,872	0.860	1,706	1.000	1,706
	90–91	329,075	32	10,284	0.860	1,794	1.000	1,794
Totals for 10 years						15,104		15,104
Dir./Coord.	80–81	337,086	1,711	197				
	81–82	350,340	1,711	205	0.730	61	0.400	24
	82–83	366,941	1,711	214	0.730	64	0.400	26

	83–84	385,198	1,711	225	0.730	69	0.400	28
	84–85	406,059	1,711	237	0.730	73	0.400	29
	85–86	426,646	1,711	249	0.730	76	0.400	30
	86–87	449,203	1,711	263	0.730	81	0.400	32
	87–88	472,300	1,711	276	0.730	84	0.400	34
	88–89	495,131	1,711	289	0.730	88	0.400	35
	89–90	518,913	1,711	303	0.730	92	0.400	37
	90–91	545,082	1,711	319	0.730	98	0,400	39
Totals for 10 years						786		314
Sec. Principal	80–81	138,938	852	163				
	81–82	140,467	860	163	0.830	28	0.330	9
	82–83	145,074	870	167	0.830	32	0.330	11
	83–84	151,515	880	172	0.830	33	0.330	11
	84–85	157,617	890	177	0.830	34	0.330	11
	85–86	164,511	900	183	0.830	36	0.330	12
	86–87	172,740	910	190	0.830	38	0.330	13
	87–88	181,393	920	197	0.830	39	0.330	13
	88–89	191,301	930	206	0.830	42	0.330	14
	89–90	202,999	940	216	0.830	45	0.330	15
	90–91	216,007	950	227	0.830	46	0.330	16
Totals for 10 years						375		125

Exhibit 11.3

External Supply of Labor for Management Positions

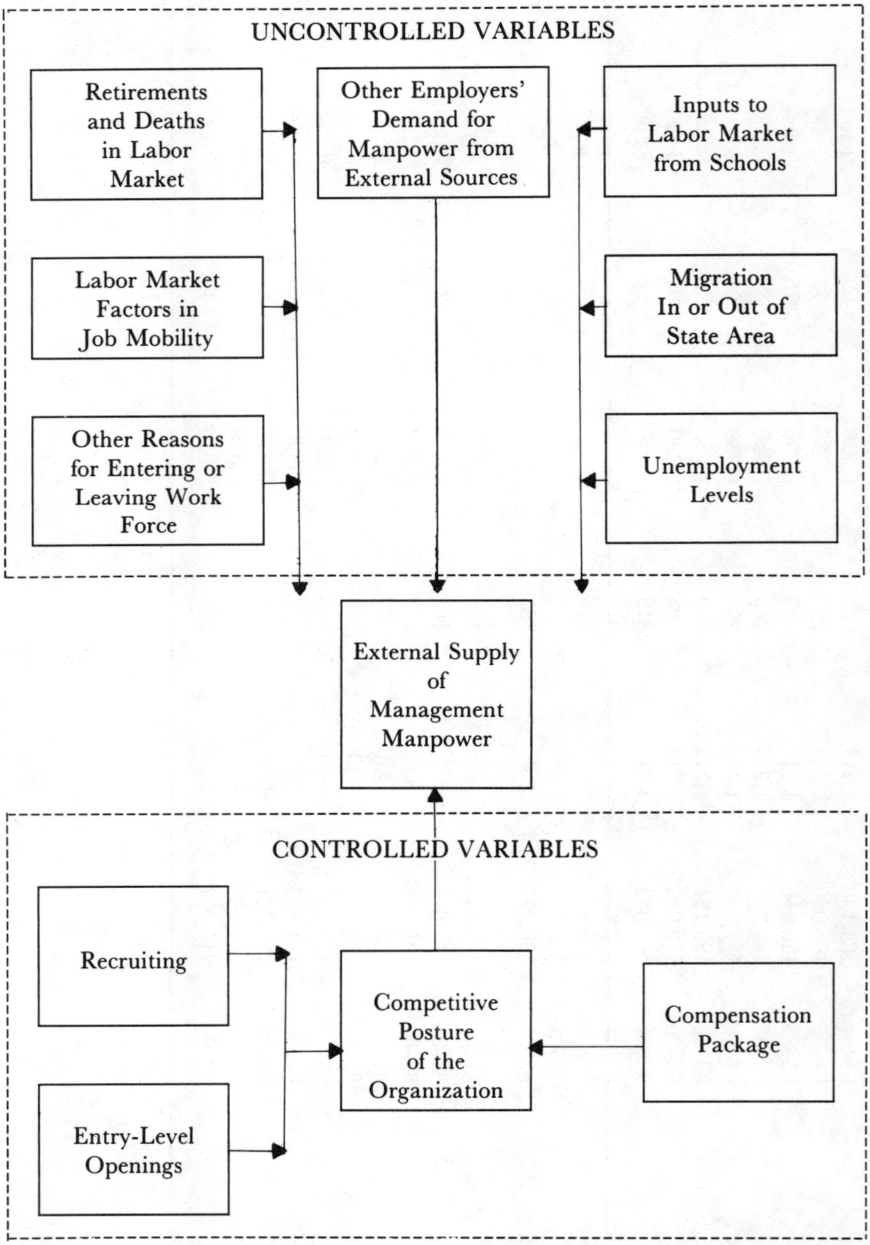

Source: George E. Biles and Stevan R. Holmberg, *Strategic Human Resource Planning* (Glen Ridge, N.J.: Thomas Horton and Daughters, 1980), pp. 152–153. Reprinted by permission.

employees nationally or regionally, technical employees regionally or locally, and clerical and blue-collar employees locally (see Heneman et al. 1980, pp. 212–213). School districts recruit bus drivers, clerk/typists, groundskeepers, and maintenance men almost exclusively from the local labor market. On the other hand, if a district is attempting to recruit a director of buildings and grounds, it would not be unusual for that recruiting effort to expand to the region. Though the surplus of teachers has reduced recruiting activities, it is still not uncommon for recruiters to look nationwide for teachers in specialized fields. Recruiters tend to develop rapport with various placement officials on college campuses and focus recruiting efforts on particular campuses where yield ratios are likely to be high.

There are significant costs to the recruitment process and it is important that recruiters maximize the return on their efforts. When planning recruitment procedures, recruiters must consider questions of where and how to look for applicants. Most school organizations have a number of direct applications—the so-called walk-ins. People new to the area or who wish to move to the area are often job hunting and visit the personnel office of the local school district to see what employment opportunities exist. This represents an excellent source of classified personnel for most school systems, and when the demand for teachers is not especially great, school districts can often fill their needs for professional personnel through walk-in applicants.

In addition, there are employee referrals. Candidates are referred by or are recruited by current employees; the notice of a job opening is spread by word of mouth, and candidates appear. Often, these applicants are indistinguishable from walk-in candidates, but hiring from walk-in and employee referral candidates is relatively inexpensive.

Some organizations advertise available positions in want ads. Classified employee positions are usually advertised in local newspapers, and advertisements for professional positions are usually placed in professional association newsletters and technical trade publications. Over time, the *New York Times, Wall Street Journal*, and *Christian Science Monitor* have become favorites because they have large employment want-ad sections for professional employees. Private schools tend to rely heavily on advertising as a way of recruiting employees.

Among professional positions it is more typical for advertisements to be prepared for administrative positions. Principalships, assistant superintendencies, and the like are often advertised in professional journals and the national press. When districts seek superintendents, they often advertise by direct mail.

Because many employees in education require formal training, schools of education represent a major source of applicants. Some recruiters prefer to visit campus personally to recruit candidates. Many other school systems regularly send notices of job openings to placement offices and deans of schools of education for posting on job bulletin boards. For high-level administrative positions it has become a frequent practice in recent years to engage consultants or executive search firms to recruit and screen candidates.

The recruiter's job is not simply to alert those in the labor pool of the job opportunities in a particular school district but also to take on the task of "selling" the applicant on working in the school district. Recruiters need to be knowledgeable about the organization and its opportunities and they must be personable because the candidates who are being recruited often get their first impression about the school or school system from the recruiter. Also, the development of "catchy" ads that portray the advantages of employment in the school district are often helpful in making those job opportunities more attractive than others that may be listed in the same location.

Legal Restrictions and Problems

In recent years both federal and state governments have passed legislation dealing with employment opportunities. These acts prohibit districts from discriminating against or from taking any action that would indirectly discriminate against applicants in so-called protected classes. In other words, districts cannot rule out applicants because of their race, sex, or age or if they are physically handicapped.[3] In some cases school districts have developed affirmative action plans to attempt to redress the imbalance in staffing that has come about over the years wherein women and minorities have not received an equal share of employment and promotion opportunities.

Selecting

The purpose of the selection process is to choose from the pool of candidates who have been recruited for any position those individuals who will likely perform effectively in the job. In a sense, the process of selection is the process of predicting performance in the job from available data collected about each candidate.

The selection process is intimately associated with the recruitment process for two reasons: (1) it is limited by the applicant pool acquired during recruitment, and (2) much of the information that selection decisions are based on is collected as a part of the application procedures associated with recruitment.

Industrial psychologists tell us that performance results from the interaction of ability, motivation, and opportunity.[4] This function is written as $P =$

---

3. For a good discussion of the principles and specific applications of federal employment law regarding discrimination, see Player (1981).
4. For an overview of the motivation and ability factors determining performance, see Lawler (1973, esp. chap. 1).

$A \times M \times O$. An individual with very high motivation but low-level ability will probably not perform well. Likewise, a teacher with exceptional classroom skills who is bored with teaching is not likely to perform effectively. A person who is very highly motivated may not make a very good clerk/typist without prerequisite typing skills.

Selecting Performance Predictors

In the selection process, therefore, the object is to discover a predictor or predictors that can be used to estimate the likely performance of the individual under real job conditions. In general, the predictors will be different for each class of employment. The abilities required to perform effectively as a school principal will differ from those abilities required to perform as a teacher, bus driver, or groundskeeper. In preparing the selection data profile, personnel administrators and others who are involved in the process must be very careful to identify the unique characteristics of the job and to select appropriate predictors.

Selection of predictors is based on three considerations:

1. *Reliability*—Will the information be the same each time the data are collected?
2. *Validity*—Is the indicator or measure an accurate predictor of performance on the job?
3. *Cost*—Is the predictor cost-effective? It is often possible to imagine very effective predictors that might be used, but the cost of obtaining data is very, very high. Some school districts hire hundreds of personnel each year, and the cost of obtaining elaborate measures of performance would be prohibitive. Costs of measuring certain important attributes must be considered in light of the projected costs of *not* measuring.

It is a general axiom of industrial psychologists and personnel specialists that the best predictor of future performance is past performance. As a consequence, most predictors used in the selection process in some way measure performance that occurred before a job is assumed. Resumes, grade-point averages, and other indicators provide data about the past performance of candidates in certain settings. Test performance is also a type of historical performance because it is assumed that the ability to perform well on a test taken in a preselection circumstance is a predictor of future performance on the job.

Training and Certification Effects on Selection

Among the professional positions in education there exists a multistage selection process. Candidates for teaching, administrative, and other instructional assignments in education actually go through the first selection process when they apply to colleges of education. Schools of education act to weed out those candidates who are not able to perform satisfactorily in various teaching-related activities, such as coursework or cadet teaching assignments. In public school service the pool is further reduced by state certification requirements that include passing a competency test in some states. (Generally private schools are not required to employ state-certified teachers or administrators and hence may have a larger pool from which to select.) Finally, schools apply their own selection criteria to those who survive the earlier selection stages.

There are other positions in school districts that have similar kinds of training, experience, and license requirements. For example, school bus drivers in many states must pass rigorous written tests and in some cases demonstrate their skills in safety and operation of school buses before they are awarded a valid operator's license and become eligible to be a driver.

Types of Predictors

There are a number of predictors of an applicant's ability to effectively perform a job that may be contemplated for use in the selection process. For example, *tests* may be used and are grouped generally as ability, personality and interests, and work-sample tests. Ability tests measure cognitive, mechanical, or psychomotor abilities. Personality and interest tests are sometimes used to measure personality traits thought important to effective performance or interests that may affect motivation. Work-sample tests may be of two types: (1) behavioral work sample and (2) knowledge and skill tests. Examples of a work-sample test would be typing tests or tests in which bus drivers would be asked to maneuver a school bus through a trial course. A prominent example of a knowledge and skill test is the widely used National Teacher Examination, which purports to measure knowledge of pedagogical matters. Some states require that all teacher aspirants take the National Teacher Examination, and a number of districts require that candidates take the exam and achieve a certain minimum score. An example of a combined knowledge and skill test and work-sample test would be in the assessment methods being developed by the National Association of Secondary School Principals. This two-day battery of tests and simulation exercises is being used in some parts of the country as a screening device for potential school administrators.[5]

Another class of selection predictors is *training and experience*. For professional positions in education, training and experience are often important prerequisites. Public school positions usually require certain training and experience, and private schools and universities also tend to weigh training and experience heavily during selection processes.

---

5. For a description of the National Association of Secondary School Principals' Assessment Center, see *NASSP Bulletin* (1980).

References and recommendations are also used as predictors. Many school districts use recommendation forms that are sent to references supplied by applicants. There are serious questions, however, concerning the validity of references and recommendations. Most research has shown that open-ended letters of recommendation tend to be uniformly high and therefore are not much help in discriminating among candidates (Heneman et al. 1980, p. 275; see also Harris et al. 1979, pp. 153–154). Some school districts have employed standardized reference rating forms in an attempt to force referees to be more critical and to gather the same information from all candidates' references.

Application blanks provide a variety of data about the candidates. Usually application blanks gather certain biographical data about the candidates that reflect their training and experience, skills, age, and other demographic characteristics. Some school districts will require candidates applying for professional positions to write a brief essay describing either their talents or their ideas about education.

Research on application blanks indicates that the most valid type is what is called a "weighted application blank" (Heneman et al. 1980, p. 176; see also Castetter 1981, p. 173). In this type of application blank, each item in the application related to job success is given a weighting according to the degree to which it predicts job performance. The scores for these items are then totaled to give a single prediction score. Research has shown that these data may be particularly useful in predicting turnover (see Miner and Miner 1973, pp. 278–280).

Some school districts require a *physical examination* for certain positions. Though these are primarily used in school district settings for health and safety reasons—that is, to protect children from individuals who may carry disease or who would be unable to safely carry out certain aspects of the job—they are no longer as widely used as they once were. Many school districts now only require candidates to fill out a health form and provide evidence through a Schick test or an x-ray that they do not have active tuberculosis. The tremendous cost of health examinations has led to their diminished use.

Among the most widely used devices in the selection procedure is the *interview*. Interviews differ greatly in length and in structure. Interviews for semiskilled or unskilled positions are usually brief—frequently lasting from ten to fifteen minutes. In these cases the prime objective of the interview is usually to make a quick determination as to whether the individual can fit into the work group. Interviews for teacher candidates may be longer—thirty minutes to an hour in length—and a teacher candidate may be interviewed by both the personnel director (or someone from the personnel office) and one or several principals in the school district. Some districts require interviews with multiple interviewers or a panel of interviewers.

Interviews also differ greatly in structure. Structured interviews are planned in advance and all applicants are asked the same questions in the same order. Unstructured or open-ended interviews are those in which the interviewer probes items as they arise. Not only are interviews devices for gathering data about the candidates but they are also instrumental in providing information to the candidate and "selling" the candidate on the job. This important two-way aspect of the interview may in part account for its popularity.

Certain issues of interviewing suggest that the interview and interview data need to be used very cautiously. Most studies of the reliability of interviews have indicated that intrarater reliability is quite high; the same interviewer is likely to have the same impression in two different interviews with the same individual. Interrater reliability, on the other hand, is generally low (Miner and Miner 1973, p. 276; see also Heneman et al. 1980, pp. 280–282; Harris et al. 1979, p. 156). Two different interviewers are likely to rate candidates differently. This lack of interrater reliability would suggest that the validity of interviews is low. The evidence on interviews also suggests that the validity and the interrater reliability can be improved substantially by using structured interviews (Miner and Miner 1973, pp. 278–280). Research suggests that interviewers, especially in unstructured interviews, tend to form a fairly lasting impression of the candidate within the first two or three minutes of the interview. The "accept" or "reject" decision is made early—long before all of the data from the interview are in.

Given the tendency of interviewers to form quick judgments, other data should be withheld from the interviewer to prevent the interviewer from stereotyping the applicant. Inasmuch as the interview is expected to provide data not available from other sources, the interviewer should probably not have access to rating forms, recommendations, grade-point average, and other data about the candidate prior to or during the interview session. However, the interviewer should know what other data are being collected.

Research on interviewing also suggests that where interviewers engage in multiple interviews, reaction to a given candidate will be influenced by the person interviewed immediately before (Heneman 1980; p. 281). If the preceding candidate was particularly strong, the current candidate will be rated lower. If the preceding candidate was weak, the current candidate will be rated higher. In light of available evidence, it may be that interview data are overemphasized in selection decisions. Interviews will be more valid if careful attention is given to training interviewers and structuring the process.

Validating Predictors

The validity of predictors used in selection may be determined in two ways. The first is through an analysis of the job content. In this method the job requirements are studied and the attributes of successful performers are estimated; predictors are then selected that reflect this job content. For instance, if a school has a position for a clerk/typist in which typing skills are essential, it would be appropriate to assess the typing skills of the candidates. This might be done by asking the candidates about their typing speed and accuracy or by administering a typing test. It is assumed that the better the candidate's typing performance, the more effective the candidate will be in the secretarial job.

It is also possible to validate predictors by using empirical methods. In this method predictors are correlated with criterion measures of performance. A high correlation indicates that the measure is a good predictor of job performance. Predictor–criterion correlations may be obtained in two ways. One is a concurrent validity check in which the predictor and criterion are measured simultaneously, usually using subjects already on the job. A problem with this method is that those people already performing in the job whose success can be measured may not be motivated to take the predictor test or provide predictor data with the same degree of enthusiasm as those who are applying for the job.

A second, more accurate method of validating predictors is to use a longitudinal design wherein the predictor for job applicants is measured before the personnel are selected and then a second time after the chosen candidates have been on the job. In this way it is possible to get accurate scores from applicants and to see whether those scores are useful in predicting the performance success of candidates who are chosen. The problem with this design, of course, is that only a limited number of candidates out of an applicant pool are hired. To the extent that the predictor has influenced that decision, the variance in predictor scores will be artificially narrowed.

Legal Constraints

Many federal and state statutes, court decisions, and governmental agency regulations address selection procedures. In general, the actual predictors and procedures must be nondiscriminatory, as must their consequences. Personnel managers must be prepared to show that tests are clearly job-related predictors if scores are consistently lower for minorities or if fewer minority applicants pass the test.

Predictors may not be used that discriminate by sex, age, or national origin *unless* it can be shown that the predictor clearly relates to job performance—that is, it represents a *bona fide occupational qualification.* Race may never be used as a predictor.

Selection and Other Personnel Functions

Too frequently the relationships between selection decisions and other personnel functions are not acknowledged. This is unfortunate because selection has significant meaning for other functions. For instance, selection and assessment are interactive. If selected candidates always perform well in the job, the importance of performance assessment is reduced. Conversely, if the selection process does not discriminate well among applicants, assessment becomes important because poor performers that slipped through the selection process must be identified and terminated.

In general, personnel managers will emphasize processes that are most controllable, effective, and efficient. For example, emphasis on the processes of selection, appraisal, and termination will be placed according to their difficulty, accuracy, and cost. If it is difficult to terminate employees from a given job, selection will take on more importance as personnel managers try to choose employees who will perform well. If it is difficult or costly to select with assurance, personnel managers will emphasize performance appraisals and termination.

Evaluating

A major but frequently troublesome function of personnel management is the evaluation of employees' performance. School organizations need to know how effective their personnel are for a variety of reasons: so they can provide feedback to their employees, assist in the design of systems for improving deficient performance, and make administrative decisions concerning transfer, promotion, and termination.

Purposes of Performance Appraisals

Performance appraisals can serve at least four separate purposes in school organizations. They can be done to provide objective feedback on an employee's performance for his or her own use. This is a *diagnostic* evaluation, and in it there is no intention of communicating the outcome to others within the school organization or that supervisors will use the data to form judgments about the employee's performance or worth to the organization. Microteaching methods make considerable use of this type of appraisal, in which no records are kept of evaluation findings.

Some performance appraisals are directed at providing a basis for improving employee performance, and these strategies are termed *developmental* evaluations. This type of evaluation involves collaboration between the employee and his or her supervisor, is usually conducted regularly over the work year, and the decisions and judgments become part of the personnel records.

Personnel performance appraisals that determine the worth of the employee to the organization are *administrative* evaluations. These evaluations are used as the basis for promotion, termination, and merit award decisions.

Finally, performance appraisals may be used to assess selection predictors and processes. These are termed *validation* assessments.

Performance Measurement

Generally the decisions about data to be collected for performance appraisal begin in the job analysis stage where attempts are made to define the acceptable or essential performances for given jobs. For some jobs development of performance dimensions and standards is relatively straightforward. This is more likely to be true for classified personnel within a school than it is for professional personnel whose jobs are multidimensional.

For any given job there are often multiple performance measures that can be employed. In general, measures fall into two categories: output measures and process measures. Output measures focus on outcomes; the number of classrooms cleaned by a custodian (to a standard of cleanliness) would be an example of an output measure. Another example is the performance of students on a standardized test where that measure is used as a measure of teacher performance.

In process measures of performance, information is gathered by observing the employee perform the required work. In this approach the supervisor observes the work of the employee and judges his or her performance. It is possible to gather performance data on teachers by asking students to evaluate the teacher, although these data are usually acquired from only older students. Process evaluation is the traditional method of gathering data about teacher performance. Principals usually visit a teacher's classroom for a period of forty-five minutes to an hour, and during this time they note various patterns of performance and report those to the teacher and to the school district.

Appraisal Systems

Performance appraisal systems may use several different approaches. A *comparative procedure* requires the employees to be ranked on a performance dimension. Employees under the supervisor's control may be ranked from best to worst on a particular performance dimension or set of performance dimensions. In other cases the evaluators will be asked to compare each employee with each other employee. This method is called *paired comparisons*. Evaluators may be asked to assign employees to a small number of categories on the basis of performance. Those grouped together are presumed to be equal, and employees placed in different categories are presumed to be unequal.

Although comparative procedures are not widely used in education, they have some distinct advantages: (1) they seem to yield relatively consistent rankings of employees across evaluators; that is, they seem to have relatively good reliability; (2) they are easy to use; and (3) the process itself is relatively easy to understand.

The disadvantage of comparative evaluation procedures is that they do not provide information about performance relative to absolute standards, and although employees can be ranked or compared, the system provides no data about whether the performance itself is acceptable or as high as desired. Since the procedure usually requires the evaluators to rank employees on global performance dimensions, the method provides relatively little feedback for diagnostic or developmental purposes.

Another approach to performance evaluation is through the use of *absolute standards*. These are the most common methods employed in education. Principals who evaluate teachers usually use a checklist containing a series of performance categories. The principal rates teachers' performances in each of the categories. Though these methods do not facilitate intragroup comparison, they are useful for diagnostic and developmental purposes.

There are significant disadvantages or drawbacks to the use of traditional rating scales: (1) the items representing performance dimensions are usually drawn arbitrarily and no attempt is made to weight the items; (2) because of the number of items that the evaluator usually has to deal with, there is a tendency to arrive at some global appraisal and then to create a profile reflecting that global assessment; and (3) little attention has been given to validation of the items. It is not uncommon to see a performance rating scale record where the evaluating principal has drawn a straight line down through the same category on all performance dimensions—indicating that all areas are average or above average. With most rating scales there is little to indicate that the items being measured are known to contribute directly to how well students learn.

Recently there has been experimentation with other forms of rating scales. One is the *behaviorally anchored rating scale*. This type of performance rating scale uses critical incidents to form the scale. Behavioral rating scales are constructed as follows: (1) performance dimensions are identified through a critical-incident form of job analysis, (2) the incidents are grouped into a small set of dimensions (usually four to nine) representing performance on that job, and (3) these dimensions are defined (based on the critical incidents that are assigned to each dimension) and are used in the final rating instrument (Heneman 1980, p. 127).

Another type of performance evaluation currently being used derives from *management by objectives*. In this form of performance appraisal, a small number of objectives are identified for each employee to implement during some future work period. The objectives may be set by management, they may reflect consultation between supervisors and employees, or they may be performance areas identified by employees. At the end of a performance period, the employee is evaluated according to the performance goals established at the beginning of the period. This type of performance appraisal is particularly appropriate in the case of professional personnel who are presumably capable of recognizing their own performance needs and deficiencies and of identifying goals for their own improvement. Depending on how the performance goals are established and how uniform they are across performance groups, this method may or may not be useful in making administrative judgments. If a set of performance objectives is established for each employee, it is conceivable that the performance goals would be highly variable across employees; therefore they would not lend themselves readily to comparison.

Issues in Performance Appraisal

A number of issues surround performance appraisal in education. Some are problems of the reliability and validity of performance measures. Not much useful information will be derived from performance systems that gather unreliable data or data that are irrelevant to assessing performance.

Another major problem lies in the political significance of performance appraisal within the school setting because both employee and supervisor are aware of the impact of performance appraisal on administrative judgment. The special arrangement of work in education means that a school principal cannot gather very much data about the performance of instructional personnel by observation. Teachers teach in individual classrooms, and work is not easily observed except from within the classroom. The structure of the school usually restricts the amount of observation time possible as do rules developed during collective bargaining. Appraisals are, therefore, usually based on a total observation period of one to four hours—hardly enough to gather very much data about performance on an ongoing basis.

Teachers and others in education have strongly resisted the use of output measures to assess performance. Though in many ways data from these indicators would be much easier to collect, limited understanding of the production function in education means that it is difficult to ascribe to a given teacher credit for changes in achievement; thus there is a great reluctance on the part of all concerned to use output measures instead of process measures.

And finally, there is the problem of how performance appraisals affect the relationships between supervisors and their employees within the school organization. In the use of diagnostic and developmental evaluation, for instance, all employees are aware that data collected about their performance may ultimately influence administrative decisions. Principals are asked to engage in diagnostic and developmental evaluations with their staff, and at the same time they must make administrative evaluations. Teachers are very well aware of this conflict of interests and will withhold information that might be critical to good diagnostic and developmental evaluations.

Administering Compensation

The design and execution of compensation rules is of central importance to the operation of schools. The term "compensation" as used here refers to all forms of payment and rewards that employees receive as a result of their work. It includes pay or wages, fringe benefits, and incentives that are designed to reward or encourage performance. Decisions about compensation have critical economic consequences—both to employees, who depend on wages and benefits in order to obtain a certain standard of living, and to the employer, who must keep in mind that the direct and indirect costs of compensation for employees represent 85 percent of the operating budget. Compensation has significance in schools beyond economic considerations, however. It is the central feature in the employment contract, which specifies the labor transaction and terms of compensation for employees' investment of energy and time when they work for an organization. Compensation is given to employees in return for work.

The major component of the compensation system is pay. Wage or salary payments usually account for about 65 percent of the total operating expenditure for most schools. Teachers' salaries normally account for approximately 50 percent of operating revenues, and the salaries of classified and support personnel account for perhaps another 15 percent.

In our society, pay has considerable symbolic importance. Wage rates tend to reflect the value or status of a job both within the organization and in the larger society (see Patten 1977, pp. 6–7). The more important a person is in the organization, the higher that person's wage; wages tend to reinforce the hierarchical structure within organizations.

Labor economists and industrial psychologists use the phrase "wage-effort bargain" or "psychological contract" to describe the basic component of the employment transaction or rights transfer.[6] As mentioned, employees make their labor available to an organization in exchange for compensation. The rate of exchange determines the level of effort that employees put into a particular job and is, in part, dependent on perceptions of the purchasing power associated with a given wage. Employees who believe they are being well paid will tend to invest greater energy in performing their jobs than will employees who feel they are underpaid, and hence may behave as though the organization is compensating them for a smaller share of their available energy.

Finally, rates of pay or benefits have significance to the labor market. It is generally thought that higher-ability people are attracted to higher-paying (and higher-status) occupations. Since teaching competes for talent with a number of other professions, the relative wage payment to teachers partly determines the attractiveness of teaching as a career option. Recently in the United States there has been a high demand for people trained in mathemat-

---

6. For discussions of wage-effort bargains, see Cresswell and Murphy (1980, pp. 202–209) and Patten (1977, pp. 102 and 395). For a discussion of a generalized form of psychological contract as used by industrial psychologists, see Kolb, Rubin, and McIntyre (1979), pp. 12–14).

ics and science. As a consequence of supply and demand, the wages offered to people with this kind of training have steadily increased. Mathematicians can now earn considerably more by working in private industry than by teaching mathematics in schools. The result of this labor market condition is that there is a growing shortage of mathematics and science teachers for public and private schools that are unable or unwilling to meet the wages offered in the general labor market. As long as the demand for people trained in mathematics and science substantially exceeds the supply, schools will be faced with a shortage unless they can find some way to compensate teachers of mathematics consistent with the wage price set in the free market.

In fact, the competition for labor goes well beyond the need for more mathematics and science teachers. Though mathematics and science are extremely visible examples, in reality teaching competes on college campuses for students in all areas. Students' career decisions are based on the students' perception of the desirability of the various occupations for which they can prepare. One dimension of their decision is based on the relative financial advantages of various occupations. Clearly the financial rewards for graduates in teaching are considerably less in terms of salary than they are for many other occupations, such as engineering, law, medicine, and business management. Many argue that the low wages offered in teaching force schools of education to choose among the less able students on campus.

Compensation Theories and Concepts from Economics and Behavioral Sciences

Though many wage theories have been developed by economists, compensation and particularly wage rates have long been the subjects of analysis. Many economists begin their analysis with the view that wage is the "price" of labor, which is set in much the same way as prices are set for other commodities[7]. The wage rate for a given job or occupation is determined in part by the supply and demand of labor for that particular job. The demand for labor is in turn determined by the price structure of the market and the subsequent demand for the product or service at a given cost. Wage costs are considered one cost of production or service delivery.

Some economic analyses focus on the affect of wages on employment.[8] Other things being equal, it is thought employers will hire fewer employees as wage rates rise. There are several reasons for this. One, an employer will seek to replace more costly labor with capital investment. Two, the demand

7. For a brief discussion of wage theory applied to educational organizations see Cresswell and Murphy (1980, pp. 440–443). For a more comprehensive treatment see Patten (1977, chap. 4).

8. For good discussion of wages and labor markets see Davey, Bognano, and Estenson (1982, chap. 13). See also Chamberlain and Cullen (1971, chap. 17).

for the product or service will decline as the cost of the product is pushed up by higher wage costs per unit. In public education the forces of the market do not work as clearly as they do in the private business sector. It is relatively more difficult to discover substitutes for the services offered by schools, at least in the short term, and consumers are less able to purchase an alternative product or service to accomplish or satisfy their needs for education. As a consequence, the demand for education is relatively constant, particularly because it is buttressed by legislation that requires all children between the ages of six and sixteen to participate in some form of organized schooling. In the public sector of schooling, it may be that political restraints curb the growth of educational expenditures in much the same way that market constraints control prices in the private sector, however. We are all familiar with growing taxpayer dissatisfaction and resistance—particularly in states such as Massachusetts and California.

Behavioral scientists have studied the impact of wages on various behaviors of employees. A number of theories have been developed to explain how wages and compensation affect employee behavior, particularly in the areas of motivation and performance.[9] It is sometimes assumed by managers that employees may be induced to be more productive if they are paid higher wages. Much research has shown that the relationship between pay and performance is far more complicated and that there is no simple relationship between wage and effort or wage and satisfaction. Patten (1977) has summarized the current research evidence, particularly regarding how monetary incentives motivate employee behavior. He states:

> The model of the employment exchange for performance specifies that for an incentive plan to motivate performance (1) employees must believe that good performance will lead to more pay; (2) employees must want more pay; (3) employees must not believe that good performance will lead to negative consequences; (4) employees must see that other desired rewards in addition to pay result from good performance; and (5) employees must believe that their efforts do lead to improved performance. [P. 153]

Pay is clearly only one dimension of employees' decisions about work output.

There has been much discussion of merit pay in educational institutions, particularly among teaching personnel. Many lay people and policymakers support the idea that people who perform better should be rewarded with higher pay or with bonuses. The five criteria taken from Patten suggest difficulty in using pay in educational organizations to motivate behavior. Current pay systems for teachers make it almost impossible for employees to be certain that improved performance will lead to more pay. It is also not

9. A good discussion of pay as it relates to motivation and performance can be found in Patten (1977).

clear that employees want more pay and consequently are willing to work harder to achieve more pay. A major problem lies in the linking of merit criteria to improvement in educational outcomes or other achievement factors presumably affected by teachers. It is not clear that desirable things will happen in the classroom if teachers do the things required to gain merit pay. Much judgment of performance in education reflects values, not technological considerations.

A further problem with performance-based payment schedules in education is that they tend to further erode trust between administrators and teachers. Where funds for individual performance-based payments are limited, teachers sense competition with other teachers for merit awards, and are less willing to collaborate and share ideas. Selective distribution of merit awards by principals often results in charges of favoritism.

Pay Scales

In its most basic form, a pay scale is a wage continuum for a given job. Most organizations choose to offer various pay increments (or steps) to allow employees who hold the same job over time to acquire salary increases, to let employees know their work is valued, and to encourage good employees to remain in service. On the wage scale, seniority is usually an important factor in the determination of salary, but other factors such as skill and competence may also affect wages.

More complex wage schedules such as those typically used for teachers in public schools may be developed on a wage continuum. Teachers in public schools are generally paid according to what is known as a single-salary schedule, which is a matrix of salary values constructed from steps reflecting experience and columns reflecting post-baccalaureate education. Exhibit 11.4 shows a typical schedule. The teachers' salary schedule in exhibit 11.5 may be viewed as an elaboration of the continuum, wherein the various columns represent salary scales that overlap but together define a large salary continuum. In education the progression of a teacher on the scale and from subscale to subscale is left primarily to the discretion of the individual teacher. By remaining in service, teachers will progress down each column (or subscale) by yearly increments until they reach the top or maximum salary on the scale. Presumably teachers who complete graduate courses during their career can progress from column to column until they reach the scale that contains the highest maximum wage rate.

Clearly, wage scales for teachers are designed to provide incentives to (1) remain in service in a given school district (there are frequently limitations on the amount of credit that can be transferred to other districts) and (2) continue their professional education and "stay current" with contemporary knowledge. From a salary-planning standpoint, however, this type of

Exhibit 11.4
Typical Teacher Salary Schedule

Teacher Salary Schedule 1982–83

Step	B.A. Degree	B.A. Degree 30 Hrs.	B.A. Degree 60 Hrs.	M.A. Degree	M.A. Degree 30 Hrs.	M.A. Degree 60 Hrs.
1	13,467	13,927	14,756	15,090	—	—
2	13,869	14,479	15,307	15,665	—	—
3	14,236	15,054	15,894	16,239	—	—
4	14,857	15,663	16,503	16,849	16,965	—
5	15,512	16,272	17,123	17,469	17,607	—
6	16,190	16,927	17,778	18,123	18,274	19,505
7	16,891	17,581	18,444	18,790	18,963	20,206
8	17,615	18,271	19,134	19,491	19,676	20,930
9	18,373	18,995	19,870	20,204	20,423	21,689
10	19,166	19,742	20,605	20,950	21,193	22,481
11	19,971	20,523	21,397	21,732	21,998	23,285
12	20,843	21,339	22,201	22,536	22,825	24,135
13	—	22,178	23,040	23,363	23,686	24,997
14	—	—	23,902	24,225	24,571	25,905
15	—	—	—	25,133	25,502	26,847
16	—	—	—	—	26,467	27,812

pay schedule has a serious limitation in that the employer cannot control an employee's movement on the scale and no review of performance is usually required.

Often in the classified service and for teachers in some private schools, scales are constructed wherein the movement from column to column is not automatic but rather is promotional; movement is thus a function of increased responsibility, not of increased education. Classified service distinctions among gardeners and groundskeepers are examples. There may be a Gardener 1, Gardener 2, and Head-Gardener scale. To advance on the wage scale, an employee must be promoted from Gardener 1 to Gardener 2 and may be expected to take on more responsibilities on promotion. These responsibilities may be the direction of a small work crew or care of a larger area. In the private sector, pay scales usually reflect a mix of responsibility and seniority.

Fringe Benefits

Employer-paid employee benefits add significantly to the total compensation package. Benefit costs have increased substantially in recent years to the point where benefits for professional employees now add 30 percent or more to salary costs. Benefit costs have grown for two main reasons: the number of

Exhibit 11.5
Salary Scale and Salary Continuum

Salary Continuum	B.A. Degree	B.A. Degree 30 Hours	B.A. Degree 60 Hours	M.A. Degree	M.A. Degree 30 Hours	M.A. Degree 60 Hours
13,000	13,467					
	13,869	13,927				
14,000	14,236	14,479	14,756			
	14,857					
15,000	15,512	15,054	15,307	15,090		
		15,663	15,894	15,665		
16,000	16,190	16,272	16,503	16,239	16,965	
	16,891	16,927		16,849		
17,000	17,615	17,581	17,123	17,469	17,607	
			17,778			
18,000	18,373	18,271	18,444	18,123	18,274	
		18,995		18,790	18,963	
19,000	19,166	19,742	19,134	19,491	19,676	19,505
	19,971		19,870			
20,000	20,843	20,523	20,605	20,204	20,423	20,206
				20,950		20,930
21,000		21,339	21,397	21,732	21,193	21,689
					21,998	
22,000		22,178	22,201	22,536	22,825	22,481
23,000			23,040	23,363	23,686	23,285
			23,902			
24,000				24,225	24,571	24,135
						24,997
25,000				25,133	25,502	25,905
26,000					26,467	26,847
27,000						27,812
28,000						

paid benefits has grown and the cost to schools of those benefits has increased. During the last twenty years, benefit coverage has expanded considerably; fully paid health insurance has become the norm in public school districts; dental, accident, and life insurance benefits have been added; leave benefits have been increased. The purchase cost of these benefits has increased for several reasons. Health care costs in the United States have risen dramatically, driving up health insurance premiums. Also, health and life insurance coverage has been increased in many cases, adding to the premium costs. State and federal unemployment, accident, and retirement programs have increased premiums and contribution rates to cover deficits or remain actuarially sound.

Although employee benefit costs are not significantly higher for school employers than for employers in other sectors, many school managers have nonetheless begun exploring ways to curtail escalation of benefit costs. One plan being used is called a "cafeteria" or "cost-limit" benefits plan. In this approach, employees are given a voucher with a fixed dollar value to be used for the purchase of benefits from the "menu" of benefits offered by the employer. This plan is growing in popularity for several reasons. First, each employee has different benefit needs. A teacher who is covered under a spouse's medical plan may not need or wish to have a second coverage but might want greater life insurance coverage. The cafeteria plan allows employees to tailor coverages to their needs. Second, the plan allows the employer to have better control of benefit costs. If a fixed amount is given to each employee for benefits, that amount can be more easily factored into compensation calculation and planning. Third, the plan simplifies collective bargaining relative to the compensation package. By using a cafeteria plan, union and management representatives need only to set the dollar amount of the benefit voucher, whereas under more conventional approaches they must negotiate each benefit separately. Fourth, employees often view the cafeteria benefits plan as more equitable. They can maximize the usefulness of compensation benefits by selecting the benefits they need—they do not end up with a package containing unnecessary benefits. Fifth, the plan may eventually reduce the cost of benefits to the employer. When one benefits package is applied to all employees it may have to be very broad and therefore costly. Under a cafeteria plan, the size of the benefits compensation bill may be reduced because employees can satisfy their benefit needs more efficiently.

Administering Contracts

Grievance procedures are essential to contract administration for several reasons. First, they help to preserve the balance between employee and management rights. In most work settings, including schools, it is generally held that managers have the right to direct the work force. Within certain constraints they have the rights to employ, assign, and evaluate workers and to design work processes.

Even though it is generally accepted that management's job is to organize and direct the work force, employees are not without options to object to managerial actions if they feel the actions are inconsistent with terms of the written or implied employment contract; employees can challenge management actions through the grievance system.

A second purpose of the grievance process in a school organization is to ensure a system of fairness and organizational justice—this purpose takes the first one a step farther. Organizations are goal-seeking enterprises; they set out to accomplish certain specific objectives. Usually this is to produce goods or to deliver services as efficiently as possible, and many personnel and management functions are directed toward improving organizational productivity and efficiency. In some instances, the preferences of managers as they strive for production efficiency conflict with the just treatment of employees. In the school setting there is currently a great deal of concern about incompetent teachers. Many school managers and parents believe that schools would be more effective if it were easier to rid the system of those teachers thought to be incompetent or performing at substandard levels. In most school settings managers can terminate incompetent teachers, but termination rules make the process time consuming.

Some managers would prefer to be able to dismiss teachers quickly, without being fettered by procedural requirements. But employees have discovered that to protect themselves from potentially arbitrary, capricious, or discriminatory behavior by managers they have to establish rules that govern the ability of managers to employ, assess, and terminate employees. The grievance process permits employees to challenge managerial decisions in these important areas and provides employees a basis for securing organizational justice.

A third function of the grievance process is to smooth out ambiguities and rough spots in contract language or the interpretation of a contract. Labor agreements are often lengthy and complex documents that cover in extended detail much of the work relationship. It is inevitable that managers and employees will differ in their interpretations of the meaning of contract language. It has been noted that legal systems require some mechanism for interpreting and enforcing the law, whether it be private law in the organizational setting or public law in the governmental arena. The grievance process is the mechanism by which the private law of an organization is interpreted and enforced.

And finally, the grievance mechanism helps to prevent work disputes and work disruptions. If workers in work settings without grievance mechanisms believe they have been treated unfairly under the terms of the labor agreement, their only recourse is to use power devices, such as strikes and job actions. The United States has been relatively free of wildcat strikes and other job actions over contract interpretations due to, most authorities feel, the grievance mechanism and its ability to institutionalize and resolve contract disputes peacefully.

Scope of the Grievance Procedure

A grievance is a complaint lodged by an employee or group of employees against a management practice. Most authorities agree that formal grievances should be complaints regarding interpretation or application of the written labor agreement. Most grievance arbitrators will not hear grievances that are complaints against practice not covered by the agreement. Employees can feel aggrieved because of a number of situations, not all of them rooted in contract interpretation or application. Grievances are an excellent source of information about the feelings and hostilities of employees, and school managers can use this information to help them to develop more effective relationships with employees and to correct work circumstances that lead to anger and frustration. Many students of the grievance process recommend that employees should be allowed to address any problems through the grievance procedure regardless of the source of the problems. They also believe the grievance process can be used as a problem referral mechanism as well as a system to resolve contract administration disputes in school organizations. Grievances bring problems to the attention of personnel officers and line administrators. Because they are pushed upward in the hierarchy until resolved, the problems they address receive attention.

The Grievance Process

Grievance processes are usually defined in labor agreements. In general, they consist of three to five steps, beginning with an informal discussion of the grievance at the first supervisory level and ending with a final resolution of the grievance by the school board, labor tribunal, or arbitrator. Exhibit 11.6 provides Kenneth Ostrander's (1981) excellent summary of the grievance procedure in flow-chart form.

Most grievances are resolved by employees and managers approaching the problem together in search of resolution. A few grievances are not resolvable because they involve either differences in interpretation of the contract or very fundamental disagreements about the way the contract should be applied. These basic disagreements are characteristically referred to an independent source for hearing. In the public school setting the school board may serve as the final arbitrator of grievance disputes. In most cases, however, the arbitration provisions of the school board provide for final arbitration of the disagreement by a grievance arbitrator.[10] Like an arbitrator in an interest dispute, a grievance arbitrator is a neutral third party who agrees to hear the dispute and render a decision that may be binding on the parties. The grievance arbitrator in this system becomes the judge of the behavior of managers and employees under the terms of the system of rules they have adopted.

---

10. In 1975 about 85 percent of school districts with enrollments of one thousand or more had grievance procedures containing arbitration.

Exhibit 11.6
Diagram of a General Grievance Procedure

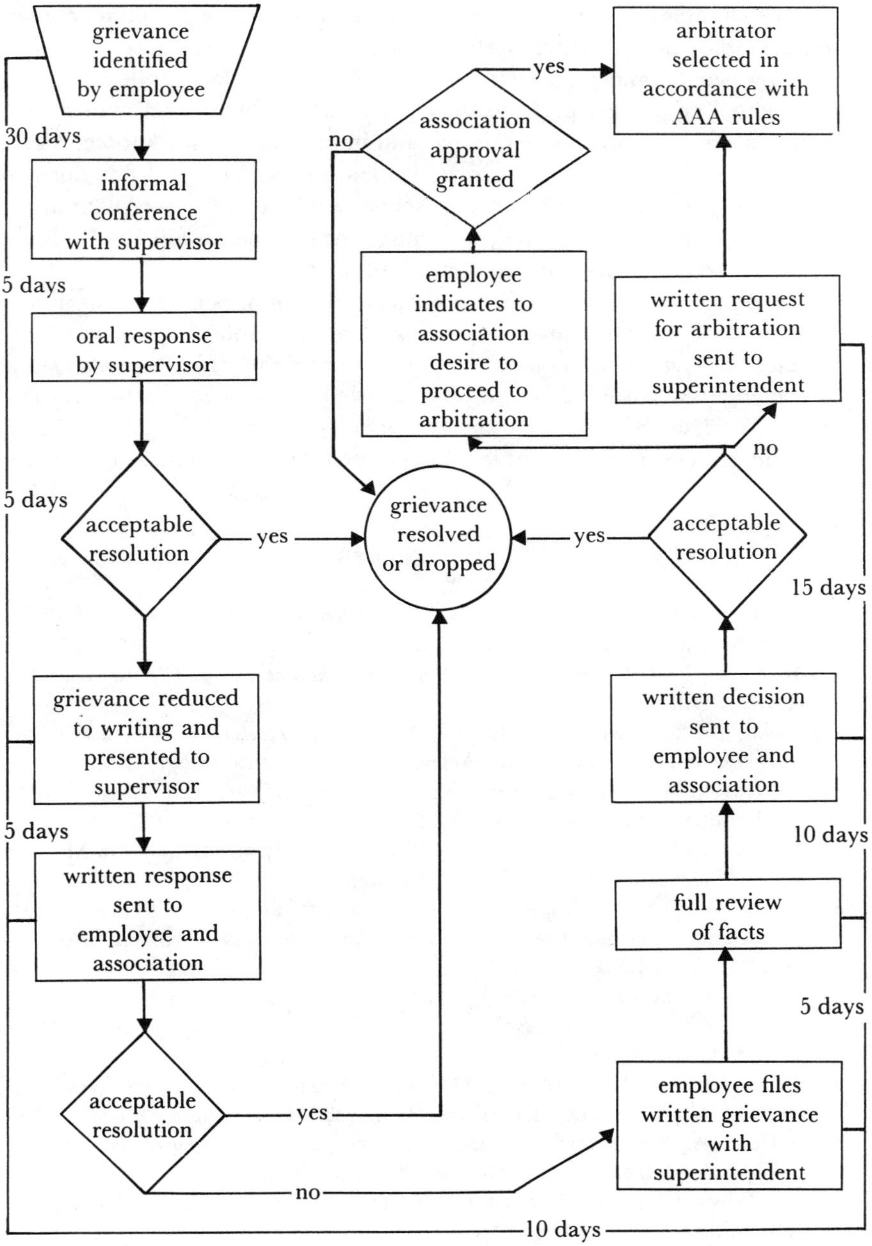

Source: Kenneth H. Ostrander, *A Grievance Arbitration Guide for Educators* (Boston: Allyn and Bacon, 1981), p. 15. Reprinted by permission.

Summary

This chapter has been concerned with the work of the personnel manager in the employment relations system of schools. Most of the work in schools is done by people, and the effectiveness of the school is largely determined by how school employees perform their jobs. Because personnel managers are instrumental in securing, sustaining, and improving the work force, theirs is a vital role. This role includes management of six personnel functions that influence personnel effectiveness in schools: human resource planning, recruiting, selecting, evaluating, administering compensation, and administering contracts (especially grievance handling).

Personnel managers' work is subject to a number of environmental influences. They are constrained by and accountable to public law as it defines employee welfare, job, and governance rights. They are also subject to private organizational law that further defines employees' and managers' rights. Work force supply-and-demand factors beyond the control of personnel managers exert considerable influence on employee quality and quantity.

References

Castetter, William B. *The Personnel Function in Educational Administration.* 3rd ed. New York: Macmillan Publishing Co., 1981.

Chamberlain, Neil W., and Cullen, Donald E. *The Labor Sector.* 2d ed. New York: McGraw-Hill, 1971.

Cresswell, Anthony M., and Murphy, Michael J. *Teachers, Unions, and Collective Bargaining in Public Education.* Berkeley: McCutchan Publishing, 1980.

Davey, Harold W.; Bognano, Marco F.; and Estenson, David L. *Contemporary Collective Bargaining.* 4th ed. Englewood Cliffs, N. J.: Prentice-Hall, 1982.

Guthrie, James W., and Zusman, Ami. "Teacher Supply and Demand in Mathematics and Science." *Phi Delta Kappan* 64:1 (September 1982): 82–83.

Halpenny, Diane. "The Impact of Collective Bargaining on California Education Code Laws Governing Teacher Tenure, Evaluations, and Dismissal." *Pacific Law Journal* 2 (April 1980) : 799–820.

Harris, Ben M.; McIntyre, Kenneth E.; Littleton, Vance C., Jr.; and Long, Daniel F. *Personnel Administration in Education: Leadership for Instructional Improvement.* Boston: Allyn & Bacon, 1979.

Heneman, Herbert C., II; Schwab, Donald P.; Fossum, John A.; and Dyer, Lee D. *Personnel/Human Resources Management.* Homewood, Ill.: Richard D. Irwin, 1980.

Kolb, David A.; Rubin, Irwin M.; and McIntyre, James M. *Organizational Psychology: An Experiential Approach.* Englewood Cliffs, N. J.: Prentice-Hall, 1979.

Lawler, Edward E., III. *Motivation in Work Organizations.* Monterey, Calif.: Brooks/Cole Publishing Co., 1973.

Miner, John B., and Miner, Mary Green. *Personnel and Industrial Relations: A Managerial Approach.* 2d ed. New York: Macmillan Publishing Co., 1973.

NASSP Bulletin 64: 438 (October 1980): 87–117.

National Center for Education Statistics. *The Condition of Education.* Washington, D.C.: U.S. Government Printing Office, 1982.

Ostrander, Kenneth H. *A Grievance Arbitration Guide for Educators.* Boston: Allyn & Bacon, 1981.

Patten, Thomas H., Jr. *Pay: Employee Compensation and Incentive Plans.* New York: The Free Press, 1977.

Player, Mack A. *Federal Law of Employment Discrimination in a Nutshell.* 2d ed. St. Paul, Minn.: West Publishing Co., 1981.

Schlecty, P., and Vance, V. "Do Academically Able Teachers Leave Education? The North Carolina Case." *Phi Delta Kappan* 63:2 (October 1981): 106–112.

Selznick, Philip. *Law, Society, and Industrial Justice.* New York: Russell Sage Foundation, 1969.

PART IV

Logistics Systems

Logistics systems provide the necessary support functions to ensure that schooling programs can be carried out. Logistics systems include, but are not limited to, transporting students to and from school, feeding them, and providing classrooms, furniture, equipment, supplies, books, and teachers. In a sense, *all* of school business administration is logistics—the school business administrator's role is to ensure that schooling services take place. This part of the book examines logistics more narrowly and more abstractly. We do not attempt to examine *every* logistical system, each with its own technology, language, problems, and purposes. Instead, we first examine the *service* characteristics of logistics systems and point out how they differ from *capital goods* characteristics. All logistics systems have elements of both kinds of characteristics, but services are evaluated differently from capital goods. Chapters 12 and 13 examine, respectively, services management and capital goods management. Chapter 14, "Energy Management," describes the idiosyncracies—technology, purposes, language, issues—of one logistics system and points out how the goods and service components of a logistics system become interlinked in practice.

12

Services Management

•

Overview

School services vary not only by type—for example, student transportation versus school lunch—but also in systems of rights associated with their provision. Some services (especially in public schools) are required and funded by higher levels of government, while others are neither required, centrally financed, nor even necessary in order to run schools, but are provided for other reasons. Analysis of pupil transportation, school lunch, and purchasing services illustrates the range of rights and incentives available to managers regarding those services and how these services vary among sectors. Two of the most fundamental and generalizable ways of evaluating services are discussed: minimizing the sum of competing costs and increasing net revenues.

• • •

Introduction

Education is a service industry. In order to produce education services, many support services must also be "produced." What makes producing a service different from producing a good? *Goods* are defined as "articles of trade, merchandise, or wares," while *services* have been described as "the organized system of apparatus, appliances, and/or employees for supplying some accommodation and activities required by the public" and as "the performance of any duties or work for another" (Sasser, Olsen, and Wyckoff 1978, p. 8). This distinction, however, is not as clear as these definitions might suggest. Almost all purchases of goods are accompanied by facilitating services, and almost every service is accompanied by facilitating goods. However, we will consider *pure* goods and *pure* services here in order to highlight how the analysis of each differs.

Support Services in Schools

School organizations provide a wide variety of services that include not only basic education services but also services that either support or complement education. Support services are required to produce educational services, and they include supply and equipment procurement services, data processing services, personnel placement services, food and transportation services, and cleaning services. Complementary services are those that extend the mix of services offered to clients by the school but do not clearly fall within the most narrow definition of the mission of the school. Examples of complementary educational services include driver education courses, continuing or adult education courses, early childhood programs, day care, music and special athletic programs, summer camps, sports camps, and performing arts productions. They may also include offering basic educational services to new segments of the market, such as preschoolers or senior citizens.

These categories of services are not pure and represent differences in degree as much as differences in kind. Sometimes it is not clear when a particular service is auxiliary and when it is central to the mission of the school. Often, however, the motivation for providing the complementary service, which is beyond the narrow mission of the school, is that the narrow mission could not be easily provided without the service (for example, personnel placement services provide the school with teachers); the service is required by law (for example, student transportation); or it generates new revenue and "goodwill" (for example, providing adult education programs to the community).

In this chapter our primary interest in these services is not with the content of the services *per se*, even though school business administrators are usually required to be quite familiar with the basic technology of each service under their control. Rather, we are interested in the *form* of the major decisions about these services—that is, in how these decisions are made and what influences the decisions. In general this implies focusing on the costs of and revenues from service decisions, which concern the school business administrator more than any other individual in the school.

Service Incentives of the School Business Administrator

As we have discussed in previous chapters, the three primary goals of the school business administrator are (1) to decrease costs while holding service levels constant (increased efficiency), (2) to increase revenues while holding costs constant (increased profitability), and (3) to increase production while holding costs constant (improved levels of service). To accomplish these often conflicting objectives, the school business administrator makes many discrete, seemingly unrelated decisions. With respect to these three fundamental incentives, however, most decisions result from two kinds of evaluations: evaluating the sum of competing costs and evaluating the interactions between costs, service levels, and revenues. These two subjects are discussed in detail later in this chapter.

Compromising, or making trade-offs, is at the heart of all decisions, and in some respects the school business administrator's trade-offs are not unlike those of other managers. The major difference is one of emphasis: the school business administrator's trade-offs are often formulated in financial terms. Although decisions by managers have important nonfinancial elements, the school business administrator's decisions have more explicit financial elements.

Services in Schools

Before turning directly to the abstract structure of these types of decisions, we need to become familiar with those services for which the school business administrator is usually responsible. Four of the most common of these services are student transportation, school lunch, purchasing, and various sales to clients who are not part of the school's traditional or primary market. These four are by no means all of the services provided in schools, but they do provide a reference point when we discuss cost reduction and revenue enhancement later in the chapter. Collectively, they provide examples of the range of services in schools as well as the evolution of the services. Some services are required and funded by state governments; some are required and funded by the federal government; some are not required by law but are necessary to operate schools; and some are neither necessary nor required but the school business administrator seeks to pursue them for other reasons.

Each service in schools requires different facilitating goods, has come into existence for different reasons, and has evolved differently in response to different sponsor demands.

Pupil Transportation Services: State Sponsorship

Public school districts have assumed responsibility for transporting pupils to and from public schools, (and, in some instances, private schools). For a variety of reasons student transportation services have grown continuously over the last century. As early as 1869, some states were passing legislation allowing the expenditure of public funds for this purpose. Pupil transportation was first used as a means of providing access to more adequate educational programs for students residing in rural areas. In many states during the first half of this century, pupil transportation was used by state programs to consolidate and reorganize small school districts into larger attendance centers.

More recently, increased busing is attributable to increases in the average size of schools, growth of population in nonmetropolitan areas, decreases in family size (causing the closing of some neighborhood schools), and the emergence of policies to use student busing to achieve racial balance in schools. Of the pupils currently transported to school by bus, over 6 percent attend private schools. Of the approximately 49 million students in schools in 1975, about 20 million were bused, about 12 million walked to school, about 12 million were transported by car, and the remainder took public transportation. The proportion of public school students transported to school at public expense (usually by bus) increased gradually from about 7 percent in 1929 to 57 percent in 1979–80. The numbers of public school children bused at public expense increased during that fifty-year period from about 1.9 million to nearly 22 million.

Current expenditures for student transportation are, on the average, over $110 per transported student per year and range from a high of over $250 per transported pupil in sparsely populated states down to about $60 in southeastern states. There is also considerable variation among states in the methods used to distribute aid for support of pupil transportation programs. These range from flat grant programs to foundation programs that equalize aid on the basis of a district's ability to pay to formulas that reimburse a specified percentage of district expenditure. In six states, funding is included in a general operating aid program. Nine states use a flat grant distribution formula. Local transportation expenditures form the basis for state funding in eleven states, and an average cost factor is used in nineteen states (McKeown 1978, p. 226).

Because student transportation is funded largely from third-party payments, the school business administrator is concerned with maximizing these payments within the constraints of desired levels of service and costs. When busing is not totally reimbursed (it rarely is), the business administrator also tries to minimize the sum of competing transportation costs. Fees are rarely charged for busing, and thus the administrator is less concerned with pricing. The decision to operate or to contract busing is one of the major student transportation decisions.

School Lunch Services: Federal Sponsorship

Feeding programs in schools have grown from modest origins not unlike those of student transportation, with the exception that federal, not state, governmental agencies have been the major sponsors (Comptroller General of the United States 1977). The evolution of the school lunch program in the Chicago public schools is illustrative. The first lunchroom in the Chicago schools was opened in 1898 at Englewood High School through the efforts of the Englewood Women's Club. In subsequent years other neighborhood women's clubs received permission to open other lunchrooms (Department of Food Service, Chicago Public Schools 1978, p. 3). Introduction of food service in the elementary schools began in 1911 with the organization of Penny Lunch Rooms in three pilot schools. The Penny Lunch Room was instituted to make certain that undernourished children received an adequate lunch. The purpose then was what it remains today: to counteract the deleterious effects of an inadequate diet on learning. The Penny Lunch Rooms were so called because children could obtain a lunch for one penny. The menu was simple, consisting of bean soup and sandwich, or a glass of milk and a sandwich, or crackers and milk. The sandwich consisted of two slices of bread with jam or syrup. By 1941, when there were 110 Penny Lunch Rooms in Chicago, the price of a full lunch was ten cents.

The growth of food services in Chicago was paralleled in other school districts and, eventually, was stimulated elsewhere by the federal government's participation in programs to combat inadequate diets. In 1933 Congress authorized the distribution of surplus agricultural commodities to schools in an effort to support farm prices. Additional legislation throughout the 1930s and early 1940s reorganized and expanded this program.

World War II provided the single largest impetus to federal support of the school lunch program, when the draft revealed that large numbers of men were unfit for service because of inadequate diet. In 1946 Congress passed the National School Lunch Act (P.L. 396) "as a measure of security to safeguard the health and well-being of the nation's children and to encourage the domestic consumption of nutritious agricultural commodities and other food" (Department of Food Services, Chicago Public Schools 1978, p. 4). Major additional pieces of federal school food service legislation that occurred during the next thirty years included authorization of the Special Milk Program in 1954; special assistance to ensure access to the school lunch programs for children from low-income families in 1961; the Nonfood Assistance Act in 1962 to support purchases of equipment; authorization of the school breakfast program in 1966; and in 1970 P.L. 91–248 emphasizing free and reduced-price meals and establishing eligibility standards (Department of Food Services, Chicago Public Schools 1978, p. 4).

As a result of the federal government's steadily increasing involvement in school lunch, school food service programs today are in effect joint enterprises of the U.S. Department of Agriculture, the states, and local school districts (or private schools). The four major subjects that bind these levels of government together in providing school lunches are the establishment of minimum nutritional standards (the "Type A" lunch); administration of the free and reduced-price lunch program; administration of donated agricultural commodities; and programs of financial assistance for purchasing nonfood items.

The Type A Lunch

The National School Lunch Act of 1946 established three lunch programs, designated as Types A, B, and C. The latter two have since been dropped; Type A is the only standard for defining a school lunch and is the basis for federal financial assistance. The Type A lunch consists of meat or a meat alternate, vegetables and fruits, bread and bread alternates, and milk; specific quantities of each are required. Currently, federal regulations specify standard minimum portions to be served to all children. However, this has resulted in considerable waste, since children are required to accept full portions of all items, regardless of their age, size, or appetite (Department of Food Services, Chicago Public Schools 1978, p. 5). In response to this problem, USDA has been testing portion patterns keyed to children's ages. If these are successful, schools may be required to serve five different-sized meals and to make certain that children receive the meal appropriate to their ages.

Another modification in the Type A requirements is the "offer-versus-serve" option. Until recently, schools were required to actually serve all food group items to every child, even if the child did not want all of them. Now, high school students must be offered all items but need to select only three. A high school Type A lunch containing any three items will qualify for reimbursement.

Free and Reduced-Price Lunch Program

Since the passage of federal legislation requiring that children from low-income families be provided with free or reduced-price lunches, the USDA has published annually an income scale for determining family income for eligibility. Eligibility guidelines in effect for the 1982–83 school year specified, for example, a $12,090 annual income for a family of four to qualify for free lunches and an annual income of $17,210 to qualify for reduced-price lunches. Income eligibility levels vary according to family size.

Typically at the beginning of each school year, building administrators receive application forms and guidelines for admission into school lunch programs. The forms are sent to and completed by parents. The federal guidelines under which local school administrators must operate specify what constitutes income, exceptions to income calculation procedures, verification of information supplied by parents, restrictions on disciplining and employing free and reduced-price lunch recipients, and prohibitions against overtly identifying free or reduced-price lunch recipients.

Donated Commodities

For almost half a century, the USDA has been donating agricultural commodities to school districts. School districts may order donated commodities annually up to a specified value, for example, twelve cents multiplied by the number of meals served. School districts may select, reject, or substitute from the list of commodities available through the USDA. The value of donated commodities to participating schools is substantial, amounting to millions of dollars annually in large city school systems. The major problem with donated commodities as seen by local administrators is the inability of the USDA to guarantee delivery dates, which frequently results in the school district having to purchase from another source a commodity already ordered from the USDA. The resulting duplication may create difficulties in planning the menus for the schools and expense in warehousing the foodstuffs. To counter these and other problems the federal government has been investigating the feasibility of permitting school districts to receive cash in lieu of donated commodities.

Nonfood Assistance

The Nonfood Assistance Program was established by Congress to enable schools to obtain equipment for the storage, preparation, transportation, and serving of food. This program provides for federal reimbursement of up to 75 percent (100 percent for needy schools) of the cost of such equipment.

Today about two-thirds of all schoolchildren in public schools participate daily in the national school lunch program, while another 12 percent participate at least weekly. The remaining fifth either do not participate that often or attend schools without programs. Participation in school lunch has declined in recent years due to declining school enrollment, higher prices charged, and stricter eligibility rules for free and reduced-price meals. The level of participation in school breakfast programs, which was less than four million during its peak year of 1981, has also declined.

The USDA contributed about $3.3 billion to various child nutrition programs in fiscal 1982, including school lunch and breakfast. As school lunch program costs have increased, the USDA has paid a larger total share.

That share declined in 1982, however, with lower payments for paid and reduced-price meals despite higher payments for free meals.

School lunch is one of the auxiliary services that currently reflects the philosophy that recipients should pay for a service to the extent that they are able. The issue of pricing and its relation to participation (demand) is one of the central financial policy decisions about school lunch that involves business administrators. Their pricing decisions reflect a compromise between desires to maintain or increase revenues and desires to increase service levels (sometimes called participation rates).

A recent study conducted by the USDA estimated that "all other things being constant, a one cent increase in the price of a school meal would lower the average daily participation rate by about one half of one percent." But price alone does not affect participation rates: all other things are not held constant. Higher participation rates generally occur in smaller schools, in rural areas, among the lower grades, where lunch periods are short, and where school lunch managers have had formal training. Other factors seem to work against high participation rates, including the availability of a la carte items, the close proximity of commercial food outlets, the use of food service management firms, and off-site preparation.

Food service, like student transportation, is organized to claim third-party payments. As a result, extensive reporting systems are created to justify claims. Unlike student transportation, price decisions must also be made. Ability to portray relationships between cost, volume, and revenue provides a means for determining prices of food service.

Purchasing Services: Regulated but Not Required

Purchasing services differ from food service and student transportation in at least two ways that are important for the school business administrator. First, it is an intermediate service. By this we mean that purchasing services are provided to teachers (operators) to enable them to provide direct services to students. Second, purchasing would take place even in the absence of any requirements that it be done, hence external monitoring of purchasing activities deals much more with how it is done than with whether it must be done.

Purchasing has always been a part of school operations. The history of its growth is less traceable to specific legislation than it is to the growth of schooling in general. The increased complexity of purchasing can perhaps be best illustrated with a description of the responsibilities of a typical purchasing department (see exhibit 12.1). From that list we see that part of the functions are specific to the technology of purchasing and part are similar to those planning and control activities required of any service manager.

Exhibit 12.1

Responsibilities of a Typical Purchasing Department

Records, data, and basic information

Maintaining general purchase records
Maintaining price records
Maintaining parts history records
Maintaining vendor records, including financial and performance
Maintaining specification files
Maintaining standards file, including MHL/JAN specifications
Maintaining catalog files

Purchasing research, analysis, and studies

Conducting market studies and trends
Conducting material studies
Conducting make-or-buy studies
Conducting price/cost analysis
Investigating supply sources
Conducting supplier-plant visits and inspections
Developing new supply sources
Developing alternate materials and sources
Participating in value studies

Purchasing

Checking authorized requisitions
Obtaining capital appropriations
Issuing requests for bid
Determing bidders' list
Preparing request for bids
Conducting pre-bid briefings
Receiving all bids
Analyzing quotations and/or proposals
Determining nonresponsive bids
Evaluating suppliers
Selecting suppliers
Determining quantity to buy
Scheduling purchases and deliveries
Determining mode of transportation and carrier
Interviewing salesmen
Determining type of contractual instrument
Negotiating contracts
Writing and issuing contractual agreement (purchase order, subcontract, blanket order, lease, rental agreement, etc.)
Developing legal conditions of contracts
Determining applicable federal, state, and local taxes or foreign duties
Following up for delivery, i.e., expediting and updating open-order status reports

Checking receipt of materials
Checking and approving invoices
Corresponding with suppliers
Negotiating adjustments with suppliers
Negotiating contract changes
Terminating contracts

Inventory management

Developing inventory classifications
Maintaining minimum stocks
Establishing economic order levels
Maintaining inventory balance
Improving inventory turnover
Establishing stock and parts numbering system
Transferring materials
Consolidating requirements
Avoiding excess stocks and obsolescence
Declaring surplus inventory
Standardizing packages and containers
Accounting for returnable containers
Accounting for demurrage charges
Making periodic reports of commitments
Maintaining property records

Managerial

Preparing and updating purchasing manuals
Assisting in department audits and reviews
Evaluating purchasing performance
Evaluating personnel performance
Performing merit reviews and salary determination
Making reports to management
Conducting training and job enrichment programs
Conducting cost improvement programs
Participating in quality and zero defects programs

Shared with other departments

Contracting for services
Purchasing consultants' and special services
Purchasing construction contracts
Determining whether to make or buy
Negotiating leases for real property and equipment
Purchasing vehicles, trucks, and off-the-road equipment
Operating garage and fleet maintenance
Operating janitorial and custodial services
Operating and maintaining record archives
Supervising reproduction equipment
Purchasing exhibit material

Exhibit 12.1, continued

Conducting scrap and surplus sales
Establishing employee purchase program
Operating cafeteria, in-plant feeding, and vending services
Purchasing computer time sharing and special outside test facilities

Source: George W. Alijan, *Purchasing Handbook*, 3d ed. (New York: McGraw-Hill, 1973), pp. 1-18–1-19. Reprinted by permission.

The eight objectives pursued by one school district's purchasing department are representative of most:

1. To support the organization with an uninterrupted flow of goods and services
2. To buy competitively and wisely
3. To keep inventory investment and losses to a minimum
4. To develop reliable allotments and sources of supply
5. To develop good vendor relationships (through honesty, integrity, and fairness)
6. To achieve maximum integration with other departments in the organization (through communications about new products, market conditions, and specifications for school needs)
7. To train and develop highly competent personnel who are motivated to make the organization successful
8. To accomplish all of the above at the least possible cost (maximize the value received for each dollar expended)

Comparing Purchasing Rights in the Public and Private Sectors.

An analysis of purchasing services is useful for comparing structural differences in rights between school business administrators in public and private schools. The differences in rights affect the behavior, if not the incentives, of the two groups of administrators. These differences in rights also reflect how purchasing activities in most public organizations differ from those in most private organizations. Perhaps the major differences between the two is the lack of secrecy surrounding purchasing in public schools: "Prices paid and sources of supply are never revealed by industry, whereas specifications, bids, puchase orders, and other public purchasing documents are matters of public record for all interested persons to see" (Aljian 1973, p. 20–12). The public nature of purchasing in public schools is of course intimately related to the issues of legislative control discussed in chapter 2. With the absence of equity claims and other self-monitoring incentives facing the public school business administrator, state legislatures feel that extensive purchasing regulations need to be created and enforced to deal with the agency problem between sponsors and operators. Differences in regulation affect the manner in which school administrators can pursue their preferences through purchasing.

The presence of extensive regulations does not ensure efficient purchasing practice, even if the business administrator desires to be efficient. Rather, the regulations purposely restrict the behavior of the public school business administrator. It is a cost that legislators are willing to pay to help control the administrator's discretionary use of public funds. The public school business administrator's purchasing role is, hence, more complex.

> In public purchasing, it is not only necessary to perform with sound business acumen, but it is essential to exercise the function in the manner and form provided by legislation. Where the statute prescribes the only mode by which the power to contract for public works or for the furnishing of public supplies shall be exercised, the mode is the measure of the power. On the contrary, private purchasing in most firms is highly flexible. Innovations can be applied immediately by a private business, whereas the public purchaser may have to wait for the amendment to the statutes before implementing new departures. [Aljian, p. 20–12]

These differences require closer scrutiny.

The authority for public school purchasing derives from laws. Therefore, public school business administrators are responsible to and are controlled by a legislative body and, by extension, are accountable to the voters who elect that body. Private school business administrators have no legal responsibility beyond the trustees of their school. Many of the statutes that govern public-sector purchasing are designed to prevent choices by school business administrators based on personal favoritism and to assure all qualified vendors an equal opportunity to bid on public school business (Westing, Fine, and Zenz 1969, p. 228). These restrictions usually require that public school districts advertise for bids. In addition, bids must be publicly opened and the award made to the lowest responsible bidder. Private schools, by contrast, may negotiate secretly, buy without competitive bidding award, contract with any vendor, and not divulge information concerning their purchases. This is not to imply that private school business administrators will act any less "honestly" or "efficiently." Rather, a number of control devices *other than laws* act to monitor and restrict their behavior.

Because all public school purchasing activities are in theory open to public scrutiny, all actions must be defensible against challenge. This requires extensive recordkeeping, which in turn increases the costs of public-sector purchasing. The effect of public knowledge of purchasing on prices is mixed:

> [It]. . . sometimes results in governmental buyers paying higher prices for comparable goods than [private sector purchasers]. Vendors know that quotations to

governmental agencies are publicly posted, revealing their offers to all competitors. Consequently, they are less inclined to cut prices to secure governmental orders than [with the private sector]. However, there is prestige, price, and advertising value in having governmental agencies use a firm's products or equipment. This is a silent testimonial, and attractive bids are sometimes submitted to public agencies, with the price reduction charged to advertising. [Westing, Fine, and Zenz 1969, p. 229]

All else equal, public school business administrators are not likely to achieve significantly lower prices. In public buying, unless all bids are rejected, the first bid submitted by each vendor is final. In the private sector it is not unusual to grant vendors a second chance to bid in order to meet lower prices quoted by competitors, which is a practice that may lead to private school business officials paying less for comparable items in comparable quantities.

School business administrators, regardless of the sector in which they work, wish to minimize the sum of competing costs. In purchasing, this is usually formulated in part as balancing the costs of ordering items against the costs associated with carrying those items (including the lost interest that would have been earned by putting money in the bank instead of using it to stock inventories of supplies). Beyond this basic similarity, the school business administrator seeks the best quoted price and must operate within the constraint of available money. Working within an annual appropriation may create incentives for the school business administrator to restrict purchases to items that will be consumed within the fiscal year. Of course, this budget limitation works in both directions. While in some instances it acts as an expenditure cap to constrain buying, in other instances it provides an upper limit that the school business administrator has strong incentives to reach before the end of the fiscal year. In this later instance where "carry-overs" are not allowed, the business administrator seeks to obligate the unexpended funds in purchases for goods that may be consumed primarily in the next fiscal period. This is more prevalent in public than in private schools where carry-over balances are encouraged.

An evaluation of the different advantages of public and private school buyers is difficult, and there are contradictory arguments. However, the results of a past study on one difference, sealed-bid procedures, may reflect generalizable differences between public and private schools. One of the premises underlying the sealed-bid procedure is that the procedure fosters competition, because awards must be made to the lowest qualified bidders. "It is assumed that all bidders will behave competitively in setting their price, since no influence other than price can be brought to bear" (ibid., p. 230). In a comparative study of public and private institutions conducted by Reck, competition was found to vary according to the commodity being purchased. Using data on bids to supply white enamel paint to the federal government, he found that:

[P]rices tended to cluster around the level of the last government purchase. This was especially true during periods of oversupply when sellers were particularly interested in the business and were willing to sell at less than full cost. They seemed to bid below the last transaction price by an amount they believed necessary to underbid competitors, with their variable costs as the floor. Sellers apparently are willing to follow this bid pattern because a low quotation on one procurement followed by a later high quotation does not prejudice their relationship with governmental buyers, as it would with . . . [private organization] buyers who would be more inclined to expect the low price to continue. In periods of short supply they tended to bid higher than the previous award price for white enamel because they did not particularly want the business. *They evidently preferred to supply their . . . [private organization] customers first. . . .* As a consequence, most enamel purchases were made from small paint companies to whom government orders were so important they were willing to compete hard for them. [Westing, Fine, and Zenz 1969, p. 230, emphasis added]

It seems that, while public buying procedures assure free competition, broad exploration of the market, pressure to lower price, and equal opportunity for suppliers to compete, there are certain inherent disadvantages, such as (1) inability to deviate from established procedures when time is important; (2) reluctance of suppliers to furnish technical advice and service, since they cannot be assured of compensation for their efforts; and (3) the inability to favor a deserving supplier who has performed exceptionally well (ibid., p. 229).

Unregulated, Nonrequired Services

More recently, school business administrators have begun pursuing revenues through the more novel (for them) approach of marketing and sale of nontraditional services. The activities of the Montclair (New Jersey) School District are indicative. On an operating budget of about $22 million, administrators have generated about $433,000 in the sale of services (Wilkin 1983, pp. 1,5). Montclair receives about $242,000 of this from tuition payments received from parents living in neighboring school districts. The school business administrator there explains: "The board of education has established several magnet schools covering everything from science and technology to the performing arts, and a lot of parents from nearby communities find these services very attractive for their children." The district also creates and markets a summer arts program and a summer computer-assisted instruction program.

In addition to serving individuals, Montclair also markets services to other school districts and municipal governments. It provides about 3,000 lunches a day to other school districts (generating net revenue of about $65,000 annually) as well as to agencies running Head Start programs. The district generates about 31,000 additional dollars per year selling computer services to nearby school districts. Finally, the district operates what amounts to "a floating garage sale" for worn out and retired equipment. District administrators argue: "If you sell used equipment such as old lawnmowers, typewriters, mimeograph machines, with care, you'd be surprised what you can pick up on stuff that has no trade-in value but which can be useful to people who need it only for light use" (Wilkin 1983, p. 5).

In many of these instances the business administrator can maximize net revenue through decisions about producing, pricing, and marketing services to individuals and to organizations. The examples described in Montclair are just that, examples of a fraction of the service enterprises that school business administrators are undertaking with the aim of producing net revenues. Meno (1983) identified a wide range of enterprise activities including, in addition to those already mentioned, leasing and selling facilities, selling transportation services, charging user fees of various types (such as for driver education or recreational swimming), and selling access to students. *Selling access* means allowing businesses into the school to operate concessions (for example, pictures, rings, vending machines, video games) in return for a fee (Meno 1983, p. 11). Some districts are even embarking on sale-leaseback ventures whereby assets are sold to for-profit entities and are then leased back. (The for-profit organization can capture the benefits of tax credits or depreciation and share those savings with the school. The sale-leaseback mechanism achieves this and is discussed in the next chapter.)

This sampler of school services indicates that education requires or is affiliated with many different services, not just with "education." The services vary in different ways, including whether they are required by law; whether they are necessary in order to operate schools; how much of their cost is borne by clients versus third parties versus the school's general fund; and whether the "client" is a K–12 student residing in the school attendance area, is some other individual, or is an organization. Despite this variety of services, the school business administrator usually evaluates them from two largely financial perspectives: efficiency improvement and revenue enhancement.

The school business administrator seeks primarily greater efficiency (output to cost) in those service areas where direct revenues are not generated through sales. These services—such as personnel, cleaning, purchasing, grounds upkeep—are cost centers, and the trade-offs facing the business manager in those areas are largely among various costs and between costs and service levels. There are incentives not to decrease service levels where this is perceived as a decline in "quality of service." Within the constraint of maintaining or improving service levels, the school business administrator attempts to reduce the sum of competing costs.

In those service areas where revenues from sales (paid either by clients or by third-party sponsors) approach or surpass the costs of service, the school business administrator evaluates the trade-offs among service levels, costs, and revenues. The objective in these instances is to increase net revenues (or reduce net operating losses). The general forms of cost reduction and revenue enhancement are the subjects of the remainder of this chapter.

Minimizing the Sum of Competing Costs

Traditionally school business administrators have been more concerned with cost minimization than with revenue maximization. Provision of any service requires decisions about the technology that will be employed to provide a given service level. The general form of these decisions is portrayed in exhibit 12.2

Exhibit 12.2

Reducing the Sum of Competing Costs for a Given Service Level

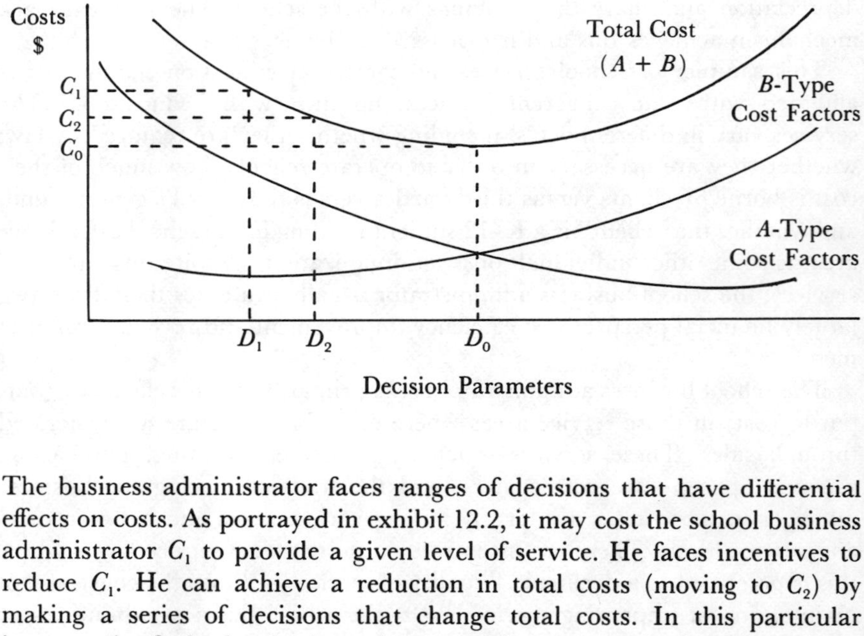

The business administrator faces ranges of decisions that have differential effects on costs. As portrayed in exhibit 12.2, it may cost the school business administrator C_1 to provide a given level of service. He faces incentives to reduce C_1. He can achieve a reduction in total costs (moving to C_2) by making a series of decisions that change total costs. In this particular instance, he finds that by incurring more *B*-type costs he is able to incur sufficiently fewer *A*-type costs to reduce total costs down to C_2. *A*-type costs and *B*-type costs are competing costs, and the school business administrator seeks to minimize their sum. An example of supply management follows.

Exhibit 12.3
Example of Competing Costs in Purchasing

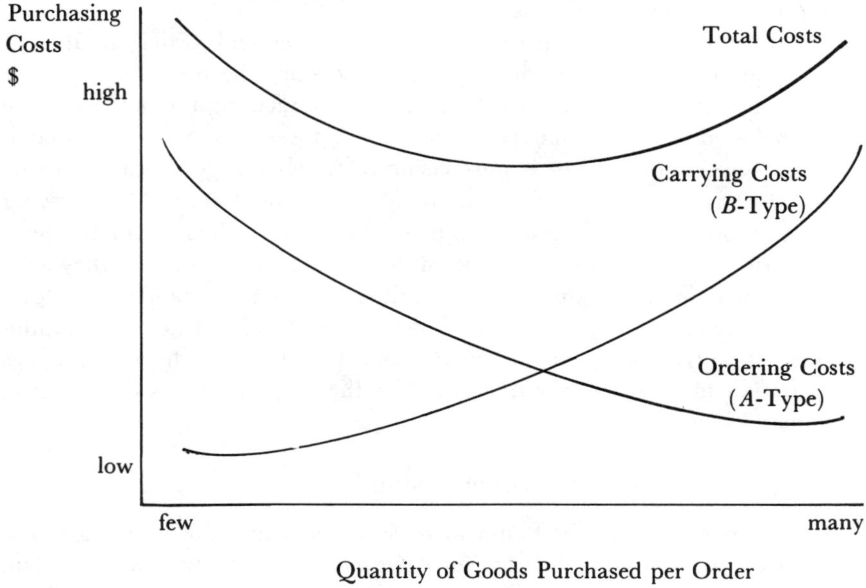

Example of Supply Management

One of the classic problems of supply management is to determine how to minimize the sum of ordering costs and carrying costs. *Ordering costs* are composed of the costs of getting an item into a school district's inventory. These costs are incurred each time an order is placed and are expressed in dollars per order. Ordering costs start with the requisition sent to the purchasing office and include the costs of issuing the purchase order and of following it up; they continue with such steps as receiving the goods and placing them into inventory; they end with the district paying the supplier. Salaries constitute the major portion of ordering costs.

Carrying costs, on the other hand, are costs incurred because the school district owns or maintains inventories of goods (which were at one time ordered). Carrying costs include lost interest on money invested in inventory; obsolescence of unused goods; storage-space costs; storage operation, including recordkeeping, taking physical inventory, and security; and additional costs such as insurance, depreciation, and deterioration. The trade-offs between ordering and carrying costs are shown in exhibit 12.3.

The decision in this instance involves the quantity of a good (or goods) to order each time an order is placed. If large quantities are ordered each time, costs of ordering are lowered because fewer orders have to be placed during the year. (In this instance, ordering costs are *A*-type costs). While ordering costs are reduced by ordering larger quantities, carrying costs increase. (Carrying costs are *B*-type costs here.)

Whether the school business administrator should order greater or smaller quantities per order depends of course where he presently is on the horizontal axis, whether all of the relevant costs affecting the decision have been included in the formulation, and whether they have been estimated reasonably accurately. If he is purchasing relatively few goods each time he orders, he has only a small supply on hand at any one time, and his carrying costs are therefore low. Because he is placing so many orders during the year, his ordering costs are quite high, and his total costs are higher than they need to be. By ordering larger quantities each time he orders, he could reduce total costs of purchasing. The opposite holds true if the school business administrator is currently at the other ("many") end of the horizontal axis. (Estimation of these costs requires use of the same concepts discussed in chapters 8 and 9.)

Other Examples

Competing costs can be found in most services in schools. Total repair costs incurred in a school district, for example, can be portrayed as the sum of two classes of competing costs: the cost of scheduled maintenance and the cost of unscheduled maintenance. The school business administrator may feel that by stepping up scheduled maintenance, the costs of costly breakdowns may be reduced by more than the resulting increases in scheduled maintenance costs. This approach, of course, can be taken too far, to where the increased costs of scheduled maintenance would be greater than the savings resulting from reduction in costs of unscheduled maintenance.

Operating costs of food preparation (labor and food but not capital costs) consist of competing costs. Food can be purchased in its most elemental form (for example, flour, sugar, sides of beef) at low prices, but extensive labor is then required to convert the food into meals. Alternatively, highly processed, pre-prepared foods (such as baked goods, casseroles) require much less labor time but cost more to purchase. Decisions are made that attempt to minimize these competing costs. (We deliberately excluded discussion of capital costs here, because they do not occur regularly like operating costs do and require a different kind of treatment. That is the subject of the next chapter.)

Optimum Versus Satisfactory Solutions

General formulations of revenue maximization and cost minimization suggest that there are or can be *optimal decisions* about how to manage services, that is decisions that will make or save the most money possible, or provide the most service for a given amount of money. Theoretically this is true, but not practically. In most decision problems of any magnitude, the school business administrator will have incomplete information and will have to make assumptions about cause and effect that may not be measurable or even true. The best that he can do is to prepare estimates of costs and benefits, the quality of which he judges sufficient for the decision. He hopes to make a decision that improves on current operations. This suggests an incremental approach to administration, that is, evaluating discrete departures from current status. Such solutions are not optimal within the narrow confines of the problem: there probably exists a better theoretical solution. However, they may be "good enough" decisions from the standpoint of the school business administrator, especially when his preferences for other things, his stock of relevant information, and the cost of acquiring additional information are added to the decision problem. The school business administrator, like any other manager, seeks to maximize his preferences, not to pursue optimal solutions.

Other formulations of problems have been developed that do yield optimal financial solutions. Various forms of mathematical programming have been applied, for example, to menu planning, student transportation, and investment of idle funds. Problems that lend themselves to mathematical programming, however, are very well-defined, limited in scope, and, frankly, constitute a very small fraction of the types of decision problems the school business administrator faces (Hentschke 1979).

Increasing Net Revenues

Most school business administrators view themselves as pursuers of revenues as well as controllers of costs. The public school business administrator pursues "yes" voters in budget and bond elections, aggressively claims reimbursements whenever possible, closely monitors the activities of invested funds, and mobilizes parent groups to visit their state capital to seek more financial aid. The private school administrator pursues tuition dollars by seeking more enrollments at higher prices, pursues donor dollars through annual giving and capital campaigns (private nonprofit), and lobbies for legislation that brings unrestricted aid to private schools. All of these activities are variations on how revenues might be pursued.

Cost, Revenue, and Production-Level Relationships

In planning for service delivery, the school business administrator evaluates relationships between production levels and associated costs and revenues. Production levels assume a given technology and a variable volume of service. Costs associated with that service are assumed to include both fixed-cost components and variable-cost components. (See chapter 9 for a

Exhibit 12.4
Cost–Volume Relationships

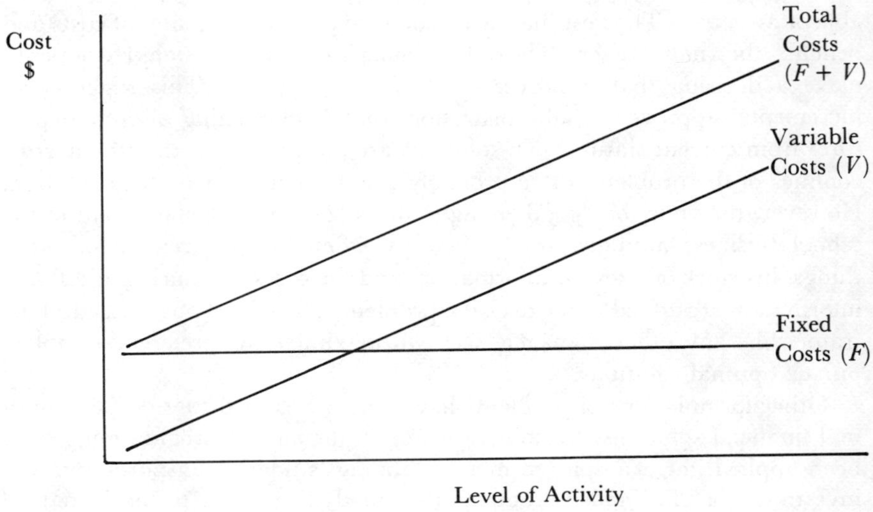

discussion about how these are measured.) Total costs of producing a given level of service are:

fixed costs + (variable cost per unit × level of activity) = total cost

These relationships are portrayed graphically in exhibit 12.4. The level of activity is measured on the horizontal axis, and fixed, variable, and total costs are measured on the vertical (cost) axis. Although variable costs per unit are constant in this exhibit, in most actual instances they will not be. (See Henry and Haynes 1978, p. 312.)

To make reasonably acceptable decisions, the school business administrator seeks to measure changes in the cost of particular items in relation to various kinds of changes in business activity. The purpose of this estimation step is to isolate incremental costs for any given decision. The second step entails measuring relationships between total costs, rates of production of service, and total revenues. When the school organization derives all of its revenue to pay for a service from direct sales of the service to clients, the price charged for the service should pay for all of the variable costs associated with one unit of service plus some of the fixed cost.

Break-even Point

The general relationships among costs, production rates, and revenues are portrayed in a typical break-even chart in exhibit 12.5. Total revenue is

Exhibit 12.5
Break-even Chart

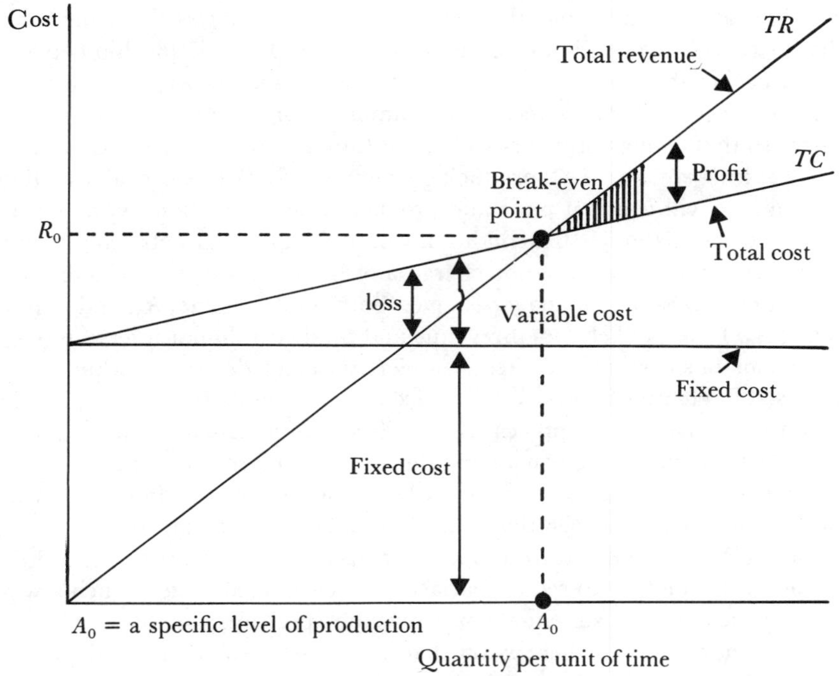

described as a straight line passing through the origin, implying that all unit prices charged are equal regardless of volume sold. (Variations on this simplifying assumption are discussed later in this chapter.) Total costs (*TC*) intersects total revenue (*TR*) at the break-even point.

The purpose of conducting a break-even analysis is only indirectly related to the break-even point. Rather, the school business administrator seeks to evaluate the profit (net revenue) and loss (net expense) that accrue to the school at various levels of output (sales) of the service. As the level of activity (volume) increases, total revenue increases at a greater rate than total costs. At point A_0 in exhibit 12.5, enough units of service have been sold to recover both the fixed and variables costs. (At this point, R_0, total revenue equals total cost.) To the extent that units beyond A_0 can be sold, the enterprises yield net revenue (shaded area).

Increasingly, school business administrators find themselves in the position of viewing some services as having to "pay their own way" or even as having to yield net revenues. Examples of services sold both inside and outside the formal organization include data-processing services, food service, office space, continuing education, even basic schooling itself in the private sectors.

Differences Between Public and Private Schools

This form of the model is the private school paradigm. Implicit in this paradigm are two decisions that are made at more or less the same time: what price to charge and at what level to produce. The relationship between these two variables requires estimates of how consumers will behave given different prices. The private school administrator attempts to set tuition (price) so that enough students will enroll (at least A_0 of them) to cover cost (*TR* is at least equal to *TC*), producing revenue of R_0. Before considering that problem, we will contrast price and production-level decisions with administrative decisions under the condition where the manager gets a lump-sum budget appropriation, may not charge any price, and does not determine production levels. The manager is given both total revenue, R_0, and enrollments, A_0. If, as is likely, total revenue and total cost do not intersect at A_0, the school business official faces a different set of decisions, which were discussed in chapter 9: how to adjust fixed and variable costs so as to make A_0 and R_0 intersect. This process is portrayed graphically in exhibit 12.6. In graph A the manager is given an enrollment of A_0 and revenue of R_0, which is his budget. Under existing technology he would be able to afford to educate only *X* students, far fewer than the A_0 number of students that he must educate. (He is prohibited from operating at a deficit.) What he must do is change his technology to reduce variable and even fixed costs in such a way that adjusted total costs equal total revenue (portrayed in the graph *B*). Although our attention here is on differences between public and private schools, the underlying difference is between selling units of service at a price and receiving a lump sum appropriation to serve a given number of clients (Hentschke 1985).

This situation is much more analogous to that faced by many public school business administrators with regard to their overall school district budgets. Their objective is to balance revenues and expenditures, but they have very little control over either the level of activity (enrollments) or the total revenue. As a result, the major decisions are influenced by possible changes in technology, which will result in changes in fixed and variable costs. (This is the problem of fiscal strain discussed at length in chapter 5.)

Relationships Between Demand and Price

While preparing a break-even analysis, the responses of consumers to prices charged for services must be estimated. In order to judge consumer behavior, the school business administrator is ultimately forced to make certain assumptions about consumer demand for services. Although in our previous discussion of break-even analysis, we decided that at least A_0 number of consumers would be willing to purchase the service at the unit price *U* (such that $U \times A_0$ revenues would accrue), this assumption might not be true in real life.

Exhibit 12.6
Public-Sector Response to Break-Even Problem

A. Given current technology, projected total cost is greater than total revenue at expected level of enrollment A_0.

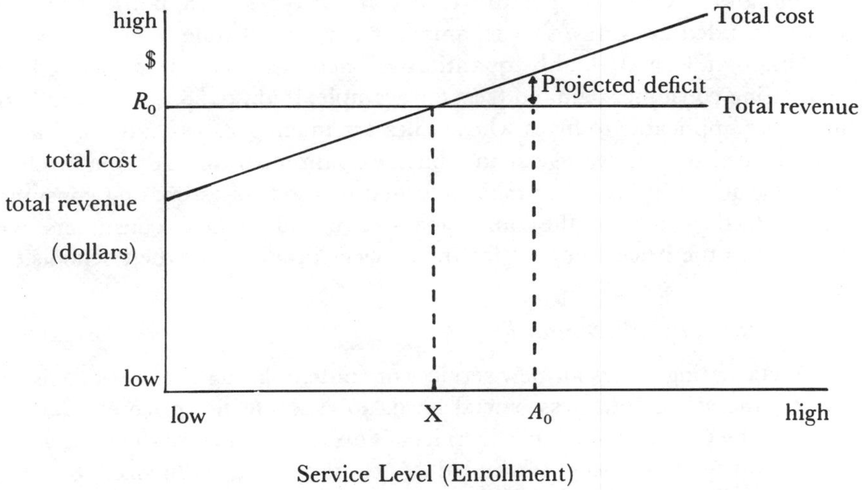

B. Technology is changed so that projected total cost is reduced to match total revenue at expected level of enrollment A_0.

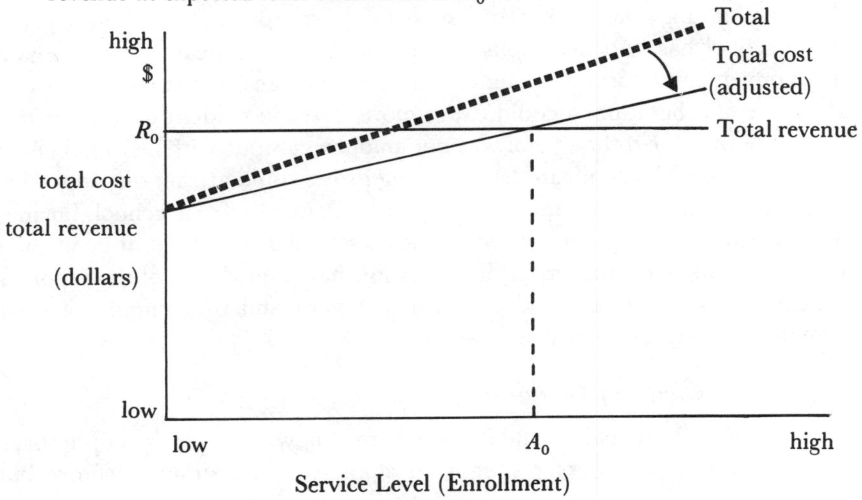

The school business administrator must consider several variables before making assumptions about consumer demand for services. To the individual consumer, demand usually implies a single quantity. To the school business administrator, on the other hand, demand is a specific relationship of various quantities per period to such variables as price, consumer incomes, existence of substitutes for services, prices of substitutes, expected future conditions, season, and availability of credit (Henry and Haynes 1978, p. 57). (Quantities demanded are rates, that is, amounts per unit of time.)

Although formal, highly quantitative methods have been derived for estimating consumer demand (see, for example, ibid., p. 58.), those methods are more applicable to firms whose sales are much greater than the "sales" experienced by the average school business administrator. Although school business administrators use more informal methods of estimating consumer demand, they pursue the same goal—to calculate how consumers will respond to the prices they set for the services provided by their schools.

Price Elasticity of Demand

When setting prices for new services or contemplating changes in existing prices, the school business official needs to estimate the price elasticity of demand by consumers for those services. This is a measure of the variation in the quantity of services demanded by consumers as influenced by price changes (assuming all other variables are constant). *Price elasticity is the ratio of percentage change in quantity of services demanded to percentage change in price.* Demand tends to be more elastic if the services offered by the school business administrator (1) compete with a greater number of close substitutes at similar prices; (2) make up greater percentages of the total expenditures of the consumers; and (3) are regarded more as luxuries than as necessities. The demand for school lunch in a school, for example, might be more elastic if the school has "open-campus" rules and is located near fast-food chains and convenience stores. Greater elasticity here means that small increases in the price of school lunch could cause more losses in student customers than would be the case if the school was not an open campus with fast-food chains nearby. (It could also mean that lowering prices could attract disproportionately more students to the lunch room). Demand for a school business administrator's computer services by other school districts might be inelastic if other sellers of computer services lack intimate knowledge of the reporting requirements of the state education department and thus could not easily provide comparable services.

Income Elasticity of Demand

Income elasticity of demand is a measure of how the quantity of purchases demanded by consumers responds to changes in consumer income. Purchases of some services change according to increases or decreases in the income of consumers. Continuing education courses in "hobby" subjects are an example. However, demand for some services may not change as dramatically with changes in income. In fact, there may be an inverse relationship between demand for a service and change in income. Continuing education courses in computer programming may be an example, because if a consumer's income decreases, the consumer might want to learn marketable skills in order to find a high-income job.

Analysis of demand requires simultaneous consideration of price, consumer income, and availability of substitutes as independent variables affecting the quantity of services purchased by consumers. This may not, however, be sufficient. People make choices for a great variety of reasons, some of which the consumer can articulate (such as because of a change in price), may not wish to state, or may not even realize. The purchaser of a fire-engine red Ferarri may not mention (but thinks to himself) that he is purchasing social status. He may also subconsciously be seeking to purchase manliness. The business administrator in school district A may have reasons that have no correspondence to price or quality for purchasing computer services from the business administrator in school district B. He may, for example, want to show goodwill to the administrator in school district B in order to get him to buy something from district A in return.

Pricing Strategies

Even after school business administrators have evaluated break-even functions and demand elasticities, they must ultimately develop a pricing strategy that they believe will most effectively help them maximize their preferences. If, for example, an administrator's objective is to maximize total revenue for a service before the eventual saturation of the market, the service may be offered initially for a relatively high price, then gradually be reduced to tap a wider and wider market. This practice is sometimes called *skimming*. Skimming is often used when introducing a product or service that is either unique or very differentiated. Schools that first offered afternoon day-care programs (from after school until dinner time) to accommodate latch-key children were able to charge higher prices because there were few desirable substitutes for some parents. (Although more and more school business administrators are entering this market, prices have not fallen appreciably because demand has also been increasing.)

An alternative strategy employed in pricing new services is *penetration pricing*, that is, where the price at introduction is lower than the price that will be maintained after the service is established in the market or after consumers have "bought in" to the service. This tactic is employed in private schools and in day-care programs where younger clients are charged less than older clients are, even though the costs of serving younger clients may be higher. The logic behind this strategy is that once you enroll the child in the entry-level grade, his or her family will have to incur some psychic and monetary costs if it enrolls the child in a different school or day-care center in following years.

In addition to (or instead of) maximizing total revenue or share of the market, the school business administrator may simply prefer to recover the full costs incurred in producing the service. The implication of *full-cost pricing* is that all categories of customers are treated alike regardless of market conditions. There are several competing reasons for the school business administrator to adopt (or reject) a full-cost pricing strategy. Full-cost pricing can be used when the school business administrator simply has no way of knowing (or even guessing) the demand for services at various prices. Also, an administrator may choose full-cost pricing due to a strong desire for "fairness" or "justice" in pricing. In addition, by allocating overhead (and any profit markup), full-cost pricing helps ensure that the school's scarce resources are not given to services that fail to carry their share of the overhead expenses and produce their share of profit. (This of course applies only to services that are supposed to achieve those objectives.)

Full-cost pricing is sometimes erroneously equated with ensuring a profitable venture by making sure the overhead, or fixed, costs as well as the variable costs of production are paid. This is not always the case, if only because there may not be sufficient demand to break even at full-cost prices.

Another alternative to pricing based on assumptions about demand is imitative or *going-rate* pricing. In these instances the school business administrator simply imitates the prices of substitutes or of comparable services offered in other schools. This is perhaps the easiest means of pricing, and it may work reasonably well under certain circumstances.

Uniform pricing using nondemand-based information is often a reasonable approach to pricing when third parties reimburse a relatively large proportion of costs or when the total cost and revenue associated with the service is small, and when the cost to the consumers is a very small proportion of their disposable income. When the opposite conditions exist, the school business administrator will have stronger incentives to implement differential pricing strategies. We have already discussed examples of differential strategies that change over time (skimming and penetration pricing). Compelling arguments can also be made in some instances to differentiate prices charged to different customers at the same time. This tactic is called price discrimination, and a brief discussion of its major tenets follows.

Price Discrimination

With skimming and penetration pricing, the price charged to the consumer varies over time, but usually all consumers pay the same price at a given point in time. Price discrimination, on the other hand, is the practice of charging different categories of consumers differential prices for the same service. Administrators who claim a philosophy of "fairness" and "equity" sometimes have difficulty defending price discrimination, although there are times when they argue for it on the grounds of equity. Price discrimination in some form is a widespread practice in schools, especially in private schools, where sales (tuition) constitutes a larger part of the total revenue.

Financial Need as a Criterion for Discrimination Pricing. Most often, administrators price discriminate on the basis of consumer need or ability to pay. Examples range from school lunch all the way up to full-tuition scholarships and living stipends at private boarding schools. The preference for reducing the price of a good or service in order to aid those in "need" is a strong one for many administrators. (As school business administrators in public schools increasingly contemplate charging student fees as one of their many attempts to maintain services, the issue of equity will become manifest.) The impetus behind price discrimination on the basis of financial need is usually motivated by a preference for affording opportunities to a certain category of students (in this case, financially poor students) who would otherwise not purchase the service.

Similar motivation may exist to reduce the cost of services to other categories of students, such as the academically or athletically talented, racial minorities, or students with siblings in the school. In any of these instances, the business administrator's preference for revenue maximization may be subordinated to other preferences. However, price discrimination is widely used to maximize sales revenue and can be used to pursue jointly both profit-increasing and nonfinancial objectives.

Maximization as a Criterion for Discrimination Pricing Revenue. School business administrators should be familiar with the revenue-maximizing arguments for price discrimination so that they can more effectively pursue that preference in jointly determined pricing decisions, especially the big dollar decisions such as tuition levels (see Prakash 1979, pp. 298–327). Discriminatory pricing enhances revenues by capturing elements of consumer surplus. In order to understand the term *consumer surplus* and how it is "captured" by discriminatory pricing, we return briefly to the concept of consumer demand.

As we mentioned earlier, the "trick" in price setting is developing reasonable estimates about the willingness of individuals to buy the service at varying prices, that is, determining the aggregate demand for the service. Aggregate demand is the sum of individual demand schedules, and an individual's consumer demand schedule is made up of the quantity of service that the consumer would purchase at each price in a range of prices. The hypothetical demand curves of six consumers are shown in exhibit 12.7.

Exhibit 12.7

Hypothetical Individual Demand Curves for a School Service

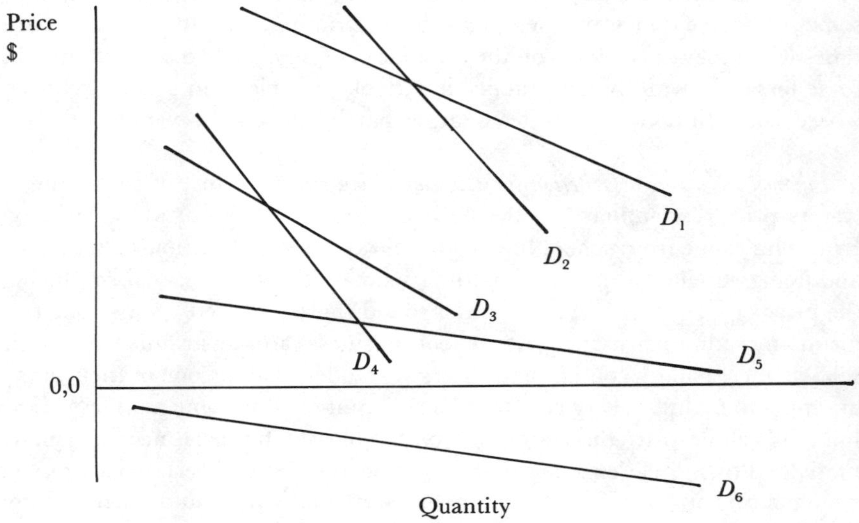

D_2 describes a consumer with relatively high and inelastic demand for the service; in other words D_2 wants more than most consumers and as the price of a service increases, the consumer purchases only a little less. (The more of these types, the better.) D_1 reflects a consumer who wants more than most consumers and is a little more sensitive to changes in price than D_2. D_4 and D_3 may be the "poor cousins" of D_2 and D_1 respectively. They will purchase less at any price and are not willing to pay high prices for a given quantity of service. (Actually, being poor is only one of many reasons for D_3 and D_4 to demand less and at lower prices.) D_5's demand is very elastic and is located in the low range of prices. Slight increases in price will cause his demand to fall off drastically. (How would you describe D_6? Is it a theoretically reasonable example?)

An aggregate demand schedule is merely a summation of the individual demand schedules of many consumers (see exhibit 12.8). If the school business administrator with this aggregate demand schedule offered services at the unit price of P_1, the administrator could expect to sell Q_1 units of that service and derive revenue equal to $P_1 \times Q_1$. Of course, more units of service could be sold by selling them at a lower price and fewer units could be sold by selling them at a higher price. (How either of these changes affect total revenues would depend on the slope of the demand schedule, that is, the elasticity of demand.)

The school business administrator has done three things by setting the price for a service at P_1 (or any other point) for all sales. First, revenue has

Exhibit 12.8

Aggregate Demand Schedule and Response of the Market to Price P_1

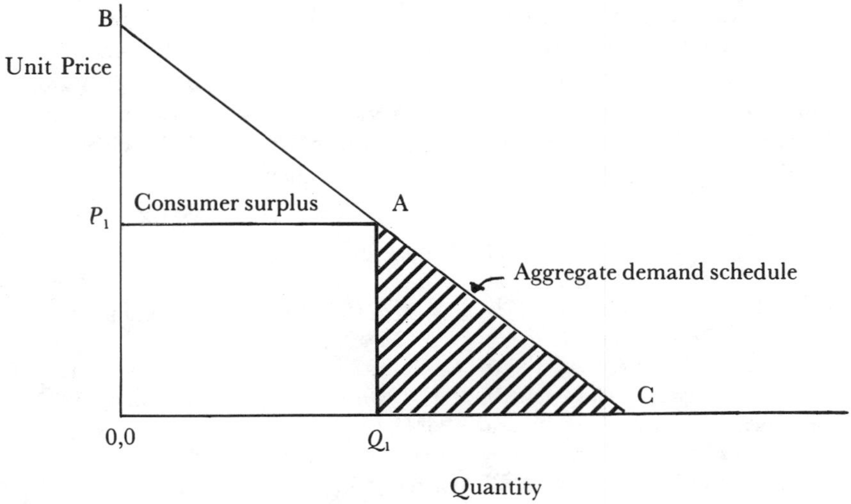

been generated equal to $P_1 \times Q_1$ or P_1–A–Q_1–O. Second, sales to those consumers (shaded area) who did not purchase at P_1 but who would have purchased at prices less than P_1 have been lost. Third, the revenue (equal to B–P_1–A) from consumers who would have been willing to pay more than P_1 for the service has been lost. This area, B–P_1–A, is defined as consumer surplus. Although controversy still surrounds the conceptual meaning of aggregate consumers' surplus, we know logically that there are some consumers who would have paid more than P_1 for the service and also that if the price were less than P_1, more people would have purchased the service.

When price setting, school business administrators usually attempt to capture the consumer surplus by setting the base price as high as possible and then providing discounts or scholarships to categories of clients whose patronage in the numbers desired may not be otherwise secured. The willingness to consider price discrimination may better enable school business administrators to pursue their preferences for clients. In most instances, however, attempts are made to discourage the impression that clients paying full price are somehow subsidizing the others.

Conclusion

In certain respects, school services are apparently similar across types of schools. For example, students need to be fed, faculty and staff need to be hired, and the lawn needs to be mowed regardless of the sector of the school.

Looking more closely, however, we see that schools in one sector provide services generally not offered by schools in another sector (such as student transportation.) Furthermore, sector location may determine whether a service is rationed by price or given away, and if it is sold, the sector may determine whether the service contributes net revenues to the school.

Perhaps the feature that most fundamentally distinguishes provision of support services among schools is the degree to which the school business administrator has to generate revenues through sales of services versus providing the service at little or no cost to the clients.

References

Aljian, George W. *Purchasing Handbook*. 3rd ed. New York: McGraw-Hill, 1973.

Comptroller General of the United States." *Impact of Federal Commodity Donations on the School Lunch Program*. Report to the Committee on Education and Labor, House of Representatives. Washington, D.C.: U.S. Government Printing Office, 1977.

Department of Food Services, Chicago Public Schools. "Report: Food Services in the Chicago Public Schools." Chicago: Board of Education, 1978.

Henry, William R., and Haynes, W. Warren. *Managerial Economics*. Dallas: Business Publications, 1978. Especially chapter 11, "Price and Nonprice Competition," and chapter 12, "Selected Topics in Pricing."

Hentschke, Guilbert C. "Implementing Management Science in a Relatively Undeveloped Field: The Case of Education." In *The Implementation of Management Science*, edited by Robert Doktor, Randall Schultz, and Dennis Slevin, pp. 205–218. Amsterdam: North Holland Publishing Co., 1979.

Hentschke, Guilbert C. "Emerging Roles of School District Administration: Implications for Planning, Budgeting, and Management." *Public Budgeting and Finance* 5: 1 (Spring 1985): 15–26.

McKeown, Mary P. "An Efficiency-Oriented Funding Formula for Pupil Transportation." *Journal of Education Finance* 4 (Fall 1978): 225–233.

Meno, Lionel R. "An Examination of the Types of Nontraditional Financing Methods and Their Present and Potential Impact on Public School Districts." Ed.D Dissertation, University of Rochester, 1983.

Prakash, Prem. "Cost-Benefit Approach to Capital Expenditure." In *Management Principles for Nonprofit Agencies and Organizations*, edited by Gerald Zaltman, pp. 291–339. New York: AMACOM, 1979.

Sasser, W. Earl; Olsen, R. Paul; and Wyckoff, D. Darryl. *Management of Service Operations*. Boston: Allyn and Bacon, 1978.

Westing, J. H.; Fine, I. V.; and Zenz, Gary Joseph. *Purchasing Management*. New York: John Wiley and Sons, 1969. Especially chapter 12, "Purchasing for Public and Nonprofit Agencies."

Wilkin, William. "Montclair, New Jersey: Educational Entrepreneur Par Excellence." *School Cost Management* 1: 9 (February 28, 1983): 1, 5.

Supplementary Reading

Fitzsimmons, James A., and Sullivan, Robert. *Service Operations Management.* New York: McGraw-Hill, 1982.

Ginzberg, Eli, and Vojta, George. "The Service Sector of the U.S. Economy." *Scientific American* 244: 3 (March 1981): 48–55.

Tersine, Richard J. *Production/Operations Management: Concepts, Structure, and Analysis.* New York: North Holland Publishing Co., 1980. Especially chapter 19, "Inventory Control Models."

13

Capital Goods Management

Overview

Because the benefits of capital goods extend over a period of years, *time* must be an integral part of models used to evaluate the costs and benefits of capital goods. Also, capital goods vary greatly in cost, replacement requirements (useful life), and how frequently the design changes. These three variables determine how much attention is given to a particular capital goods decision. Capital goods items that highlight the importance of these variables particularly well are facilities, buses, and computers. The two major decisions about capital goods involve choosing among alternative investments and determining when to replace a capital good. Each decision is discussed at length. Differences in capital goods management between public and private schools are discussed along with the impact of financing methods on capital goods decisions.

• • •

Introduction

Capital goods are physical assets that provide benefits for at least one year (Tersine 1980, p. 86). They include facilities, machinery, vehicles, and equipment but not supplies or other items consumed relatively rapidly. Despite their longer useful life, it is necessary to continually spend resources for these items because physical assets such as buildings are continually wearing out and need to be replaced; and new products and more efficient methods may render an asset obsolete even though it continues to function as designed (this is called technological obsolescence). Also, the long-run capacity of the school or school district may change, which might require different configurations of physical assets. Planning and managing changes in the physical assets of schools, like planning and managing changes in services, is complex, and methods to simplify this complexity are required in order to limit administrators' choices to a manageable number.

Because of the multiyear life of capital goods, school managers are more constrained when planning and managing them than they are when planning or managing services. Radical changes in the configuration of capital goods are, in the short run, much more costly than changes in services are. *Incremental analysis* is an important technique used more for managing capital goods than for managing services.

Incremental Analysis

The goals of school business administrators in managing assets are very much like those in managing services: to reduce costs while holding quality constant, to increase revenue while holding costs constant, and to increase quality while holding costs constant. Yet decisions about capital goods management are, even more than those decisions involving services, incremental. "Incremental" here means building on past decisions about capital goods and making sure that future decisions are compatible with and do not radically depart from current practices.

Incremental analysis in this context has three characteristics. First, differences among the alternatives being considered are compared. When cost or benefit elements are common to each alternative, they are not relevant and can be excluded from the analysis. Second, in incremental analysis, benefits and costs vary as a function of the alternatives considered. This further suggests that incremental analysis is situational, and that each situation is unique. Third, a cost may be fixed or variable, but the analysis can include benefits as well as costs in its comparisons of alternatives. However, many of the analyses prepared by the school business administrator will devote more explicit attention to cost, not benefit, comparisons (Tersine 1980, p. 82).

Explicit Consideration of Time

The major difference between managing services and managing assets is in the consideration of *time*. Services are purchased, provided, and consumed within the same, relatively short, period of time. Teacher services, for example, are usually bought, provided, and consumed within a year. (Teacher *X* can be hired again next year to do the same or a different job, but that is a separate transaction.) Capital goods, on the other hand, are usually not purchased, made available, and consumed during identical periods of time. A school building, for example, may be purchased over a twenty-year period, after three years it may be made available for use, and it may be used (consumed) during the subsequent fifty years. Debt obligations (both principal and interest) can bind the school business administrator for decades and can constitute a sizable fraction of a school's liabilities. Services can be reevaluated and changed annually to accommodate fluctuations in financial and other circumstances; but because assets require comparatively large financial commitment, they are much less easily modified from year to year.

Because the periods of purchase, availability, and consumption of capital goods are not identical and extend usually far beyond a single year, the tools for evaluating trade-offs, which we discussed in the previous chapter, require modification. When making incremental decisions about capital goods, the school business administrator must evaluate the costs and benefits of alternative *investments* of money for various opportunities; these costs and benefits have differing degrees of utility. The issue differs from our discussion of budgeting in chapter 6 primarily on the basis of the added complexities associated with the multiperiod nature of capital investment decisions. Each of the possible uses of capital funds has incremental effects on the school's revenues, costs, and services over a series of periods in the future. In attempting to maximize their own and their schools' utility, school business administrators generate investment alternatives, estimate the benefits and costs of those alternatives, and help select among alternatives.

Time affects the types of costs associated with capital goods, and hence, the selection of alternatives. Whereas *purchase price* accounts for much of the costs of services, it reflects only a fraction of the relevant costs associated with capital goods. *Operating costs* over the life of the capital good as well as the *salvage value* after its useful life also affect the total cost of a capital good. Because many of the larger capital items are so expensive, their purchase price usually must be financed, and the *cost of money* becomes part of the overall cost of the acquisition. All of these cost elements require consideration for each of the alternative investments being evaluated.

Formal Analysis of Capital Goods Decisions

Capital investment decisions usually require relatively formal analysis and merit the attention of top-level school district decision makers for several reasons. One reason is that a large amount of money is being committed. Also, the money is being committed for a long period of time, and usually decisions to purchase are not reversible without great expense. Risks and uncertainty in this area increase as the length of time the good will be used increases, and an ill-conceived decision could fundamentally harm the school. Consider, for example, the technical college in the Northeast that acquired a financially troubled liberal arts college about fifty miles away. After several years of operating both campuses and continuing to incur large operating deficits each year on the liberal arts campus, the technical college had to sell off the liberal arts campus at a substantial loss. The acquisition was in effect siphoning off the financial margin of success that the technical college had tried so hard to achieve.

In the next part of the chapter we discuss briefly the scope and major trends in the use of capital goods in schools and the types of decisions associated with three particular capital goods. By focusing on facilities, buses, and computers we highlight the ways in which decision making and analysis vary with the type of good. We next consider methods—life-cycle costing and discounting—that incorporate considerations of time in making decisions about capital goods. In the subsequent two sections we apply these methods to two categories of decisions about capital goods: (1) deciding among *alternative investments* in capital goods and (2) deciding among *alternative points in time* to replace a capital item. Following this we discuss briefly how other preferences interact with strictly monetary ones and that most decisions are not based strictly on financial criteria. Finally, we close with a discussion of the differences in capital goods management between public and private schools.

Characteristics of the Major Assets Used in Schooling

Although schooling is technically a service industry, it requires substantial amounts of physical assets (capital goods) to facilitate service delivery. School buildings, buses, and furniture are only the most manifest of these physical assets; there are a multitude of smaller, more specific capital goods and associated decisions about their acquisition, upgrading, and disposal of the larger items. Before discussing the evaluation models that school business administrators apply when making decisions about physical assets, it would be helpful to briefly mention trends in the use of three major capital expenditure items in schools—buildings, buses, and computing equipment. Each of these capital goods illustrates different characteristics of the issues involved in capital goods management: facilities, because of their high cost and long duration; buses, because considerations about their replacement recur often; and computers, because of their rapidly changing technology.

School Facilities

The physical accommodations within which school programs operate have changed dramatically over the last forty years. In 1940 there were over 223,000 elementary and secondary schools. By 1977 the number had fallen to less than half that to about 106,000. By far the largest deline over this period was in the number of one-teacher elementary schools, which declined from about 108,000 in 1940 to about 1,000 today. Nonpublic elementary and secondary schools constituted about 15,000 of the schools in 1940, while there are about 17,000 today (U.S. Bureau of Census 1979, p. 134).

The two major costs associated with acquiring assets, especially "large ticket" items like buildings, are the expenditures for the assets themselves and the costs associated with financing those expenditures. Expenditures for construction of new facilities are the single largest capital outlay item. The combined costs of all new school facilities in the United States are large enough to affect national economic activity. The long-run trends in school construction have greatly affected the national economy in general and the construction industry in particular. Each $1 billion spent on school construction during 1977 would have generated the equivalent of about 36,700 year-long jobs throughout the economy (Olsen 1979, p. 39). In turn, schools have been influenced by changes in construction technology as well as by changes in pedagogical theory, as reflected in the programming of educational services. For example, expenditure patterns for building construction are shifting from materials, built-in equipment, and supplies to on-site wages and salaries, contractor's equipment, overhead, and profit.

Increased use of capital equipment reflects the increasing economies of scale possible as the average size of newly constructed schools has increased over time. The average school built in 1959 had twenty-one classrooms, but thirteen years later the average had jumped to over thirty-one (ibid., p. 41). The increasing size of schools has made evident several of the conflicting preferences of the school administrator. Larger schools are preferred because savings result in other areas. For example, if fewer schools are built because each is larger, then fewer principals would need to be hired. Also, larger buildings can accommodate specialized programs that might not otherwise be affordable. Administrators' preferences for smaller schools might result from the sense of "belonging" that students in these schools enjoy as well as from the greater administrative control within the school. Despite the trade-offs, more administrators seem to prefer larger schools over smaller ones.

The lack of a uniform, directly correlated relationship between assets and services is illustrated by comparing changes in operating budgets with changes in expenditures for construction over time. New school construction declined during the 1970s along with enrollment. Since 84 percent of capital outlay was for land and buildings in 1973–74, it is not surprising that annual capital outlay decreased by more than 50 percent in real terms over the decade—from $13.0 billion in 1970–71 to $6.1 billion in 1980–81 (Frankel 1978, p. 95), while real spending for services did not decline.

Although school buildings will continue to be built because old buildings must be replaced, students migrate, and overcrowded and unsatisfactory classrooms are being reduced, it is expected that capital outlay will continue to decline through the late 1980s. After the 1980s, however, increasing enrollments will force increased outlays for facilities (ibid., p. 95).

As mentioned earlier, a major cost associated with capital outlays is the interest charged to finance long-term debts. Interest charges, however, distort relationships between cost and usage. For example, expenditures for interest in real terms by public school systems decreased from $2.8 billion in 1970–71 to $2.1 billion 1980–81. However, interest did not decline as rapidly as capital outlay for construction did because interest expenditures continue twenty years or more after the actual construction. As a result, debt incurred during the growth years of the 1950s and early 1960s kept interest expenditures high during the 1970s, when construction declined significantly.

Much of the existing and future demand for spending on facilities is, accordingly, associated with rehabilitation of existing facilities, which includes repair of structural and systems deficiencies as well as accommodation to changes in educational practices. Many of the buildings constructed during the population increase of the 1950s and 1960s were designed to keep purchase costs as low as possible, but they are requiring increasing maintenance and operation costs today. Consider, for example, the observations of a leading architect of school facilities:

> [I]t was very inexpensive to spray asbestos on steel for fire-proofing. I've seen gymnasiums with exposed steel structures that had been sprayed with asbestos which had been hit so many times with a basketball that whole chunks of asbestos are coming down, (requiring extensive maintenance and repair costs). . . .
>
> [In economizing efforts] pipes were buried under concrete slabs. . . after thirty years pipes fill up and you have to replace them. In order to do that, you have to tear up the floor or put in a whole new plumbing system someplace else. [Leggett 1983, p. 13.]

Program changes will also require alteration of school facilities. Some apparent trends include pulling the ninth grade, and in some cases the eighth grade, into the high school, moving the sixth and seventh grades into the middle schools, and adding specialized spaces in all schools. If there is increased cooperation between schools and businesses, it may mean that space for vocational and occupational education may not be as necessary in the high school (Green 1983, p. 10). Of all capital goods, facilities are the most fundamentally important in that they consume most of the capital goods dollars and most severely constrain instructional service options.

School Buses

After expenditures for buildings and grounds, the largest capital investment for most school districts is buses. Nationally about 236,000 school buses are used to transport students over 2.6 billion miles. The dollar value of these assets is in the billions. In New York State, for example, there are about 14,000 school buses, both privately and publicly owned, representing a capital investment of over a quarter billion dollars (Kelly 1979, p. 1). The major historical developments in this field were discussed in the previous chapter in conjunction with student transportation services. As described there, demand for buses continues to increase despite enrollment delines. The short life cycle of buses (compared to buildings) of seven to twelve years makes them a recurring annual cost item in most school districts. Methods for evaluating bus replacement are examined in more detail later in this chapter.

Computing Equipment

Increasingly schools are investing heavily in computing equipment. Precise data on the number of computers in schools are difficult to find, in part because they are changing rapidly. Within the last few decades, operational computers have progressed from being virtually nonexistent to becoming a basic extension of human capability (not unlike the telephone). In 1944 the first digital computer was put into use at Harvard University. Six years later there were only twelve computers in the United States, but by 1960 there were six thousand (Hentschke 1982). By 1980 there were fifty thousand general-purpose computers in the United States. Today the number of computers in schools, both general-purpose mainframe computers and microcomputers, is increasing daily.

The characteristic of computers that makes them particularly challenging capital goods items to purchase or upgrade is the rapid and unpredictable rate of increase in the productivity of computing equipment. The increasingly popular microcomputer of today has a larger computing capacity than the first computer built just a few decades ago and is twenty times faster and thousands of times more reliable. These quantum improvements in productivity show little sign of dramatically slowing down. Compared to these changes, changes in the technology of school buildings and school buses over the same period are virtually nonexistent. The cost of comparable computer operations is falling dramatically and is likely to fall further. This is not true with buildings and buses.

Capital goods with rapidly changing technologies, such as computers, require disproportionately *conservative* estimates of useful life and salvage value. All other things being equal, it is not likely that a given computer acquisition will be as cost-effective in the future as it is today, because it will rapidly become more cost-effective to upgrade relatively quickly.

Incorporating the Effects of Time when Deciding Among Alternative Investments

When deciding whether to purchase new capital goods—be they buildings, buses, or computers—school business administrators cannot consider only low bids for the purchase price of the item. Capital goods usually include two types of costs (aside from the cost of money): (1) costs associated with the *value* of the item, such as purchase price and salvage value, and (2) costs associated with the operation of the item, such as labor, fuel, and repair costs. Brand *A* of a particular type of capital good may cost little to purchase, cost a lot to operate, and not last long. Brand *B*, while costing more initially, may cost less to operate and last longer. Consider, for example, the choice between gasoline-powered and diesel-powered school buses. Diesel buses are about $4,000 to $5,000 more expensive, use fuel more efficiently, require slightly less-expensive fuel, and last about three years longer than buses that use regular gasoline (*Education U.S.A.* 1981, p. 147). Which type of bus is the most cost-effective purchase? The technique of life-cycle costing helps the school business administrator answer this question.

Life-Cycle Costing

Life-cycle costs include all costs associated with the system or equipment, including costs for research and development, investment, operation and maintenance, and phaseout. Costs are estimated by year for major equipment and associated support goods. These estimates are derived from a combination of accounting records (historical data), bid prices, and predictions and are arrayed as a *cost stream*, or *cost profile*, such as the one for capital good *X* in exhibit 13.1.

The utility of life-cycle costing lies in incorporating the *stream of costs* that the capital good generates, whether the costs be associated with purchase price, financing cost, or operating or repair costs. Despite its usefulness, life-cycle costing does not *by itself* help the school business administrator to directly compare costs of alternative capital expenditures. Cost streams of different configurations are, by themselves, difficult to compare. For example, consider the two cost streams in exhibit 13.2. Which represents the desirable economic choice? It is hard to tell by inspection even if the total dollars spent on each were summed.

Estimates of life-cycle costs must be transformed into forms that make different cost streams directly comparable. This is particularly the case in the evaluation of alternative proposals where comparisons must be made on an equivalent basis. The process of transforming cost streams entails discounting them to a measure of their value *at present*.

Exhibit 13.1
Sample Cost Stream

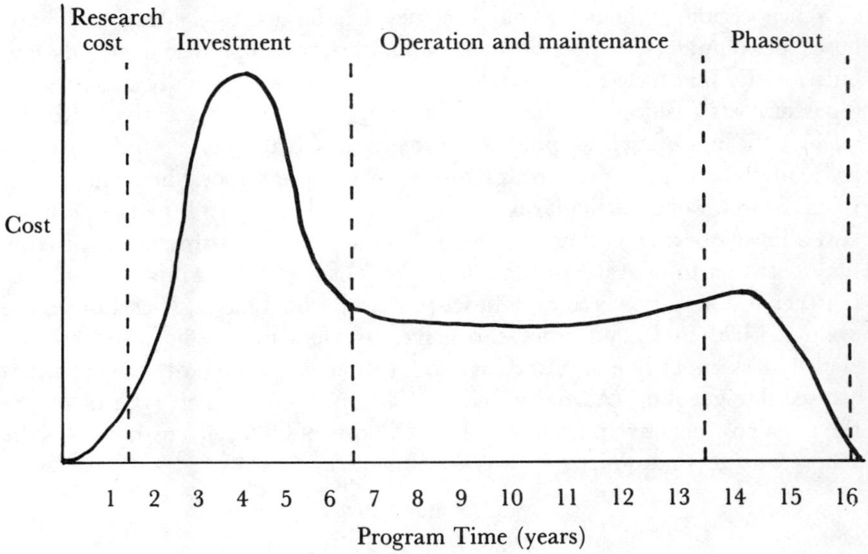

Exhibit 13.2
Comparing Alternative Investments in Capital Goods

	Good *A*	Good *B*
Purchase Price	$10,000	$10,000
Useful Life	5 years	5 years
Projected Savings		
in year: 1	$1,000	$6,000
2	$2,000	$2,000
3	$3,000	$2,000
4	$4,000	$2,000
5	$6,000	$2,000

Discounting to Present Value

Discounting in this context is the application of a discount (or interest) rate, chosen by the school business administrator, to measure the difference between dollars spent (or received) in the present and dollars spent (or received) at various points in the future. Discounting allows for the evaluation of various alternative configurations of cost streams as if they occur at one point in time (the present) rather than as if they were spaced over the life of the items.

The fundamental assumption when considering present value is that receiving $100 today is preferable to the absolute assurance of receiving $100 one year from now. When making payments, the reverse holds true: in most instances we would rather pay a $100 debt a year from now than today. What must be determined is how much $100 will equal a year from now ($105? $110? $120? if we are paying the money; $85? $90? $95? if we are receiving the money). The difference, that is, the degree to which future dollars are more or less valuable than present dollars, is attributable to the administrator's determination of the discount rate. (We focus here on the paying, or expenditure, issue.)

The discount rate is a function of a number of factors; one factor is the demand for and supply of loanable money, which is reflected in interest rates. It involves, in addition, the manager's perception of the degree of certainty that future payments will be made (risk), as well as assumptions about the alternative uses to which the money could be put if it were presently available (opportunity costs). (See Barish 1962, pp. 217–236 for a discussion of different factors considered in the cost of money.) While it is difficult to objectively evaluate the contribution that each of these factors plays in determining a manager's discount rate, the point remains that, all else being equal, future expenditures are preferable to current expenditures of equal amount, and current income is preferable to assurances of future income of equal amount. Many managers use the current cost (interest rate) of short-term borrowing as their discount rate.

Discounting is applied to life-cycle costs to "bring back" those figures to a single value at present. For purposes of illustration, assume that costs are determined for a capital good with a life cycle of five years. Although costs actually occur either continually or at discrete points throughout each year, they are usually treated (discounted) either at the beginning or at the end of the applicable time period. In this example, the costs are determined at the end of each year throughout the life cycle (see exhibit 13.3). The object of discounting is to translate these costs into "today's" value, since this is the point in time when the decision is made to invest in the good. Exhibit 13.3 is a simple illustration of a good's life cycle each year for five years, which must be conveyed in terms of its present value.

For the first year, costs are estimated for each applicable item and are represented at point A. The question is, "What is the value of that total cost at point A in terms of the decision point?" (The *decision point* is when a decision is made whether to purchase a capital good.) This can be determined from the following single-payment present-value expression:

Exhibit 13.3
Capital Good Life-Cycle Costs

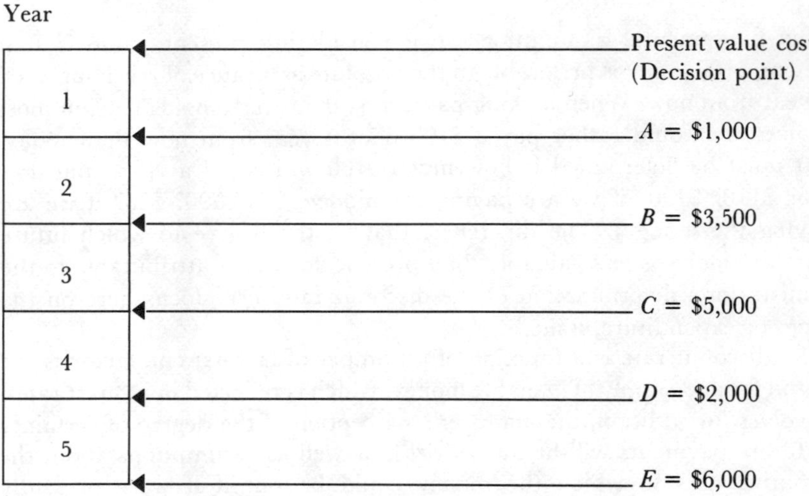

$$P = F\left[\frac{1}{(1+r)^n}\right],$$

where P equals present value or present principal sum, F equals future sum at some interest period hence, r equals the annual interest rate, and n equals the interest period. Assuming an interest rate of 10 percent, the present-value cost at point A is

$$P = \$1{,}000\left[\frac{1}{(1+0.1)}\right] = \$909.09. \tag{1}$$

For point B, this value becomes

$$P = \$3{,}500\left[\frac{1}{(1+0.1)^2}\right] = \$2{,}892.56 \tag{2}$$

Next, consider the present value of the costs at point A and point B combined. This is calculated from the expression

$$P = F_A\left[\frac{1}{(1+r)}\right] + F_B\left[\frac{1}{(1+r)^2}\right]. \tag{3}$$

Assuming the undiscounted estimates of \$1,000 and \$3,500 at points A and B respectively, the present value is

$$P = \$1{,}000\left[\frac{1}{(1+0.1)}\right] + \$3{,}500\left[\frac{1}{(1+0.1)^2}\right] \qquad (4)$$

$$= \$3{,}801.65$$

This continues until the costs for each year in the system life cycle are discounted to the present value and totaled. The total present-value cost for this system is $12,649.74. (The undiscounted total value is $17,500.00.) When costs are different for each year in the life cycle, the present-value expression is a continuation of equations 1–4, or

$$P = F_A\left[\frac{1}{(1+r)}\right] + F_B\left[\frac{1}{(1+r)^2}\right] + F_C\left[\frac{1}{(1+r)^2}\right] + \cdots + F_N\left[\frac{1}{(1+r)^n}\right].$$

Incorporating the Effects of Time into Replacement Decisions (Decisions Among Points in Time)*

In the previous discussion about present value, we considered examples where the school business administrator had to compare alternative investments and then select one. The flows of costs and benefits over time were reduced to estimations that could be directly compared. Often, the school business administrator faces a variant of this general capital investment problem—the problem of replacing a capital good. In deciding whether to replace a capital item, the administrator must compare the costs and benefits of current equipment with those associated with purchasing new equipment.

The replacement problem is roughly like the types of cost-balancing problems we discussed in the previous chapter: when we sought to balance competing costs of services, our decision involved the mix of services. With the replacement problem, which involves balancing competing costs of physical assets that vary over time, our decision involves time, that is the point in time when a capital good should be replaced so as to minimize long-run costs to the school. Although we are looking at acquisition of capital goods in a slightly different manner here, we are considering the same variables as we did in life-cycle costing: costs associated with the value of the item over time and costs associated with the operation of the item over time.

The replacement problem is really a special case of the cost-minimizing problem we discussed in the previous chapter. The decision parameter in this

* Special thanks to Robert Kelly, Mobile Oil Corporation, from whose work the empirical example in this section was drawn.

instance happens to be *time itself*, and the competing costs are the annualized purchase price of the capital good versus the annual cost of operating and maintaining the capital good. *Annualized capital cost* (sometimes called the capital recovery factor) is an estimation of the imputed annual costs of an investment when the useful life of the item and the interest rate can be reasonably determined. Rather than assuming that a physical asset has a useful life of *x* years and costs *y* dollars to buy, we seek a way to represent the item as a function of its useful life. That is, we want to see how the average cost of the item varies with changes in assumptions about its useful life. This can be represented as follows:

$$K(+) = V(+) \left[\frac{r\,(1 + r)^t}{(1 + r)^t - 1} \right]$$

where $K(+)$ = annualized capital goods
$V(+)$ = initial cost of the investment
r = interest rate
t = the year under consideration; t ranges from 1 to n.
n = life of the investment

Interest Rates and Useful Life Estimates

Annualized capital cost is sensitive to the interest rate and the life of the investment. Consider the differences in annualized capital cost for a $22,000 school bus when its useful life varies from seven to twelve years and the cost of capital to finance it varies from 5 to 15 percent. As shown in exhibit 13.4, the resulting computations range from a low of $2,482 to a high of $5,287 per year.

Exhibit 13.4
Annualized Capital Costs for a School Bus

Interest Rate (r)	Useful Life 7 years	 10 years	 12 years
5%	$3,802	$2,849	$2,482
10%	$4,519	$3,580	$3,228
15%	$5,287	$4,380	$4,058

As the interest rate goes up, the annualized cost of capital for the investment also goes up. As the length of useful life is extended, annualized costs go down. To make a replacement decision, the interest rate is decided upon and held constant as the effects of changes in useful life are examined. The same general issues of determining interest rate apply here as when comparing alternative investments.

By using the capital recovery factor to determine the time-adjusted average cash flows, we can compare investments in assets where different useful lives are expected. *The general replacement rule is to replace the capital good now if in the coming year the operation and maintenance costs of the good are expected to be equal to or greater than the average annual cost of financing, maintaining, and operating it over t years.* More specifically, replace if:

$$W(t) \geq \bar{W}(t) + \bar{k}(t)$$

$W(t)$ is the cost of operation and maintenance in year t for $t = 1,n$

$\bar{W}(t)$ is the average cost of operation and maintenance in year t for $t = 1,n$

$\bar{K}(t)$ is the annualized cost of the capital good in year t for $t = 1,n$

The relationships between these functions is shown in exhibit 13.5. Line $W(t)$ represents the actual operating costs that would be incurred each period—costs that are assumed to rise as the bus ages. The $\bar{W}(t)$, lying below it, shows the time-adjusted average annual operating costs. The time-adjusted average annual operating cost is the present value of the operating costs per period up to period t converted to a uniform flow by means of the capital recovery factor. These costs also increase with time but do so more slowly each additional year due to the discounting effects of time and the fact that these are averages.

The $\bar{k}(t)$ curve represents the time-adjusted average cost of capital, that is, the purchase price of the bus converted to a flow by the capital recovery period. This cost falls steadily with age as is the case when any fixed cost is spread over longer periods. The curve $TC(t)$ represents the sum of $\bar{W}(t)$ and $\bar{k}(t)$. Given assumptions about the behavior of $\bar{W}(t)$ and $\bar{K}(t)$, $TC(t)$ *must* be U-shaped.

The goal of the school business manager is to select the optimum replacement cycle t^* for which $TC(t^*)$ is minimized. This is the point where $\bar{w}(t^*) = TC(t^*)$, that is, where $W(t)$ crosses $T\bar{C}(t)$.

To Estimate W

Both the initial investment in the capital good and the interest rate are relatively easy to estimate. To make a reasonable estimate of operating and maintenance costs, it is necessary to keep records and to analyze the resulting data. The goal here is to derive a reasonable estimate of the general effect of aging on the operating and maintenance costs of the capital goods. A simple technique is to run a least squares regression with operating and maintenance costs as the dependent variable and age as the independent variable. Since common sense indicates that this relationship is probably a

Exhibit 13.5

Graphic Portrayal of the Replacement Decision

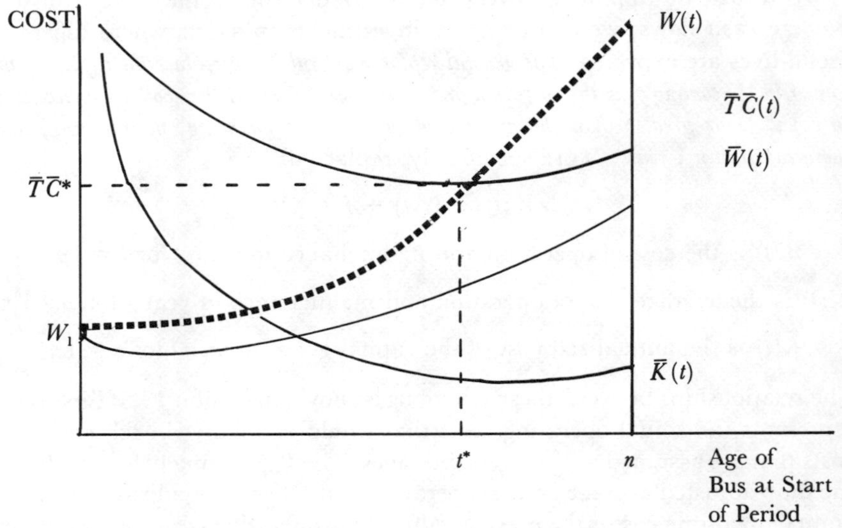

$\overline{TC}$ (t) – the sum of $\overline{W}$(t) and $\overline{K}$(t)
$\overline{K}$(t) – time = adjusted average cost of capital
$\overline{W}$(t) – time = adjusted average operating costs
Wt – actual operating costs incurred each period
t* – optimum replacement cycle
n = life of the investment

curve rather than linear, we add a second independent variable to the regression model that represents the square of the age.

Disincentives to Financial Optimization

The financial models discussed in this chapter are structured to yield a *financially* optimum result. As we discussed in chapter 2, the business administrator has multiple, sometimes conflicting preferences. Very often, financial savings are not the only (sometimes not even the major) preference. For example, under conditions of fiscal strain, it is tempting to postpone the purchase of school buses and other capital items to future years even when the school business administrator realizes that such a decision will increase total costs to the school. Or, in districts where bond issues are used to finance capital acquisitions, the voters may not approve the bonds. Investments that will help to save on total costs (such as installing energy-saving insulation) may then have to be postponed.

Other instances where financial preferences are suppressed involve inaccurate financial modeling, as when significant cost factors are not considered. In-house maintenance capability, for example, sometimes creates the impression of fixed and sunk (already committed) costs. Hence, school administrators feel they save money by keeping capital goods, such as buses, far beyond their theoretical replacement period. Their rationale is that since they have extensive garage facilities and a staff of mechanics, it would be foolish not to use them to full advantage. This view of the replacement issue places greater importance on costs of acquiring capital equipment and does not consider the full costs of operation and maintenance.

In other instances, school managers face incentives to replace *earlier* than the theoretically most cost-effective point in time. Often, replacement is associated with minor "upgrades" that are seen as desirable. Were the added features on the new model not desired, the old model would be likely retained longer. In addition, the uncertainties associated with operating failures are less with newer equipment, which by itself causes managers to want to replace equipment sooner than would otherwise be necessary. Few managers want the grief associated with reduced service due to equipment failure.

In short, the financial models described in this chapter suggest optimum decisions only as "optimum" is defined by the model. In these instances, "optimum" is synonymous with "minimizing financial expenditure, holding quality constant." The models indicate financially optimal decisions, but not necessarily the overall "best" thing for the business administrators' schools.

Differences Between Public and Private Schools

As we discussed in chapter 4, the broad financial parameters of financing capital expenditures are usually mapped out in specially designated funds, such as "capital" or "equipment" or "building" funds. These funds represent actions of the school business administrator to receive money to spend on capital items. All managers can to varying degrees resort to borrowing for capital improvements and hence pass on to future periods the costs as well as the benefits of capital goods. The basic methods and opportunities for acquiring and spending such money vary from school to school, but general similarities can be found across sectors. In the public sector this often entails the sale and repayment of bonds coupled with infusions of money from the operating fund. Public-sector managers face statutory limits on the amount of money they can raise (usually a percentage of the assessed valuation in their district), and they often must secure voter approval.

In the private sectors, money for capital improvements is usually raised by securing and paying off a single debt instrument, such as a mortgage, as well as by transferring into this fund money from the operating fund or from the endowment fund. In private nonprofit schools, money may also be raised in donor markets through a capital fund drive. The school administrator of the private for-profit school has in addition the right to depreciate the value of capital goods for tax purposes and to do so at rates greater than reflected by actual usage. All of the "traditional" methods of financing capital goods shape school business administrators' preferences as they make investment and replacement decisions.

The Search for Revenues from Non-traditional Sources

When administrators make capital investment decisions, the methods of financing are usually given. Because the cost streams of major capital investment alternatives are usually of the same order of magnitude, the method of financing is usually the same for any alternative chosen. Two trends, however, are forcing the school business administrator to increasingly consider financing as a variable and not a constant, and to pursue newer, less traditional methods of raising money. First, many schools have less easy access to their traditional sources of money for capital projects. Many public school districts are at their bonding limit or have had bond issues increasingly voted down in local elections. Banks are less willing to make large financial commitments to many private schools where demand for their services has softened and their financial position has become more precarious. Schools and school districts in these situations often have to resort to leasing mechanisms regardless of whether or not they are more costly. Second, some school business administrators have incorporated methods of financing as a variable, because they suspect that this may save them significant amounts of money.

Methods of financing are evaluated exactly like capital expenditures—that is, there are comparable alternatives, each of which has a unique stream of costs and benefits. Most often the alternatives considered are a "traditional" one and a relatively novel mechanism. For example, private school administrators have relied on public-sector grants and subsidies for the financing of some capital improvements. Public school managers have pursued donor markets for the same reason. A brief description of one of the most popular alternatives to capital goods financing in the public and private nonprofit sectors—sale-leaseback—follows.

Sale-Leaseback

Sale-leaseback is the term applied to a variety of practices used by managers of public and private nonprofit organizations to raise money in which they acquire the depreciation right enjoyed by investors in the private for-profit sector. The application of this method as an alternative to traditional bond sales approaches is described briefly here with reference to one public school district's requirements for three new buildings.

Sale-leaseback in this example represents a set of arrangements between the school administrator and a private, for-profit legal entity. (The structure of the for-profit entity may vary; it could be a corporation, partnership, or sole proprietorship, for example.) The school manager desires to acquire a capital good. The for-profit entity buys that item and leases it to the school manager. (Assume here, for simplicity, that both organizations would have to pay the same purchase price for the item.) The for-profit entity is able to depreciate that capital good on its ledger sheets, which shelters from taxes the profits earned in other enterprises. Because of this, the cost of the capital good to the private for-profit entity is less than the cost of the same good to the school manager.

The for-profit entity recovers its cost of the good through lease payments from the school district. And, after a fixed number of years, the school district would likely have the option to assume ownership of the good by paying one dollar for it. The lease payments have to cover the cost of the capital good paid by the for-profit entity plus profit. Because the net cost of the capital good to the for-profit entity is less than that which the school administrator would have paid, some of those "savings" can be passed on to the school district. The remainder of the "savings" is retained by the for-profit entity as profit (including the cost of performing the service). The underlying goal here is to use tax law to facilitate the procurement of capital goods by public and private nonprofit schools. This kind of arrangement is used when it is less expensive than more traditional bond selling arrangements as well as when those arrangements are not available.

The sale-leaseback arrangement involving the Jefferson County, Colorado, school district is illustrative (Heard 1982, p. 6.). That district has used sale-leaseback arrangements developed by E. F. Hutton and Company to allow it to build three new schools without holding a bond election. The plan allows the district to raise $23 million for construction of the schools by selling about $26 million worth of certificates of participation in a lease on the school to E. F. Hutton, which will then resell the certificates to an investment group. For ten years the investors will be "nominal owners" of the buildings, and the district will buy the buildings with lease payments of about $3.3 million per year. Money for the lease payments will come from the district's capital reserve fund, which the school district maintains to provide for the construction, repair, and replacement of buildings.

The fund takes in about $7 million per year through a 4-mill tax levy, the highest levy permitted for a capital reserve fund under Colorado state law. Since only half of each year's capital reserve fund would be required to make the annual lease payments, there would be no need for a tax increase or drawing off revenues from its general fund or its bond fund. (This arrangement required a change in Colorado law that prohibited the use of the bond fund for any other purpose than making payments for general-obligation bonds.)

This particular arrangement was designed to save the district $5.5 million over the cost of paying off bonds of comparable worth. E. F. Hutton clears a profit through the sale of certificates of participation to investors. Investors' return on investment is both in cash and in "tax losses" associated with depreciation of the buildings, which they can declare on personal income tax statements.

As school business administrators pursue their preferences, they seek alternative financing arrangements that will permit them to spend within their budgets in more preferred ways. *How* they do this varies from sector to sector.

Conclusion

School business administrators, regardless of sector, approach management of capital goods by attempting to reconcile differences in duration between paying for and using those goods and by recognizing the need for more formal analysis of alternatives than is required in managing services. These generalizations across sectors are counterbalanced by the sector-specific advantages and problems inherent in managing capital goods.

Public school administrators rely heavily on legislative or voter approval of resources for capital improvements. At the same time, they attempt, through sale-leaseback and other mechanisms, to capture some of the advantages available to administrators in the private for-profit sector. Private nonprofit administrators rely more than administrators in the other sectors on pursuit of donor dollars for facilities, and they often acquire a donated capital good in exchange for long-term recognition of the donor (as by naming the new building after the donor). Private for-profit administrators have the additional benefit of deducting depreciation of capital goods as an operating expense of the business. How capital goods are managed in the long run is accordingly shaped by the sector in which school business administrators work.

References

Barish, Norman. *Economic Analysis for Engineering and Managerial Decision-Making.* New York: McGraw-Hill, 1962, especially chapter 17, "The Economy of Replacement and Retirement (Economic Life)."

Education U.S.A. "School Buses, Longer Life." *Education U.S.A.* 23:19 (January 5, 1981): 147.

Frankel, Martin M., ed. *Projections of Education Statistics to 1986–87.* Washington D.C.: National Center for Education Statistics, 1978.

Green, Alan. "History Repeats Itself." *American School and University*, April 1983, pp. 10–13.

Heard, Alex. "Colorado District Turns to Private Financing of Construction." *Education Week* 2:7 (October 26, 1982): 6.

Hentschke, Guilbert C. "Information Management and Computing." In *Encyclopedia of Educational Research, Fifth Edition,* edited by Harold E. Mitzel, vol. 2, pp. 874–882. New York: The Free Press, 1982.

Kelly, Robert. "School Buses: The Replacement Decision." Course paper, "Management Operations in Education." Graduate School of Education and Human Development, University of Rochester, 1979.

Leggett, Stan. Quoted in "History Repeats Itself." *Americal School and University,* April 1983, pp. 10–13.

Olsen, John G. "Labor and Material Requirements for New School Construction." *Monthly Labor Review,* April 1979, pp. 38–41.

Tersine, Richard J. *Production/Operations Management: Concepts, Structure, and Analysis.* New York: North Holland, 1980, especially chapter 4, "Cost and Capital Analysis."

U.S. Bureau of Census. *Statistical Abstracts,* Vol. 100. Washington, D.C.: U.S. Government Printing Office, 1979.

Supplementary Readings

"College Seeks Savings by Leasing Its Campus." *New York Times,* April 4, 1983, p. A16.

Colley, John L. Jr.; Landel, Robert D.; and Fair, Robert R. *Production, Operations, Planning, and Control.* San Francisco: Holden-Day, 1977, especially chapter 2, "Facilities Planning."

Frankel, Martin M., and Gerald, Debra E., eds. *Projections of Education Statistics to 1988–89.* Washington, D.C.: National Center for Education Statistics, 1979.

"Labor Requirements for School Construction." *Montly Labor Review,* July 1961, pp. 724–730.

"Labor Requirements for School Construction." *Montly Labor Review,* August 1968, pp. 40–43.

Olsen, John G. "Labor and Material Requirements for New School Construction." *Monthly Labor Review,* April 1979, pp. 38–41.

14

Energy Management

by Shirley J. Hansen

•

Overview

Many general topics mentioned in the other chapters in this volume are discussed in this chapter with specific consideration given to managing energy use in schools. Energy management is focused on for several reasons: (1) energy is a major and growing cost in schooling, (2) the logistics of supplying energy require specialized technical knowledge, and (3) controlling energy costs usually requires influencing the behavior of many individuals. This chapter addresses these reasons within the context of the school business administrator pursuing a cost-effective energy management policy, which includes tasks such as collecting and evaluating data, developing alternative courses of action, and finding the "best" alternatives. Specialized terms are defined both in the text and in the glossary at the end of the chapter.

• • •

Energy management has become an increasingly important task of the school administrator. With energy costs estimated to run as high as $680 per pupil by 2000, economic considerations will force energy management to the forefront of school business administrators' responsibilities; therefore, school officials who can effectively manage a system's energy needs will be in great demand. The best instructional leaders will have difficulty serving students' needs unless actions are taken to prevent education dollars from going up the smokestack of inefficient energy use.

Managing energy use is no longer a short-term, "crisis" responsibility. Attention to energy use has become an essential and a continuing component of sound business management. A 1982–83 poll of school superintendents found 88 percent reporting they currently had major budget and finance problems or felt such problems were likely in the near future, and the most frequently cited cause of these problems (by 82 percent) was "increased costs of fuel for heating/cooling" (American Association of School Administrators 1983a).

Education's Fiscal Profile and Energy Implications

School budgets are peculiarly and particularly affected in an unstable economy such as the United States experienced during the early 1980s. The moves away from local support to state aid—from funding acquired primarily through property tax to funding received through income tax—have made the schools even more vulnerable to budget cuts. Fluctuations in income levels and changing political climates make budget planning even more precarious. In a financial situation where the combined levels of government are providing proportionally less support for education, escalating energy costs can have a devastating effect (U.S. Dept. of Education 1983).

In America's inflationary economy during the 1970s, energy costs outpaced those of all other commodities. The President's Commission for a National Agenda for the Eighties for Energy reported, "The Consumer Price Index, starting at a base of 100 in 1967, increased to 217.4 at the end of 1979; the energy component of that index, also starting at 100 in 1967, reached 275.9. The Producer Price Index, a measure of wholesale prices, rose from 100 to 236.3 over the same period; its energy component jumped to 409.1" (President's Commission for a National Agenda for the Eighties 1981).

The 15 percent of the typical school budget that does not go to personnel costs is generally referred to as the "discretionary" portion. This is clearly a misnomer because there is little discretion involved in how the money is spent, particularly as energy costs take an ever bigger bite. In 1976 energy costs required 12.5 percent of the discretionary budget. By 1978 the national average had grown to 25 percent. By the early 1980s it had reached 32 percent.

A survey conducted by the Federal Energy Administration (FEA) in 1975–76 found that in 1972–73 the schools paid approximately $20 per pupil for fuel. At the time of the FEA survey the costs had risen to $29 per pupil. By the fall of 1978 the costs per pupil were $57—nearly three times the

1973 figure (Educational Facilities Laboratories 1981). At the beginning of the 1980s the cost of energy averaged over $100 per pupil (Educational Facilities Laboratories 1981; Educational Research Service 1984). Average energy costs per pupil are expected to be about $180 in 1985, $270 in 1990, and $680 in 2000 (U.S. Dept. of Energy 1984). Actual costs per pupil vary with the source of fuel, the region of the country, the size of the district, and the level of conservation in effect.

Although oil prices decreased in the early 1980s, energy costs to the schools unfortunately did not. Natural gas costs continued to climb, and since 60 percent of the nation's schools depend on natural gas as their primary heating fuel, their gas bills continued to climb as well. DOE projects an 80 percent increase in the cost of natural gas by 2000 (U.S. Dept. of Energy 1984). In addition, schools that use natural gas are apt to find that the utilities who supply their electricity do too; thus schools' electricity bills also increase.

The public schools constitute the only sector of the economy that cannot pass on higher energy costs to the consumer. The schools must go to the voters for more revenues, or they must cut programs. Private schools have the painful task of either raising tuition or cutting programs to pay the fuel bill. The one alternative both public and private schools have to this dilemma is to cut energy use.

Fortunately, school administrators have already made great strides in reducing energy consumption. A national study in 1981 reported a drop of more than 40 percent in energy consumption by schools from the 1973 FEA figures (American Association of School Administrators 1981). Without this reduction, energy costs to the schools in 1980 would have been $1.5 billion higher than they were.

Unfortunately, however, most public school buildings in use today were built in the late 1950s or early 1960s when space was critical and energy was cheap. These post-World War II "baby boom" buildings are energy sieves—they are a tremendous energy burden to education and to the nation. Although reduction of energy use in these buildings has been significant, experience shows there is a potential for saving much more.

It should be reemphasized to education's financial planners, however, that even with concerted conservation efforts energy costs have continued to mount. Exhibit 14.1 shows natural gas costs versus consumption for the Lincoln, Nebraska, public schools through the 1970s. Even this district, which has an exemplary energy management program and has achieved a significant reduction in energy use, has had increasingly higher costs. Consider, however, what the costs to the district would have been without a reduction in consumption. By multiplying energy consumption in an earlier (base) year by today's energy prices, school administrators can figure what they would have been paying. By subtracting current costs from that figure, the money saved, or costs avoided, can be determined.

Building an Energy Background

Many school business administrators have found energy responsibilities thrust on them almost overnight. Conflicting news stories about supply and a great deal of rhetoric, often without much substance, at workshops, conferences, and conventions have left many of education's business officials aware of a growing problem but ill-equipped to handle it.

Probably the greatest deterrent to finding a way to tackle the schools' energy problem is the wave of new energy jargon. Isaac Asimov once observed, "Every small segment of the culture develops its own vocabulary for the sake of forming an in-group. There are a million verbal walls behind which fools cower." His comment is extremely appropriate with regards to energy. Schoolpeople have been besieged by "experts" with the ideal "black box" solutions—experts that a couple of years earlier didn't know a Btu from a cup of coffee. Generally speaking, there is an inverse ratio between the amount of energy jargon used and how much the speaker knows. Too often the idea is to impress and intimidate the potential customer.

The school administrator would do well to remember that the district is the customer and has the right and the obligation to insist on understandable language. Legitimate salespeople or consultants will be pleased to rephrase their energy messages. A glossary of some of the more common energy-related terms has been provided at the end of this chapter. Very often such terms are a shorthand way of addressing rather cumbersome topics and often give a flavor to the concept of energy management. It is useful to have a feel for these words, but a command of all of them is not essential.

A sound rule in energy management is to recognize that school business administrators should not be expected to know everything about energy—and should be willing to admit they do not. Rather, administrators should undertand enough so they can acknowledge what they do not know, and they should be aware of when and whom to ask for advice.

Such a task is not as awesome as it first seems. There are reasonable parameters within which a school business administrator can operate. The verbiage can be pared away and the whole situation put in perspective by recognizing that energy has only two dimensions—price and availability. If energy were still cheap and abundant, there would be no "energy problem" for the schools, or for anyone else.

The availability of energy is sporadically a problem of great importance. The availability concept and the need for contingency planning to meet energy shortages will be addressed later. The more prevalent and persistent concern, however, is price. To maintain an appropriate learning environment, lights must be turned on, fans must run, air must be conditioned, and so on. With every "must" there is a price tag, and the utility bills must be paid. As the price goes higher, so does the desire to use less energy; therefore, energy management is primarily an economic concern.

Exhibit 14.1
Natural Gas* Costs Versus Consumption

Lincoln Public Schools—Energy Management Program
History of School District Energy Use

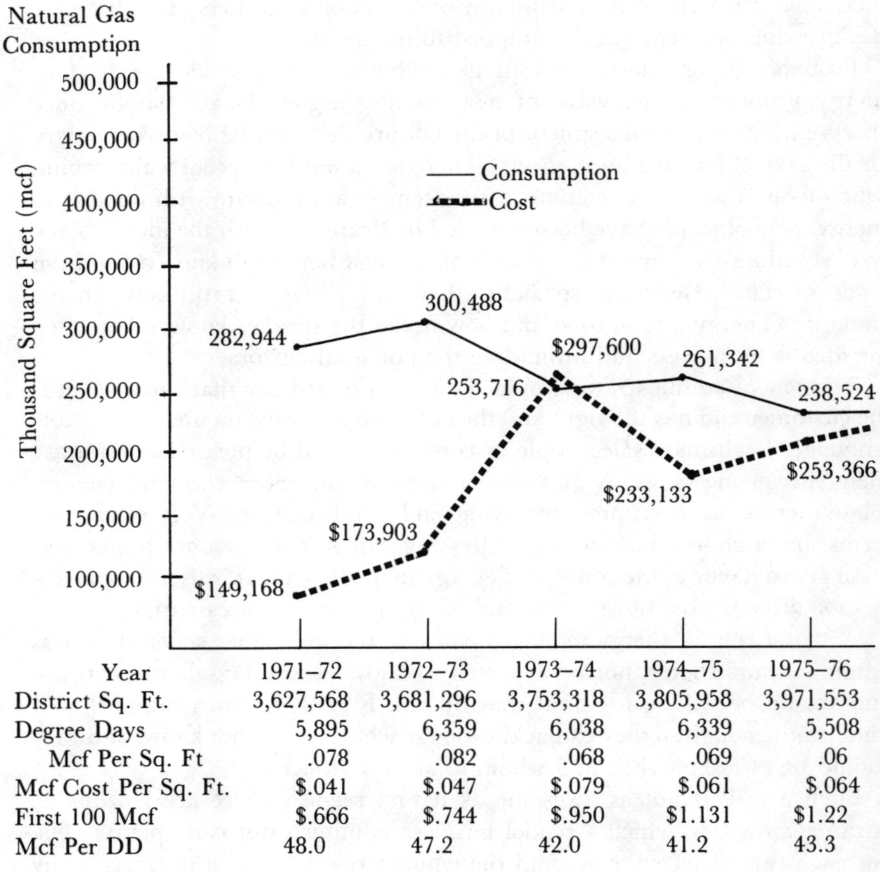

Year	1971–72	1972–73	1973–74	1974–75	1975–76
District Sq. Ft.	3,627,568	3,681,296	3,753,318	3,805,958	3,971,553
Degree Days	5,895	6,359	6,038	6,339	5,508
Mcf Per Sq. Ft	.078	.082	.068	.069	.06
Mcf Cost Per Sq. Ft.	$.041	$.047	$.079	$.061	$.064
First 100 Mcf	$.666	$.744	$.950	$1.131	$1.22
Mcf Per DD	48.0	47.2	42.0	41.2	43.3

*Firm Interruptible Gas
Prepared By:
John M. Romishor, Administrative Assistant
Division of Business Affairs

Prepared for:
Robert Den Hartog, Associate Superintendent
Division of Business Affairs

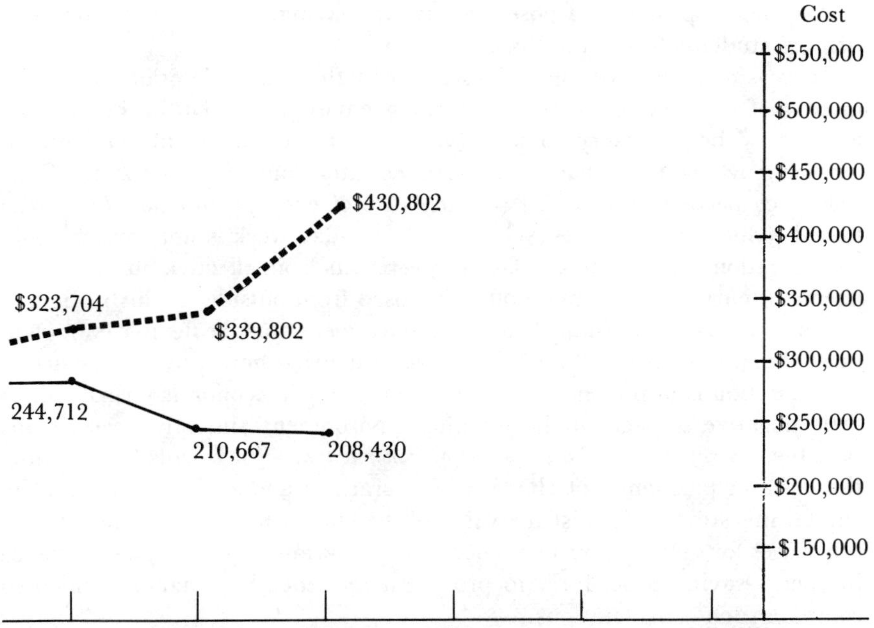

1976–77	1977–78	1978–79	1979–80	1980–81	1981–82
3,998,741	4,005,090	4,021,565			
6,042	6,980	7,113			
.061	.053	.052			
$.081	$.085	$.107			
$1.67	$2.04	$2.33			
40.5	30.2	29.3			

1982–83
Rudy J. Bauer, Director
Operations and Maintenance

Energy Report No.20
1/30/80

World supplies or national energy needs, as important as they are, are not the school business administrator's immediate or primary concern. Arguments over "how much oil we have left" distracted schoolpeople for years from their more immediate challenge of how to cost-effectively reduce the energy demands of their schools—*the goal is to use essential energy as efficiently as possible.* The school business administrator, however, should never lose sight of the school's primary purpose—education. Saving energy at the expense of helping students learn is not conservation.

Increasing costs of energy or its scarcity might cause a deterioration in the quality of the services or in the learning environment. Cutbacks in some areas may be necessary to preserve other, more important services. In assessing where to cutback, the administrator must be cognizant of the difference between *conservation* (efficient use of energy) and *curtailment* (the forced reduction of services). Going to a four-day week is not conservation. Conservation—using energy efficiently—results from effective internal management; curtailment is more often imposed from outside the institution.

Any universal definition of energy management must be flexible enough to meet the unique needs of a given school or district; however, the essence of the definition is improvement of energy efficiency in economic terms with as little negative impact on the learning environment and other services as possible. *Energy management is a series of economic trade-offs.* It calls for weighing the costs of personnel, of changes in operations and maintenance, and of capital investments against the value of the energy to be saved and against other uses for that money. The schools have now amassed enough experience in energy-saving procedures to provide a reference base against which to compare such considerations.

By cutting away the more esoteric concerns of world and national energy problems and by considering just the economics of energy efficiency, the schools' energy problems can be reduced to manageable terms: How much energy is consumed, how much does it cost, how is it used (or wasted), and what cost-effective means can be used to reduce consumption?

Determining how much of what type of fuel is used in each building and its cost is the first order of business. This information constitutes the data base for further analyses. An energy accounting system is essential to knowing where you were, where you are, and where you are going. Program effectiveness cannot be gauged without it.

Building a Data Base

The data base should incorporate historical, current, and projected energy consumption and cost patterns. A data base should contain a record of the costs and consumption figures for each fuel and for their combined use in each building and in the entire school system. It should also establish a log, by building, of what energy conservation work has been done and the results and recommendations of any audits that may have been conducted.

Energy Costs

Cost information is needed to plan budgets and to communicate the impact of energy costs on school operations to the staff and to the legislators and taxpayers. Trends in price increases are useful in anticipating the budget needs for the coming school year and for succeeding years. Long-range planning for new construction or for modifying existing buildings is facilitated when trends are analyzed.

Analyzing Energy Costs

One of the first steps a school business administrator can take to analyze energy use is to develop simple energy accounting forms for each building and for the entire system. In addition to identifying the building and related information such as square footage, these forms should track consumption by fuel unit and by cost for each type of fuel used by the month or by the billing period. The number of days in the billing period is not always the same and should be recorded so that comparisons are not distorted. The costs of the fuels should be combined to determine the building's total energy demand by month and by year. Calculating an Energy Cost Index (ECI) by dividing annual energy cost by the square footage can help point out those facilities with the greatest economic needs.

Energy consumption of all fuels must also be found for each building. In order to add kilowatt-hours to gallons or to natural gas mcfs, a common denominator is needed—the energy value of each fuel is measured in British thermal units (Btus). The conversion of each fuel to Btus to calculate combined consumption is discussed later in the chapter.

Building a data base also requires a look at the entire budget to find what areas money has been taken from to pay the fuel bill. School systems have been able to cut energy consumption initially by the more obvious means: turning off lights, lowering the thermostat, making minor automatic control adjustments, and the like. Unfortunately, the second strategy for saving money has often been deferred maintenance. The "maintenance gap" in the nation's schools has been conservatively estimated at $25 billion (American Association of School Administrators 1983b). Deferred maintenance borrows from the future budget because maintenance costs are higher later on, and fuel bills are higher in the interim because the buildings are less energy efficient.

Energy considerations are forcing schools to do better long-range planning. Schoolpeople are finally breaking away from the low bid, first cost bind that generally looked good initially, but too often meant the schools would have to eventually pay more. Later in this chapter, life-cycle costing as a more realistic way of comparing alternative measures will be discussed. Life-cycle costing recognizes recurring costs and helps place deferred maintenance in perspective.

Finally, in relation to budget planning and to help determine the relative value of making energy management investments now, future energy costs should be considered. The data base for *internal planning*, but not for publication, should include the national, regional, and local projections. It is well to remember that there is no uniform price or prediction that can hold for all schools. National averages make good talking points and can serve as bases of comparison; however, they can be misleading. Per-pupil energy costs can vary dramatically by region, by district size, or by fuel source. Exhibit 14.2 shows the ranges of per-pupil energy costs in 1984.

In order to assess future energy costs, the local school official must look at how the electricity for the district is generated. The price of electricity runs higher than other energy costs (per Btu) due to losses during electrical generation and transmission. It takes 11,600 Btus to generate and transmit a kilowatt-hour (kWh), and the Btu value drops to 3,413 kWh by the time it reaches the site. This two-thirds loss in Btu value means that a major increase in the cost of the fuel used to produce electric power results in even higher electricity costs to the consumer. The southern school administrator who thinks that increases in the price of gas is essentially a northern heating problem has usually not considered how the schools' electricity is generated—natural gas is often used to generate electricity in the south.

When analyzing fuel costs, a school business administrator must also consider the energy policies of the federal government. For example, the Natural Gas Policy Act of 1978 set controls on the price of "new" natural gas (gas discovered after 1977). These controls held the price of natural gas down through the early 1980s and accounted for some of the regional discrepancies shown in exhibit 14.2. Fuel sources by federal energy region are shown in exhibits 14.3 and 14.4. While the regional designations are not the same on the two tables, the relationship between natural gas dependency and energy costs is evident. For example, Federal Energy Regions 1, 2, and 3 (New England and the Mideast) rely heavily on oil, while Regions 6 and 9 (Southwest) rely primarily on natural gas. As shown in exhibit 14.2, the energy expenditures in the oil-dependent New England and Mideast areas range from $135.00 to $151.00 per pupil, while in the Southwest the energy costs average $116.00 per pupil. As oil prices dropped and natural gas prices continued to rise in the early 1980s, these discrepancies were virtually eliminated.

Natural gas prices are expected to continue to rise more rapidly than are oil prices. Exhibit 14.5 compares, to the end of the century, the projected

Exhibit 14.2

Mean Budgeted Energy Expenditures: Fiscal Year 1984–85
(heating and cooling fuel plus all other utilities except telephone)

	Expenditure per Pupil	Percentage of Current Expenditures
Total—All Reporting Districts	$127.43	4.11%
Enrollment Group:		
25,000 or more	113.27	3.87
10,000 to 24,999	118.43	4.06
2,500 to 9,999	128.40	4.20
300 to 2,499	132.31	4.08
Per-Pupil Expenditure Group:		
$3,500 or more	175.14	3.84
$3,000 to $3,499	128.71	3.99
$2,500 to $2,999	111.45	4.05
$2.000 to $2,499	95.32	4.16
Less than $2,000	86.70	4.71
Region:		
New England	135.28	4.01
Mideast	151.56	3.84
Southeast	99.52	4.08
Great Lakes	141.87	4.87
Plains	116.27	3.90
Southwest	116.09	4.21
Rocky Mountains	141.10	4.17
Far West	105.88	3.05
Community Type:		
Large urban	126.55	3.72
Medium urban	112.34	3.68
Suburban	146.31	4.11
Small town	115.02	4.31
Rural	124.18	4.10
County district—mix of community types	127.23	4.36

Source: Educational Research Service, Arlington, Virginia 22209. The data were compiled during Fall 1984 from approximately 1,000 school districts as part of the annual ERS Local School Budget Profiles project. Districts that participate receive a computer-generated report that compares a district's budget to those of 18 other districts. Reprinted by permission.

Exhibit 14.3

Types of Fuel Used in Schools in 1979 (by Federal Energy Regions)

Federal Energy Regions	Fuel Type (by percentage)					
	Natural Gas	Oil	Electricity		Propane	Coal
			Heating & Cooling	Heating Only		
1	1.0	86.2	3.2	6.4	2.5	-0-
2	24.1	58.7	2.4	11.9	0.7	2.0
3	31.1	55.5	5.7	2.9	3.8	1.1
4	68.8	11.0	8.9	3.6	2.5	3.2
5	67.1	13.5	4.6	9.1	0.7	4.4
6	92.4	-0-	3.9	1.4	1.0	-0-
7	65.5	9.8	7.0	6.7	10.5	0.5
8	74.6	3.7	2.1	9.0	5.7	4.1
9	78.7	0.7	15.3	3.7	1.5	-0-
10	25.9	55.6	1.6	14.5	0.7	0.5
National Average	63.6	19.1	6.7	5.9	2.2	1.6

Source: American Association of School Administrators, *AASA Energy Use Study, 1980* (Arlington, Va.: American Association of School Administrators, 1980).

per-pupil energy costs for schools using gas-fired boilers with the costs for schools that use oil-fired boilers. Cost calculations are based on a 15 percent electrical usage (excluding electrical heating and cooling), the DOE projected energy cost increases, and a 6 percent per annum inflation rate (U.S. Department of Energy 1984). The progressive increase in the costs of all fuels, as shown in exhibit 14.5, will place a greater financial burden on the schools. An important aspect of energy management is to anticipate and prepare for these increased costs.

Although general energy cost projections are critical to long-range financial planning and cost-effectiveness calculations and are essential to communicating energy needs and accomplishments to the staff and to the public, they should not be used to compare building or district energy consumption. This is because, as already suggested, price changes cause distortions. Furthermore, fuels do not cost the same per Btu. These variations in cost and in energy mix make it impossible to track progress in reducing consumption by fuel cost.

Energy Consumption

In order to make any legitimate comparison of the amount of energy consumed, a common denominator must be used. Some districts attempt to make this comparison by units of fuel, that is, by gallons, therms, kWh, and the like. Although this is better than comparing by price because the measure is consistent, it still gives pieces of information and not a comprehensive figure. The best unit of measure to use for comparing energy use is the Btu per square foot.

Computing Btus

The process for calculating Btus used is not complex once the units of energy are known. Conversion factors have been established and are shown in exhibit 14.6. Btu conversion factors may vary by grade of coal or type of oil, and if school administrators are in doubt, they should ask the supplier about these variations.

The units of fuel consumed in a building multiplied by the conversion factor provides the Btu consumption for a given fuel for that building. The Btu consumption should be computed for every fuel used in a given building and then totaled. This figure is the Btu consumption for that building for a given period of time. Unless otherwise stated, the period of time is usually a year.

In order to compare buildings of different sizes, the total Btu consumption should be divided by the gross square footage, which yields Btu per square foot—the standard unit of measure for energy consumption. Exhibit 14.7 depicts a sample worksheet. A five-by-eight-inch index card works well.

As a basis of comparison, exhibit 14.8 shows the average Btu per square foot consumption for various regions of the country during 1978, 1979, and 1980. The data in exhibit 14.8 are not climate corrected by calculating Btus per square foot per degree days, which will be explained in the next section. It will be noted that the areas that use more Btus per square foot have the more severe climates. Exhibit 14.8 also reveals the remarkable strides the schools have made in reducing consumption.

Degree Days

Under some conditions it is advisable to qualify the Btus per square foot measurement to allow for the influence of outside temperatures on energy consumption. The common practice is to refer to degree days (DD), which are calculated by determining the difference between an established reference temperature (usually 65° F) and the mean daily temperature. The mean daily temperature is obtained by finding the average of all the outside temperature readings taken over a twenty-four-hour period. Degree day information for a given locality can be obtained from the National Oceanic

Exhibit 14.4
Federal Energy Office—Regions

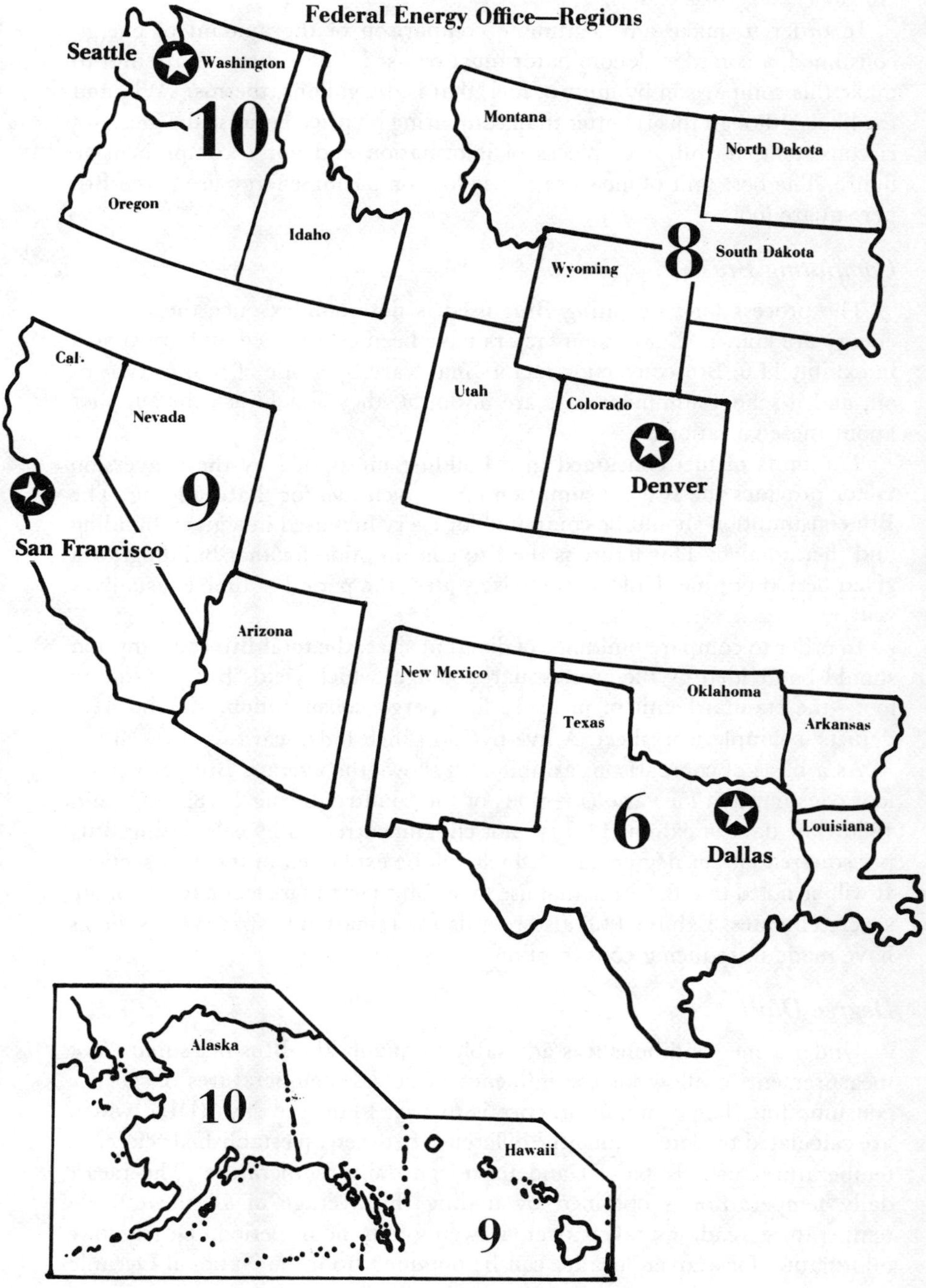

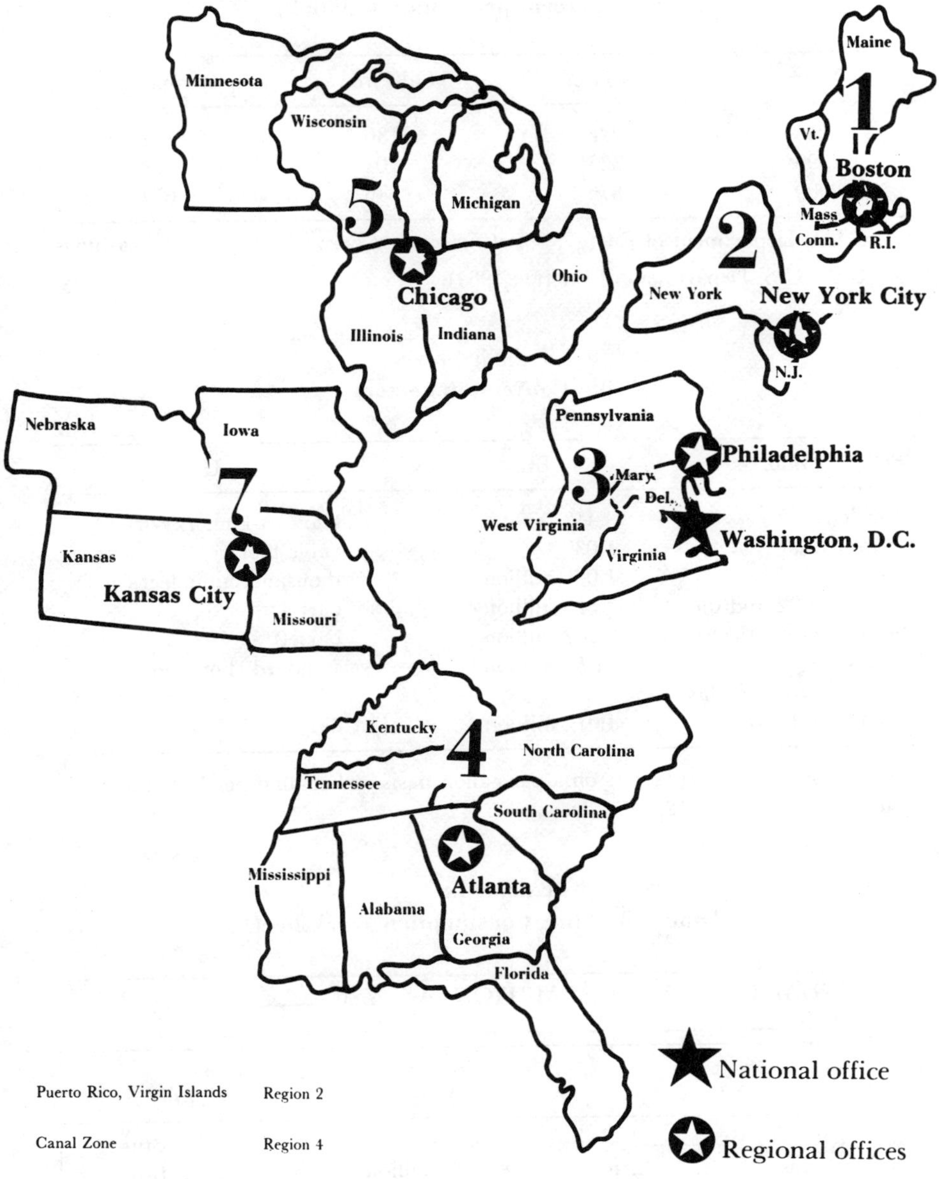

Puerto Rico, Virgin Islands	Region 2
Canal Zone	Region 4
America Samoa, Guam Trust Territory of The Pacific Islands	Region 9

Exhibit 14.5

Projected Average Per-Pupil Energy Costs (with 6 percent per annum inflation)

Year	Gas-Fired	Oil-Fired	Composite
1985	$228	$130	$184
1990	335	204	268
2000	876	546	677

Source: U.S Department of Energy, *School Finance and Energy Through 2000.* Washington, D.C.: U.S. Department of Energy, 1984).

Exhibit 14.6

Btu Conversion Factors

Source	Btu	Unit
Electricity	3,413 (site)	kilowatt-hour (kWh)
Natural Gas	1,030	cubic foot
or	1.03 million	thousand cubic feet (mcf)
Distillate (#2 and diesel)	5.825 million	barrel*
Residual (#4, #5, #6)	6.287 million	barrel*
Coal	24.5 million	standard short ton
Liquid Petroleum Gas (Butane & Propane)	4.01 million	barrel*

* To obtain conversion factors on a per gallon basis rather than per barrel for liquid fuels, divide by 42.

Exhibit 14.7

Annual Building Consumption Worksheet

ANNUAL ENERGY CONSUMPTION Year ____________
Building ______________________________ Sq.Ft. ____________

Source	Unit		Conversion Factor		Btus
Electricity	________	kWh	× 3,413	=	____ Btus
Natural Gas	________	mcf	× 1.03 million	=	____ Btus
Oil #____	________	barrel	. . .		. . .
			. . .		. . .

Total Annual Btu Consumption ______Btus
Total Btus divided by sq.ft. ______Btu/sq.ft.

Exhibit 14.8
Median Consumption of All Fuels

Federal Energy Region	Btus per Square Foot 1980	1979	1978	Percentage Change 1978 to 1979	1979 to 1980
1	85,203	107,719	114,999	− 6.3%	−20.9%
2	85,146	101,167	109,687	− 7.8	−15.8
3	115,633	94,522	111,241	−15.0	+22.3
4	59,008	65,286	75,604	−13.6	− 9.6
5	87,113	109,695	110,488	− 0.006	−20.6
6	57,594	61,735	77,907	−20.8	− 6.7
7	88,442	109,277	117,766	− 7.2	−19.1
8	105,627	122,165	120,103	+ 1.7	−13.5
9	57,279	74,929	66,523	+12.6	−23.6
10	73,189	91,988	85,978	+ 6.9	−20.4
National	85,260	102,060	104,445	− 2.3	−16.5

Source: American Association of School Administrators, *AASA Energy Use Study, 1981.* (Arlington, Va.: American Association of School Administrators, 1981).

and Atmospheric Administration (NOAA), commonly referred to as the national weather service. Other sources of degree day data are the local utility company or a nearby airport. To obtain the degree day data, it is best to go to the source where weather conditions most closely resemble those at the institution.

In order to use degree days in relation to Btus per square foot, the total degree days must be for the same period of time as that used in measuring the units of fuel; for example, by week, month, or year. The Btus per square foot per degree days can be determined by dividing the Btus per square foot by the total degree days for the specified time.

The use of degree days is optional, and it may be inappropriate or not worth the trouble for several reasons. First, degree days are a measure of the difference between the average temperature and a fixed reference temperature, usually 65° F, for a twenty-four-hour period. If the inside temperature is not equal to the reference temperature or the equipment does not operate twenty-four hours a day, calculations are made against an unrepresentative reference base. If degree days are being used as only a gross measure of the severity of the weather from year to year for the same facility, these factors are not significant. However, if temperature changes are considered important in the calculations, the degree day value should be adjusted to represent actual conditions. If the value is not adjusted, then some qualification should appear with the reported data. Second, degree day information is often represented as "weather data" and Btus per square foot per degree days as "climate corrected." In some circumstances, humidity or wind are more significant factors than temperature is. The inclusion of degree days in such instances may mislead people into believing weather conditions were sufficiently treated. Finally, under some conditions, outside temperature variations may have such a small proportional effect on consumption that it's not worth obtaining the data and including them in the Btu equation. For example, in a building with a good thermal resistance in the shell and a high internal load, which may result from a high concentration of people, outside temperature variations may have a relatively small effect.

The procedures outlined above to determine current consumption should be repeated for the preceding years. At least two years of history is preferable, particularly if the data are not climate corrected. Using the average of two or three years can help to correct for climate variations and can serve as a base year against which program success can be measured.

Work Logs

The third component in assessing energy needs, in addition to the cost and consumption records, is a work log. Energy-related operations and maintenance (o&m) and capital modifications should be entered by the nature of the work done with space to indicate the date completed.

The log should include the school name, location, principal or contact person, pertinent building characteristics, fuel sources (and options), current and past Btus per square foot figures, and an o&m checklist. The building characteristics that should be included in the log are: (1) the configuration and construction of the walls and roof and (2) the type of heating, ventilating, and air-conditioning (HVAC) system. It should be noted if an audit has been done, and the audit report or a summary page with cross-file citing should be attached. The summary page should show the kind of audit conducted, the o&m recommendations, capital modifications recommended, and the projected costs and payback periods of the capital modifications.

From the building schedules, a master schedule for the district or other group of schools, such as Catholic schools within a diocese, should be set up. For school business administrators in charge of multiple buildings, this schedule should be devised to show what are the most cost-effective procedures and investments that can be made (in personnel time and capital investments) throughout the system. This not only will help to determine the allocation of the system's limited resources, in terms of both manpower use and purchases, but it will also aid in long-range planning. The schedule will also serve as a valuable tool in documenting and explaining energy needs to the superintendent, headmaster, board, parents, public, and school principals.

Experience has shown that the most cost-effective energy conservation efforts are in the o&m area. In fact, energy cost comparisons before and after o&m time has been expended usually provide effective data to defend against cuts in o&m staff.

Computer-Based Accounting

The greatest advantages of using a computer to record energy data are the computer's data storage and recall capacity and the resultant speed and sophistication with which the data can be treated. A computer is valuable for logging data; however, it is even more valuable for analyzing data. Data gathering, which tracks consumption, often reveals problems. The sooner the data are available for analysis, the sooner the problems can be addressed.

Energy accounting systems do not require a mainframe computer. If a computerized financial accounting system is already in use, the energy information can easily be "piggy-backed"; that is, the information can be entered as part of the normal billing process. Accessiblity to the data is a critical consideration; therefore, it is usually better to use a small microprocessor and locate it in the offices of those directly responsible for building operations. If the energy data are swallowed by the financial apparatus or if burdens on the system cause an output lag, energy problems will not be caught as promptly if the energy data are not readily accessible.

A number of software packages to assist in energy accounting are now on the market. This software is compatible with microprocessors such as the Apple IIc. Each school system administrator should determine what needs to be known and then should work with a computer specialist to adapt a packaged program or create the system's own procedures. Care should be exercised that the value of the desired information is balanced against the cost of maintaining the data bank and accessing the information. Too many computer-based accounting systems suffer from data glut.

Data Analysis

Assembled data are of no value unless the information is used and analyzed. The manner in which data are kept should be dictated by the way they will be used and analyzed. Analyses of energy data often center on comparisons. The following are common bases of comparison:

Individual buildings; current consumption compared to—

1. the same month in the prior year or a base year;
2. current year to date versus the same period in the prior year or a base year;
3. an acceptable consumption range (to create an exceptions list to flag problems);
4. design or target goals;

5. other units or buildings within the administrative unit by institution-wide ranking; and
6. other similar units by their specific functions; for example, research.

Multiple building or institution-wide; consumption comparisons of—

1. total consumption and cost for all units or buildings to the previous year or to the same month in the prior or base year;
2. subgroups to other subgroups; for example, laboratories to athletic facilities, secondary schools to elementary schools, and so on;
3. buildings with special activities to ones without; for example, after-school facility use; and
4. buildings with energy retrofits to those without.

Specialized interests comparing—

1. variable-load electric needs to estimate the efficiency of various cooling systems;
2. demand billings on facilities with and without demand limiters; and
3. multiyear trends.

Data analysis should, at the very least, do three things: (1) flag problems, (2) help measure the degree to which past endeavors are working, and (3) provide a basis for charting future efforts.

The Energy Management Team

The energy management team forms the nucleus of any institution's energy conservation efforts. The key person is the energy manager. To be effective, he or she must have the commitment and full support of the superintendent, headmaster, board, and any other supervisors.

A policy statement from the board speaking to the need for commitment is essential. Board action to designate certain responsibilities to specific personnel and to supply an appropriate budget is a tangible commitment—and is more likely to obtain results. An institution-wide committee and building-level teams will aid in more comprehensive planning, extend support and involvement, and increase communications.

The Energy Manager

Every educational organization, no matter how small, should designate someone who has primary responsibility for the institution's energy concerns. That person should have the time (proportionate to the extent of responsibility) and training to carry out the energy management plan. A rough rule of thumb is if the system can put in place (from within-staff or by hiring) an energy manager with the necessary support personnel, space, and equipment for 10 percent of the fuel budget, then it cannot afford not to. Any system with an annual energy budget over half a million dollars should carefully consider the costs and benefits of a full-time position. Smaller districts and schools should judge the economic trade-offs of costs and savings and devote as much to energy conservation as they think is required. Smaller districts and schools should also consider the advantages of using the services of a regional service agency.

The qualifications of an effective energy manager will vary with the school system's size, existing expertise, and energy plans. Generally, however, the supposition that this person should be a professional engineer is false. In fact, the single most important quality for an energy manager to have is the ability to work with people in a manner that will stimulate their involvement and support. This implies a willingness to learn about the problem and the ability to articulate it.

Most schools' staffs and the general public have been confused and "turned off" by the conflicting reports and aimless rhetoric that have surrounded the energy issue. They are skeptical about how "real" the problem is. They therefore tend to resist energy conservation efforts. An energy manager must overcome this resistance by translating energy costs into relevant economic terms, that is, dollars—dollars that could buy teaching supplies, athletic equipment, and so forth. Investment in energy conservation is good business. It can create a positive cash flow. It can prevent educational dollars from going up the smokestack of energy waste. The energy manager must convey these ideas to the teacher who would rather have new books, to the board that sets policy and budget, or to the reluctant taxpayer who is inclined to vote "no."

Other skills that an energy manager should have are the ability to perceive what data are needed and to be able to assimilate and synthesize the data so others can readily understand the problems. The energy manager must be aware of the available options and be able to articulate them to others. A rudimentary understanding of thermodynamics and economics is of great importance, but this information can be learned.

Energy managers are not born or magically given special understanding—they must learn the trade. If a school system does not hire a person with the required background and training, then it must train the person hired or someone chosen from the staff. The board and top administration should recognize the need to provide the experiences or training necessary for effective implementation of an energy program.

The quickest and often most economical way for a new manager to get initial help is to visit other schools or districts with successful programs. Help in identifying such districts might come from the state energy office or national educational associations such as the American Association of School

Administrators or the Association of School Business Officials—or their state affiliates. The new manager should not hesitate to go beyond the state's borders. The price of an airline ticket is very small when compared with the potential savings.

Workshops, conferences, and university seminars are now being provided to help educate energy managers. As in any group effort, these courses may not serve an individual's particular needs. However, they can provide some basics that may be adapted to local needs. Interaction with other participants with similar problems can also be very helpful. All too often new managers attempt to learn energy management piecemeal from various salespeople. This is an inefficient use of time and seldom provides balanced or comprehensive information.

Energy Committee

The committee approach provides broad input regarding the impact various possible actions may have throughout the system. It also creates conduits to disseminate the reasons for the plan and how it will be implemented. In some private schools the buildings and grounds committees have assumed responsibility for energy management.

A district-level committee should be formed on an ongoing basis only if the energy manager has sufficient time to staff the committee and believes it is sound use of his or her time. To be effective, members of the committee should be people of influence within the system. Their time is valuable too. A nonfunctioning committee can drag down, even discredit, the energy effort.

One alternative is to form an ad hoc committee to set up the initial energy plan. Although disbanding the committee once its task is done frees up some time for the energy manager and the committee members, disbanding can cause the plan to lose its ongoing support as well as the continual input for evaluation and revisions. The ad hoc approach can leave the false impression that energy management is a one-time effort rather than a constant one.

However the committee is constituted, its responsibilities should be clearly defined by the board and administration. Within clearly defined parameters, it should be a decision-making body, not an advisory one. Its makeup should be representative of the staff and draw from the diverse strengths of the community when appropriate.

The Energy Team

Depending on the size of the district and its organizational structure, the energy committee may be of sufficient force to follow through to the building level. If the district is large or diverse, an energy team in each bulding will strengthen the energy effort. The building energy team should include an administrator, teacher, head custodian, those representing special services or needs, a parent, and, if appropriate, a student.

The inherent danger in forming committees or teams is the implication that those not part of such a group do not have any responsibility in the issue, but every person in the system has an important role to play. A concerted effort to ensure appropriate widespread involvement should be made.

The energy manager, the energy committee, and the energy team must know and share with others what managing energy is all about. New members are apt to shy away from seeking an understanding because they believe energy management issues are too complex. A "short course" in thermodynamics will put managing energy in perspective. Following is a brief guide to understanding energy conservation; school systems are encouraged to provide an adaptation of it to their staff who work in the area of energy management.

Understanding Energy Conservation

An understanding of energy conservation is based on this basic axiom: heat always seeks the cold; that is, heat flows toward the colder air or material by means of radiation, conduction, or convection. If you hold your hand about a quarter of an inch from your face, you can feel your cheek become warmer—that's radiation. If you put one end of a metal rod in the fire while you hold the other end, you will feel the end you are holding become warmer—that's conduction. The mass movement of air can be one form of convection.

There are only four sources of heat in a building and only six ways energy can be used or lost.

Heat sources	*Heat use and lost*
1. sun	1. infiltration
2. people	2. ventilation
3. light	3. transmission
4. heating plant	4. illumination, electrical needs
	5. system inefficiencies
	6. hot water

Heat Sources

Body heat from people in a room, in and of itself, is neither a help nor a hindrance. The value of such heat depends on the desired air temperature. If the air is being heated, body heat is an added benefit. If the air is being cooled, body heat increases the amount of energy needed to cool the room.

We have all been in a crowded room that quickly became too warm; yet we seldom think of body heat as helping to heat the air in a building. Young, active bodies can produce a significant amount of heat, and in a space as densely populated as a schoolroom, bodies are a major heat source. Some HVAC people believe the schools in even the country's northern regions use more energy to expel excess heat than they do to heat the air. This is a significant factor in determining whether or not schools should be closed to save energy during a supply disruption. Closing schools will be discussed further under contingency planning.

Recognizing the implications of heat flow can help school administrators understand the complexities of engineering trade-offs. For example, eliminating windows will reduce heat loss in the winter months, but the heat gain from the sun (passive solar) is also lost. When measures of such magnitude are considered, the services of a professional engineer or architect to weigh the possible trade-offs is generally a sound investment.

Energy Losses

Most energy is expended to condition a building's air, which either seeps in uncontrolled from the outside (infiltration) or is deliberately brought in (ventilation). Unless the outside air is at the desired indoor temperature, it must be heated or cooled. State codes set requirements for the amount of induced outside air in cubic feet per minute (cfm) per occupant. Years ago when energy was not a factor, codes were set on the assumption that if a little fresh air was good, a lot of fresh air was even better. In some states the codes called for as much as thirty cfm per occupant of fresh air. In most states the requirements are now four or five cfm per occupant. Many unit ventilators still need to be adjusted to this lower intake level.

The Audit

Managing energy is predicated on understanding the sources of heat, how it moves, how it is lost, and how energy is used. The energy audit consists of both the application of this knowledge and of common sense. Understanding audits and their function and value is the backbone of energy conservation.

The many names assigned to audits have proved confusing. It helps to remember that an audit is no more than an inspection of a building to identify opportunities for conserving energy. Audits vary in intensity, comprehensiveness, preciseness of findings, and the credentials of the auditors.

A mini-audit, often referred to as a "walk-through audit" or the "energy audit" in the federal energy grants program, commonly called the Schools and Hospitals Program, is an elementary inspection that takes a few hours and uses little instrumentation, limited auditor training, and often a checklist or workbook. It is relatively inexpensive and the findings are generally recommendations for operations and maintenance procedures or low-cost "quick-fix" measures. The auditor for the walk-through audit usually has some training but seldom has a professional license. Recommendations usually do not include precise cost-effectiveness figures. Because of its limitations, school administrators should not use mini-audit information as a basis for recommending capital investments.

In contrast, the maxi-audit is comprehensive, instrumented, often computer-based, considers all envelope components and all energy-consuming subsystems (unless otherwise directed by the owner), and is more expensive. The findings are based on the professional judgment of the auditor, who is professionally licensed, and the recommendations are accompanied by precise calculations—initial investment costs, energy savings per measure, and projected payback are all spelled out. These major audits also go by various names, including verification audit and investigatory audit; in the Schools and Hospitals Program this type of audit is referred to as a Technical Assistance (TA) analysis. Since the federal energy grants program came along early in the evolution of the energy audit, the last description is becoming more commonplace.

Energy Management Plans and Implementation

The basics of energy management previously described need to be applied to specific conditions and molded into a comprehensive plan. The best energy plan is one that helps a school system identify what it can do for itself, schedule a way to do it, evaluate it, and know when to call for outside help.

An energy management plan will evolve from a careful review of the data base, the audit results, and the interaction of the planners. Costs for energy, the opportunity to use less energy, the potential return on energy-saving investments, and available resources will dictate much of the educational organization's plans. There are some concerns common to most districts or private schools that warrant special attention, including level of effort, auditing needs, staff training, judging retrofit options, life-cycle costing, demand billing, energy education, contingency planning, and communications and public relations.

Level of Effort

When a school business administrator launches an energy management program, there seems to be a great temptation to try to do everything at once. Generally, this generates false expectations and frustrations, and it is seldom the most efficient way to use available resources. The wise use of limited resources requires a plan that identifies the most cost-effective measures and then implements and evaluates the measures before addressing other concerns.

In a situation where no concerted effort has been made to conserve energy, the following steps should be taken after the data base is established:

Step 1. Through the analysis of the data, rank the buildings by Btus per square foot consumption. Look at those buildings using a disproportionate amount of energy—the "energy hogs." Eliminate any building where the reasons for the high discrepancies in consumption are known; for example, if it is the only air-conditioned building in the system, if it is a facility used extensively outside of regular school hours, and the like.

Step 2. Do a walk-through energy audit. Inspect the energy hogs first. The audit should have a checklist to identify the possible energy-conserving operations and maintenance procedures and should have space to log completion of the procedures. In other words, the energy audit checklist and the work log can be the same document. This audit should also gauge whether there is a potential to save significant amounts of energy through capital investments. This assessment is crucial, for it is quite possible to pay more for a comprehensive audit than is warranted by the potential for saving energy.

Step 3. Gather together the recommended changes for energy conservation in operations and maintenance procedures and the low-cost energy conservation recommendations for the high-consumption buildings identified in step 1. Make an interim master schedule for conservation measures that serves only these buildings.

Step 4. Implement those recommendations that are educationally and economically feasible. This step can save the most money. (Experience shows that institutions with energy retrofits that maintain their energy-conserving operations and maintenance save five times as much as those institutions that make only the capital investments.) Implementation of energy-efficient o&m procedures requires that the o&m staff be trained to carry out this function. If they are not, a one- or two-day workshop should be held to provide this training. (See the following section on staff training.)

Step 5. Gather new data on energy consumption and assess whether the buildings are still out of line. If they are, review the energy audits regarding the value of building modifications. Weigh the recommendations against criteria such as the age of the building, the building's function, and the potential to save energy; then, determine if a more comprehensive audit is warranted. Rank those buildings where a professional audit appears desirable.

Step 6. Secure the services of an engineer or of an engineer and architect team with energy conservation experience. Ask for and check references. In order of priority, audit those buildings identified in step 5.

The requirements for a Technical Assistance analysis under the National Energy Conservation Policy Act, Title III, serve as a good guide. (It is wise to actually satisfy such requirements if a school may ultimately be considered for a grant under the federal program or a similar state program.)

Step 7. All the comprehensive audits should be reviewed and the recommendations weighed in terms of the resources available and the criteria listed in the following section on judging retrofit applicability. If all other conditions are approximately equal, the recommendations should be ranked by payback, and the school system should go as far down the list as resources allow.

Step 8. As the energy conservation measures are completed, new consumption data should be gathered to determine whether additional work on a given building is justified or if attention should be turned to other buildings in the system.

Across all these steps communication is critical. Everyone affected should know what is being done and why. Care should be exercised that no building-level personnel feel threatened or criticized by having their building inspected. It is not a fault-finding mission but an effort to identify *opportunities* to conserve.

Clearly the steps outlined in the previous list are not as discrete or as sequential as numbering them might suggest. Operations and maintenance work continues; it is not signed off at step 4 and forgotten. Some buildings may be ready for a professional audit or for energy modifications while others are having further operations and maintenance work done. Availability of materials and equipment, the nature of the modification, and whether or not it can be done while the school is occupied or under prevailing weather conditions all may affect progress through the steps.

The underlying theme is that the simple, less costly things are done first and are then assessed. It is not good business nor cost-effective to jump ahead and sign a contract, as one district nearly did, to have all buildings professionally audited as the very first step in an energy management program. To put it in education parlance, we need to cope with *See Spot Run* before we tackle *War and Peace.*

Staff Training

Experience has shown that acquiring and installing the best of the energy conservation hardware is less than half the battle. Energy is, in large measure, saved by people who understand energy conservation and their building and its systems.

Training custodians and o&m people is particularly important. Training principals as building managers is also highly desirable. As indicated previously in step 4, a one- or two-day workshop to acquire an energy sensitivity and some technological "know-how" is critical. It is undoubtedly the single most cost-effective energy effort the school system can undertake.

An energy management plan is of only limited value if it does not provide for training the people who have the ultimate responsibility for implementing the plan. Energy is not saved by a memo or a plan but by the person who turns the valve or flips the switch. Unless a school system is fortunate enough to have staff with considerable energy management expertise, the staff training should be provided by outside consultants. Ongoing technical reenforcement, if treated concertedly and conscientiously, can often be handled internally. For example, custodians in the Lincoln Public Schools in Nebraska routinely audit each other's buildings.

Judging Retrofit Applicability

Assuming that all the energy-conserving o&m procedures and low-cost recommendations have been implemented, the next step is to determine what, if any, energy conservation measures (ECMs) should be implemented. The criteria for evaluating the merits of the various potential measures should include (not necessarily in order of priority):

1. Payback—How cost-effective is it? How soon will the initial cost be recovered through the energy saved?
2. Educational soundness—Will the installation process or the resulting modifications have any negative impact on the learning environment?
3. Effect of fuel—Would a switch in fuels put the school system in a better position because of availability or price?
4. Aesthetically pleasing, or at least not unattractive.
5. Resources to do the job—personnel and funds to cover initial expenditures.
6. Relationship to other nonenergy jobs that must be done; for example, increasing insulation during reroofing.
7. Potential life and use of the building.
8. Relationship to other measures under consideration—the contemplated ECM may be more or less attractive if done jointly with other energy modifications.
9. Other factors deemed important by local school officials.

While this list is not intended to suggest which criteria are most important, the first criterion listed, payback (initial cost divided by the annual value of energy saved), is often the most important consideration when evaluating an ECM. The economics of an ECM are especially key in tight budget situations. Furthermore, the agents responsible for allocating funds can often be "sold" on the energy-conserving modifications because these measures have a good return on investment.

In addition to the previous criteria, there are some potential ECMs that deserve further elaboration.

Solar Energy

When considering major retrofits, active solar systems should be included. Unfortunately, in most areas of the country active solar is not cost-effective for existing buildings because the paybacks are apt to extend beyond the life of the buildings. Generally, many measures are more economically attractive, although active solar for new construction in some parts of the country is becoming more economically feasible. Anyone contemplating active solar should also consider the recurring costs associated with maintaining a system. It is wise to talk with other administrators in the area who have active solar—their experiences should be helpful. The state energy office can provide sources of information and often the names of places with solar installations.

As other fuels increase in cost, solar will improve as an alternative energy source. With increased demand, the technology and the materials' cost will put it more within reach. Periodic reevaluation of the cost-effectiveness of solar should be an ongoing part of an energy management plan.

These observations pertain to *active* solar, which involves the installation of solar collectors and thermal storage systems. *Passive* solar—gaining solar energy benefits through building orientation, configuration, and structure—is already an economically attractive energy source in many localities, particularly in new construction.

In addition to cost considerations, active and passive solar do provide greater energy independence. Solar is somewhat weather dependent; however, unlike fossil fuels, international and national political and economic concerns do not influence its availability. Reliance on solar and other renewable resources reduces the schools' vulnerability to shortages in nonrenewable fuels.

Structural Considerations

Modifications can change other factors affecting a building. For example, increasing roof insulation on buildings in the northern states will improve the insulation properties, reduce snow melt, and increase the weight that load-bearing walls may have to carry. Any roof insulation project in heavy snowfall areas should also consider the structural load.

Lighting

Under the broader rubric of judging energy conservation measures, lighting needs very special attention. Lighting seems as simple as the flick of a switch—it is not. Well-intentioned but misguided efforts may save a little energy but, at the same time, may detract from the learning environment.

Most schools entered the 1970s overilluminated. When administrators saw their utility bills zooming upwards, they started removing the bulbs or tubes, both referred to as "lamps" in the trade. Suddenly foisted into a new "energy" world, most schoolpeople did not discriminate between the amount and the quality of light. They took out every other lamp or emptied every other fixture without regard to the available light or the uneven

Exhibit 14.9

Annual Kwh Required to Light a Facility by Lamp Type (10,000 Sq. Ft. to 100 Footcandles for 4,000 Hrs./Yr.)

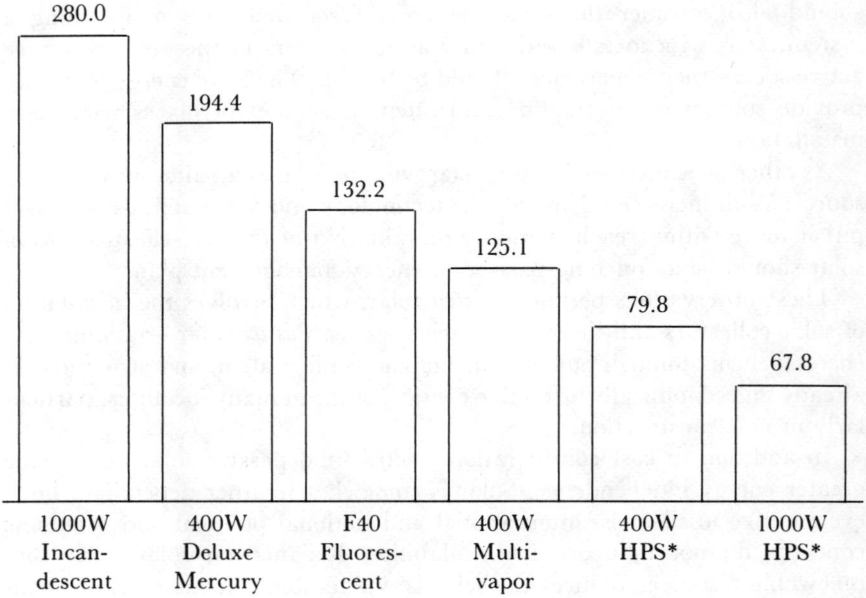

* High Pressure Sodium

Source: General Electric Company

lighting patterns that resulted from those actions. Few administrators owned or used a light meter. Too often they left the energy-draining ballast in place.

Today administrators better understand the importance of measuring light to be sure it is adequate for learning activities, and they recognize that some lamps are more energy efficient than others. Exhibit 14.9 shows the number of kilowatt hours it takes to create the same level of illumination with various lamps.

Exhibit 14.9 shows that incandescent lamps use twice the power as standard fluorescent lamps to provide the same illumination. When operating costs are factored in, replacing incandescent general lighting with fluorescent will reduce costs about 70 percent. Using the watt-reduced fluorescent (not shown in the exhibit) will reduce the amount of available light, or lumens, generated by about 3 percent, but will cut costs by up to 14 percent over standard fluorescents. This efficiency is further enhanced by installing energy-efficient ballasts.

High-pressure sodium (HPS) is presently the most efficient lamp on the market; however, its color rendition is not true. Using it for gymnasiums or outdoor lighting will reduce operating costs 80 percent over incandescent, 50 percent over mercury, and 30 percent over fluorescent. However, *HPS is not recommended for classroom use.*

Another way of saving energy through better lighting design is to provide flexibility with multiple switches so that the teacher will use only the lighting necessary. Very often the bank of lights by the windows need not be turned on, while others farther away from the window are needed. Twenty footcandles of natural light is equal to fifty footcandles of mechanically produced light.

Assessing Cost-Effectiveness

Cost-effectiveness is not static as long as fuel prices are fluctuating. ECMs that do not seem cost-effective at one time should be reexamined at a later date. As energy costs increase, the sliding scale of what is cost-effective also goes up. Conversely, if energy costs drop, the payback period becomes longer. At any given time, the conservation measures should be judged against a common denominator such as the payback period. The simple payback period as a criterion to determine what measures to cut first is a quick and useful yardstick; however, it does not address all costs associated with the measure. Life-cycle costing is a more comprehensive procedure that also reduces all the variables to a single common measure of effectiveness.

Life-Cycle Costing (LCC)

As a public trust, the schools have abided by certain procedures to ensure funds are spent without bias or favoritism. The "low-bid" procedure emphasized first cost (initial cost of a purchase), but this practice dissuaded careful consideration of the full cost (additional costs that might arise) of any purchase over its life.

Increasing energy costs call for more careful scrutiny of these procedures, and administrators are increasingly recognizing the importance of identifying all costs related to the purchase and maintenance of energy-saving items. Therefore, an energy management plan should incorporate some aspects of LCC in appraising the value of potential energy conservation measures.

LCC is a means of evaluating all relevant costs that might occur over the life of the equipment. (This concept was discussed in greater detail in the preceding chapter.) In addition to the initial investment costs, future replacement costs, and operations and maintenance costs, salvage and resale values are adjusted to a consistent time basis and combined into one measure of cost-effectiveness so alternative projects can be compared.

Because of its consideration of future costs, LCC is a tool particularly appropriate for judging the effectiveness of energy conservation measures against future energy savings. A formula suggested in the guide *Life-Cycle Cost*

Manual for the Federal Energy Management Program, developed by the National Bureau of Standards (1980) for the federal government's own use, helps put the various significant dollar costs related to a project into a usable sequence:

Total life-cycle costs		Investment costs		Salvage value		Maintenance and operations (nonfuel)		Replacement costs		Energy costs
TLCC	=	I	−	S	+	M	+	R	+	E

Calculations are made using present value (or present worth). The goal is to establish a time-equivalent value of past, present, or future costs for an item or project related to a specified time, such as a base year. This process is designed to avoid mixing present dollars with tomorrow's inflated dollars and then attempting to make comparisons with two such discrepant values.

Demand Billing and School–Utility Relations

Energy management may include procedures that do not necessarily save energy, but do save dollars. Such is the case with electrical demand charges. Carsie Denning, former Assistant Controller for the Support Services of the North Carolina State Board of Education, has reported that districts may spend an additional twenty to thirty thousand dollars over a two-year period because of the amount of energy they used in one fifteen-minute period of peak demand (Denning 1981).

Approximately 70 percent of the school systems are on some kind of demand billing, but the percentage of school administrators that know how to read electricity rate schedules is abysmally low. The section on buying power in the chapter "Accounting for Energy" in *Managing Energy Efficient Schools* (Hansen 1984) can help school administrators become familiar with the intricacies of a rate schedule and its implications for school operations.

The school business administrator should be sure the energy manager also looks over utility bills every month. Both the energy manager and the person paying the utility bill should be on a first-name basis with their utility representative. The representative should "walk through" the rate schedule and the billing procedure with the schoolpeople until they can identify exactly how charges are established and billed. The schoolpeople should then consider the implications of the rate schedule for school operations.

The utility company is not the adversary. Too often it is the school administrator's own ignorance that creates misunderstanding. In many cases demand charges are a penalty for poor management. Given the chance, most utilities will work closely with the schools to bring demand down—this is a potential partnership that the wise school official should not pass up.

If demand billing is a costly problem, the school system should consider some demand-limiting procedure that will shut off equipment when the system is about to move into the higher cost brackets. The most effective way to accomplish demand limiting is with an automated energy management system.

Energy Management Systems (EMSs)

The cheapest, most effective way to save energy is to shut things off when they are not needed. Due to human fallibility, good intentions do not always mean correct actions will be taken. Logistics also get in the way. The cost of personnel and their proximity to the switches, particularly for more sophisticated on and off timing such as duty cycling, contribute to making very desirable manual-control procedures too cumbersome and costly. However, as the cost of microprocessor systems continues to come down, computer-based EMSs are being used more often to mechanically control the equipment. The potential to save energy is so great that the original investment often pays back within a year. Yet schoolpeople are often disappointed with their EMSs. This disappointment is usually fostered by the tendency to think about hardware long before needs, functions, and software.

Before discussing specific concerns and capabilities, it's important to stress that a computer-based system can aid the facility's operations and maintenance team but cannot replace it. An EMS is no substitute for on-site judgment. Nor does it make up for sloppy maintenance. It can, however, make an efficient system operate even better.

The first step is to analyze how the buildings use energy and what strategies can most effectively be used to reduce consumption. These strategies will need to be translated into customized software that will control energy-consuming equipment. Exhibit 14.10 provides a list of typical EMS software strategies.

Once the desired strategies have been identified, developing the right specifications will make a great difference. They should be specific enough to protect the system from a low bid that would provide less service than needed, but general enough to allow for differences between vendors. One of the first rules in EMS specifications is "write to the point," since the sensor and control points read the situation and give the orders (see exhibit 14.11). Some points are musts, others offer nonenergy benefits, and some fit in the "sure-would-be-nice" category. An EMS cannot neglect the "must" points without compromising the value of the system, and avoiding unnecessary points can control costs. Consulting engineers can really earn their keep in designing the right number of points.

Exhibit 14.10

Typical EMS Software Strategies

- **Start/Stop (S/S)**—a lot of energy can be saved by just being sure equipment runs only enough to meet needs and is *Off* when not needed. Multiple S/S with 24-hour programs will start and stop lights, fans, boilers, air conditioners, and the like at designated times. Holiday scheduling should be included.
- **Optimized start/stop**—warm-up and early shut down allows variable scheduling to condition a building just before occupancy and begins to shut down heating/cooling before people leave, allowing the building to "coast."
- **Enthalpy control**—a "free" cooling strategy that uses dry bulb and dew point temperatures to measure indoor and outdoor air heat content (enthalpy). It opens damper to allow outside air to enter when it's less than indoor air enthalpy. This economizer function allows cool, dry outside air to replace a certain amount of mechanically cooled air. (Requires an analog output signal that could increase costs.)
- **Demand limiting**—monitors utility meters, calculates demand (rate, measured in kw), and compares it to the peak in computer memory. As demand approaches peak, selected loads are turned off on a priority schedule. Demand charges can be up to 40 percent of the electric bill; so demand limiting can mean substantial savings used with duty cycling (see below), and *Off* times can be staggered for even greater savings.
- **Duty cycling**—selected loads are shut off for a percentage of time in a preset period since many schools have overdesigned equipment; duty cycling can shut them off for short periods without loss of comfort. Software should allow for *On/Off* times to be adjustable and to compensate if temperatures exceed preset upper or lower limits. Variable duty cycling is an enhancement of duty cycling where the relative On/Off periods are adjusted according to some sensor condition. Load distribution in duty cycling permits loads to be distributed to prevent all loads being cycled together, thereby reducing demand.
- **Minimum On/Minimum Off**—establishes minimum time for equipment to be *On* or *Off*; prevents excessive duty cycling.
- **Self-diagnosis**—the EMS dianoses itself and indicates what, if anything, is wrong with it.
- **Override switch monitoring**—the override switches are necessary for safety and maintenance functions, but can lead to EMS abuse. Program should monitor use of switches.
- **Special functions**—user-generated print programs, restart routines, equipment status checking, error detection.

Exhibit 14.11

Guidelines in Point Selection

Controlled Equipment and Device	Necessary Points	Possible Points
Sensors—Environmental	1 outdoor dry bulb (heating, cooling)	1 outdoor dew point or relative humidity (enthalpy program)
	1 indoor dry bulb (monitor space conditions; operation of heating and cooling; night set back)	Return air dry bulb and dew point (enthalpy)
		Percent oxygen and temperature of stack gasses (boiler efficiency)*
		Measurement of mixed air and supply air temperature at each fan (advance sensing of problems)
		Chilled water temperature supply and return, and chiller operating amps to calculate efficiency
Sensors—Facility	Watt transducer if utility signal not available (transducer from utility meter is most accurate)	Submetering of partial loads
		Flow verification, fans and pumps
		Compressor operation verification
		Filter status (sense fan maintenance needs)
Fan Units	Start/stop, each supply fan	Damper control at fan

exhibit 14.11, *continued*

Controlled Equipment and Device	Necessary Points	Possible Points
		Damper operation verification
		Start/stop on independently operated return fans
Boilers	Start/stop	
Air-Conditioning Units (Chillers and Cooling Towers)	Start/stop of AC unit	Alarm if safety switches trip
Pumps	Start/stop	

*For district above 4,000 heating degree days, this becomes a necessary point.

At this stage, a check with equipment manufacturers for advice on control strategies and warranty protections can prevent headaches later. For example, duty cycling (see exhibit 14.10) reportedly shortens equipment life, and it may pay to check for guidelines from such groups as the National Electrical Manufacturers Association. Systems that ensure minimum *off* and *on* times are available and should be considered. Energy savings may compensate for shorter motor or compressor life.

Specific system configurations and hardware should be considered after software and control point needs have been determined. Desired performance specifications can usually also serve as specifications for the hardware. The school system can also protect itself by listing acceptable equipment and installers.

An EMS has applications beyond the control of energy-consumer devices and equipment. The two most prevalent adjuncts to an EMS are fire and security procedures. A system can be used to monitor smoke detectors, fire control system water-flow rates, and intrusion alarms and to count the number of times an area is entered. When outfitted with a communications interface and autodialing modem (automatic telephone), the system can even call a fire or police department. Since the EMS is already connected to air handlers (which distribute heated and cooled air to the conditioned areas through ducts), it can shut them off when smoke is detected.

An EMS can also serve as an excellent management tool. It can maintain an equipment status log, keep an inventory of equipment and spare parts, report faulty equipment, log equipment repair, and schedule preventive maintenance. The system can analyze incoming data for alarm conditions, trip audible and visible alarms, and log the alarms. It can also provide consumption data directly to the energy accounting system—storing, rejecting, or synthesizing as programmed.

In addition to the initial installation considerations, always check to see how easily the system can be expanded, what kind of service and maintenance is provided, and what kind of personnel training and follow-up support is offered. Unless the school system has someone trained and responsible for operating the system as well as solid maintenance procedures, an EMS is nothing more than a glorified time clock.

Energy Education

Energy managers, o&m personnel, custodians, and others responsible for reducing consumption are inclined to worry about the school plants, and in the process they overlook a key group that can provide much help in conserving energy—the students.

There is no better time for the students to learn about energy conservation than when the walls and systems around them are being changed to reduce energy consumption. The schoolhouse makes an excellent laboratory for learning about energy. As students learn, they help reduce consumption, and in addition, the teachers develop a greater appreciation of what the energy manager and his team are trying to do and often contribute to the energy conservation effort.

Tenneco (1981) has a free booklet available to schoolpeople, called "Something Special for Teachers." Building on the experiences from its Schoolhouse Energy Efficiency Demonstration Project, Tenneco has designed the booklet to provide teachers with some background information on energy, a survey form so students can audit a school building themselves (recommended for eighth grade and above), and lesson plans to teach students about energy and energy conservation.

An energy management plan should recognize the importance of all facets of energy education (not only conservation), should encourage an integration of energy management activities with curriculum activities, and should structure teacher-student involvement in the school system's energy efforts.

Contingency Plans

Part of managing a district or a private school's energy needs is knowing how to run the schools with less energy during supply disruptions, and central to such contingency planning is an understanding of energy availability. Contrary to the impression often given by the press, the availability of any fuel does not depend on any one factor; rather, there are three: (1) undiscovered resources—those likely to exist; (2) proven reserves—tapped, sitting, or moving; and (3) deliverability—receiving the energy when it's needed.

There is very little likelihood in the near future that the nation is going to run out of any kind of fuel. Areas of the country may *temporarily* run low on *specific* fuels. (This chapter does not address a complete cutoff of imports, which is another scenario of such magnitude that it cannot be adequately dealt with here.) What is important in this discussion is to emphasize planning for any substantial reduction either in imports or domestic production or in the nation's ability to assure deliverability under such conditions.

State energy offices have exhorted industries to make their own contingency plans to reduce economic disruption. Schoolpeople need to make contingency plans as well because it is unwise to count on someone else developing a rational plan for the school or district. The data base will show how much of a certain kind of fuel is being used in the system. The contingency plan should include measures to operate on 10 percent less and 20 percent less *of each fuel* consumed, and it should describe how to implement an orderly shutdown procedure, particularly for winter shutdown in the northern states where freezing temperature could cause building or equipment deterioration. Unless carefully planned, unanticipated closings could prove an expensive problem.

When there is a supply disruption, closing schools seems to be the easy remedy. Closer scrutiny suggests that this action is simplistic and perhaps counterproductive. Collectively, students give off a considerable amount of heat. When school is dismissed, that collective benefit is lost. In order to keep schools from deteriorating while shut down in cold weather, they must be heated to between 50° and 55°. Body heat can make up much of the difference between 55°F and the thermostat setting of 68°F. Both the North Carolina and New York state departments of education did studies that concluded that closing schools to save energy was probably counterproductive. With half the mothers of school-age children working outside the home, many homes are vacant during the day. Closing the school not only means economic disruption for the mothers or fathers (nationally, 18 percent of the schoolchildren come from single-parent families), but also that the energy demand in the home goes up.

Energy is not derived from a single fuel. The North Carolina and New York studies tell only part of the story. We will not be short of "energy," but rather of a specific fuel. The school or district plan must develop a contingency plan for shortages of *each* fuel. If a school building is burning natural gas and there is a disruption in the gas supply, then it is important to know how many homes, occupied and unoccupied during the day, in that attendance area also burn gas—and what the impact would be on the community supply if the students were sent home.

Under a federal law that is now lapsed, the state energy offices were required to make contingency plans for an energy shortage. By the mid-1980s, only nine states had contingency plans that provided for education in any fashion, and some of these treated energy as a single fuel. In other words, the plan could call for a shutdown of all schools during an *oil* shortage—even if some of the schools burned natural gas.

To this end, it is well to remember that schools can better control their destiny under a supply disruption and also gain the opportunity to "fuel shop" if fuel option boilers are installed. Boilers that burn oil or gas are readily available. Small fluidized bed boilers that offer coal as a third option are now available as well. If a facility warrants boiler work, fuel option should be one of the alternatives considered.

School administrators and their state associations need to work with state education and energy officials to develop rational allocation procedures that account for various levels of cutbacks for each type of fuel. If school business administrators do not become involved, someone at the state level who does not understand the local situation will decide when to close the local schools. Of course, this assumes the state is able to obtain the scarce fuel, which leads us to the other facets of availability.

Generally, most energy watchers agree the fuel will be there in the foreseeable future—if we are willing to pay for it. In the pattern for the rest of the 1980s and probably the 1990s two factors will prevail: in the long run fuel will cost more and additional resources will not be immediately available. In the meantime, the schools could have some hard years ahead. President Reagan's plan to allocate by price, that is, let the marketplace determine availability, suggests that tight supplies will mean more and more expensive energy. The schools' unique governance and financing structure makes it exceedingly difficult for them to compete in the marketplace, and the more optimistic energy projections continue to indicate that school systems must have contingency plans in hand.

Availability concerns must also be part of financial planning. Schools that are shut due to a fuel shortage may lose the state aid that is paid on the basis of school attendance. Furthermore, experience has shown that start-up and repair costs after shutdowns can be significant.

Schoolpeople must exercise a voice in a decision to close a school. To do so, they should know whether closing a school will save a certain fuel at the plant or in transportation, and, if so, what kind and how much. Monitoring consumption during a holiday such as Christmas vacation can supply a comparative data base. They should also have some estimation of whether or not closing a school would save a given fuel in the community as a whole. Finally, they should have in hand some calculations as to what it would cost the local taxpayer to maintain and reopen the schools should they close.

Communications and Public Relations

In order for either a public or a private educational organization to implement an effective energy management plan, it must include a means of communicating with the various groups of people, both inside and outside its walls, who have an interest in the organization. Even the best of plans, if not communicated in a fashion to win support and encourage involvement, is just so much paper.

The essence of effective communication comes in knowing: (1) the target audience (or source); (2) the purpose of the message (or question); (3) what and how much the audience needs to know (or can supply); and (4) the most effective time, format, and approach to reach them. For example, an energy manager might ask why teachers should care that the school is moving from a gas-fired to an electrically driven chiller and that EMS controls are being installed. He or she should realize that information shared early may discourage teachers' resentment that the funds did not go into a pay raise or supplies. The message might convey that reducing energy costs may be the best way to assure that future supplies and pay raises will be possible. Care should be taken, however, to focus on general economic equivalents and not to promise specific deliverables.

1. *The target audiences*. The various audiences to be reached can be grouped as external and internal.
   a. *External audience*. The relations with the external audience may not rest with the energy manager, but it should clearly be his or her responsibility to keep those responsible for school communications informed of contemplated or proposed activities and to share energy achievements.
   b. *Internal audience*. The primary purpose of the energy committee and the building team is to provide conduits for internal communications. They are available to hear input from the different groups inside the organization regarding the various energy activities being contemplated, to inform staff of energy plans, and to elicit support for the energy program. The key to reaching the total staff and the specific groups on staff is to decide what each group needs to know and to tailor the content and approach to those groups.
2. *Purpose of the message*. All communications should have a purpose. *Why* should certain information be shared or sought? The internal energy network is only a mechanism, and until its purposes are supported with well-thought-out content, it is an empty conduit. It can easily be

misused and become useless. Clogged by trivia and obstructed by those who speak but fail to listen, the process can collapse. Clear purpose is essential to clear communication.

3. *The need to know.* The seeking or dispensing of information is generally predicated on a need or desire to inform or to be informed. How much is passed along depends on how critical the details are and on the listener's receptivity. An individual's willingness to listen is influenced by catching his or her attention at the right time and in the right way.

   Recognizing the need is basic. "Empty conduit" stories are often the focal point of disaster scenarios in energy management. Take the example of the school custodian who religiously flipped a switch each evening and flipped it back each morning because "he was told to." But no one ever bothered to tell him why—that it was a manual night setback. During an energy audit, the engineers discovered it was not connected, and, checking the records, found it hadn't been for twelve years. The school had been running wide open, full tilt, round the clock, in a very cold climate all those years—a sad but true story.
4. *Time, format, and approach.* Many an important message falls on "deaf ears" because the timing and the presentation or approach were wrong. A few communications guidelines can help to avoid situations where the intended recipient hears but does not listen, or sees but does not understand.
   a. *Level of content, vocabulary, and the like.* These should be geared to the recipient's level of readiness and receptivity. Complex schematics will probably not help marginally skilled maintenance people to adjust equipment.
   b. *Speak to the listener's or reader's interests.* The question to ask is "Why should they care?" As an example, how many on the staff know what the school's energy bill is this year? How many real dollars would it yield to the operating budget if energy costs were cut by 20 percent? What might that mean in supplies—or in salaries?
   c. *Be honest, realistic, and concise.* Once lost, credibility is hard to restore. False expectations can destroy future receptivity. Don't hide problems; the staff just might help solve them. Wordy, too frequent, or unnecessary memos will gain a reputation for lining the circular file.
   d. *Recognize achievements and contributions.* Good ideas and results can encourage the contributor and others if they are appropriately recognized. Publicizing accomplishments in the newsletter, on a bulletin board, traveling trophies, banners, and the like may seem trite, but these types of recognition do work and have for a long time.

      A carrot *and* stick approach that some administrators have found valuable is making energy achievement part of a job performance review.

e. *Printed material should capture the audience's attention.* Material should be attractive, easy to read, and probably broken up (or spiced up) with some graphics. A little humor often makes the point best of all.
f. *Be attentive.* The best strategy for disseminating information still turns on the old adage, "If you want to be heard, listen."

The above guidelines are not new. They bear repeating because various audiences have over the years built up a gigantic resistance to the topic of energy. Most people are tired of hearing about "energy." They heard about the "crisis" *ad nauseum.* They were told over and over again how we were "running out," but in 1983 the oil glut made front-page news. Skepticism today is real and often justified.

In the final analysis, the school system's energy problem is an economic one. Talk money. Everyone has an interest in greenbacks. Talk benefits to school programs, to the staff's working conditions. Translating "energy" into *real dollars* will overcome energy rhetoric fatigue.

To summarize, the importance of school business administrator leadership and the inherent communications function of the position can best be illustrated by considering the energy audit. The audit is a valuable tool. But audits do not save energy, people do. The audit report unattended gathers dust. Only when it is read, discussed, and implemented can its energy savings be realized. The difference between dust and energy savings is people. And, it is effective communication that will encourage the people to make it work.

Resources

Unfortunately, implementing an energy management plan takes time and money. And, as some clever fellow once said, "Time is money." So, it all boils down to money. Money for the energy manager position and for his or her staff and operations. Money for the operations and maintenance personnel to do their energy-conserving work. Money to do audits. Money to buy and install energy conservation measures. Money—*ad infinitum.*

There are six places the school business administrator can go for financial assistance: existing internal resources, community resources, voter authority for additional revenues, state aid, federal grants, and private-sector alternate financing procedures.

Existing Internal Resources

With declining revenues, higher prices on goods and services, and escalating energy costs, schools today seldom have the internal resources they need to launch an energy program. Ironically, it is energy costs that have so badly depleted many school budgets.

A careful assessment of the school's energy situation, however, will usually reveal the economic justification for cutting back something else in order to make available the money needed to start controlling energy dollars. Business administrators who do not take this step could easily find that the energy drain can take away permanently those things that might have been cut only temporarily.

Community Resources

Very often the local utility or an industry in the community can share someone with energy expertise to help the system begin to cut back on its energy consumption and costs. Retired engineers and others with some knowledge or experience in the field may be willing to assist on a part-time basis at no cost. Also, the local parent group or civic group may plant windbreaks or fund needed instruments such as light meters.

Voter Revenue Authority

Public school districts have not been overwhelmingly effective in recent years in gaining voter authority to assess more taxes or sell bonds. The school business administrator, however, is more apt to get a favorable vote by giving well-documented economic reasons for reducing energy consumption rather than by giving a reason such as, "to raise my salary!" Investing to control energy costs is good business. A school district that can show what it has done on a shoestring with positive results and can show further quick returns on investments is more likely to get the authority to spend the money.

State Aid

Some states, such as Maine and Nebraska, have passed special legislation to provide financial assistance to help schools help themselves. Other states, such as California, have approriated monies to help the local school systems take advantage of the federal energy grants program. School administrators and their state associations should ascertain if such help is available or if the state legislatures might be receptive to requests for this kind of assistance.

Many states now have a great financial interest in containing the public schools' energy dollar. In 1982–83, most states supplied over 50 percent of the public schools' financial support. The cost of energy to the public schools is projected to reach $11 billion by 1990 and $31 billion by 2000. Over half of that is expected to come out of the states' pocketbooks. Reducing school energy consumption is definitely in the states' financial interests.

Federal Grants

The National Energy Conservation Policy Act, Title III, provided funds for Technical Assistance (audits) and Energy Conservation Measure grants to public and private nonprofit schools, institutions of higher education, and hospitals. The law provided funds to match by 50 percent the amount spent by the schools, except in cases of hardship where the federal share may go as high as 90 percent.

Grant cycles follow the federal fiscal year. School business administrators wishing to participate may secure applications and guidelines from their state energy office. The completed applications are submitted to the state energy office for ranking, and recommendations are made to the U.S. Department of Energy. Funds are sent directly from the department to the grant recipient.

Alternate Financing

Alternate financing refers to any source or method of financing other than federal or state education appropriations or local revenues obtained through the normal capital budgeting procedures.

Energy efficiency improvements are increasingly viewed as investments with attractive returns. As a result, outside investors are making capital for retrofits available to school systems through various financing procedures.

Alternate Financing Opportunities and Cautions

In the face of capital constraints, public school administrators must take an agressive approach to developing their ability to save on energy costs. Accessing private capital to improve energy efficiency can

1. Generate immediate positive cash flow;
2. Relieve the tax burden of funding from state and local budgets;
3. Free scarce resources for other educational purposes while preserving the borrowing capacity for other needs;
4. Capitalize on the opportunity value of district money not diverted to energy investments;
5. Avoid the costs of delay that could be incurred through higher energy costs and efforts to maintain old, inefficient equipment; and
6. Make use of private sector energy management expertise.

Many aspects of alternate financing are in their formative stages. Some state laws or guidelines may preclude certain of the following financing procedures. Alternatives for financing have not been fully standardized, and few guidelines are available. As in any new field, firms may venture in without sufficient assurance to the school system that they will survive.

First, the school business administrator should realize that the procedures are set up so that an outside firm will make a profit by investing in energy-efficient improvements for the school system. In almost every instance, the schools could accrue those same financial benefits if they had the initial capital in hand. The cost of delay—losses in potential energy cost savings—will generally exceed the private sector's share if the school system goes through its usual time-consuming bonding and acquisition procedures. In considering any alternate financing scheme, the school administrator needs to weigh the cost of the "interest" on the capital against the availability of the initial investment funds, the cost of the expertise, the maintenance benefits offered, the advantages of obtaining capital without incurring greater indebtedness, and opportunity to use the investment capital for other educational needs.

If alternate financing seems desirable, the institution should seek outside independent consultation before any commitment is made. Consultation sources include state energy offices, workshops on alternative financing, and energy management consulting firms. As with any such agreement, particularly in a relatively new field, certain precautions are warranted. They include:

1. Securing and checking the references of the firm offering alternate financing
2. Establishing the base year after conducting a low-cost audit to be sure the simple energy-conserving operations and maintenance items such as caulking doors and windows, reducing lighting, and calibrating thermostats have been done
3. Determining parameters of comfort levels (the boundaries within which the school system can turn over heating, cooling, and lighting control)
4. Understanding exactly how the formula for determining energy saved and the associated dollar value are calculated and how adjustments in occupancy, functions, or climate are treated
5. Establishing termination provisions, including a user buy-out clause or removal provisions
6. Monitoring the energy savings independent of contractor figures by separate periodic checks or individual metering and working through the formulas
7. Incorporating performance bonding into the contract provisions
8. Having the school system's lawyer review the contract before signing

Financing procedures that can make private capital available to improve energy efficiency include tax-exempt bonds, municipal leasing, cost sharing, shared savings, third-party or joint venture, and general energy services contracts. Because of their size and governance structure, school systems usually exercise one of three options: municipal leasing, cost sharing, and shared savings.

Municipal Leasing. In many states both the public and the nonprofit private schools can enter into a municipal-leasing agreement. This agreement is often structured like a simple loan. It is, in essence, a lease-purchase agreement. The procedure is attractive to the lessor because the interest income is tax-exempt. At the end of the lease, ownership of the property passes to the lessee. Municipal leasing is not generally considered a long-term debt, so concerns regarding voter authority or reduced borrowing capacity are usually not issues.

School districts generally need to include a clause in the agreement limiting their obligation to make lease payments within any single fiscal period. The statement generally stipulates that the lessee will be obligated to make every effort to secure the funds for lease payments. The clause, however, satisfies the common restriction against multiyear liabilities.

Sound energy projects, where a positive cash flow can be anticipated, help secure the agreement. Energy projects are particularly attractive for municipal leasing, especially if the lease payments are structured to be less than the projected savings on energy costs.

Cost Sharing. Schools may enter into an arrangement with the energy equipment supplier to pay the cost of the equipment from the projected savings. The supplier usually takes about 80 percent of the avoided costs until the equipment is paid for. The institution enjoys the 20 percent benefit without any capital investment. The clause discussed under municipal leasing is sometimes desirable for public schools since it limits the district's obligations and satisfies multiyear liabilities. Cost sharing is usually viewed as a lease-purchase agreement and may not be treated as an incurred debt.

In this procedure, the district or the school, of course, is limited to buying the equipment from the vendor offering cost-sharing arrangements. However, many firms, especially those selling computerized energy management systems, now offer such financing opportunities.

Shared Savings. At the end of 1984 shared savings programs were being used with increasing frequency in public and private schools as a means of alternate financing. A private firm audits the buildings to determine the potential for energy savings. Using its expertise and its capital, the firm then modifies the building and installs equipment to reduce energy consumption. The school system and the private firm split the avoided energy costs by using a predetermined formula.

At the end of the contract period, the installed equipment may belong to the institution. More commonly the shared savings company retains ownership. If the firm continues to own the equipment at the end of the contract, the company will generally enter into a subsequent agreement with the schools, offering a split in the savings that is more favorable to the schools.

General Energy Services Contract. A step beyond shared savings and with some of the nuances of third-party financing is the energy services contract. The company delivers the end product for a fee. The package includes lighting at specified levels, electricity for motors and fans, and conditioned air within specified parameters (thermostat settings) established by the school system. Financial arrangements are based on some predetermined service fee plus a penalty factor for any energy consumed over a certain quantity.

The outside firm supplies the energy and assures its most efficient use. The firm usually provides audits, equipment, and site maintenance to help assure the building's energy efficiency. The level of efficiency affects the institution's costs and the firm's profits.

Availability of alternate financing reaffirms that energy conservation is good business. It also means that the scarcity of capital should not deter a system from realizing the benefits of improving energy efficiency in its schools.

Revenues for education will remain tight in the foreseeable future, and energy costs to the nation's schools are expected to continue to climb. Managing energy use will become a progressively more attractive, even essential, way to free up dollars in the school budget. Whether energy conservation funds are made available in the traditional way, with federal grants, or through alternate financing, the investment can facilitate sound business practices in the schools.

Summary

Energy management is primarily a series of economic trade-offs. Weighing those trade-offs requires good data and a careful review of local conditions backed by an understanding of energy conservation.

To meet the energy predicament head on, some tough decisions may have to be made. If all else fails, the school business administrator may have to lobby for less colored paper in kindergarten in exchange for new energy-efficient lamps, or to request a cut in night football to convert a boiler—some unpopular decisions may have to be made. But, if they are not and the energy situation goes unchecked, it could mean no kindergarten or no football at all.

In 1983, when oil prices were fairly low, it cost thirty-five dollars for a *delivered* barrel of oil but only eight dollars for a *conserved* barrel of oil. The inevitable conclusion that must be reached and conveyed is that putting off energy-conserving efforts only makes the matter worse. Materials and equipment to reduce consumption are increasing in cost. The longer a district waits to act, the longer it is apt to pay higher energy costs—and for energy it may not have needed at all. Installing or implementing an energy-conserving measure requires a single major expenditure, but the savings accumulate year after year. For education, the energy problem will be persistent, pervasive, and perhaps pernicious. Managing energy could well become the school business administrator's most critical responsibility.

As energy costs take an ever higher toll, the most prevalent question in the nation may become, "Where will we get the money to pay the fuel bill?" For education, the question may be rephrased: "Where do we get the money to educate the child?" The answer may lie in how well the school system manages its energy concerns.

Glossary of Commonly Used Energy Terms

Barrel—liquid measure of oil, most often crude oil; equals forty-two gallons.

Barrel of oil equivalent—a way to equate other energy sources to a barrel of crude oil; 5.8 million in Btu equivalents.

Boiler capacity—the rate of heat output in Btus per hour measured at boiler outlet, at the design pressure or temperature, and rates fuel input at the site elevation.

Btu (British thermal unit)—a standard unit of measure for heat energy. Equal to the amount of heat energy required to raise the temperature of one pound of water one degree Fahrenheit (specifically 62°F to 63°F). Generally abbreviated Btu (also BTU and B.T.U.).

Building envelope—the building shell; the elements of a building that enclose conditioned spaces. That portion of a building through which thermal energy may be transferred to or from the exterior.

Ccf—a hundred cubic feet. A standard measure of natural gas used for billing purposes. Natural gas is also measured in mcf (thousand cubic feet), and therms.

Cfm—cubic feet per minute. A measure of air change.

Chimney effect—the tendency of cold, denser air to displace the less dense heated air. Refers to the tendency of heated air to rise in ducts, vertical passages, or multistory buildings and the tendency of the cold, denser outside air to replace the heated air through penetrations such as doors, cracks, fireplaces, and the like.

Degree days—a method of measuring temperature variations for any given day. It is the difference between 65°F and the mean daily temperature. Heating degree days refers to when the mean is below 65°F, and cooling degree days refers to when the mean is above 65°F. Cumulatively, it is one measure of the severity of the climate for the season.

Demand load—the electrical energy requirements measured in cycles, usually 15- or 30-minute segments. Most utilities base the price of electricity on this demand level.

Delta temperature—the difference between the desired indoor temperature and the outdoor temperature for a certain locality at a given time. It is often signified by the Greek delta and a subscript *T*.

Efficiency—the ratio of useful work (energy output) to total work (energy input).

Energy—that which does or is capable of doing work. Takes a number of forms and can be transferred from one to another; for example, mechanical (work) to thermal (heat). It is measured in terms of the work it is capable of doing.

Energy audit—an examination of a building's architectural and mechanical drawings, energy history, and use patterns to identify ways to reduce energy consumption. Usually includes an on-site inspection of the building's structure and energy-using systems.

Energy conservation measure (ECM)—a modification to a building requiring capital investment for the purposes of reducing energy consumption.

Environment—the sum of all external conditions and influences affecting the life and survival of an organism.

Footcandles—a measurement of the *amount*, not necessarily quality, of light at a given location; the energy of light one foot from a standard candle.

Glazing—another term used for glass in windows. Windows are also referred to as fenestration.

Gross square feet (GSF)—total square feet in a building envelope using the floor area as a basis. Derived by multiplying the dimensions for each floor.

Heat loss/gain—the quantity of heat passing through a section of material and not available for work, expressed in Btus per hour.

Heat transfer—the movement of heat from a hot substance to a cooler substance by radiation, conduction, or convection.

HVAC—the heating, ventilating, and air-conditioning system; includes heating or chilling equipment, controls, and distribution systems.

Infiltration—the unintended flow of air into a building.

Insulation—a material used as a component part of the building envelope, around piping, or in any fashion to increase resistance to heat flow.

Learning environment—the conditions necessary for satisfactory learning.

Life-cycle costing (LCC)—a method used to determine the total cost of equipment over its lifetime (or a set number of years) calculated in present worth; includes initial cost, anticipated maintenance and operation costs, and replacement costs, as well as salvage or resale values.

Lumen—A measure of light generated by a luminous source. One lumen across one square foot equals one footcandle.

R value—a measure of resistance to the flow of heat. All envelope components have an R value, generally used to measure insulation materials in units of square feet per hour; the higher the R value, the greater the resistance. Also called an R factor.

Simple payback period—the length of time required for an initial investment to pay for itself in the current value of the energy saved.

Therm—a unit of natural gas fuel containing 100,000 Btus.

U value—a coefficient expressing the thermal conductance of a composite structure in Btus/sq. ft./hr./Δ_T.

Ventilation—outside air deliberately induced into a contained space; any related air change equipment and processes.

References

American Association of School Administrators. *AASA Energy Use Study, 1981*. Arlington, Va.: American Association of School Administrators, 1981.

American Association of School Administrators. *1982–1983 Member Survey of Status and Opinions*. Arlington, Virginia: American Association of School Administrators, 1983. (a)

American Association of School Administrators (with the National School Boards Association and the Council of Great City Schools). *The Maintenance Gap*. Arlington, Va.: American Association of School Administrators, 1983. (b)

Denning, Carsie. "Economies Through Electric Load Management: How to Program Electric Power Efficiently." A presentation to the American Association of School Administrators Annual Convention, Atlanta, 1981.

Educational Facilities Laboratories, Academy of Educational Development, New York. Personal conversations, 1981.

Educational Research Service. Data from the annual ERS Local School Budget project, 1984.

Hansen, Shirley, J. *Managing Energy Efficient Schools*. Austin, Texas: Energy Efficiency Division of the Public Utility Commission of Texas, 1984.

National Bureau of Standards. *Life-Cycle Cost Manual for the Federal Energy Management Program*. Washington, D.C.: United States Department of Commerce, 1980.

President's Commission for a National Agenda for the Eighties. *Energy, Natural Resources, and the Environment in the Eighties*. Washington, D.C.: Superintendent of Documents (81–649, AACR 2), 1981.

Tenneco, Inc. *Something Special for Teachers*. Schoolhouse Energy Efficiency Demonstration (SEED) Project. Houston, Texas: Tenneco, Inc., 1981.

United States Department of Education. *The Condition of Education, 1982 Edition*. Washington, D.C.: National Center for Education Statistics, 1983.

United States Department of Energy. *School Finance and Energy Through 2000*. Prepared by Shirley Hansen Associates under a Department of Energy contract. Washington, D.C.: U.S. Department of Energy, 1984.

Supplementary Reading

Hansen, Shirley J. *Energy Efficient Operations and Maintenance for Schools*. Austin, Texas: Energy Efficiency Division of the Texas Public Utility Commission, 1983.

Hansen, Shirley J. "Selecting and Specing Energy Management Systems (EMS)." *The School Administrator*. Arlington, Va.: American Association of School Administrators, 1983.

Stephan, Edward. "Solar Energy in Schools—Real Answer or Fad?" Presentation to the American Association of School Superintendents Annual Convention, 1981.

The Electrification Council. *Energy Management in Educational Facilities*. Washington, D.C.: The Electrification Council, 1983.

United States Department of Education. *School Finance Project*. Vol. I. Washington, D.C.: U.S. Department of Education, 1983.

PART V

Information Systems

Information enables the school business administrator to plan and control, and the quality of information can make the difference between a good and a bad decision. It is no wonder that the school business administrator allocates large amounts of time and resources to collecting, storing, modifying, retrieving, and reporting information. In schools today, computers are used to manage the bulk of information, and as a consequence, issues of information are also issues of computer hardware, software, and associated personnel. Chapter 15 emphasizes processes for creating and modifying management information systems. Chapter 16 focuses on how general-purpose software in tandem with low-cost microcomputers has rapidly increased the school business administrator's ability to automate information handling, which often increases the usefulness of information while reducing its cost.

15

Managing Information Requirements

by Richard P. Vigilante

During the past decade, school districts have had to deal with a number of critical educational issues arising out of a dynamic social and political environment. Compliance with integration laws, fiscal constraints, declining enrollments, and low achievements have all imposed great demands on districts' decision-making capabilities. As a result, educational administrators have been repeatedly faced with the need for accurate, detailed, and timely information for a variety of analyses, operations, and reports. Such situations, which are becoming increasingly more frequent, call for both high levels of technical expertise and clear lines of organizational authority to provide the necessary information.

This chapter will introduce administrators to the basic concepts and procedures necessary to successfully implement school computer systems. Emphasis will be placed on *information*—how to gather it, maintain it, and project it—rather than on *systems*; consequently, those aspects of computer technology that are more often the function of the analyst, such as data file structure programming, will not be discussed. The topics covered are therefore based primarily on their relevancy to the educational administrator as the user of an information system.

Educational Computing: A Crash Course

The Latin word *computare* means "to compute." Therefore, any device that helps a person do computations—such as a slide rule, adding machine, or pocket electronic calculator—might technically be called a computer. However, today the word *computer* is almost always used to refer to an electronic, digital computer. Computers are basically tools for doing jobs better, and their advantages include fundamental features such as speed of processing, accuracy, and access to data.

Computer Fundamentals

The features that distinguish an electronic computer from other computing devices are speed, internal memory, and automatic execution of a program stored in the computer's memory. The speed of an electronic computer results from electronic circuitry. The internal memory of a computer is used to store both data and instructions. A sequence of instructions (such as an entire payroll calculation) is carried out automatically, without human intervention. In contrast, a calculator requires human direction (by means of a keyboard) at each step in a computational routine.

There are two basic types of computers: analog and digital. An *analog computer* operates on data that vary continuously, such as voltage, pressure, and temperature. A *digital computer* is basically a counting device that operates on discrete data or numbers. Since most educational data are in discrete form (either numerical or alphabetical), the digital computer is readily adaptable to both administrative and instructional data-processing applications.

All applications of a computer to education, regardless of their complexity, require a *computer system* for their operation. A computer system consists of the *hardware* and *software* through which the application is processed. As the name implies, hardware is physical equipment such as the mechanical, electronic, and magnetic units in a computer. Software is the set of computer programs that causes the computer to produce the desired results. To understand the purpose of each of these units, one must know what operations a computer must perform in order to solve a problem.

Suppose a school administrator wished to compare the salaries of twenty teachers in a school and find the arithmetic mean. To accomplish this task manually, the following steps might be performed:

1. Write the annual salaries of the twenty teachers in a column on a sheet of paper.
2. Add the twenty salaries together to obtain their sum.
3. Divide the sum by twenty to obtain the mean of the salaries.
4. Record the answer or communicate it to someone else.

Now consider how a computer might accomplish the task without any outside assistance or intervention during the calculations. First, there are two steps that would have to be performed by a human being:

1. A set of instructions would have to be prepared to direct the computer to perform each step in the calculation. Such a set of instructions is called a *program*. The program must be prepared in a language or form that the computer can understand.
2. The twenty salaries would have to be prepared or made available in a form suitable for entry into the computer (for example, they might be punched into cards).

To solve a problem on the computer, it is necessary to create a computer program and to prepare the input data. If such a program has been prepared to compute the arithmetic mean of twenty salaries, and this program has been stored in the computer, the program will direct the computer to perform the following steps:

1. Read the twenty salaries into the computer.
2. Compute the sum of the salaries.
3. Divide the sum by twenty.
4. Write or display the result.

In this example, as in most computer applications, the computer must be able to *read* or *input* data, and it must be able to *write* or *output* results. It must have a *memory* to store program instructions as well as the data that are being processed. Since the computer is directed by a program, it must have a unit that interprets the program instructions and supervises their execution. These functions are performed by a *control unit.* Finally, the computer requires a unit that can add, divide, and perform other arithmetic operations. This unit is called an *arithmetic and logic unit*, since it can also perform logical operations. These various units and their functions are described in more detail.

Central Processing Unit

In most computers the memory, control unit, and arithmetic/logic unit are integrated into a single device called the *central processing unit* (*CPU*), which is usually contained in a single cabinet. Continual advances in modern electronics technology result in ever smaller, faster, and more reliable central processing units. This has made possible the development of tiny processing units contained on a single semiconductor chip called a *microprocessor*. Microprocessors perform many of the CPU functions in most computers, from the smallest *microcomputer* to the largest *mainframe* computer.

Memory. Program instructions and required data are stored in the memory unit of the CPU. Data and instructions are kept in areas called *locations*; each location in the memory unit has an *address* so that data can be located. The capacity of the main memory depends on the size of the computer, which can range from a few thousand locations in a small microcomputer to several million locations in a mainframe computer. Since memory is relatively expensive, it is often not feasible to store all of the data used in large processing applications in the CPU. Instead, less-expensive *mass* (or *secondary*) storage devices such as tape and disk drives are used for storing large data files.

Control Unit. The control unit supervises all activities of the computer under the direction of a stored program. First, the control unit determines which instruction is to be executed next by the computer. The control unit then fetches this instruction from the memory and interprets the instruction, which is then executed by the other computer units. For example, the control unit may cause two numbers to be added by the arithmetic/logic unit. Other instructions may cause data to be read into the memory or to be displayed on a printer.

Arithmetic/Logic Unit. The arithmetic/logic unit of the CPU performs arithmetic operations as directed by the control unit. For example, an instruction to add causes two or more numbers to be transferred to the arithmetic/logic unit. The addition is performed by this unit, and the result is then returned to the memory. As well as performing the four basic arithmetic operations, the arithmetic/logic unit also performs logical operations. A typical logical operation involves comparing two numbers, then selecting one of two program paths depending on the result of the comparison.

Input/Output Units

Most educational data-processing applications require the preparation and input of large amounts of data that accrue from the school district's various transactions. These data must be converted to a machine-readable form before they can be input into the computer. As a result, costs of preparing data for input may represent a significant percentage of the total operating budget of a typical computer center. In addition, the number of data-processing jobs that can be handled daily is often limited by input/output operations rather than by internal computer-processing speeds.

A large number of devices and media are used for input and output of data. These may be categorized according to the type of medium used. For low input and output volumes, devices using paper media (punched cards and printed outputs) may be used. For fast but limited data entry and display, keyboard printers and video display terminals are often used. Magnetic media (magnetic tape, disk, and diskette) provide very high-speed input and output and are used in high-volume applications. Some of the more important input/output devices and their advantages and disadvantages are summarized in exhibit 15.1.

Exhibit 15.1

Principal Input/Output Media and Devices

Media/Device	Advantages	Disadvantages
Card (Input)	— Human readable — Easy to change	— Cumbersome and easily damaged — Slow and expensive input
Tape (Input)	— Faster input than cards — Compact and inexpensive	— Only machine readable — Sequential data access
Disk (Input)	— Faster input than tape — Random data access	— Expensive for limited use — Requires tape back-up
Printer (Output)	— Human readable — Multiple copies	— Slow output — Space consuming
Video (Output)	— Compact and cheap — Interactive	— Slow output — Limited display size
Microform (Output) — includes both film and fiche	— Very cheap and compact — Very fast output	— Needs reader/printer — Needs careful indexing

Computer Software

Before problems can be solved on a computer, they must be stated as a program, which is a concise set of instructions to the computer. In the early days of computing, it was necessary to state problems in a highly complex machine language that consisted of octal or hexadecimal number system codes. This was very difficult and tedious, and the number of successful applications was quite limited.

To overcome these problems, a body of computer programs and techniques called software has been developed. Software includes programming languages and translators, and computer operating systems. It also includes *application* programs designed to solve problems for a particular user. Supporting documents and training programs are often considered part of software.

Software systems greatly improve the efficiency of computer use. Well-designed systems can promote use of the computer and reduce programming time and cost. They decrease the dependence of the computer on human action and judgment, thereby increasing productivity. To a large extent, the rapid increase in data-processing applications in recent years can be attributed to improved software systems.

A computer performs a given task by executing a series of instructions stored in its memory. These instructions are prepared (or coded) by a programmer. While relatively simple tasks can be written by a single programmer, many of the applications for education described in the following section require the development of a complex sequence of programs that represents the efforts of both individuals with technical skills and the user.

Computer Applications in Education

Very few institutions and organizations today are unaffected by computer technology. In the past decade educators have become increasingly interested in how they might realize some of the benefits that computers offer. Many schools and school districts already use computers to some extent; however, a great number have not yet explored the possibilities of what computers can do for them and their students.

The basic applications for using computers in schools are shown in exhibit 15.2. As the diagram illustrates, computing is used in three areas of education: administration, research, and instruction.

Administrative Applications

As with almost every other organization today, the average school district has experienced an increase in the number and variety of accounting and record-keeping tasks. The large data-handling and fast data-processing capabilities of computers have found wide applicability in such areas of educational administration as student accounting (for generating attendance data, report cards, and student schedules), budget and finance (for line-item or program budgeting, encumbrance accounting, and financial analyses), payroll and personnel (for producing paychecks, earnings statements, and employee profiles), and career guidance (for student access to occupational, educational, and financial-aid data banks).

Research Applications

Research within a school district can run the gamut from basic statistical analyses of descriptive characteristics (registers, attendance, class size) to fairly sophisticated enrollment forecasts and evaluations of educational programs. Computers not only support such studies by providing statistical programs to analyze data, but they also make the data themselves readily

Exhibit 15.2
Computers in Education

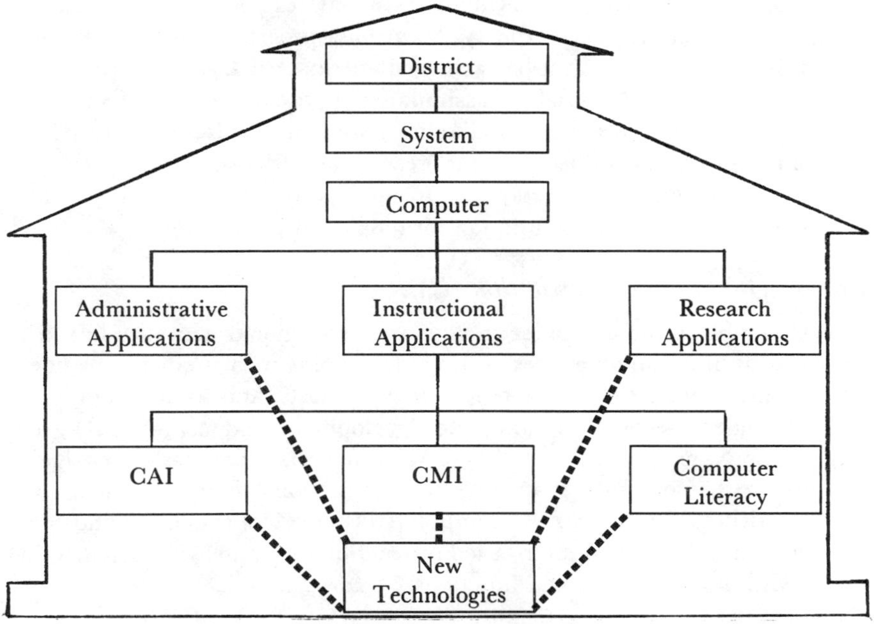

available through the creation and maintenance of detailed and longitudinal data files on students, personnel, programs, and facilities.

The more recent innovations in educational computing involve computers as a tool for or subject of instruction. Instructional computing is a method of automating part of the teaching-learning process. The same storage and processing capabilities used in the more traditional computing applications are also used to store and present instructional material to a student. It is in this application that some questions and misconceptions arise about computers. For example, the idea that the impersonal computer in some way will replace the teacher is sometimes heard. Actually, computer-assisted and computer-managed instruction properly integrated into the curriculum should help both the teacher and the supervisor to be more effective. It can, for example, enable a teacher to provide a student with specialized instruction that otherwise might not be available. A computer can give the slow student additional instruction, and it can help the fast student progress at a speed closer to his or her capability.

Computer-Assisted Instruction (CAI)

CAI uses the capabilities of the computer to provide individualized instruction by complementing other educational methods and materials such as lectures, textbooks, films, and television. The ability of CAI to analyze and feed back information on a student's progress makes it a sophisticated teaching tool. The computer evaluates student responses and adjusts the presentation of material accordingly. Many CAI programs call for branching to new levels when a student has achieved adequate skills in a given subject or for remediation of material not assimilated by the student. CAI techniques include drill and practice (individual student drills with response-adjustment), tutorial (subject content presented in a dialogue mode), simulation (user-computer interaction with models of real situations), and problem-solving (student solution of formulas and problems).

Computer-Managed Instruction (CMI)

CMI employs the computer to support instructional activities linked to educational program objectives, to provide ongoing measurement of student performance with criterion-referenced mastery tests, and to maintain longitudinal student records. At first, the development and use of CMI were largely motivated by the fact that CMI functions were less expensive to perform in the computer than were the instructional functions themselves (such as drill and practice). As computers become less expensive and more powerful, most large computer-based instructional systems will include CMI along with other instructional functions.

Computer Literacy

Increasingly, the computer itself has become a subject of instruction because of its widespread use in business, government, and the professions. There are very few students in school today who will not, at some time in their careers, require some knowledge of computers and their operation. The impact of recent advances in information technology is expected to be felt throughout society. Andrew Molnar of the National Science Foundation writes that in an information society "a computer-literate populace is as important as energy or raw materials are to an industrial society" (Molnar 1978, p. 35). He emphasizes that computers should be part of the curriculum from kindergarten to the university. Computer-literacy programs can be offered at an awareness level (introduction to computer concepts, terminologies, and applications), a functional level (hands-on proficiency in basic computer operations and programming), and a professional level (detailed technical, economic, and organizational knowledge of computer systems).

New Technologies

Five years ago the continuing advances in the miniaturization of computer hardware resulted in the widespread availability of the microcomputer. These small personal computers typically include a relatively powerful microprocessor chip, some primary memory for data and program storage, a keyboard, and a video monitor or small printer for data output. The recent development of the more powerful 16- and 32-bit microcomputers such as the IBM Personal Computer and the Apple MacIntosh has made possible a wide range of administrative data-processing applications. With their hard disk drives, letter-quality printers, professional software, and telecommunications modems, these new microcomputers provide educational administrators with much of the power of a 1970s' minicomputer system at a fraction of the purchase and operating cost. Appropriately configured, professional microcomputers will allow administrators to support and integrate many of the school district's data-processing, word-processing, and communications requirements.

Management Information Systems

Data processing is a term that often connotes a room full of blinking computers, spinning tape reels, and hard-working technicians. Although this may well be an accurate picture of what data processing represents in many instances, data processing does not necessarily require a computer. *Data processing*, more generally and accurately defined, simply means the manipulation of data to achieve a desired result. Viewed from this perspective, computing is only one of many ways to manipulate data.

To provide an additional dimension to the term *data processing*, the word *system* can be added. A system is simply an organized way of doing something. Thus, a data-processing system is an organized way of manipulating data to achieve a desired result. When that desired result is information to be used in the management of organizations, the organized manipulation of data can be called a *management information system.*

Information-System Concepts

Information can be thought of as the end result of some data-manipulation activity. *Data* are facts—the raw materials from which information is made. Data are facts about people and their activities, places, and things. These unorganized facts, or raw data, are transformed by some process into an arranged, ordered, and usable form—information. In a stricter sense, data may consist of numbers and letters that can be restructured by an information system in a way that will increase their usefulness. The processing or restructuring of data into usable information may take place in many ways. However, raw data are not randomly manipulated and then formulated into usable information. Instead, data are manipulated according to a predetermined procedure to achieve a desired result.

Exhibit 15.3 shows the sequence of steps by which data become information in a management information system. *Original data* (1) are gathered on a written transaction form or are input by means of a computer terminal and delivered to the computer center. *Data editing* (2) means both manual checks for completeness and basic accuracy and computerized checks for total arithmetic accuracy and internal logic. *Data processing* (3) involves manipulation of the data—sorting, classifying, computing—into the final desired and usable format. *Information* (4) consists of the various reports, terminal displays, and graphics that are given to the intended users within the organization.

It is often assumed, by both the computer specialist and the administrative user, that the generation of information in step 4 is the end of the process. But the very definition of information, data that have been transformed into something useful, belies this assumption. As with any system, information systems should change according to changing needs, circumstances, and conditions. Such change requires the introduction of a formal feedback mechanism. Steps 5 through 8 in exhibit 15.3 show how such feedback might affect an information system.

In addition to the various reports produced in step 4, it is likely that some of the information produced must be saved and used in the next processing cycle. A monthly payroll that must accumulate year-to-date salary and deductions for annual tax preparation is such an example. Therefore, *data files* (5) that store the information produced are a useful component in an information system. In each successive processing cycle, the new data collected in step 1 and edited in step 2 are joined in step 3 by cumulative data stored from previous processing cycles, and consequently the information generated in step 4 consists of manipulations of both current and historical data.

A more significant feedback process, however, is shown in steps 6, 7, and 8. Users need to assess the usefulness of information that a system has produced for them. *User evaluation* (6) is a continuing process and begins with the production of the first report. If the user finds the generated data useful, then the system can complete subsequent operating cycles without change. At some point, however, the user will likely find the information to be less than what was originally desired (or is presently required), and system changes will have to be made. *New programs* (7) will be needed if the processing manipulations or report formats have to be changed. Although these changes will involve some expense and time, they are primarily the concern of the computer staff and user and do not necessarily affect the larger organization. *New data* (8), however, will involve not only reprogramming but also changes in the forms, procedures, and edits used to gather the data. Since collecting new data may likely involve the retraining of staff outside of the user's organizational unit, this type of system change will involve greater expense and time.

Exhibit 15.3
Components of an Information System

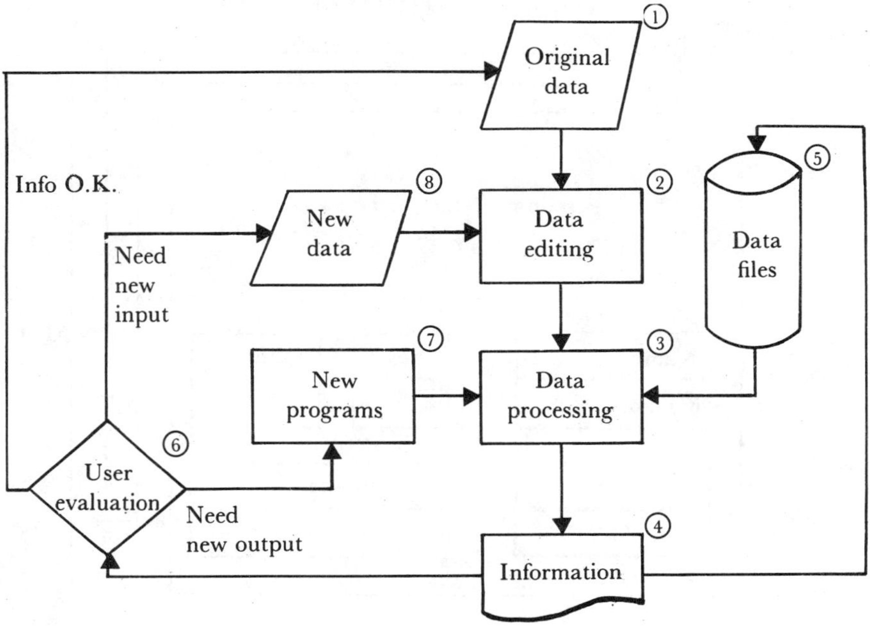

Modifying an information system to accommodate unanticipated, new, or restated needs is frequently costly and sometimes impossible. Thus, an information system can become a constraint on decision making because of its inflexibility. This rigidity can have serious effects. Information systems can, quite inadvertently, prevent accessibility of needed information because of the effort involved in trying to process or alter data lodged within the system's files in a manner never envisioned by the system's designers. Given the likelihood for change at some point in an information system's lifetime, system flexibility becomes an important consideration.

Data Files and Data Bases

Many school district administrators have difficulty fully managing and using their educational data for reasons that are largely historical. Because of the rapid growth of computer technology, management of data has developed in a haphazard and laggard fashion over the years. A general, more comprehensive, approach to data organization has emerged only very recently; consequently, most educational information systems and their data files are highly specialized, and they are designed for a specific operational use or for a specialized staff function.

Exhibit 15.4
Hierarchical Levels of Data

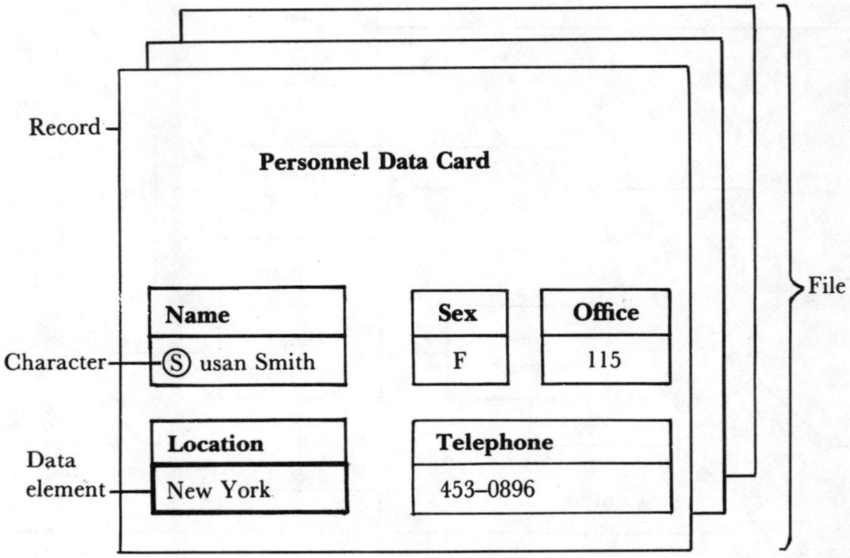

Data used in an information system are organized in a hierarchy of levels, as shown in exhibit 15.4. The most discrete level of data is the *character* (also called the *byte*) and consists of a single number, letter, or special symbol that, by itself, has little or no meaning. One or more characters make up a *data element* (or *variable* or *field*) that represents specific and meaningful attributes such as a person's name, social security number, or sex. All of the data elements that pertain to an individual person, place, or thing constitute a *record* (or *observation* or *case*). A group of records that are related by function, type, or use compose a *file*. Common data files in education include payroll, personnel, student, and achievement files.

In the early days of school district computerization, the limited memory and capabilities of the hardware and software in turn limited the scope of programming and the amount of data needed for any given application. In effect, this reinforced the practice of creating and maintaining separate files for each educational application. Although the later generations of computers had considerably more power, many school districts still organized and coded their data along first-generation computer lines, that is, by specific files and programs.

Hence, the administration of data has continued to develop in a fragmented fashion and at rather low organizational levels. This traditional approach to educational data processing used by most school systems in-

Exhibit 15.5
Components of a Data File System

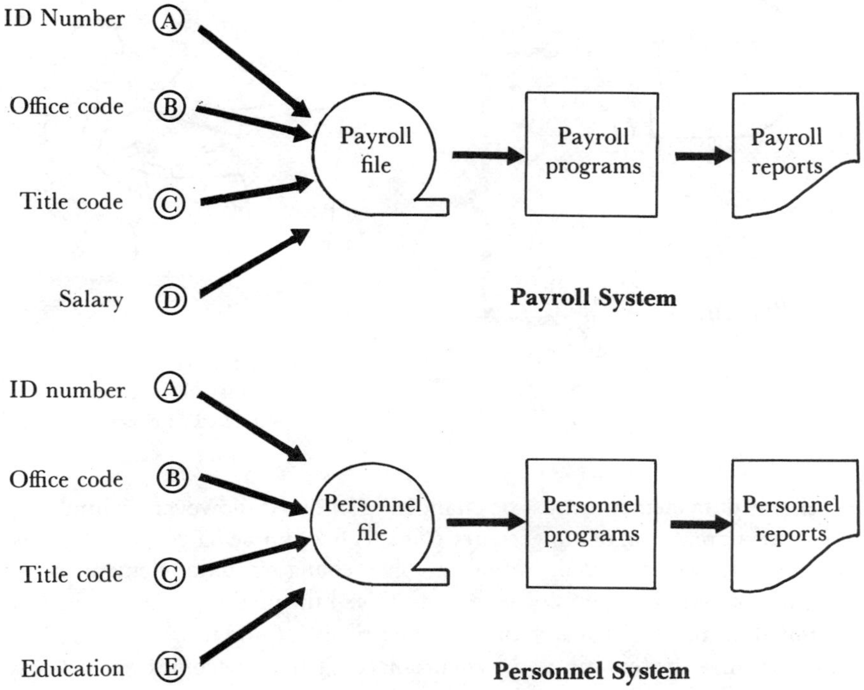

volves collecting, editing, and coding data for specific computer systems, and consequently linking them more or less permanently and exclusively to these systems as well as to the district offices or units that create and maintain them. This type of data structure—separate data files feeding into specialized reporting systems—severely limits the utility of these data for management (Hussain 1973, pp. 135–136).

Exhibit 15.5 shows an oversimplified and hypothetical model of two educational data systems—payroll and personnel—that are structured along the traditional approach. The payroll file consists of four separate data elements or characteristics on each employee: identification number (A), office code (B), employee title code (C), and salary (D). The personnel file also contains four data elements per employee: identification number (A), office code (B), title code (C), and employee education level (E). Notice that data elements A, B, and C are common to both files.

The redundancy of data is obvious. In this simplified example, six out of eight (75 percent) of the data elements in the files are redundant. During the initial operation of data systems, redundancy does not cause much trouble.

Exhibit 15.6
Data File System Update Problems

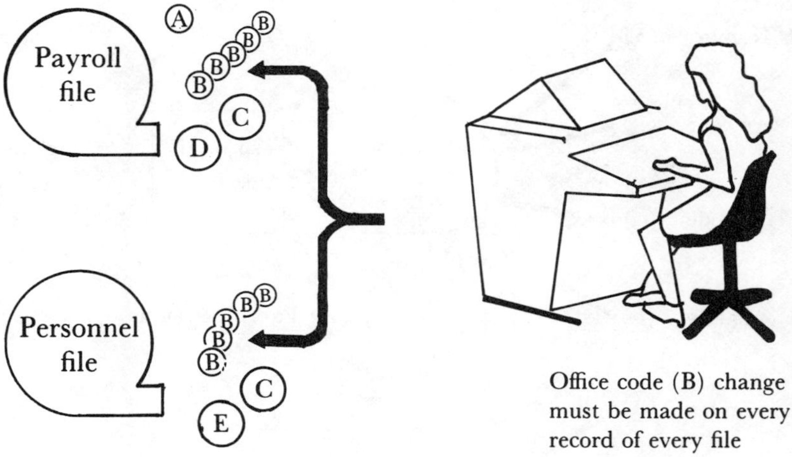

Office code (B) change must be made on every record of every file

As soon as data elements must be changed or updated, however, redundancy can cause a great deal of unnecessary effort. A few simple office code changes, as shown in exhibit 15.6, would involve changing data element B on hundreds of individual employee records. Given the plethora of separate data systems that many districts maintain, the process of updating all the redundant files in a systematic and synchronized fashion becomes exceedingly difficult and costly.

The traditional data structure also severely limits the ability of districts to combine and analyze data elements from separate data files. For example, exhibit 15.7 shows that employee salary (element D) and employee education (element E) are contained in two different data files. If one wanted to analyze the statistical relationship between these two variables, it would be necessary to first perform employee-by-employee editing of each record and then employee-by-emloyee sorting and matching from each of the two files (while identifying and correcting all manner of data errors and coding inconsistencies in the process) in order to produce a new data file containing data elements A, B, C, D, and E. The time and effort required to do this often discourages requests for such analyses or leads to a manual computation of the data from printouts. As a result, the school district's own data have become a frozen asset—a highly constrained resource—analogous to funds that may be used to purchase only one type of instructional supply.

Today, school administrators need access to information that can be generated from only properly structured, cross-functional data files that incorporate data from the specialized applications and activities located

Exhibit 15.7
Data File System Merge Problems

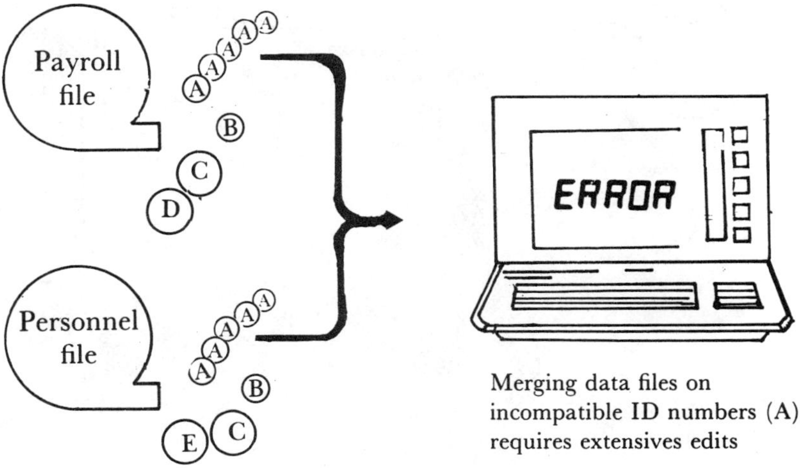

Merging data files on incompatible ID numbers (A) requires extensives edits

throughout the district's organizational hierarchy. For management purposes, school administrators must have consistent data that can be used in conjunction with flexible reporting systems to generate information on a broader and more comprehensive scale than the single, isolated application files and systems.

The information needs of school administrators have given rise to the concept of a district-wide data base. The data-base concept has two key aspects:

1. The data (for example, student, payroll/personnel, budget/finance) that computer programs use are considered an independent resource in themselves, separate from the computer programs.
2. There is an optimal approach to managing and structuring the school district's data as a whole so that they constitute a resource available to the entire district for broad-ranging applications, especially on an ad hoc basis (Josephson 1975, pp. 106–107).

As shown in exhibit 15.8, the data-base concept hierarchically structures and combines the payroll and personnel data files into a common pool. Note that no files appear, since the pool of data elements constitutes the general file for the school district (at least, for this example, employee salary and personnel data), and the specific files are for the most part unnecessary. In the data-base approach, an interface called the data-base management system exists between the data and the various reporting systems for accessing the data elements and producing reports. The data base enables the

Exhibit 15.8

Components of a Data-Base Management System

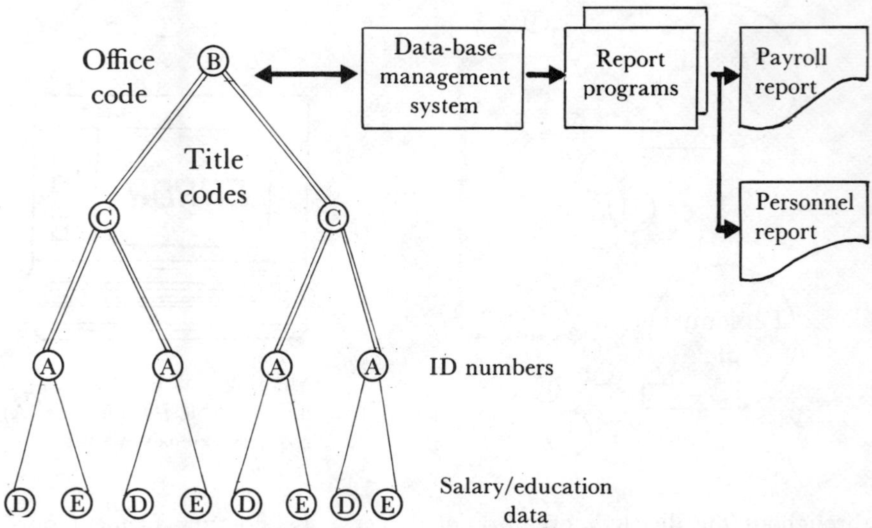

district to organize and structure the data elements in a way that minimizes redundancy and inconsistencies and maximizes data accessibility.

The use of data-base management systems to maintain and access information will provide school administrators with more flexibility. In the previous office code change example, a data-base system would change only the affected B data elements and not the hundreds of employee data records (data element C) that a data-file system would necessitate. The data base would automatically associate each class code change with all of their respective student records.

The creation of data bases requires a new position within the district organization: the data-base administrator. The data-base administrator is the custodian of the data and is responsible for its security and control (see sections below on data control and data confidentiality). The administrator has an overall knowledge of the district's data, encourages standardization of data items, and determines what data structures and layouts will be best for the data users as a whole. Within a school district the data-base administrator's job is a rare combination of technology and organizational politics (Martin 1976, pp. 6–7).

Information-Systems Implementation

The process of developing even a modest educational information system is likely to involve the efforts of dozens of individuals over many months or even years. Both the complex nature of the task and the wide range of technical and administrative activities that must be coordinated make proper management of the total process a prerequisite for success. Only through the appropriate participation of the administrator can the promises of the computer staff and the expectations of the educational user be fully realized. Although even elementary discussion of the systems implementation process is far beyond the scope of this chapter, an outline of the various steps involved may prove useful. Exhibit 15.9 shows the major steps in the implementation of a management information system. Each step is identified with a managerial, technical, or shared level of responsibility and with one of the four phases—definition, design, development, or operations—that make up the overall implementation process.

Definition Phase

This phase, and the entire implementation process, begins when the district's management *identifies the need* (1) for an information system due to a change in district goals, programs, structure, or requirements. To ascertain whether and what kind of a system would meet the anticipated information need, a *feasibility study* (2) is conducted by a team of administrators, educators, and technical specialists. The feasibility study identifies basic information objectives, policy issues, and resource constraints, and it evaluates some alternative approaches to meeting the stated needs. The completed study is *evaluated* (3) by district management to determine whether the effort should be terminated, revised and restudied with different objectives or constraints, or deemed satisfactory. In the last case a commitment is made to proceed to the *design phase* (4).

Design Phase

This phase will transform the general technical and administrative parameters of the system that were identified by the feasibility study into specific input, processing, and output specifications. A formal *project management* (5) unit of both administrative and technical staff is established to assume direct operating responsibility for the system-implementation effort until it is declared *operational* (17). A major design consideration that will involve administrators is the type of *data structure* (6) the system is to use. A conventional data-file structure should not impose too many changes upon the district's organizational structure or procedures, but a data-base system may have a profound impact on the *data-administration* (7) functions, which will be discussed in the next section of this paper. Completion of all system-design specifications leads to the complex *system-development phase* (8).

Exhibit 15.9

Implementation of a Management Information System

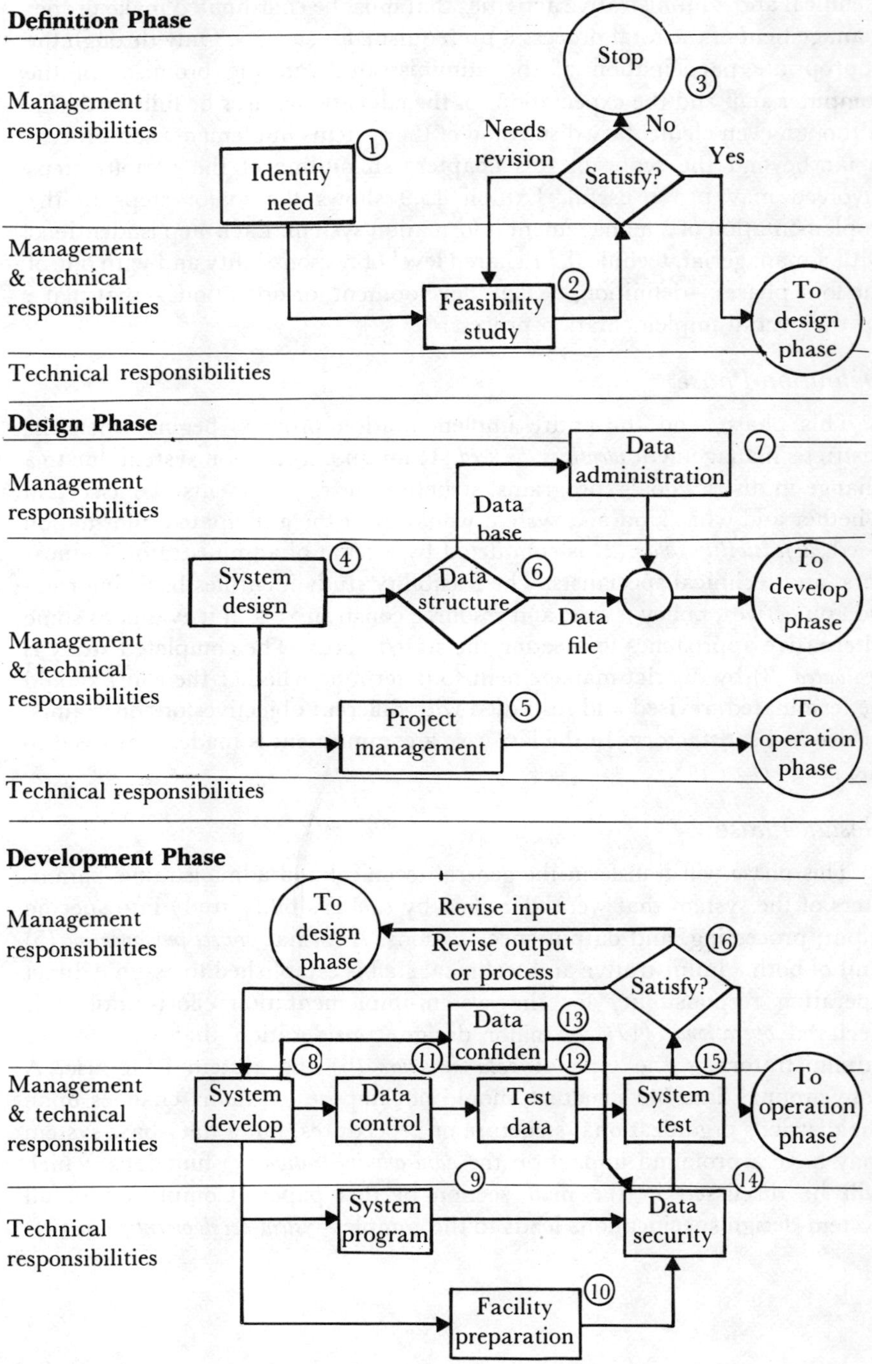

Exhibit 15.9. *continued*

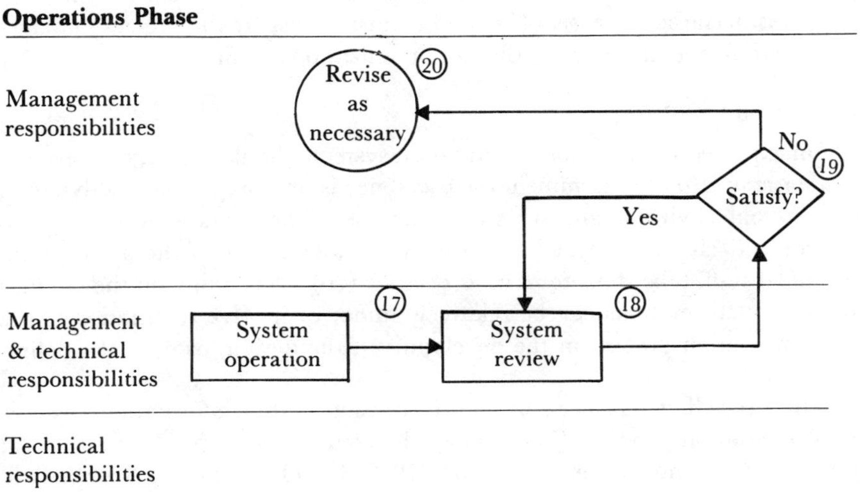

Development Phase

This phase involves many simultaneous efforts at all organizational levels of the district. On the technical level the completed design specifications are used for *facilities preparation* (10)—selecting, contracting, preparing, and installing the necessary work space and electrical, computer, data-entry, and support equipment—and for *system programming* (9)—writing all of the computer programs and documentation for the system. During this period, selected administrative and technical staff should be formulating a *data-control* (11) procedure and policy under which the system will operate. A joint group of administrators and technicians will also prepare *test data and procedures* (12) and evaluate the system's programs and procedures. A group of management and policy personnel will establish the *data-confidentiality* (13) policies that the system may require. Once formulated, these policies on data access are used by technical staff to develop *data security* (14) procedures and mechanisms. When all of these developmental activities have been completed, an integrated *system test* (15) is conducted to run the system under operating conditions, either on a partial basis or parallel to the existing system. The system test provides both technical and managerial staff with a clear indication of how well the new hardware, software, procedures, and organizational staff work together. Following a few months of system testing, a formal management *evaluation* (16) is made to assess whether the users are satisfied with the system. At this point, any need to revise input, process, or output parameters is identified and acted on. If the users' expectations are met, the system is declared *operational* (17) and is turned over by the project management staff to the appropriate district organizational units.

Operations Phase

Once placed in operation, information systems should undergo a periodic *system review* (18) to determine if the users' needs, in the context of a dynamic educational environment, are still being met. The users *evaluate* (19) the system and either confirm its adequacy or, together with the appropriate technical staff, take steps to *revise as necessary* (20). Depending on the circumstances, such revisions can be relatively minor or involve reinitiation of the implementation process in the development, the design, or even the definition phase.

The preceding has been a brief discussion of the information systems implementation process. (For a more detailed analysis, see Hussain 1973, pp. 173–341, and Lucas 1978, pp. 219–278.) The following section will investigate those aspects of the implementation process that call for direct participation and decision making by educational administrators.

Computer-System Issues For Administrators

The flow of educational data is the administrative lifeblood of school districts. This data flow is a constantly changing record of the many pertinent factors that affect the successful operation of a district. A major responsibility of school managers is the development of mechanisms for the administration, control, and dissemination of critical information from this flood of data that will facilitate effective decision making. Information management is—or, more properly, should be—such a mechanism. In this section a number of issues that affect the successful implementation of management information systems are examined.

Data Control

The primary function of management information systems is to provide accurate, timely, and comprehensive educational information in a way that minimizes the cost to the school districts. Essential to the management and control of this information is careful coordination of the collection of data required by federal, state, and district educational offices. A plethora of survey forms that have never been reviewed and approved through a common data-control procedure are described in information-systems terminology as fragmented or nonintegrated. To cope with this phenomenon, integrated information systems require structured or orderly data collection procedures that identify and approve all relevant data acquisition activities according to established criteria.

During the late 1970s, both federal agencies and a number of state education departments created procedures for coordinating the collection of educational data. Excessive government paperwork that cost school districts time and money, which could have been better spent educating students, prompted Congress to create the Federal Education Data Acquisition Council (FEDAC). FEDAC is responsible for coordinating the activities of all federal agencies that collect educational data and for ensuring that the data are collected as efficiently as possible. The intent is to reduce the federally imposed burden of paperwork by eliminating excessive detail and redundancy in information requests.

The procedures employed by FEDAC were described in a National Center for Education Statistics report as follows:

> To carry out its purpose, FEDAC annually prepares the federal education data acquisition plan and inventory. The plan identifies federal instruments used to request education information from 10 or more persons. It includes questionnaires, telephone and personal interviews, guides, and any other types of forms used for grant applications, research and evaluation studies, statistical surveys, financial and performance reports, and other management reports. FEDAC prepares the plan by coordinating requests proposed by federal agencies and reviewing them for redundancy, costs, overall burden, and the use of standard terminology and definitions. [1980, p. 3]

A review of the data-collection procedures used by the federal and various state education agencies has identified a basic data-collection model that should be of great use to school-district administrators. The following is a description of the procedures for this model as they might be established for a school district. The flow of procedures for the model is shown in exhibit 15.10.

1. *Data-Request Submission.* All requests to collect data by district offices, and by city, state, or federal agencies are submitted to the district's data-base administrator. School district offices must prepare a data review and approval document providing information concerning the justification for and pertinent details of (for example, respondents, frequency, data elements, completion time) the data-collection activity. State and federal agencies must provide notification of prior approval by the appropriate authority (for example, United States Office of Management and Budget, FEDAC, state education department).

2. *Data-Request Review.* The district's data-base administrator will evaluate requests for student data using criteria for review and approval that fall within two major categories: (1) justification, and (2) technical analysis. In special circumstances, data requests not based directly on law or regulation may be authorized on an emergency basis when such data are critical to the

Exhibit 15.10
District Data-Collection Approval Process

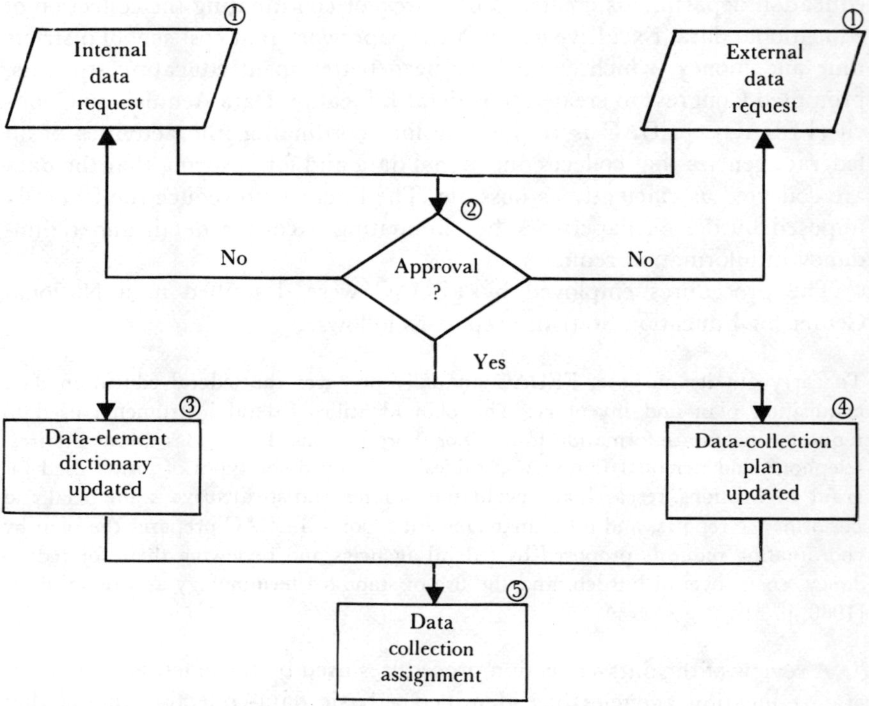

school district's operations and when delay would seriously jeopardize mandated activities. Based on the evaluation, a data request will be either disapproved, conditionally approved (upon completing required modifications), or approved.

3. *Data-Element Dictionary Updated.* When a data-collection activity is approved, the data-element dictionary will be updated by the data-base administrator to include new data elements and an identification of new users of existing data elements. The dictionary defines the characteristics of data elements available within the school district and is used to build a common data base and provide detailed descriptions of each item of relevant data to aid in retrieval. There would be an annual review of the dictionary to determine if data elements should be deleted or modified to show changes in current usage. The dictionary would be distributed throughout the school district to allow all users ready selection of data elements that have been defined and to inform users of where a specific data element can be located at the district office.

4. *Annual Data-Collection Plan Updated.* After a data-collection activity has been approved, the district's schools and offices should have advance knowledge of when they can expect to receive the survey forms. Advance notice is one of the primary reasons for the data-base administrator's creation and continual updating of an annual data-collection plan. The plan is a publication of the approved data-collection activities scheduled for implementation during a given school year. It would list by month the justification for, and the types of, data survey forms that would collect the data. The plan would be distributed in the spring prior to the school year in question and would be updated during the school year by addendum notices.

5. *Data-Collection Assignment.* The data-base administrator would review all approved data-collection activities and, through a feasibility analysis, assign the data-gathering activity to the appropriate district unit. This determination of assignment would be based on the potential interface between the data collection forms and the data base. Where necessary, the feasibility analysis would define from the data user's viewpoint the requirements of the data-collection activity by information flow, output documents, input data, and data processing.

The result of a uniform and mandated set of data-collection procedures is a management information system that can provide for one-time collection of data, easy retrieval of stored data, and ready access to existing data. In order to be effective, however, these procedures must be authorized by policies established by the district superintendent and the school board. The establishment of the following policies regarding data-collection procedures would therefore be necessary:

1. No instruments shall be authorized and used to collect data from schools, districts units, or offices unless they follow the standard data-collection procedures of the school district and are approved by the data-base administrator.
2. No office or unit within the school district shall collect data or authorize collection of data directly from schools unless they coordinate their needs with the data-base administrator.
3. No state or federal agency or their contractors shall collect data directly from schools without having first routed their request through the data-base administrator.
4. No school or district office shall be required to complete a data-collection form prepared by a city, state, or federal agency that has not been reviewed and approved by the data-base administrator.

When the data-base administrator approves a data-collection activity, a control number and date of expiration would be assigned to the data form. The data-base administrator would then provide a standard letter of authorization that must be attached to the actual data form. This, coupled with the annual data-collection plan, would ensure the adherence to item 4 in the preceding policy statement and would provide school and district personnel with an appropriate authorization check.

Data Confidentiality

The successful development and implementation of student and personnel information systems will create a host of policy and technical issues concerning the confidentiality and security of the personal information thus collected and maintained. Computerized data files may be more difficult to access than manual files—or, at least, fewer people have the ability to access such files. However, once computerized files are penetrated, more data can be obtained in less time with less effort. Even where access is stringently controlled, legitimate copies of information extracted from a computer system compound the problems of protection and confidentiality.

Safeguarding personal information that is protected by statute or by policies of confidentiality and privacy is an integral part of information management. Unauthorized disclosure or use of personal and privileged information can be seriously detrimental to students or personnel. Adequate safeguards are necessary to protect confidentiality as well as to ensure cooperation in the accurate and timely flow of student and staff information needed to support educational operations. Although legal or administrative safeguards may exist, it is the responsibility of the school district to ensure that adequate procedures and physical measures are implemented. Measures must address unauthorized or inadvertent disclosure and the destruction, diversion, or alteration of confidential data.

Protective measures must not, however, impede the authorized exchange of student and staff information with other agencies outside the school district. Such exchange is essential to meet the data requirements of state and federal programs and to minimize the duplication of data required from respondents. However, the agencies that either acquire or exchange data must provide adequate protection of confidentiality, or the transfer as well as the collection of the required personal information could be hindered.

When considering student information systems, the confidentiality of the student data that are collected and maintained by the school district determines not only what information may be withheld from public disclosure but also the extent to which that information may or may not be shared with other agencies. Accordingly, it is essential that administrators be familiar with relevant confidentiality laws when they formulate student information policies. Presently, confidentiality of student information is most affected by two laws: The Family Educational Rights and Privacy Act (1976) and the Freedom of Information Act (1974).

In view of the broad range of information likely to be supported by a student data base and the unique problems of privacy and security created by computerization of the information, a thorough review and revision of existing school-district regulations and policies and the establishment of new and appropriate standards of confidentiality and access are matters of high priority. In analyzing the body of student information to be maintained by a data-base system, the superintendent and school board should establish a formal mechanism to formulate and reexamine present and future standards of confidentiality of student data based on the following criteria:

1. The public interest, which can be served by student-data disclosure by—
    a. helping the school district to fulfill its functions and accomplish its objectives.
    b. providing information to the public as required by law.
    c. facilitating intergovernmental sharing of data and reducing duplication of effort.
2. The potential harm that both public and private interests could experience, through the release of student information by—
    a. adversely affecting the collection and the quality of such data in the future due to a lack of confidentiality guarantees.
    b. constituting a clearly unwarranted invasion of privacy.
3. The alternatives to full disclosure that could protect both private and public interests, such as removing identifying characteristics or codes prior to the public release of student data or providing limited information to other agencies rather than full public disclosure.

Because the issues generated from use of an expanding student data base will undoubtedly be persistent, the criteria proposed above should be implemented by a standing committee on student-information policy. This committee, chaired by the data-base administrator and including representatives of the district's teachers, principals, and office administrators, would meet on a regular basis. The committee should have the following responsibilities regarding the implementation and use of computerized student information:

1. Revise current regulations and policies, promulgate and implement new regulations and policies governing computerized student information, and base policies on the principles established in existing law and along guidelines that allow the broadest, most feasible dissemination of public information while providing the necessary safeguards to ensure the protection of the rights and privacy of students and parents.
2. Whenever new student data are collected, inform student information sources and information respondents of the school district's legal authority and technical ability to guarantee confidentiality; the specific data that will be safeguarded; and the extent, if any, to which data disclosures will be made (for example, what data will be designated as directory information).

3. Determine the appropriate organizational levels of staff access (superintendent, principal, counselor, teacher, and aide) to the various kinds of information in the student data base, and establish guidelines encompassing the management and technical safeguards for computerized student information.
4. Review and evaluate on an individual basis all requests by outside parties, organizations, institutions, or governmental agencies for access to and use of any portion of the student data base for any informational, statistical, survey, or research purpose not already prohibited by existing policy, regulation, or statute.

Data Administration

One final information-management issue that must be addressed by school administrators is the location of the data-processing function within the district's organizational hierarchy. The most appropriate location will depend in part on the size of the central administrative office, the number and kind of educational applications to be computerized, and the importance given to management information by the chief district administrators. Basically, there are three possible locations for a district's data-processing unit: as a business subunit, as a service center, and as a major line unit (Sanders and Birkin 1980, pp. 245–247).

Data Processing (DP) as a Business Subunit

The small memory, slow speed, and complex programming of the Garvy computers limited the first computer applications to relatively simple and straightforward tasks such as payrolls and accounting statements. Since most of these early applications were financial, the computer and its staff were most often placed under the control of the district's business administrator. Even as the computer operation expanded to include nonbusiness functions such as personnel and instruction, its location in the organization remained unchanged. Experience in many school districts, however, identified a number of serious disadvantages with this business-area location. Since the computer staff reported to the business administrator, users who needed data processing for nonbusiness functions were often given lower priority than were users with business applications, perhaps despite the greater importance of nonbusiness functions to the district. Also, many of the computer staff were likely to have backgrounds and orientations that clearly favored the business side of the district's operations.

DP as a Service Center

In an effort to avoid bias in setting data-processing priorities for particular functions, some districts have located their computer facility as a "service center" not directly responsible to any single district office. Each district activity is provided with appropriate access to the computer and priority for its systems within a given overall district policy and within the limitations of the computer staff and facility. While the service-center concept appears sound, it usually suffers from a lack of coherent direction because of its ambiguous position on the periphery of the main district organization. The DP manager, therefore, has little organizational status or authority, and the development of new application systems often proceeds along a fragmented, "free-for-all" approach.

DP as a Major Line Unit

Given the general lack of satisfaction with the two previously described DP organizational locations and an increasing awareness on the part of educational administrators that management of information has become a basic function of the district, some school districts have established their computer centers as independent departments equal in organizational rank to such traditional line-management operations as business, personnel, and instruction. Such a placement provides the DP director with sufficient status in the organization to determine broad information-management policies for the district and with the ability to work directly with the chief district administrators. This, in turn, will make possible both the development of integrated data-base management systems and the resolution of data-control and confidentiality issues.

Conclusion

Many educational administrators still view a computerized information system as a product with precise and unchanging input, processing, and output specifications. Users are asked to specify their information needs, and a system is designed and delivered around these requirements. Experience has shown, however, that information systems developed through this conventional approach have frequently failed to meet the high expectations of their users. Educators are often unable to completely specify their information needs a priori. When situations change and new needs emerge, which they invariably will, demands for information must change.

The alternative conception of an information system advocated in this paper is one of process: the system should include an ongoing and integrated set of activities for acquiring data and producing information. This view differs from the product view in that the specifications for input data, processing operations, and output report formats are not frozen at any time. In the process-oriented system, all of these system components are expected to change continually.

Certain functional requirements that follow from this process view should be incorporated into the design of the information system. Since school administrators cannot specify their complete information needs, the system's data should be stored within a disaggregated but integrated data base so that future needs to use the data in ways not initially anticipated can be met. Furthermore, the data-handling capacity of the system should be large enough so that any information required to support future management needs can be stored.

In considering the costs of educational information systems, the services provided by the system should not be separated from the functional activities it would support. The costs of developing a highly flexible process-oriented system are necessarily higher than are those for a fixed product-oriented system. The temptation to reduce development costs of a system at the expense of flexibility is always strong. However, failure to resist that temptation totally defeats the purposes of an effective information system.

In the end, it must be remembered that an educational information system, by itself, has no reason for existence. Therefore, the costs of its development cannot be the measure of its effectiveness. The value of an information system cannot be determined in isolation from the functional activities that it was designed to serve. True measures of effectiveness—those related to educational and administrative objectives—can be defined and evaluated only for the management activities themselves.

References

Hussain, Khateeb M. *Development of an Information System for Education.* Englewood Cliffs, N. J.: Prentice-Hall, 1973.

Josephson, Ben, Jr., et al. *The Comprehensive Instructional Management System.* New York: Riverside Research Institute, 1975.

Lucas, Henry C., Jr. *Information Systems Concepts for Management.* New York: McGraw-Hill, 1978.

Martin, James. *Principles of Data Base Management.* Englewood Cliffs, N. J.: Prentice-Hall, 1976.

Molnar, Andrew R. "The New Great Crisis in American Education: Computer Literacy." *T.H.E. Journal* 5 (1978): 35–39.

National Center for Education Statistics. *The Condition of Education: 1980.* Washington, D.C.: U.S. Government Printing Office, 1980.

Sanders, Donald H., and Birkin, Stanley J. *Computers and Management in a Changing Society.* New York: McGraw-Hill, 1980.

Supplementary Reading

Frates, Jeffrey, and Moldrup, William. *Introduction to the Computer.* Englewood Cliffs, N. J.: Prentice-Hall, 1980.

16

Emerging Technologies in Information Management

by James H. Faux

•

Overview

As computers become more "user friendly," school business administrators can more easily develop application programs tailored to their specific needs. Administrators are increasingly using four types of software packages to design applications: word processing, spreadsheet, data-base management, and graphics generation. By themselves or in combination, these packages are being used to enhance the information-processing power of the school business administrator.

• • •

Introduction

During the second half of the twentieth century, the role of the school business administrator has significantly evolved from that of a financial recordkeeper to that of a central figure in negotiations, personnel, budgeting, curricular planning, and, at least through the early 1970s, building expansion. Since the middle 1970s, the school business administrator has worked in a period of declining student enrollments, program cutbacks, and curtailing revenue sources. During this entire period, the school business administrator has also assumed greater importance in the overall operation of school district affairs. Nowhere is this more evident than in the area of information management and control. The school business administrator is expected to be able to generate data, analyze relationships, and submit carefully documented proposals to the school superintendent and the school board.

The methods the school business administrator has used to gather data and analyze relationships have undergone a dramatic revolution since the 1950s. The environment of paper and pencils and a desktop mechanical adding machine has given way to a sophisticated electronic environment. The 1960s saw the arrival of large mainframe computers to assist the data-processing requirements of public education, and in the late 1970s and early 1980s minicomputers and microcomputers exploded into use in the school business offices. The challenge before the school business administrator is to maximize use of the available technology in order to provide the district's leadership team with the best information with which to make decisions.

There is a basic and distinct difference between data collection and information processing, and one needs only to compare a file cabinet of purchase orders with a monthly computerized printout that summarizes those orders to see how much more easily information may be acquired by using a computer. The data the school business administrator needs access to must be maintained in an information system in the school district that allows for easy retrieval of the data. If the information is not easily accessible, the school business administrator might be thought of as a highly paid account clerk.

In the late 1970s the New York State Association of School Business Officials Research Committee surveyed school business officials in eastern New York State in an attempt to identify both the immediate and the long-term computer needs of school business administrators. The top ten computer needs were:

1. Generation of all state aid forms by a computer
2. Ability to project employee retirement, FICA, insurance, and other fringe costs
3. End-of-year budget projections
4. Complete personnel management system
5. Salary projections for negotiations
6. Ability to project budget impact of changes in key areas
7. Ability to project estimated budget
8. Ability to project costs and display trends
9. Cash-flow reports
10. Inventory control

These perceived computer needs apply to many of the school business administrators' responsibilities discussed in the previous chapters. In this chapter we will discuss how school business administrators may best use microcomputers to undertake these responsibilities.

The Revolution in Computer Technology

Computerized data processing was introduced into the public and private schools during the late 1950s and early 1960s. These early-generation IBM, Univac, DEC, and Burroughs mainframe computers were powerful, large, and expensive. Input was of the classic "IBM card" variety. These mainframes either served large school systems or were owned and used cooperatively by neighboring school districts. They were primarily used in the business office for payroll and accounting purposes. Many of these mainframes are still in service throughout the nation and are very adequately performing the functions for which they were designed.

The technological advances of the mid- to late 1970s resulted in the development of relatively inexpensive minicomputers and of the even less expensive microcomputers. These machines could perform many of the administrative and business functions of the older and much larger mainframes. As with most new technology, these new computers brought both good news and bad news. The positive effect was that electronic data processing could be located much closer to the school user at a very low cost. The negative effect was that many of these powerful low-priced computers were bought with no regard to linking them to existing computers or planning for long-range data-processing requirements (Edwards 1983; Heintz 1983; Stewart 1983; "Word Processor Special" 1982).

The initial computer software that accompanied the mainframes required a degree in data processing to use it. This is no longer the case, and much of the available software for micros is easily used by people who are not computer scientists. This software evolution has been a significant factor in the acceptance of microcomputers in the school business office. But the use of microcomputers in the school is not limited to the business office. In many schools, computers are being used as instructional tools in the classroom. In fact, computer literacy and even elementary programming are now part of an elementary school education. Many children are entering kindergarten classes with an awareness of computers and the ability to use computer software.

Neither the mainframe computers nor dedicated word processors have had as much of an impact on the school office environment as the microcomputers or minicomputers have. Business officials are finally getting full control of their computing power and are able to provide decision-making data to superintendents and boards of education with unprecedented speed. Microcomputers are being used in numerous ways: as stand-alone computers, distributed "analysis" workstations, word-processing systems, data-entry stations connected to mini- or mainframe computers, or full business systems. The major microcomputer applications are:

1. *Word processing*—report preparation, list processing, data-based mailings

2. *Electronic spreadsheets*—financial analyses, budget reports, budget and program modeling and simulations, cash flow, and so on
3. *Data-base management*—personnel systems, inventory control
4. *Graphics generation*—full-screen and hard-copy bar, line, or pie charts

These applications are discussed in more depth later in this chapter.

The Evolution of the Powerful Microcomputers

The first electronic computers were developed in Germany, Britain, and the United States during World War II. By 1946, ENIAC (Electronic Numerical Integrator and Calculator) had arrived as the first sophisticated computer. Its 20,000 vacuum tubes consumed 200,000 watts of electricity. Shortly afterward, scientists at Bell Laboratories invented the transistor, which could do what the vacuum tube could do using less power. By the late fifties the transistor had replaced the tube, which resulted in smaller and cheaper (hundreds of thousands instead of millions of dollars) computers.

In the early 1960s scientists devised a way to integrate several transistors onto a tiny silicon chip. The result was the minicomputer, a $20,000 to $30,000 machine no larger than a two-drawer file cabinet. In the seventies the most significant development was the microprocessor. This is a silicon integrated-circuit chip with several thousand microscopic circuits that form the nerve center of every modern microcomputer.

By the late 1970s several companies had begun marketing low-cost hobby and personal microcomputers. The literature is replete with stories about the birth of the Apple microcomputer in a garage in California. The Radio Shack TRS-80s and the Apples were the first computers to gain mass acceptance across the country in home and educational settings. These early micros were characterized as follows:

—*Main memory*: 16–48 K bytes of built-in memory
—*Mass storage*: cassette storage
—*Operating systems*: single user only; eight-bit microprocessor
—*Software*: limited and programmer oriented

The next few years saw the introduction of an improved Apple—the Apple II Plus. This micro featured an automatic operating system that started up when the Apple was turned on. Also, the marketplace became flooded with excellent management software to operate on the micros. Many companies sprang up instantly to fill the demand for "user-friendly" programs that did not require a degree in computer science to use. These companies developed many excellent software packages for the Apple, TRS–80, Pet, and other popular micros, and a number of these were very suitable for use in the school business office. We will examine some of these in depth in the next section. Suffice it to say that words like *Visicalc*, *DB Master*,

PFS, and *Word Star* became as common in many business circles as *B.A.N.* and *cash flow*.

On August 12, 1981, IBM introduced the next generation of micros—the IBM-PC. The PC had significant improvements over the Apple and the TRS models:

—*Memory*: 64–256K RAM memory (additional capacity to ten to twenty Meg.); 40K permanent memory
—*Microprocessor*: High-speed chip; sixteen-bit microprocessor
—*Keyboard*: Eighty-three keys on a detached keyboard (six-foot cord); ten programmable function keys; ten-key numeric pad
—*Communications*: asynchronous protocol (single-character transmission to minis and mainframes); up to 9,600 bits per second

Perhaps the most significant feature of the PC is its ability to interface with the IBM mainframes that are used in many of the regional and city computer centers. The IBM environment supports the ability of the IBM-PC to upload and download data to and from the larger IBM mainframes. This allows the PC to be an excellent dual-purpose micro. Within one year after its introduction, there were over twelve hundred software packages and hardware peripheral devices available for the IBM-PC.

On January 18, 1983, Apple Corporation introduced its long-awaited improved version of the highly successful Apple II Plus—the Apple IIe (*e* for enhanced). The IIe had 64 K of on-board memory, a sixty-three key keyboard accessing the full 128 ASCII character set, an inexpensive eighty-column card, an improved 6502A chip, and 31 chips in the motherboard instead of 109. The software that helped make the Apple so popular in educational and business settings was also compatible on the new IIe.

At the same time, Apple introduced the Lisa, which was a significant advancement in the state of the art of the microcomputers. At its introduction, the Lisa was priced in the $7,000 to $10,000 range—definitely at the high end of the market. The basic machine consists of three separate pieces: a main console containing the videoscreen and and two floppy disk drives, a detached typewriter-style keyboard, and an innovative palm-sized box called the "mouse," which controls the Lisa.

The designers of the Lisa focused on three characteristics that set their micro apart from the other personal computers. First, the Lisa was designed so that the computer user would feel assured that the system would operate in a consistent and predictable manner. The Lisa was not the first computer to use graphic symbols and a mouse control. (The Xerox Star, which was introduced in the mid seventies, cost over $15,000 and was not a commercial success.) However, with the Lisa all the menu options appear on the screen at one time and you use the mouse to choose the option you want. Second, whether you are editing text, drawing graphs, creating spreadsheets, or copying files, many of the necessary operations are similar. While there were literally hundreds of well-documented software packages for the Apple, IBM, TRS, and so on, each program had a unique system of control keys and procedures, which made it awkward to use different programs and next to impossible to transfer data files between programs. The Lisa is designed to avoid this. The third goal of the Lisa's designers was to provide an integrated system. Because this computer does not operate unrelated programs, data can be moved back and forth between documents and application programs without the need for awkward conversion programs. You can easily "cut and paste," on the computer, a spreadsheet table or a graph into a body of text.

In spring 1984 Apple Corporation introduced the sleek IIc, the successor to the IIe. This portable personal computer had a standard 128K bytes of RAM (random access memory) and a built-in disk drive. While this new Apple II was still based on the original Apple II Plus technology, it was an instant success for personal use.

Simultaneously, Apple introduced the Macintosh. This new microcomputer was designed around the Lisa's advanced 32/16-bit microprocessor. The "Mac" is a 23-pound micro, which classifies it as a transportable machine. The operating system is a streamlined version of the Lisa and has mouse-controlled cursor positioning, icons, and pull-down menus. The Mac comes with a standard 128K of RAM memory and is expandable to 512K and beyond with expansion hard disk drives. Since its introduction in 1984, software manufacturers have begun producing business applications that take advantage of the Mac's powerful and technologically advanced features.

The Macintosh's success in the business world will depend on software and hardware manufacturers' ability to take advantage of the Mac's MC 68000 processor, the 3 1/2-inch variable-speed disk drive, the high-resolution display, the advanced operating system and user interface, and its excellent graphics capabilities.

However innovative Apple's newest microcomputer may be, the standard in the business environment has been the IBM-PC. The IBM-PC has proved to be extremely reliable and versatile. Many other manufacturers have introduced IBM look-alikes that claim to be able to run most of the IBM software. Companies such as AT&T, Compaq, and Hypernion have challenged the IBM-PC. IBM has responded by introducing a portable PC with 256-512K bytes of memory and their innovative IBM AT with a hard disk drive. At the time this book goes to press, the IBM-PC is the business office workhorse against which other microcomputers are measured.

Applications of the Microcomputer to School Business Administration

The school business administrator has a wider variety of responsibilities than any other person in a school system except the superintendent. In order to explore the possible areas in school business administration where microcomputers can be of value, it would be in order to examine the responsibilities of the school business administrator. The Association of School Business Officials of the United States has compiled a comprehensive listing of the kinds of responsibilities that may be assigned to a school business administrator. Exhibit 16.1 is not inclusive, but it is illustrative. We have categorized the four primary microcomputer application areas as word processing, electronic spreadsheets, data-base management, and graphics representation. In the exhibit we have indicated to the right of each responsibility which applications would apply to that responsibility. An in-depth discussion of the four microcomputer applications follows.

Word Processing

The arrival of word processors has eliminated a big question writers often face: Is the change worth having the whole page retyped? With word-processing programs, writers can delete and change words, paragraphs, or even whole pages. The better word processors will automatically adjust the text body to accommodate the changes.

The first computers were designed to "crunch" numbers. As the electronic technology advanced, designers realized that the machines could be built to "crunch" words as well; that is, perform arithmetic and mathematical operations at fractions of a second. When microcomputers became widely used in the early eighties, software companies began marketing word-processing programs to be used on the micros. The larger computer firms, such as Xerox, IBM, and Wang, also developed dedicated single-purpose word-processing machines. These machines, however, have seen limited use in school business offices because they are relatively expensive — at least twice as expensive as an Apple II or IBM-PC—and cannot be used for the wide variety of activities that occur in the typical business office.

The quality of "professional" word-processing software available for the microcomputers varies greatly. Some programs are very complex, and their instruction manuals are inadequately written. Other programs will run only with micros equipped with extra hardware, such as RAM cards, Z-80 cards, CP/M, 80-column cards, and the like. However, of the wide variety of commercial software available, many, such as The Word Handler, Apple Writer II, Word Star, and Multi-Mate, will function very well on a micro.

How can word processing be used in the business office? The executive secretary to the school business administrator should definitely have access to either a dedicated word processor or a micro with word-processing capabilities. If the school business administrator is involved in writing memos and letters, drafting multipage reports or regulations, or preparing position papers, then he or she should also consider using a word processor—regardless of handwriting ability.

Exhibit 16.1

Responsibilities of the School Business Administrator

Key

Application	Code
Word processing	1
Spreadsheets	2
Data base	3
Graphics	4

Responsibilities		Microcomputer Applications
I.	Financial Planning and Budgeting	
	A. Budget compilation, in coordination with educational planning	1, 2, 3, 4
	B. Long-term fiscal planning; operating budget	2, 3, 4
	C. Estimating	2
	1. Receipts	
	2. Disbursements	
	D. Budget control	2, 3, 4
	E. Fiscal relationships with other government units	2
	F. Use of systems analysis and PPBES	1, 2
	G. Cash-flow management	2
II.	Accounting	
	A. General fund	2, 3
	B. Capital reserve fund, trust funds, and special-purpose grants	2
	C. Construction funds	2
	D. Internal accounts	2
	E. Student activity funds	2, 3
	F. Voucher and payroll preparation	3
	G. Inventory	2, 3
	H. Attendance, census, tax-roll accounting	2, 3
	I. Government tax and pension accounting; categorical aids	2, 3
	J. Special trust funds	2, 3
	K. Cost accounting; cost analysis; unit and comparative costs; cost distribution	2, 3, 4
	L. Student stores, bookstores	2
	M. Source documentation	1
	N. PPBES — ERM concepts and procedures	1
	O. Employer-benefits accounting—vacations, sick leave, seniority status	2, 3, 4
	P. Petty-cash funds	2
III.	Debt Service and Capital Fund Management	
	A. Long- and Short-term financing	2

Exhibit 16.1, continued

	B. Maturities and debt payments	2
	C. Long-range capital programs	2
	D. Investments and cash flow	2, 4
	E. Reporting	1, 2
	F. Bond and note register	2
	G. Debt-service payment procedures	1, 2
	H. Short-term debt management	1, 2
	I. Revenue anticipation loans; emergency loans	1, 2
	J. Bond prospectus	1
	K. Credit data — credit ratings	2
IV.	Auditing	
	A. Preaudit, or internal, procedures	1
	B. Determination that prepared statements present fairly the financial position	
	C. Propriety, legality, and accuracy of financial transactions	
	D. Proper recording of all financial transactions	2
	E. Postaudit procedures	1
	F. External audits	
	G. Reconciliation of internal and external audits	1, 2
	H. Legal advertising and reporting	
V.	Purchasing and Supply Management	
	A. Ethics in purchasing	1
	B. Official purchasing-agent designation	1
	C. Legal aspects of purchasing and contracting	1
	D. Purchase methods—seasonal and off-season buying	
	E. Stock requisition and buying cycles	1
	F. Standards and specifications	1, 3
	G. Requisition and purchase orders	3
	H. Purchase bids	3
	I. Cooperative purchasing—state contracts, local contracts	3
	J. Testing and value analysis	2
	K. Purchases of supplies and equipment	1, 3
	L. Warehousing and distribution procedures	2, 3
	M. Storage, delivery, and trucking services	2, 3
	N. Inventory controls	2, 3
	O. Management of supplies, furniture, and equipment	2, 3
	P. Computerized purchasing and supply management	2, 3
VI.	School Plant Planning and Construction	
	A. Establishment of educational standards for sites, buildings, and equipment	1

Exhibit 16.1, continued

Key	
Application	Code
Word processing	1
Spreadsheets	2
Data base	3
Graphics	4

Responsibilities		Microcomputer Applications
	B. Plant utilization studies	1, 2
	C. Projections of facility needs	1
	D. Design, construction, and equipment of plant	3
	E. Safety standards	
	F. Contracts management	
	G. Architect selection	
VII.	Operation of Plant—Custodial, Gardening, and Engineering Services	
	A. Standards and frequency of work	
	B. Manpower allocations	2
	C. Scheduling	2, 3
	D. Inspection and evaluation of services	1
	E. Relationship with educational staff	
	F. Operating of related school-community facilities, such as recreation, park, museum, library programs, and so on	3
	G. Community use of facilities	3
	H. Protection of plant and property	
	I. Security and police forces	
	J. Salvage, surplus and waste disposal	
VIII.	Maintenance of Plant	
	A. Repair of buildings and equipment	3
	B. Upkeep of grounds	3
	C. Maintenance policies, standards, and frequency of maintenance	1
	D. Scheduling and allocation of funds and manpower	2, 3
	E. Modernization and rehabilitation versus replacement	
IX.	Real Estate Management	
	A. Site acquisition and sales	1
	B. Rentals, leases	1
	C. Rights-of-way and easements	
	D. Assessments and taxes	2, 3
	E. After-school use of buildings	3
	F. Dormitories, student unions, and concessions	

Exhibit 16.1, continued

X.	Personnel Management	
	A. Records	
	1. Probationary and tenure status of employees	1, 2, 3, 4
	2. Sick leave and leave of absence	1, 3, 4
	3. Official notices of appointments and salaries	1, 2, 3
	4. Retirement data and deductions	2, 3
	5. Salary schedules and payments	2, 3
	6. Individual earnings records	2, 3
	7. Withholding, tax, and group insurance or fringe benefits	2, 3
	8. Civil Service and Social Security	2, 3
	9. Substitute and part-time employees	2, 3
	10. Dues checkoffs	3
	B. Supervision of noninstructional staff	
	1. Recruitment	1
	2. Selection	1
	3. Placement	1
	4. Training	
	5. Advancement	
	6. Working conditions	
	7. Disciplinary action	
	8. Termination of services	
	C. Relationship to instructional staff	
	1. Good will and service concept	
	2. Cooperation in procurement	
	3. Cooperation in budget preparation	
	4. Information on pay and retirement	
	5. Personnel records and reports	
XI.	Permanent Property Records and Custody of Legal Papers	
	A. Security and preservation of records	1
	B. Maintenance of storage files	
	C. Purging of records no longer legally required	
XII.	Transportation of Pupils	
	A. Policies, rules, regulations, and procedures	1
	B. Contract versus district-owned equipment	2
	C. Routing and scheduling	3
	D. Inspection and maintenance	3
	E. Staff supervision and training	
	F. Utilization and evaluation of services	
	G. Standards and specifications	1
XIII.	Food Service Operations	
	A. Policies, rules, regulations, and procedures	1

Exhibit 16.1, continued

Key

Application	Code
Word processing	1
Spreadsheets	2
Data base	3
Graphics	4

Responsibilities		Microcomputer Applications
	B. Staffing and supervision	3
	C. Menus, prices, and portion controls	2, 3
	D. Purchasing, storage, and distribution	2, 3
	E. Accounting, reporting, and cost analysis	2, 3
	F. In-service training	
	G. Coordination with educational program	1
	H. Procurement and operation of contract services	1
XIV.	Insurance	
	A. Insurance policies	
	B. Insurable values—buildings and contents	
	C. Coverages to be provided	
	D. Claims and reporting	1, 3
	E. Insurance and procurement procedures	1
	F. Insurance and claims record	2, 3
	G. Distribution of insurance to companies, agents, and brokers	
XV.	Cost Analysis	
	A. Unit costs	2, 4
	B. Comparative costs	2, 4
	C. Cost-distribution studies	2, 4
XVI.	Reporting	
	A. Local financial and statistical reports	1, 2, 4
	B. State financial and statistical reports	1, 2, 4
	C. Federal financial and statistical reports	1, 2, 4
	D. Miscellaneous reports	1, 2, 4
	E. Required legal advertising	
	F. Relationships with public information media	1, 4
XVII.	Collective Negotiations	
	A. Service on management team when required	1, 2, 3, 4
	B. Preparation of pertinent fiscal data for management team	2, 3, 4

Exhibit 16.1, continued

	C. Development of techniques and strategies of collective negotiations	2, 4
	D. Sharing of proper information with employee units	1, 2, 3, 4
	E. Use of outside negotiations and agencies	
	F. Mediation, arbitration, and grievances	2, 3
XVIII.	Data Processing	
	A. Selection of system	1
	B. Programming	1-4
	C. Utilization of systems analysis	1-4
	D. Forms preparation	1, 2, 3
	E. Broad use of equipment for all pertinent applications	1-4
XIX.	School-board Policies and Administrative Procedures as Related to Fiscal and Noninstructional Matters	1
XX.	Responsibilities for Elections and Bond Referenda	
XXI.	Responsibilities for School Assessment, Levy and Tax-Collection Procedures as May Be Set by Law	1, 2

Some of the more useful features of word processors are as follows:

1. Word wrap—When you reach the end of a line during text entry, the next word automatically begins on the next line; there is no need to use a return key.
2. Block moves—This allows you to move paragraphs from one part of a document to another by using a few commands.
3. Search and replace—you can find any word or phrase in the document and replace it with another.
4. Screen-oriented—These programs display on the video monitor exactly what you will see on the printed page.
5. Form letters—This is the ability to process a form letter by inserting name and address data into specific places in the form letter.
6. Spelling checkers—Disk dictionaries are used to check the spelling of common words.
7. Other important features—centering, justification, proportional spacing, underlining, and so on.

Before buying a particular software package, a school business administrator should review the many valuable articles and sources on this subject and should also talk with others who have used particular programs.

Electronic Spreadsheets

It has been stated many times that Visicalc, the original electronic spreadsheet program for micros, has sold more microcomputers than any other software package. Visicalc, a product of Visicorp, was the most popular micro software program through the late seventies and the early eighties, but at $200 for a copy, it is not particularly cheap. Although its features have been improved with newer software, it was a programming marvel. It was the first truly "user-friendly" software package that allowed the user to develop, among other things, personnel, negotiations, and financial formats or templates. These applications were all characterized by repetitious numerical computations.

Visicalc, Supercalc, Mathcalc, and the similar electronic spreadsheet programs are essentially computerized replacements for the quantitative paper-and-pencil calculations of the business office. In Visicalc, the "worksheet" is composed of a large sheet of memory 254 rows long and 63 columns wide. Each memory location, or cell, is identified by a set of X, Y coordinates. Thus, cell B-4 is located in the second column and the fourth row, and cell BK-254 is located in the bottom right corner of the spreadsheet. These memory cells can hold numbers, words, labels, and formulas. Although a 64K microcomputer will not have enough memory to fill every cell, it will have more than sufficient space for a trendline data chart, a negotations salary grid, or a monthly attendance file for 225 teachers. The users of a 256K IBM or an Apple with a memory expansion board will have considerably more space to hold data.

The responsibilities of the school business administrator lend themselves particularly well to the numerous applications of electronic spreadsheet software. Some of the features of a program such as Visicalc that make it useful for the business official are as follows:

1. A "wall-sized" worksheet of 63 columns by 254 rows.
2. A powerful recalculation feature allows you to change any number or formula, and the computer immediately changes all the numbers affected by that number or formula.
3. A replicate command allows you to duplicate any number, label, or formula through the worksheet.
4. A window feature splits the worksheet into two parts to view separate areas of the worksheet.
5. Variable formatting lets you set any or every number to integer, dollars and cents, left or right justification.
6. A complete set of mathematical function options.

With several hours of training, a school business administrator can learn to generate reporting formats, or templates, that can be used for revising periodic reports.

Exhibit 16.2
School Historical Data

GENERAL FUND BUDGETS AND TRUE VALUE TAX RATES

1974-75 TO 1985-86

A.S.B . 01-Aug-85

YEAR	TOTAL GEN.FUND BUDGET	INCREASE FROM PREV.YEAR	C.P.I. INCREASE	ADJUSTED C.P.I. BUDGET	TAX RATE ON TRUE VALUATION	INCREASE/ DECREASE
1974-75	$8,451,089	-	10.40	$8,451,089	$20.63	
1975-76	9,208,321	$757,232	9.50	$9,330,002	20.14	($0.49)
1976-77	9,606,547	398,226	6.30	10,216,352	19.05	(1.09)
1977-78	10,008,304	401,757	5.00	10,859,983	18.88	(0.17)
1978-79	10,717,703	709,399	4.80	11,402,982	18.40	(0.48)
1979-80	11,340,246	622,543	11.40	11,950,325	17.49	(0.91)
1980-81	12,537,083	1,196,837	10.30	13,312,662	16.30	(1.19)
1981-82	13,778,229	1,241,146	6.50	14,683,866	16.72	0.42
1982-83	14,502,703	724,474	5.10	15,638,317	16.68	(0.04)
1983-84	15,463,268	960,565	6.60	16,435,872	17.94	1.26
1984-85	16,177,024	713,756	4.30	17,520,639	17.81	(0.13)
1985-86	17,491,761	1,314,737	-	18,274,027	18.40	0.59
1974-85 INCREASE		$7,725,935	91.42%	$9,069,550		($2.82)
AVE. INCREASE		$772,594	9.14%	$906,955		($0.28)

A School Financial Model

Exhibit 16.2 illustrates historical school budget data over an eleven-year period. This file would take up about twenty-five rows and seven columns as a Visicalc template. The data in columns 3, 4, and 6 are calculated by formulas you must type in. For example, suppose that the second data entry in the second column, $8,451,089, is located in cell B-10. Then the second data entry in the third column, $1,136,173, would be automatically calculated using this formula: B-10 – B-9. This formula would be repeated to find each number in the third column. The entries in columns 4 and 6 would be automatically calculated by typing in and repeating similar formulas. While these calculations could certainly be accomplished with paper and pencil, the speed and accuracy of a computer are undeniably appealing.

A School's Salary Schedule

The area of employee salary negotiations is an excellent one in which to develop expertise with this type of software. The teacher salary grid in exhibit 16.3 was created by using a spreadsheet file.

In the upper left corner of the table is the base salary. Each of the grid cells contains the formula:

base × index of step

Exhibit 16.3

Salary Level Progressions

BASE SALARY :$14,200

LEVEL	B	B+5	B+10	B+15	B+20	B+25	B+30	B+35	M	M+5	M+10	M+15	M+20	M+25	M+30
1	$14,200	$14,413	$14,626	$14,839	$15,052	$15,265	$15,478	$15,691	$15,904	$16,117	$16,330	$16,543	$16,756	$16,969	$17,182
2	14,860	15,073	15,286	15,499	15,712	15,925	16,138	16,351	16,564	16,777	16,990	17,203	17,416	17,629	17,842
3	15,521	15,734	15,947	16,160	16,373	16,586	16,898	17,111	17,324	17,537	17,750	17,963	18,176	18,389	18,602
4	16,181	16,394	16,607	16,820	17,033	17,246	17,608	17,821	18,034	18,247	18,460	18,673	18,886	19,099	19,312
5	16,962	17,175	17,388	17,601	17,814	18,027	18,460	18,673	18,886	19,099	19,312	19,525	19,738	19,951	20,164
6	17,814	18,027	18,240	18,453	18,666	18,879	19,312	19,525	19,738	19,951	20,164	20,377	20,590	20,803	21,016
7	18,666	18,879	19,092	19,305	19,518	19,731	20,164	20,377	20,590	20,803	21,016	21,229	21,442	21,655	21,868
8	19,518	19,731	19,944	20,157	20,370	20,583	21,016	21,229	21,442	21,655	21,868	22,081	22,294	22,507	22,720
9	20,370	20,583	20,796	21,009	21,222	21,435	21,868	22,081	22,294	22,507	22,720	22,933	23,146	23,359	23,572
10	21,222	21,435	21,648	21,861	22,074	22,287	22,720	22,933	23,146	23,359	23,572	23,785	23,998	24,211	24,424
11	22,074	22,287	22,500	22,713	22,926	23,139	23,572	23,785	23,998	24,211	24,424	24,637	24,850	25,063	25,276
12							24,282	24,495	24,708	24,921	25,134	25,347	25,560	25,773	25,986
13							24,992	25,205	25,418	25,631	25,844	26,057	26,270	26,483	26,696
14								25,915	26,128	26,341	26,554	26,767	26,980	27,193	27,406
15									26,928	27,141	27,354	27,567	27,780	27,993	28,206
16										27,941	28,154	28,367	29,180	28,793	29,006
17												29,167	29,380	29,593	29,806
18														30,393	30,606

By changing the dollar amount in the base cell, an entirely new salary grid is generated. A computer can replace thirty to forty-five minutes of hand calculations with five seconds of "number crunching."

When a school official is in the midst of serious teacher or support staff negotiations, it often seems that the cost data requested is endless. Much time and energy can be saved if the time is taken to prepare Visicalc formats that can be used in a particular school district. The printout in Exhibit 16.4 is a variation of the same file used in exhibit 16.3. The entries in columns 2, 3, and 4 are automatically computed each time a new base salary is entered, as in the previous example. For example, suppose the level-one salary is in row 10 and that the 1983–1984 salaries are in column A, and so on. Then, $1,160, the salary increase in cell C-11, is automatically calculated if cell C-11 contains the formula: B-11 − A-10. In this example the entry in C-11 ($1,160) is obtained by subtracting the entry in cell A-10 ($13,700) from the entry in B-11 ($14,860).

The following is a development outline for a negotiations file. The key entry is the base salary cell, and new data would be calculated following a progression from left to right in the Visicalc file.

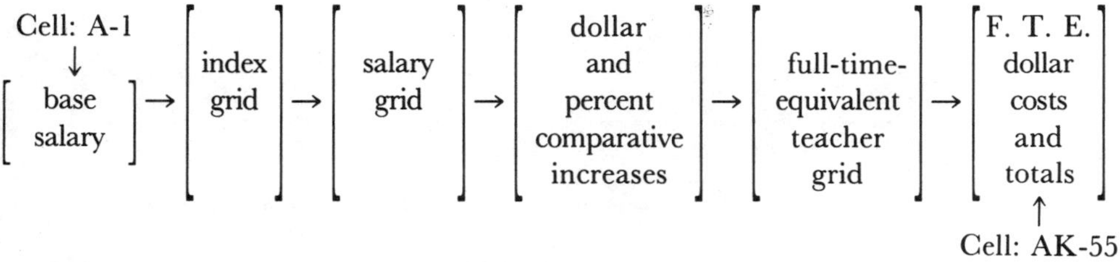

Exhibit 16.4
Salary Schedule

LEVEL	1983-84 B	1984-85 B	LEVEL INC.	PERCENT INC.	1983-84 B+30	1984-85 B+30	LEVEL INC.	PERCENT INC.
1	$13,700	$14,200	-	-	$14,933	$15,478	-	-
2	14,337	14,860	$1,160	8.47%	15,618	16,138	$1,205	8.07%
3	14,974	15,521	1,184	8.26%	16,303	16,898	1,280	8.20%
4	15,611	16,181	1,207	8.06%	16,988	17,608	1,305	8.00%
5	16,365	16,962	1,351	8.65%	17,810	18,460	1,472	8.66%
6	17,187	17,814	1,449	8.85%	18,632	19,312	1,502	8.43%
7	18,009	18,666	1,479	8.60%	19,454	20,164	1,532	8.22%
8	18,831	19,518	1,509	8.38%	20,276	21,016	1,562	8.03%
9	19,653	20,370	1,539	8.17%	21,098	21,868	1,592	7.85%
10	20,475	21,222	1,569	7.98%	21,920	22,720	1,622	7.69%
11	21,297	22,074	1,599	7.81%	22,742	23,572	1,652	7.54%
12					23,427	24,282	1,540	6.77%
13					24,112	24,992	1,565	6.68%
14								
15								
16								
17								
18								
	AVERAGE	INCREASE :	$1,277	7.57%	AVERAGE	INCREASE :	$1,339	7.34%

Exhibit 16.5

Spencerport School District Tax Rates

1984–1985

TAX LEVY-$ 5609611 DATE: 8/1/84

TOWN	TENTATIVE EQUAL.RATE	ASSESSED VALUATION	TRUE VALUATION	PERCENT TRUE VALUE	TAXES TO BE RAISED	TAX RATE PER $1000
OGDEN	.6104	89100373	145970467	46.36	2600383.52	29.1848781
GATES	.1403	13550746	96584077	30.67	1720592.17	126.973981
GREECE	.1432	4854047	33896976	10.76	603855.97	124.402581
PARMA	.1362	5235466	38439545	12.21	684779.33	130.796252
TOTALS		112740632	314891065	100.00	5609611.00	

COMPARATIVE TAX RATES

TOWN	RATE ON ASSESSED VALUATION 1983-1984	RATE ON ASSESSED VALUATION 1984-1985	INCREASE/ DECREASE AMOUNT ($/1000)	INCREASE/ DECREASE PERCENT
OGDEN	28.70	29.18	0.48	1.69
GATES	123.06	126.97	3.91	3.18
GREECE	119.13	124.40	5.27	4.43
PARMA	126.62	130.80	4.18	3.30

TRUE VALUE

TAX RATE ON TRUE VALUATION '84-85	17.81
TAX RATE ON TRUE VALUATION '83-84	17.94
INCREASE $	-0.13
INCREASE %	-0.70

TAX LEVY

TAXES'84-85	5609611
TAXES'83-84	5278344
INCREASE $	331267
INCREASE %	6.28

1984-1985 PROJECTED TAX RATES

TOWN	AVERAGE ASSESSMENT	TAX RATE INCREASE PER $1000	INCREASED COST TO AVE HOMEOWNER	PERCENT INCREASE
OGDEN	25000	0.48	12.00	1.69
GATES	7000	3.91	27.37	3.18
GREECE	6000	5.27	31.62	4.43
PARMA	6000	4.18	25.08	3.30

A Tax Levy File

In designing a tax levy file, it is desirable to have the formulas and labels arranged so that the printouts fit on one page and look orderly. The tax levy file in exhibit 16.5 occupies sixty-four lines and six columns that just fit on a single sheet of paper. The generated data are tax information common to all school districts, depending on the number of towns that constitute the school area. The key cell is the "tax levy" figure ($5,609,611). When that entry is changed, every other entry based on the tax levy changes. Calculating and checking the information presented in exhibit 16.5 would take the better part of an hour with a hand calculator—it took six seconds on an Apple. The appendix contains more examples that illustrate how a spreadsheet program can increase the productivity of the school business administrator.

Data-Base Management

Visicalc was the business software sensation of the late seventies and early eighties, but in the opinion of many leading data-processing experts, data-base management systems will be the ultimate management tool of the 1980s.

A data-base management system (DBMS) may be defined as a centralized collection of data stored for use in one or more applications, and it uses computer hardware and software capabilities to organize information in a video display or hard-copy format. However, a DBMS does have different meanings for different people. A school business administrator with general ledger, inventory, personnel, or salary requirements will probably look on the management of a data base in more formal terms than would the homeowner who uses a DBMS to keep track of the dates on which meat cuts are purchased for storage in the home freezer.

A data base essentially consists of fields, records, and files. A *field* is a basic unit of information, such as an employee's name. The *record* consists of a number of related fields, such as the three fields containing an employee's name, address, and phone number. A file is a group of related records, such as a personnel file. Thus, a micro-based data-base management system is a file of records consisting of associated fields.

A good data-base system includes the following features:

1. Documentation—a well-written, easy-to-follow, illustrated manual with examples is a must unless your degree is in data processing
2. Ease of use—a menu design with user-oriented operating features.
3. Flexibility—options for input and output formats.
4. Data-sequencing ability—the ability to sort numerically and alphabetically in ascending and descending order.
5. Report capability—the capability for video display and hard-copy options, subtotals, final totals, variable headings, and labels.
6. Expandability—the ability to adjust the field or record file after the file has been created.
7. Default options—options to allow automatic input of common data and to speed up input and output procedures.
8. Look-up features—the ability to search for records defined by multiple criteria.

Exhibit 16.6

Spencerport Central School District Support Staff
(Bernabi School)
1984–1985

****

UNIT	LAST NAME	FIRST NAME	HRS/ DAY	STARTING TIME	FINISHING TIME	DAYS/ WEEK
ADMIN	PARKER	WAYNE		7:30	4:00	ALL
CLERICAL	BUTTNER	L. CHRISTINE	7.50	8:00	4:00	ALL
	KNAPP	GENE	7.50	7:45	3:45	ALL
	MCLELLAN	JUDITH	7.50	8:00	4:00	ALL
NURSES	MOHNKERN	KATHLEEN	7.25	8:15	4:00	1 OUT 3
POM	DATES	WILLIAM	8.00	2:30	10:30	ALL
	EBERLIN	DORIS	8.00	2:30	10:30	ALL
	OPALENIK	JOSEPH	8.00	6:30	3:00	ALL
SCHOOL AIDE	ERWIN	BETTE	1.00	8:00	9:00	ALL
	HOTCHKISS	LOIS	2.00	11:15	1:15	ALL
	VAN SLOOTEN	CHARLENE	2.00	11:15	1:15	ALL
SCHOOL LUNCH	BLANCHARD	ETHEL	3.00	10:15	1:30	ALL
	CANNAN	LORRAINE	6.25	7:15	1:30	ALL
	ERWIN	BETTE	4.00	9:15	1:30	ALL
	GRANDY	GAYLE	6.25	7:15	1:30	ALL
	PISKOROWSKI	AGNES	4.00	9:15	1:30	ALL
TCHG ASSTS	CULBERT	LINDA	1.00	9:40	10:40	ALL
	HARRIS	JANICE	3.50	8:15	2:45	MWTH
	LENNON	BONNIE	6.00	8:15	2:45	ALL
	NOXON	VIRGINIA	3.50	8:15	1:15	MTWTH
TCHR AIDES	BERARDICURTI	FRANCES	6.50	8:00	3:00	ALL
	CRAFTS	ELLEN	4.00	8:30	2:00	TWTHF
	RINAS	ELEANOR	6.25	8:30	3:15	ALL
	SWETZ	MARY ELLEN	3.00	8:30	11:30	ALL
	YOUNGJOHN	MARIE	5.00	8:00	1:00	ALL
TRANSPORTATION	MULLINS	LYNNE	8.00	5:30	2:00	ALL

Among the wide variety of data-base management systems on the market, Personal Filing System and Power Base are particularly useful for school business management, especially for beginners learning the basics of DBMS. The experienced micro user will find it more beneficial to acquire a more powerful and complicated system, such as DB Master, D Base III, R-Base 5000, or Condor. Exhibit 16.6 illustrates a support staff data-base file sorted by school building and subsorted alphabetically by employee unit and then by name. This file was created using Power Base, which is possibly the best all-around DBMS for the IBM-PC.

With some DBMS, you can calculate fields in binary fashion only. That is, a yearly salary field would be computed by multiplying the hourly rate by the

Exhibit 16.7

Screen for a School District Support Staff Personnel System

```
LASTNAME   _______________    UNIT     TRANSPORTATION     DATE ________
FIRSTNAME  _______________    BLDG.    _______________
ADDRESS 1  _______________    C.S.TL.  _______________    ST.TIME ___________
ADDRESS 2  _______________    D.O.B.   ________           FN.TIME ___________
CITY       SPENCERPRT         S.S. #   ___ - ___- ____    DAYS    _______
STATE      NY  ZIP   14559
PHONE # ( 716) ________

WORK YR(MO) 10                OLD MERIT     Ø             LONG 1    Ø     ADJ.HR.
HRS / DAY   ____              NEW MERIT     Ø             LONG 2    Ø    RATE:   $Ø.ØØ
DAYS / YR   26Ø               STIPEND 1     Ø             LONG 3    Ø
HR. RATE    ______            STIPEND 2     Ø             LONG 4    Ø
BASE SALARY        $Ø.ØØ      NGT.SHIFT     Ø             TOT.SALARY        $Ø.ØØ

HEALTH INS.  _                NYS RET.    _               DIST.RET.DATE ________
DENTAL INS.  _                RETIRE. #   _________       SEN.LAST 6/3Ø _____
MAJ.MED.INS. _                TIER #      _               VAC.DAYS ___   YR 1984/85
                              DATE JOIN   ________        BUD.CODE ________ % 1ØØ.ØØ
COMMENT: __________________________________________       BUD.CODE ________ % _____
```

number of hours worked during the year. You could not multiply together three previously defined fields, such as hours per day, number of days worked, and hourly rate to obtain the same yearly salary.

With many of the better DBMS packages, you can create your own custom input screens and a wide variety of formats for the output. For example, the IBM-PC Power Base, data-base management system mentioned above, would allow you to do this. The screen in exhibit 16.7 illustrates a school district support staff personnel system with forty-nine fields. The fields with entries in them contain the default values (where the computer picks the value unless you enter in another one). A field such as "base salary" is a computed field. Specifically, it is the product of hours per day, days per year, and hourly rate. Exhibit 16.6 is just one type of report easily generated by this data-base system.

A Physical Assets Inventory Data Base

As was pointed out in exhibit 16.1, the school business administrator is responsible for ensuring the currency and accuracy of the district's physical assets inventories. This is necessary for insurance purposes and to minimize the possibility of the theft or misplacement of school district property.

With most schools, it is difficult to keep track of musical instruments from year to year—many instruments seem to disappear over the years. Exhibit 16.8 illustrates a district's instrumental music inventory sorted by individual school buildings.

A Comparative School Budget Data Base

A final example of a DBMS application is a comparative study of the school budgets in a county in New York State. The data base was set up on a

Exhibit 16.8

Instrumental Music Instruments Inventory

INSTRUMENT	MAKE	LOANED TO	CONDITION
	--TOWN LINE	MUSIC INSTRUMENTS--	
OBOE	LINTON	NOT IN USE	FAIR
BASSOON	MOENIG	NOT IN USE	AVERAGE
ALTO CLARINET	SELMAR	USED IN SCHOOL	POOR
BASS CLARINET	SELMAR	NOT IN USE	POOR
BASS CLARINET	LEBLANC	USED IN SCHOOL	FAIR
TENOR SAXOPHONE	SELMAR	GINA LOCIANO	FAIR
TENOR SAXOPHONE	CONN	DANNY SMITH	GOOD
TENOR SAXOPHONE	YAMAHA	MIKE IRVING	NEW
BARITONE SAXOPHONE	VITO	USED IN SCHOOL	GOOD
FRENCH HORN F	CLEVELAND	NOT IN USE	BAD
FRENCH HORN F	CONN	NICOLE GRIGG	GOOD
FRENCH HORN F	REYNOLDS	NOT IN USE	SCRAP
TROMBONE	REYNOLDS	NOT IN USE	AVERAGE
BARITONE HORN	CONN	HEATHER HARSTER	GOOD
BARITONE HORN	CONN	RON HART	GOOD
BARITONE HORN	HOLTON	ADAM GALLAGHER	EXCELLENT
BARITONE HORN	REYNOLDS	KEITH NATALE	FAIR
BARITONE HORN	REYNOLDS	JASON ARNOLD	FAIR
TUBA	MIRAPHONE	BEN WARD	GOOD
TUBA	MIRAPHONE	RAY LALLY	GOOD
SOUSAPHONE	KING	USED IN SCHOOL	GOOD
TYMPANI	ROGERS	USED IN SCHOOL	GOOD
TYMPANI	ROGERS	USED IN SCHOOL	GOOD
BASS DRUM	ROGERS	USED IN SCHOOL	GOOD
SNARE DRUM (CONCERT)	LUDWIG	USED IN SCHOOL	BAD
SNARE DRUM (CONCERT)	LUDWIG	USED IN SCHOOL	BAD
SNARE DRUM (CONCERT)	LUDWIG	USED IN SCHOOL	BAD
SNARE DRUM (CONCERT)	LUDWIG	USED IN SCHOOL	GOOD
SNARE DRUM	SLINGERLAND	USED IN SCHOOL	NEW
CRASH CYMBALS	ZILDJIAN	USED IN SCHOOL	FAIR
SUSPENDED CYMBAL	ZILDJIAN	USED IN SCHOOL	GOOD
CONCERT BELLS	MUSSER	USED IN SCHOOL	GOOD
FRENCH HORN	SANSONE	MICHELLE BRODIE	GOOD
FRENCH HORN	CONN	GENNI WARD	GOOD
FRENCH HORN	HOLTON	E.J.ARNOLD	GOOD
FRENCH HORN	HOLTON	CONNIE BROTT	GOOD
FRENCH HORN	CONN	JENNIFER FAUX	GOOD

school-by-school basis, with each school file containing about fifty of its budget's account appropriations. The report was designed to divide the second column (the school's budget) by the first (the school's enrollment) and then print the schools in the order of descending cost per pupil. As you can see in exhibit 16.9, a hand-calculated report would require much repetitious division and then per-pupil cost sorting after finding the per-pupil costs. But a computer can produce these calculations instantly; the basic file was created on an Apple DBMS (Data Factory 6.0). The yearly budget amounts and enrollments are entered each fall, and a new cost per pupil is calculated.

Graphics Generation

A tremendous amount of information flows from the office of the school business administrator to various offices in a school community. In many

Exhibit 16.9
SBM-1 Study for 1984–85
Total General Fund Appropriation
(A9999)

SCHOOL	ENROLLMENT	BUDGET	COST/PUPIL
1. BRIGHTON	3223	19948077	6189.29
2. RUSH-HENRIETTA	6134	35754683	5828.94
3. EAST IRONDEQUOIT	2537	14530090	5727.27
4. WHEATLAND-CHILI	1000	5720978	5720.98
5. PITTSFORD	5150	28972259	5625.68
6. EAST ROCHESTER	1359	7294926	5367.86
7. PENFIELD	4082	21852625	5353.41
8. GATES CHILI	5025	25534373	5081.47
9. WEBSTER	6036	30282438	5016.97
10. CITY OF ROCHESTER	33155	165840682	5001.98
AVERAGE COST			4981.25
11. GREECE	10973	54046263	4925.39
12. HONEOYE FALLS LIMA	1909	9173524	4805.41
13. SPENCERPORT	3442	16177024	4699.89
14. WEST IRONDEQUOIT	3498	16388371	4685.07
15. HILTON	3617	16288471	4503.31
16. CHURCHVILLE-CHILI	3555	15789404	4441.46
17. FAIRPORT	7096	31448691	4431.89
18. KENDALL	1131	4644531	4106.57
19. BROCKPORT	4248	17376274	4090.46
20. HOLLEY	1229	4942591	4021.64

cases a graphic representation of the data can illustrate relationships much better than words or numbers can. Several excellent business graphics packages are on the market for use on microcomputers, including PFS Graph, Chartmaster, and Chartman. These programs allow you to produce various types of graphs quickly and easily.

The following are some of the major features of this type of software:

1. A variety of display formats: bar, area, line, pie, scatter, hi-lo charts
2. Automatic and manual scaling of the axes
3. Ease of data entry
4. Ability to overlay graphs for more than one data series

Exhibit 16.10
Summary of a Budget Distribution

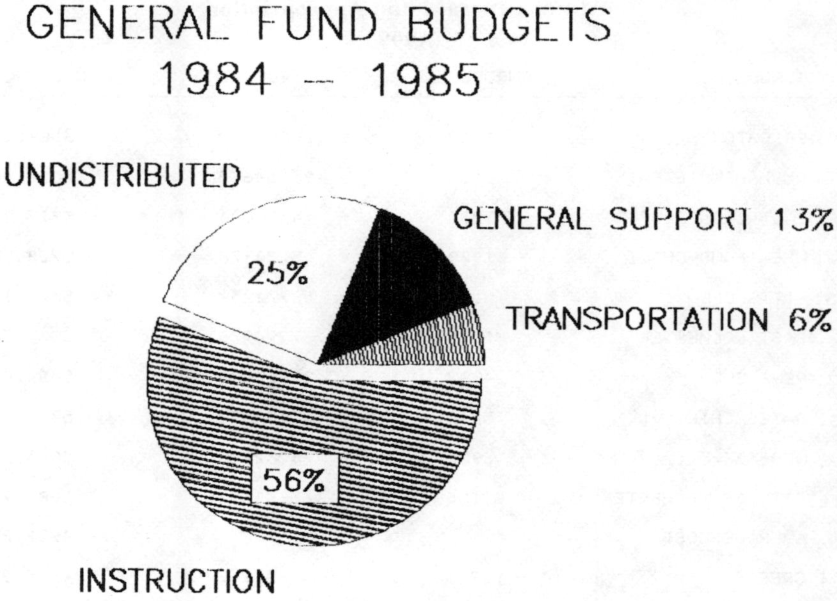

5. Split bar graphs for side-by-side comparsions
6. Flexible labeling on the chart and on the axes

A County Budget Study

When the data for the county budget study mentioned in the last section were compiled on the DBMS, summary data were generated using LOTUS 1-2-3. That summary data were then depicted on a pie chart, shown in exhibit 16.10, using Chart master. The summary data are shown in exhibit 16.11.

An Energy Conservation Project

The Spencerport School District in Spencerport, New York, undertook an $800,000 energy conservation project during the summer of 1980. The split bar chart in exhibit 16.12 indicates the energy use by building before and after the energy project. Exhibit 16.13 compares the energy use on a therms-per-day basis; exhibit 16.14 compares the energy use on a therms-per-day-per-square foot basis; and exhibit 16.15 compares the energy cost on a dollars-per-degree-day basis. These graphs were produced from an energy management data base on LOTUS 1-2-3.

Graphics for Salary Negotiations

In the course of negotiations, the school business administrator must often present salary data to different audiences. The following two Chartman graphs depict the identical salary offer during negotiations with teachers. The difference was the unit of measure on the Y-axis. One graph was presented to the teachers (exhibit 16.16) and the other was given to the school board (exhibit 16.17). Exhibit 16.16 indicates the increased dollars payable to teachers who have more years of service, while exhibit 16.17 indicates cost containment at the upper salary levels.

Initial Microcomputer Applications (Where to Start)

Although many possible micro-based applications can be imagined, it is less obvious which applications should be undertaken first and why. Typically, the first applications are associated with a single-purpose type of software and have relatively few input data requirements. More often than not, the school business administrator will start by first developing competence with electronic spreadsheet software and then applying this skill to areas such as tax levies, cash flow, short-term investments, monthly revenue, and appropriation reports. These applications require relatively little computer literacy, save relatively large amounts of time, improve error control, and are used regularly and frequently.

The second phase of applying a computer system would be the use of data-base management software. With well-documented software, the business office could automate the school district's personnel directory and the various mailing lists maintained and used by the district.

Subsequent applications include one or more of the following: (1) more ambitious applications using existing software that build on the competence gained in developing more simple applications, for example, using the electronic spreadsheet program for salary negotiations; (2) combining the features of two or more of the software packages into one application, for example, combining spreadsheet and graphics software to produce energy-use charts (as in exhibits 16.12–16.15); (3) acquiring new software packages to use in new applications, for example, purchasing word-processing software for report writing. From the viewpoint of the school business administrator, the relative usefulness of generic software packages, in order of decreasing importance, is as follows: electronic spreadsheets, data-base management, graphics, word processing, and others.

In the early 1980s software manufacturers recognized the need for microcomputer software that combined application areas and minimized the different operating commands. The most successful of these was LOTUS 1-2-3 produced by LOTUS Development Corporation.

Exhibit 16.11

Summary of a Budget Study

BUDGET CATEGORY	GENERAL SUPPORT		INSTRUCTION		TRANSPORTATION		COMMUNITY SERVICES		UNDISTRIBUTED		TOTAL GENERAL FUND APPROPRIATIONS
SCHOOL DISTRICT	BUDGET AMOUNT	PERCENT	BUDGET AMOUNT	PERCENT	BUDGET AMOUNT	PERCENT	BUDGET AMOUNT	PERCENT	BUDGET AMOUNT	PERCENT	GRAND TOTAL
BRIGHTON	$3,029,454	15.19%	$11,222,660	56.26%	$692,091	3.47%	$4,600	0.02%	$4,999,272	25.06%	$19,948,077
BROCKPORT	$2,252,596	12.96%	$9,926,486	57.13%	$1,102,984	6.35%	$5,800	0.03%	$4,088,408	23.53%	$17,376,274
CHURCH.-CHILI	$1,907,202	12.08%	$8,837,103	55.97%	$1,226,527	7.77%	$1,895	0.01%	$3,816,677	24.17%	$15,789,404
E.IRONDEQUOIT	$2,137,316	14.71%	$7,998,341	55.05%	$1,456,365	10.02%	$0	0.00%	$2,938,068	20.22%	$14,530,090
E.ROCHESTER	$1,188,529	16.29%	$4,269,383	58.53%	$294,000	4.03%	$20,000	0.27%	$1,523,014	20.88%	$7,294,926
FAIRPORT	$3,397,457	10.80%	$19,396,629	61.68%	$1,291,963	4.11%	$34,545	0.11%	$7,328,097	23.30%	$31,449,691
GATES-CHILI	$3,573,738	14.00%	$14,737,749	57.72%	$1,400,532	5.48%	$36,835	0.14%	$5,785,519	22.66%	$25,534,373
GREECE	$8,045,271	14.89%	$30,868,743	57.12%	$2,366,449	4.38%	$11,600	0.02%	$12,754,200	23.60%	$54,046,263
HILTON	$2,162,733	13.28%	$9,041,695	55.51%	$1,002,450	6.15%	$85,563	0.53%	$3,996,030	24.53%	$16,288,471
HOLLY	$671,938	13.59%	$2,704,144	54.71%	$329,316	6.66%	$2,095	0.04%	$1,235,098	24.99%	$4,942,591
HON.FL.-LIMA	$1,070,284	11.67%	$5,018,413	54.71%	$623,867	6.80%	$37,185	0.41%	$2,423,775	26.42%	$9,173,524

KENDALL	$539,380	11.61%	$2,640,656	56.86%	$291,506	6.28%	$1,672	0.04%	$1,171,317	25.22%	$4,644,531
PENFIELD	$2,757,245	12.62%	$12,327,785	56.41%	$1,210,045	5.54%	$7,855	0.04%	$5,549,695	25.40%	$21,852,625
PITTSFORD	$3,368,230	11.63%	$16,555,585	57.14%	$1,488,369	5.14%	$40,550	0.14%	$7,519,525	25.95%	$28,972,259
ROCHESTER	$20,327,562	12.26%	$93,131,620	56.16%	$12,028,006	7.25%	$176,015	0.11%	$40,177,479	24.23%	$165,840,682
RUSH-HEN.	$4,917,897	13.75%	$20,074,416	56.14%	$2,403,850	6.72%	$20,500	0.06%	$8,338,020	23.32%	$35,754,683
SPENCERPORT	$1,972,529	12.19%	$9,186,051	56.78%	$1,067,923	6.60%	$0	0.00%	$3,950,521	24.42%	$16,177,024
WEBSTER	$3,841,564	12.69%	$17,144,616	56.62%	$1,675,175	5.53%	$21,000	0.07%	$7,600,083	25.10%	$30,282,438
W.IRONDEQUOIT	$2,005,221	12.24%	$10,132,400	61.83%	$553,002	3.37%	$3,600	0.02%	$3,694,148	22.54%	$16,388,371
WHEAT.-CHILI	$673,902	11.78%	$3,069,005	53.64%	$312,708	5.47%	$1,000	0.02%	$1,664,363	29.09%	$5,720,978
84/85 TOTALS	$69,840,048	12.89%	$308,283,480	56.88%	$32,817,128	6.05%	$512,310	0.09%	$130,553,309	24.09%	$542,006,275
83/84 TOTALS	$67,421,219	13.34%	$283,416,169	56.07%	$32,276,611	6.39%	$407,973	0.08%	$121,967,574	24.13%	$505,489,546
$ INCREASE	$2,418,829		$24,867,311		$540,517		$104,337		$8,585,735		$36,516,729
% INCREASE	3.59%		8.77%		1.67%		25.57%		7.04%		7.22%

Exhibit 16.12
Split Bar Chart

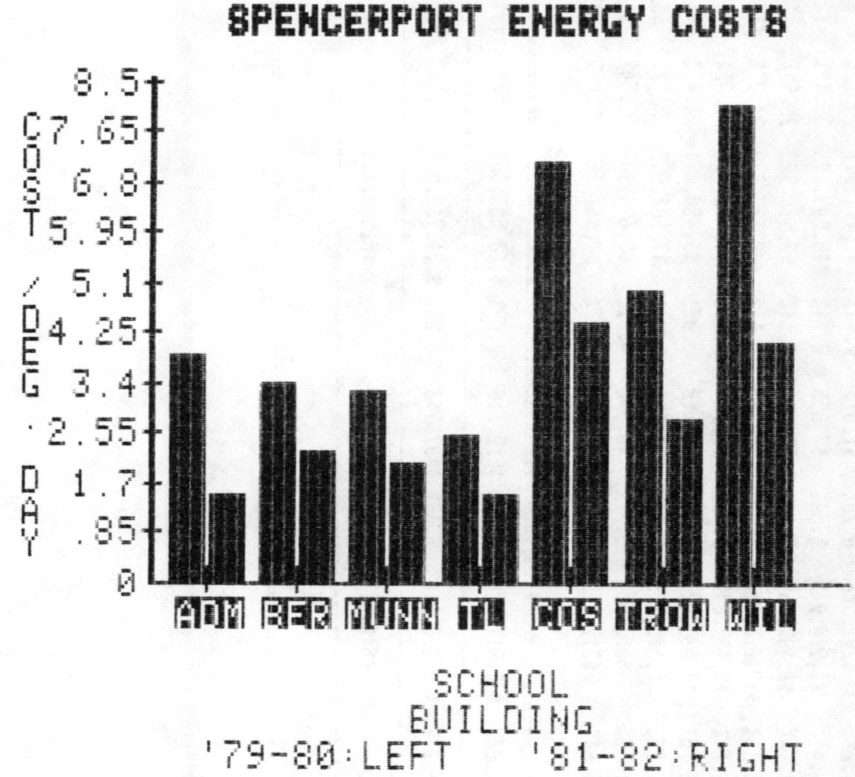

LOTUS 1-2-3 is an integrated package for the IBM and IBM compatibles that combines spreadsheet, data-base, and graphics capabilities into one well-designed program. In the mid-1980s LOTUS enhanced the immensely popular 1-2-3 by introducing Symphony, which added word-processing and telecommunications capabilities to 1-2-3. Ashton-Tate developed Framework, which integrated spreadsheets, word processing, business graphics, outline processing, and communications. Apple introduced Appleworks, which contained spreadsheet, word-processing, and data-base applications.

An integrated software package, such as LOTUS 1-2-3, is relatively easy to learn and contains the software a school business administrator most often uses.

Exhibit 16.13

Comparison of Energy on a Therms-per-Degree-Day Basis

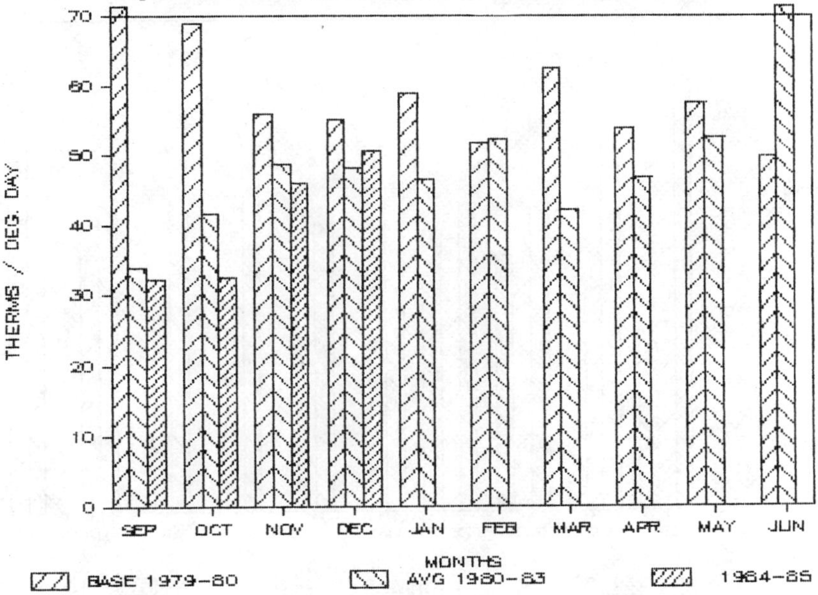

Exhibit 16.14

Building-to-Building Comparison of Energy Use on a Therms-per-Degree-Day-per Square-Foot Basis

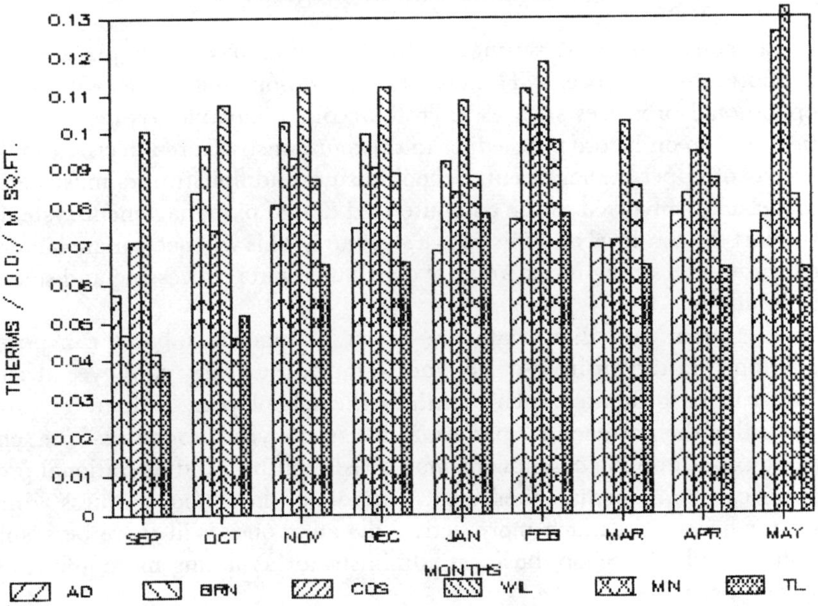

Exhibit 16.15

Comparison of Energy Use on a Dollars-per-Degree-Day Basis

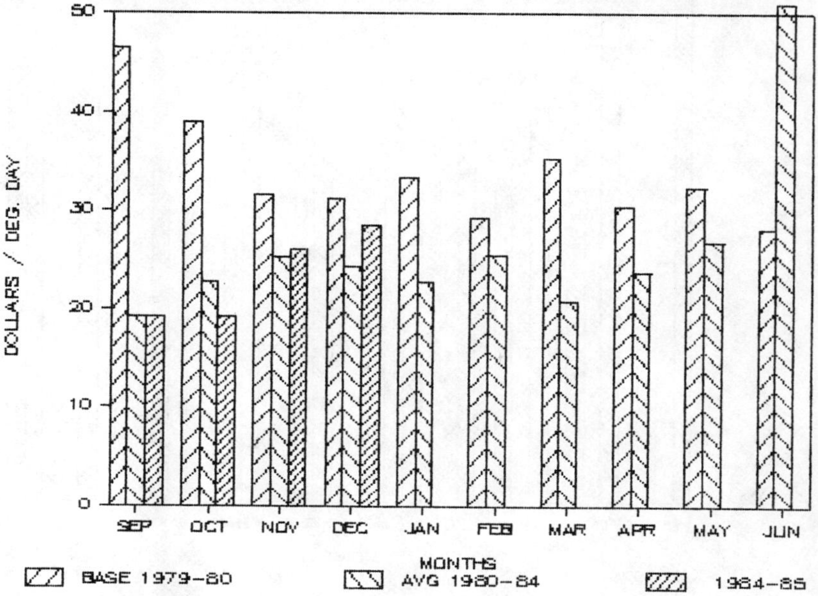

The Future Role of the School Business Administrator in Information Management

In many industrial settings computerization has taken place through a "bottom-up" process. That is, mechanization first starts with routine operational processes such as payroll, accounts payable, typing, reproduction, and so on before proceeding to the more unstructured decision-making arenas of upper management. School business administrators must become increasingly involved in the computerized design of management systems to support the top-level administrative structure. This will necessitate increased educational training in the areas of distributed data processing and software capabilities.

It is often said that "data are power." Huge data bases can now be developed in the business office. For example, the yearly employee absentee data can be generated each month of the school year. Employees can be advised of their attendance pattern as the school year progresses. The school energy consumption can now be monitored monthly, and operational procedures can be immediately effected. The role of the school business administrator becomes a much more active, dynamic one. Will there be a subtle shift towards the school business administrator assuming more influence in school districts?

Exhibit 16.16

Graph Depicting Salary Increases by Dollar

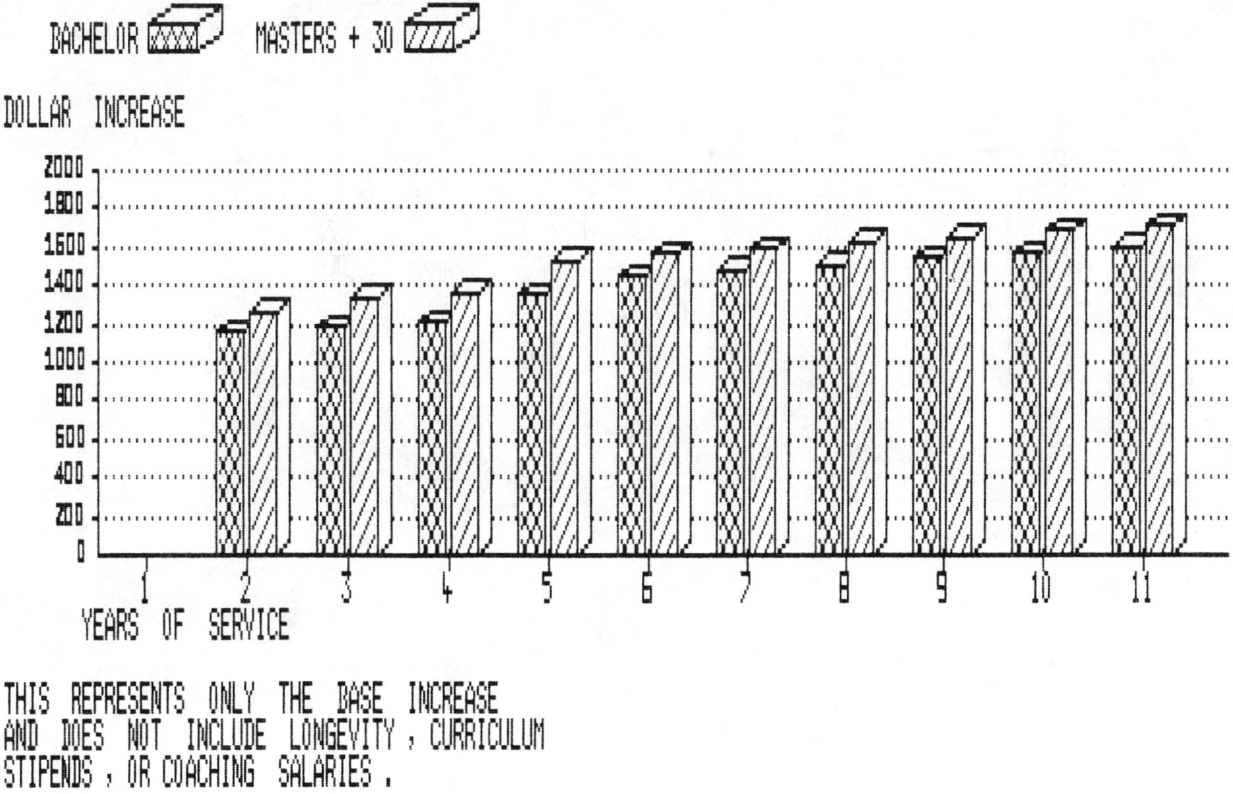

Exhibit 16.17

Graph Depicting Salary Increases by Percentage

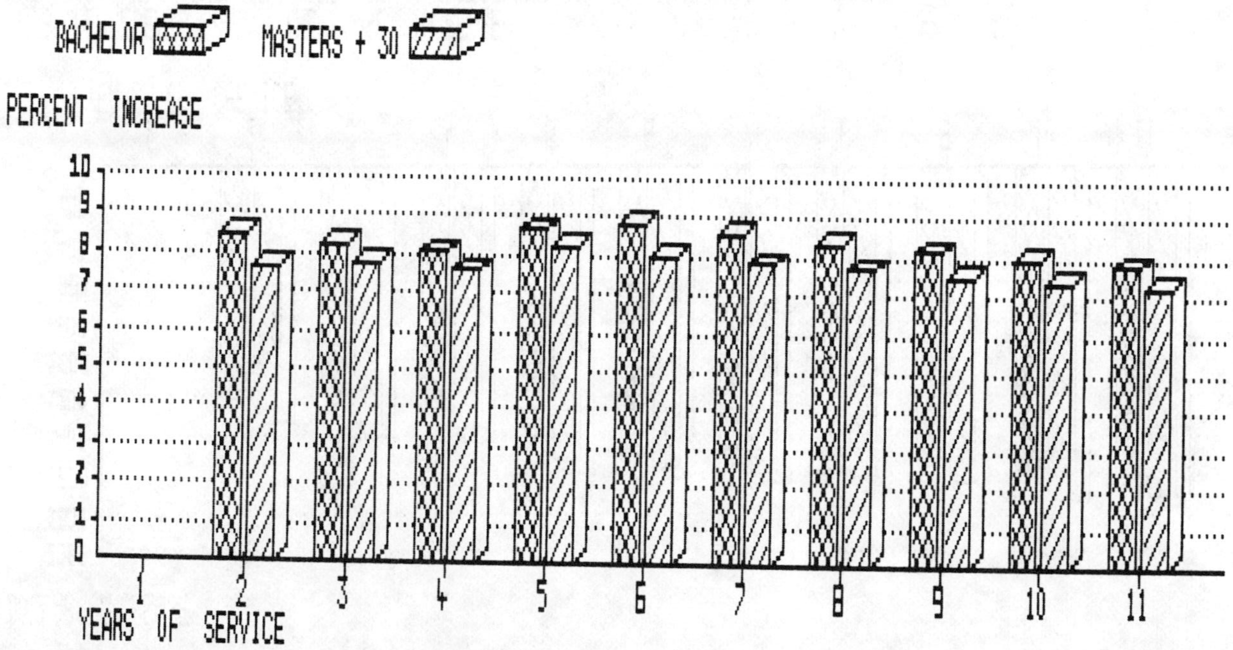

THIS REPRESENTS ONLY THE BASE INCREASE
AND DOES NOT INCLUDE LONGEVITY, CURRICULUM
STIPENDS, OR COACHING SALARIES.

A closer look will also have to be taken at the working relationship between individuals. Which tasks should be reallocated to the school business administrator and which to the secretaries? How will administrators with access to micros interact with those district administrators who still use a pocket calculator?

Most people define administration through words such as "accomplishing goals through the efforts of others." What will be the impact of this technology on traditional approaches to problem solving? It is our belief that a successful school business administrator must be an active agent for change in this revolution in school administration.

The impact of the microcomputer revolution is really twofold. First, it brought the cost of computing down to a level that was affordable for many. Second, this large market made it economically feasible for companies to mass-produce broadly useful software. Now, with relatively little investment of time and money, school business administrators can significantly enhance their productivity with a micro.

A hint of what this all means in the short run was shown in exhibit 16.1. The major responsibilities of the school business administrator are presented there along with the types of micro applications that are most likely to be relevant. All of the general headings in that table are discussed throughout this text, and it is likely that micro applications can enhance administrators' productivity in most future responsibilities.

Equally important is the fact that these four generic software applications—electronic spreadsheets, data-base management systems, word processing, and graphics—have been integrated into a single package. "Integrated" capabilities imply the ability to move from mode to mode with little effort and to be able to pursue a problem on information collecting, analyzing, or reporting unconstrained by incompatible software packages. This capability already exists in the integrated software such as LOTUS 1-2-3, Framework, Enable, Appleworks, and so on. These business software systems will be the norm in the future.

School Business Administrator: A Manager of Information

The importance to the school business administrator of information management cannot be overstated. One of the basic themes running throughout this text is that managers pursue preferences through the combined activities of analyzing information and exercising rights. The school business administrator as a manager of information influences the behavior of others through the data he or she collects, analyzes, and presents. The technology of information management, including microcomputing, is as important to the school business administrator as it is to any other educator.

Periodicals

Apple Orchard, 908 George Street, Santa Clara, CA 95050
Business Software, 2464 Embarcadero Way, Palo Alto, CA 94303
Byte, 70 Main St., Peterborough, NH 03458
Computerworld, Box 880, 375 Cochituate Road, Framingham, MA 01701
Creative Computing, P.O. Box 789-M, Morristown, NJ 07960
Desktop Computing, 80 Pine St., Peterborough, NH 03458
Interface Age/Computing for Business, 7330 Adams St., Paramount, CA 90723
Micro Co-op Newsletter, P.O. Box 714, St. Charles, IL 60174
Nibble, P.O. Box 325, Lincoln, MA 01773
PC World, 555 De Haro St., San Francisco, CA 94107
Personal Computing, 50 Essex St., Rochelle Park, NJ 07662
School Business Affairs, 720 Gordon St., Park Ridge, IL 60068

References

Edwards, John. "Apple IIe." *Popular Computing* 2:5 (March 1983): 108–110.
Heintz, Carl. "Guide to Database System Software." *Interface Age* 8: 2 (February 1983): 52–64.
Stewart, George. "A First Look at Lisa." *Popular Computing* 2: 5 (March 1983): 84–92.
"Word Processor Special." *Peelings II* 3: 6 (July 1982): 6–42.

Appendix 16.1: Business Administration Management Tasks

This is an example of a LOTUS spreadsheet application outlining the week-by-week tasks of a school business administrator each year. Obviously others arise, but these are typical.

BUSINESS
ADMINISTRATION
MANAGEMENT
TASKS

MONTH	JULY
WEEK ONE	ADULT EDUCATION REPORT BUDGET MEMO TO ADM. COUNCIL ANNUAL CIVIL SERVICE SALARY ROSTER ORDER TAX ENVELOPES /ROCK PRESS BOOKSTORE INVENTORY FROM HIGH SCH. ORGANIZE SUMMER TASKS CHECK ON STATE AID FORMS RECEIVE STATE AID INFORMATION FROM DIRECTORS AGENDA ITEMS TO SUPERINTENDENT
WEEK TWO	CORNERSTONE ARTICLES WRITTEN SCHOOL BOARD ORGANIZATIONAL MTG. SCHOOL BOARD MEETING COMPLETE SA-1Ø3[TEXTBOOK AID] RECEIVE EXTRA-CLASSROOM REPORT SUBMIT BOARD CANDIDATES REPORTS ADVERTISE FOR SUPPORT POSITIONS
WEEK THREE	ADMINISTRATIVE COUNCIL COMPLETE STATE AID FORMS SUBMIT DISTRICT OFFICERS REPORT REPORT: STATE AID LOSS /R.A.N.S UPDATE VISICALC REPORT FILES INTERNAL AUDITORS AGENDA ITEMS TO SUPERINTENDENT PREPARE CHAPTER II GRANT PROPOSAL ASBO MEETING REPORTS:REVENUE & APPROPRIATIONS BUDGET TRANSFERS REPORT:BOARD BUILDING INSPECTIONS
WEEK FOUR	SCHOOL BOARD MEETING BOARD WARRANTS MEETINGS CALL TN ASSESSORS FOR ASSESSMENTS INTERNAL AUDITORS REPORT:REVENUE/EXPENDITURES REVIEW SUBMIT ASBESTOS REPORT TO S.E.D.

BUSINESS ADMINISTRATION MANAGEMENT TASKS	BUSINESS ADMINISTRATION MANAGEMENT TASKS
AUGUST	SEPTEMBER
UPDATE THIS MANAGEMENT CHART	
SUBMIT STATE AID REPORTS	SUBMIT SA-32
SEND COPIES OF STATE AID FORMS TO DIRECTORS	
ANNUAL SUPPORT SUBSTITUTE LISTS	
SEND EMPLOYEE CONTRACTS TO ADM.CL.	
INTERNAL AUDITORS	
ST-3 REPORT	
REPORT: ANNUAL SCHOOL LUNCH	
AGENDA ITEMS TO SUPERINTENDENT	AGENDA ITEMS TO SUPERINTENDENT
REPORT:STATE AID PROJECTIONS	
CORNERSTONE ARTICLES WRITTEN	CORNERSTONE ARTICLES WRITTEN
CALL FOR FINAL EQUALIZATION RATES	MEETINGS WITH ASSN. PRESIDENTS
SCHOOL BOARD MEETING	SCHOOL BOARD MEETING
REPORT: ANNUAL VANDALISM	
MEMO ON R.A.N. BORROWING FOR YEAR	
INTERNAL AUDITORS	
PREPARE NEW TAX RATES AND REPORT	
DEVELOP M.B.O.S FOR THE NEW YEAR	
DEVELOP COMPUTER EDUCATION GOALS	
DEVELOP NEW YEAR'S CASH FLOW CHART	
ADMINISTRATIVE COUNCIL	ADMINISTRATIVE COUNCIL
FINALIZE THE ST-3	PREPARE ANNUAL AUDIT RESPONSES
SUBMIT THE ANNUAL NEWSPAPER REPORT ON THE ST- 3	NEW YEAR'S BUDGET CALENDER TO BOARD
AGENDA ITEMS TO SUPERINTENDENT	AGENDA ITEMS TO SUPERINTENDENT
ASBO MEETING	ASBO MEETING
REPORTS:REVENUE & APPROPRIATIONS	REPORTS:REVENUE & APPROPRIATIONS
BUDGET TRANSFERS	BUDGET TRANSFERS
REPORT:INVESTMENT INCOME	PREPARE BID AWARDS
REPORT:FUND BALANCE	
SCHOOL BOARD MEETING	SCHOOL BOARD MEETING
BOARD WARRANTS MEETINGS	BOARD WARRANTS MEETINGS
SUBMIT ST-3 TO S.E.D.	ANNUAL AUDIT
FINAL PREPARATIONS FOR OPENING SCH.	

BUSINESS ADMINISTRATION MANAGEMENT TASKS	BUSINESS ADMINISTRATION MANAGEMENT TASKS
OCTOBER	NOVEMBER
REVISE NEW BUDGET GUIDLINES DEVELOP NEW BUDGET PARAMETERS	
AGENDA ITEMS TO SUPERINTENDENT	AGENDA ITEMS TO SUPERINTENDENT
CORNERSTONE ARTICLES WRITTEN SCHOOL BOARD MEETING	CORNERSTONE ARTICLES WRITTEN SUBMIT SA-19 DATA TO S.E.D. SCHOOL BOARD MEETING BEGIN "EARLY LOOK AT NEXT YEAR'S BUDGET"
ADMINISTRATIVE COUNCIL PREPARE NEXT YEAR'S SA-120,121,122 REVISE MOODY'S REPORT	ADMINISTRATIVE COUNCIL
AGENDA ITEMS TO SUPERINTENDENT	AGENDA ITEMS TO SUPERINTENDENT REPORT: FALL'S PROP. TAX COLLECTION
ASBO MEETING REPORTS: REVENUE & APPROPRIATIONS BUDGET TRANSFERS PREPARE BID AWARDS	ASBO MEETING REPORTS: REVENUE & APPROPRIATIONS BUDGET TRANSFERS PREPARE BID AWARDS
SCHOOL BOARD MEETING BOARD WARRANTS MEETINGS	SCHOOL BOARD MEETING BOARD WARRANTS MEETINGS

BUSINESS ADMINISTRATION MANAGEMENT TASKS	BUSINESS ADMINISTRATION MANAGEMENT TASKS
DECEMBER	JANUARY
SEND OUT AIDE/ASST. EVALUATIONS SEND OUT CLERICAL EVALUATIONS SUBMIT FIRE INSPECTION REPORTS	NEW BUDGET DEVELOPMENT
AGENDA ITEMS TO SUPERINTENDENT	AGENDA ITEMS TO SUPERINTENDENT
CORNERSTONE ARTICLES WRITTEN MEETINGS WITH ASSN. PRESIDENTS SCHOOL BOARD MEETING REVIEW SA-129I FORMS TO DATE	CORNERSTONE ARTICLES WRITTEN SCHOOL BOARD MEETING
ADMINISTRATIVE COUNCIL REVIEW PAST DUE INVOICES TO DIST. SUBMIT:EARLY LOOK AT NEXT BUDGET	ADMINISTRATIVE COUNCIL
AGENDA ITEMS TO SUPERINTENDENT	AGENDA ITEMS TO SUPERINTENDENT
ASBO MEETING REPORTS:REVENUE & APPROPRIATIONS BUDGET TRANSFERS PREPARE BID AWARDS	ASBO MEETING REPORTS:REVENUE & APPROPRIATIONS BUDGET TRANSFERS PREPARE BID AWARDS
SCHOOL BOARD MEETING BOARD WARRANTS MEETINGS	SCHOOL BOARD MEETING BOARD WARRANTS MEETINGS REVIEW EVALUATIONS FOR RETENTION OF AIDES/TEACHING ASSISTANTS

BUSINESS ADMINISTRATION MANAGEMENT TASKS	BUSINESS ADMINISTRATION MANAGEMENT TASKS
FEBRUARY	MARCH
SUBMIT SA-1Ø3[TEXTBOOK AID] COMPLETE INDIRECT AID DATA	SUBMIT SA-133,135 FOR B.A.N. AID PROCESS TEACH.RET.CREDIT: A-632
REPORT: SCHOOL LUNCH[1ST SEMESTER] SUBMIT NEW BUDGET: DEBT SERVICE,EMPLOYEE BENEFITS	SUBMIT NEW BUDGET: GENERAL SUPPORT,TRANSPORTATION, P.O.M.
AGENDA ITEMS TO SUPERINTENDENT	AGENDA ITEMS TO SUPERINTENDENT
CORNERSTONE ARTICLES WRITTEN	CORNERSTONE ARTICLES WRITTEN
SCHOOL BOARD MEETING	SCHOOL BOARD MEETING ESTABLISH NEW AUDITING SCHEDULE WITH DISTRICT'S AUDIT FIRM
ADMINISTRATIVE COUNCIL WRITE ASSESSORS FOR TAX CHANGES	ADMINISTRATIVE COUNCIL MEMO ON NEW BUS PURCHASES
AGENDA ITEMS TO SUPERINTENDENT	AGENDA ITEMS TO SUPERINTENDENT
ASBO MEETING REPORTS:REVENUE & APPROPRIATIONS BUDGET TRANSFERS PREPARE BID AWARDS PREPARE FOR R.A.N. BORROWING	ASBO MEETING REPORTS:REVENUE & APPROPRIATIONS BUDGET TRANSFERS PREPARE BID AWARDS
SCHOOL BOARD MEETING BOARD WARRANTS MEETINGS R.A.N. AUTHORIZATION	SCHOOL BOARD MEETING BOARD WARRANTS MEETINGS

BUSINESS ADMINISTRATION MANAGEMENT TASKS	BUSINESS ADMINISTRATION MANAGEMENT TASKS

****

APRIL	MAY

****

PREPARE FOR LEGAL NOTICE ADS.	
SUBMIT NEW BUDGET: INSTRUCTION,ALL OTHERS SUMMARY TOTALS	
AGENDA ITEMS TO SUPERINTENDENT	AGENDA ITEMS TO SUPERINTENDENT

****

CORNERSTONE ARTICLES WRITTEN	CORNERSTONE ARTICLES WRITTEN
SCHOOL BOARD MEETING SEND OUT AID/ASST. EVALUATIONS SEND OUT CLERICAL EVALUATIONS	SCHOOL BOARD MEETING

****

ADMINISTRATIVE COUNCIL SUBMIT SA-1Ø3[TEXTBOOK AID] SUBMIT NEW BUDGET: REVENUES,TOTALS	ADMINISTRATIVE COUNCIL PREPARE NEW SBM-1
AGENDA ITEMS TO SUPERINTENDENT	AGENDA ITEMS TO SUPERINTENDENT
ASBO MEETING REPORTS:REVENUE & APPROPRIATIONS BUDGET TRANSFERS PREPARE BID AWARDS PREPARE APPT.TELLERS,CLERKS,SUBS. FOR ANNUAL MEETING	ASBO MEETING REPORTS:REVENUE & APPROPRIATIONS BUDGET TRANSFERS PREPARE BID AWARDS

****

SCHOOL BOARD MEETING BOARD WARRANTS MEETINGS	SCHOOL BOARD MEETING BOARD WARRANTS MEETINGS SCHOOL BUDGET INFORMATIONAL MTG.

****
****

ADMINISTRATION
MANAGEMENT
TASKS

****

JUNE

****

MEETINGS WITH ASSN. PRESIDENTS
WRITE BANKS FOR 6/30 STATEMENTS
REMIND ADMINISTRATORS FOR STATE AID
WORKSHEET DATA TO B.O.
BOCES PUPIL COUNTS TO PPS DIRECTOR
SUBMIT NEW BUS SBM-16 TO S.E.D.
ANNUAL MEETING
ANNUAL VOTE
AGENDA ITEMS TO SUPERINTENDENT
PREPARE SALARIES FOR NON-UNIT STAFF
****
CORNERSTONE ARTICLES WRITTEN
PREPARE NEW YEAR'S CASH FLOW DATA
SCHOOL BOARD MEETING
DEVELOP JULY'S ORGANIZATIONAL MTG.
AGENDA
SUBMIT NEW SBM-1 TO S.E.D.

****
ADMINISTRATIVE COUNCIL
INDEPENDENT AUDITORS
REVISE MEMO ON B.O. PROCEDURES
TO ADMINISTRATORS

AGENDA ITEMS TO SUPERINTENDENT

ASBO MEETING
REPORTS:REVENUE & APPROPRIATIONS
BUDGET TRANSFERS
PREPARE BID AWARDS

****

SCHOOL BOARD MEETING
BOARD WARRANTS MEETINGS

****
****

Appendix 16.2: Samples of Computer Applications

LOTUS 1-2-3 Chart

1985-86 PROPOSED BUDGET

INSTRUCTION

BUDGET SUMMARY

PERSONAL SERVICES, PROFESSIONAL STAFF	BUDGET 1984-1985	PROPOSED BUDGET 1985-1986	DOLLAR INCREASE/ DECREASE	PERCENT INCREASE/ DECREASE
A2010.150 CURRICULUM DEVELOPMENT	$56,343	$60,567	$4,224	7.50%
A2020.150 SUPERVISION	470,108	516,131	46,023	9.79%
A2110.110 TEACHERS, 1/2 K	126,900	148,329	21,429	16.89%
A2110.120 TEACHERS, 1-6	2,012,500	2,220,504	208,004	10.34%
A2110.130 TEACHERS, 7-12	2,671,500	2,832,590	161,090	6.03%
A2110.132 SUMMER CURRICULUM	23,242	30,500	7,258	31.23%
A2110.140 TEACHERS, SUBSTITUTES	117,255	126,050	8,795	7.50%
A2250.150 HANDICAPPED PROGRAMS	328,592	319,390	(9,202)	-2.80%
A2270.150 PSEN, CHAPTER 241	194,116	210,742	16,626	8.56%
A2330.150 CONTINUING EDUCATION	47,510	47,891	381	0.80%
A2610.120 LIBRARIANS, K-6	75,629	82,932	7,303	9.66%
A2610.130 LIBRARIANS, 7-12	40,191	42,556	2,365	5.88%
A2805.150 ATTENDANCE	23,388	25,259	1,871	8.00%
A2810.150 GUIDANCE, 7-12	163,567	175,531	11,964	7.31%
A2816.150 DIAGNOSTIC	0	27,591	27,591	-
A2820.150 PSYCHOLOGICAL	30,920	14,736	(16,184)	-52.34%
A2855.150 COACHES	67,140	68,618	1,478	2.20%

TOTAL PROFESSIONAL SALARIES :	$6,448,901	$6,949,917	$501,016	7.77%
PERSONAL SERVICES, SUPPORT STAFF				
A2010.160 CURRICULUM DEVELOPMENT	$13,858	$18,854	$4,996	36.05%
A2020.160 SUPERVISION	188,477	207,169	18,692	9.92%
A2110.160 MONITORS AND AIDES	180,534	178,839	(1,695)	-0.94%
A2250.160 HANDICAPPED PROGRAMS	66,977	81,572	14,595	21.79%
A2270.160 PSEN, CHAPTER 241	46,064	49,327	3,263	7.08%
A2330.160 CONTINUING EDUCATION	500	600	100	20.00%
A2610.160 LIBRARY AIDES	41,339	41,188	(151)	-0.37%
A2805.160 ATTENDANCE	5,187	9,367	4,180	80.59%
A2810.160 GUIDANCE	54,116	51,724	(2,392)	-4.42%
A2815.160 HEALTH	54,021	51,955	(2,066)	-3.82%
A2816.160 DIAGNOSTIC	0	6,779	6,779	-
A2820.160 PSYCHOLOGICAL	8,800	9,799	999	11.35%
TOTAL SUPPORT SALARIES :	$659,873	$707,173	$47,300	7.17%
TOTAL PERSONNEL	$7,108,774	$7,657,090	$548,316	7.71%

LOTUS 1-2-3 Chart

ALTERNATE METHODS OF COMPENSATION

	A	B	C	D	E	F
X	Y = 4*X+100	Y = .16*X^2+100	Y = [1+.0281]^X*100	Y = [10000+1200*X]^.5	Y = [100000+18627*X]^.4	Y = [1000000+280509*X]^.333
0.00	100.00	100.00	100.00	100.00	100.00	100.00
0.25	101.00	100.01	100.70	101.49	101.84	102.28
0.50	102.00	100.04	101.40	102.96	103.63	104.47
0.75	103.00	100.09	102.10	104.40	105.37	106.57
1.00	104.00	100.16	102.81	105.83	107.07	108.59
1.25	105.00	100.25	103.52	107.24	108.73	110.54
1.50	106.00	100.36		108.63		
22.50	190.00	181.00		192.35	193.24	194.09
22.75		182.81	187.85		193.93	194.71
23.00			189.15	193.91	194.62	195.32
	193.00	186.49	190.47	194.68	195.31	195.93
	194.00	188.36	191.79	195.45	195.99	196.54
23.75	195.00	190.25	193.13	196.21	196.66	197.14
24.00	196.00	192.16	194.47	196.98	197.34	197.74
24.25	197.00	194.09	195.82	197.74	198.01	198.34
24.50	198.00	196.04	197.18	198.49	198.67	198.93
24.75	199.00	198.01	198.55	199.25	199.34	199.52
25.00	200.00	200.00	199.93	200.00	200.00	200.11
CUM.TO	1400.00	984.00	1256.26	1538.64	1604.46	1669.11

LOTUS 1-2-3 Chart

Investment
Schedule
July 1,1984 - June 30,1985

Date: 26-Feb-85

DATE INV.	DATE DUE	SOURCE OF FUNDS	BK. DEP.	PRINCIPAL AMOUNT	INTEREST RATE	NUMBER OF DAYS	INTEREST INCOME	TOTAL INVESTMENT INCOME
5/14	7/6	ST.AID	S.T.	$100,000	0.10200	53	$1,501.67	$416.67
5/14	7/20	ST.AID	S.T.	$100,000	0.10200	67	$1,898.33	$2,315.00
5/14	8/3	ST.AID	S.T.	$100,000	0.10200	81	$2,295.00	$4,610.00
5/14	7/13	ST.AID	S.T.	$100,000	0.10300	60	$841.88	$5,451.88
6/29	8/20	FD.BAL	S.T.	$700,000	0.10400	52	$10,515.56	$15,967.44
9/7	9/17	TAXES	S.T.	$290,000	0.10350	10	$833.75	$16,801.19
9/7	9/14	TAXES	S.T.	$100,000	0.10350	7	$201.25	$17,002.44
9/7	9/17	TAXES	S.T.	$100,000	0.10350	10	$287.50	$17,289.94
9/7	9/18	TAXES	S.T.	$101,000	0.10350	11	$319.41	$17,609.35
9/7	2/19	R.A.N.	M.M.	$2,900,000	0.11450	165	$152,189.58	$169,798.93
9/1	9/21	TAXES	S.T.	$109,000	0.10000	5	$151.39	$169,950.32
9/18	9/28	ST.AID	S.T.	$250,000	0.10250	10	$711.81	$170,662.13
9/21	9/28	TAXES	S.T.	$420,000	0.10125	7	$826.88	$171,489.00
9/25	10/2	TAXES	S.T.	$150,000	0.10000	7	$291.67	$171,780.67
9/25	10/3	TAXES	S.T.	$100,000	0.10000	8	$222.22	$172,002.89
9/25	10/4	TAXES	S.T.	$120,000	0.10000	9	$300.00	$172,302.89
10/3	10/12	TAXES	S.T.	$100,000	0.10250	9	$256.25	$172,559.14
10/3	10/15	TAXES	S.T.	$100,000	0.10250	12	$341.67	$172,900.81
10/3	10/16	TAXES	S.T.	$100,000	0.10250	13	$370.14	$173,270.95
10/3	10/17	TAXES	S.T.	$100,000	0.10300	14	$400.56	$173,671.50
10/3	10/26	TAXES	S.T.	$100,000	0.10300	23	$658.06	$174,329.56
10/3	11/1	TAXES	S.T.	$160,000	0.10400	29	$1,340.44	$175,670.00
10/3	11/12	TAXES	S.T.	$200,000	0.10400	40	$2,311.11	$177,981.11
10/5	10/19	TAXES	S.T.	$300,000	0.10200	14	$1,190.00	$179,171.11
10/5	10/29	TAXES	S.T.	$100,000	0.10300	24	$686.67	$179,857.78
10/5	10/30	TAXES	S.T.	$100,000	0.10300	25	$715.28	$180,573.06
10/5	10/31	TAXES	S.T.	$100,000	0.10300	26	$743.89	$181,316.95
10/5	11/01	TAXES	S.T.	$100,000	0.10300	27	$772.50	$182,089.45
10/5	11/02	TAXES	S.T.	$100,000	0.10300	28	$801.11	$182,890.56
10/5	11/05	TAXES	S.T.	$100,000	0.10375	31	$893.40	$183,783.96
10/5	11/09	TAXES	S.T.	$100,000	0.10375	35	$1,008.68	$184,792.64
10/5	11/13	TAXES	S.T.	$100,000	0.10400	43	$1,242.22	$186,034.86
10/5	11/21	TAXES	S.T.	$200,000	0.10400	47	$2,715.56	$188,750.42
10/5	11/23	TAXES	S.T.	$100,000	0.10400	49	$1,415.56	$190,165.97

LOTUS 1-2-3 Chart

APPROPRIATIONS STATUS REPORT
1984 -- 1985 PERIOD ENDING : 5/31/85

FUNCTION	84-85 BUDGET	BUDGET ADJUSTMENT	ADJUSTED BUDGET	ENCUMBERED	EXPENDED	UNENCUMBERED	ESTIMATED EXPENSE	ESTIMATED BALANCE
BOARD OF EDUCATION	$22,848	($582)	$22,266	$1,785	$14,836	$5,645	$2,245	$3,400
CENTRAL ADMINISTRATION	108,718	1,846	110,564	7,998	101,144	1,422	722	700
FINANCE	175,442	8,869	184,311	16,751	162,461	5,099	3,099	2,000
STAFF	38,359	5,369	43,728	7,577	31,953	4,198	48	4,150
CENTRAL SERVICES	1,461,445	1,250	1,462,695	145,414	1,169,260	148,021	28,021	120,000
SPECIAL ITEMS	165,717	1,965	167,682	29,608	135,970	2,104	404	1,700
INSTRUCTION								
CURR.DEV.&SUP.	75,801	843	76,644	5,692	70,827	125	125	0
SUPERVISION	698,975	(7,036)	691,939	54,139	633,155	4,645	1,445	3,200
RESEARCH	8,000	0	8,000	0	0	8,000	0	8,000

TEACHING	6,421,833	(7,195)	6,414,638	970,292	5,387,915	56,431	2,431	54,000
HANDICAPPED	977,650	(4,494)	973,156	142,313	684,663	146,180	21,180	125,000
PSEN	247,180	(9,505)	237,675	23,372	198,253	16,050	350	15,700
SPECIAL SCHOOLS	53,430	799	54,229	968	41,420	11,841	841	11,000
LIBRARY	201,575	(4,298)	197,277	16,255	172,350	8,672	672	8,000
COMPUTER ASST.INST.	0	52,674	52,674	738	49,572	2,364	(4,336)	6,700
ATTENDANCE	29,063	2,236	31,299	2,735	28,165	399	(601)	1,000
GUIDANCE	221,596	1,943	223,539	37,335	184,905	1,299	(2,701)	4,000
HEALTH	94,867	234	95,101	4,059	85,904	5,138	(5,862)	11,000
PSYCH. SERVICES	41,175	(2,287)	38,888	1,924	31,037	5,927	(1,073)	7,000
CO-CURR.ACT.	1,200	0	1,200	0	765	435	435	0
INTERSCH. ATHLET.	113,706	2,661	116,367	8,274	90,152	17,941	6,941	11,000
						0		
TRANSPORTATIION	1,067,923	467	1,068,390	43,470	892,759	132,161	50,161	82,000
EMPLOYEE BENEFITS	2,829,443	(13,637)	2,815,806	498,902	2,205,442	111,462	1,462	110,000
INTERFUND TRANSFERS	0	40,000	40,000	0	0	40,000	40,000	0
DEBT SERVICE								
BUILDING BONDS	976,078	0	976,078	478,718	497,360	0	0	0
REVENUE ANT. NOTES	145,000	30,000	175,000	0	0	175,000	173,234	1,766

****

	$16,177,024	$102,122	$16,279,146	$2,498,319	$12,870,268	$910,559	$319,243	$591,316

****

PERCENT CHANGE 3.66

****

LOTUS 1-2-3 Chart

BUDGET TO BUDGET AND PROPOSED BUDGET TO ESTIMATED EXPENDITURES

A.S.B. 25-Apr-85

CODE	FUNCTION	(1) ACTUAL EXPENDITURES 1983-84	(2) BUDGET 1984-85	(3) ESTIMATED EXPENDITURES 1984-85	(4) PROPOSED BUDGET 1985-86	(5) BUDGET TO BUDGET INC./DEC. (4-2)	(6) BUDGET TO BUDGET % CHANGE (5/2)	(7) 84/84 EST.EXP. TO 85/86 BUDGET INC./DEC. (4-3)	(8) 84/84 EST.EXP. TO 85/86 BUDGET % CHANGE (7/3)
A2210.11	PERSONAL SER.,K	$111,917	$126,900	$137,049	$148,329	$21,429	16.9%	$11,280	8.2%
A2110.12	PERSONAL SER.,1-6	1,954,810	2,012,500	2,035,192	2,220,504	208,004	10.3%	185,312	9.1%
A2110.13	PERSONAL SER.,7-12	2,555,617	2,671,500	2,608,191	2,832,590	161,090	6.0%	224,399	8.6%
A2110.132	PER. SER.,SUMM.CURR.	39,758	23,242	33,000	30,500	7,258	31.2%	(2,500)	-7.6%
A2110.14	PER. SER.,TCHR.SUBS.	137,227	117,255	118,000	126,050	8,795	7.5%	8,050	6.8%
A2110.16	SUPPORT SERVICES	171,490	180,534	176,000	178,839	(1,695)	-0.9%	2,839	1.6%
A2110.2	EQUIPMENT	116,077	118,598	61,912	65,723	(52,875)	-44.6%	3,811	6.2%
A2110.4	CONTRACTUAL	124,157	157,776	151,000	161,310	3,534	2.2%	10,310	6.8%
A2110.47	TUITION	14,862	19,000	17,000	19,000	0	0.0%	2,000	11.8%
A2110.48	K-12 TEXTBOOKS	93,408	96,250	109,000	99,050	2,800	2.9%	(9,950)	-9.1%
A2110.49	BOCES SERVICES	722,572	749,434	734,719	692,725	(56,709)	-7.6%	(41,994)	-5.7%
A2110.5	MATERIALS&SUPPLIES	125,644	148,844	130,800	161,904	13,060	8.8%	31,104	23.8%
	TOTAL A2110.0	$6,167,539	$6,421,833	$6,311,863	$6,736,524	$314,691	4.9%	$424,661	6.7%

NOTE : INCLUDES SWIMMING POOL (A2189) BUDGETS AND EXPENDITURES

IBM Chartmaster

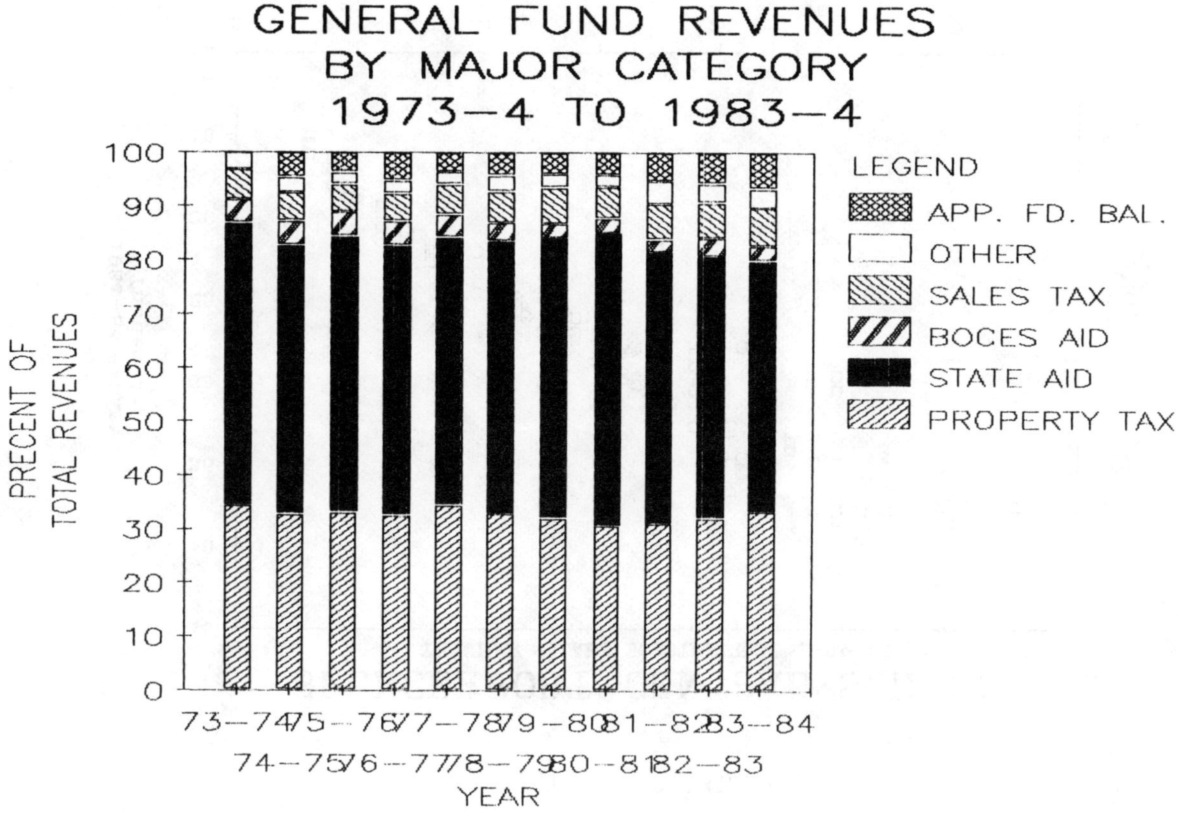

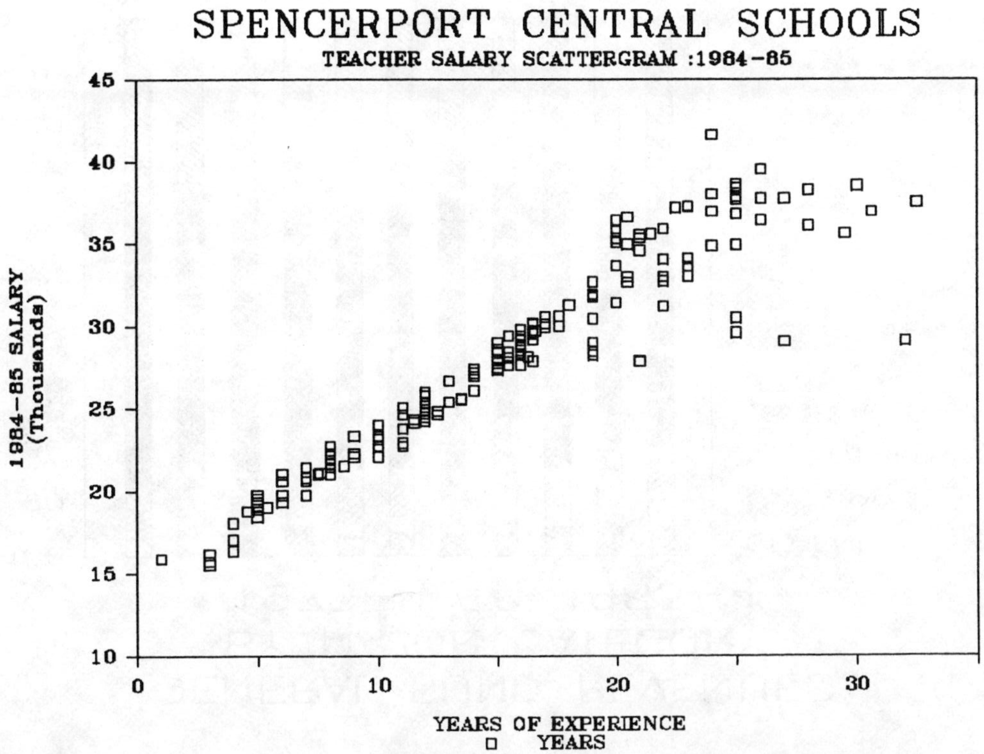
SPENCERPORT CENTRAL SCHOOLS
TEACHER SALARY SCATTERGRAM :1984-85
1984-85 SALARY
(Thousands)
45
40
35
30
25
20
15
10
0
10
20
30
YEARS OF EXPERIENCE
YEARS

LOTUS 1-2-3 Graphics

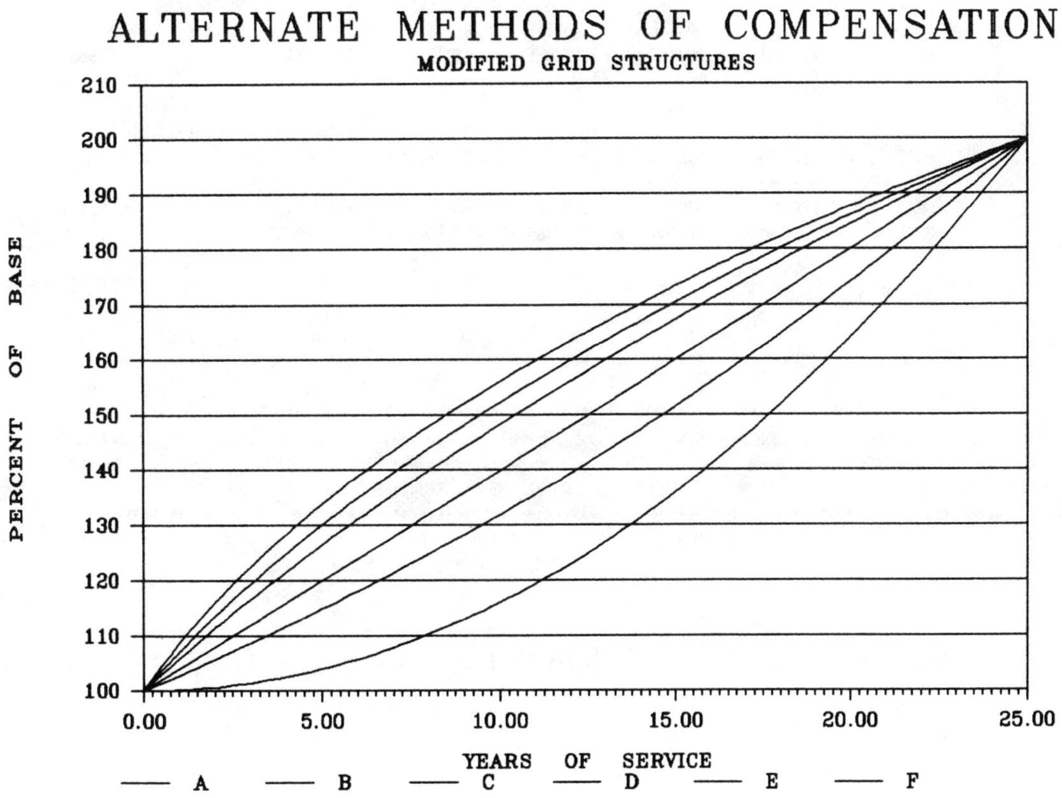

LOTUS 1-2-3 Chart

REVENUE STATUS REPORT

1984 -- 1985 PERIOD ENDING: 4/31/85

REVENUE CATEGORY	RECEIVED TO DATE	ESTIMATE TO RECEIVE 1984-85	ESTIMATED TOTAL 1984-85	SCHOOL BUDGET 1984-85	INC/DEC FROM BUDGET	PERCENT CHANGE
PROPERTY TAXES						
	$5,610,209	$0	$5,610,209	$5,609,611	$598	0.01
PERCENT	100.00	0.00	100.00			
STATE AID						
GENERAL	$5,601,632	$1,989,564	$7,591,196	$7,499,894	$91,302	1.22
TEXTBOOK	92,898	8,902	101,800	94,875	6,925	7.30
TOTAL	$5,694,530	$1,998,466	$7,692,996	$7,594,769	$98,227	8.52
PERCENT	74.02	25.98	100.00			
BOCES AID						
BASIC	$317,269	$109,564	$426,833	$430,000	($3,167)	-0.74
REFUND-PRIOR YEAR	41,942	0	41,942	18,000	23,942	133.01
FACILITY REPAYMT.	0	(19,065)	(19,065)	(19,065)	0	0.00
TOTAL	$359,211	$90,499	$449,710	$428,935	$20,775	4.84
PERCENT	79.88	20.12	100.00			

OTHER REVENUES

SALES TAX	$889,701	$330,299	$1,220,000	$1,168,742	$51,258	4.39
ADULT EDUCATION	46,364	636	47,000	53,430	(6,430)	-12.03
INTEREST/INVESTMENTS	371,918	58,082	430,000	300,000	130,000	43.33
ADMISSIONS	5,307	193	5,500	5,500	0	0.00
TUITION/HEALTH SER.	8,175	8,825	17,000	17,000	0	0.00
SALES OF BUSES	6,862	0	6,862	5,000	1,862	37.24
INSURANCE RECOVERIES	2,285	215	2,500	2,500	0	0.00
SALES OF INST. MAT.	982	18	1,000	700	300	42.86
SALES- VENDING	16	9	25	50	(25)	-50.00
TELEPHONE	147	3	150	75	75	100.00
PANASOTE LIEU /TAXES	25,166	0	25,166	4,800	20,366	424.29
FAC.USE-OUTSIDE GP.	4,624	2,376	7,000	7,000	0	0.00
BUS RENTAL(SUMMER)	540	2,960	3,500	3,500	0	0.00
RUS RENTAL(BOCES)	383	2,617	3,000	3,000	0	0.00
RM.RNT.-BOCES SPEC	9,600	21,400	31,000	30,900	100	0.32
RM.RNT.-BOCES-ADM.	0	13,468	13,468	13,468	0	0.00
RM.RNT.-STA-COSGR.	416	0	416	416	0	0.00
RM.RNT.-ADM./CRED.U.	0	577	577	0	577	-
RM.RNT.-ADM./SHER.	10,832	5,416	16,248	0	16,248	-
RM.RNT.-SHER.CUST.	0	2,000	2,000	2,000	0	0.00
RM.RNT.-SHER.UTIL.	0	1,500	1,500	1,500	0	0.00
SABB.REF-L.REED	3,828	0	3,828	3,828	0	0.00
NYS SOC.SEC. INT.	4,218	0	4,218	5,300	(1,082)	-20.42
MISCELLANEOUS	20,429	4,571	25,000	15,000	10,000	66.67
TOTAL	$1,411,793	$455,165	$1,866,958	$1,643,709	$223,249	13.58
PERCENT	75.62	24.38	100.00			
TOTAL REVENUES	$13,075,743	$2,544,130	$15,619,873	$15,277,024	$342,849	2.24
APPROP. FUND BALANCE				$900,000		
TOTAL BUDGET 1983-84				$16,177,024		

PART VI

Conclusion

17

School Business Administration: Toward Improved Understanding and Continued Improvement

with Lionel Meno

•

Overview

Throughout this book we have described the major job differences among school business administrators in the different sectors of schooling. We began by contrasting the pure-form characteristics of the public, private nonprofit, and private for-profit school administrators. Differences in rights, which are indicated by differences in sector, shape school business administration and, we feel, define the most important dimensions of a specific school business position. Rights or sector differences do *not*, however, suggest that managers are "prisoners" of the sector in which they work. Indeed, the opposite is true. The enterprising school business administrator seeks to alter systems of rights in personally beneficial ways. We give an example in this chapter by describing how public school business administrators can set up a nonprofit organization to improve their yields on investment of idle funds.

• • •

Introduction

Throughout this book has run the underlying theme that individuals' rights can often help to explain their behavior. More precisely, systems of rights vary among schooling organizations; the sector of a school (such as the public sector) describes much of the systems of rights of that organization. Therefore, the behavior of educational administrators in schools will vary due in part to the sector in which they are employed. If we take this statement as unalterable fact, then, we should be able to quickly sum up the previous chapters by defining the major differences in administrator behavior that vary according to the sector. Although this "cause-and-effect" relationship between sector and behavior is the first topic of this concluding chapter, it is not really a satisfactory conclusion to a book on management for managers. To follow such a rigid explanation of administrators' behavior would be to suggest that individual administrators are rather like prisoners of their sectors and cannot help the way they behave. Our intent is to promote the opposite conclusion: managers can alter systems of rights, and this ability is one of the most important arrows in the manager's quiver. The second part of this chapter examines some of the basic ways in which managers, especially those in the public sector, "break out" of their pure-form organizations, and we give a major reason for why this benefits them—that is, scale economies. We conclude in the third part with an extended description of an example of how managers have achieved objectives by altering systems of rights. This example demonstrates how public school business officials can create a nonprofit organization to improve yield from investments of idle cash.

Contrasting Public, Private Nonprofit, and Private For-Profit Sectors

In our analyses of the business functions of schooling organizations, we have focused on how, in general, business functions are carried out in schooling organizations. Within the context of these generalizations we have also seen how differences in behavior appear to be linked to differences in systems of rights as exemplified by differences in sector location. Because these differences are imbedded in each of the major functional areas, they may appear indiosyncratic and unrelated to each other. Yet, when taken together, they add up to fundamentally different jobs of management. At a relatively crude level of generalization, we have three archetypal managers in education: the public school manager ("Public"), the private, nonprofit school manager ("Nonprofit"), and the private for-profit manager ("Profit"). Each manages fiscal, human resource, logistics, and information systems, but each does so differently from the administrators in the other sectors. Whether these are differences in emphasis or differences in kind is for the reader to judge.

The Public School Manager—"Public"

To operate *fiscal systems* effectively, Public relies heavily on lobbying legislators and building political consensus among voters. To secure revenues, Public develops and implements complex, formal, and extensively documented planning and budgeting processes and stresses broad participation. Through these processes as well as more direct lobbying attempts, Public persuades sponsors (voters and legislative bodies) to appropriate sums of money to public schools. To secure the requisite proportion of "yes" votes from these sponsors, Public promises to provide a wide range of services that will be made available to clients (ideally) at zero price. (After money has been allocated, sponsors use Public's budgets and planning documents, along with required reports, to monitor Public's behavior and to help assure sponsors that Public has provided the services promised.) For Public, planning is more operational than strategic, because Public has very little discretion over the schools' mission or service mix.

Public reports (directly or indirectly) to a board composed of individuals with a wide variety of preferences. Their diversity reflects in part the highly diverse mission and service mix provided in Public's schools. Public spends a large proportion of time preparing for board meetings and dealing with school board members. Extensive meetings with the board and the often intense differences among board members cause Public to be both bound by and highly subject to the direction of shifting coalitions of board members. Public counters this disadvantage with an extensive knowledge of the system of rights that determines to a large extent what is legally possible in Public's schools.

Public works hard to raise revenues and to spend them in preferred ways. In order to successfully argue for revenues, Public describes extensive "unmet needs," warns that reducing valuable programs must be avoided, pleads for maintenance of quality programs, and advocates the desirability of ensuring equal educational opportunity for all children. Public seeks to maximize school budgets. In order for Public's sponsors to assure themselves that Public's behavior corresponds with his or her arguments, sponsors seek to impose constraints on Public through regulations (laws, statutes, advisory opinions, policies) and devices designed to monitor compliance (required reports, audits, freedom-of-information laws). Public's accounting requirements are designed more to assure Public's compliance with the sponsors' preferences than to inform Public's decisions. Public exercises relatively little discretion over the size, expenditure level, and service mix in the schools. Public's strategic imperative is to manage capacity (shrink and enlarge the school district to accommodate changes in enrollments) and to alter service levels in response to externally imposed fiscal and programmatic constraints and changes in demographics. Performing "well" for Public means being able to manage schooling services within these constraints.

Sponsors constrain Public's discretion over *human resources* in much the same way and for the same reasons as they constrain discretion over fiscal resources. Public has relatively little discretion over the pool of labor hired and fired. Public's supervisory rights emphasize professional development but not financial compensation or working conditions. Those decisions are negotiated by groups of employees far removed from Public.

Public manages the school's *logistics systems* much like the fiscal and human resource systems, because, like the other two systems, there is relatively little opportunity for independent judgment. Public often exercises buy-or-make decisions over noninstructional services, but restrictions placed by sponsors on Public's *purchasing* behavior often increase the cost of the "buy" alternative. Decision rights over capital goods are structured by the imperative to change capacity to match demographic demand.

Within these highly constrained rights, Public has incentives to operate efficiently and effectively, much like any other consumer with unlimited desires and a limited budget. Overall budget constraints and mandated services force Public to consider new and better ways of providing services, but logistical and legal constraints limit the extent to which Public can act on those incentives and be innovative.

Public develops *information systems* as much in response to sponsors' demands for monitoring as to provide Public with better information. Sponsors use reporting as a means of control, and data are required in order to confirm compliance with required processes as well as to ascertain schooling outcomes, such as test scores.

The Private Nonprofit School Manager—"Nonprofit"

Nonprofit behaves quite differently from Public. To operate *fiscal systems* effectively, Nonprofit relies heavily on inducing individual client-sponsors to purchase schooling services as well as on inducing sponsors to contribute resources to further the relatively narrow mission of Nonprofit's schools. Planning and budgeting procedures and documents are important for management decisions but play secondary roles in the pursuit of revenues from sponsors. Instead, Nonprofit relies on other activities, namely recruiting and fund raising, that are specifically designed to generate revenues. Less attention is paid to formal relations between goals, programs, and expenditures, although more attention is given to defining the relationships between expenditures and sources of revenue.

Nonprofit spends a lot of time determining what services to offer and how much to charge for them as well as what management activities to undertake and how much to spend on them. Knowledge of demand and price relationships is critically important. The financial benefits of, for example, an all-day kindergarten have to be weighed against the increased cost of providing the service; the costs of a special recruitment drive for students have to be weighed against the benefits that might result from more and better applicants; the benefits of doubling the amount of scholarship money for needy students have to be weighed against the potential for lost revenue. Nonprofit tries to maximize net income, whereas Public tries to maximize expenditures. Nonprofit, however, must not move so far from the school's mission in pursuit of net income that the organization's nonprofit status is jeopardized or sponsor-donors are alienated. Nonetheless, Nonprofit operates with much more freedom than Public does.

Unlike Public, Nonprofit seeks to keep the mission of the schooling organization relatively narrow in order for the school to be sufficiently attractive to a relatively small but financially sufficient segment of the schooling market. Nonprofit has no incentive to be all things to all people. Furthermore, Nonprofit has no incentive to argue for money based on the *problems* associated with teaching students. On the contrary, Nonprofit promotes his school as a high-quality institution: the school is the "best" of its kind; it is "special"; it is "uniquely well suited" to do what it does. If problems exist, there are no incentives to broadcast their presence.

Like Public, Nonprofit operates under a school board that represents clients and other sponsors. However, because the spectrum of individual preferences on that board is relatively narrow, differences of opinion are not so fundamental. Nonprofit's board meets less frequently, and discussion at board meetings is characterized by more consensus. Still, the board acts to constrain Nonprofit's behavior to a degree.

Nonprofit has more decision rights over *human resource systems* than Public does. Nonprofit can hire from a broader range of personnel, can dismiss personnel more easily and selectively, and can differentiate the compensation levels and work assignments of employees with greater ease. Similarly, when managing *logistics systems*, Nonprofit has more freedom over the ways in which related services and goods can be acquired. Any limitations are associated more with limits on revenue-raising ability than with legal restrictions. Nonprofit develops *information systems* that are most likely to aid in decisions as opposed to those required for external reporting to outside regulatory agencies. For example, Nonprofit more likely values donor rosters complete with contribution history than he values certification data on teachers, and Nonprofit's information systems reflect these preferences.

The Private For-Profit School Manager—"For-Profit"

For-Profit has the greatest discretion over changes in mission and revenue-generating activities. He reports to no governing board (although he may chair the annual stockholders' meeting) and is not legally constrained to pursuing activities solely related to specific kinds of schooling. Like Nonprofit, For-Profit pursues net revenues, but, unlike Nonprofit, For-Profit is likely to provide a cluster of services that are *economically* integrated as opposed to *programmatically* integrated. For example, For-Profits's service mix may include drop-out prevention, adult literacy, SAT preparation, computer literacy, and instructional software. These services, seemingly unrelated programmatically, may all represent For-Profit's capital commitment to instructional computing hardware, software development, and instructional space.

For-Profit has strong incentives to modify the school's mission and service mix whenever it appears to result in increased net revenues. Revenues may be from sponsors acting as individuals (for example, paying students) or as agents for other organizations (for example, governments). For-Profit will provide services when demand is high and the cost of entry into the field is not prohibitive. For-Profit has incentives to be efficient because he is a residual claimant—that is, For-Profit is likely to own all or part of the organization. As owner, For-Profit seeks to protect his financial investment in the organization while at the same time drawing as much from it for himself as possible.

Comparing Pure Forms

We have sketched the pure forms of managers' rights and behavior in the public, nonprofit, and for-profit sectors. These representations should not suggest that schools in one sector are categorically better than those in another—no more than, say, rugby teams are "better" than football teams. We have been comparing organizations composed of different individuals who are playing under different sets of rules.

However, because sector location influences what managers do, schools in one sector may be more likely to accomplish *some tasks* more effectively and efficiently under *certain* conditions than schools in another sector are able to. What those tasks and conditions are varies, but the notion is theoretically "in line" with earlier propositions. To make our analysis less complex, we will consider differences between public schools on the one hand and private schools (both private sectors) on the other.

Public-sector schools may provide schooling more effectively under conditions where uniformity of mission and service mix is desired, where one "best" service mix is recognized, and where services are relatively unchanging in content and process. Public schools may work particularly well when revenue sources are stable and relatively plentiful, because effectiveness in the public sector seems to require more resources. Schools in the private sectors, on the other hand, specialize their missions and mixes of services to a much greater degree than do schools in the public sector. They are more likely to innovate (for example, they might provide all-day kindergartens) and to innovate in ways that improve net revenue. In addition, private organizations generally are able to provide comparable services at less cost (Bennett and Johnson 1981, pp. 37–75; Poole 1979; Savas 1982, pp. 89–111), so they become more attractive as public-sector revenues decline and public schools cut back on services. At the risk of oversimplification, the fundamental trade-offs between public and private schools seem to be uniformity (quality and quantity) and comprehensiveness of service at high cost versus specialization of service and greater variability of quality at somewhat less cost. However, insufficient research exists at present to conclusively support these speculations.

Implications for the Individual Manager

In order to make this analysis more relevant for the individual manager, we need to depart from a rigid comparison of sectors. As we pointed out in the beginning of the book, we want to look at sector differences because they provide a useful way to contrast different systems of rights. However, there are limits to this structure. First, there are great variations in systems of rights *within* each sector. We have focused our attention only on the most basic and gross differences among sectors. Second, we have not discussed the implications for the individual school administrator, who, after all, must work within only one of the sectors. We return now to a discussion of the individual manager and why the systems-of-rights perspective can be useful.

It is a useful perspective for the individual administrator, not because rights vary across sectors but because individual administrators are in a position to change the systems of rights of the sector in which they work. Throughout this book and earlier in this chapter we have focused our attention on three pure forms of schooling organizations: public, private nonprofit, and private for-profit. Among these pure forms are a variety of alternative ways to organize schooling and other public services, and each embodies a different system of rights and engenders different incentives (Savas 1982). The individual administrator is often in a position to alter organizational forms for providing schooling whether the organization is a public one (government) or a private one (nonprofit or for-profit).

Managers in Public Organizations

The manager in the public organization can provide services by hiring employees or by contracting with other managers. One unit of government can hire or pay another government office to supply a service. A local school district without its own high school often arranges to send its pupils to the high school in a neighboring town. These *intergovernmental agreements* exist for a wide range of municipal services. Over half of the municipalities in the United States have agreements for the provision of services to their citizens by other governmental units. Over 40 percent of all cities produce services for other units of government (Savas 1982, p. 59).

Managers in government also *contract with private firms* (for-profit and nonprofit) to deliver goods and services. The list in exhibit 17.1 suggests the breadth of "public" services that some public-sector managers have contracted out to private managers. Additional contracted *social services* include day care, foster-home care, group-home care, adoption, institutional care, rehabilitative services, family counseling, child protection, homemaker services, and legal aid for impoverished defendants (Fisk, Kiesling, and Muller 1978). Examples of contracted *educational* services include programs for potential school dropouts, special education programs for the physically and psychologically handicapped, home school services, and test preparation.

Government managers also *award franchises* as an alternative to direct provision. An exclusive franchise is an award of monopoly privileges to a private firm to supply a particular service, usually with price regulation by a government agency. Nonexclusive and multiple franchises are also awarded; an example is taxicab service. Cab owners buy the franchise rights from government and then charge riders (consumers) for the service. A franchise differs from contracted services in that the government pays the producer for contracted services, but the consumer pays the producer for the franchise service. Examples of franchises include utilities (electricity, gas, and water distribution), telephone service, cable television, bus transportation, and concessions in parks and other public properties.

Government managers also encourage consumption by provision of services through *grants*. Under a grant, the subsidy is given by government to a private producer in the form of money or tax-exempt status. Examples of this arrangement include government-supported provision of low-cost housing by private real estate firms and subsidized mass transit, as well as higher education, health care, and cultural and performing arts. With the grant mechanism, the producer is a private firm and usually both the government and the client–consumer make payments to the producer.

Vouchers represent another attempt by government managers to encourage consumption of public goods by particular classes of consumers. The voucher system subsidizes consumers, permitting them to exercise relatively free choice in the marketplace. This is unlike the grant mechanism, which subsidizes the producer and restricts consumers' choice to the subsidized producers only. As an example in housing, rent vouchers are contrasted with low-cost housing supplied by grants. Other examples of vouchers include food stamps, the G-I Bill of Rights after World War II, Medicaid and Medicare enrollment cards, and various programs to foster consumption of cultural activities (Savas 1982, p. 69).

Exhibit 17.1

The Number of Cities Using Private Firms to Supply Municipal Services Under Contract

Service	Number of Cities Contracting with Private Firms
Refuse Collection	339
Street Lighting	309
Electricity Supply	258
Engineering Services	253
Legal Services	187
Ambulance Services	169
Solid Waste Disposal	143
Utility Billing	104
Animal Control	99
Planning	92
Water Supply	84
Mapping	74
Water Distribution System	67
Payroll	65
Street Construction and Maintenance	63
Hospitals	57
Special Transportation Services	49
Cemeteries	47
Microfilm Services	47
Nursing Services	34
Assessing	31
Public Relations	30
Bridge Construction and Maintenance	25
Industrial Development	24
Tax Collection	24
Mental Health	22
Sewage Disposal	21
Management Service for Publicly Owned Transit	18
Electrical and Plumbing Inspection	17
Libraries	17
Zoning and Subdivision Control	16
Sewer Lines	14
Treasury Functions	14
All Fire Services	13
Mosquito Control	12
Museums	12
General Development	10
Alcoholic Rehabilitation	9
Records Maintenance	9

Exhibit 17.1 continued

Service	Number of Cities Contracting with Private Firms
Election Administration	8
Police Communications	8
Building and Mechanical Inspection	7
Fire Communications	7
Housing	7
Recreational Facilities	7
Personnel Services	6
Urban Renewal	6
Crime Laboratory	5
Irrigation	5
Parks	5
Traffic Control	5
Water Pollution Abatement	5
All Public Health Services	4
Juvenile Delinquency Program	4
Licensing	4
Soil Conversion	4
Civil Defence Communications	2
Fire Prevention	2
Noise Abatement	2
Patrol Services	2
Registration of Voters	2
Training of Firemen	2
Air Pollution Abatement	1
Jails and Detention Homes	1
Welfare	1

Note: Based on responses of 2,375 cities to a mail survey in 1973.

Source: E. S. Savas, *Privatizing the Public Sector*. Chatham, N. J.: Chatham House Publishers, 1982, pp. 63–64. Derived from *The Challenge of Local Governmental Reorganization*, vol. 3 (Washington, D.C.: U.S. Government Printing Office, Advisory Comission on Intergovernmental Relations, February 1974), appendix table 3.A.

For the Manager in Private Organizations

In our discussion of "pure-form" managers, the private nonprofit and private for-profit firms dealt entirely with nongovernment consumers and sponsors. But just as public-sector managers can incorporate private-sector features into their service delivery, so too can private-sector managers incorporate public-sector features into their service delivery. Here we are actually looking at the same contracting discussion from the private side instead of from the public or government side. Private-sector managers can and do contract with governments in the variety of ways discussed previously.

Reasons for Contracting

Although managers often choose to produce a good or deliver a service by hiring their own people and watching over their work to make sure it is done correctly and at the least possible cost, they occasionally choose *not* to for a number of reasons. Managers may have to pay higher wages in their own organizations than they would have to pay by contracting. Or, the conditions of employment in their organizations are such that they would not have sufficient control over employees once they are hired. Or, some other firm may have acquired valuable experience and expertise that would be very expensive to duplicate. Or, it may be easier to adjust to changes in volume by contracting than by hiring and firing. All of these reasons show that differences in systems of rights influence decisions.

Scale Economies

Another reason for public-sector managers to contract, especially at the municipal level, is the probable mismatch between city size and the "best size" for a particular service—the economy-of-scale argument. The notion that for a given industry there is an optimum firm size comes into play as municipalities contract to firms whose size varies from that of the municipality. Most public jurisdictions are sometimes not of optimum size for provision of most public services (see Bennett and Johnson 1981, pp. 32–35). Private firms are free to adjust the scale of operations and mix of services and goods so that the minumum cost of production can be achieved. As a consequence, some industries are characterized by relatively few firms that serve relatively large markets—such as aluminum smelting or automobile stamping—while other industries are characterized by many small firms—barbershops, laundries, gift shops. In an industry where firms experience extensive scale economies, they may serve national or even worldwide markets. At the other end, a small firm may serve a market limited to a few square miles or to a few city blocks.

Even when a political jurisdiction may be the ideal size for the production of a particular good or service, it is impossible for the public sector to produce all goods and services at lowest cost. Optimum size varies as much across "public goods" as across all other goods and services. The scale-economies argument applies to financing as well as to production of a good or service. A political jurisdiction may be too small to use cost-cutting techniques, to collect fees for a service, or to get favorable terms for borrowing to finance capital equipment (Bennett and Johnson 1981, p. 34).

Experience with consolidation of police services (that is, two or more cities sharing the same service) is illustrative. Certain functions of police service decrease in unit cost as the scope of police service increases (up to a point); examples are twenty-four-hour phone answering, radio dispatching, training programs, a crime lab, and prisoner-holding facilities. The intuitively appealing conclusion of consolidation of all services is, however, not necessarily warranted. Above about 250,000 population the costs of coordinating the services begin to overcome those scale economies. Many small- and medium-sized cities are consolidating not entire police departments but only costly support services. For example, adjacent police departments in towns may share the costs of one radio dispatcher. This type of functional (not departmental) consolidation fosters scale economies without incurring the concurrent costs of total consolidation. Departments in one municipality that provide contract services to another municipality usually price their service (such as the provision of additional cars and officers) above the marginal cost but less than the average cost. Thus, both municipalities achieve some savings.

The scale-economies approach serves as a major means of reducing costs faced by public managers if only because the size (scale) of public jurisdictions has remained relatively fixed for so long. Private-sector firms have enjoyed much greater freedom to modify scale and missions. Increasingly, public-sector firms are resorting to outside markets as less costly alternatives to internal provision of some services. In some respects this runs counter to the history of public-sector firms (Williamson 1981).

Modifying Systems of Rights in School District Cash Management

Educational administrators in any of the three sectors have opportunities to alter systems of rights (or to create new organizational relationships) and on occasion will do so if such action would result in more cost-beneficial policies than the current systems do. School business administrators are able to effect improvements in the efficiency and effectiveness of the financial, human service, logistical, and information systems over which they have responsibility.

One of the best current examples is in the area of cash management. Some public school business officials have created separate private nonprofit organizations that they contract with in order to improve the efficiency and effectiveness of their cash management tasks. A description of this innovation follows.

The organizational modifications (revised system of rights) presented in the following outline grow out of the cash management activities that were described in chapter 7; we present this example to convey the impact that new organizational forms can have on school business administration. School business administrators seek to improve yields from investments of idle cash (see chapter 7), and some have seen benefits to redefining the "existing organization" from one school district to a consortium or federation of school districts. Such action involves the creation of a new organizational form designed specifically to help public school business officials to invest idle funds (see Hentschke 1984).

Pioneers of this idea, such as Linford Moyer, saw the theoretical benefits (and costs) that were likely to accrue from creating a new organization that would allow school districts to federate for purposes of investing idle funds. Some benefits follow.

1. A federation would have a larger pool of investable funds and could invest in instruments of larger denominations, thereby producing a higher investment yield.
2. The scale economies of professional management are large. Professional management seeks the same information for fifty school districts as it would for one district. In other words, the costs per district of investing—costs associated with rate shopping, execution of purchases, evaluation of investment quality, economic and interest rate forecasts, cash-flow projection, and maturity selection—fall dramatically when funds are pooled.
3. Bookkeeping and operating procedures normally associated with multiple direct investments could be reduced.
4. The investment pooling nature of a federation enables each school district, in effect, to have a more diversified portfolio than it could obtain as an individual investor without sacrificing yield.
5. With a sufficiently large federation of school districts, no single district action would be of sufficient magnitude to affect the overall operation of the pool. This makes possible several additional benefits:
   a. School districts in the pool would not have to schedule the maturities of their investments to coincide with estimated cash-flow requirements.
   b. There need be no minimum periods of investment and no penalties upon withdrawal.
   c. Each district can keep its funds invested at the higher yield available to pooled investments, thereby minimizing float. [Pennsylvania School District Liquid Asset Fund (PSDLA) 1982]

The largely economic benefits available through pooling idle cash are achieved through the design and creation of a new organization. The ability of the new organization to achieve the theoretical economic benefits depends on the rights and resulting incentives partitioned out to various actors.

The Pennsylvania School District Liquid Asset Fund

A few pooling federations have been in operation for several years (they are in Pennsylvania and Michigan); others are on the verge of becoming operational (for example, in New York); and still other school districts are participating in general government pooling federations (Florida, Illinois, and Wisconsin are states where this is occurring). The forms of organization vary from state to state. The structure of the Pennsylvania School District Liquid Asset Fund (the Fund) is, nonetheless, illustrative of how school business administrators can redefine systems of rights and set up incentives to maximize the investment preferences of member school districts.

The Fund was created as a private, nonprofit organization under the laws of the Commonwealth of Pennsylvania in January 1982. Among its many advantages, such an organizational form permits (as you recall from chapter 2) continual accounting surpluses (profits) while avoiding tax costs. All of the particulars of the Fund are published in the "Information Statement" of the Pennsylvania School District Liquid Asset Fund. Rights have been partitioned among four actors in order to make the fund work to the advantage of school business administrators.

Trustees

Trustees (from whose number officers are elected) have "full, exclusive, and absolute control and authority" over the business of the Fund. They oversee, review, and supervise the activities of the investment adviser, the co-administrators, the custodian, and the Fund's other consultants and professional advisers. The articles of incorporation require that three of the initial seven trustees be individuals who are business officials of member school districts, three must be board members of member districts, and one may be either a school business official or a board member of a member district. The same proportional composition of the board of trustees, with respect to school business officials and school board members, must be maintained in the event the number of individuals serving as trustees is changed.

The trustees serve without compensation, but they are reimbursed by the Fund for reasonable travel and other out-of-pocket expenses incurred in connection with their duties as trustees. The trustees are not required to devote their entire time to the affairs of the Fund. Officers are elected annually.

Investment Adviser

The investment adviser provides the Fund with paid expertise in short-term, fixed-income management as well as economic and credit analysis. The Fund does not (cannot) engage in trading investment instruments with or through the investment adviser.

The investment adviser is paid a fee at an annual rate equal to 0.15 percent of the first $250 million of the Fund's average daily net assets, 0.125 percent of its second $250 million, and 0.10 percent over $500 million. The fee is calculated daily and paid monthly. The agreement between the investment adviser and the Fund requires annual approval by the trustees or by a majority of participating school districts. It is not assignable and may be terminated without penalty on sixty days' written notice at the option of either party.

Currently the investment adviser is Brown Brothers Harriman and Company, the oldest and largest private bank in America. As of 1982 it managed over $2 billion for corporations and large discretionary money market pools and had total assets in excess of $775 million, $40 million of which was equity capital. They supply the following staff to the Fund: four short-term portfolio managers, seven fixed-income advisers, four credit analysts, four economists, and twenty research analysts (PSDLAF 1982, p. 5). This level of expertise is, of course, *far* beyond the reach of any one school district, even the largest.

Administrators

The role of the administrator is to service all member school district accounts in the Fund; determine and allocate income of the Fund; provide written confirmation of each investment and withdrawal of funds by a member school district; provide administrative personnel, equipment, and office space to the Fund; determine the net asset value of the Fund on a daily basis; and perform all related administrative services for the Fund. In addition, on a quarterly basis, administrators provide the trustees with a detailed evaluation of the performance of the Fund, including a comparative analysis of the Fund's investment results as compared with various industry standards.

The administrators pay the Fund's expenses for printing documents; the administrative costs of the Fund such as postage, telephone charges, and computer expenses; the fees of the Fund's independent accountants; and the costs of appropriate insurance for the Fund and its trustees. As in the case with the investment advisors, the Fund does not engage in the trading of investment instruments with or through the administrators. Administrators are paid a combined fee at the annual rate of 0.25 percent of the first $250 million of the Fund's average daily net assets, 0.20 percent of its second $250 million, and 0.15 percent of its average daily net assets in excess of $500 million.

Currently the Fund is co-administered by E. F. Hutton and Company, Inc., and WTS Consulting Services, Inc. As of 1982 E. F. Hutton performed similar services for over $10 billion, had 274 sales offices (nine in Pennsylvania), and possessed total capital over $448 million of which $259 was equity capital. WTS Consulting Services, Inc., has developed cash-mobilization plans for the State of West Virginia, the Arizona Teachers' Retirement System, and the Permanent Fund of the State of Texas.

The co-administrators' agreement with the Fund is renewable annually by the trustees or by a majority of member districts. The agreement is not assignable and may be terminated without penalty on sixty days' written notice at the option of either party.

Custodian

The custodian acts as safekeeping agent for the Fund's investment portfolio and serves as the depository in connection with the direct transfer investment and withdrawal mechanisms. The custodian does not participate in the Fund's investment decision-making process. The Fund may invest in obligations of the custodian and buy and sell legally permitted investments from and to it. The agreement must be renewed annually by the trustees or by a majority of member school districts. It is revocable without penalty on sixty days' written notice at the option of either party. Custodian fees are a function of the quantity and kind of transactions the custodian is instructed to undertake.

The Pennsylvania School District Liquid Asset Fund is deliberately structured so that the actors will *want* to act in such a way as to maximize the investment income of the member districts. The investment adviser and the administrator cannot benefit from "churning" the Fund because they are compensated on the basis of net asset value, not transaction volume. The custodian is paid on the basis of transaction volume, but cannot benefit from "churning" because it does not participate in investment decisions. Other checks are built in. For example, the administrator monitors and reports on the Fund's performance (the responsibility of the investment adviser). All in all, this creative improvement may well yield millions of additional dollars in revenue for member school districts, and it points out the difference between simply *carrying out* school business functions and *improving* business functions.

Improving School Business Administration

School business administrators require a vast array of specialized knowledge in order to carry out the many school business functions that they supervise. The contents of all of the earlier chapters represent only the most elementary and generalizable of those functions. Of all of the areas of expertise discussed, the most important area of competence, that which separates the proverbial sheep from the goats, is how to *improve* business systems. This is, unfortunately, easier said than done.

There are many, many ways to improve each of the business functions of schools, including to automate accounting, reduce costs of food service, schedule buses more efficiently, and develop a personnel promotion system. The range of technical competence and alternative choices for improvement is so large that school business administrators cannot possibly involve themselves deeply and personally in all the areas under their jurisdiction. The information and time requirements are simply much more than a single individual can manage. So, what to do? The very best (and only) way that school business administators can *improve* the efficiency and effectiveness of schools as businesses is to modify their own systems of rights and those of others in such a way that other people will be *able* (competent) as well as be *willing* to act in accord with the business administrator's preferences.

Therefore, the way in which the school business administrator structures and modifies the systems of rights of others is likely to have the greatest long-run impact (either positive or negative) on his unit's performance. To do that well, the school business administrator's good grasp of the technology of various business functions needs to be complemented by some sense of how rights systems affect the incentives and behavior of others and whether changes in these rights could yield improvements in their behavior.

Although we have given a lot of attention in this book to the technical dimensions of school business administration, we close with the observation that an interesting frontier of school business administration is to explore new ways of organizing through changes in systems of rights in order to improve these technical dimensions and, hence, improve schools. The example we discussed in this chapter is but one form of these exciting possibilities. Other examples discussed earlier in the book include contracting with private for-profit firms for instruction and for sale-leaseback of capital goods and creation of private-nonprofit public education funds to pursue donor dollars for public schools.

These possibilities, in turn, point up the fundamental conflict inherent in school business administrators' roles. On the one hand, school business administrators are in one of the best positions to create, design, and carry out bold new ventures in school management. On the other hand, they are the guardians, the fiscal conservators, the careful custodians of finances, who facilitate the policies and strategies of others. Thus, the revenue-producing entrepreneur conflicts with the cost-conscious steward.

Conclusion

A noted sociologist commented once, "all social science researchers can be divided into two camps—'lumpers' and 'splitters'." By "lumpers" he meant people who analyze seemingly disparate, idiosyncratic, discontinuous, independent phenomena and draw from them single, unifying, continuous themes. Their work may be summarized abstractly as follows: "All of the so-called radical changes we saw in *X* are merely variations in the long-run historical development of *Y*." Or, "Careful examination of *A, D, M,* and *F* reveals that all followed pattern *P* in their behavior."

By "splitters" he meant those people who examine a single subject, phenomenon, or issue and see differences within—differences not in degree but in kind. An abstract summary of their work is the following: "By looking sufficiently closely at *Q* we see that *Q* is really made up of *R* and *S*, which are fundamentally different from each other." Or, "Although we have historically thought of *Q* as being influenced by *R* and *S*, the advent of *L* has radically changed our conceptions of *Q* and *R* and *S*." Our analysis of school business administration in this book first followed the perspective of the lumpers; then we put on the mantle of the splitters; and we conclude here with a return to the viewpoint of the lumpers!

First Lumper Perspective. All formal efforts to provide formal elementary and secondary educational programs to youth constitute a single industry. Despite substantial variation and competition among firms in this industry, the firms *collectively* provide those educational services to young people that society compels them to receive. Despite the fact that most of these services are currently financed and provided publicly, the industry is composed of firms with a variety of organizational forms. This was the message in the first chapters.

Splitter Perspective. Among firms in the compulsory education industry there exist fundamental differences in the systems of rights that educators face. These differences in rights, coupled with assumptions about individual human motivation (preferences), create different sets of incentives that cause differences in behavior. Specifically, behavior of the prototypical public-sector educator is fundamentally different from that of the private nonprofit educator, and those two categories of people behave unlike private for-profit educators. Although our focus has been on individual behavior, differences across sectors in systems of rights of individuals portray how it may appear that *organizations* behave in ways that can be attributed to their sector location. This has been the central theme throughout most of the book.

Second Lumper Perspective. Differences in the behavior of educators in different sectors of the industry are, in effect, only variations of the unifying perspective of property rights. There are no inherent qualities in the individual sectors other than differences in systems of rights that make behavior so different. With this second lumper perspective, the focus then shifts again from differences in behavior associated with sector location to the unifying theme: systems of rights, regardless of sector, greatly influence behavior.

A potentially productive area of future research and improvement in educational practice is not, then, how sector location influences behavior. Sector location is only a handy device to get a rough feel for the impact on behavior of differences in rights. This position is supported by looking within sectors and at the systems of rights that cross sector lines.

The manager in a large for-profit corporation who receives a lump-sum budget from a higher level manager and who has no control over the volume of service to be supplied (for example, the director of a personnel department or of a large corporate training program) may well face certain systems of rights and consequently behave much like our prototypical public administrator. Personnel services or educational programs may be given away, not sold, and the director may have to argue for the budget on the basis of unmet needs and problems that will arise if the budget is not approved. On the other hand, the public school administrator who has the task of generating revenue through sales of vending rights, adult education classes, food service, excess classroom space, obsolete school equipment, computer services, and the like may behave much like his private-sector counterparts. In brief, there are instances where budget maximizing can occur in the private sectors and seeking to maximize the present value of future net revenues can occur in the public sector.

Policy Development for Schooling. Policy directions follow from this perspective: educators maximize personal utility; educator behavior is explained by the incentives educators face; incentives are determined by rights and personal preferences; changes in the behavior of educators occur according to the rights (and, hence, the incentives) that educators face. The implications of this point of view suggest that policies that are merely statements of desired changes in educator behavior and that do not change educators' incentives will have limited impact at best.

To date, policy debates on schooling reform have been replete with statements of dissatisfaction with the current outcomes of schooling and what the desired outcomes should be. Little has been done to analyze the incentives of today's educators and identify changes in the systems of rights that will change behavior in desired ways. (The debates on public versus private schooling have been generally superficial and do not carefully consider the causes of behavior within and across sectors.) In order to make significant improvements in the industry of elementary and secondary schooling in America it will be necessary to examine the incentives of educators more carefully and ultimately to change systems of rights in such a way as to cause educators to *want* to behave in new and desired ways.

References

Bennett, James T., and Johnson, Manuel H. *Better Government at Half the Price.* Ottawa, Ill., and Ossining, N.Y.: Caroline House Publishers, 1981.

Fisk, Donald; Kiesling, Herbert; and Muller, Thomas. *Private Provision of Public Services: An Overview*. Washington, D.C.: Urban Institute, May 1978.

Hentschke, Guilbert C. "Chapter Four: Fiscal Management—Investments." In *Managing Limited Resources: New Demands on Public School Business Management*, edited by Van Mueller and L. Dean Webb. Cambridge, Mass.: Ballinger Press, 1984.

Levine, Marsha, and Doyle, Dennis P. "Private Meets Public: An Examination of Contemporary Education." In *Meeting Human Needs: Toward a New Public Philosophy*, edited by Jack A. Meyer, pp. 272–329. Washington, D.C.: American Enterprise Institute for Public Policy Research, 1982.

Pennsylvania School District Liquid Asset Fund. "Information Statement." February 24, 1982.

Poole, Robert W., Jr., *Cutting Back City Hall*, New York, Universe Books, 1979.

Savas, E. S. *Privatizing the Public Sector*. Chatham, N. J.: Chatham House Publishers, 1982.

Williamson, Oliver E. "The Modern Corporation: Origins, Evolution, Attributes." *Journal of Economic Literature* 19 (December 1981): 1537–1568.

Author Index

Subject Index